Naples

www.timeout.com

Time Out Digital Ltd
4th Floor
125 Shaftesbury Avenue
London WC2H 8AD
United Kingdom
Tel: +44 (0)20 7813 3000
Fax: +44 (0)20 7813 6001
Email: guides@timeout.com
www.timeout.com

Published by Time Out Digital Ltd, a wholly owned subsidiary
of Time Out Group Ltd. Time Out and the Time Out logo are
trademarks of Time Out Group Ltd.

© Time Out Group Ltd 2016
Previous editions 2000, 2002, 2005, 2007, 2009.

10 9 8 7 6 5 4 3 2 1

This edition first published in Great Britain in 2016 by Ebury Publishing.
20 Vauxhall Bridge Road, London SW1V 2SA

Ebury Publishing is part of the Penguin Random House group of companies
whose addresses can be found at global.penguinrandomhouse.com

Distributed in the US and Latin America by Publishers Group West
(1-510-809-3700)

For further distribution details, see www.timeout.com.

ISBN: 978-1-84670-357-7

A CIP catalogue record for this book is available from the British Library.

Printed and bound in China by Leo Paper Products Ltd.

Penguin Random House is committed to a sustainable future for our
business, our readers and our planet. This book is made from Forest
Stewardship Council® certified paper.

MIX
Paper from
responsible sources
FSC® C018179
www.fsc.org

Contents

229

55

20

10

Time Out **Naples**

Editorial
Editor Nicky Swallow
Copy Editor Dominic Earle
Proofreader Jo Willacy

Editorial Director Sarah Guy
Group Finance Manager Margaret Wright

Design
Art Editor Christie Webster
Group Commercial Senior Designer Jason Tansley

Picture Desk
Picture Editor Jael Marschner
Deputy Picture Editor Ben Rowe
Picture Researcher Lizzy Owen

Advertising
Managing Director St John Betteridge

Marketing
Senior Publishing Brand Manager Luthfa Begum
Head of Circulation Dan Collins

Production
Production Controller Katie Mulhern-Bhudia

Time Out Group
Founder Tony Elliott
Executive Chairman Julio Bruno
Chief Executive Officer Noel Penzer
Publisher Alex Batho

Contributors
Naples Today Alfredo Cafasso Vitale. **Explore** Nicky Swallow, Bonnie Alberts (Campi Flegrei). **Children** Nicky Swallow. **Film** Nicky Swallow. **Gay & Lesbian** Nicky Swallow. **Nightlife** Jimmy della Corte, Anthony Mastroianni. **Escapes & Excursions** Nicky Swallow, Bonnie Alberts (Ischia, Pompeii, Vesuvius). **Getting Around, Resources** Bonnie Alberts.

The Editor would like to thank Bonnie Alberts, Kate Bolton, Julio Cesar Bustos Cardoza, Carla Celestino, Vito Cinque, Carmen Davolo, Rosario di Meglio, Pietro Fusella, Benedetta Gargano, Crescenzo Gargano, Sophy Leys Johnston, Gennaro Marciante, Lee Marshall, Luca Moggi, Nicoletta Rondinella, Fiona Sutherland-Beatson and all contributors to previous editions whose work forms the basis for parts of this book.

Maps JS Graphics Ltd (john@jsgraphics.co.uk)

Cover Photography Michele Falzone/AWL Images

Back Cover Photography Clockwise from top left: Courtesy Grand Hotel Quisisana, Capri; Sandro MIchahelles Fotografo; Francesco R. Iacomino/Shutterstock.com; S-F/Shutterstock.com.

Photography pages 5 (bottom left), 20/21 (top) Greta Gabaglio/Shutterstock.com; 7, 16, 17, 19, 28/29 (bottom), 31 (bottom), 82, 83, 123, 142, 262/263, 264, 266 (left) Gianluca Moggi; 11 Liberonapoli/Wikimedia Commons; 13, 28/29 (top), 95 Vladimir Korostyshevskiy/Shutterstock.com; 15 Barrosh.m/Wikimedia Commons; 20/21 (bottom), 56/57 Yulia Grigoryeva/Shutterstock.com; 21, 32/33 eFesenko/Shutterstock.com; 22, 31 (top), 44, 76 Armando Mancini/Wikimedia Commons; 23 (left) alterdimaggio1957/Wikimedia Commons; 23 (right), 88, 98 Miguel Hermoso Cuesta/Wikimedia Commons; 26 Mess/Wikimedia Commons; 46 Maurizio rea/Wikimedia Commons; 46/47 GTS Productions/Shutterstock.com; 69 MM/Wikimedia Commons; 72 © José Luiz Bernardes Ribeiro/Wikimedia Commons; 74 Mattia Luigi Nappi/Wikimedia Commons; 77, 248/249, 250, 257, 259, 260/261 Wikimedia Commons; 84 Lalupa/Wikimedia Commons; 90 Giuseppe D'Anna; 92/93 Velvet/Wikimedia Commons; 106, 150 Luciano Romano; 112/113 Baloncici/Shutterstock.com; 120 Ververidis Vasilis/Shutterstock.com; 120/121 Pinotto992/Wikimedia Commons; 124/125, 148 photogolfer/Shutterstock.com; 126 Matyas Rehak/Shutterstock.com; 127 Giuseppe Senese - Direzione Centrale Media - Gruppo FS; 129 mari27454/Wikimedia Commons; 131 Francesco Squeglia; 132 Giffoni Film Festival; 133 Miramax/Everett/REX Shutterstock; 134 PFMphotostock/Shutterstock.com; 135 Sergio Siano; 145 Laura Ferrari/Archivio Napoli Teatro Festival Italia/Wikimedia Commons; 146 Carla Buccin/Wikimedia Commons; 149 Felipe Castaño; 151 Sailko/Wikimedia Commons; 156 Eugene Sergeev/Shutterstock.com; 172 Vogel/Shutterstock.com; 176, 186 Gino Cianci/Fototeca ENIT; 196 Vito Arcomano/Fototeca ENIT; 204 Chris Hadfield @ NASA/Wikimedia Commons; 208, 219 Fondazione Sorrento Collection/Carlo Alfaro; 214 Mihael Grmek/Wikimedia Commons; 222 Vito Fusco; 226, 227 Sandro MIchahelles; 234 Enrico Capuano; 241 Mauro Fiorese; 246/247, 306/307 Paola Ghirotti/Fototeca ENIT; 253 De Agostini/Getty Images; 255 Tancredi Scarpelli/Wikimedia Commons; 256 Raffaele Esposito/Wikimedia Commons; 265, 266 (right), 267 Wikimedia Commons; 268/269 Roberto De Martino/Wikimedia Commons; 271 IlSistemone/Wikimedia Commons; 276 Richard Bryant/arcaidimages.com; 283 Roberto Bonardi

The following images were supplied by the featured establishments: 5 (top), 20, 27, 30, 54, 64, 86, 104, 110, 119, 128, 130, 138, 141, 143, 158, 159, 160, 163, 164, 165, 178, 179, 182, 191, 211, 225, 230/231, 244, 245, 274/275, 277, 278, 279, 281, 284, 287, 288, 289

About the Guide

GETTING AROUND

Each sightseeing chapter contains a street map of the area marked with the locations of sights and museums (❶), restaurants (❶), cafés, bars and gelaterie (❶) and shops (❶). There are also street maps of Naples at the back of the book, along with an overview map of the city. In addition, there is a detachable fold-out street map.

THE ESSENTIALS

For practical information, including visas, disabled access, emergency numbers, lost property and local transport, see Essential Information. It begins on page 274.

THE LISTINGS

Addresses, phone numbers, websites, transport information, hours and prices are all included in our listings, as are selected other facilities. All were checked and correct at press time. However, business owners can alter their arrangements at any time, and fluctuating economic conditions can cause prices to change rapidly. The very best venues in the city, the must-sees and must-dos in every category, have been marked with a red star (★). In the sightseeing chapters, we've also marked venues with free admission with a FREE symbol.

THE LANGUAGE

Naples is getting used to receiving many more tourists these days and you'll find English (or a version of it, at least) spoken much more widely than in the past. You'll find a primer on page 300 to get you started, along with some help with restaurant ordering. There is also a glossary on page 299.

PHONE NUMBERS

The area code for Naples is 081. This includes Pozzuoli, Ischia, Capri, Sorrento and Pompeii. It doesn't include Positano and Amalfi, which are in the Salerno province (area code 089). When calling within Naples you need to dial the area code even if you are calling from the same area. From outside Italy, dial your country's access code (00 from the UK, 011 from the US) or a plus symbol, followed by the Italy country code (39), then 081 for Naples and the number. So, to reach the Museo di Capodimonte, dial + 39 081 749 9111. For more on phones, see page 297.

FEEDBACK

We welcome feedback on this guide, both on the venues we've included and on any other locations that you'd like to see featured in future editions. Please email us at guides@ timeout.com.

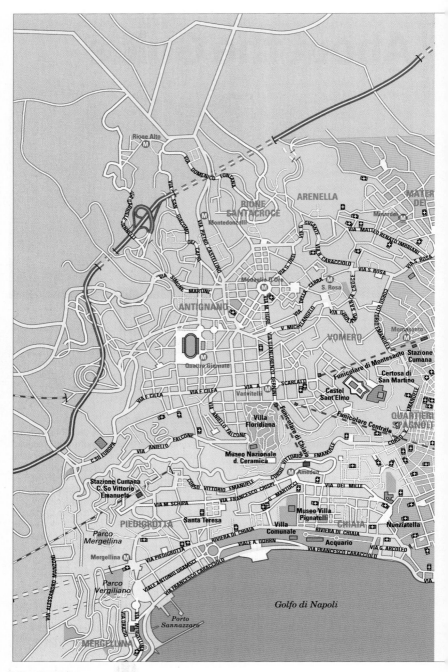

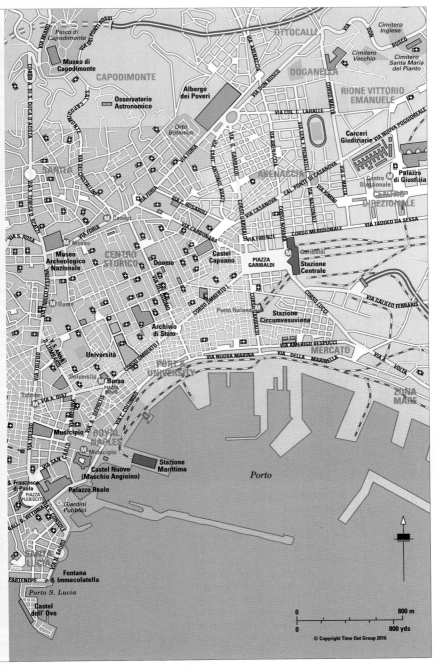

Naples'
Top 20

*From pizza to palazzi,
we count down the
city's finest.*

1 Museo Archeologico Nazionale
(page 82)

Naples' archaeological museum houses
one of the world's finest collections of
ancient art and artefacts. The layout,
lighting and labelling leave much to
be desired, but that doesn't diminish
the impact of pieces such as the *Toro
Farnese*, the bronze *Athletes* from Villa
Papiri and the fabulous collection of
mosaics from Pompeii. You'll need at
least half a day to take it all in.

2 Spaccanapoli
(pages 58-65)

Slicing through the heart of the old city, straight as an arrow, the so-called Spaccanapoli follows the path of the ancient Roman *decumanus inferior*. A walk along this narrow, buzzing street today reveals once-glorious *palazzi* and art-filled churches jostling for space with shops selling tourist tat and religious memorabilia and stalls touting *pizza fritta*.

3 Cappella Sansevero
(page 58)

Although the big draw at the funerary chapel of the Di Sango family is Giuseppe Sammartino's show-stopping *Cristo Velato* with its virtuosic draping, the other sculptures, such as Francesco Queirolo's *Disillusion*, don't disappoint either. Afterwards, take a look at what's in the basement: Naples at its most ghoulish.

4 Teatro San Carlo
(page 148)

The Teatro San Carlo, a gloriously over-the-top confection of red velvet and gilt, is one of the best opera houses in Italy; many of the greatest operas have had their debuts here – among them *La Donna del Lago*, *Lucia di Lammermoor* and *Luisa Miller*. Its season features world-class singers and conductors: splash out on a box or bag a cheap ticket in the gods. If you can't catch a performance, you can join a guided tour of the building.

⑤

5 Cimitero delle Fontanelle (page 84)

If the idea of seeing the stacked remains of some 40,000 souls doesn't spook you, a visit to the Cimitero delle Fontanelle is not to be missed. Carved out of the underbelly of the Rione della Sanità, this vast cavern was used as an open grave for the victims of plagues, cholera and poverty from the 17th century onwards. After World War II, grieving parents took up the practice of adopting skulls in memory of sons killed in action.

6 Museo di Capodimonte (page 90)

King Carlo III's expanded ex-hunting lodge may be hard to get to, but it's home to a superb collection of paintings. The vast, deep-red building is set in extensive parkland on a hill to the north of the city centre, its elegant rooms hung with masterpieces that range from glowing medieval altarpieces to prime examples of Neapolitan painting in all their gory glory, including Caravaggio's *Flagellation* and Pietro Cavallino's *St Cecilia In Ecstasy*.

④

7 The Duomo (page 67)

The rather bland, neo-Gothic façade of Naples' cathedral does little to prepare the visitor for the glittering splendours within. Highlights include the stunning Cappella di San Gennaro, the gilded coffered ceiling and the remains of Santa Restituta with its fourth-century baptistery.

8 Caravaggio's Seven Acts of Mercy
(page 68)

There's something special about seeing a great painting in its original setting (rather than hanging in an art gallery), and the icing on the cake is that you might have the place to yourself. Caravaggio's great altarpiece painted for the Pio Monte della Misericordia chapel, with its dramatic chiaroscuro effects, is all this and more.

9 Orto Botanico
(page 193)

A perfect antidote to the grimy, noisy city, this botanical garden was founded in 1807 by Joseph Bonaparte and is one of Europe's earliest examples. It's home to some 9,000 species of palms, aquatic plants, cacti, shrubs and ferns, all clearly labelled and beautifully laid out. An hour's stroll around here is the perfect way to recharge the batteries.

10 Napoli Sotterranea
(page 68)

Naples is a multi-layered city with many hidden secrets. The fascinating Napoli Sotterranea tour leads you through the complicated network of underground aqueducts, tunnels and cisterns that date from the dawn of the Greek city of Neapolis. Not one for claustrophobics.

11 Pignasecca market
(page 82)

This is where the locals stock up each morning from stalls piled with seasonal fruit and veg, and trays and buckets of

still-wriggling sea creatures. You can also pick up fake Prada sunglasses, pirated DVDs and cut-price perfumes. It's noisy, messy, crowded and Neapolitan to the core.

12 Metro Art Tour
(page 19)

The price of a single metro ticket will buy you access to what is probably the most extensive collection of contemporary art and architecture in Italy. The latest openings on the city's metro system are among the most impressive: Karim Rashid's bubblegum colours at Università, Oscar Tusquets Blanca's soaring mosaics at Toledo, and Alvaro Siza and Edoardo Souto de Moura's clean, sober lines at Municipio.

13 Certosa-Museo di San Martino
(page 94)

The sweeping views of the city and bay would be reason enough to visit, but there's lots more besides: a lavish Neapolitan Baroque church; an art gallery; museums showcasing boats, Christmas cribs and carriages; and two sunny cloisters.

14 Pizza
(page 66)

Once the food of kings (or queens, to be more accurate), the pizza margherita was created in Naples for Queen Margherita in 1889. For such a simple dish, it's hard to get right – each Neapolitan has his or her own favourite *pizzaiolo*. This is no time for fancy gourmet versions: if you only eat one, make it Da Michele.

15 San Lorenzo Maggiore
(page 69)

A triumph of Angevin Gothic hidden behind a tiny, weathered Baroque façade, this church houses a splendid cross-vaulted apse and the tomb of Catherine of Austria by Tino da Camaino. It was built on the site of the Roman *macellum* (food market) and you can also visit this astonishing throwback to Graeco-Roman Neapolis – excavations have revealed streets as they were some 2,000 years ago, complete with a butcher's, a bakery and a porticoed arcade.

16 Catacombe di San Gaudioso
(page 86)

Tunnelled into the Capodimonte hillside during Roman times, these labyrinthine catacombs house fragments of fifth- and sixth-century mosaics, as well as early frescoes. A fascinating range of burial techniques were

18 Campi Flegrei
(pages 112-119)

Part of Naples' ugly, sprawling western suburbs, the 'Burning Fields' area is fascinating for its air of mystery and myth, as well as weird geological phenomena such as the steaming Solfatara and the rising/falling water levels at the Serapeo in Pozzuoli. Add in a 40,000-seater Roman amphitheatre, the small but beautiful Museo Archeologico at Baia and a fishy lunch, and you have the perfect day trip.

19 Mozzarella
(page 105)

Your first taste of Campanian mozzarella will be a gastronomic epiphany. Soft, yet resistant to the knife, milky and slightly salty, mozzarella here comes from either Paestum or Battipaglia to the south. Muu has a good selection to eat in or take away.

20 Funicular rides
(page 290)

Four trundling funicular railways provide links between Vomero and the city centre. Chiaia was built in 1889, followed by Montesanto. The Centrale – one of the world's longest and busiest – came next and, finally, Mergellina. Hop on board for the slow ascent up the hill, whistling the ditty 'Funiculì-Funiculà' as you go.

used here, including one where the upright corpse had its head cemented into the rear wall while bodily fluids drained away. The Baroque church of Santa Maria della Sanità above provides light relief.

17 Rione della Sanità
(pages 85-87)

The evocative, densely populated neighbourhood of Sanità – crammed with ancient burial sites, architectural gems such as the Palazzo dello Spagnolo, lively street markets and several of the best pizzerias in the city – is no longer off limits to tourists, during daylight hours at least. If you want a feel for 'real' Naples, this is the place to come. To get a local's take on it, sign up for one of the Sunday Miglio Sacro guided tours.

Naples Today

I t's all too easy to apply stereotypes to Naples, but they don't begin to capture the social and cultural complexity of this ancient metropolis. This is a city riven with contradictions. There's third-world-style traffic congestion, but also a state-of-the-art metro with beautiful stations designed by contemporary artists and architects. Forgotten, dilapidated neighbourhoods share city space with a cutting-edge, high-rise business district; there are gypsy encampments and splendid palaces. The state of all-out warfare between drug-dealing clans is matched by the passion of countless volunteers who care for the city's monuments, do voluntary social work and protest fearlessly against the Camorra.

THE FAILURE OF LOCAL POLITICS

For the most part, both local politicians and the national government have failed the city and its 960,000-odd inhabitants in recent years. In 1993, when Antonio Bassolino became mayor, it looked as if Naples would experience a renaissance, but this optimism was sadly short-lived and political inactivity resumed with the election of mayor Rosa Russo Iervolino, who took over when Bassolino became governor of the region of Campania in 2001.

The current mayor, Luigi De Magistris, elected in 2011, has also failed to effectively address the deterioration of the city and its infrastructure, further contributing to the negative image of Naples in both the national and international media. It seems that little of note will remain of his tenure except, perhaps, the improved system of rubbish collection and recycling in central neighbourhoods, which has reduced the huge amounts of waste that famously fouled the streets in the past. Reduced but not removed: the problem is ongoing and will remain a key issue for the council after the local elections in 2016.

In the light of such failings, the Neapolitans have learned the hard way that they need to rely on their own resources and creativity to improve not only their own lives, but also the life of the city around them.

HISTORY AND POROSITY

Diverse outside influences made their mark on the city through the centuries, shaping its appearance today. Built according to the design of a Greek architect and pupil of Pythagoras, Neapolis was an important commercial centre where the Greek language and customs were long maintained. For the Romans, it was a paragon of Greek civilisation, much favoured by the Empire's highly cultured aristocracy; this was brought to light particularly vividly in the archaeological digs at San Lorenzo Maggiore. Then there's the influence of three centuries of Spanish domination, which left an indelible imprint on Naples' layout and urban planning. The best-known example of this is the Quartieri Spagnoli, the grid of narrow *vicoli* (lanes) overshadowed by the medieval Castel Sant' Elmo. Many noble *palazzi* (mansions) were built in this area, which once served as quarters for the Spanish troops.

The vibrant street life of Naples has always intrigued visitors, and it was Walter Benjamin who first defined the city as 'porous' – much like the tufa and the black piperno volcanic rock of Vesuvius on which it rests. It's in the Quartieri Spagnoli – focus of rehabilitation projects during Bassolino's tenure – that this porosity is most obvious. Here, the ground floors of the *palazzi* were made up of *bassi* (one-room apartments where the poorest inhabitants lived), while the upper floors housed the wealthier *signori*. Even now, these two diverse groups of people still co-exist in the same buildings in an everyday dynamic unknown in any other city. Today, though, a much more varied population (a mix of Neapolitans and immigrants from African, Asian and eastern European countries) shares life in the *bassi*.

For visitors, the sheer difference from the European or American norm makes these streets fascinating. And thanks to the influx of B&Bs in the area, more and more tourists are venturing into these labyrinthine lanes, experiencing the street life and dodging buzzing scooters – ridden by two or three women squeezed on to one saddle, perhaps. They'll also need to dodge those locals determined on the infamous *scippo* (scooter-propelled purse-snatching), as tourists are especially easy targets.

'A PARADISE INHABITED BY DEVILS'

This expression, wrongly attributed to Goethe, was first used by Bernardino Daniello, a 16th-century commentator known for his work on Dante. But it captures a grain of truth about the city today, because areas such as La Sanità, Forcella, Ponticelli and Scampia still cope with the strong presence of the Camorra.

Father Alex Zanotelli, a local priest working in the Sanità, points out that the social decay in much of Naples means that young people are easily recruited to a life of crime. 'Here in La Sanità there are 70,000 people living in five square kilometres, without a single nursery or junior school, and with a secondary school that is ranked the second worst in the

Università, one of Naples' *stazione dell'arte*.

country. Where are kids going to end up, if not in the clutches of the Camorra?'

Following a recent increase in the number of shootings in the area, Roberto Saviano, author of *Gomorrah*, the best-selling exposé of the Camorra, dismissed the promise of extra police as 'a political pantomime'.

But there are glimmers of hope. In Sanità, some of these young people are now at the centre of an interesting project that promotes the area's sights – such as the San Gennaro catacombs and the Fontanelle cemetery – to tourists. Others have joined the theatre school of the excellent Nuovo Teatro Sanità.

Even in the troubled neighbourhood of Scampia – a place that shows what poverty looks like when Corbusian city planners try to impose their Utopias on people's lives – important initiatives are afoot involving local teenagers. One outstanding example is Arrevuoto, a theatre project where some of Italy's best-known actors and directors are attempting to provide local youngsters with some tools for their future.

'MANGIA, MANGIA!'

'Eat, Eat!' This typical plea of Neapolitan mothers could be a suitable anthem for the city as a whole, with its infinite variety of markets and street-food stands, trattorias and classy restaurants. A recent addition to the food scene is the 'home restaurant', a similar idea to the guerrilla eateries that first sprung up in New York, where any keen cook can host friends, acquaintances and strangers for a meal around their dining table. This type of conviviality – which transcends social class and status – is typically Neapolitan.

There are fish markets across the city, and going to the *mercato* to choose fish for Sunday lunch, listening to the droning sales pitch of the fishmongers, perfected over centuries, is a ritual that Neapolitan men still follow. The men not only select the fish but, if only on this one day of the week, also painstakingly prepare it for their families.

FROM BAROQUE TO CONTEMPORARY

Baroque may be the defining style of art in Naples, but a strong dialogue with contemporary culture has developed here since the late 1970s, when the enlightened art dealer Lucio Amelio brought Andy Warhol and Joseph Beuys to the city.

Antonio Bassolino, during his years as governor of Campania, promoted the Metro dell'Arte, the innovative scheme to use underground metro stations as platforms for contemporary art installations. It has become one of the most talked-about projects in Italy. And above ground, the MADRe contemporary art gallery, housed in Palazzo Donnaregina and redesigned in 2004 by Portuguese architect Alvaro Siza Vieira, was one of the first of a new generation of museums in Italy.

The city's increasing reputation for contemporary art has also attracted exciting private galleries and dealers: the Lia Rumma gallery, with its cutting-edge agenda, is now a Naples institution; and Artecinema, an important international festival of films on contemporary art directed by curator Laura Trisorio, will celebrate its 20th year in 2016.

THE STRUGGLE FOR SUSTAINABILITY

A constant struggle for a more sustainable way of living, especially in terms of traffic and pollution (*viabilità*, as it's known), is a central theme of everyday life in Naples. Once the major roadworks in Piazza Garibaldi and Piazza Municipio are finished, things should improve significantly, especially if the Neapolitans are willing to make greater use of the metro system now that it's almost complete. But the reduction of car traffic in the city centre due to the ZTL (limited traffic zone) has been controversial for its commercial implications, and is less effective than might be imagined because the locals use scooters so extensively. Major 'unfinished business' includes the transformation of the waterfront area near the Molo Beverello and the conclusion of the restoration of the vast Real Albergo dei Poveri on Via Foria.

LOOKING TO THE FUTURE

The political future of Naples is uncertain, to say the least. If the Neapolitans continue to look for a saviour rather than taking responsibility themselves, it's difficult to imagine that there will be any social improvement. Naples is also the cultural and economic capital of the Mezzogiorno (southern Italy); the city needs to revive itself before there can be any real progress in the fortunes of this very significant part of the country.

METRO ART

How the contemporary art scene went underground.

The innovative idea of creating a public art project within the stations of the Naples metro was born in the 1980s, but it wasn't until 2001 that the first *stazione dell'arte* – Museo – was opened. Curated by Achille Bonito and largely funded by EU money, the ongoing project has involved more than 100 artists and architects to date who have been commissioned to transform the stations into a city-wide museum for the 160,000 daily passengers. You can access this world-class collection for a mere €1.50, the price of a 90-minute metro ticket. All the stations mentioned below are on Line 1. For more details on the artworks, visit www.anm.it.

Start at **Garibaldi**, completed in 2013 by French architect Dominique Perrault. Here, the vast space is intersected by suspended escalators, at the bottom of which are Michelangelo Pistoletto's steel-and-mirror panels with images of waiting passengers.

Università (*pictured*) is the next stop, where Anglo-Egyptian Karim Rashid's joyous riot of bubble-gum colours, psychedelic designs and mirrors was inaugurated in 2011, a nod to the youthful energy of the students from the nearby university.

The newest station, **Municipio** (partially opened in June 2015), has been entrusted to Portuguese duo Álvaro Siza and Eduardo Souto de Moura, who have created a serene, minimalist space in dark grey and white using local volcanic stone. It incorporates the base of one of the round towers of the adjacent Castel Nuovo and will eventually be connected to the Stazione Marittima via a long corridor, which will hold finds from the Roman remains uncovered during the building work. It's due to be completed by the end of 2016.

Toledo (opened in 2013), designed by Catalan architect Oscar Tusquets Blanca, has been called one of the world's most beautiful stations. Here, the descent into the bowels of the city involves a jaw-dropping escalator ride that passes under Blanca's towering *Crater de luz* mosaic with a twinkling LED installation by Robert Wilson.

At **Dante** (2002), you're struck by Joseph Kosuth's neon-lit *Queste cose visibili* and then, at the bottom of the escalator, Jannis Kounellis's untitled piece where train tracks bisect the wall, crushing toy trains and abandoned shoes as they go. At Gae Aulenti's **Museo** stop (2001), the highlight is the Stazione Neapolis exhibition, showing Greek and Roman artefacts unearthed during the expansion of the metro system.

Materdei station houses a hotchpotch of pieces from Sol LeWitt's bright geometric murals and curvaceous plastic stalagmites to Luigi Ontani's fantastic mosaic at the exit. Next stop is **Salvator Rosa**, where works include Perino & Vele's weird, life-sized, veiled Fiat 500s. **Quattro Giornate** shows current Neapolitan artists. Look out for the image by artist Betty Bee peering out of a lightbox above one escalator.

Vettor Pisani's line of prehistoric animals occupies the mezzanine of **Vanvitelli** station, with two mosaics by Isabella Ducrot on the platforms. Descending the escalator into the station, you pass Mario Merz's final work: a spiral neon light representing the Fibonacci sequence.

Rione Alto, three stops away, is a bit of a trek, but its 120-metre (394-foot) corridor is an ideal space for lightbox installations by Bianco and Valente; polychrome panels by David Tremlett brighten up the mezzanine. Images by local artists cover the walls leading to the platforms; to complete the tour, leave the station to admire Antonio Tammaro's bronze statue and a fountain mosaic by Achille Cevoli.

Itineraries

Plot your perfect trip to Naples with our step-by-step planner.

9.30AM

11AM

2.30PM

Day 1

9.30AM Gird yourself for some serious sightseeing on your first day in Naples with a frothy cappuccino and flaky *sfogliatella* at **Gran Caffè Gambrinus** (p42, the grand dame of the city's cafés. Don't linger too long on the terrace, though, as the first major sight awaits in the shape of the splendid **Palazzo Reale** (p40) – before you go in, admire the statues of past kings of Naples that line the long façade.

11AM Opera buffs could then catch a tour of the world-famous **Teatro San Carlo** (p42) or, alternatively, you could follow in Alfonso I's footsteps and pass beneath the splendid, carved marble triumphal arch of the **Castel Nuovo** (p40) before taking the lift up one of the towers for views that take in the whole waterfront. Walk through the newly pristine **Piazza del Municipio** (p36) and past the restless **Fontana di Nettuno** (p41) en route to Via Toledo and a bit of window shopping.

2.30PM

Clockwise from left: **Gran Caffè Gambrinus**; **Toledo metro station**; **San Lorenzo Maggiore**; **Gesù Nuovo**.

Nip into **Palazzo Zevallos Stigliano** (p77) for a look at Caravaggio's last painting before going underground to ogle Oscar Tusquets Blanca's jaw-dropping **Toledo metro station** (p19). There's just time for a wander round the vibrant Pignasecca market for a touch of Neapolitan vernacular before lunch.

1.30PM The homely **Taverna del Buongustaio** (p80), which is hidden away down an alleyway behind lines of drying laundry, will provide a cheap, cheerful meal before heading into the ancient Centro Storico.

2.30PM Start in the church of **Gesù Nuovo** (p58), located at the western end of the Spaccanapoli (see p58), for an overdose of Neapolitan Baroque. By comparison, the church of **Santa Chiara** (p59), just to the east, is positively naked, although it has a florid maijolica-tiled cloister. Lively Piazza San Domenico sports one of Naples' ornate *guglie* spires and is also home to the famous **Scaturchio** *pasticceria* (p63). Further on, you'll see three brass skulls atop the railings outside **Santa Maria delle Amine del Purgatorio ad Arco** (p70): the hypogeum still contains a pile of venerated bones.

Next up is Via San Gregorio Armeno, which is packed with shops selling Christmas crib paraphernalia, even in August. You should be able to fit in a visit to the treasure-filled **Duomo** (p67) before walking back along Via dei Tribunali. The archaeological site under the church of **San Lorenzo Maggiore** (p69) reveals the fascinating remains of the old city, and the other must-see sight in the area is Sammartino's *Cristo Velato* in the **Cappella San Severo** (p58).

4.30PM There's time for a quick, restorative coffee at **Mexico** (p85) in Piazza Dante before hot-footing it to the **Museo Archeologico Nazionale** (p82; last entry is 6.30pm) for an ancient art feast.

7PM Aperitivo time: Piazza Bellini is the social hub of this area, so grab a café terrace table – **Intramoenia** (p71) is a good bet – and order a well-earned spritz. Hungry by now? For a blow-out dinner, book into Michelin-starred **Palazzo Petrucci** (p62). Alternatively, head back to Via dei Tribunali and the more down-to-earth Carmine. Either way, you're well placed to sample the after-dinner buzz in Piazza San Domenico.

Day 2

9.30AM Start the day up on Vomero hill with a visit to the huge **Certosa-Museo di San Martino** (p94); aside from its glorious art treasures, it also offers magnificent views. The nearby **Villa Floridiana** (p95) with its lovely park is another attraction up here. Peckish? Drop into **Frigittoria Vomero** (p98) for a deep-fried snack.

11.30AM Now catch the metro (line 1) from Vanvitelli to Museo (taking in more artwork en route) and then bus 168, R4 or C63 up to the church of **Santa Maria della Sanità** and the fascinating **Catacombe di San Gaudioso** (p86) where various early burial techniques are revealed.

1PM A pizza has to be involved at some point in any visit to Naples. **Pizzeria Oliva** (p87) serves one of the best in town and is a short walk through the heart of the sensory overload that is La Sanità. On your way back to the Cavour metro stop, pause to admire Ferdinando Sanfelice's trademark 'flying

staircase' at **Palazzo dello Spagnolo** (p85). Take the metro (line 2) to Amedeo and the upmarket, arty neighbourhood of Chiaia.

3PM Check out what's on offer at **PAN** (p102) before taking a stroll past the smart boutiques in Via dei Mille and Via dei Filangieri. **La Torteria** (p106) is a good place for a coffee-and-cake break. From here, it's not far to the Lungomare, Naples' sunny waterfront drag that extends past the **Castel dell'Ovo** (see p44). Huddling at its base is the pretty Borgo Marinari and the yacht marina.

5PM Time to head back to Chiaia and the network of attractive lanes to the west of Piazza dei Martiri for a spot of boutique shopping. Stop off at **Marinella** (p108) to drool over the gorgeous silk ties and then dive into **Feltrinelli** (p137) to pick up a copy of Elena Ferrante's bestselling *Neapolitan Novels*, before moving on to **Sapori e Dintorni** (p108) for local foodie treats. For clothes, have a look at the knitwear at **Amina Rubinacci** (p107) or Italian cashmere at **Capua** (p107), and then head to **Idem** (p108) for an interesting selection of clothes and accessories with a stylish, ethnic slant. **Ciro Ricci** (p107) is the place for handmade sandals.

7PM Chiaia, and its ever-shifting bar scene, is the place to be for an aperitivo. Established favourites include the likes of **Ba-bar** (p143), **Enoteca Belledonne** (p144) or **Happening** (p144), but you can also just dip into the place that most takes your

9.30AM

1PM

NAPLES FOR FREE
More sights, less euros.

HEAVENLY DEALS
Unlike several other important Italian tourist destinations (Venice and Florence, for example), Naples hasn't yet started charging for entry into its churches and there's an awful lot of them. Most are packed with art, so you could keep yourself happy for several days visiting not only the famous ones such as the Duomo, Santa Chiara and San Lorenzo, but also lesser-known gems like San Giovanni a Carbonara and Santa Maria della Sanità.

CUT-PRICE CULTURE
If your visit coincides with the first Sunday of the month, you can get into all the state museums in Naples (and, indeed, throughout Italy) free of charge. The only problem is that lots of locals will also be taking advantage of these free visits, so you may find endless queues.

GREEN SPACES
Naples has some wonderful public parks to escape to when city life becomes too much, and most of them are free. So stock up on goodies for a delicious picnic and head to the Villa Comunale, the Parco della Floridiana or the huge park surrounding the Museo di Capodimonte to wind down with an al fresco lunch and a snooze on the grass.

METRO ART
In Naples, your €1.50 metro ticket buys you entrance to a city-wide underground museum of contemporary art and architecture. Many of the metro stations are enhanced by site-specific works of art from such high-profile names as Gae Aulenti, Karim Rashid, Oscar Tusquets Blanca and William Kentridge. You get 90 minutes to tour the lot.

fancy. Some of the *aperitivi* buffets are substantial enough to make dinner, but if you're still hungry, try the fishy specialities at **Pescheria Mattiucci** (p105) or tuck into a plate of pasta at classic **Umberto** (p105).

10PM The bar scene in Chiaia morphs into a more clubby atmosphere as evening becomes night, but for something a little more low-key, wander back down to the Via Partenope waterfront with its many bars, restaurants and *gelaterie* and the moonlit seascape as a backdrop.

Left: **Villa Floridiana.**
Above: **Palazzo dello Spagnolo**.

Diary

*Plan your perfect
weekend with our
year-round guide.*

Naples loves a party and, as often as not in this deeply faith-driven city, it's the festivals with religious roots that prompt the most extravagant celebrations. Easter and the period between Christmas and Epiphany are hugely important, as are the thrice-yearly rituals involving the 'liquefaction' of the blood of San Gennaro (the city's patron saint). The celebrations for the feast day of the Madonna of Piedigrotta have developed way beyond religious rituals to include concerts, parades of allegorical floats and a singing contest. Secular events range from Wine & the City and the Pozzuoli Jazz Festival to the Napoli Teatro Festival Italia and Napoli Film Festival. May's Maggio dei Monumenti, which goes from strength to strength, allows a rare peek inside some of the city's most fascinating places, while the Naples Marathon gives fitness fiends something to work for. Events tend to come and go in this anarchic city, so confirm as close as possible to the scheduled date.

Settimana Santa.

Spring

Napoli Marathon
www.napolimarathon.it. **Date** late Feb/
early Mar.
Runners take to the streets for a full marathon, half
marathon, 4km fun run or leisurely walk.

Settimana Santa
*Various locations (081 557 4111,www.chiesa
dinapoli.it).* **Date** late Mar/Apr.
Easter week means processions and passion plays in
the streets and piazzas.

Festa di San Gennaro
*Duomo, Via del Duomo 147 (081 557 4111,
www.chiesadinapoli.it). Bus E1, R2.* **Date** 1st Sat
in May. **Map** p312 N7.
The first of three dates each year when the patron
saint's preserved blood is said to liquefy. Enormous
crowds gather to witness the phenomenon. *See also
p 72* **City of Blood**.

Wine & the City
Various locations (www.wineandthecity.it).
Date mid May.
The 2015 edition of this brilliant two-week festival
involved 130 venues across the whole city, from historic *palazzi* to boats, from hotels to churches and
architects' studios. The focus is wine tasting, of
course, but there are also food events, book readings,
lectures, tours, video installations and more.

Maggio dei Monumenti
*Various locations (Tourist office 081 410 7211,
www.comune.napoli.it).* **Date** May.
An impressive calendar of events, including tours,
lectures, concerts, exhibitions and access to monuments that are normally closed to the public. Many
of the events are free.

Vitigno Italia
Castel dell'Ovo (081 794 4608, www.vitignoitalia.it).
Date late May. **Map** p316 K15.
This major trade show attracts plenty of buyers
and producers from all over Italy for three days of
wine tastings.

Summer

Independent Film Show
*Museo Nitsch, Vico Lungo Pontecorvo 29D
(081 564 1655, www.em-arts.org). Metro Dante.*
Date late June. **Map** p312 K8.
This three-day international festival showcases
some three dozen independent films and videos.

Napoli Teatro Festival Italia
*Various locations (081 1956 0383, www.napoli
teatrofestival.it).* **Date** June-July.

PUBLIC HOLIDAYS

New Year's Day (Capodanno)
1 Jan

Epiphany (La Befana)
6 Jan

Easter Monday (Pasquetta)

Liberation Day (Festa della Liberazione)
25 Apr

Labour Day (Festa del Lavoro)
1 May

Republic Day (Festa della Repubblica)
2 June

Feast of the Assumption (Ferragosto)
15 Aug

**Feast of Saint Gennaro
(Festa di San Gennaro)**
19 Sept

All Saints' Day (Ognissanti)
1 Nov

**Feast of the Immaculate
Conception (L'Immacolata)**
8 Dec

Christmas Day (Natale)
25 Dec

Boxing Day (Santo Stefano)
26 Dec

Theatre, dance and musical shows, starring local and international performers, take place in venues across town.

Open Estate a Napoli
Various locations (Tourist office 081 410 7211, www.comune.napoli.it). **Date** June-Sept.
Open-air films, plays and concerts are on the agenda for the 'Summer in Naples' season; around 100 free events are staged across greater Naples.

Pozzuoli Jazz Festival
Various locations, Campi Flegrei (www. pozzuolijazzfestival.it). **Date** late June/July.
Three weeks of summer jazz, blues and soul from a range of Italian and international artists at venues in and around Pozzuoli and the Campi Flegrei, including the Solfatara, Tempio di Nettuno and Rione Terra.

Brividi d'Estate
Orto Botanico, Via Foria 223 (081 542 2088, www.ilpozzoeilpendolo.it). Metro Cavour or Museo, or bus 182,184, 201, C47. **Date** July, Sept. **Map** p313 O5.
Outdoor musical theatre performances, usually on a mystery or thriller theme, are staged in the Botanical Gardens most nights at 9pm.

Santa Maria del Carmine
Piazza del Carmine 2 (081 557 4111, www.chiesa dinapoli.it). Metro Porta Nolana, or bus 116, 154, 475, E2. **Date** 16 July. **Map** p313 P9.
Santa Maria del Carmine's well-attended feast day is celebrated with fireworks lighting up the belltower of the church.

Ferragosto
Various locations (Tourist office 081 410 7211, www.chiesadinapoli.it). **Date** 15 Aug.
The Feast of the Assumption is celebrated across the region; in Pozzuoli there's a slippery pole contest, followed by fireworks.

Autumn

Festa della Madonna di Piedigrotta
Various locations (081 214 0813, www.festa dipiedigrotta.it). **Date** early-mid Sept.
Although this is an important religious festival, there's also a ten-day programme of parades, floats, music, dancing, street festivals and performances to celebrate the feast day of the Madonna of Piedigrotta on 7 September.

Festa di San Gennaro
For listings, see p25. **Date** 19 Sept.
The blood of Naples' patron saint is said to liquefy once again during the Festa di San Gennaro, amid frantic praying in the Duomo.

Napoli Film Festival

Various locations (081 588 5688, www.napoli filmfestival.it). **Date** late Sept/early Oct.
The film festival's venue and duration vary from year to year; check online for the latest information. Tickets are modestly priced, ranging from €4 for a single film to €20 for a festival pass.

Piano City

Various locations (337 108 3100, www. pianocitynapoli.it). **Date** mid Oct.
Hundreds of concerts and events across three days celebrate the piano in a multitude of venues – some unusual (Stazione Centrale, the arrivals terminal at the airport, the *polidinico*), others more mainstream. House concerts are held in private living rooms.

Winter

Natale a Napoli

Various locations (081 557 4111, www.chiesa dinapoli.it). **Date** Nov-Dec.
Christmas is celebrated with a rich programme of free events, ranging from concerts and exhibitions to plays and parades. Few churches are without a crib; the 18th-century examples in the Certosa-Museo di San Martino (*see p94*) and the Palazzo Reale (*see p40*) are particularly fine.

Festa di San Gennaro

For listings, see p25. **Date** 16 Dec.
The blood of Naples' patron saint allegedly liquefies for a third time on 16 December, this time within the heightened cultural context brought on by the annual Christmas festivities.

Capodanno (New Year's Eve)

Piazza del Plebiscito (081 542 2090, www. comune.napoli.it). Metro Municipio, or bus C25, R2, E6. **Date** 31 Dec. **Map** p316 K13.
A concert of classical, traditional and rock music welcomes in the New Year, lasting well into the morning. There are fireworks over Castel dell'Ovo.

La Befana (Epiphany)

Piazza del Plebiscito (081 542 2090, www. comune.napoli.it). Bus C25, R2, E6. **Date** 6 Jan. **Map** p316 K13.
The old hag who brings gifts to good children and leaves charcoal in the shoes of bad ones descends from the sky to distribute her presents in Piazza del Plebiscito. There's also a free concert, held in a different venue each year.

'O Cippo di Sant'Antonio

Various locations. **Date** 17 Jan.
In many neighbourhoods, Neapolitans clear out all their unwanted belongings, pile them in the streets and piazzas and proceed to set them on fire (a *cippo* is a bonfire).

Carnevale

Various locations (081 542 2090, www.comune. napoli.it). **Date** Feb.
This masked celebration before the start of Lent is a shadow of its formerly riotous self, but children still don fancy dress and proudly parade around town.

Piano City.

Naples' Best

There's something for everyone with our hand-picked highlights.

Fontana dell'Immacolatella.

Sightseeing

VIEWS

Certosa-Museo di San Martino p94
Commanding vistas of the whole city and beyond.

Castel Nuovo p40
Bird's-eye view over the busy port area from the turrets.

Grand Hotel Vesuvio p277
Full-on views of the Castel dell'Ovo from the front rooms.

Hotel San Francesco al Monte p287
Views from all the rooms, plus a rooftop garden and pool.

Fontana dell' Immacolatella p44
The views take in the bay, Vesuvius, the Sorrentine peninsula all the way to Capri; best at sunrise.

ART

Museo di Capodimonte p90
The Farnese's fabulous haul.

Pinacoteca dei Girolamini p67
An under-visited gallery hung with works by the Neapolitan greats.

Pio Monte della Misericordia p68
Caravaggio's masterful *Seven Acts of Mercy* dominates a modest chapel.

Palazzo Zevallos Stigliano p77
Caravaggio's last painting hangs in splendid isolation on the top floor of a former bank.

Cimitero delle Fontanelle.

Metro stations p19
A city-wide gallery of world-class contemporary art and architecture.
MADRe p87
Naples' contemporary art museum is well worth a visit.
Hermann Nitsch Museum p77
Nitsch's splatter paintings and the relics of his mock crucifixions are housed in an a former power station.

CHURCHES
Duomo p67
Naples' magnificent cathedral dedicated to San Gennaro.
San Lorenzo Maggiore p69
A masterpiece of Angevin Gothic architecture.
San Gregorio Armeno p68
For over-the-top Neapolitan Baroque swagger.
San Giovanni a Carbonara p87
A little-visited church hiding some superb sculpture and charming frescoes.
Gesù Nuovo p58
Forbidding façade hides a lavish Baroque interior.

CLASSIC SIGHTS
Museo Archeologico p82
One of the world's great collections of ancient art and artefacts.
Cristo Velato p58
Sammartino's virtuosic sculpture.
Castel dell'Ovo p44
A Neapolitan icon.
Castel Nuovo p40
The Angevin stronghold that today houses the municipal offices.
Palazzo Reale p40
Splendid seat of Neapolitan Kings.
Certosa-Museo di San Martino p94
Hilltop monastery complex.

WHAT LIES BENEATH
Catacombe di San Gennaro p90
San Gennaro's burial place.
San Lorenzo archaeological site p68
Discover the layers of Naples' history.
Napoli Sotteranea p68
Explore a fascinating maze of underground tunnels, water cisterns and aqueducts.
Cimitero delle Fontanelle p84
An underground burial chamber that houses 40,000 skeletons.

CHILDREN
Stazione Zoologica p102
A delightfully old-fashioned aquarium.
Liberty City Fun p127
Trampolines, carousels and pirate boats in the suburbs.
The Solfatara p115
Hissing fumaroles and bubbling mud in the Campi Flegrei.
Città della Scienza p127
A brilliant hands-on science museum.
A swim in the sea p128
When temperatures rise in the city, take the kids to the beach.

Eating & Drinking

FISHY FAVOURITES
Baccalaria p302
A temple to salt cod.
Pescheria Mattiucci p105
A bright and breezy hole-in-the-wall with a daily-changing menu.
Mimì alla Ferrovia p49
A Neapolitan stalwart with reliable classics.

Il Commandante

Crudo Rè p104
Platters of *crudo* (raw fish) and spaghetti with razor clams.
Dora p105
A tiny restaurant where the no-fuss fish dishes are as good as they get.
Il Piccolo Ristoro p55
This port-side place offers one of the cheapest fish deals in town.

CHEAP & CHEERFUL NEAPOLITAN
Osteria Da Tonino p105
Traditional food and plenty of atmosphere.
Nennella p80
Good home cooking in the Quartieri Spagnoli.
Antica Trattoria da Carmine p70
Wholesome food and central location are the strong points at this family-run place.
Osteria Donna Teresa p95
Exemplary home cooking on Vomero hill.
Friggitoria-Pizzeria Giuliano p62
For delicious, sizzling hot deep-fried goodies.

PIZZA
Da Michele p49
No frills but this is one of Naples' best.
50 Kalò p109
Ciro Salvo claims that his pizza is more digestible than most.
Concettina ai Tre Santi-Pizzeria Oliva p87
Dynamic young *pizzaiolo* Ciro Oliva's Sanità outpost.
Pizzeria Starita p87
This historic pizzeria featured in *L'Oro di Napoli.*
Sorbillo p70
For Gino Sorbillo's near-perfect pizza.

WITH A CREATIVE TWIST
Veritas p105
Campanian dishes with a light touch and creative edge.
Ristorante dell'Avvocato p45
Seriously good inventive dishes at this cozy Santa Lucia address.
La Stanza del Gusto p71
Mario Avallone's Tasting Room was one of the first true gourmet outposts in the city.

Anhelo p104
Stylish little tapas bar and bistro with excellent coffee to boot.

PUSH THE BOAT OUT
Sud p123
Marianna Vitale works Michelin-starred miracles in the boondocks.
Palazzo Petrucci p62
Lino Scarello's seriously good, inventive cooking has won him a Michelin star.
Il Commandante p55
Two Michelin-starred; Salvatore Bianco's culinary pyrotechnics plus all the bells and whistles.

COFFEE
Buona Merenda p62
This buzzy modern coffee bar serves up Anhelo's own-roast beans.
Mexico p85
A Naples institution, the retro Mexico makes one of the best *espressi* in the city.
Gran Caffè Gambrinus p42
The coffee at this celebrated watering hole comes with large lashings of belle époque elegance.

FOR A SWEET TOOTH
Attanasio Sfogliatelle Calde p52
Stupendous *sfogliatelle* near the station.
La Tortiera p106
Be tempted by delicious ice cream-stuffed fruit and frozen cakes.
Moccia p106
A Chiaia classic: try the *fungo al cioccolato.*
Gelateria della Scimmia p80
Chocolate-covered banana *gelato* is the speciality of popular ice-cream parlour the Monkey.

Shopping

FOOD & DRINK

Mercato Pignasecca p82
A rowdy and exuberant slice
of Neapolitan life.
Sapori e Dintorni p108
An excellent food and
wine emporium.
Enoteca Dante p85
For a good selection of
keenly-priced wines from
Campania and beyond.
Leopoldo p81
This is where to buy the
best *taralli* in Naples.
Caseari Cautero p80
Top-notch gourmet goodies
from all over Italy.
Gay-Odin p63
Wonderful old chocolate
and confectionery shop.

GIFTS & SOUVENIRS

Marinella p108
Bespoke silk ties favoured
by kings and presidents.
Mario Talarico p81
Handmade brollies that
will last a lifetime.
Fratelli Tramontano p43
Quality, handmade leather
goods from a family firm.
Scriptura p65
Handbags and leather
accessories, plus leather-
bound books and albums.

Museum Shop p64
The place to come for museum-
related souvenirs.
Contemporastudio p107
Funky modern jewellery often
with a Neapolitan theme.
Campobasso p107
Beautiful antique *presepii*.
**Via San Gregorio
Armeno** p67
Everything you'll need
for a Neapolitan-style
nativity extravaganza.

Nightlife

APERITIVO BARS

Ba-bar p105
Cosy café-restaurant by
day, cocktail and music bar
by night.
Libreria Berisio p139
Cocktails and dancing among
the bookshelves.
Cammarota Spritz p140
Tiny Quartieri Spagnoli
drinking dive with cheap-
as-chips spritz.
Enoteca Belledonne p144
An old favourite for
wine buffs.

CLUBS & LATE BARS

Galleria 19 p139
A cool club in the
Centro Storico.

Gran Caffè Gambrinus.

Happening p144
Slick bar with DJ and dancing.
Be Bop p144
Vintage vibe and sounds.
Nabilah p141
Classy summer hangout and
club down on the beach.
Arenile p141
Year-round waterside club.

LIVE MUSIC

Bourbon Street p140
Classic jazz venue.
Lanificio25 p139
Performance space in
an ex-convent close to
Porta Capuana.
Pozzuoli Jazz Festival p145
Jazz performances in the
Burning Fields.
Galleria Toledo p140
An innovative theatre with
regular live music slots.

Performing Arts

Teatro San Carlo p148
Catch a performance at Italy's
most lavish opera house.
Associazione Scarlatti p149
Follow this excellent series of
classical music concerts.
Napoli Teatro Festival p150
Itinerant theatre and
dance festival with some
performances in their
original language.

Mercato Pignasecca.

Explore

Royal Naples & Monte Echia

EXPLORE

Naples is one of the oldest cities in the western world and it was here, on the tiny island of Megaris, now occupied by the Castel dell'Ovo, that Parthenope – later Neapolis – was founded more than 2,500 years ago. Legend has it that sailors found the body of the siren Parthenope washed up on this shore after she drowned herself, having been jilted by Ulysses. The mariners buried her on the rock, and the settlement was established. For over a thousand years, this was the centre of monarchic power. Now it has become a mishmash of historical sites, hotels, shops and low-rent housing. Still, there's no better spot to watch the sun rise behind Vesuvius than by the Fontana dell'Immacolatella.

Castel Nuovo.

Don't Miss

1 Castel Nuovo The civic museum and the serene Capella Palatina (p40).

2 Palazzo Reale Sumptuous apartments and hanging gardens (p40).

3 Teatro San Carlo One of the finest opera houses in Italy (p42).

4 Castel dell'Ovo Naples' oldest castle and an ancient fishing hamlet (p44).

5 Evening stroll along the seafront Essential to any Naples visit (p44).

EXPLORE

ROYAL NAPLES

Start at the vast, neoclassical **Piazza del Plebiscito**, one of the most splendid *piazze* in Italy, if not Europe. Until 1994, it was a grimy, oil-streaked expanse of tarmac used as a bus depot and car park. Restored to its former glory, complete with a new surface of local volcanic cobblestones, it's now traffic-free. This is a key site for major events: concerts, political rallies, New Year's Eve parties, an annual Christmas art installation and a horse show in May.

The piazza is dominated by the church of **San Francesco di Paola** (*see p41*) and the **Palazzo Reale** (*see p40*). The semicircular colonnade with Doric columns that adorns this stately piazza was begun in 1809 under French ruler Joaquim Murat; San Francesco di Paola was added later by the restored Bourbon monarchy in thanks for the end of the French occupation. The bronze equestrian statues of Bourbon kings Carlo III and Ferdinando I are by Antonio Canova.

Adjoining Piazza del Plebiscito to the north-east, Piazza Trieste e Trento is home to Naples' most elegant watering hole, the **Gambrinus** – a favourite of Oscar Wilde. Guided tours of the 16th-century underground water system, the **Acquedotto Carmignano**, depart from here. Also in the square is the church of **San Ferdinando** (open 8am-noon, 5-7pm Mon-Sat; 9.30am-1pm Sun), which has scenes from the lives of illustrious Jesuits on its ceiling and some fine 19th-century marblework by Tito Angelini and the Vaccaros in the chapel in the left transept.

Leading west out of the square, Via Chiaia is packed with clothes shops of varying quality, cheap ice-cream parlours and, a new phenomenon in Naples, chip bars. Amorous athlete and supreme self-publicist Giacomo Casanova, and the infinitely more serious German poet Johann Wolfgang von Goethe, both stayed at the imposing **Palazzo Cellamare** (no.149; closed to the public) in the 18th century – though not at the same time.

Pedestrianised, shop-lined Via Toledo leads north from the square; on its right-hand side is the entrance to the magnificent **Galleria Umberto I**. This steel-and-glass cross-shaped arcade was completed in 1890, and generally compares favourably with its slightly older counterpart, the Galleria Vittorio Emanuele II in Milan; unlike its Milanese twin, the mosaic bull under the central dome has no testicles. During a World War II air raid, all the glass was blown out of the massive dome. The former sleazy air of the place has diminished, allowing visitors to better enjoy the elaborate neo-Renaissance decorations and fine engineering. Tragically, a 14-year old boy was killed here by falling masonary in July 2014, which prompted the authorities to undertake major engineering work to secure the building and make sure that such an event never happens again.

Heading east out of Piazza Trieste e Trento, Via San Carlo leads past the illustrious **Teatro San Carlo** royal opera house (*see p42*) and the gardens of the **Palazzo Reale**, and into the **Piazza del Municipio**. On the southern side of the piazza rise the darkly majestic towers of the 13th-century **Castel Nuovo**.

At its northern end, the early 19th-century **Palazzo San Giacomo** was built to house the massive bureaucracy of the Bourbon monarchs. Today, it's the headquarters of the Naples city council, and a magnet for all kinds of protesters.

A large arched, wrought-iron gate to the right of the municipal headquarters leads to the charmingly royalist 16th-century church of **San Giacomo degli Spagnoli**. Behind the altar, the tomb of Spanish viceroy Don Pedro di Toledo sits amid the crumbling remains of a very theatrical chapel. If you can find the sacristan, ask him for the keys.

The centre of Piazza del Municipio has long been a mess of construction and archaeological digs. Work on the new metro line has been going on for years; in 2004, workmen turned up the remains of the old Roman harbour and three ancient ships, which slowed things down even more. However, the massive urban renewal plan drawn up by Portuguese architect Alvaro Siza is now partially complete. The upper part of the vast piazza has been beautifully remodelled and now has as its centrepiece the famously wandering 15th-century **Fontana Nettuno** (*see p41* **In the Know**): the finished square will incorporate part of the excavations for all to see. The first phase of the long-awaited Municipio metro station opened in June 2015; it will eventually be connected to the Stazione Marittima via a long, subterranean museum-gallery where artefacts recovered from the archaeological site (including several of the boats) will be displayed.

On the western side of Via Medina stands the deconsecrated church of **Santa Maria Incoronata** (open 9am-6pm Mon-Sat). Adapted from a courthouse in the 14th century to commemorate the coronation of Angevin Queen Joan I, the church was reputedly a favourite with Petrarch, Boccaccio and Giotto. Inside, frescoes by Giotto's pupil Roberto Oderisi show scenes from the coronation.

On the opposite side of the street, the **Pietà dei Turchini** church (081 552 0457 open 7.15am-1.45pm, 5-8pm daily) started life as a poorhouse, where children were dressed in turquoise shifts. The imposing police headquarters (*Questura*), at the end of the street on the left, dates from the Fascist era, as does the post office beyond.

In front of the Castel Nuovo is the main port, Beverello, and the 1930s **Stazione Marittima** – the departure point for ferries to Sicily, Sardinia, North Africa and elsewhere. From the port, public transport heads west past the military

WALK A RIGHT ROYAL PROMENADE

Begin at the **Castel Nuovo** (see p40). Don't miss the chance for a dip underground to see the spectacular new Municipio metro station. Head north out of Piazza del Municipio and along Via Santa Brigida, ducking into the massive **Galleria Umberto I** (see p36), and on to the famous **Teatro San Carlo** (see p42).

From here, a short stroll will take you into Piazza Trieste e Trento with its grand watering hole, **Gran Caffè Gambrinus** (see p42), and on past the **Palazzo Reale** (see p40), where you can visit the Royal Apartments or check out the gardens. Swing around to the front of the palace, where you'll feel dwarfed by the kingly effigies sitting in niches along its façade, as well as by the wide sweep of Piazza del Plebiscito. After a peek into the church of **San Francesco di Paola** (see p41), cross the square to Via Cesario Console. Here,

a narrow park looks over the Giardini Pubblici and across the bay to Mount Vesuvius.

Take Via Nazario Sauro along the seafront, and you'll arrive at the scene of the classic Naples *passeggiata*: past luxury hotels, the **Castel dell'Ovo** (see p44) and **Megaris** (see p44), then ranks of waterside restaurants and on to the gardens of the **Villa Comunale** (see p104), rife with classical statuary.

When you come to the **Acquario** (see p102), follow Via San Pasquale a Chiaia into the upmarket district of **Chiaia** (see p102). Keep heading up until you get to picturesque Piazza Amedeo. From here, you can take the *funicolare* up to the **Vomero** neighbourhood (see p92) or, alternatively, stroll back along chic Via dei Mille to Piazza dei Martiri, and eventually back to Piazza del Plebiscito and on into the Centro Storico.

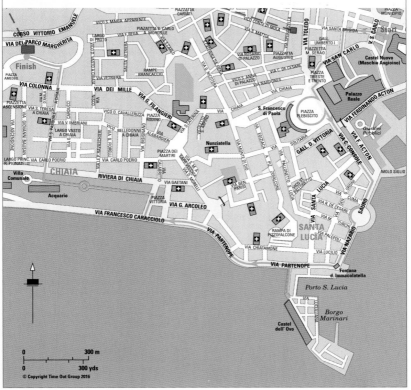

© Copyright Time Out Group 2016

EXPLORE

EXPLORE

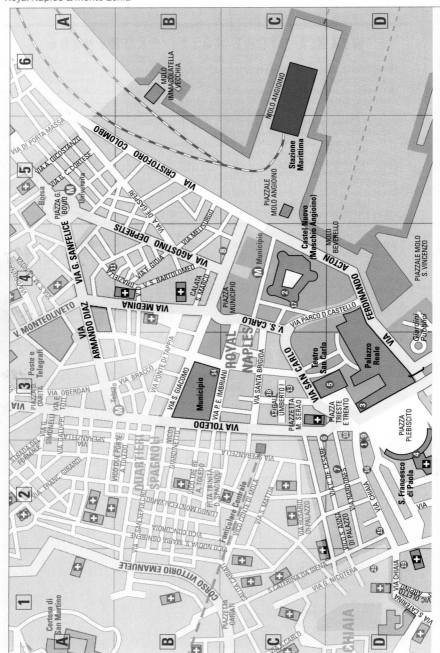

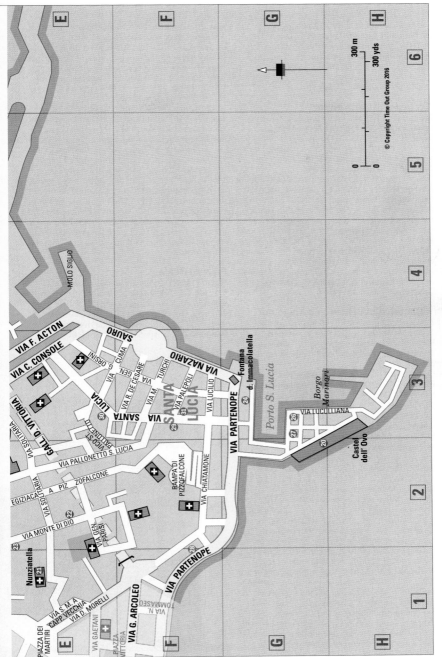

EXPLORE

© Copyright Time Out Group 2016

and tourist harbour and run-down public gardens, and through the smoggy Galleria della Vittoria tunnel. Hop out at the end by the offices of *Il Mattino*, Naples' newspaper, and head into the Santa Lucia neighbourhood (*see p45*).

Sights & Museums

Acquedotto Carmignano

Bar Gambrinus, Via Chiaia 1-2 (081 400256, www.lanapolisotterranea.it). Metro Municipio, or bus R2, C25, 140, 154. **Open** *Guided tours only* 9pm Thur; 10am, noon, 6pm Sat; 10am, 11am, noon, 6pm Sun. **Admission** €10; €5 reductions. **No credit cards. Map** p38 D2 ❶

Naples' historic infrastructure extends for miles beneath the city centre, at a depth of 40m (130ft) or more. A maze of water ducts and cisterns dug into the rock during the 16th and 17th centuries, the Carmignano drainage system was developed under the Spanish viceroys; the volcanic *tufa* rock that was extracted was used to build the houses above. The tunnels were in use until the disastrous cholera epidemic of 1884, and also acted as air-raid shelters during World War II. The guided tour lasts around an hour, but isn't suitable for claustrophobes. Advance booking not required.

★ Castel Nuovo (Maschio Angioino)

Piazza del Municipio (081 795 58778). Metro Municipio, or bus R2, C25, 140, 154. **Open** 9am-7pm Mon-Sat (last entry 6pm). **Admission** €6; free under-18s & over-65s. **No credit cards. Map** p38 C4 ❷

Called *nuovo* (new) to distinguish it from the older Castel dell'Ovo, this castle is better known locally as the Maschio Angioino (Angevin stronghold). It was built in 1279 by Charles of Anjou and used by subsequent Angevin monarchs as a royal residence and fortress. It also became a centre of arts and literature, attracting such illustrious characters as Petrarch, Boccaccio (some of the best tales of the *Decameron* are set in Naples) and Giotto, who frescoed the main hall and chapel around 1330.

Precious little of Giotto's work remains. The castle's current appearance is the result of radical alterations that were carried out by the Aragonese monarchs in the mid 15th century; the splendid triumphal arch was added for the entry into the city of Alfonso I 'the Magnanimous' of Aragon in 1443, a scene that is depicted in the relief above the portal. Subsequent changes to the interior decoration of the palace occurred during the reign of the Viceroy.

The castle has housed Naples' *museo civico* since 1992, with access via an internal courtyard after the ticket office. In the far left-hand corner of the enclosure, an area of glass flooring allows visitors to examine a number of ancient finds that include the foundations and cemetery areas (replete with skeletons) of a convent that considerably pre-dates the castle itself. From the courtyard – which is

now graced with a monumental bronze helmet by Mimmo Paladino – an adjacent staircase leads to the Sala dei Baroni, named after the mutinous barons arrested here while conspiring against King Ferrante in 1486. Giotto's frescoes may have disappeared; not so the unusual, umbrella-vaulted ceiling that now hovers dramatically over Naples City Council meetings.

The plain yet elegant Cappella Palatina, also shorn of its Giottos (bar tiny traces in the embrasure of the right-hand apsidal window), is the only section of the castle that remains from the Angevin period.

The *museo civico* is housed on two floors. The first floor contains paintings from the 15th century to the 18th century, with much local colour; the second floor houses 19th- and 20th-century works by Neapolitan artists. There's also a fine bronze door, commissioned in 1475 by the Aragonese to commemorate their victory over the Angevins (the embedded cannonball probably dates from a sea battle off Genoa in 1495, when the door was being shipped to France). Don't miss the views from the fortress towers.

Palazzo Reale

Piazza Trieste e Trento & Piazza del Plebiscito 1 (081 580 8111, 081 400547, www.palazzoreale napoli.it). Metro Municipio, or bus R2, R4, C25, 140, 152. **Open** 9am-8pm Mon, Tue, Thur-Sun (last entry 7pm). **Admission** €4; €3 reductions; free under-18s & over-65s. **Map** p38 D3 ❸

Castel Nuovo.

Work on the Royal Palace started in 1600, under the rule of the Spanish viceroys, by Neapolitan architect Domenico Fontana. The bulk of the palazzo was completed in two years, although a number of features (such as the staircase) were added 50 years later. The Bourbon monarchs had the building extended eastwards in the mid 18th century, when niches were added to the façade. Under French rule in the early 19th century, the interior took on its current neoclassical appearance, and the hanging gardens and statues of Naples' kings were added later that century.

The ticket office is on the left-hand side of the portico that skirts Piazza del Plebescito, with access to the 30 royal apartments through the bookshop. The apartments, overwhelming in size and number, house a collection of paintings, frescoes, tapestries, chandeliers and furniture from the 17th to the 19th centuries. The gilt-and-stucco ceilings are impressive, as is the gloriously ornate Teatrino di Corte (1768), a private theatre. The pleasant roof garden features flowerbeds, fountains and neoclassical benches.

The Palazzo Reale also houses the Biblioteca Nazionale (081 781 9111, www.bnnonline.it) national library, with its grand reading rooms and collections of manuscripts and musty books, some dating to the fifth century. There's also a tourist office just off the Cortile d'Onore, open on weekdays only and stocked with excellent leaflets. The gardens within the palace complex, dotted with modern sculpture, offer a quieter alternative to the nearby Giardini Publici (open 8.30am-7pm Mon-Fri, 8.30am-1.30pm Sat).

IN THE KNOW ON THE MOVE

Built in 1601, the **Fontana Nettuno** in Piazza del Municipio has a history of restless wandering. It was originally in the Arsenale in the port area, but in 1629 was moved to Piazza del Plebiscito. It then upped sticks to Borgo Santa Lucia. Next stop was Via Medina where it was damaged in the 1647 Masaniello revolt. There then followed two more centuries of itinerant life before the fountain was dismantled in 1886. Two years later, it was reassembled in Piazza Bovio where it remained until 2000. After another stint in Via Medina, it was moved in 2015 to what will hopefully be its final resting place.

FREE San Francesco di Paola

Piazza del Plebiscito (346 270 2576, www.santuario paola.it). Metro Municipio, or bus R2, R4, C25, 140, 152. **Open** *Apr-June, Sept, Oct* 6.30am-7pm daily. *July, Aug* 6.30am-8pm daily. *Nov-Mar* 6.30am-6pm daily. **Admission** free. **Map** p38 D2 ❹

One of the few neoclassical buildings in Naples, the church of San Francesco was commissioned by King Ferdinando in 1817 in thanks for the repossession of his kingdom after the period of French rule, and designed by Swiss architect Pietro Bianchi. Flanked by a hemicycle of curving colonnades reminiscent

EXPLORE

EXPLORE

IN THE KNOW VIRGIL'S EGG

The Castel dell'Ovo gets its name from a local legend concerning the poet Virgil. When he stayed here during the first century BC, it's said that he placed an egg (*uovo*) in a glass carafe and then locked the carafe in a cage suspended from the roof of a tunnel below the castle. The poet predicted that when the egg broke disaster would strike.

of Saint Peter's square, the church itself is an imitation of Rome's Pantheon. It takes its name from a saint who, conveniently, came from the town of Paola in Calabria, near to where Joaquim Murat – Napoleon's brother-in-law and Naples' king from 1808 to 1815 – had been shot by Ferdinando's police after an ill-fated attempt to lead an Italian uprising. The apex of the dome stands 53m (174ft) above the ground – ten metres higher than its Roman counterpart.

★ Teatro San Carlo
For listings, see p149. **Map** p38 D3 **5**
One of Italy's grandest opera houses, the original San Carlo theatre was built in 1737 in just eight months, to a design by Giovanni Medrano; after it burned down in 1816, it was rebuilt in less than a year. Second in prestige only to Milan's La Scala, the San Carlo has lavish decor with acres of red velvet and intricate gilded stucco moulding, and an unusual revolving clock in the vault of the proscenium arch. A century and a half ago, foreign tourists complained of the noise during performances – the local aristocracy would chat, eat meals and play cards in the boxes. Guided tours in English and Italian (booking advised) are offered daily (081 797 2468, €3-€6) subject to rehearsals and performances. Alternatively, get dressed up in your poshest togs and catch a performance.

Restaurants

€ Pizza Fritta Sorbillo
Piazza Trieste e Trento 53 (081 416306, www. sorbillo.it). Metro Municipio, or bus 140, 152, C25, R2, R4. **Open** 11.30am-10pm Mon-Fri; 11.30am-11pm Sat, Sun. **Average** €5. **Map** p38 C3 **6** *Pizzeria*
It's standing room only at celebrity *pizzaiuolo* Gino Sorbillo's tiny latest opening, so the fried pizza-munching crowds spill on to the pavement at peak times. *Pizza fritta* is a Neapolitan fast-food speciality that must be tried at least once, so throw caution (and calorie-counting) to the wind and dig in. Top-notch ingredients go into the folded-over dough that's stuffed with the likes of *ciccioli* (pancetta bits), mozzarella, ricotta, provola and tomato, and then deep-fried. Healthy? No. Tasty? Very.

Trattoria San Ferdinando
Via Nardones 117, Piazza Trieste e Trento (081 421964). Metro Municipio, or bus R2, R4, C25, 140, 152. **Open** 12.30-3pm Mon, Sat; 12.30-3pm, 7.30-11pm Tue-Fri. Closed 3wks Aug. **Average** €35. **Map** p38 D2 **7** *Trattoria*
The Bruno family's delightful little trattoria is popular among locals, as well as musicians performing at the nearby Teatro San Carlo (check out the opera memorabilia hanging from the yellow walls). The handwritten, regularly-changing menu might include a classic (but excellent) *spaghetti alle vongole* or risotto with asparagus and prawns among the *primi*, followed by the house speciality, *baccalà* (salt cod), or stuffed squid. Homemade desserts – pear and ricotta tart, perhaps – are delicious, and there are some fine local wines on offer.

Cafés, Bars & Gelaterie

Il Chicco d'Oro
Piazza Municipio 73 (081 1890 8296, www. ilchiccodoro.it). Metro Municipio, or bus 151, 154. **Open** 5.30am-2am daily. **Map** p38 C4 **8**
This large, smart new bar matches large, smart new Piazza Municipio. Its pre-dawn opening time makes it a good breakfast place if you're catching an early ferry; the coffee is delicious and there's a wide choice of fresh cakes and pastries. Later on, there's a menu of hot and cold dishes, and a help-yourself salad bar. There's free Wi-Fi too.

Gran Caffè Gambrinus
Via Chiaia 1-2 (081 417582, www.grancaffe gambrinus.it). Metro Municipio or Toledo, or bus R2, E6. **Open** 7am-1am Mon-Thur, Sun; 7am-2am Fri, Sat. **Map** p38 D3 **9**
This grand café has a gloriously flouncy art nouveau interior, an elegant pavement terrace and a distinguished history. Established over a century ago, former clients include Oscar Wilde. In the 1930s, the government closed down certain rooms that were the haunt of left-wing intellectuals, but these days you'll find more fur coats than anti-fascists. It's expensive and service can be brusque, but it's a classic spot for a coffee or an *aperitivo* and the location is very convenient, especially if you're headed for the Teatro San Carlo (*see left*).

Il Vero Bar del Professore
Piazza Trieste e Trento 46 (081 403041, www. ilverobardelprofessore.com). Metro Municipio or Toledo, or bus R2, E6. **Open** 6.30am-2am Mon-Fri, Sun; 6.30am-3am Sat. **Map** p38 D3 **10**
A cheap-and-cheerful alternative to Gambrinus (*see above*), this famous place may have somewhat cramped tables outside, but there are 63 types of coffee on offer, including house specialities *caffè alla nocciola* (hazelnut coffee) and *caffè al cioccolato* (chocolate coffee). One of the delicious *sfogliatelle* makes a perfect accompaniment.

Shops & Services

L'Antico
*Vico Graziella 14 (081 551 0582). Metro Università
or Municipio, or bus C25, R2, R4.* **Open** 7am-3pm
Mon-Fri; 7am-noon Sat. Closed Aug. **No credit
cards. Map** p38 A4 ⑪ **Antiques**
On a dingy alley lined with metal-working ateliers,
L'Antico's cavernous premises are stuffed with
antiques (both repro and genuine) of every description, from Greco-Roman bronzes to Capodimonte
porcelains. Quality is high and prices are low.

Ascione
*Piazzetta Matilde Serao 19, Galleria Umberto I
(081 421 1111, www.ascione.it). Metro Municipio
or Toledo, or bus R1, R2, R4, C25.* **Open** 4-7.30pm
Mon; 10.30am-2pm, 4-7.30pm Tue-Sat. Closed 3wks
Aug. **Map** p38 C3 ⑫ **Jewellery**
Since 1855, the Ascione family has been one of the
region's pre-eminent makers of coral jewellery. Some
of the finest examples are showcased at this exclusive shop. Call ahead for an appointment to view the
store's private collection, a veritable museum.

Box Office
*Galleria Umberto I 17 (081 551 9188, www.
boxofficenapoli.it). Metro Municipio or Toledo,
or funicular Centrale to Augusteo, or bus C25,
R2, E6.* **Open** 9am-8pm Mon-Fri; 10am-1.30pm,
4.30-8pm Sat. Closed 1wk Aug. **Map** p38 C3
⑬ **Ticket agency**
A convenient place to pick up tickets for concerts
and opera, theatre, sports events and just about
everything else that happens in Naples.

Farmacia d'Arti
*Piazza Municipio 15 (081 552 4237). Metro
Municipio, or bus R2, C25, 140, 154.* **Open** 8.30am-
2pm, 3-8pm Mon-Fri & every other Sat. Closed 2wks
Aug. **Map** p38 B3 ⑭ **Health & beauty**
Homeopathic products are a speciality at this well-
stocked pharmacy and the staff speak English.

Fratelli Tramontano
*Via Chiaia 142-143 (081 414837, www.aldo
tramontano.it). Metro Toledo, or bus C25, R4.*
Open 10am-1.30pm, 4-8pm Mon-Fri; 10am-2pm
Sat. **Map** p38 D2 ⑮ **Accessories**
This is the place to come for quality handmade
leather goods: handbags and luggage, shoes, wallets,
belts and other accessories.

Galleria Fonti
*Via Chiaia 229 (081 411409, www.galleriafonti.it).
Metro Toledo, or bus C25, R4.* **Open** 4.30-7.30pm
Tue-Fri. Closed Aug. **Map** p38 D2 ⑯ **Gallery**
Giangi Fonti's small upstairs space is located on bus-
tling, pedestrianised Via Chiaia. Artists on display
include conceptualist Piero Golia, a Neapolitan who
lives in Los Angeles.

Mercato dei Fiori
*Castel Nuovo, nr Piazza Municipio. Metro
Municipio, or bus R2, C25, 140, 154.* **Open**
dawn-9am daily. **Map** p38 C4 ⑰ **Market**
Tucked beside the Castel Nuovo, this early morning
market features verdant displays of flowers and
plants. Florists shop here and bargains abound.

Sephora
*Galleria Umberto I 31-33 (081 420 2165, 081
552 6677, www.sephora.com). Metro Municipio
or Toledo, or funicular Centrale to Augusteo,
bus C25, R2, E6.* **Open** 9.30am-8pm Mon-Sat.
Map p38 C3 ⑱ **Health & beauty**
Try out perfume, eyeshadow and powders to your
heart's content at this branch of Sephora.

Siola
*Via Chiaia 111-115 (081 412580, 081 415036).
Metro Toledo, or bus C25, R4.* **Open** 9.30am-8pm
Mon-Sat; 10am-1.30pm, 5-8pm Sun. **Map** p38 D1
⑲ **Children's fashion**
Expect upmarket children's clothes, with price tags
to match: top Italian brands such as Blumarine and
I Pinco Pallino, as well as Armani Junior & Twin Set.

MONTE ECHIA & AROUND

The remains of the crater rim of an extinct volcano
– and the site of ancient Paleopolis – **Monte
Echia** rises to the south-west behind Piazza del
Plebiscito. A 20-minute walk from the piazza, up
Via Egiziaca a Pizzofalcone and steep salita Echia,
brings you to the scruffy public gardens at the top.
From here, you can see the sinister observation
posts of the modern police headquarters, as well
as bask in a rather cluttered but glorious view of
one of the cradles of Western civilisation.

On the northern side of the hill, Pizzofalcone is
home to more military and police establishments,
including the huge, red-painted citadel of the
Nunziatella military academy, with its Baroque
church. Founded in 1787 to produce officers for
the kingdom of Naples, La Nunziatella is Italy's
oldest military academy and still trains cadets,
both men and women. Here, too, is the rather
melancholic Palazzo Serra di Cassano and the
early 17th-century churches of **Santa Maria
degli Angeli** (Largo Santa Maria degli Angeli,
081 440756, open 8am-2pm, 5-8pm Mon-Sat,
8am-2pm Sun) and **Santa Maria Egiziaca a
Pizzofalcone** (Via Egiziaca, 081 764 5199, open
10am-1pm, 5.30-7.30pm Mon-Sat; 5.30-7.30pm
Sun). The former has an enormous dome (not
immediately visible from the road), a splendid
barrel-vaulted ceiling and, in the first chapel on
the right, two marble reliefs by Tito Angelini.

From Monte Echia, the rampa di Pizzofalcone
zigzags down towards the Castel dell'Ovo. You
can savour Naples' briny side as you inhale
seafood smells wafting from the waterfront

EXPLORE

restaurants and admire the yachts packed into the marina on the island of **Megaris**. On the seafront, newly pedestrianised Via Partenope and Via Sauro skirt the Santa Lucia district, then pass by Pietro Bernini and Michelangelo Naccherino's **Fontana dell'Immacolatella** (1601) and back to Piazza del Plebiscito.

Sights & Museums

ᴵᴿᴱᴱ Castel dell'Ovo
Via Eldorado 3, Borgo Marinari & Via Partenope (081 795 4593, www.castel-dell-ovo.com). Bus 140, C25, 151. **Open** 9am-7.30pm Mon-Sat; 9am-2pm Sun. **Admission** free. **Map** p39 G2 ⓴
Castel dell'Ovo lies on the tiny island of Megaris. The Aragonese gave the fortress its present look in the 16th century. Prior to that, it was home to a monastic community. Earlier still, it was part of the estate of Roman general Lucullus. After crossing the bridge from Via Partenope, pass through the main portal and either climb up to the right or bear left along to the far end of the *mole* (breakwater), where the gun emplacements used to stand. It's a strangely deserted spot, with Naples almost completely hidden from view by the castle. The rooms leading off the long climb up the ramp inside the castle itself are a mix of offices and exhibition areas; some are still being excavated and restored and are only visible through glass.

At the foot of the castle lie the yacht marina and the picturesque fishing hamlet of Borgo Marinari,

Palazzo Serra di Cassano.

with its cluster of bars and restaurants. Feeling light years away from the city centre chaos, it makes a romantic spot for *aperitivi* and dinner.
► *Watch out for Vitigno Italia, the annual wine event held here each May (www.vitignoitalia.it).*

ᴵᴿᴱᴱ La Nunziatella
Via Generale Parisi 16 (081 764 1520). Metro Toledo, or bus E6. **Open** Mass 9-10am Sun; other times by appt. **Admission** free. **Map** p39 E1 ㉑
This pocket-sized Baroque jewel belongs to the adjacent military academy, which was founded by the Bourbon royal family in 1787. Originally built in the 16th century, La Nunziatella was redesigned by Ferdinando Sanfelice in 1737, gaining a harmonious blend of painting, sculpture and inlaid marble. Note the marble altar by Giuseppe Sammartino.

ᴵᴿᴱᴱ Palazzo Serra di Cassano
Via Monte di Dio 14 (081 245 2150). Metro Toledo, or bus E6. **Open** by appt only. **Admission** free. **Map** p39 E2 ㉒
It's hard to get a proper view of the trim façade of this 18th-century palazzo, hemmed in as it is by other buildings. One of the high points in Ferdinando Sanfelice's architectural career, it has a no-nonsense double stairway in cool grey volcanic stone, with a beautifully cut marble-pillared balustrade. The apartments feature fine frescoes and original furniture, and the palazzo is now the headquarters of the Italian Institute for Philosophical Studies.

Restaurants

Amici Miei
Via Monte di Dio 78 (081 764 4981, 081 764 6063, www.ristoranteamicimiei.com). Bus 140, 151, E6. **Open** noon-3pm, 7.30pm-midnight Mon-Sat; noon-3pm Sun. Closed July, Aug. **Average** €30. **Map** p39 E2 ㉓ Ristorante
Amici Miei is an old-fashioned, family-run joint. It's the perfect antidote to all that fish: there's none on the menu. Come instead for the likes of stupendous *paccheri Amici Miei* (pasta with aubergine and gorgonzola sauce), fillet steak with green peppercorn sauce, seasonal vegetables and cheeses. Delicious homemade *dolci* include *crema pasticciera* served with brandied chestnuts. The wine list, with plenty of local labels, is good value.

La Bersagliera

Borgo Marinari 10-11 (081 764 6016). Bus E6, 128, 140. **Open** noon-3.30pm, 7.30pm-midnight Mon, Wed-Sun. Closed 1wk Jan. **Average** €60. **Map** p39 G3 ㉔ **Ristorante**
This belle époque jewel has a fine view of the harbour: it's a delightful spot for a long, lazy lunch. Attracting a sophisticated clientele (and celebs from the five-star hotels nearby), it serves predominantly fish-based cuisine: try the house speciality of mussel and clam soup or *orata* (gilthead bream) baked in a salt crust.

€ La Mattonella

Via Nicotera 13 (081 416541). Bus 140, 151, E6. **Open** 12.30-4pm, 7.30-11.30pm Mon-Sat; 12.30-3.30pm Sun. Closed 2wks Aug. **Average** €20. **Map** p38 D1 ㉕ **Osteria**
This tiny, family-run *osteria* has a delightfully old-fashioned atmosphere and takes its name from the colourful ceramic tiles (*mattonelle*) that decorate the walls. Authentic Neapolitan home cooking is the focus here: classic *pasta e ceci* (thick pasta and chickpea soup) and *penne a la Genovese* (with meat and onion sauce) are exemplary. Good *vino locale* is served in ceramic jugs from Vietri on the Amalfi Coast.

Transatlantico

Borgo Marinari, Santa Lucia (081 764 9201, www.transatlanticonapoli.com). Bus E6, 128, 140. **Open** 12.30-3.30pm, 7pm-midnight Mon, Wed-Sun. **Average** *Ristorante* €40. *Pizzeria* €15. **Map** p39 G3 ㉖ **Ristorante/pizzeria**
In a prime location by the yacht marina, this smart restaurant enjoys a fine view of Vesuvius and has a wonderful terrace. The fish and meat dishes are pricey but good: pizza is a more affordable option (try the one with seafood). Service is slick, and there's a smart bar next door if you want to linger.

★ € Trattoria Castel dell'Ovo

Via Luculliana 28, Borgo Marinari (081 764 6352). Bus E6, 128, 140. **Open** 1-3pm, 7.30pm-midnight Mon-Wed, Fri-Sun. **Average** €20. **No credit cards**. **Map** p39 G3 ㉗ **Trattoria**
The Conte family's authentic trattoria charges half the price of its upmarket neighbours and is a lovely spot in which to sit and savour simple, tasty seafood such as *spaghetti alle vongole* or *alici fritti* (fried fresh anchovies). Try for a table on the quayside. When there's a football match, the TV will be on full volume.

Cafés, Bars & Gelaterie

ROL Gelateria

Via Partenope 12/M (081 764 8393, www.rolgelateria.it). Bus 14, 128, E6. **Open** 11am-2am daily. **Map** p39 F1 ㉘
This superb *gelateria* is unusual as there's no table service charge, so you can enjoy the sea views from the terrace free with your ice-cream. Ingredients are natural and mostly local.

SANTA LUCIA

Via Santa Lucia and Via Chiatamone wind through **Santa Lucia**, where the backstreets of the old fishermen's quarter, the **Pallonetto**, rise up towards Pizzofalcone. There's a whiff of 'old Naples' in the air here, and the pavement cafés and restaurants make it an appealing shortcut between Castel dell'Ovo and Piazza del Plebiscito.

The church of **Santa Lucia a Mare** on Via Santa Lucia (081 764 0943, open 7.30am-noon, 5-7pm daily) was rebuilt after its 19th-century predecessor was bombed during World War II; a church has stood on this site since the ninth century. Further up the street on the right is the tiny **Santa Maria della Catena** (Via Santa Lucia 12, open 8-10.30am Mon-Sat, 8.30am-1pm Sun, but often closed). To the left of the altar is the tomb of Francesco Caracciolo; one of the leaders of the Parthenopean Republic, he was hanged on the orders of Admiral Nelson.

Restaurants

€ Da Marino

Via Santa Lucia 118 (081 764 0280). Bus E6, 128, 141. **Open** 12.30-4.30pm, 7.30pm-midnight Tue-Sun. Closed 2wks Aug. **Average** *Pizzeria* €10. *Trattoria* €25. **Map** p39 F3 ㉙ **Trattoria/pizzeria**
This reliable place has a large, bright dining room inside and plenty of outside tables in summer. There's a fresh fish counter in the middle of the room, and the antipasti and seafood dishes are pretty good. Pizzas are classic – try the tasty Anastasia.

€ Ettore

Via Santa Lucia 56 (081 764 0498, www.ristorante ettore.it). Bus E6, 128, 141. **Open** 12.30-3pm, 7.30pm-midnight Mon-Sat. Closed Aug. **Average** *Pizzeria* €15. *Trattoria* €30. **Map** p39 E3 ㉚ **Trattoria/pizzeria**
Local favourite Ettore pairs simple, rustic decor with a wide-ranging, traditional menu. Tuck into a plate of *spaghetti alle vongole* (with clams) or the extravagant *linguine all'astice* (with lobster), or order one of the renowned pizzas. Another speciality is *pagnottielli* – rolled pizza dough stuffed with tasty fillings such as sausage or *friarielli* greens.

★ Ristorantino dell'Avvocato

Via Santa Lucia 115/117 (081 032 0047, www.ilristorantinodellavvocato.it). Bus E6, 128, 141. **Open** 12.30-3.30pm Mon, Sun; 12.30-3.30pm, 7.30-11.30pm Tue-Sat. **Average** €50. **Map** p39 F3 ㉛ **Ristorante**
Lawyer (*avvocato*)-turned-chef Raffaelle Cardillo's passion for seasonal, local ingredients shine through in his renderings of traditional Neapolitan cuisine such as *gnocchetti* with seafood, pistacchios and lemon zest. The menu is inviting for carnivores too: try lamb shanks with jerusalem artichoke fondue.

EXPLORE

The Port & University

Wedged between the Centro Storico and the sea, the dishevelled swathe of Naples that includes the insalubrious Port area, the university and the 1960s Stazione Centrale may not seem like the most inviting neighbourhood, but even here there are some fascinating corners to be explored: a clutch of interesting churches, the ancient university and its quirky museums, and the colourful theatre of the Mercato di Porta Nolana fish market. In recent years, the area has been at risk of being totally engulfed by the snarling traffic chaos along four-lane Corso Umberto I and Via Cristoforo Colombo that skirts the port, but this should be alleviated somewhat once major work on Piazza Garibaldi is completed and the final phase of the new underground system is up and running. After years of hold-ups, the station area will be linked to the rest of the city.

Santa Maria del Carmine.

Don't Miss

1 Mercato di Porta Nolana
One of Europe's most vibrant markets (p53).

2 Centro Musei Scienze Naturali Quirky university museums (p48).

3 Sfogliatelle from Attanasio Among the very best in the city (p52).

4 Santa Maria del Carmine Site of miracles and murky goings-on (p53).

5 Il Commandante
Spectacular food worth busting the budget for (p55).

EXPLORE

CORSO UMBERTO & THE UNIVERSITÀ

Arrow-straight Corso Umberto I was built in 1884 to modernise Naples and isolate the city from the cholera-ridden port. Known locally as il Rettifilo, it runs from **Piazza Garibaldi** to **Piazza Bovio**. The former is a vast, rather unwelcoming car and bus interchange – also home to the Stazione Centrale train station – with an early 20th-century monument to Giuseppe Garibaldi at one end. In recent years, it has been reduced to a vast building site thanks to work on the new underground line. But the end is in sight, it seems. Meanwhile, work on Piazza Bovio has finished and the brand-new Università metro station – complete with some stunning artwork (*see p19* **Metro Art**) – is up and running.

At first glance, Corso Umberto seems like little more than an array of tacky clothes shops and wall-to-wall street vendors. In fact, there's plenty to see, including the university area, the ill-famed Forcella district, and the colourful street market around Porta Nolana.

On the northern side of Corso Umberto, the **Università di Napoli Federico II** was founded in 1224. Although its faculties are dotted around the city, the area just east of Piazza Bovio remains the nucleus. West of the main building stands the headquarters of the 16th-century Università Orientale, so called because its first students came from China for religious training. A host of churches (many perpetually closed for renovation) and splendid *palazzi* (some, alas, quite derelict) cluster around the two universities, making this an interesting area to explore.

On Via Monteoliveto, north-west of Piazza Bovio, **Palazzo Gravina** (no.3, open during university term time, Sept-July) houses the architecture faculty; its 16th-century façade was restored after being destroyed by Swiss troops trying to flush out Italian patriots in 1848. North of the busy crossroads overlooked by the *questura* (police station), **Via Santa Maria la Nova** leads to the church of the same name, whose Renaissance façade matches that of Palazzo Gravina. Part of a convent complex dating from the 13th century, the church is no longer used for religious services but is now part of a museum (Largo Santa Maria la Nova 44, 081 552 1597, open 9.30am-3pm Mon-Fri, 10am-1pm Sat, admission €5) that includes the **Chiostro di San Giacomo della Marca** – its vaults are entirely covered with 15th-century frescoes attributed to Simone Papa, with a section dedicated to *presepii* (nativity scenes).

Via Santa Maria la Nova leads to Piazza Teodoro Monticelli, where the petite, early 15th-century **Palazzo Penne** (no.11, closed to the public) is one of Naples' last surviving houses from that era.

In Largo San Giovanni Maggiore, the chapel of **San Giovanni Pappacoda** has a splendid early 15th-century ogival portal, a rare example of Gothic decoration in Naples. Now deconsecrated, the church only opens for university graduation ceremonies. Opposite stands **Palazzo Giusso** (no.30, open during university term time, Sept-July), seat of the Università Orientale. The church of **San Giovanni Maggiore** (no.29, closed for restoration) was probably built on top of the ruins of a pagan temple in the fourth century, then rebuilt in the 17th and 18th centuries.

The main entrance to the Università di Napoli is on Corso Umberto, but an entrance further up Via Mezzocannone gives easier access to the **Centro Musei Scienze Naturali**. Through the university buildings in Via Paladino, the church of **Gesù Vecchio** (no.38, 081 552 6639, open 7.30am-12.30pm daily) dates from the late 16th century.

Further east, in Piazza Grande Archivio, the **Archivio di Stato** (Corso Umberto 5) was once the convent of the adjoining church of **Santi Severino e Sossio** (closed for restoration).

Near the station, the 13th-century church of **San Pietro ad Aram** stands guard over the notorious **Forcella** district. More than any other downtown area, Forcella lives up to the stereotype of lowlife Naples: racketeering, rip-off joints, gangland activity and petty crime. Above all, it has a long history of crushing poverty and neglect. Unwanted children, or children whose parents couldn't afford to care for them, ended up in the infamous foundling wheel beside the church of **Santissima Annunziata**, and women were 'saved' in the convent of **Santa Maria Egiziaca** (now the Ascalesi Hospital, Via Egiziaca a Forcella 31). Even today, there's often an uneasy tension on the streets.

On the southern side of Corso Umberto, 50 metres from Piazza Garibaldi, pedestrianised Via Nolana leads to Porta Nolana. Beyond this 15th-century city gate lies the Circumvesuviana station. But before the gate, the scene explodes into a mass of colour and smells as you enter **Vicolo Sopramuro**, home to one of the most vibrant street markets in Europe. The **Mercato di Porta Nolana** has produce and fish spilling out of shops and stalls, as well as stores dealing in specialist merchandise such as leather or fabrics.

Sights & Museums

★ Centro Musei Scienze Naturali

Via Mezzocannone 8, Largo San Marcellino 10 (081 253 7516, www.cmsnf.it). Metro Garibaldi, Università, or bus E1, R2, 202. **Open** 9am-1.30pm, 2.30-4.50pm Mon, Thur; 9am-1.30pm Tue, Wed, Fri. Closed Aug. **Admission** *All museums* €4.50; €3 reductions. *One museum* €2.50; €1.50 reductions. **No credit cards. Map** p50 B4 ❶

These four delightful little museums – known collectively as the Centro Musei Scienze Naturali – are all located in and around the enormous Università di Napoli Federico II. Although the main entrance faces Corso Umberto, the easiest access to the museums is from Via Mezzocannone. The museums (in order of appearance) are: the Mineralogy and Geology Museum; the refurbished Anthropology Museum (on the first floor across the courtyard); the Zoology Museum (a favourite with kids); and the Palaeontology Museum, occupying the magnificent ex-Basilian convent and cloisters around the corner in Largo San Marcellino.

FREE San Pietro ad Aram

Corso Umberto I 292 (366 247 1637). Metro Garibaldi, or bus R2. **Open** *Church* 8.15-11.30am, 5-7.30pm Mon-Fri; 7am-1pm Sun. **Admission** free. **Map** p51 E2 ②

In the first century AD, the sea almost reached the current site of the Stazione Centrale, lapping against what would later become the estates of the convent of San Pietro ad Aram. It was here, according to local legend, that St Peter was driven ashore by a storm that stopped him from reaching Pozzuoli in AD 44. Undaunted, Peter seized the opportunity to convert Asprenus (who became the first bishop of Naples) and Candida, both of whom were eventually canonised. Although there's no evidence that St Peter ever came to Naples, a cult celebrating his presence here was born and inspired centuries of restorations and expansions to his church. Inside the church is the altar where St Peter is said to have performed mass. The crypt (currently closed), possibly an ancient church itself, is a site of local worship of the souls of the dead. Today's complex is the product of 17th-century restorations and the demolition of two great cloisters to make way for the Rettifilo (Corso Umberto).

FREE Santissima Annunziata

Via dell'Annunziata 34 (081 283017, 339 271 8901). Metro Garibaldi, or bus R21. **Open** *Church* 9am-noon, 5-6pm Mon-Sat; 9.15am-noon Sun. *Wheel* 9.30am-6pm Mon-Sat. **Admission** free. **Map** p51 E2 ③

The church owes its current appearance to Carlo Vanvitelli's mid 18th-century design. However, the whole Annunziata complex, which includes a courtyard and fountain and a foundling wheel (*ruota*), dates from the 14th century. Such wheels were once common throughout Italy and Spain. Women would place their unwanted newborn babies in them under the cover of darkness, and the babies would generally be reared by nuns; here, an adjoining orphanage (now a hospital) was set up for their care. Astonishingly, this particular wheel remained in use right up until the 1970s. It's not a tourist attraction for Neapolitans, but a reminder of very recent, very harsh times; don't mistake the stoicism with which this symbol is borne for indifference. Anyone with the surname Esposito,

from *expositus*, meaning 'laid before' the mercy of God, is a descendant of one of the foundlings.

Dominated by a large bell tower with a majolica clock, the entrance features a splendid carved marble portal (c1500) by Tommaso Malvito; in the apex, a Madonna gathers children under her cloak. The fine wooden doors (by Belverte and Da Nola) are also from the early 16th century. At 67m (220ft), the church's dome is one of the highest in the city.

Restaurants

★ Baccalaria

Piazzetta di Porto 4 (081 012 0049, www.baccalaria.it). Metro Università, or bus C25, 151, 154. **Open** 12.30-3.30pm, 7.30-11.30pm Mon-Sat; 12.30-3.30pm Sun. **Average** €30. **Map** p50 B5 ④ Osteria

Done out in mod nautical style, this new generation *osteria* stands on a small square behind Piazza della Borsa. The name gives the game away: the menu is dedicated to *baccalà* (salt cod) and *stoccafisso* (stockfish). If you're not a fan of these strong-tasting ingredients, don't bother (although there are a few non-cod dishes on the menu). If you are a fan, though, you're in for a treat (the owner has a *baccalà* processing business, so quality is guaranteed). You can order it every which way: boiled, deep-fried, roasted with a dill pesto, in a club sandwich, in a hearty soup with *scarola* and beans, stuffed into *cappelacci, livornese*-style with tomato sauce, or rolled into *polpettine* spiked with star anise. No time to sit down? Drop by for a glass of wine and a *baccalà*-themed snack; a crisp Campania white makes the perfect accompaniment.

★ € Da Michele

Via Sersale 1 (081 553 9204). Metro Garibaldi, or bus R2. **Open** 11am-11pm Mon-Sat. Closed 2wks Aug. **Average** €10. **No credit cards.** **Map** p50 D2 ⑤ Pizzeria

Don't let the no-frills decor at this traditional pizzeria fool you: Da Michele serves one of the best pizzas in the city. There are only two types (margherita or marinara), and drinks are limited to beer, Coca-Cola or water. But service is friendly and fast, and the pizzas are enormous, delicious and unbelievably cheap. Take a number at the door before joining the queue, and let the theatrical *pizzaiolo*, staff and punters entertain you while you wait.

★ Mimì alla Ferrovia

Via Alfonso d'Aragona 19/21 (081 289004). Metro Garibaldi, or bus C30, R2. **Open** noon-4pm, 7-11.30pm Mon-Sat. Closed 1wk Aug. **Average** €35. **Map** p51 E1 ⑥ Ristorante

Something of a Neapolitan institution, this restaurant is located near the law courts and has attracted numerous celebrities and bigwigs over the years – as you'll see from the photos adorning the walls. A perfect foil to the chaos of nearby Piazza Garibaldi, the place is filled with punters feasting on platter after

EXPLORE

EXPLORE

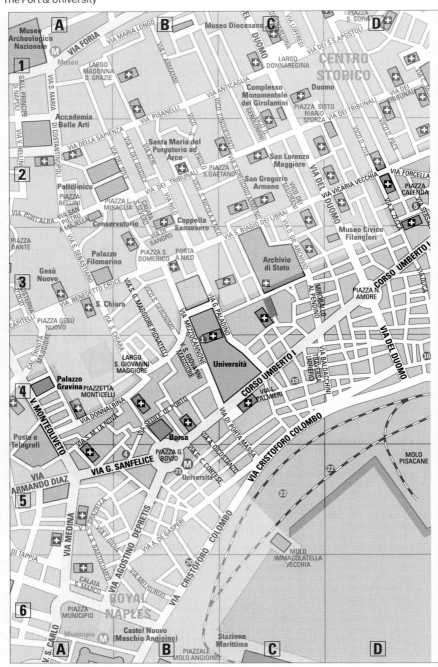

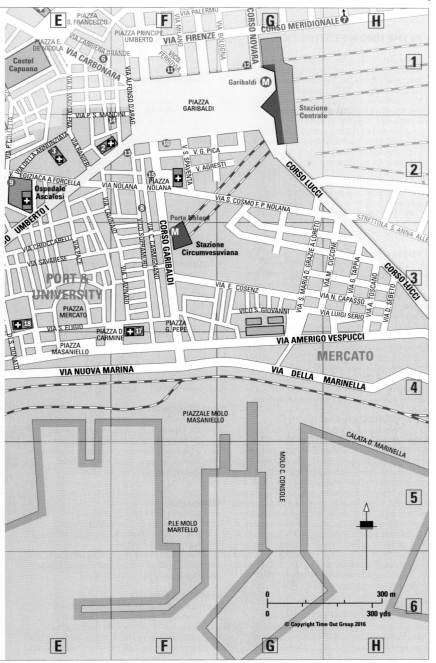

EXPLORE

platter of delicious seafood. The mixed antipasto is almost a meal in itself, while other temptations include exemplary *spaghetti alle vongole* and a sizzling *fritto misto*. An impressive wine list plus old-school decor and service complete the picture.

€ Pizzeria Pellone al Vasto

Via Nazionale 93 (081 553 8614). Metro Garibaldi. **Open** noon-3.30pm, 6.30pm-midnight Mon-Sat. Closed 1wk Aug. **Average** €10. **Map** p51 H1 **7** Pizzeria
A short walk from the station, the ever-popular Pellone is very much a neighbourhood pizzeria: queues are immense in the evenings, although the extension on Via Bari has improved matters slightly. A vast oil painting of the Bay of Naples dominates the entrance to the dining room. It's tempting to start your meal with a selection of *fritto* (fried antipasto), but be warned: the award-winning pizzas are huge. If you haven't got time to sit down, you can always grab a snack-sized pizza from the street counter.

★ € Trattoria Da Giovanni

Via Soppramuro a Porta Nolana 9/10 (081 268320). Metro Garibaldi, Porta Nolana. **Open** 9am-11pm Mon-Sat. **Average** €20. **Map** p51 F2 **8** Trattoria
At this very traditional trattoria, the Graziano family have been serving up homely Neapolitan cooking with great warmth and charm since 1936. Set in the context of the colourful Mercato di Porta Nolana (*see p53*), with a wide-ranging cast of characters that eat here regularly, the menu is based on what's available from the market stalls outside: tender *insalata di polpo* (squid), piles of steaming *spaghetti ai frutti di mare*, perfectly grilled swordfish steaks. There's a fantastic choice of seasonal vegetables, plus meat dishes (*polpettine*, rabbit, *salsiccie*) if you don't want fish. Prices are ridiculously low, making this one of the city's genuine gastronomic bargains.

€ Trianon

Via Colletta Pietro 46 (081 553 9426, www. pizzeriatrianon.it). Metro Garibaldi, or bus R2. **Open** 11.30am-3.30pm, 6.30-11.30pm daily. **Average** €10. **Map** p51 E2 **9** Pizzeria

This vast pizzeria, with its marble tabletops and faded frescoes, is a Neapolitan institution dating from 1923 and offers fantastic pizzas for next to nothing. It's practically across the street from Da Michele (*see p49*). One big difference is that there's never a queue here, as it accommodates 450; the other is that there's a wide choice of pizzas. Service is snappy and the old-world atmosphere unique.

Cafés, Bars & Gelaterie

Il Caffè

Piazza Garibaldi 134 (081 204905). Metro Garibaldi, or bus R2. **Open** 6am-8.30pm Mon-Fri; 6am-7pm Sat; 6am-1pm Sun. **No credit cards. Map** p51 F2 **10**
One of many Illy concept stores cropping up in Italian cities, this tiny haven is a useful place for coffee if you're catching a train. Courteous staff serve a consummate espresso and a pretty decent cappuccino.

Shops & Services

★ Attanasio Sfogliatelle Calde

Vico Ferrovia 2/4 (081 285675, www.sfogliatelle attanasio.it). Metro Garibaldi, or bus R2. **Open** 6.30am-7.30pm Tue-Sun. Closed 2wks July. **Map** p51 F1 **11** Patisserie
At this *pasticceria*, hidden away in the backstreets near the station, the Attanasio family have been turning out some of the best *sfogliatelle* in the city since 1928 – fluffy, sweet ricotta cheese with a touch of spice wrapped in flaky pastry, hot out of the oven – heaven. The only dilemma is which type: clam-shaped, mille-feuille-style *riccia* or little mounds of ricotta-stuffed *pasta frolla* (shortcrust pastry)? Try both.

Fusco Profumeria

Corso Novara 1B (081 283421). Metro Garibaldi, or bus R2. **Open** 8.30am-8pm Mon-Sat. Closed 1wk Aug. **Map** p51 G1 **12** Health & beauty
Fusco Profumeria stocks a good range of perfumes and cosmetics, at prices that are hard to beat. **Other location** Corso Luci Arnaldo 110 (081 267618).

Intimissimi

Corso Umberto I 393 (081 264663, www. intimissimi.com). Metro Garibaldi, or bus R2, R4. **Open** 9.30am-7.30pm Mon-Sat. Closed 2wks Aug. **Map** p51 F2 **13** Fashion
Intimissimi stocks basic, well-priced underwear and pyjamas for men and women, plus flouncy lingerie. **Other locations** throughout the city.

Mercato di Forcella

Near train station, between Corso Umberto & Piazza Garibaldi. Metro Garibaldi, or bus R2. **Open** 9am-noon daily. **Map** p51 F2 **14** Market
A veritable treasure trove of shoes, leather goods, booze, perfume, crafts, knick-knacks and knock-offs.

Mercato di Porta Nolana
Nr Piazza Garibaldi. Metro Garibaldi, Porta Nolana, or bus R2, E2. **Open** 7am-1.30pm daily. **Map** p51 F2 ⑮ **Market**
Everyone (including the city's best restaurants) shops here for the freshest fish delivered daily from the local boats, so come early for the best selection.

THE WATERFRONT

Via Nuova Marina (also known as La Marina) cuts along the port past **Piazza del Mercato**. Now a car park, the piazza lives up to its name (*mercato* means market) with shops selling a staggering array of toys, furniture, clothes and household items. The southern prospect over the sea is obstructed by a hideous modern construction. There's little to indicate that this was the site of the public burning, hanging and beheading of wrongdoers down the ages, including King Conradin of Swabia in 1268 and the leaders of the Parthenopean Republic in 1799.

The executions took place beside the easternmost obelisk, and the names of the Parthenopean leaders are listed in sombre fashion just inside the church of **Santa Maria del Carmine** in the adjacent piazza of the same name. Traffic streams to and from the motorway exit, past the two remaining piers of the 14th-century **Porta del Carmine** gate (white with black piperno stone highlights) and the two towers from the same period – all that's left of the fifth castle in Naples' medieval defence system; the rest was demolished in 1906.

Naples' waterfront was subjected to heavy bombardment during World War II and just two wonderful but little-known medieval churches – **Sant'Eligio Maggiore** and **San Giovanni a Mare** – remain amid the semi-derelict old buildings and new office blocks.

The area south of Corso Umberto, between Piazza Bovio and Piazza Nicola Amore, is known as **I Quattro Palazzi**, after its four fine late 19th-century buildings. Within this area, the **Borgo degli orefici** (goldsmiths' district) still features an age-old community of silversmiths and goldsmiths, and *orefice* (goldsmith) often features in street names.

Further west, off Via Nuova Marina in Via Porta di Massa, the Faculty of Letters occupies the former convent of **San Pietro Martire** (open during university term time, Sept-July), with its fine cloisters and church. Built in the late 13th century as a bulwark against portside vice, the church was remodelled in the 18th century. Portside vice, however, lives on – mainly in the form of clandestine goods from all over the world smuggled into the Port of Naples.

Via Marina continues past the notorious container port. Opposite the 16th-century church of **Santa Maria di Portosalvo** (closed for restoration), the Immacolatella quayside area – which lies between the 18th-century **Capitaneria di Porto** (harbour master's office) and the fascist-era **Stazione Marittima** – has been the subject of an on-off development project designed to redevelop the seedy port area. At the moment it's most definitely 'off', so the area remains a messy hotchpotch of lorry and car parks, bollards and makeshift ticket offices.

Incongruously, this neighbourhood is also home to one of the city's most upmarket hotels, the glass-and-steel Kenzo Tange-designed **Romeo** (*see p277*), which occupies the ex-headquarters of Lauro shipping lines.

The ferry port facilities on the western **Molo Beverello** dock – once a decidedly seedy place – have now been cleaned up and are comparatively efficient. Sailing times are clearly indicated and there are a couple of moderately priced bars.

Sights & Museums

FREE San Giovanni a Mare
Via San Giovanni a Mare 8 (081 553 8429). Bus E2, 151, 154, or tram 1, 4. **Open** 9am-noon daily or by appt. **Admission** free. **Map** p50 D4 ⑯
So-called because the sea (*il mare*) used to lap against its walls, this 12th-century building is the only surviving Norman church in Naples. The foundations of the original apse can be viewed at the junction of the nave and the 13th-century transept. The first side altar on the left – with an unusual cambered arch – contains an exhibition of photos documenting restoration work. If you can't find anyone to let you into the church, ask at Sant'Eligio Maggiore (*see p55*).

★ FREE Santa Maria del Carmine
Piazza del Carmine 2 (081 201196). Bus E2, 151, 154, or tram 1, 4. **Open** 7am-noon, 4.45-7.30pm Mon-Sat; 7am-1pm, 4.30-7.30pm Sun. **Admission** free. **Map** p51 F3 ⑰
With its 75m (246ft) bell tower – the tallest in the city – this church is part of an ancient complex. Restructured and expanded at the end of the 13th century, it includes a convent that still provides succour for the needy and homeless. In the transept is a monument to Corradino di Swabia, who was executed in 1268 at the age of 16 for having led an unsuccessful attempt to reclaim the kingdom of Sicily. His remains are believed to be underneath, although the SS agents sent by Hitler in 1943 to search for the remains of the early German leader found nothing. Opposite the monument stands the pulpit from where, in 1647, 27-year old Tommaso Aniello (known as Masaniello) gave a speech inciting the people to rise against the city's Spanish occupiers. He was later assassinated in the convent and buried here in an unmarked tomb.

Legend has it that during Alfonso of Aragon's 1439 siege of the city, a cannonball penetrated the wall of the church and headed straight for a 14th-century wooden crucifix under the transept

EXPLORE

CAFFE CULTURE
Coffee is a sacred ritual in Naples.

Bets are settled and friendships are acknowledged by the phrase '*ti offro un caffè*', and after eating out, Neapolitans will often make a beeline to the nearest bar where superior coffee is served. Amid the numerous varieties on offer, the one that really counts is the espresso, which is served piping hot in a lip-scalding cup. The ground coffee is pressed down in a coffee machine, which heats purified water to 90-95°C. This then filters slowly through to fill less than half of the tiny cup.

Coffee in Naples is often served *zuccherato*, with sugar heaped into the cup to create a thick paste at the bottom; if you don't want your coffee too sweet, ask for '*amaro*' or '*non-zuccherato*', or don't stir. You'll also be given a glass of water, to clear your palate of foreign tastes prior to the coffee experience.

Most coffee is taken standing at the bar, in a quick in-and-out process, but the phrase '*prendiamo un caffè insieme*' ('let's have a coffee together') is more than just a simple, polite offer. It is rather an invitation to chat, to do business or to forge a closer relationship – the local equivalent of 'let's do lunch' – so all but the smallest cafés or bars have at least a few tables. (Beware: you can be charged up to three times more for your coffee at these.)

If you take the standing option, pay at the cash register first, elbow your way to the counter, and slap down your receipt with a 10¢ or 20¢ coin, an almost compulsory tip here. Don't expect bar staff to ask what you'd like: you'll wait all day. Instead, summon up all the assertiveness (not rudeness) you can muster, and ask for *due cappuccini* or *due caffè* (variations on 'please' or 'may I have' are unnecessary). Another tradition, peculiar to Naples (although not as common as it used to be) is '*pago un caffè sospeso*', where you pay for two coffees: one is drunk, and the other is 'offered' to the next down-and-out to pass through the door.

If you are invited to a Neapolitan's house, you'll immediately be offered a coffee, which in the old days would have been prepared in a *caffettiera napoletana*. The story goes that a Neapolitan gentleman was preparing a coffee for Milanese engineer Luigi Bezzera and complained about the slowness of his coffeemaker. In response, Bezzera invented the *caffettiera napoletana* in 1901 – although it has now been replaced by the more efficient Moka. When it comes to good coffee, there's no room for sentimentality.

WHERE TO TAKE A TAZZINA
Buona Merenda (*see p62*). Small Spaccanapoli café with a young vibe and Anhelo's excellent in-house roasted beans.
Gran Caffè Gambrinus (*see p42*). Good coffee in sumptuous, old-world surroundings.
Mexico (*see p85*). Superb espressos, sinful iced coffees.

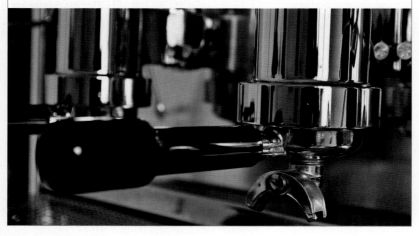

IN THE KNOW THE ORIGINAL ASPIRIN?

Now incorporated into the vast Palazzo Borsa (Stock Exchange) just off Piazza Bovio, the eighth-century church of Sant' Aspreno al Porto was built on the site of a legendary cave said to have been inhabited by Saint Aspren. The altar in the ancient crypt has a square hole in it and was believed to have curative properties: if you were suffering from a headache, you'd kneel down and stick your head into the hole, while invoking the saint's name, and the pain would miraculously disappear. Saint Aspren was the first bishop of Naples and was particularly good at curing headaches – a gift, some say, that was due to his having been beheaded for converting to Christianity. It seems that drug company Bayer was inspired by Saint Aspren when they first marketed their painkilling drug in 1899, giving it the name 'Aspirin'.

arch. The statue miraculously ducked its head and the crown of thrones fell off, never to be recovered. Yet more miracles are associated with the image of the Madonna del Carmine (or Bruna as she's known locally) behind the main altar, and on 16 July the faithful flock to see the magnificent bell tower almost ablaze with fireworks celebrating her feast day.

FREE Sant'Eligio Maggiore

Via Sant'Eligio (081 553 8429). Bus E2, 151, 154, or tram 1,4. **Open** 9am-2pm daily. **Admission** free. **Map** p51 E3 ⑬

This extraordinary 13th-century church was badly damaged in 1943; subsequent restoration work uncovered much of the original building. Sant'Eligio was the first church built in Naples by the Angevin monarchs. The leaping vertical height of the interior is accentuated by ribs and groin vaults. Outside, the fine Gothic archway and bell tower date from the 15th century; the clock is a 16th-century addition.

Restaurants

€ Antica Pizzeria del Borgo Orefeci

Via Luigi Palmieri 13 (081 552 0996). Metro Università, or bus E2, 151, 154, or tram 1,4. **Open** noon-3.30pm, 7-10.30pm Mon-Sat. Closed Aug. **Average** €10. **No credit cards**. **Map** p50 C4 ⑲ Pizzeria

This simple, authentic pizzeria is tucked away on a side street in the old goldsmiths' quarter (now pedestrianised and gentrified). Excellent pizzas – try the *friarielli e salsiccia* (local bitter greens and sausage) – and a great range of fresh fish dishes are served at tables both inside and out.

★ Il Commandante

Hotel Romeo, Via Cristoforo Colombo 45 (081 017 5001, www.romeohotel.it). Metro Università, or bus 151, 154, or tram 1,4. **Open** 7.30-10.30pm Mon, Wed-Sun. **Average** €80. **Map** p50 B6 ⑳ Ristorante

Dinner at the top-floor restaurant of the strikingly contemporary Hotel Romeo (*see p277*) is an experience: the memorable views over the tourist port to Vesuvius; the palate-teasing amuse-bouches served with *aperitivi;* the fantastic selection of home-baked breads with whipped buffalo butter; the five different kinds of salt; the exquisite chocolates and petits fours that close the meal. Then there's the main event – the clever, technical yet convincing food, firmly rooted in local traditions, that has won young chef Salvatore Bianco a Michelin star. An extravagant treat.

Europeo di Mattozzi

Via Marchese Campodisola 4 (081 552 1323). Metro Università, or bus R2, R4. **Open** noon-4pm, 8-11.30pm Mon-Sat. Closed 2wks Aug. **Average** €15. Ristorante €40. **Map** p50 B5 ㉑ Ristorante/pizzeria

Sepia photographs, copper pots and colourful ceramics jostle for wall space at this reassuringly old-fashioned restaurant, which has been going since 1930. Popular with business folk, it serves textbook versions of local classics such as *paccheri* pasta with potatoes and provola cheese or soup with fava beans and mussels. The fish is excellent: if you come in the summer months, try the *fragaglie* (tiny, fried newborn fish). The pizzas are excellent too.

€ Il Piccolo Ristoro

Calata Porto di Massa in Porto (349 192 9074). Bus 151, 154, or tram 1, 4. **Open** noon-3pm Mon-Fri, Sun; noon-3pm, 7.30pm-midnight Sat. Closed 2wks Aug. **Average** €20. **No credit cards**. **Map** p50 D5 ㉒ Trattoria

To find one of Naples' best-kept secrets, enter the port through Varco Pisacane or head east for about 200m from the main port. Il Piccolo Ristoro is housed in little more than a shack, with no sign outside (look for the green-and-white canopy), but serves delicious fish that's freshly caught each day. Family-run, it's one of the best bargains in the city; even the lobster pasta is affordable.

Cafés, Bars & Gelaterie

Dolcezze Siciliane

Piazzale Immacolatella Vecchia (081 552 1990). Metro Municipio, or bus 151, 154, or tram 1, 4. **Open** 7am-7pm Tue-Sat; 7am-2pm Sun. Closed June-Aug. **No credit cards**. **Map** p50 C5 ㉓

This bar and pastry shop is located inside the port area, near the quay where boats from Ischia and Capri dock. Enter from Piazza Municipio, turn left and keep walking – it's worth it for the fresh Sicilian *dolci* that arrive here from Palermo by boat every morning.

Centro Storico

EXPLORE

The heart of Naples, both in body and soul, is the Centro Storico (historic centre), a UNESCO World Heritage site since 1995. Nowhere else in the city is the past so alive in the present, and no other area offers such a heady sense of what Naples is today. Here, Greek and Roman history rub shoulders with the modern city within the layout of the three ancient *decumani* (main streets) that run arrow-straight from east to west, intersected from north to south by the *cardines*. The Spaccanapoli is the *decumanus inferior*, which lay at the heart of Neapolis; where tourists now tread, Romans once walked, and Greeks before them. The Angevins concentrated their construction efforts here when Naples became their capital in the 13th century, building soaring churches. Today, the area is packed with sightseers, university students and locals simply getting on with their daily lives.

The Duomo.

Don't Miss

1 Spaccanapoli The heart of old Naples (p58).

2 Cappella Sansevero Home to Giuseppe Sammartino's extraordinary *Veiled Christ* (p58).

3 The Duomo Naples' great cathedral houses glorious treasures (p67).

4 San Lorenzo Maggiore Explore the city's ancient history in depth (p68).

5 Street food Join the crowds for *pizza fritta*, *arancini* and more (p73).

SPACCANAPOLI

Spaccanapoli is the central axis of old Naples, changing its name as it runs straight as a die from Via Domenico Capitelli in the west, through Via Benedetto Croce and Via San Biagio dei Librai, to Via Vicaria Vecchia in the east. It effectively splits the Centro Storico district in two, hence its name (*spaccare* means 'to split'). Most of the street is pedestrianised and crowded with a mix of tourists and students. A mishmash of bookshops, jewellery stores, souvenir shops, fast food outlets, neighbourhood grocers and local *trattorie* fight for space along the way, while once-elegant *palazzi* look on, their magnificent courtyards crumbling and overgrown.

Towards the western end of Spaccanapoli, Piazza del Gesù features a towering rococo obelisk, the marvellously ornate **Guglia dell'Immacolata** (1747-50). The piazza is surrounded by elegant *palazzi* (Degas was a frequent visitor to the private Palazzo Pignatelli di Monteleone at Calata Trinità Maggiore 53) and is overlooked by the unusual façade of the church of **Gesù Nuovo** and the curiously squared-off bell tower of **Santa Chiara**.

The short stretch of Spaccanapoli called Via Benedetto Croce – after the Neapolitan philosopher and historian (1866-1952) – is crammed with prestigious *palazzi*, a few of which are in decent shape. Croce's own home, **Palazzo Filomarino** (no.12), has two 14th-century arches walled into the left-hand staircase, and a courtyard portico that dates from the 16th century. Look out for the late 16th-century doorway at the **Palazzo Carafa della Spina** (no.45), guarded by a pair of marble, lion-like creatures (their open mouths were used to snuff out torches), with fauns merrily frolicking above the portal.

Work on the **Guglia di San Domenico** in Piazza San Domenico began in 1658 in thanks for the end of a plague epidemic, but was only completed 99 years later. The piazza is dominated by the 13th-century church of **San Domenico Maggiore** and a series of very fine 16th- and 17th-century *palazzi* (closed to the public), including the red-ochre **Palazzo Corigliano** at no.12 (part of the University of Naples), **Palazzo Casacalenda** (no.16) and **Palazzo Sangro di Sansevero** (no.9). A short jaunt north past the Guglia to Vico San Domenico leads to the funerary chapel of **Cappella Sansevero**, home of Giuseppe Sanmartino's sublime *Veiled Christ* along with some creepy anatomical artefacts.

Before becoming Via San Biagio dei Librai, Spaccanapoli crosses piazzetta Nilo, site of the little church of **Sant'Angelo a Nilo**, which houses a tomb partly carved by Donatello, his only work in Naples. In a small square by the church stands a revered statue of the Nile god.

Further down Via San Biagio dei Librai, at no.114, the **Monte di Pietà** chapel contains statues of *Safety* and *Charity* by Pietro Bernini in its façade, and a 17th-century frescoed ceiling by Belisario Corenzio. At no.39 is the **Palazzo Marigliano**, with a carefully renovated façade from 1513 and a fine coat of arms; steps at the back of the courtyard lead to an 'invisible' garden (currently closed).

The massive bulk of the church of **San Giorgio Maggiore** stands where Spaccanapoli crosses Via Duomo. To the north, at Via Duomo 288, is the **Museo Civico Filangieri**, which reopened in 2012 after years of closure.

East of Via del Duomo, Spaccanapoli becomes Via Vicaria Vecchia, and passes the pretty church of **Sant'Agrippino** (no.86). It was almost destroyed during World War II, but the delicate 13th-century arches in the apse have been salvaged, and furnishings from the now-derelict Santa Maria a Piazza (Via Forcella 12), which stands opposite, have been moved here.

Sights & Museums

★ Cappella Sansevero

Via Francesco de Sanctis 19 (081 551 8470, www.museosansevero.it). Metro Dante or Toledo, or bus E1. **Open** 9.30am-6.30pm Mon, Wed-Sat; 9.30am-2pm Sun. **Admission** €7; €5 reductions; free under-10s. **No credit cards. Map** p60 C4 ❶
The funerary chapel of the Di Sangro family was built in 1590, but took on its current appearance in 1749-66, thanks to the eccentric prince of Sansevero, Raimondo di Sangro, who hired the leading sculptors of the day to decorate it. The high altar is carved in accordance with the then-fashionable 'picture hewn out of stone' criterion; the statues have titles such as *Domination of Self-will, The Pleasures of Marriage* and *Shyness*. The celebrated 'Cristo Velato' or *Veiled Christ* (1753), by Giuseppe Sammartino, is uncanny in its realism; so impressed was neoclassical sculptor Antonio Canova when he visited the chapel that he tried to buy it. The figures in the crypt, meanwhile, are downright macabre.

FREE Gesù Nuovo

Piazza Gesù Nuovo (081 557 8111, www.gesu nuovo.it). Metro Dante or Toledo, or bus E1. **Open** 7am-12.30pm, 4-7.30pm Mon-Sat; 7am-12.30pm, 4-8.45pm Sun. **Admission** free. **Map** p60 B5 ❷
Embellished with diamond-shaped stonework, the façade of this extraordinary church was part of a 15th-century palazzo, before being transformed into a church for the Jesuit order at the end of the 16th century. The portals, windows and external decorations date from the conversion. Inside is a stupendous barrel-vaulted ceiling, and a dome that has been rebuilt several times. The inner façade has a large fresco (1725) by Francesco Solimena, and the ceilings and walls are a treasury of frescoes and

paintings, with works by Giuseppe Ribera and Luca Giordano and marble statues by Cosimo Fanzago. A large, busy room on the right-hand side of the church is dedicated to Giuseppe Moscati (1880-1927), who was canonised in 1987. The ex-votos covering the chapel walls give an indication of local faith in the miracle-working doctor, who treated the poor for free and cured a man with terminal meningitis.

Museo Civico Filangieri
Via Duomo 288 (081 203175, www.salviamoil museofilangieri.org). Metro Cavour, or bus E1, E2. **Open** 9am-6pm Tue-Sat. **Admission** €5. **Map** p61 E4 ③
Solid, Florentine-style Palazzo Como houses the remnants of the once much larger, but nevertheless still intriguing, private collection of art connoisseur Prince Gaetano Filangieri (1824-1892). The palazzo was torn down to make way for Via Duomo, but was painstakingly reconstructed by the Prince in 1879 and filled with his eclectic haul of paintings, furniture, weapons and costumes, donated to the state in 1888. A devastating fire during World War II seriously depleted the collection, but what remains is housed in a series of salons and includes paintings by Neapolitan masters such as Solimena, Ribera and Francesca Jerace. There's also a library of 30,000-odd volumes, some of which date back to the 13th century. The vast entrance hall with its dark wood carvings is used for temporary exhibitions.

FREE San Domenico Maggiore
Piazza San Domenico Maggiore (081 459188, treasury 081 442 0039, www.parteneapolis.it). Metro Dante or Toledo, or bus E1. **Open** *Church* 8.30am-12.30pm, 4-7pm daily. *Treasury* 9.30am-noon Tue-Thur, Sun; 9.30am-noon, 4.30-7pm Fri, Sat. **Admission** *Church* free. *Treasury* €3. **Map** p60 C4 ④
This vast, castellated church has a grand rear entrance with a wide flight of steps leading up from the piazza. However, it's best entered from the side street, Vico San Domenico. Here, the porticoed entrance dates from the late 13th century, when the church was built, incorporating the pre-existing church of Sant'Angelo a Morfisa. The chapels include some fine works of art: 13th-century marble tombstones (the first chapel on the right); 14th-century frescoes by the great and unjustly neglected Roman artist Pietro Cavallini (second on the right); and a couple of paintings by Mattia Preti (fourth on the right).

As the Neapolitan headquarters of the Dominican order, the monastery played host to the hermeticist philosopher Giordano Bruno (burnt at the stake for heresy in Rome in 1600), who studied here, and St Thomas Aquinas, to whom the sixth chapel on the right is dedicated. The figure of Jesus in the 13th-century Crucifixion over the altar is said to have spoken to Thomas, offering him anything he wanted in return for the nice things the saint had written about Him. To this, Thomas replied: 'Nothing, if not You.'

The luminous sacristy has a fine ceiling fresco by Francesco Solimena and a bizarre set of coffins; their contents include the decapitated body of a victim of the barons' conspiracy of 1486. An elaborately carved door leads to the Treasury – which is said to have once housed the hearts of Kings Charles II of Anjou, Alfonso I and Ferdinand I.

FREE San Giorgio Maggiore
Via del Duomo 237A (081 287932). Bus E1, E2. **Open** 8am-noon, 5-8pm Mon-Sat; 8.30am-1pm Sun. **Admission** free. **Map** p61 E4 ⑤
The original fourth-century basilica was built by St Severus (364-410), when this area of Naples was occupied by descendants of families driven out of their homes by the AD 79 eruption of Vesuvius. Severus's relics are behind the altar; his splendid marble throne is to the right of the main aisle. The vestibule, with its three Byzantine-Roman arches (at the entrance in Piazzetta Crocelle ai Mannesi), was the apse of the original basilica, and the only part that survived an earthquake in 1640. Subsequently, architect Cosimo Fanzago rotated the floorplan by 180°, placing the 17th-century apse and main altar at the opposite end of the church.

★ FREE Santa Chiara
Via Benedetto Croce (081 797 1235, museum 081 551 6673, www.monasterodisantachiara. com). Metro Dante or Toledo, or bus E1. **Open** *Church* 7.30am-1pm, 4.30-8pm daily. *Museum & cloister* 9.30am-5.30pm Mon-Sat; 10am-2pm Sun. **Admission** *Church* free. *Museum & cloister* €4; €4.50 reductions. **Map** p60 B5 ⑥
The church and convent of Santa Chiara was built for Robert of Anjou's wife, Sancia, in the early 14th century and is Naples' most significant monument in Angevin Gothic style. Its Gothic features were hidden by Baroque restructuring during the mid 18th century, before a direct hit in an air raid in August 1943. In the 1950s, the rose window, portal, chapel arches, mullion windows, exterior flying buttresses, and some altars and shrines were salvaged or faithfully copied, and the church was rebuilt along its original Gothic lines. The interior contains many royal tombs, including the towering monument to Robert of Anjou himself, carved by the Florentine Bertini brothers in the mid 1300s. To the right of the altar, the tomb of Carlo, Duke of Calabria was carved by another Florentine, the great Tino da Camaino, who also made the tomb of Carlo's wife, Marie de Valois. It was his last work. Walk around the left-hand side of the church to the small gate that leads into Naples' most famous cloister. The Choistro delle Clarisse is decorated with bright majolica tiles made in the mid 18th century. Beyond this, the Museo dell'Opera has bits and pieces salvaged from the air raid, including some superb 14th-century friezes and busts, plus an archaeological area revealing a gymnasium and baths from the old Roman city, unearthed during the post-war restoration.

EXPLORE

Centro Storico

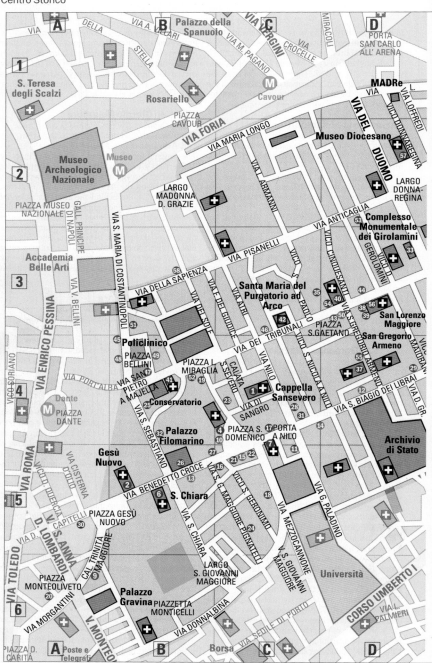

EXPLORE

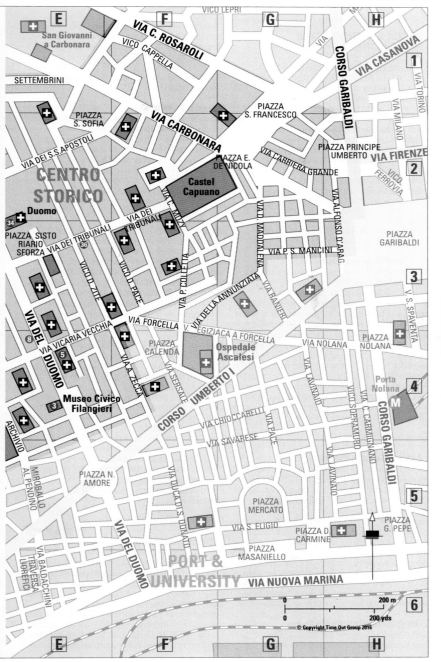

IN THE KNOW MURDER MOST HORRID

Carlo Gesualdo, Prince of Venosa (1566-1613), was a prolific Neapolitan composer of madrigals and church music. His defining moment came on 6 October 1590 – not thanks to a particularly beautiful composition, but because he caught his wife Maria and her lover, the handsome Duke of Andria, 'in flagrante' in his apartment in Palazzo Sangro di Sansevero (Piazza San Domanico 9) and brutally murdered them in a frenzy of jealous rage. Gesualdo is known in musical circles for bending the Renaissance rules of harmony to such an extent that his compositions sound almost atonal, but his hideous crime caught the public imagination at the time and has continued to fascinate ever since.

FREE Sant'Angelo a Nilo

Piazzetta Nilo. Metro Dante or Toledo, or bus E1. **Open** 9am-1pm, 4.30-7pm Mon-Sat; 9am-1pm Sun. **Admission** free. **Map** p60 C4 **❼**
With its striking red-and-grey façade, this small church was built in 1385 for the Brancaccio family but was given a makeover in the 18th century. A chapel to the right of the altar houses the beautiful marble funerary monument of Cardinal Rinaldo Brancaccio, which was made in Pisa in 1427 and shipped to Naples. The fine bas-relief portraying the Assumption on the front of the tomb, the cardinal's head and the right-hand caryatid (a column shaped like a person) are the only works by Tuscan artist Donatello. There's a delicate bell tower, but it's quite difficult to see from the narrow street.

Restaurants

€ Antica Osteria Pisano

Piazzetta Crocelle ai Mannesi 1, corner of Via Duomo & Spaccanapoli (081 554 8325). Metro Dante or Cavour, or bus E1, E2. **Open** noon-4pm, 6.30-11pm Mon-Sat. Closed Aug. **Average** €20. **Map** p61 E4 **❽** Neapolitan
Run by the Pisano family for some 70 years, this excellent little trattoria has a limited lunchtime menu and a more elaborate selection in the evening. Traditional favourites such as *pasta al sugo* or *alla genovese* are a particular forte, and the *contorni* are abundant and fresh – a fine substitute for a main course. The kitchen opens on to the restaurant, and staff are more than happy for you to have a gander. Pisano is popular but tiny, so be prepared to wait.

€ Friggitoria-Pizzeria Giuliano

Calata Trinità Maggiore 33 (081 551 0986, www.pizzeriagiuliano.com). Metro Toledo or
Università, or bus E1. **Open** 10am-11pm Mon-Sat. Closed Aug. **Average** €5. **No credit cards**. **Map** p60 A6 **❾** Friggitoria/pizzeria
In business since 1959, this place serves some of the best *pizzette* (snack-sized pizzas) in town. The potato croquettes and *zeppole* (deep-fried dough balls) are crisp and fresh too.

Palazzo Petrucci

Piazza San Domenico Maggiore 4 (081 552 4068, www.palazzopetrucci.it). Metro Dante or Toledo, or bus E1. **Open** 7.30-10.45pm Mon; noon-2.45pm, 7.30-10.45pm Tue-Sat; noon-2.45pm Sun. Closed 3wks Aug. **Average** €85. **Map** p60 C4 **❿** Contemporary Italian
Located in the former stables of handsome Palazzo Petrucci, this restaurant was awarded a Michelin star in 2008. Chef Lino Scarallo serves up Neapolitan nouvelle cuisine with a regularly changing menu that features unusual – but convincing – combinations such as risotto of almonds and clams with a hint of thyme, lemon and turmeric root; and lamb served with preserved apricots, pecorino cheese and mint. The spartan room with its soaring ceilings and unadorned walls is rather cold, but the food makes up for it.
▶ *Looking for something cheaper? Try the nextdoor Pizzeria Palazzo Petrucci: the gourmet pizzas are delicious and the terrace tables are great for watching the lively goings-on in the piazza.*

€ Tandem

Via Paladino 51 (081 1900 2468, www.tandem.napoli.it). Metro Dante or Toledo, or bus E1. **Open** 12.30-3.30pm, 7-11.30pm Mon, Tue, Wed-Sun (daily during July & Aug). **Average** €15. **Map** p60 C5 **⓫** Neapolitan
The highlight at this tiny, bright trattoria just off Piazzetta del Nilo is the intense, simmered-for-hours ragù (*'rrau'* in dialect), which comes in both meat and vegetarian versions. It's served on a variety of pasta shapes, sometimes with the addition of ricotta or provola cheese. You can even order the moreish sauce by itself in a little bowl with chunks of bread to dunk (known as *'fare la scarpetta'* in Italian). Portions are generous enough to make a meal, but if you want more there are also grilled meats with chips and salad.

Cafés, Bars & Gelaterie

★ Buona Merenda

Via San Biagio dei Librai 19 (081 580 2274, www.buonamerenda.it). Metro Dante or Toledo, or bus E1. **Open** 8am-7pm daily. **Map** p60 D4 **⓬**
There's a constantly evolving bar and café scene along narrow, bustling Spaccanapoli, but this small, contemporary space is a cut above the rest – both in terms of its classy, New York-style decor and the quality of its coffee. Opened in December 2013 by the owner of Anhelo, it serves up excellent own-roasted coffee, fresh pastries and muffins,

made-to-order gourmet sandwiches, wines by the glass and artisan beers. It's crowded at lunch with students from the nearby university faculties and is a popular stop on the *aperitivo* trail too.

▶ *The same owner's stylish deli and tapas bar, Jamon, sits at the top of Piazza San Domenico.*

★ Gay-Odin
Via Benedetto Croce 61 (081 551 0794, www. gay-odin.it). Metro Dante or Toledo, or bus E1. **Open** 9.30am-8pm Mon-Sat; 10am-1.30pm Sun. Closed Aug. **Map** p60 B5 ⑬

This small temple of top-notch *gelato* and chocolate in the heart of the Centro Storico is an outpost of the revered, old-school Gay-Odin chocolate factory. The *gelato* achieves a perfect balance between creamy and light, with the best chocolate flavours in town: try white chocolate and hazelnut or *cioccolato al rhum*, or the ice-cream truffles. **Other locations** throughout the city.

Gu Shu
Via San Biagio dei Librai 121 (081 193 7142). Metro Dante or Toledo, or bus E1. **Open** 4-8pm Tue-Sun. **Map** p60 C4 ⑭

A calm, quiet, ordered oasis in the chaotic Centro Storico, Gu Shu offers 70-odd varieties of tea – some of them very rare indeed – from China, Sri Lanka, Nepal, India, Japan and Taiwan. To a background track of vinyl jazz, the tea is prepared and served as it would be in China: a slow, ritualistic process that forces you to calm down and savour every sip.

▶ *You can buy the tea itself from nearby Qualcosa di Te (see p65), under the same ownership.*

Scaturchio
Piazza San Domenico Maggiore 19 (081 551 6944, www.scaturchio.it). Metro Dante or Toledo, or bus E1. **Open** 7.20am-8.40pm daily. Closed 1wk Aug. **Map** p60 C5 ⑮

Set on bustling Piazza San Domenico Maggiore, historic Scaturchio's one-time reputation for producing the best *sfogliatelle* in the city means that the place is often jammed with tourists. Those days are gone and the locals know differently, but the speciality *ministeriale* (rich, dark chocolate cake filled with rum-infused cream) is a superb concoction, only produced from September to May. There are tables on the piazza.

Shops & Services

★ Affaitati
Via Benedetto Croce 21 (081 444427). Metro Dante or Toledo, or bus E1. **Open** 10am-1.30pm, 4.30-7.30pm Mon-Sat; 10am-1.30pm Sun. Closed Aug. **Map** p60 C5 ⑮ Antiques

Family-run since 1885, this museum-like shop offers a compendium of the best Neapolitan furnishings, reflecting the Baroque period, Empire style and much more. Prices are fair, considering the quality.

Alfonso Artiaco
Palazzo di Sangro, Piazzetta Nilo 7 (081 497 6072, www.alfonsoartiaco.com). Metro Dante. **Open** *June-Sept* 10am-8pm Mon-Fri. *Oct-May* 10am-8pm Mon-Sat. Closed Aug. **Map** p60 C4 ⑰ Gallery

This well-regarded gallery, which has now relocated to the Centro Storico, shows a mix of high-profile and emerging artists: the likes of Jannis Kounellis, Sol LeWitt, Gilbert & George, David Tremlett and Wolfgang Laib, as well as young locals. *Photo p64.*

Carrefour Express
Via Mezzocannone 99A/B (081 552 7438, www.carrefour.it). Metro Università, or bus E1, R2. **Open** 8am-8pm Mon-Sat; 9am-1.30pm Sun. **Map** p60 C5 ⑱ Food & drink

This is a handily located outpost of the French supermarket chain.

La Casa Brutta
Vico San Domenico 19 (081 1933 1638, www. lacasabrutta.it). Metro Dante or Toledo, or bus E1. **Open** 10.30am-2pm, 4-8pm Tue-Sat. **Map** p60 B4 ⑲ Homewares

This little haven of up-to-the-minute industrial and vintage design sells recycled and reconditioned objects and furniture, along with pieces from established names such as Tolix, Jieldé and Frama.

Dedalus Centroviaggi
Piazza Monteoliveto 2 (081 551 0643, www.dedalus centroviaggi.it). Metro Toledo or Università. **Open** 9.30am-1.30pm, 3.30-7pm Mon-Fri; 9.30am-1.30pm Sat. **Map** p60 A6 ⑳ Travel agent

Paride and his English-speaking team can make train, ferry, hotel and flight bookings, and recommend inexpensive accommodation.

Eboli
Via Benedetto Croce 35-37 (081 551 6363). Metro Dante or Toledo, or bus E1. **Open** 10am-7.30pm Mon-Fri; 10am-1pm Sat. Closed 3wks Aug. **Map** p60 C5 ㉑ Gifts & souvenirs

This street is crammed with jewellery shops specialising in silver ex-votos, offered to saints as thanks for 'divine' healings. The silver arms, legs, tummies, breasts, heads and bodies make intriguing gifts; Eboli also stocks silver animals, so you can give thanks on behalf of your pet. Items start at around €10.

Eder
Via Benedetto Croce 44 (081 551 7081). Metro Dante or Toledo, or bus E1. **Open** 9am-8pm Mon-Sat; 9am-3pm Sun. **Map** p60 C5 ㉒ Food & drink

The eye-catching window displays of this tiny Spaccanapoli shop will lure you in to discover local pastas, buffalo mozzarella and other cheeses from Campania, jars of marinated vegetables, and orange and aniseed liqueur (a speciality).

EXPLORE

Alfonso Artiaco. *See p63.*

Kiphy
Vico San Domenico 3 (340 284 9691, www. kiphy.it). Metro Dante or Toledo, or bus E1. **Open** 10.30am-2pm, 3-7.30pm Tue-Sat. **Map** p60 C4 ㉓ Health & beauty
A bright, modern shop selling organic, vegetable-based artisan soaps, essential oils, scrubs and bath salts, and all sorts of other indulgent goodies.

Lavanderia Santa Chiara
Via San Giovanni Maggiore Pignatelli 36-37 (081 551 8460). Metro Dante or Toledo. **Open** 9am-1.30pm, 3-8pm Mon-Fri; 9am-2pm Sat. Closed 2wks Aug. **No credit cards. Map** p60 C5 ㉔ Dry-cleaners
A reliable washing, ironing and dry-cleaning service.

IN THE KNOW PRINCE OF GHOULS

Raimondo di Sangro, seventh Prince of Sansevero (1710-1731), commissioned the exquisite sculptures in his family's funerary chapel, but he had a darker side. Obsessed with embalming, the prince supposedly carried out experiments on defunct domestics, injecting their bodies with chemical substances to preserve them: local lore has it that they weren't always dead when the operations took place. Two of these figures are on display in the crypt.

Loveri Strumenti Musicali
Via San Sebastiano 8/10/66/72/74/75 (081 296755, www.loveri.com). Metro Dante, or bus E1. **Open** 10am-1.30pm, 4-8pm Mon-Fri; 10am-1.30pm Sat. **Map** p60 B4 ㉕ Musical instruments
Loveri has everything from traditional Neapolitan mandolins to modern synths and guitars. Its premises are on Naples' celebrated 'music alley'.

Matermatuta
Via Benedetto Croce 12 (081 1981 0439). Metro Dante or Toledo, or bus E1. **Open** 10am-2pm, 4-8pm Mon-Sat. Closed 2wks Aug. **Map** p60 B5 ㉖ Jewellery
Mostly designed and made up in-house, the affordable jewellery here uses semi-precious stones and pearls, silver, copper and other metals. There's another shop just across the road at no.38.

Melinoi
Via Benedetto Croce 34 (081 552 1204). Metro Dante or Toledo, or bus E1. **Open** *July-mid Aug* 10am-2pm, 4.30-7.30pm Mon-Sat. *Sept-June* 10am-2pm, 4.30-7.30pm Mon-Sat; 10am-2pm Sun. Closed 2wks Aug. **Map** p60 B5 ㉗ Fashion
Labels at this boutique are sourced from as far afield as Iceland; European designers are also well represented. The designs are elegant but unusual.

Museum Shop
Via Benedetto Croce 12 (081 360 4228, www. museumshop.it). Metro Dante or Toledo, or bus E1. **Open** 9am-7pm Mon-Sat. Closed 2wks Aug. **Map** p60 C4 ㉘ Gifts & souvenirs

Housed on the ground floor of philosopher Croce's family palazzo, this shop offers a good range of high-quality, pricey museum repros (custom orders taken) and souvenirs.

★ Ospedale delle Bambole
Via San Biagio dei Librai 46 (081 203067, www.ospedaledellebambole.it). Metro Cavour or Università, or bus E1. **Open** 10.30am-3pm Mon-Fri. Closed 10 July-10 Sept. **No credit cards.** **Map** p60 D4 ㉙ Gifts & souvenirs
Naples' famous 'doll hospital' is a tiny shop and museum filled with dolls, figurines and traditional toys. Ask about visiting hours at the hospital where the 'operations' take place, in a nearby palazzo.

Ottica Sacco
Via Domenico Capitelli 35-37, off Piazza Gesù Nuovo (081 552 2631, www.otticasacco.it). Metro Dante or Toledo, or bus E1. **Open** 9am-1.30pm, 4.30-8pm Mon-Sat. Closed 2wks Aug. **Map** p60 A5 ㉚ Opticians
Prescriptions can be made up in an hour.

★ Qualcosa di Te
Via San Biagio dei Librai 1 (081 552 3158, www.qualcosadite.com). Metro Dante or Toledo, or bus E1. Open 10am-2pm, 4-8pm Mon-Sat. **Map** p60 C4 ㉛ Food & drink
Giuseppe Musella is passionate about tea and travels regularly to China to source a wide variety of artisanal blends for his little shop. Connoisseurs will be familiar with names such as Dongfang Meiran and Gong Ting Pu'er, but for many of us buying tea here is a voyage of discovery. There's a lovely choice of tea-related accessories too. If you want to taste before buying, nip round to the Gu Shu tearoom just up the road (*see p63*).
Other location Via Massimo Stazione 2F, Vomero (081 1980 6338).

Scriptura
Via San Sebastiano 22 (081 299226). Metro Dante or Toledo, or bus E1. **Open** 3-8pm Mon; 10.30am-8pm Tue-Sat. **Map** p60 B4 ㉜ Accessories
This small, family-run shop sells hand-crafted leather goods made from top-quality Tuscan leather, including satchels and handbags, wallets and belts, leather-bound albums and notebooks. There's a wide range of colours and styles, and prices are very reasonable.

THE CITY WALLS

Considering the sprawling chaos of modern Naples, it's hard to believe the city remained neatly confined within its walls from its Greek beginnings until the middle of the 17th century – yet remarkably, the city limits around the Centro Storico remained more or less unchanged for 2,000 years. In the early 15th century, King Ferdinando I had them extended by a few hundred metres, and

16th-century Spanish viceroy Don Pedro de Toledo beefed up defences by stringing walls or ditches between the city's five castles: Carmine (now gone), Capuano, Sant'Elmo, Nuovo and dell'Ovo.

A few minutes' walk from the eastern end of Spaccanapoli, the impressive **Porta Capuana** gate, with its carved marble triumphal arch and dark towers, dates from 1484. On nearby Via Muzy is **Castel Capuano**, the Hall of Justice, which today houses municipal offices. Built as a palace in the late 12th century, it owes its Renaissance appearance to 16th-century modifications. The façade is strikingly decorated with white plaster, contrasting with the ubiquitous black *piperno* stone. Between castle and gate is the early 16th-century **Santa Caterina a Formiello** (open 8am-8pm daily), considered one of the city's most beautiful Renaissance churches. Inside there's a magnificent organ loft built in 1718 by Giuseppe de Martino, as well as a glorious dome and frescoes by Paolo De Matteis.

The street that heads north-east from the church, Via Carbonara, was where the city's rubbish was once burnt, hence its name; ten minutes up the street on the right is the lovely **San Giovanni a Carbonara** (*see p87*).

VIA DEI TRIBUNALI

Via dei Tribunali, the *decumanus maior* of Greek Neapolis, has maintained a commercial flavour since ancient times, and is lined with small shops and street stalls.

Beginning at the eastern end of Via dei Tribunali and heading west from the Castel Capuano, Piazza Cardinale Sisto Riario Sforza is home to another monumental *guglia*, this one dedicated to **San Gennaro**. Residents erected it in thanks to the city's patron saint, after Naples escaped destruction by an eruption of Vesuvius in 1631. Opposite the monument, the 17th-century church of **Pio Monte della Misericordia** contains Caravaggio's spellbinding *Seven Acts of Mercy*. In the church's *pinacoteca* (gallery) is a small but choice collection that includes works by Giuseppe Ribera and Luca Giordano.

From here, you can't miss the **Duomo**, Naples' cathedral; the main entrance is just down Via Duomo. Across the street is the monumental complex of the **Girolamini** with its *quadreria*, where there's a modest but lovely array of religious paintings.

Back on Via dei Tribunali, an incline leads up past the white façade of the early 17th-century church of the Girolamini, recently reopened after restoration. Beyond it stands the medieval church of **San Lorenzo Maggiore**, and an extraordinary archaeological site revealing the streets of ancient Naples, which have been painstakingly unearthed.

DREAMY DOUGH

You'll be spoilt for choice in Naples, pizza capital of the world.

Pizza has existed for thousands of years. It's said that at the height of the Persian Empire, the soldiers of Darius the Great (521-486 BC) baked a kind of flatbread on their shields, then added cheese and dates. Virgil (70-19 BC) describes how 'we devour the plates on which we fed' and there's evidence that an early form of pizza was baked in ancient Pompeii. Opinions on the etymology differ: it comes either from the Latin *pinsere*, meaning to pound or press, or the Greek *pitta*.

By the 18th century, pizza was a staple food of the poorer classes. Pizza-makers stood on street corners with large vats of boiling fat, frying pizza for passers-by: tomatoes were an extravagant extra. Today, such stalls have all but disappeared, but the more traditional pizzerias often have takeaway counters on the street for snacks on the run. The oldest pizzeria in the city, and indeed the world, is Pizzeria Port'Alba, dating from 1830.

The margherita was created by Raffaele Esposito in 1889. Working for Pizzeria Brandi (still in business today), he was summoned to the Royal Palace to prepare pizza for King Umberto I and Queen Margherita. The Queen's favourite was based on the Italian tricolore flag – red tomatoes, white mozzarella and green basil – and afterwards named in her honour.

Pizza is a simple dish, but extremely difficult to produce well. The *pizzaiolo* is justly proud of his position and a good pizza chef can command a high wage. Until very recently, the art of the *pizzaiolo* has been a strictly male domain but, in 2015, a Neapolitan

woman became world pizza champion, beating some 500 competitors from all over the world. Dough is freshly made each morning: after being kneaded for around 20 minutes until it has the desired non-sticky, elastic consistency, it's worked into balls, placed in wooden trays and left to rest for six to eight hours.

In 2004, the ministry for agriculture issued regulations outlining how a real Neapolitan pizza, *pizza verace napoletana*, should be made. The pizza must be round, no more than 35cm in diameter and no thicker than 0.3cm in the middle with a crust of 1-2cm. The dough is shaped by hand on a flour-covered marble work surface, then the topping added. A large metal spatula is used to place the pizza in the wood-fired oven (*forno a legna*), at a temperature of 485°C, for 60 to 90 seconds. It should be served without delay.

Look for the VPN sign outside pizzerias to sample one of the three authentic types: *pizza napoletana marinara* (San Marzano tomatoes from Vesuvius's slopes, garlic, oregano and olive oil), *pizza napoletana margherita* or *pizza napoletana margherita DOC* (with buffalo mozzarella).

For decades, the pizza scene in Naples has been dominated by traditional pizzerias churning out the same old (albeit very delicious) product, day in and day out. But recently, a new generation of *pizzaioli* have been transporting the humble pizza to new gourmet heights by working on more digestible doughs, sourcing top-notch local ingredients and using some unusual flavour combination as toppings.

A left turn off Via dei Tribunali, Via San Gregorio Armeno is home to the 16th-century church of **San Gregorio Armeno**. The street itself is famous for its Christmas nativity scenes; even in midsummer, crowds line up to buy this much-loved Neapolitan art form.

Returning to Via dei Tribunali, you can't miss the imposing bulk of the church of **San Paolo Maggiore**, which stands above Piazza San Gaetano; beside the church is the entrance to the series of subterranean archaeological sites known as **Napoli Sotterranea**.

The palazzo at no.339 (closed to the public) was built in the 13th century for Philip of Anjou; it has its original, sturdy four-span portico and a 13th-century portal. Opposite is the church of **Santa Maria del Purgatorio ad Arco**, infamous for its skeletal proclivities. Not far away, the Baroque **Santa Maria Maggiore** (closed to the public) has a pretty Romanesque bell tower known as the 'Pietrasanta'. The adjacent **Cappella Pontano** (081 292316, open 9am-1pm Mon-Sat) is a Renaissance work from 1492, though the interior had a Baroque makeover.

Nearby is the small, bare 16th-century church of **Croce di Lucca** (open 9am-1pm Mon-Sat), saved from demolition by writer and philosopher Benedetto Croce, which still bears an unusual Fascist emblem on one external wall.

Continuing along Via dei Tribunali, the splendid church of San Pietro a Maiella stands next to the **Conservatorio di Musica** (*see p69*), illustrious alma mater of such musicians as Scarlatti and Pergolesi. Finally, the street reaches Piazza Bellini: with its abundant trees, beautiful architecture and sunny outdoor cafés, this is the most appealing square in the city.

Sights & Museums

★ Complesso Monumentale dei Girolamini

Via del Duomo 142 (081 294444). Metro Dante or Cavour, or bus E1, E2. **Open** 8.30am-7pm Mon, Tue, Thur, Fri; 8.30am-2pm Sat, Sun. **Admission** €5; €2.50 reductions. **No credit cards. Map** p60 D3 ⑬

The monumental complex of the Girolamini incorporates a vast church, an oratorio, several chapels, a *quadreria* (picture gallery), a library and two cloisters. Built by the Oratorian Fathers (a secular order founded in Rome by San Filippo Neri) during the rule of the Spanish Viceroys, it was designed by Florentine architect Giovanni Antonio Dosio. The church, built on a Latin cross design in high Baroque style with lashings of marble and gold leaf, is dedicated to San Filippo Neri and stands on unremarkable Piazza dei Girolamini (the entrance to the whole compound is round the corner on Via Duomo). The smaller of the two cloisters leads to the church, which is filled with paintings by the greatest Neapolitan masters. Don't miss Luca Giordano's

Christ Expelling the Traders from the Temple on the back wall and Giuseppe Sammartino's *Angels*. On either side of the main altar are two magnificent organ lofts. The larger of the two cloisters, a serene grey-and-white space planted with orange trees and approached via a flight of steps from the entrance, leads to the *quadreria*. This art gallery may be small, but it's thoroughly rewarding, not least because few visitors find their way up here. Consequently you may be alone with paintings by some of the greatest masters of the 16th to 18th centuries. The pick of the crop hang in the penultimate room: Battista Caracciolo's superb *chiaroscuro Baptism of Christ* and other works, Andrea Vaccaro's *Adoration of the Shepherds*, Luca Giordano's stirring *Mourning the Death of Christ*, and five paintings bearing the typical grotesque features of Giuseppe Ribera's school. Along the side walls are works by Neapolitan stalwarts Paolo de Matteis and Francesco Solimena. The 150,000-volume library is renowned, but closed to all but the most insistent.

▶ *For more on painting in Naples, see pp262-267.*

★ FREE Duomo

Via del Duomo 147 (Duomo 081 449097, Museo del Tesoro 081 294980, www.museosangennaro. com). Metro Duomo, or bus E1, E2. **Open** *Church* 8.30am-1.30pm, 2.30-8pm Mon-Sat; 8.30am-1.30pm Sun. Archaeological area closed. *Baptistery* 9am-12.30pm, 2-6.30pm Mon-Sat. *Museo del Tesoro* 9am-5.30pm daily. **Admission** *Church* free. *Baptistery* €1.50. *Museo del Tesoro* €5; €3 reductions. **No credit cards. Map** p61 E3 ㉞

Naples' cathedral dates from the fourth century, when the basilica of Santa Restituta was founded. In the late 600s, the cathedral of Santa Stefania was constructed perpendicular to the original basilica, and at the end of the 13th century the current Duomo was built over Santa Stefania, incorporating Santa Restituta as a side chapel. The bland, 19th-century neo-Gothic façade is tucked away in an unprepossessing, heavily congested side street, so little prepares the visitor for the splendours within.

The gloom of the 100m (328ft) Latin cross interior fails to obscure the fine gilt coffered ceiling (1621) and the paintings by Luca Giordano and his school. The large chapel on the right is the Cappella di San Gennaro, or Museo del Tesoro, which contains the relics of San Gennaro and a large number of bronze and silver statues of saints (many others are kept in the sacristy, and are only put on public display in May and September).

The most famous remains of all are kept in a 14th-century French silver bust and two vials in a strongbox behind the altar. The bust contains Gennaro's skull, the vials his congealed blood. Three times a year the blood allegedly liquefies, most dramatically on Gennaro's feast day, 19 September (*see p72* **City of Blood**). The chapel has a magnificent gilded bronze gate by Cosimo Fanzago (1668), and some fine frescoes by Domenichino (1631-43)

EXPLORE

depicting miraculous episodes from the saint's life. Above the right-hand altar, San Gennaro emerges unscathed from a fiery furnace in a painting by Giuseppe Ribera.

Back in the main church, to the right of the high altar, the chapel of Sant'Aspreno and the Minutolo family chapel have original Gothic decorations. Below the high altar, a magnificent late 16th-century *succorpo* or *confessio* (small chapel) by Tommaso Malvito houses a fine statue of a kneeling Cardinal Carafa and an urn containing more of San Gennaro's bones. The entrance to Santa Restituta is on the left side of the nave; inside, the ceiling painting is attributed to Luca Giordano. Carry on into the fourth-century baptistery – the oldest building of its kind in the West. Beneath the baptistery, the archaeological area showcases Greek and Roman walls, columns and roads, along with early Christian mosaics from the original Santa Stefania cathedral.
▶ *Naples' leading artists vied for the privilege of decorating the Cappella de San Gennaro – and not everyone played fair.*

★ Napoli Sotterranea

Piazza San Gaetano 68 (081 296944, 340 460 6045, 334 366 2841, www.napolisotterranea.org). Metro Dante or Cavour, or bus E1, E2. **Open** *Guided tours* every hour 10am-6pm (Italian); every 2hrs 10am-6pm (English) daily. **Admission** €10. **No credit cards. Map** p60 C3 ❸

A visit to Underground Naples is a fascinating experience and gives a deeper understanding of the complex history of the city. Lying some 35m (123ft) below street level, the series of tunnels, aqueducts and chambers date from the dawn of the city of Neapolis in the fourth century BC, when the Greeks – and later the Romans – excavated the volcanic tuff stone to build the city walls and temples. They also excavated extensive areas to be used as burial chambers. Gradually incorporated into Naples' labyrinthine water supply system, the vast complex remained in use until the cholera epidemic of 1884. During World War II, it was used as bomb shelters. The tunnels, some of them barely passable, stretch for almost 450km (270 miles): the excellent guided tour (available in several languages) covers a kilometre of this, but should be avoided if you're claustrophobic.

★ Pio Monte della Misericordia

Via dei Tribunali 253 (081 446944, www.piomonte dellamisericordia.it). Metro Dante or Cavour, or bus E1, E2. **Open** *Church & Gallery* 9am-2pm Mon, Tue, Thur-Sat. **Admission** €7; €4-€5 reductions. **No credit cards. Map** p61 E3 ❸

Caravaggio's 1607 *Seven Acts of Mercy*, one of the most important artworks in Naples, is housed in this modest, octagonal chapel. It was commissioned by a confraternity of seven Neapolitan nobles whose purpose was to provide interest-free loans to the needy: borrowers would leave items as security, which could be auctioned if the loans were not repaid. The confraternity still exists today, and donates funds to schools, churches and hospitals. Caravaggio's seminal painting, famous for its use of *chiaroscuro* (light and dark), hangs above the chapel's high altar and shows the Virgin and Child being borne asunder by winged angels to a background of a gritty Spaccanapoli street scene. The adjacent picture gallery houses works by Luca Giordano, Giuseppe Ribera, Massimo Stanzione and other 17th- and 18th-century Neapolitan masters. The room where the original confraternity used to meet still holds the seven-sided conference table.

FREE San Gregorio Armeno

Via San Gregorio Armeno 1 (081 552 0186). Metro Dante or Toledo, or bus E1, E2. **Open** 9.30am-noon Mon-Fri, 9.30am-12.30pm Sat, Sun. **Admission** free. **Map** p60 D4 ❸

Built on the site of a Roman temple to the fertility goddess Ceres, the 16th-century church of San Gregorio owes its unflagging popularity to the cult of Santa Patrizia, whose relics are conserved here and whose blood allegedly liquefies not only on her feast day (25 August), when impressive celebrations are held, but also every Tuesday.

Patrizia might well have been Naples' patron saint, had the closed order of nuns that brought her relics from her native Constantinople in the eighth century not kept them secret. For many years only women were allowed to see them, but they're now on view to all in a chapel to the right of the altar. The church is preceded by a porticoed vestibule, and the interior is rich with Neapolitan Baroque. There are paintings and frescoes by Luca Giordano and Paolo de Matteis, and a 17th-century marble altar by Dionisio Lazzari.

To reach the adjacent convent and cloisters, continue up Via San Gregorio, under the arch, and turn left into Via Maffei; the gate will be ajar during opening hours. Still visible by the entrance are the bronze drums through which supplies were passed to the nuns. The lovely cloisters, with their orange trees and pretty fountain, provide a tranquil refuge.

★ San Lorenzo Maggiore (archaeological site)

Via dei Tribunali 316 (081 211 0860, www. laneapolissotterrata.it). Metro Dante or Cavour, or bus E1, E2. **Open** 9.30am-5.30pm daily. **Admission** €9; €6-€7 reductions. **Map** p60 D3 ❸

CONSERVATORIO SAN PIETRO A MAIELLA
Explore the city's musical roots.

A walk from leafy Piazza Bellini along the first part of the ancient *decumanus maior* may well be accompanied by the sounds of music drifting from the halls of the **Conservatorio San Pietro a Maiella** (Via San Pietro a Maiella 35, 081 564 4411, www.sanpietro amajella.it). The word '*conservatorio*' was originally applied to institutions where orphans and young children were looked after ('*conservato*') and educated, and musical training played an important role.

Naples' centre for musical excellence has its roots in a group of four orphanages founded in the 16th and 17th centuries, the most famous of which, La Pietà dei Turchini (named after the turquoise uniforms worn by pupils) was founded in 1592. The four orphanages merged in 1807 to form the Conservatorio di San Sebastiano, which moved to its current location in the late 13th-century monastic complex of San Pietro a Maiella in 1826, changing its name en route. Over the centuries, illustrious musicians such as Alessandro Scarlatti, Domenico Cimarosa, Vincenzo Bellini and, more recently, Riccardo Muti have all worked within these walls. Today, the conservatory is one of the most distinguished in Italy.

To gain access to the small museum and library housing 'millions of pages' of manuscripts, you have to arrange a guided tour (write to the director at direttore@ sanpietroamajella.it), but anyone can pop

through the entrance portico for a look at the lovely cloister, where the sounds of students leave you in no doubt as to where you are.

For anyone even slightly interested in the history of music in Naples, a visit is highly recommended for the remarkable collection of manuscripts, instruments and musical memorabilia. It was once obligatory for composers to deposit a copy of any new opera they produced in the conservatory before it was published, hence the huge archive of original manuscripts housed here. Some go back to the 16th century, but most date from the 1700s and 1800s and include Monteverdi's *Incoronazione di Poppea*, the complete operas of Scarlatti and Porpora, and string quartets by Verdi. Other curiosities include a pair of Bellini's braces, a lock of Donizetti's hair, Paisiello's glasses and a small harp by Stradivarius.

REGIO CONSERVATORIO DI MUSICA

EXPLORE

At the heart of the most densely populated city in Europe, you can stand in silence and feel as if you've been whisked back to Greco-Roman Neapolis. Excavations of this astonishing archaeological site are still ongoing, but have so far revealed sections of the city streets as they were 2,000 years ago, complete with a butcher's, a dyer's, a bakery and a porticoed arcade. Admission includes a visit to the Museo dell'Opera, a small museum with displays that span the site's long history.

★ FREE San Lorenzo Maggiore (church)
Via dei Tribunali 316 (081 211 0860, www. laneapolissotterrata.it). Metro Dante or Cavour, or bus E1, E2. **Admission** free. **Map** p60 D3 ③⑨

More or less returned to its original 13th-century appearance thanks to post-war restoration work, the vast, luminous, plain interior of this much-used

church is in stark contrast to the tiny Baroque façade (1742), which was designed by Ferdinando Sanfelice. It was here, in 1334, that the *Decameron*'s Boccaccio fell in love with Fiammetta; Petrarch stayed in the adjoining convent, which served as the headquarters of the Parthenopean government in 1799.

Some traces of 17th- and 18th-century Baroque remain inside, notably in the third chapel on the right. On the high altar is an early 16th-century relief sculpture of Naples by Giovanni da Nola, and the left-hand transept chapel has two paintings by Caravaggio's disciple Mattia Preti. Sections of the original mosaic flooring are preserved under glass in the transept. Look out, too, for the magnificent Gothic arch that leads into the delicate, cross-vaulted apse.

FREE San Paolo Maggiore
Via dei Tribunali (081 454048, www.sanpaolo maggiore.it). Metro Dante or Cavour, or bus E1, E2. **Open** *Church* 10am-6pm Mon-Sat; 10am-

1pm Sun. *Crypt* 7.30am-noon, 5-7.30pm Mon-Sat; 5-7.30pm Sun. **Admission** free. **Map** p60 D3 ⑩
This lofty, majestic church, dating from the end of the 16th century, stands on the site of a Roman temple to Castor and Pollux. In front of the façade are two tall, white fluted pillars from the temple. Entered via the narrow lane to the right of the church, the interior is notable for the colossal size of its Latin cross interior, and the sacristy has fine frescoes by Francesco de Maria. The adjoining ex-convent at Via San Paolo 14 is an archive of legal documents from the 15th century onwards. The church's crypt, accessible from San Paolo's right aisle or directly from the piazza outside, is dedicated to San Gaetano.

FREE San Pietro a Maiella

Piazza Luigi Miraglia 393 (081 459008). Metro Dante, or bus E1. **Open** 7.30am-noon Mon-Sat; 10am-noon Sun. **Admission** free. **Map** p60 B4 ㊶
Approached from Via dei Tribunali, San Pietro looks for all the world like an English country church, with its cusp-shaped spire of tufa stone. Dating from the early 14th century, the interior has preserved many of its original Angevin features. The round and pointed arches contrast with the elaborate coffered ceiling, adorned with 17th-century paintings by Mattia Preti. There's a superb stained-glass window behind the high altar, and a fresco fragment between the arches on the left of the altar show a rare depiction of the Madonna breastfeeding by an anonymous 15th-century artist. Other lavish works include a fine Madonna appearing to Celestinus V by Massimo Stanzione in the fourth chapel on the right.

FREE Santa Maria delle Anime del Purgatorio ad Arco

Via dei Tribunali 39 (081 440438, www.purgatorio adarco.it). Metro Dante, or bus E1. **Open** 10am-2pm Mon-Fri; 10am-5pm Sat. *Guided tours of church & hypogeum* half-hourly 10.30am-1pm Mon-Sat. **Admission** *Church* free. *Guided tour & hypogeum* €4. **No credit cards. Map** p60 C3 ㊷
The three bronze skulls on the railings (a fourth was stolen in the 1950s), and its popular name, *cap 'e morte* ('death's head'), are clues to why this 17th-century church has such a hold over Neapolitans. This was the centre of a death cult, in which people would adopt and look after the cache of skulls in the *hypogeum* (underground chamber). Inside the church, a winged skull and crossbones in marble (representing the liberation of the soul after death) overlooks the altar, and there are several Baroque paintings, including a circular *Madonna and Child* that some experts attribute to Giotto. Underneath, the *hypogeum* still contains piles of venerated bones and the dusty remains of gifts left by those who practised the cult. Access to the *hypogeum* is only via lively, informative guided tours, some of which are in English (call for information).
▶ *The Church banned the practice of bone worship in 1969, although it's said to live on.*

Restaurants

€ Antica Trattoria da Carmine

Via dei Tribunali 330 (081 294383). Metro Dante, or bus E1. **Open** noon-4pm Tue, Sun; noon-4pm, 7-11pm Wed-Sat. **Average** €20. **Map** p60 D3 ㊹ Neapolitan
The Romano family's bright trattoria is a good spot for a bite between the sights of the Centro Storico. Crowded with locals and visitors, who all appreciate the solid home cooking and modest prices, it serves up traditional staples such as a particularly delicious *melanzane alla parmigiana*, legendary *mpepata 'e cozze* (sautéed mussels), and *spaghetti alle vongole*.

€ Di Matteo

Via dei Tribunali 94 (081 455262). Metro Dante, or bus E1. **Open** 9am-midnight Mon-Sat (open daily Dec). Closed 2wks Aug. **Average** €7. **No credit cards. Map** p60 D3 ㊹ Pizzeria
The decor may be unimpressive, but the pizzas are fabulous at this tiny, highly popular establishment – at lunchtimes, there's always a crowd of people munching pizza on the street. Di Matteo is one of the few places where the *ripieno fritto* (fried calzone pizza) is to be recommended. Delicious deep-fried snacks (*frittura*) can be nibbled to keep hunger at bay while you wait; eat in or take away.

€ L'Etto

Via Santa Maria di Costantinopoli 102 (081 1932 0967). Metro Dante or Museo. **Open** 12.30-3.15pm, 7.30-11pm Mon-Fri; 12.30-3.30pm, 7.30pm-midnight Fri, Sat. **Average** €15. **Map** p60 B4 ㊺ Italian
'*Un etto*' is a measure of weight in Italian (100g to be precise), and in this brilliant new restaurant you help yourself from a buffet of tempting dishes and take your plate to be weighed – each 100g costs €2.50. In a bright, modern space with stripped wood and white paintwork, the emphasis is on healthy eating and you'll find a choice of meat, chicken, fish and pasta or rice dishes, plus soups, vegetables, flans and delicious desserts. For €20, you can fill your boots.

★ € Sorbillo

Via dei Tribunali 32 (081 446643). Metro Dante, or bus E1. **Open** noon-3.30pm, 7-11.30pm Mon-Sat. Closed 3wks Aug. **Average** €6. **Map** p60 C3 ㊻ Pizzeria
Sorbillo's original Centro Storico outpost is the best, according to locals, and shouldn't be confused with the other pizzeria of the same name just along the street. Run by the energetic and media-savvy Gino, a third-generation *pizzaiuolo*, this two-level squeeze of a space has a quick turnover and an ever-present crowd of punters on the street waiting to be served. The wide choice of pizza is based on a superb, puffy dough and the very best local tomatoes and mozzarella; you can order a classic margherita or something a little more exotic – Vittorio is topped with local red tuna, olives and wild oregano.

Gino Sorbillo now has a branch on the seafront and a pizza fritta shop in Piazza Trieste e Trento.

€ Un Sorriso Integrale

Vico San Pietro a Majella, Piazza Bellini 6 (081 455026, www.sorriso integrale.com). Metro Dante or Museo. **Open** noon-4pm, 7.30pm-midnight daily (7.30pm-midnight daily Aug). **Average** €15. **Map** p60 B4 ⓴ **Vegetarian**

This longstanding bastion of vegetarian, vegan and organic cuisine with a Mediterranean bent is tucked away in a quiet courtyard just off Piazza Bellini. Modestly priced, it's popular with students and has a friendly vibe at its communal tables. The pasta and soup options change daily, and the mixed platter specials are fresh and wholesome. After lunch, stock up on organic produce from the shop.

★ La Stanza del Gusto

Via Santa Maria di Costantinopoli 100 (081 401578, www.lastanzadelgusto.com) Metro Dante or Museo. **Open** noon-11pm Mon-Sat. Closed lunch in Aug. **Average** €40. **Map** p60 B4 ⓸ **Contemporary Neapolitan**

Trailblazing chef Mario Avallone is a pioneer of contemporary Neapolitan cuisine, having founded the 'Officine Gastronomiche Partenopee' cultural association – dedicated to good food and the eating of it – in 1991. He soon made a name for himself as a master of creative cuisine, and in 2007 moved his famous restaurant to its present location near Piazza Bellini. The restaurant is on two levels: a colourful, bistro-style room looking on to the street, ideal for a quick 'working lunch' (a snip at €13); and a more relaxed restaurant upstairs. The menu, showcasing the best regional produce, is the same at both and ranges from snacks such as *cunzato* (a kind of panino, maybe with mozzarella and grilled aubergines), salads and soups to the sort of eclectic dishes that made Mario's name: lamb tagine, *calamaro croccante* (crispy squid) with smoked provola cheese, and pork shank cooked with beer. To sample Mario's cooking at its creative best, go for the tasting menu (€65) and let him get on with it.

IN THE KNOW BANKSY IN NAPLES

Scruffy Piazza dei Girolamini is home to one of two works that elusive graffiti artist Banksy has left in Naples. At the base of the wall to the right of the entrance to the church of San Girolamini (see p67) is his image of the Holy Virgin, surmounted by a pistol. Banksy's other Neapolitan work was painted on the wall opposite the church of Santa Chiara in Via Benedetto Croce but has been more or less obliterated by graffiti from a rival artist.

Cafés, Bars & Gelaterie

★ Intramoenia Caffè Letterario

Piazza Bellini 70 (081 451652, www.intramoenia.it). Metro Dante or Museo. **Open** 10am-2am daily. **Map** p60 B4 ⓵

This handsome, welcoming spot overlooking Naples' most beautiful piazza is a cultural club and café all in one. The snack menu includes panini and bruschettas, salads, and platters of cheese and meat. It's great for meeting friends or just passing time with a good book and eyeing up Naples' intellectual hipsters.

Pastisseria Capriccio di Salvatore Capparelli

Via dei Tribunali 325 (081 454310). Metro Dante. **Open** 7am-8.30pm Tue-Sun. Closed last wk Aug. **Map** p60 D3 ⓾

The few tables on the Via dei Tribunali make for prime people-watching potential. The *gelato* is of the *produzione artigianale* (home-made) variety, and fresh, piping-hot *babà* (cake in rum syrup) and *sfogliatelle* are delivered regularly from the bakery next door.

Shops & Services

Antica Libreria Regina

Via Santa Maria di Costantinopoli 51/103 (081 290925, 081 459983, www.libreriaregina.it). Metro Dante or Museo. **Open** 9am-8pm Mon-Sat. Closed Sat July & 3wks Aug. **Map** p60 B3 ⓾ **Books & antiques**

This specialist bookshop stocks a good selection of 19th-century gouache paintings of the Bay of Naples, as well as books on Neapolitan culture and history.

★ Colonnese

Via San Pietro a Maiella 33 (081 459858, www.colonnese.it). Metro Dante or Museo. **Open** 9am-1.30pm, 4-7.30pm Mon-Sat. Closed 2wks Aug. **Map** p60 B4 ⓾ **Antiques**

A publishing house, cultural gathering place and bookshop, Colonnese is a hotspot for the local literati. Tomes tackle Neapolitan history in the 19th and early 20th centuries, and there are old postcards, prints and rare books to browse. Look out for book readings and literary events.

Fondazione Morra Greco

Largo Avellino 17, off Via Anticaglia (081 210690, www.fondazionemorragreco.it). Metro Cavour or Museo. **Open** 10am-2pm, 3-7pm Mon-Fri; 11am-2pm, 3-7pm Sat. Closed Aug. **No credit cards. Map** p60 D2 ⓾ **Gallery**

Dental surgeon and art collector Maurizio Morra Greco began using the gutted Palazzo Caracciolo d'Avellino in 2006 to exhibit artists such as German Gregor Schneider. Another show was devoted to intimate video portraits by Estonian Mark Raidpere, with an installation about sea navigation by Sven Johne upstairs.

EXPLORE

CITY OF BLOOD
Superstitions are rife in Naples – along with a taste for the macabre.

To an outsider, everyday life in Naples appears to involve a tangled fabric of superstitions. Take the hand gesture for warding off the *malocchio* (evil eye): if a funeral procession should pass by, or if someone should be so foolhardy as to mention illness or misfortune, Neapolitans will inevitably make horns with their index and little fingers and point at the ground – in addition, most probably, to crossing themselves.

Not for nothing is Naples known as *urbs sanguinum* (city of blood). Consider the city's patron saint, San Gennaro. After he was beheaded in 305, his blood was brought to what became the catacombs of San Gennaro (see p90). About a century later, the first miraculous liquefication of Gennaro's dried blood is said to have taken place, although the first official record of the miracle dates back only as far as 1389.

Gennaro's blood is said to bubble into action at the Duomo (see p67) three times a year: on the Saturday before the first Sunday in May, on 19 September (his feast day) and on 16 December, when crowds of devotees flock to witness the phenomenon. It usually takes between two minutes and an hour for the blood to liquefy, accompanied by the faithful's fervent prayers. In 1980, the miracle failed to occur – the very year that a devastating earthquake rocked southern Italy. Saintly blood is something of a Neapolitan theme; Santa Patrizia's also liquefies, in the church of San Gregorio Armeno (see p68).

Neapolitans are also obsessed with death; just take a look at the bronze skulls at Santa Maria delle Anime del Purgatorio ad Arco (see p70), polished by the constant caresses of locals. Such things are taken very seriously, although few will admit it. 'It's not true,' they'll tell you, 'but I believe it anyway.'

There does seem to be a particular obsession with Purgatory, however. Along Via San Gregorio Armeno (see p67), in addition to the crib figures and omnipresent Pulcinellas, you'll find painted figurines of various souls in flames: priests, gamblers, soccer players and even Berlusconi.

For other local fetishes, a quick look inside the chapel on the right in Gesù Nuovo (see p58) will confirm that the tradition of ex-votos endures. Silver icons of bodies and body parts cover the walls, and all sorts of designs are sold in Spaccanapoli's jewellery shops. In the Museo Archeologico Nazionale (see p82), compare the ancient Roman terracotta breasts, penises and testicles to realise just how ancient and deeply held this belief is.

That brings us to another ever-present talisman: the *corno*. In its modern embodiment it looks like a red pepper, but there seems little doubt that this popular amulet is a surrogate phallus, and derives from the ancient custom of men touching their genitals (*testis* is Latin for 'witness') when making an oath, seeking protection from evil or calling on unseen powers for a stroke of luck.

★ Limoné

*Piazza San Gaetano 72 (081 299429, www.
limoncellodinapoli.it). Metro Dante or Cavour,
or bus E1, E2.* **Open** 10.45am-8.30pm daily.
Map p60 D3 ㊿ **Food & drink**
Free tastes and tours are offered at this friendly limoncello shop, where an organic version of the ubiquitous lemon liqueur is made on site. Other boozy temptations include liqueurs made from rocket, fennel and liquorice, and jars of *babà* soaked in limoncello.

Il Mondo dei Pastori

*Via San Gregorio Armeno 46 (081 551 6205,
www.ilmondodeipastori.it). Metro Dante or Museo,
or bus E1.* **Open** 9am-7.30pm Mon-Sat. Closed
1wk Aug. **Map** p60 D4 ㊿ **Gifts & souvenirs**
Neapolitans take their Christmas nativity displays very seriously. This street is where they come to buy new heads and limbs, or to undertake major expansions. Ugo Esposito is a master of the art. He also produces hand-painted terracotta Pulcinellas, as well as various souls burning in the flames of Purgatory.

★ T293

*Via Tribunali 293 (081 295882, www.t293.it).
Metro Dante or Cavour.* **Open** Oct-mid July noon-7pm Tue-Fri; other times by appt. Closed mid July-Aug. **No credit cards. Map** p60 D3 ㊿ **Gallery**
Opened in 2002 in a cool, tranquil space in a decaying palazzo, T293 is run by young curators Paola Guadagnino and Marco Altavilla. It moved its headquarters to Rome in 2010, but the Naples gallery continues to show thought-provoking conceptual work.

THE DECUMANUS SUPERIOR

The third ancient *decumanus* runs parallel to Via dei Tribunali to the north, starting at Via Santa Sofia opposite the church of **San Giovanni a Carbonara** (*see p87*). It passes the towering church of the **Santissimi Apostoli** (open 8-11.30am, 5.30-8pm Mon-Sat, 8.30am-1pm Sun), believed to have been built over a Roman temple to Mercury. The street then changes its name to Via dei Santissimi Apostoli, passing the 17th-century Baroque church of **Santa Maria Donnaregina Nuova**. Behind the church, on Vico Donnaregina, stands the original 14th-century church of the same name; both churches are now incorporated into the **Museo Diocesano Napoli**. After the church, the street changes its name to Via dell'Anticaglia. A little further on, you'll reach two Roman brick archways that once joined a theatre on the south of the street to baths on the north.

Sights & Museums

Museo Diocesano Napoli

*Largo Donnaregina (081 557 1365, www.museo
diocesanonapoli.it). Metro Dante or Cavour, or*

bus E1. **Open** 9.30am-4.30pm Mon, Wed-Sat; 9.30am-2pm Sun. **Admission** €6; €4 reductions. **No credit cards. Map** p60 D2 ㊿
The collection of art housed in this museum is an accumulation of paintings and other treasures salvaged from many of the city's once art-rich but now defunct or abandoned churches. Inaugurated in 2007, the museum occupies a monastic complex that includes the beautifully restored church of Santa Maria Donnaregina Nuova, a masterpiece of Neapolitan Baroque that was once connected to the adjacent 13th-century church of Santamaria Donnaregina Vecchia. While the newer church houses works by the likes of Solimena, Luca Giordano and Massimo Stanzione – as well as a rare, 12th-century reliquary cross that enshrines a fragment of wood believed to come from Christ's Cross – it's the deconsecrated older church that's the real draw here. The bare interior has delicate fan vaults that, like the walls, bear traces of 14th-century Giotto-style frescoes. Tino da Camaino's magnificent marble tomb of Queen Mary of Hungary (1323), wife of Charles II of Anjou, is against the left-hand wall, and the nun's choir (which you can climb up to) has a coffered ceiling and 14th-century frescoes by Pietro Cavallini. Depicting biblical scenes, saints and contemporary nobles, these are the most complete frescoes of their era in Naples.

Restaurants

★ € La Cantina di Via Sapienza

*Via della Sapienza 40 (081 459078). Metro Museo
or Dante.* **Open** noon-3.30pm Mon-Sat. Closed
3wks Aug. **Average** €13. **No credit cards.**
Map p60 B3 ㊿ **Neapolitan**
This little family-run place is only open at lunchtimes and the dozen tables are usually packed with doctors and nurses from the neighbouring Policlinico hospital who come for some of the best (and cheapest) home cooking in the city. Daily specials might include *pasta alla siciliana* (with aubergines, tomato and mozzarella), *pasta al ragù* or an outstanding *parmigiana di melanzane*. Expect friendly service, fine desserts and good *vino locale*.

Via Toledo & La Sanità

From the flashy shops and elegant *palazzi* of Via Toledo to the earthy, densely populated area of La Sanità – rich in folklore, catacombs and burial sites – this chapter covers a lot of ground. Via Toledo is central Naples' main drag, stretching from Piazza Trieste e Trento in the south to the magnificent Museo Archeologico Nazionale in the north, and channelling a hugely varied cast of characters, from bankers to beggars (plus lots of tourists), along the way. The once-notorious Quartieri Spagnoli lie just to the west, the dense grid of streets now adorned with bunting inviting visitors to cross the threshold. Traffic-clogged Via Foria converges with Via Toledo at its most northerly point, the two roads effectively creating the northern and western boundaries of the Centro Storico. To the east lies the lush oasis of the Orto Botanico and, beyond that, the missed opportunity that is the vast Albergo dei Poveri.

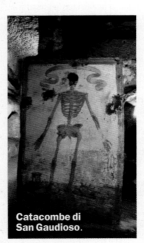

Catacombe di San Gaudioso.

Don't Miss

1 Museo Archeologico Nazionale Relics aplenty at this world-class museum (p82).

2 MADRe Contemporary art in a converted palazzo (p87).

3 Catacombe di San Gaudioso What lies beneath (p86).

4 Pizzeria Starita Some of the finest pizza in the city (p87).

5 Mexico Exceptional espresso (p85).

VIA TOLEDO & THE QUARTIERI SPAGNOLI

Created in the early 16th century by Spanish viceroy Don Pedro di Toledo, **Via Toledo** was rechristened Via Roma when Naples became part of the Italian republic in 1860. A recent return to its original name can be confusing and you may hear it called both.

Forming a link between the Quartieri Spagnoli and the old city to the east, the road was lined with elegant *palazzi* and lauded as one of Europe's most impressive streets. Where the homes of nobles and bankers once dazzled visitors, clothing retailers now hold sway. The *palazzi* are still there, though, visible above the shopfronts and from the *cortili* (courtyards) that can be glimpsed through impressive entrances.

The street's pedestrianised area ends at the junction with Via Armando Diaz. East along Via Diaz, modern Piazza Matteotti is dominated by the vast, Fascist-era façade of the 1930s post office, the **Palazzo delle Poste e Telegrafi**. Towering over the square from behind the modern Questura (police headquarters) is the 30-storey Jolly Hotel, a hugely unpopular eyesore that received planning permission from the city council in the 1950s.

North of the post office in Piazza Monteoliveto, the 15th-century church of **Sant'Anna dei Lombardi** was once part of a much larger convent. Some of the complex has since been incorporated into the adjacent Carabinieri (police station) – scene of the *mani pulite* ('clean hands') anti-corruption enquiries of the 1990s.

Further north, the grim 20th-century façade of the church of **Spirito Santo** (no.409, open 9-11.30am Mon-Sat, 10.30am-noon Sun) masks a lofty, cool grey-and-white interior, above which looms one of the largest domes in the city.

The grid of streets on the slope west of Via Toledo constitutes the **Quartieri Spagnoli**, built to house Spanish troops during Don Pedro di Toledo's flourish of urban expansion in the 16th century. Cramped from the start, the Quartieri became home to some of the poorest of Naples' poor; buildings that were scarcely fit for Spanish horses 400 years ago became the damp, exhaust-filled dwellings of wretched human beings. Many still are, and the Quartieri holds some unenviable records: Europe's highest rates of unemployment and respiratory disease are just two of them.

Yet there's something fascinating – for the visitor – about this warren of streets which has been cleaned up and almost gentrified in recent years. It used to be a no-go area (and you should still be careful after dark), but it's now much more geared up to receive tourists, selling itself as a quaint visitor attraction. One draw is the delightful **Via Pignasecca**, home to a chaotic street market. With the market in full swing, crowds of people streaming towards the city

Palazzo Zevallos Stigliano.

centre by funicular railway and ambulances screaming around the Pellegrini hospital, the swirling inferno is as loud as it is mesmerising.

Sights & Museums

★ Hermann Nitsch Museum

Vico Lungo Pontecorvo 29D (081 564 1655, www.museonitsch.org). Metro Dante. **Open** 10am-7pm Mon-Fri; 10am-2pm Sat. Closed Aug. **Admission** €10; €5 reductions; under-18s (EU citizens) free. **No credit cards. Map** p78 D2 ❶

Set in a former electricity plant, with magnificent views that stretch as far as Vesuvius and Capri, this museum and archive was opened in 2008 by the Fondazione Morra. It's dedicated to Viennese 'actionist' artist Hermann Nitsch's splatter paintings, and the relics of his orgiastic, bloody, theatrical mock crucifixions (by now more than 100). His work is strangely in keeping with the religious rites and iconography of the teeming Neapolitan streets, such as the 'miraculous' flowing of San Gennaro's blood in the Duomo three times a year (*see p72* **City of Blood**). Collector Peppe Morra has sponsored Nitsch's performances since the 1970s; one, Lehraktion, took place in 1996 within view of the museum, at a hilltop vineyard owned by Morra.

Palazzo Zevallos Stigliano

Via Toledo 185 (800 454229, www.gallerie ditalia.com). Metro Toledo, or funicular Centrale

to *Augusteo, or bus C25, R2.* **Open** 10am-6pm Tue-Fri; 10am-8pm Sat, Sun. **Admission** €5; €3 reductions. **Map** p79 H2 ❷

Caravaggio's final work, *The Martyrdom of St Ursula* (1610), hangs in the 17th-century Palazzo Zevallos Stigliano, which was once the opulent headquarters of a bank – the ground floor, now used for concerts and conferences, still retains the wonderful carved wood counters. The art collection of the Banca Intesa San Paolo hangs in a series of beautifully lit galleries on the top floor, and includes works by Luca Giordano, Artemesia Gentileschi and Francesco Solimena. The star turn – the Caravaggio – hangs in splendid isolation in a small blue room decorated with stucco work.

FREE Sant'Anna dei Lombardi

Piazza Monteoliveto 44 (081 551 3333). Metro Dante or Museo, or bus 201, E1, R4. **Open** 10am-1.30pm, 2-4pm Mon-Thur; 10am-1.20pm, 2-6pm Fri, Sat. **Admission** free. **Map** p79 F3 ❸

Sant'Anna dates from the early 15th century, but it was refurbished in the 17th century and rebuilt after wartime bombing. Inside, its Renaissance sculptures include an extraordinary group of terracotta statues, *Mourning the Death of Christ*, by Guido Mazzoni (1492). In the Correale chapel is a bas-relief of the Annunciation by Florentine Renaissance master Benedetto da Maiano (closed for restoration) and the sacristy has a fine ceiling frescoed by Giorgio Vasari in 1544; the unusual inlaid wooden wall panels are from the same period.

Restaurants

Ciro a Santa Brigida

Via Santa Brigida 71/73 (081 552 4072, www.ciroasantabrigida.com). Metro Municipio, or funicular Centrale to Augusteo, or bus C25, R2. **Open** 12.30-3.30pm, 7.30pm-1am Mon-Sat. Closed 1wk Aug. **Average** *Pizzeria* €20. *Ristorante* €50. **Map** p79 H3 ❹ Ristorante/pizzeria

Set over two floors (head upstairs for a seat overlooking the street; if you strain you can see Vesuvius), Ciro offers pizzas and a huge list of seasonal *contorni* – you might find *carciofi* (artichokes), *scarola* (lettuce) or aubergine. The fish – *pesce spada* (swordfish), perhaps, or prawns – is excellent.

Il Garum

Piazza Monteoliveto 2A (081 542 3228, www.ristoranteilgarum.it). Metro Dante or Museo, or bus 201, E1, R4. **Open** noon-3.30pm, 7-11.30pm daily. Closed 2wks Aug. **Average** €35. **Map** p79 F3 ❺ Ristorante

This well-regarded osteria, which is named after the salty anchovy extract that the ancient Romans used in their cooking, has tables outside on lovely Piazza Monteoliveto. The chef creates Neapolitan cuisine with innovative touches such as *paccheri*

EXPLORE

EXPLORE

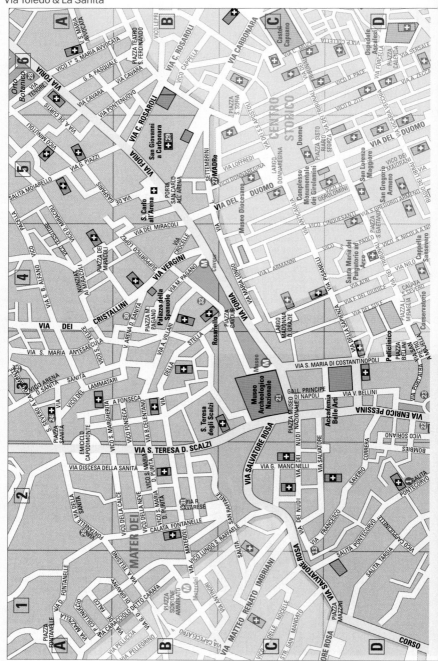

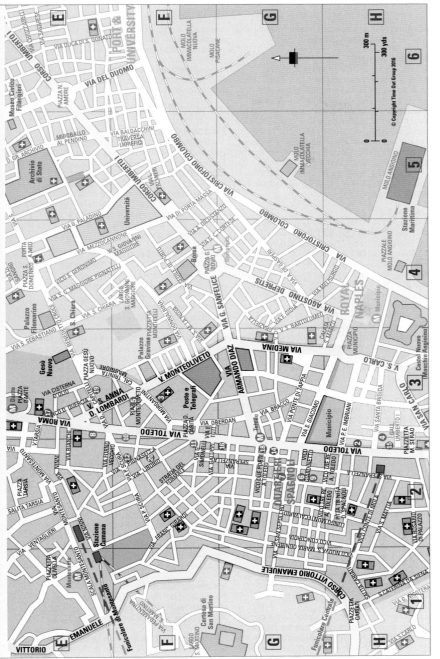

EXPLORE

with tuna roe or grilled octopus with balsamic vinegar. The set lunch menu is great value.

Hosteria Toledo

Vico Giardinetto a Toledo 78 (081 421257).
Metro Toledo, or funicular Centrale to Augusteo.
Open noon-3pm, 6.30pm-midnight Mon, Wed-Sun; noon-3pm Tue. Closed 2wks Aug. **Average**
€25. **Map** p79 G2 ➏ **Trattoria**

Quality cuisine in the Quartieri Spagnoli, with traditional fare and generous portions. The minty *courgette alla scapece* (sweet and sour) is delicious, as is the vermicelli with mussels, courgette flowers and pecorino cheese. There's a fine *melanzane alla parmigiana* and good fish, too, but leave some space for the home-made *dolci*. Weekday lunches are particularly good value.

€ Nennella

Vico Lungo Teatro Nuovo 103 (081 414338).
Metro Dante, or bus C25, R2. **Open** noon-3.30pm, 7.30-11.30pm. Closed 15 Aug-1 Sept. **Average**
€12. **Map** p79 G2 ➐ **Trattoria**

This Quartieri Spagnoli classic has been serving delicious, wholesome food at rock-bottom prices since 1949. You can't book and there's almost always a long queue of people waiting to tuck into plates of *pasta e ceci*, *spaghetti alla puttanesca*, golden deep-fried anchovies and *polpettine* (meatballs). The menu changes daily according to what's available and good at the market. This is no place to linger, but you won't get better value in Naples.

€ La Taverna del Buongustaio

Via Basilio Puoti 8 (081 551 2626). Metro Toledo or Dante, or bus 201, R4. **Open** 12.30-3.30pm, 7pm-midnight Mon-Sat; 12.30-3.30pm Sun. Closed 2wks Aug. **Average** €15. **No credit cards. Map** p79 E3 ➒ **Trattoria**

It's easy to miss this excellent, no-frills trattoria, which is hidden down a side street criss-crossed with washing lines. The white-tiled walls and waxed tablecloths, plus the homely quality of the food, all give the impression that you're eating in someone's kitchen. A written menu exists, but the waiter will rattle off the day's fish and meat dishes at a quick-fire pace: try the delicious *pasta alla puttanesca* (with tomato, capers and black olives) or the deep fried anchovies. The *torta caprese* (chocolate and almond cake) is a great final flourish.

Valù

Vico Lungo del Gelso (081 038 1139, www.valu.it). Metro Toledo, or funicular Centrale to Augusteo. **Open** noon-3pm, 6.30pm-midnight Mon-Sat. Closed 2wks Aug. **Average** €25. **Map** p79 G2 ➒ **Trattoria**

Valù, with its contemporary decor and menu of risottos and grilled meats, is rather unexpected in the Quartieri Spagnoli. Around 20 risottos are on the menu each day, and they're delicious: there's some

seasonal variation, but you can expect combinations such as taleggio cheese, pear and port, or walnut and gorgonzola. The succulent chargrilled meats are excellent and there's a good wine list. Bag a table on the small terrace and watch life go by in the colourful Quartieri. Prices are lower at lunchtimes, but there's less choice available.

Cafés, Bars & Gelaterie

Fantasia Gelati

Via Toledo 381 (081 551 1212, www.fantasia gelati.it). Metro Toledo or Dante, or bus 201, R4. **Open** 7am-midnight daily. **No credit cards. Map** p79 F3 ➓

Fantasia serves up an amazing array of creamy *gelati*, ranging from classic *cioccolato* to creative Benevento (nougat and chocolate chunks). The cakes are to die for, and there's also a tempting assortment of fruit and nuts filled with *gelato*, a southern Italian speciality.

Gelateria della Scimmia

Piazza Carità 4 (081 552 0272, www.gelateria dellascimmia.it). Metro Dante or Montesanto, or bus 201, R4. **Open** *Jan-Mar, Nov* 11am-9pm Mon-Fri; 11am-midnight Sat, Sun. *Apr-Sept* 10am-midnight daily. *Oct, Dec* 10am-9pm Mon-Fri; 10am-midnight Sat, Sun. **No credit cards. Map** p79 F2 ⓫

One of the city's oldest (it opened in 1933) and most renowned *gelaterie*, this wonderfully retro place is usually very busy. Go for the basic flavours and you won't be sorry (strawberry and lemon is an excellent combination) or try the intensely sweet house speciality – a chocolate-coated banana *gelato* on a stick. The bonbons, ice-cream sandwiches and *semi-freddi* are equally tempting.

Shops & Services

Antiche Delizie

Via Pasquale Scura 14, Toledo (081 551 3088). Metro Dante or Montesanto, or bus 201, R4. **Open** *July, Aug* 8am-2.30pm, 3-8pm Mon-Wed, Fri, Sat; 8am-3pm Thur. *Sept-June* 8am-2.30pm, 3-8pm Mon-Wed, Fri, Sat; 8am-3pm Thur; 9am-2pm Sun. Closed 1wk Aug. **Map** p79 F2 ⓬ **Food & drink**

Along with superb cheeses, Antiche Delizie stocks a mouthwatering selection of meats and preserves. Try the *caprignetti* (soft goat's cheese in herbs) or cheese with *tartufo* (truffles). There are local wines and home-made pasta dishes too.

★ Caseari Cautero

Piazzetta Pontecorvo (081 1917 9449). Metro Museo, or bus 139, C16, C47. **Open** 8am-8pm Mon-Wed, Fri, Sat; 8am-2pm Thur. **Map** p78 C2 ⓭ **Food & drink**

Salvatore Cautero's *gastronomia* (delicatessen) may be hard to reach, but the quality of the products he stocks justifies the effort. His small shop is stuffed with the best Italy has to offer, including a fabulous range of cheeses, superb cured meats, olive oils, vinegars and a fine selection of wines.

Disney Store

Via Toledo 129 (081 790 1377). Metro Toledo. **Open** 10am-8pm Mon-Sat; 10am-2pm, 4.30-8pm Sun. **Map** p79 G2 ⓮ **Children's toys**
Familiar characters abound at the Naples outpost of the Disney empire.

Gay-Odin

Via Toledo 214 (081 551 3491, www.gay-odin.it). Metro Dante, or funicular Centrale to Augusteo, or bus 201, R4. **Open** 9.30am-8.30pm Mon-Sat. Closed 2wks Aug. **Map** p79 H2 ⓯ **Food & drink**
Luscious piles of pralines and deliciously flaky Foresta chocolate bars are among the delicacies at this venerable Via Toledo chocolate shop. The *gelati* are equally delicious.
Other locations throughout the city.
► *Visit the small, charming factory in Chiaia (Via Vetriera 12, 081 417843) to see the Willy Wonka-style production line in action.*

Leonetti

Via Toledo 350-351 (081 412765, www.leonetti gioccattoli.com). Metro Toledo, or bus 201, R4. **Open** 10am-2pm, 3.30-8.30pm Mon-Sat. **Map** p79 G2 ⓰ **Children's toys**
A monthly visit to Leonetti is a long-established tradition for Neapolitan children. It stocks a vast selection of toys and games, both classic and modern.

★ Leopoldo

Via Toledo 8 (081 551 2909, www.leopoldo.it). Metro Dante, or bus 139, 201, R4. **Open** 7.30am-9pm daily. **Map** p79 E3 ⓱ **Food & drink**
Tarallificio Leopoldo has been baking its *taralli* (breadsticks) since 1940 and, according to locals, they're the best in Naples. There's a wide choice of other baked goods, both sweet and savoury, plus fresh handmade pasta.

★ Mario Talarico

Vico Due Porte a Toledo 4B (081 407723, www. mariotalarico.it). Metro Toledo, or funicular Centrale to Augusteo, or bus C25, R2. **Open** 8am-8pm Mon-Sat. **Map** p79 G2 ⓲ **Accessories**
In his tiny workshop, Mario Talarico constructs the finest umbrellas in the city.

Maurizio di Cesare

Via Domenico Capitelli 19, off Piazza Gesù Nuovo (081 551 3114, www.mauriziodicesare. com). Metro Dante, or bus 201, E4, R1. **Open** 9.30am-1.30pm, 4.30-7.30pm Mon-Fri; 9.30am-1.30pm Sat. Closed 2wks Aug. **Map** p79 E3 ⓳ **Photography**
A well organised and friendly photo service.

SAVING SANITÀ
Providing hope for the future.

Of the many underrated artistic treasures hidden among the ancient streets of the Rione Sanità, the San Gennaro catacombs (see p90) are among the most important. In 2009, they only received 6,000 visitors; by 2015 that number had risen to 60,000 and is still climbing. This impressive statistic is all down to a group of young, local men and women who realised that the artistic legacy of their crumbling, over-populated yet endlessly fascinating neighbourhood was being all but ignored.

Among the many issues, sites such as the Cimitero delle Fontanelle (see p86) were being kept closed by staff shortages, so in 2006 the group founded La Paranza, a not-for-profit association designed to not only take on the restoration and running of sites such as the catacombs and the Fontanelle, but also to address the crippling social problems of an area with 60 per cent youth unemployment and crushing poverty.

'The Sanità has been abandoned by the authorities, but it has so much potential,' says Vincenzio Porzio, spokesman for the group. 'Our young people need to work and they need to feel proud of their home'. So they put the two together: understaffed visitor attractions plus a huge labour pool equals putting these fantastic treasures back on the tourist map. Since its foundation, La Paranza has managed to secure major funding from both Italy and the EU, and is collaborating with projects such as the Sanità Ensemble youth orchestra and the Centro di Aggregazione initiative, set up by Don Antonio Loffredo, which opened up several church-owned properties to local kids as a safe haven for homework and other activities.

Projects such as these have created a feeling of community in the area, and with that comes real hope for the future. 'Our dream is to attract so many visitors to the Sanità that we can make an impact on the unemployment figures,' says Porzio. 'If we can get this far in ten years, just imagine what the future may hold.'

For information on the brilliant guided tours to the catacombs and the Cimitero delle Fontanelle and on the Miglio Sacro walking tours of the Sanità (all led by local guides), see www.catacombedinapoli.it.

EXPLORE

Mercato di Pignasecca.

EXPLORE

★ Mercato di Pignasecca

Via Pignasecca & surrounding streets. Metro Toledo or Montesanto, or bus 201, R4. **Open** 8am-1pm daily. **Map** p79 F2 ⑳ **Food & drink**
This is one of the city's oldest markets, a real slice of Neapolitan street life. The bustling Pignasecca sells all manner of goods: fish, vegetables, deli goods, cut-price perfume, fashion and linen, and cheap and cheerful kitchenware.

PIAZZA DANTE

Piazza Dante is situated at the point where Via Toledo turns into Via Enrico Pessina. Restored to glory for the 2002 opening of its metro station, the piazza is defined by the crescent-shaped **Convitto Nazionale**, originally a state-funded boarding school for poor children from outside Naples. Designed in the mid 18th century by Luigi Vanvitelli, the Convitto has 26 statues representing the many virtues of Carlo III. At its northern end is the Port'Alba arch, which was built in the early 17th century and rebuilt 150 years later. A second-hand book market rambles between the Porta and Via Santa Maria di Costantinopoli. The Piazza Dante metro station is also of interest, thanks to its impressive array of modern art.

The magnificent **Museo Archeologico Nazionale**, home to some of Italy's greatest

treasures, is further north on the smoggy, noisy Via Pessina. En route, in Via Bellini, stands the **Accademia delle Belle Arti** (081 441900, 081441887, www.accademiadinapoli.it, open 10am-2pm Tue, 2-6pm Fri, €5), with its mid 19th-century façade in tufa stone and fine art collection. From the northern end of Via Bellini, the rather sleazy Galleria Principe di Napoli leads to Piazza Museo.

Beyond the museum on Via Santa Teresa degli Scalzi stands **Santa Teresa degli Scalzi** (no.43, open 10am-12.30pm Sun), built in the 17th century and reworked in the 18th century. The church has been largely neglected, its fickle congregation having decamped to the Gesù Nuovo (*see p58*). It's now run by a different order, which hopes to establish regular opening hours.

Piazza Cavour, with its busy underground station and public gardens, leads east out of Piazza Museo. The restored **Porta San Gennaro**, with a 17th-century fresco by Mattia Preti, formed part of the original 15th-century city walls.

Sights & Museums

★ Museo Archeologico Nazionale

Piazza Museo 19 (081 442 2149, http://cir. campania.beniculturali.it/museoarcheologico nazionale). Metro Cavour or Museo, or bus 168, 178, R4. **Open** 9am-7.30pm Mon,

Wed-Sun (last admission 1hr before closing).
Admission €8; €4 reductions; free under-18s.
Exhibitions vary. **Map** p78 C3 ❷

In 1777, King Ferdinando I selected this early 17th-century palazzo as the perfect home for the immense collection of ancient artefacts he inherited from his grandmother, Elisabetta Farnese. Discoveries from Pompeii, Stabiae and Herculaneum were later added, making this one of the finest archaeological museums in the world.

It should be noted, however, that restoration work means there are often gaps in the collection, and pieces may not be where they should be. Due to reduced staffing, some rooms are unmanned or even closed, and queues are common. For this reason, the best day to visit is Sunday.

The museum is laid out over four floors. The basement holds the Egyptian section, with objects imported into Italy during the Roman period and unearthed in excavations in Rome and the Campania region. There's a large collection of obelisks, busts, funerary statues, jewellery and sarcophagi from the Hellenic and Ptolemaic periods, and the obligatory mummy, once part of the Borgia collection.

The meandering ground floor houses the collection assembled by the powerful Farnese family (although the paintings are in the Museo di Capodimonte, *see p90*). Most of the pieces were filched from ancient sites in Rome during the 16th century, when Alessandro Farnese ruled as Pope Paul III (1534-49). In room 1, on the right of the entrance hall, are the *Tirannicidi* (tyrant-killers Armodios and Aristogitones, who did away with the cruel Athenian rulers Hippia and Hipparchos in 514 BC); it's a Roman copy of the fifth century BC Greek original. In the same room is a Roman copy of Polycletus's *Doriforo*. Elsewhere on this floor are a series of busts and statues, some of which are simply enormous. There's the powerful *Ercole Farnese* (Farnese Hercules) between room 11 and 12, and the recently restored *Toro Farnese* (Farnese Bull) in room 16, a large marble group from the early third century AD. In room 8, the graceful Roman copy of a Greek Venus, *Venere Callipige*, glances backwards at her reflection in the water as she slips off her clothes.

Room 10 contains the delicate *Tazza Farnese*, a tiny dish made in Egypt during the Ptolemaic period. Consisting of four layers of sardonyx agate, it's renowned for its transparent beauty. The mezzanine floor houses mosaics, including a large-scale depiction of the battle between Alexander the Great and Darius from the House of the Faun in Pompeii in Room 61.

Also here is the *Gabinetto segreto*, a collection of ancient pornography uncovered at Pompeii and Herculaneum. The explicit paintings and sculptures include a vast range of phallus talismans – some winged, some jingling with bells, some with hats on. One item approaches the subject in pre-Freudian fashion, depicting a frantic struggle between the member and its owner. The high (or low) point is a sculpted Pan, caught in the act with a nanny-goat. This collection has attracted controversy over the ages and was only reopened to the public in 2000.

The first floor contains artefacts from Pompeii, Herculaneum and other southern Italian sites. On the walls of the vast, echoing Sala Meridiana hang rare paintings on archaeological themes from the Farnese collection. On its floor, a line marks a zodiacal meridian; around noon, an oval bead of light snakes in through a hole high in the corner of the room, striking the meridian in the appropriate zodiacal sign.

To the left as you enter the Sala, rooms 85 to 89 contain glassware, silver and pottery from Pompeii, and rooms 66 to 78 have friezes and frescoes from Herculaneum and Stabiae. To the right as you enter, the first entrance leads to rooms 114 to 117, with artefacts from the Villa dei Papiri in Herculaneum; note the pair of bronze athletes poised to take flight in room 116 and the lovely bronze Hermes in room 117. The second series of right-hand rooms (130 to 140) contain vases, bowls and funerary offerings from Greek and Roman Paestum, and other sites around Magna Graecia (ancient southern Italy).

The pre- and proto-historical sections are reached from the third corridor on the right. The upper mezzanine floor displays Palaeolithic, Neolithic and Early Bronze Age finds from the Campania region (rooms 148 and 149), and the lower mezzanine (rooms 145 and 146) houses finds from the Middle and Late Bronze Ages.

EXPLORE

EXPLORE

CHAMBER OF HORRORS
The grim story of Le Fontanelle.

Situated in the underbelly of the Sanità neighbourhood and reopened in 2011 after a long period of closure and restoration, the **Cimitero delle Fontanelle** (*see p86*) was once an ancient quarry for tufa building stone. This series of vast chambers and caverns was first used for mass burials in the 16th and 17th centuries, when Naples experienced a devastating series of earthquakes, famine and epidemics: the 1656 plague alone killed some 250,000 of the city's 400,000 residents.

The church cemeteries were overflowing, and bodies were exhumed by gravediggers at night and thrown into the Fontanelle quarry along with plague victims. When there was a particularly heavy storm, the torrents of water rushing down the hill from Capodimonte would wash the bodies into the street, resulting in scenes of dystopian horror. The last mass deposit of bodies seems to have been in the aftermath of the 1835 cholera epidemic. At its fullest, O Campusanto de Funtanelle (as it's known in local dialect)

may have held up to eight million skeletons. In 1872, a priest by the name of Father Gaetano Barbati attempted to organise the chaotic burial chamber, exhuming many skeletons, and stacking skulls and bones against the walls and in makeshift crypts. Now that the remains were in full sight, the cult of the dead – in which Neapolitans would 'adopt' an unnamed skull (a *capuzzella*) – developed. People would clean and care for their *capuzzella*, make little pillows for it and heap it with flowers and gifts. In return, the souls belonging to the skulls would protect their living caretakers. This practice was banned by the church in 1968.

A visit to the cemetery is an extraordinary and humbling experience, particularly if you find yourself alone in the three vast caverns. At the end of the left-hand aisle is a cave known as the '*tribuna*' where the Camorra godfathers would hold their initiation rites and issue death warrants. A bus goes right past the Fontanelle, but you should be careful in this area after dark.

The main section (rooms 124 to 127) is arranged according to place, not time, and includes Palaeolithic bones and flints found on Capri (room 127); the Iron Age is best represented, with eighth- and ninth-century funerary relics from a number of necropolises, from Capua to Ischia.

Cafés, Bars & Gelaterie

★ Mexico

Piazza Dante 86 (081 549 9330). Metro Dante, or bus 201, C63, R1, R4. **Open** 7am-8.30pm Mon-Sat. **Map** p78 D3 ㉖

Along with what's arguably the best espresso in Naples, Mexico also sells a wide range of excellent, freshly roasted coffee in gorgeous 1950s-style packaging; try the Harem or Moana blends. The *frappe di caffè* (iced coffee whisked up to pure froth) is a real treat.

Other locations throughout the city.

Shops & Services

Enoteca Dante

Piazza Dante 18 (081 549 9689). Metro Dante, or bus 201, C63, R1, R4. **Open** 9am-2pm, 3-8pm Mon-Sat. **Map** p79 D3 ㉓ **Food & drink**

This excellent shop sells wines from all over Italy, with a particular slant towards Campania. Prices are pretty reasonable.

LA SANITÀ & BEYOND

Between Via Foria, Via Santa Teresa degli Scalzi and the hill of Capodimonte is an area made up of three districts: **La Sanità** ('healthy', because it lay outside the old city walls), **I Miracoli** (thanks to the miracles wrought around saintly inmates of the catacombs) and **Le Vergini** (named after a pre-Christian, no-sex-please, Greek religious group).

Now densely populated and *folkloristico* (a plaque marks the house where dearly loved Neapolitan comedian Totò was born at Via Antesaecula 109), the area is honeycombed with underground burial places: the early Christian **Catacombe di San Gaudioso** under **Santa Maria della Sanità**, the **Catacombe di San Severo**, and the comparatively new **Cimitero delle Fontanelle**. The area was popular for burials as it remained outside the city walls until the 18th century; burial within the walls was forbidden for public health reasons.

Along with its incredible catacombs, the neighbourhood contains two architectural gems (visible from the outside only) by 18th-century architect Ferdinando Sanfelice. **Palazzo Sanfelice** (Via Sanità 2 and 6), which was the architect's own home, is now sadly dilapidated, but the magnificent 'flying'

staircase in **Palazzo dello Spagnolo** (Via dei Vergini 19) has recently been restored to its former glory. Further east, pine tree-lined Piazza Miracoli is home to the 17th-century **Santa Maria dei Miracoli** (Largo dei Miracoli 35, 081 440189, open 5-7.30pm Mon-Sat).

These lively districts are home to congested street markets, where locals clamour for fresh produce and household items. La Sanità, in particular, buzzes with all manner of activity. Note the number of scooter drivers without helmets; locals know that they must *fa' canosce* – make sure their faces are visible so they're recognised and won't be mistaken for an outsider threatening the neighbourhood turf. Needless to say, visits to La Sanità, I Miracole and Le Vergini are best made during daylight hours.

Beyond Porta San Gennaro, just off Via del Duomo, is the **Museo d'Arte Contemporanea Donna Regina Napoli**, or MADRe, a relatively new contemporary art museum. Back on the Via Foria, the traffic crawls relentlessly along, past the lush **Orto Botanico** to Piazza Carlo III, dominated by the fearsome bulk of the **Albergo dei Poveri**. Carlo III commissioned the poorhouse to shelter the homeless and destitute, keeping them out of sight and mind; rumour had it that once inside, you left only in a coffin.

Construction began in 1751 and was finally completed in 1829. Vast as it is – the façade measures 354 metres (1,239 feet) and the building covers 103,000 square metres (26 acres) – the Albergo is only one fifth the size of Ferdinando Fuga's original design. In 2000, a project began to repair serious damage from general decay and the effects of the 1980 earthquake. It was originally due for completion in 2006 – wishful thinking for such an enormous endeavour, especially in Naples. To date, despite many millions of euros having been sunk into the project (including 140 million euros from the EU), only the façade has been restored. Inside, work on creating office space, conference facilities, a library and so on has ground to a halt: office furniture remains in its packaging gathering dust, electrical wires hang from sockets, sinks and toilets have been installed in bathrooms but not plumbed in. The accessible spaces are occasionally used for temporary exhibitions, and in October 2015 (in an ironic twist of fate) a plan was approved by the city council to open a centre for the homeless. But don't hold your breath.

Via Santi Giovanni e Paolo runs north-east out of the eastern end of Piazza Carlo III. The great tenor Enrico Caruso (1873-1921) was born at No.6, and a dingy plaque on the wall introduces this as the house 'where the world first heard his voice'. Naples itself heard little more of it; slated by Neapolitan critics early in his career, Caruso left the city and never came back.

EXPLORE

Pizzeria Oliva.

Sights & Museums

★ Catacombe di San Gaudioso/ Santa Maria della Sanità

Via della Sanità 124 (081 744 3714, www. catacombedinapoli.it). Metro Piazza Cavour or Museo, or bus C51, C52, R4. **Open** 10am-1pm daily. *Guided tours* 10am, 11am, noon, 1pm daily. **Admission** €8. **Map** p78 A3 ㉔

Tunnelled out of the Capodimonte hillside in Roman times for use as water cisterns, these labyrinthine catacombs were used as a burial site from the fifth century onwards. In 452, the burial of St Gaudiosus – a North African bishop and hermit – made the site an important shrine. The damp, musty caves have patches of fifth- and sixth-century mosaics, and frescoes from the fifth, 17th and 18th centuries. A fascinating range of burial techniques is in evidence. Note the method used from 1620 to 1650: the corpse was walled upright in a niche with its head cemented into the rear wall. After the bodily fluids had drained away (the malediction *'puozza sculà'* – may you drain away – is still in use), the headless body was buried and the skull removed, to be repositioned over a frescoed portrait of the illustrious deceased. The remains of St Gaudiosus and the skulls were all transferred to the nearby Cimitero delle Fontanelle (*see below*) during the cholera epidemic of 1974.

In the 17th century, the Dominican friars that tended the chapel of San Gaudioso in the catacombs built the Greek cross-plan basilica of Santa Maria della Sanità above it. There's a fine *Madonna and child with St Hyacinth, St Rosa of Lima and St Agnes* by Luca Giordano in the second chapel on the right.

From the transept, steps lead down to the fifth-century Cappella di San Gaudioso, which was rebuilt in the tenth and 15th centuries. The church is home to a painting of Mary, found nearby. Rumour has it that after it was discovered, the plague ceased and Mary brought *sanità* (health) to the area. Another, less comforting, local story has it that Camorra *giuramenti* (blood oaths) took place in the catacombs – a tale not mentioned on the guided tour, although the Sanità is a Camorra stronghold. The hour-long tours leave from the basilica; call ahead for an English-speaking guide.

FREE Catacombe di San Severo

Piazzetta San Severo a Capodimonte 81 (081 544 1305). Metro Piazza Cavour or Museo, or bus R4. **Open** *Church* 9am-noon Sat, Sun. *Catacombs* closed for restoration. **Admission** free. **Map** p78 A3 ㉕

Built in 1573, the church stands on the site of a monastery complex and much earlier church, founded by Naples' first bishop, Severus. For now, the site is closed for restoration: call 081 744 3714 for information.

★ FREE Cimitero delle Fontanelle

Via delle Fontanelle 154 (081 1970 3197). Metro Materdei, or bus C51. **Open** 10am-5pm daily. **Admission** free. **Map** p78 A2 ㉖
See p84 **Chamber of Horrors**.

★ Museo d'Arte Contemporanea Donna Regina Napoli (MADRe)

Via Settembrini 79 (081 1931 3016, www.museo madre.it). Metro Cavour or Museo, or bus 182, 184, E1, E2. **Open** 10am-7.30pm Mon, Wed-Sat; 10am-8pm Sun (last entry 1hr before closing). **Admission** €7; €3.50 reductions; free to all Mon. **No credit cards. Map** p78 B5 ➋

For years, Naples lacked a proper contemporary art gallery – but 2005 saw the opening of two large-scale, publicly funded galleries, PAN (*see p102*) and MADRe. The palazzo that houses this pleasant, well-appointed museum was completely overhauled by Portuguese architect Alvaro Siza, who created a main display space on the ground floor and three upper floors of smaller connecting rooms.

It's looking in need of a little TLC these days (funding problems threatened closure in 2012) and it's no Guggenheim Bilbao or Tate Modern, but it is a highly functional space. The first floor hosts installations by artists such as Jeff Koons and Richard Serra; highlights include Anish Kapoor's marvellously illusory blue space and Rebecca Horn's *Spirits* (2005), mirrored skulls that recall Naples' cult of the dead. Neapolitan-in-exile Francesco Clemente also returned to fresco two rooms in their entirety. The subject matter is Naples itself and the superstitions that make the city tick. Staff are knowledgeable.

The upper floors are given over to temporary exhibitions; artists have included Jannis Kounellis (featuring his notorious dozen live horses), Rachel Whiteread and Robert Rauschenberg. There's also a bar, but opening times are rather irregular.

★ FREE Orto Botanico

Via Foria 223 (081 253 3937, www.ortobotanico. unina.it). Metro Cavour, or bus 182, 184, 201, C47. **Open** 9am-2pm Mon-Fri (by appt only). **Admission** free. **Map** p78 A6 ➋

A stroll around the city's botanical gardens makes for a refreshing change of pace. Note that visits are by appointment only. Calling to book on the same day is generally fine; you leave your details when you phone, and on arrival your name will be crossed off the list.

★ FREE San Giovanni a Carbonara

Via Carbonara 5 (081 295873). Metro Cavour or Museo, or bus 182, 184, E1, E2. **Open** 9am-5pm daily. **Admission** free. **Map** p78 B5 ➋

This 14th-century church stands at the top of a dramatic double flight of curving steps that were added in 1707 by Ferdinando Sanfelice. At the head of the staircase, the chapel of Santa Monica (closed to the public) has a marble Gothic portal; the church entrance is up a few more steps to the left of this portal. Inside is an astonishing collection of sculptures, most notably the 18m (63ft) monument and tomb of King Ladislas (1428) behind the main altar that shows Renaissance touches in its mainly Gothic design. The round chapel behind the altar has a complex

majolica-tiled floor, 15th-century frescoes portraying the lives of the hermits, and the tomb of Sergianni Caracciolo (1433), the much-hated lover of Ladislas's sister and successor, Queen Joan II.

Restaurants

Pizzeria Oliva

Via Arena alla Sanità 7B (081 290037, www. pizzeriaoliva.it). Metro Cavour, or bus C51, C52. **Open** 10.30am-11.30pm Mon-Sat; noon-4pm Sun. **Average** €12. **Map** p78 B4 ➌ **Pizzeria**

Twenty-something dynamo Ciro Oliva completely revamped his family pizzeria a couple of years ago and is making waves with superb pizzas, using top-notch ingredients such as piennolo tomatoes from the slopes of Vesuvius, and anchovies from Cetara on the Amalfi Coast. Oliva thought up the idea of the *pizza sospesa* (rather than the more usual '*caffè sosp-eso*'), where customers can offer a pizza to someone who can't afford it.

★ Pizzeria Starita

Via Matterdei 27-28 (081 557 3682, www.pizzeria starita.it). Metro Matterdei, or bus C53, C63, R4. **Open** noon-3.30pm, 7pm-midnight Tue-Sun. **Average** €12. **Map** p78 B2 ➌ **Pizzeria**

Opened in 1901, one of the claims to fame of Antonio Starita's pizzeria is that it featured in the 1954 film *L'Oro di Napoli* starring Sophia Loren. Another is that it produces some of the best pizza in the city. The place is always full and there's inevitably a queue outside (in spite of having seating for more than 100). The Materdei neighbourhood is a little iffy, so a taxi might be the best transport at night.

Cafés, Bars & Gelaterie

Pasticceria Mignone

Piazza Cavour 145 (081 293074). Metro Cavour, or bus 182, 184, E1. **Open** 7.30am-8pm Tue-Sun. Closed 3wks Aug. **Map** p78 B4 ➌

It's worth hopping off the metro at Cavour, especially to sample Mignone's cakes and pastries: from classic *sfogliatelle* and *cornetti* (sweet croissants) to *babà* and *torta caprese*, they're all delicious.

Capodimonte

Once the hunting ground of King Carlo III, the verdant Parco di Capodimonte sits atop a hill a few miles north of the *Centro Storico*, a green escape from the heat and crowds far below. With its magnificent views over the city and the Bay of Naples beyond, the park was founded as a hunting reserve in the 18th century, but the king soon decided to construct a magnificent royal palace here and surround it with splendid grounds. The result is the massive scarlet palace that you see today, home to the Museo di Capodimonte and a formidable art collection. The vast parkland is popular with families at weekends. The fascinating Catacombe di San Gennaro, with their ancient tombs, mosaics and frescoes, are another draw. Finally, the stately 19th-century observatory is open for guided tours.

The City Sightseeing tour bus stops at the Catacombe di San Gennaro and Capodimonte before descending back to the city centre. Although the Museo di Capodimonte and its park are a haven of high culture and peace, the surrounding area can be a bit dodgy, so it's best to stick to the tourist sites.

Caravaggio's *Flagellation*.

Don't Miss

1 Bellini's *Transfiguration* Room 8, Museo di Capodimonte (p90).

2 Titian's *Danaë* Room 11, Museo di Capodimonte.

3 Parmigianino's *Antea* Room 12, Museo di Capodimonte.

4 Simone Martini's *St Louis of Toulouse* Room 65, Museo di Capodimonte.

5 Caravaggio's *Flagellation* Room 78, Museo di Capodimonte.

EXPLORE

Catacombe di San Gennaro.

INTRODUCING THE AREA

The main reason to make the trek up to this corner of Naples is the **Museo di Capodimonte**. But don't ignore the ex-royal hunting ground of the **Reale Bosco** (Royal Woodland), one of Italy's largest urban green spaces. Although the area around the museum teems with visitors on sunny Sundays, the rest of the park is often strangely deserted – it's easy to find a quiet, isolated spot for a picnic. Laid out in the mid 18th century to a design drawn up by Ferdinando Sanfelice, five tree-lined avenues radiate from a hub near the palace. The smaller buildings scattered across the grounds include the **Reale Fabbrica delle Porcellane** (Royal Porcelain Factory). Work in the factory came to a halt in 1759, as Carlo shifted the whole operation to his native Spain when he returned to take the crown; it's now a craft school.

Nearby attractions include the fascinating yet little-visited **Catacombe di San Gennaro**. South-west of the park on Via Capodimonte, the pseudo-classical 20th-century church of **Madre del Buon Consiglio** (open 8am-12.30pm, 4.30-7.30pm daily) is a bombastic imitation of St Peter's in Rome. The **Osservatorio Astronomico**, south-east of the park, bears witness to scientific progress made during the Bourbon Restoration. On the road curving down from Capodimonte's Porta Grande is the **Ponti Rossi**, the well-preserved remains of an aqueduct built during the reign of Emperor Claudius (AD 41-54) to bring fresh water to Naples from the mountains near Avellino.

Sights & Museums

★ Catacombe di San Gennaro

Via Capodimonte 16 (081 744 3714). Bus 168, 178, R4. **Open** *Guided tours only (on the hour)* 10am-5pm Mon-Sat; 10am-1pm Sun. **Admission** €8; €5 reductions.

From a pleasant garden (its entrance is to the left of the church) overlooking the Sanità, steps lead down into the two-level catacombs with their fascinating frescoes, many of which have been recently restored.

After the body of San Gennaro (St Januarius) was brought here from Pozzuoli in the fifth century, it became an important place of pilgrimage. Fine *arcosolia* (sarcophagi carved into tufa walls and topped with arched, frescoed niches) fill the upper levels in the main ambulatory, with fifth-century mosaics and frescoes from the second century in the vestibule, one possibly portraying Adam and Eve. The lower level has an eighth-century baptismal tub and a chapel dedicated to Sant'Agrippino, which is still in use today. The tour (which lasts around 45 minutes) winds up in the paleo-Christian basilica of San Gennaro Extra Moenia (outside the walls).

★ Museo di Capodimonte

Porta Piccola, Via Miano 2 (081 749 9111, www.museocapodimonte.beniculturali.it). Bus C63, C66, R4. **Open** *Museum* 8.30am-7.30pm Mon, Tue, Thur-Sun (last entry 6.30pm). *Park* 8am-1hr before sunset daily. **Admission** *Museum* €7.50 (€6.50 after 2pm); €3.75 reductions; free under-18s, over-65s. *Park* free. **No credit cards**.

When construction began in 1738 on the palace that now houses one of Italy's largest and most artistically rich museums, King Carlo III envisaged no more than a hunting lodge. Seduced by plans for something far grander – and hard pushed to find space for the vast art collection he had inherited from his mother, Elisabetta Farnese – a monumental three-storey *palazzo reale* went up in the heart of a magnificent park covering 7sq km. Although it would be 100 years before the finishing touches were put to the building, the Farnese collection was installed by 1759; acquisitions by Carlo and later Bourbon monarchs enriched the gallery, and porcelain and weaponry were added in the late 19th century. Over the years the palace has acted as a repository for the royal collections, the main seat of the court, and a royal summer holiday home.

The main entrance is a regal affair. Cool, cavernous porticos on the ground floor hide bars and shops. The Farnese collection, along with the Bourbon collection, is upstairs, as are the smaller Borgia, porcelain and contemporary collections, and the armoury. There's information about the individual works of art (in English) in each room.

Italian art makes up the bulk of the Farnese collection. It starts in room 2 with groundbreaking portraits by Raphael and Titian. Umbrian and Tuscan schools are represented by Masaccio (the 15th-century *Crucifixion* from a now-dismantled altarpiece in room 3 is one of the few additions to the collection since Unification in 1861). In room 5 you'll find a copy by Marcello Venusti of Michelangelo's original (uncensored) *Last Judgment*, and an early work by Botticelli, the *Madonna with Child and Two Angels* in room 6. The prime representatives of the 15th-century Veneto tradition are Andrea Mantegna's *Portrait of Young Francesco Gonzaga* (room 8) and *St Euphemia* (room 7) and Giovanni Bellini's *Transfiguration* (room 8); note the blend of religious mysticism and realistic rural Veneto setting.

CARAVAGGIO ON CANVAS

The extraordinary life and works of the other Michelangelo.

Although Michelangelo Merisi da Caravaggio spent less than four years in Naples, he left a rich artistic legacy. Having made his name in Rome in the late 1590s, Caravaggio was as famous for his innovative compositions and extraordinary ability to recreate lifelike detail as for his unconventional behaviour. He fled Rome in 1606 with a price on his head, having killed a thuggish playboy, Ranuccio Tomassoni, in a duel.

He ended up in Naples: at the time it was the wealthiest city in Italy, and home to the powerful Colonna family, his longstanding patrons. Local artists and collectors flocked to meet the man who had caused such a stir in Rome, and Caravaggio held informal court at the Taverno del Cerriglio on Via Sanfelice, a haunt of gamblers, prostitutes, poets and artists on the make.

Although the last few years of Caravaggio's life, prior to his death in 1610 at the age of 39, are among the most mysterious, he did at least paint during this time. Of the works he painted in Naples, three remain in the city. *Seven Acts of Mercy* hangs in the Pio Monte della Misericordia (see p68). Depicting the acts of mercy described by St Matthew, the painting is life-sized, dark and chaotic – like a snapshot of Neapolitan life along darkest Via Tribunali. A pair of angels look as if they're fighting and about to fall out of a window. Below them, an innkeeper offers hospitality, a rich man cuts his cloak in two and offers half of it to a naked beggar, a dead body is carried through the chaos, and a woman suckles an old man at her breast.

The *Flagellation*, painted for the church of San Domenico (a copy of it, by Luca Giordano, still hangs there), is now in the Museo di Capodimonte (see p90). Again, there's something very Neapolitan about the scene: a shaft of light illuminates Christ's extraordinarily lifelike form, tormented by a pair of dodgy-looking characters.

The recently restored *Martyrdom of St Ursula* can be seen in the Palazzo Zevallos (see p77), the main branch of Banca Intesa Sanpaolo. It has a similarly photographic quality, despite a slightly smudgy finish: Marcantonio Doria, who commissioned it, put it out in the sun to dry when the paint was still wet, 'because Caravaggio puts it on thick', and the paint melted. Its figures loom almost three-dimensionally out of the dark background, while Saint Ursula looks at her wound with untheatrical surprise.

EXPLORE

Titian's masterpiece, *Danaë*, is in room 11. In it, Danaë, daughter of King Argos, is seduced by Jupiter in the form of golden rain; the courtesan who modelled for the painting was probably the lover of a Farnese cardinal. El Greco's *El Soplon*, a version of a work mentioned by Pliny, is in the same room.

Sixteenth- and 17th-century works from the Farnese family's former duchy in the Emilia region are plentiful. Works by Correggio include the *Mystic Marriage of St Catherine* (1517) in room 12. Parmigianino's virginal *Antea* is also in room 12; Annibale Carracci's *Mystic Marriage of St Catherine* is in room 19, and his allegorical *Hercules at the Crossroads* is in room 20; Guido Reni's *Atlanta and Hippomenes* is in room 22. Not to be overlooked in this galaxy of Italian talent are Brueghel's two enigmatic pieces, *The Parable of the Blind* and *The Misanthrope*, both in room 17.

Also on the first floor are the royal apartments, including Queen Maria Amalia's boudoir (packed with Capodimonte porcelain), the magnificent ballroom, the dainty Pompeian drawing room, and a range of French furniture and paintings.

The second floor features works produced in Naples from the 13th to 19th centuries. All the greats are here, from Simone Martini's *St Louis of Toulouse* (room 65) to Caravaggio's *Flagellation* (room 78), which influenced generations of Neapolitan painters. Massimo Stanzione's *Moses' Sacrifice* is in room 89, his *Madonna and Child* in Room 93; Giuseppe Ribera's *St Jerome and the Angel* and the allegorical *Drunken Silenus* are in rooms 90 and 91; Bernardo Cavallino's *St Cecilia in Ecstasy* is in room 94; Luca Giordano's *Madonna of the Canopy* is in room 103; and, in room 104, Francesco Solimena's *Aeneas and Dido* inspired his friend Alessandro Scarlatti to set the subject to music in 1696. A third-floor attic houses modern and contemporary paintings, including Warhol's *Vesuvius*. In rooms 106-111 there are three works by Artemesia Gentileschi, including *Judith Beheading Holofernes*.

Osservatorio Astronomico

Salita Moiariello 16 (081 557 5111, www.na. astro.it). Bus C63, R4. **Open** Guided tours only. **Admission** €5.

This magnificent neoclassical building dates from 1819, and was commissioned by King Ferdinando I. The first observatory in Italy, it contains a fine collection of equipment, historical and modern, some of which may be demonstrated during the tour.

Vomero

Vomero perches on a hill behind the city centre, aloof from the claustrophobic goings-on below. It's home to two flagship monuments, Castel Sant'Elmo (which takes its name from the small church that stood here during the tenth century, St Erasmus – corrupted over the centuries to St Elmo) and the San Martino monastery, plus verdant Parco della Floridiana with its fine ceramics museum. This one-time hilltop village, where families would come for Sunday picnics, is now more of a satellite town to Naples, a genteel and self-contained residential neighbourhood. There are good restaurants, smart shops and elegant cafés, and visitors who choose to stay up here will find the streets cleaner (and, it must be said, safer) and the air a little cooler than down below. But Vomero is missing something: the edginess and vibrant street life that makes Naples so unique is absent and life up here seems a little tame. However, a trip up the hill on one of the three historic funiculars that connect downtown Naples to this bourgeois enclave is a must, not least for the superlative views.

Certosa-Museo di San Martino.

Don't Miss

1 Certosa-Museo di San Martino Neapolitan art aplenty (p94).

2 Museo Nazionale della Ceramica Duca di Martina Porcelain perfection (p95).

3 Otranto Scoop some great *gelato* (p99).

4 Frigittoria Vomero Naughty but very, very nice (p98).

5 Pizzeria Gorizia 100 years of dreamy dough (p98).

EXPLORE

INTRODUCING THE AREA

At the heart of the district is the diamond-shaped **Piazza Vanvitelli**. Here, the tree-lined, partly pedestrianised Via Scarlatti, whose *struscio* or *passeggiata* rivals that on Via Toledo, meets the traffic hell of Via Bernini. With elegant café tables spilling out on to pavements packed with well-heeled residents, Piazza Vanvitelli epitomises the district's middle-class air.

Three of Naples' four funicular railways lead up to Vomero. The **Funicolare di Montesanto** brings you closest to its star attractions: the **Certosa-Museo di San Martino** and the **Castel Sant'Elmo**. The top station of the **Funicolare di Chiaia** on Via Cimarosa lies on the same road as the main entrance to Vomero's other crowd-puller, the green, almost wild **Parco della Floridiana**, which is home to the **Museo Nazionale della Ceramica Duca di Martina**.

Sights & Museums

Castel Sant'Elmo

Via Tito Angelini 22 (081 229404). Funicular Chiaia to Via Cimarosa, Centrale to Piazzetta Fuga or Montesanto to Via Morghen, or bus V1. **Open** 8.30am-7.30pm Mon, Wed-Sun. **Admission** €5; €2.50 reductions; free with Certosa ticket. **No credit cards. Map** p97 E5 ❶

Castel Sant'Elmo takes its name from the small church that stood here during the tenth century, St Erasmus – corrupted over the centuries to St Elmo. A castle has stood here since 1329, when King Robert of Anjou modified a pre-existing Norman watch-tower using the artists, architects and builders who were working on the adjacent monastery of San Martino. The castle acquired its massive six-pointed star shape in the mid 16th century, during an extensive reorganisation of the city's defences. In 1587, the ammunition dump was struck by lightning – the castle was badly damaged and 150 people died.

Over the years, the dungeon has held many illustrious inmates, including heroes of the 1799 Parthenopean Republic, and it was a military prison until the mid 1970s. That might explain why the castle has never been a popular destination for Neapolitans. The ground floor of the castle is closed to the public, although its gloomy interior can occasionally be glimpsed through the glass panels on the first floor – which is only opened during major exhibitions.

Piazza d'Armi, as the top floor is called, is actually the roof of the building and is best reached by lift; the view over Naples is sublime. The walkway around the battlements is splendid, and a gently sloping path inside the castle leads you back down across the drawbridge, passing beneath the coat of arms of Carlo V.

★ Certosa-Museo di San Martino

Piazzale San Martino 5 (081 229 4502). Funicular Chiaia to Via Cimarosa, Centrale to Piazzetta Fuga or Montesanto to Via Morghen, or bus V1. **Open**

8.30am-7.30pm Mon, Tue, Thur-Sun. **Admission** (includes Castel Sant'Elmo) €6; €3 reductions. *Audioguide* €4. **No credit cards. Map** p97 F6 ❷

This Carthusian monastery complex was founded in 1325, although its present appearance is the result of much 16th-century reworking. Renowned for its priceless architectural and artistic assets, San Martino was dissolved under French rule (1806-15); the monks returned only briefly before the *certosa* (charterhouse) was wrested from them again in the wake of Italian Unification in 1861. State-of-the-art visitor facilities, airy rooms and terraced gardens with sweeping views over the Naples waterfront make the Certosa a must-see.

The church's late 17th-century façade, opposite the ticket barrier, is by Cosimo Fanzago; it conceals remnants of the Gothic original, such as the pointed arches and cross-vaulted ceiling in the *pronaos* (projecting vestibule), which features 17th-century frescoes by Micco Spadaro depicting the persecution of Carthusians in England during Henry VIII's reign.

The church's interior contains as complete an array of Neapolitan art as you could hope to see. Massimo Stanzione's *Deposition* (1638) dominates the inner façade, flanked by two fine portraits by Giuseppe Ribera, who is also responsible for the 12 paintings of prophets (1638-43) tucked into the spandrels of the arches. The delicate 18th-century marble altar balustrade is by Giuseppe Sammartino. The walls and side chapels feature paintings by the Vaccaros, Francesco Solimena and Stanzione. In the vaulted ceiling are frescoes (1637-40) by Giovanni Lanfranco: *Ascension with Angels, Apostles* and *Saints*. Bonaventura Presti used material already prepared by Fanzago for his intricate inlaid marble floor (1664).

The choir features Ribera's *Communion of the Apostles*, Guido Reni's *Adoration of the Shepherds* (1642) and Battista Caracciolo's *Washing of Feet* (1622), and the sacristy has some exquisite marquetry; on the cupboards, 56 panels depict biblical scenes. In the Cappella del Tesoro are Ribera's *Pietà* and frescoes by Luca Giordano; the *parlatorio* and chapter room (where there are several works by Battista Caracciolo) are also essential viewing.

A long passageway leads left out of the small *chiostro dei procuratori* into the *chiostro grande* (great cloister) – one of Italy's finest. This bright, sunny area was created in the 16th century by Giovanni Antonio Dosio; Cosimo Fanzago added the small monks' graveyard (note the skulls) and the busts and statues above the pillared portico, as well as the grotesque faces animating the well.

The Museo dell'Opera art gallery is beautifully laid out around the main cloister. The majority of the 17th- and 18th-century works, originally created for the monastery, are now housed in the prior's quarters in the southern wing (rooms 17 to 23). The collection includes works by Ribera (*Sts Jerome and Sebastian*), Lanfranco (*Our Lady of the Rosary*) and Stanzione (*Baptism of Christ*). Spadaro created the ceilings in rooms 14, 15 and 16. Room 8 contains a

Certosa-Museo di San Martino.

remarkable sculpture, *Madonna and Child with the Infant John the Baptist*, by Pietro Bernini (father of the more famous Gianlorenzo).

The *certosa*, the Carthusian order and the history of Naples are constant themes in the works. There are splendid maps and landscape paintings, ranging from the anonymous *Tavola Strozzi* with its detailed depiction of 15th-century Naples in room 32, and Didier Barra's bird's-eye view of Naples at the end of the 16th century, to a fine series of late 17th-century paintings by Gaspar Van Wittel in room 40. On the first floor are 19th-century paintings by local artists.

Another section is devoted to Nativity scenes, including a vast *presepe* (crib) with rare 18th-century pieces. You'll also find displays on theatre, shipping and, in the former pharmacy, glassware and porcelain.

★ Parco della Floridiana/Museo Nazionale della Ceramica Duca di Martina

Via Cimarosa 77 (081 578 8418). Funicular Chiaia to Via Cimarosa, Centrale to Piazzetta Fuga or Montesanto to Via Morghen, or bus E4, V1. **Open** *Park* 8.30am-1hr before sunset daily. *Museum* 8.30am-2pm Mon, Wed-Sun. **Admission** €2; €1 reductions. **No credit cards. Map** p97 G3 **❸**

In 1815, King Ferdinando returned to Naples after ten years of French rule, accompanied by his second wife – Lucia Migliaccio, Duchess of Floridia – who was presented with this splendid villa and garden. In the 1920s, it was purchased by the Italian government; the park was opened to the public and the villa became a museum.

The museum's basement showcases ceramics from China's Ming and Qing dynasties. The Meiping vase in the shape of a phoenix is particularly rare. The collection of Japanese porcelain includes pieces from the Edo period (1603-1867).

The ground floor has majolica pieces from the Middle Ages onwards. Room 21 has a walking stick with a glass top; inside it is a portrait of the King's second wife (wags joked that this was the only way he could get the unpopular lady into the court).

The first floor houses European ceramics. There's an early 18th-century picture frame from Sicily in room 2; the fine *Capodimonte Dedaration* by Gricci in room 5; some splendid Meissen porcelain in room 6; pieces by Ginori (including *Three Putti with a Goat*) in room 9; china from Sèvres and Saint-Cloud in room 10; and an odd Meissen clock-cum-inkstand in room 14.

Restaurants

Cantina La Barbera

Via Morghen 36A (081 229 2357, www.cantina labarbera.it). Metro Vanvitelli, or funicular Chiaia to Via Cimarosa or Centrale to Piazza Fuga. **Open** varies. **Average** €30. **Map** p97 E4 **❹** Ristorante

The stylish Barbera is a versatile space with a summer terrace that functions as a cocktail and wine bar, restaurant, and live music venue. The menu covers all bases: *stuzzichini* (small snacks), filled *focacce*, salads, platters of cheese and cured meats, pasta dishes and, the house speciality, chargrilled meat.

La Cantina di Sica

Via Bernini 17 (081 556 7520, www.lacantina disica.it). Metro Vanvitelli, or funicular Chiaia to Via Cimarosa or Centrale to Piazza Fuga, or bus C28, C31, C32, V1. **Open** noon-3.30pm, 7pm-midnight Tue-Sat; noon-3.30pm Sun. Closed 2wks Aug. **Average** €25. **Map** p97 F3 **❺** Trattoria

You can't go far wrong with time-honoured dishes such as *ziti alla genovese* (pasta with beef sauce), albeit at slightly higher prices than the average trattoria. There's an interesting choice of fresh fish and meat, and truly delicious *contorni*: try the *parmigiana di melanzane*. There's an excellent wine list, and the bar downstairs often has live jazz or Neapolitan folk.

★ € Osteria Donna Teresa

Via Kerbaker 58 (081 556 7070). Funicular Chiaia to Via Cimarosa or Centrale to Piazza Fuga, or bus C28, C31, C32, V1. **Open** 1-3pm, 8-11pm Mon-Sat. Closed 3wks Aug. **Average** €15. **No credit cards. Map** p97 F4 **❻** Osteria

EXPLORE

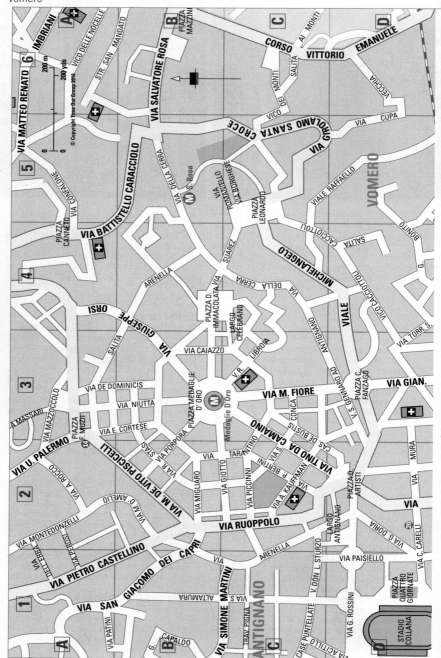

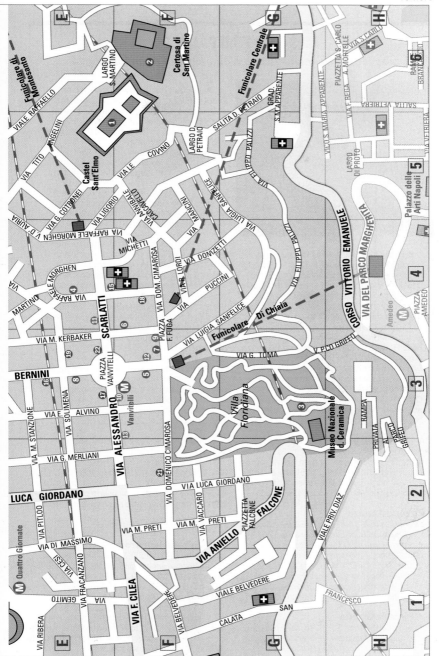

EXPLORE

STEPPING OUT
Skip the funicular and take the stairs down for a panoramic treat.

Castello Aselmeyer.

Before the funiculars were built, getting to Vomero involved scaling long flights of steps. Poorly signposted, and decidedly strenuous if tackled from the bottom up, they're a much more panoramic way to get back down to the city centre than the funicular. Beware, though: it's not advisable to tackle them after dark.

To reach the westernmost flight – the Calata San Francesco – cut through the Parco della Floridiana. Enter via the top gate on Via Cimarosa and exit on to Via Aniello Falcone from the western gate, halfway down. Head west along Via Falcone and turn left down the steep *calata*. Cut across Via Tasso and Corso Vittorio Emanuele, stopping to peek at Lamont Young's Castello Aselmeyer.

Incongruously perched at no.166, it marries Tudor elements (bow windows, loggias) so dear to the English upper-middle class with Gothic picturesque. Carry on down Via Arco Mirelli until you get to Chiaia and the western end of the Villa Comunale.

For a more panoramic but less genteel descent, take Via Pedamentino San Martino, which starts from Largo San Martino in front of the Certosa-Museo di San Martino. On reaching Corso Vittorio Emanuele, turn left and you'll see a set of steps heading down, opposite the Montesanto funicular station. These will eventually bring you out on to busy Montesanto, a major transport hub.

If, instead, you continue past the funicular station along Corso Vittorio Emanuele and take the steps up Via Cupa Vecchia on the left, you'll discover one of the few patches of inner-city greenery open to the public: the small Parco Viviani. Almost opposite, where the steps of Via Pedamentino San Martino meet Corso Vittorio Emanuele, is Vico Trinità delle Monache, which leads down to Parco dei Quartieri Spagnoli (closed all Mon & Sun pm), opened as part of a project to redevelop a one-time military hospital. However, the ambitious plans to create a complex housing a natural history museum, sports facilities and concert spaces came to a grinding halt after the first phase, leaving this semi-abandoned public park and play area.

Tiny Donna Teresa (there are only nine tables) offers exemplary home cooking, and the fixed lunch is a bargain. Try *polpette* (meatballs) in tomato sauce or *involtini di carne* (thin slices of meat wrapped round a sweet/savoury mix of pine nuts, raisins, cheese and parsley), washed down with the house red.

€ Pizzeria Acunzo
Via Cimarosa 60/62 (081 578 5362, www.pizzeria ristoranteacunzo.it). Funicular Chiaia to Via Cimarosa or Centrale to Piazza Fuga, or bus V1. **Open** 1-3.30pm, 7.30pm-midnight daily. **Average** *Pizza* €10. *Trattoria* €25. **Map** p97 F3 **7** Pizzeria
This simple place serves exemplary pizza, as well as excellent *spaghetti alle vongole, melanzane alla parmigiana* and casseroled *polpi* (small octopus).

★ € Pizzeria Gorizia
Via Bernini 29/31 (081 578 2248, www.pizzeria gorizia.it). Metro Vanvitelli, or funicular Chiaia to Via Cimarosa or Centrale to Piazza Fuga,

or bus C28, C31, C32, V1. **Open** 11.30am-4pm, 7pm-midnight daily. **Average** *Pizza* €10. *Trattoria* €20. **Map** p97 E3 **8** Pizzeria
This classic pizzeria has been making superb pizzas for a century. As well as the usual suspects, the menu includes the summery Crudaiola, a piping hot base topped with what amounts to an *insalata caprese*.

Cafés, Bars & Gelaterie

★ Friggitoria Vomero
Via Cimarosa 44 (081 578 3130). Funicular Chiaia to Via Cimarosa or Centrale to Piazza Fuga, or bus V1. **Open** 9.30am-2.30pm, 5-9.30pm Mon-Fri; 9.30am-2.30pm, 5-11pm Sat. Closed Aug. **Average** €7. **No credit cards. Map** p97 F3 **9**
This old-fashioned *friggitoria* is great for breakfast: the wonderful *graffe* (light doughnuts) are available from 9.30am. A host of other fried goodies are ready from 10am, including *zeppole* (deep-fried dough balls) and aubergines fried in batter.

Mennella

Via Scarlatti 97 (081 558 0171). Metro Vanvitelli, or funicular Chiaia to Via Cimarosa or Centrale to Piazza Fuga. **Open** 10.30am-11pm daily. **Map** p97 F3 ⑩
Originally from Torre del Greco at the foot of Vesuvius, renowned *pasticceria* Mennella is making waves with its artisanal *gelato*.

Otranto

Via Scarlatti 78 (081 1981 0303, www.gelateria oltranto.it). Metro Vanvitelli, or funicular Chiaia to Via Cimarosa, or bus V1. **Open** *Apr-Oct* 10.30am-10pm daily. *Nov-Mar* 10am-9pm Tue-Sun. **No credit cards.** **Map** p97 E4 ⑪
Don't let the no-frills furnishings and lack of atmosphere put you off: ice-cream connoisseurs consider Otranto one of the finest suppliers in the city.

Serafino

Via Bernini 8 (081 1900 4582). Metro Vanvitelli, or funicular Chiaia to Via Cimarosa or Centrale to Piazza Fuga. **Open** 11.30am-midnight Mon-Sat; 11.30am-3pm, 6pm-midnight Sun. **Average** €10. **Map** p97 F3 ⑫
This stylish, contemporary gourmet *friggitoria* serves up fast food Sicilian-style. The speciality of the house is *cuoppo di pesce fritto* (mixed fried fish served, sizzling hot, in a paper cone). The deliciously fresh, homemade *granita* finishes things off nicely.

Soave Prodotti Freschi del Latte

Via Scarlatti 130 (081 556 7411). Metro Vanvitelli, or funicuolar Chiaia to Via Cimarosa, or bus V1. **Open** 9am-2pm, 4-8.30pm daily. **Map** p97 F3 ⑬
It's not hip, but this rock-solid traditional *gelateria* produces the goods: using only the freshest fruit in season, it serves the best *fragolina di bosco* (tiny wild strawberries) ice-cream in Naples.

Shops & Services

Bellavia

Piazza Muzii 27 (081 558 4475, www. pasticceriabellavia.it). Metro Medaglie d'Oro, or bus V1. **Open** 7am-9pm Mon-Fri; 7.30am-10pm Sat, Sun. **Map** p96 A2 ⑭ **Food & drink**
Look out for the trail of people carrying large, impressively wrapped packages on a Sunday morning and you'll soon find Bellavia. Vomero's best-known *pasticceria* is renowned for its birthday cakes. If you're around at Easter, try the *pastiera* – a traditional cake made from ricotta cheese and rice-like *grano* (wheatgrain).

Carrefour

Via Morghen 28 (081 556 3282, www.carrefour.it). Metro Vanvitelli, or funicular Chiaia to Via Cimarosa or Centrale to Piazza Fuga. **Open** 24 hours daily. **Map** p97 E4 ⑮ **Supermarket**
The 24/7 Vomero branch of the French supermarket chain. This one has a big car park too.

Ciccolella

Via Bernini 57 (081 1956 9157, www.ciccolella.it). Metro Vanvitelli, or funicular Chiaia to Via Cimarosa or Centrale to Piazza Fuga, or bus C28, C31. **Open** 10am-1.30pm, 4.30-8pm Mon-Sat. Closed 2wks Aug. **Map** p97 E3 ⑯ **Homewares**
Ciccolella has a superb range of glass, crystal, porcelain and silverware from the likes of Lalique, Baccarat, Christofle, Rosenthal and Venini.

Coin

Via Scarlatti 90/98, Vomero (081 578 0111, www.coin.it). Funicular Chiaia to Via Cimarosa or Centrale to Piazza Fuga, or bus C36. **Open** 10am-8pm Mon-Sat; 10am-2pm, 4.30-8.30pm Sun. **Map** p97 E3 ⑰ **Department store**
This branch is useful for men's and women's clothing and accessories, household goods and cosmetics.

Fonoteca

Via Morghen 31C-E (081 556 0338, www.fonoteca. net). Metro Vanvitelli, or funicular Chiaia to Via Cimarosa or Centrale to Piazza Fuga. **Open** noon-1am Mon-Thur; noon-2am Fri, Sat; 6.30pm-1.30am Sun. Closed 2wks Aug. **Map** p97 F4 ⑱ **Music**
The stock (CDs and vinyl, both new and second-hand) in this music store is brilliantly eclectic. Staff will let you listen before buying.

Helianthus

Via Solimena 41 (081 578 2953, www.erboristeria helianthus.com). Metro Vanvitelli, or funicular Chiaia to Via Cimarosa or Centrale to Piazza Fuga, or bus C21, C28, C36. **Open** 9.30am-1.30pm, 4.30-8pm Mon-Sat. Closed Aug. **Map** p97 E3 ⑲ **Health & beauty**
This welcoming shop has a large selection of natural remedies, health foods and beauty products.

Mercatino di Antignano

Piazza Antignano. Metro Medaglie d'Oro, or bus R1. **Open** 8am-2pm Mon-Sat. **Map** p96 D2 ⑳ **Market**
Snap up bargain-priced kitchenware, bags, clothes, jewellery, shoes, towels, linen and lots more.

Photoexpert

Via Cimarosa 166 (081 040 3236, www. photoexpert.it). Metro Vanvitelli, or funicular Chiaia to Via Cimarosa or Centrale to Piazza Fuga, or bus C36. **Open** 9.30am-1.30pm, 4.30-8pm Mon-Fri; 9.30am-2pm Sat. Closed 2wks Aug. **Map** p97 F2 ㉑ **Photography**
The ever-obliging Luigi and Sergio will help with all your photographic kit.

R-Store

Via Scarlatti 76/78 (no phone, www.rstore.it). Metro Vanvitelli, or funicular Chiaia to Via Cimarosa or Centrale to Piazza Fuga. **Open** 10am-2pm, 4-8pm Mon-Sat. **Map** p97 E3 ㉒ **Electronics**
For all your Apple needs.

EXPLORE

Chiaia to Posillipo

Worlds away from the characterful chaos of the Centro Storico and bordering the sea, Chiaia is a highly desirable neighbourhood defined by the wide arc of the Riviera; the long, narrow Villa Comunale park; and a network of attractive, narrow lanes that fill to bursting point with revellers from *aperitivo* hour onwards. This is the Naples recalled in the descriptions of Goethe, where the Romantic poets and grand tourists would head before continuing westwards to Posillipo with its grandiose villas and sweeping vistas. From the pine-clad Posillipo hill, the Bay of Naples is laid out in all its glory, the city spread out to the side, Vesuvius slumbering restlessly to the south and the Sorrentine peninsula and Capri on the horizon. Little remains of the German poet's idyll today, but there's much to attract the visitor in this western stretch of the city.

Villa Comunale.

Don't Miss

1 Villa Comunale Escape the city bustle at this peaceful park (p104).

2 Villa Pignatelli Grand villa and gardens (p104).

3 Chiaia nightlife Kick off with an *aperitivo* and take it from there (p143).

4 Lunch in Mergellina Tuck into a seaside piscine feast in the sun (p109).

5 Muu Eat your fill of the best mozzarella in the world (p105).

CHIAIA

Elegant, wedge-shaped **Piazza dei Martiri** is a good place to start exploring Chiaia. It's dominated by four stone lions guarding an obelisk celebrating Victory. The square is flanked by two splendid *palazzi* (both closed to the public): the 19th-century, neoclassical **Palazzo Partanna** (no.58), with its original, mid 18th-century portal; and **Palazzo Calabritto** (no.30), with a fluted column portal by Luigi Vanvitelli.

Leading out of the south-western corner of the piazza is Via Calibritto, lined with designer fashion shops. Across the piazza, Vico Santa Maria a Cappella Vecchia was once home to British Ambassador Sir William Hamilton, his wife Emma and her soulmate Admiral Horatio Nelson. A nearby archway, dated 1506, leads into the courtyard of what was a Benedictine abbey until 1788, after which it was rented out to a string of notables, including the Hamiltons. Under a second archway (no.31) is the house where Nelson was introduced to Emma in 1793.

Via Morelli leads into the cavernous Via Chiatamone, which was the road closest to the coast until the late 19th century, when parallel Via Partenope, dotted with luxury hotels, was built. Via Chiatamone attracted the best and worst of Neapolitan tourism: in 1770, Giacomo Casanova visited a club in the 17th-century palazzo (now nos.26-30) to drum up business for a smart new brothel on Posillipo run by Irish madam Sarah Goudar.

To the west, tyres speed over cobbles along the once-picturesque **Riviera di Chiaia**, threatening anyone rash enough to attempt the crossing to the sole – but nonetheless lovely – park in this area, **Villa Comunale**, home to the tiny **Acquario**. Percy Shelley and his wife Mary stayed at no.250 from 1818 to 1819. During this period they took a child to the church of **San Giuseppe a Chiaia** (081 681898, open 5-8pm Mon-Sat, 10am-noon Sun) to be christened; the child's identity remains a mystery to this day. John Keats was less fortunate: around the same time, he spent three weeks stuck on a ship moored in the bay opposite. The sea was too rough to allow a landing and Keats was left feverish and violently seasick. **Villa Pignatelli** was built for Ferdinand Acton, the son of King Ferdinand I's prime minister, Sir John Acton.

A detour north from the Riviera di Chiaia along **Via Santa Maria in Portico** leads to the church of the same name (081 669294, open 7.45am-1.30pm, 5.45-8pm daily), which has a life-size Nativity scene (1647) to the left of the altar. From here, Via Giuseppe Martucci leads into Piazza Amedeo, a transport hub with a metro station, bus stop and funicular. A rather scruffy traffic island is at the centre of the tree-lined, cobbled square, incongruously overlooked by splendid *stile* Liberty (art nouveau) *palazzi*.

At no.14, **Palazzo Regina Margherita** (closed to the public) has a lovely, faded majolica-tiled façade with mullioned windows. South from Piazza Amedeo, Via Ascensione – or parallel Via Bausan – is where playwright Eduardo de Filippo was born (controversy still rages over the exact location). In nearby Piazzetta Ascensione, the church of the **Ascensione** (081 411657, open 8-11.30am, 5-7.30pm Mon-Sat, 8am-1.30pm Sun) is a mid 17th-century Cosimo Fanzago creation.

Heading east out of Piazza Amedeo, Via Vittoria Colonna, Via dei Mille and Via Filangieri form Naples' most exclusive shopping strip. Via Colonna is home to the church of **Santa Teresa a Chiaia** (081 414263, open 8-10am, 6-7.30pm Mon-Sat, 9am-12.30pm, 6-8pm Sun), designed by Fanzago in 1650. At Via dei Mille 60, among the clothing and jewellery shops, is 17th-century Palazzo Rocella. It houses the Palazzo delle Arti Napoli, better known as **PAN**. The area just south of Via dei Mille teems with the young and chic on weekend nights.

Sights & Museums

FREE Palazzo delle Arti Napoli (PAN)

Centro per le Arti Contemporanee, Palazzo Rocella, Via dei Mille 60 (081 795 8605, www.palazzoarti napoli.net). Funicular Chiaia to Piazza Amedeo, or bus 151, C25, E6. **Open** 9.30am-7.30pm Mon, Wed-Sat; 9.30am-2.30pm Sun. **Admission** free. **Map** p103 B4 ❶

The pink-hued PAN has no permanent collection, but instead describes itself as a 'centre for arts and documentation'. There are regular exhibitions, as well as film screenings, book presentations, lectures, discussions and theatre events. More off-the-wall shows have included a screening of Pink Floyd's 1971 *Live at Pompeii* with a photo tribute to the band.

Stazione Zoologica (Acquario)

Villa Comunale (081 583 3111, www.szn.it). Bus 140, 151. **Open** *Mar-Oct* 9.30am-6pm Tue-Sun; *Nov-Feb* 9am-5pm Tue-Sun. **Admission** €1.50. **No credit cards. Map** p103 C4 ❷

German naturalist Anton Dohrn founded this aquarium in 1872, making it one of Europe's oldest. The ground floor still contains the original 24 tanks, housing sea creatures from the Bay of Naples: coral, jellyfish, turtles, sea horses, an octopus or two, lobsters and starfish. Water for the tanks is brought in from 300m (1,050ft) out in the bay. Legend has it that the entire contents of the aquarium were boiled up to make a massive fish soup during the famine that struck the city in 1944; the less than philanthropic truth is that its contents were cooked up for the British Allied Commander Field Marshal Henry Maitland Wilson, after the liberation of the city in the same year. The aquarium was closed for maintenance work at the time of going to press, but it's expected to reopen in early 2016.

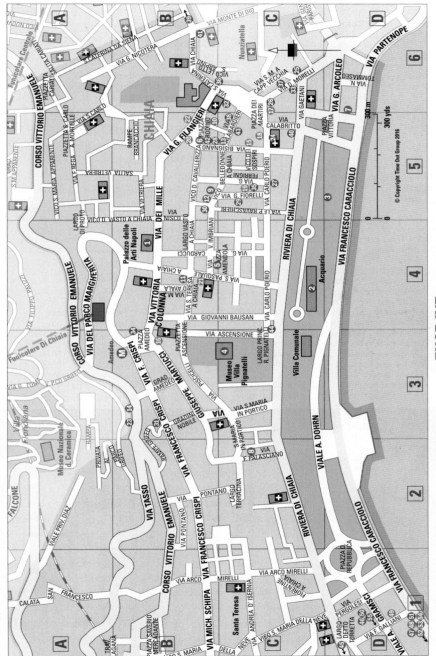

EXPLORE

300 m
300 yds
© Copyright Time Out Group 2016

★ FREE Villa Comunale

Riviera di Chiaia & Via Caracciolo (081 761 1131). Bus 140, 151. **Open** *May-Oct* 7am-midnight daily. *Nov-Apr* 7am-10pm daily. **Admission** free. **Map** p103 D5 ❸

Swathes of historic buildings were demolished to make way for this royal park. It was inaugurated in 1781 as the *giardini reali* (royal gardens) and originally only opened to the public once a year, on the feast of the Virgin Mary's nativity (8 Sept). The massive Toro Farnese – now in the Museo Archeologico Nazionale (*see p82*) – stood here until 1825, when it was replaced by a large bowl found in Paestum. Now surrounded by four lions, the bowl is the centrepiece of the Fontana delle Paparelle. The villa itself was restored for the 1994 G8 conference. There's a magnificent bandstand, built in 1887, and the Stazione Zoologica aquarium (*see p102*).

★ Villa Pignatelli

Riviera di Chiaia 200 (081 761 2356). Bus 140, 151. **Open** 8.30am-1.30pm Mon, Wed, Thur-Sun. **Admission** €2; €1 reductions. **No credit cards**. **Map** p103 C3 ❹

Built in 1826 for Ferdinand Acton, the son of Naples' prime minister Sir John Acton, this villa is a mishmash of styles. The Rothschild family bought and enlarged the villa in 1841; it then passed to the Pignatellis in 1867, and to the Italian state in 1952. Its magnificent ground-floor rooms include the ballroom, dining room, library and a series of 'coloured rooms'; the green room has a priceless collection of 17th- to 19th-century porcelain and majolica pieces. Room 1 displays works by 19th-century sculptor Vincenzo Gemito; room 2 has the collection's finest piece, Francesco Guarino's *St George* (c1650); and there are superb 18th- and 19th-century landscapes in room 6.

Restaurants

16 Libbre

Via Vittorio Imbriani 10 (081 415168). Metro Amedeo. **Open** 9.30am-midnight Mon-Thur, Sun; 9.30am-1am Fri, Sat. **Average** *Café* €20. *Restaurant* €35. **Map** p103 C4 ❺ **Ristorante/café**

This slick new restaurant/café/bar/bakery hybrid starts the day with a breakfast of excellent, freshly baked breads and pastries, before moving on to lunch (salads, filled baguettes, pasta dishes) and a full evening restaurant menu.

★ Anhelo

Via Bisignano 3 (081 402432, www.anhelo napoli.it). Metro Amedeo, or bus C25, 151. **Open** 5pm-midnight Mon-Fri; 10am-midnight Sat. Closed Aug. **Map** p103 B5 ❻ **Tapas**

This stylish little tapas bar opens in time for *aperitivi*, which are served with an interesting selection of tapas: smoked trout with apple carpaccio, perhaps, or toast with butter and salted anchovies. You can follow this with an octopus kebab or hamburger. Breakfast and lunch are also served on Saturdays.

Crudo Re

Piazza Vittoria 11/12 (081 764 5295, www. crudore.it). Bus 128, 140, C12, C18, R7. **Open** 12.30-4pm, 7pm-1am daily. **Average** €60. **Map** p103 D6 ❼ **Ristorante**

Locals come to this smart little restaurant to tuck into vast platters of fresh *crudo* (raw fish and seafood) such as oysters, scampi, tuna, salt cod and lobster. If you don't fancy eating raw fish, try tempura of prawns, salt cod or *spaghetti aglio, olio, pepperoncino e cannolicchi* (razor clams). Follow this with a whole fish baked in a salt crust or '*agli agrumi*'

137A. *See p106.*

(flavoured with citrus fruits): you can choose your victim from the wet fish counter. The weighty wine list includes some 700 labels from all over Italy.

Dora
Via Ferdinando Palasciano 30 (081 680519). Metro Amedeo, or bus 140, 151. **Open** *1-2.30pm, 8pm-midnight Mon-Sat. Closed 10 days Aug.* **Average** €70. **Map** p103 C2 ❻ **Ristorante**
A small restaurant with nautical decor and a big reputation, Dora's menu of no-frills specialities relies on exceptionally fresh local fish and seafood. There's nowhere to hide behind *primi* such as *spaghetti alle vongole* or *linguine alla Dora* (with lobster and tomatoes), but they do a great job. The *crudo di crostacei* (raw crustaceans) is a local favourite. Prices are high for Naples, but the great food and jolly atmosphere justify it. Booking is essential.

€ La Focaccia
Vico Belledonne a Chiaia 31 (081 412277). Metro Amedeo, or bus C25, 140, 151. **Open** *11.30am-2am daily. Closed Aug.* **Average** €5. **No credit cards. Map** p103 B5 ❾ **Pizza**
Choose from a delicious selection of pizza slices and focaccia. Try the *peperoni e patata* (peppers and potato) or *margherita al filetto* (cherry tomatoes and mozzarella). There's a huge range of beers, plus wine by the glass or bottle. The TV is usually blaring; if you're a footie fan, it's a good spot to watch the match.

Muu
Vico 2 Alabardieri 7 (081 405370, www.muu muuzzarellalounge.it). Metro Amedeo, or bus 140, 151. **Open** *12.30-4pm, 7.30pm-1am Tue-Sat; 7.30pm-1am Sun.* **Average** €30. **Map** p103 B5 ❿ **Ristorante**
The menu at fun, cow-themed Muu revolves around mozzarella di bufala ('muuzzarella' in dialect) and offers a choice of dishes based around the pillowy white stuff. You can have it sharing a plate with prosciutto, enveloped in chicken and speck, melted over a hamburger, or in a classic *mozzarella in carrozza* sandwich. The bar is popular at *aperitivo* time.

Osteria da Tonino
Via Santa Teresa a Chiaia 47 (081 421533). Metro Amedeo, or funicular Chiaia to Parco Margherita, or bus C25, 140, 151. **Open** *12.30-4pm Mon-Thur, Sun; 12.30-4pm, 7pm-1am Fri, Sat. Closed 2wks Aug.* **Average** *Lunch* €15. *Dinner* €25. **Map** p103 B4 ⓫ **Osteria**
Personable host Tonino rules the roost at this bustling osteria, which has been in business since 1880. Lunchtimes are particularly popular with a mix of business folk, shoppers and tourists, while dinner is a little calmer (booking advised). Classic pasta dishes with chickpeas or lentils are followed by the likes of *baccalà alla siciliana* (salt cod in a tomato and black olive sauce) or *provola alla pizzaiola* (cheese with tomato and basil sauce); it's authentic and delicious.

★ Pescheria Mattiucci
Vico Belledonne a Chiaia 27 (081 251 2215, www.pescheriamattiucci.com). Metro Amedeo, or funicular Chiaia to Parco Margherita, or bus 140, 151. **Open** *1-3pm, 7.30-10.30pm Tue-Sat; 1-3pm Sun.* **Average** €30. **Map** p103 B5 ⓬ **Trattoria**
Calling itself a 'fish boutique', this simple hole-in-the-wall place is first and foremost a fishmonger's, but you can eat here too. It's not a place to linger –many people eat standing up – although you can perch at the counter. The plates of fishy goodies that appear from the tiny kitchen are all delicious and based on what comes in on the owner's fishing boat each day. Expect the likes of calamari stuffed with prawns and courgettes in tomato sauce, *crudo mediterraneo* (raw fish), and a fishy riff on a traditional *parmigiana di melanzane*. *Aperitivo* time, from 7pm, is popular too.

Umberto
Via Alabardieri 30/31 (081 418555, www. umberto.it). Metro Amedeo, or bus C25, 140, 151. **Open** *7pm-midnight Mon; 12.30-3.30pm, 7.30pm-midnight Tue-Sun. Closed 3wks Aug.* **Average** €35. **Map** p103 C5 ⓭ **Ristorante/pizzeria**
The Di Porzio family have been serving up reliable local classics – and truly excellent pizzas – at this Neapolitan institution since 1916. The walls are covered in black-and-white photos from the 1950s and the clientele is a mixture of business folk, shoppers (it's well placed for Chiaia's boutiques) and tourists. Classic dishes such as *spaghetti alle vongole* are delicious, but there are more creative choices, too, such as swordfish gratin with panko and lime.

★ Veritas
Corso Vittorio Emanuele 141 (081 660595, www.veritasrestaurant.it). Funicular Chiaia to Corso Vittorio Emanuele, or bus C16, C27, 128. **Open** *June-Sept 8-11pm Mon-Sat. Oct-May 8-11pm Tue-Sat, 12.30-3pm Sun.* **Average** €50. **Map** p103 B3 ⓮ **Ristorante**
A bit of a trek from the city centre, Veritas started life as a wine bar but is now a seriously good restaurant. In a contemporary, minimalist setting, chef Gianluca d'Agostino's elegant dishes never stray too far from his Campanian roots, but a lightness of touch and creative twist give them a modern edge. The short menu changes regularly, but expect the likes of *insalata di mare* with green beans and pecorino mayonnaise, aubergine ravioli in an onion and smoked eel broth with mozzarella, and lamb with *zucchini alla scapece* (mint). Desserts are equally delicious. Breads are all baked in house and there's an interesting wine list showcasing labels from Campania.

Cafés, Bars & Gelaterie

Ba-Bar
Via Bisignano 20 (081 764 3525, www.ba-bar.it). Metro Amedeo, or bus C25, 151. **Open** *9am-4am daily.* **Closed** *Aug.* **Map** p103 C5 ⓯

EXPLORE

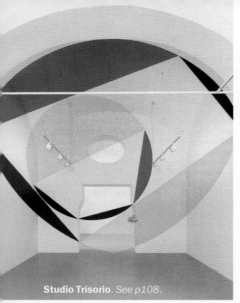
Studio Trisorio. *See p108.*

EXPLORE

Drogheria Fiorelli

Via Fiorelli 10 (081 764 1737). Metro Amedeo, or funicular Chiaia to Parco Margherita, or bus 140, 151. **Open** 10am-2pm Mon; 10am-10pm Tue-Thur; 10am-midnight Fri, Sat; 10am-2pm Sun. **Map** p103 C5 ⑲
This bar-deli occupies a long room lined with shelves stacked with goodies and wines. There's excellent coffee and home-made cakes, platters of cheeses and cold meats, plus salads, bruschettas and pâtés.

Gran Caffè Cimmino

Via Filangieri 12-13 (081 418303). Metro Amedeo, or funicular Chiaia to Parco Margherita, or bus C25. **Open** 7am-10pm Mon-Fri, Sun; 7am-midnight Sat. Closed 1wk Aug. **No credit cards. Map** p103 B5 ⑳
Crowded with lawyers and yuppies, who descend en masse for post-work *aperitivi*, this café also produces delicious cakes and pastries (try the *torta al cioccolato bianco*). Getting a seat can prove tricky. **Other location** Via Petrarca 147, Posillipo (081 575 7697).

★ Moccia

Via San Pasquale a Chiaia 21-22 (081 411348). Metro Amedeo, or bus C25. **Open** 7am-8.30pm Mon, Wed-Sun. Closed Aug. **Map** p103 B4 ㉑
This is one of the most famous cake shops in the city, with prices to match. Try the *fungo al cioccolato* (a mushroom-shaped choux pastry filled with chocolate) or a slice of the excellent *pastiera*. The own-made ice-cream is delicious too.

La Torteria

Via Filangieri 75 (081 405221). Metro Amedeo, or funicular Chiaia to Parco Margherita, or bus C25. **Open** 7am-9pm Mon; 7am-10pm Tue-Fri; 7am-midnight Sat; 7am-11pm Sun. Closed 1wk Aug. **Map** p103 B5 ㉒
Start by drooling over La Torteria's superb cakes and ice-cream cakes (made in-house) and then take a seat on the terrace across the road to enjoy your purchases. One of the specialities is fruit-flavoured ice-cream packed into the peel or shell of the fruit – the ice-cream apples and mandarins look exquisite and taste fantastic. The handmade chocolates are delicious too.

Shops & Services

137A

Corso Vittorio Emanuele 137A (081 060 7045, www.137a.it). Funicular Chiaia to Corso Vittorio Emanuele, or bus C16, C27, 128. **Open** 9.30am-6.30pm Mon-Fri. **Map** p103 B3 ㉓ **Gallery/studio**
This dynamic design studio sees architects, artists, designers and photographers sharing floor space in what was once City Hall, a former nightspot that hosted the famous meeting between Andy Warhol and Joseph Beuys, as well as performances from the likes of Chet Baker, Dizzy Gillespie and Stan Getz. While each member follows his or her individual

A relatively new arrival, cosy Ba-Bar is a buzzing nightlife venue (*see p143*). But it kicks off the day with breakfast and serves drinks and snacks through the day. There's a menu of daily specials at lunchtime.

Caffè Amadeus

Piazza Amedeo 5 (081 761 3023). Metro Amedeo, or funicular Chiaia to Parco Margherita. **Open** 7am-1.30am Mon-Thur; 7am-3am Fri, Sat; 8am-1.30am Sun. **Map** p103 B3 ⑯
There's no seating inside Caffè Amadeus, but plenty of tables set out on busy Piazza Amedeo. The art of the cappuccino is deftly demonstrated by the barista, who will inscribe the foam with any message you like.

★ La Caffettiera

Piazza dei Martiri 30 (081 764 4243). Metro Amedeo, or bus C25, 151. **Open** 7.30am-11.30pm Mon-Fri; 7.30am-1am Sat; 8.30am-11.30pm Sun. **Map** p103 C6 ⑰
With its elegant decor, old-school service and well-heeled clientele, La Caffettiera has a feel of the coffee-houses of the past. The large, canopy-shaded terrace is surrounded by designer shops, and customers look as if they've either just jumped off a yacht or are about to clinch a major deal.

Cambiovita

Via Poerio 100A (081 1957 0395, www.cambiovitastore.it). Bus 140, 151. **Open** 8.30am-8pm Mon-Thur, Sat; 8.30am-11pm Fri. **Map** p103 C5 ⑱
A friendly, bright little place with fresh flowers on stripped wood tables, Cambiovita offers a menu of freshly squeezed juices, tisanes, snacks and light, healthy meals. It also stocks a selection of health foods and alternative remedies.

106 Time Out Naples

projects, they regularly team up to present workshops, shows and seminars: above all, this is an excellent reference point for anyone interested in contemporary art and design in the city. *Photo p104*.

Amina Rubinacci
Via Carlo Poerio 10 (081 415672, www.anna rubinacci.it). Metro Amedeo, or bus C25. **Open** 4.30-8pm Mon; 10am-1.30pm Tue-Sat. Closed 2wks Aug. **Map** p103 C5 ㉔ **Fashion**
This Neapolitan designer is known for her chic, soft knitwear in lovely colours, but you'll also find crisp white shirts, tailored jackets and trousers, and a small selection of accessories.

★ Arte Antica
Via Domenico Morelli 45 (081 764 6897). Metro Piazza Amedeo, or bus C25. **Open** 10.30am-1.30pm, 4.30-8pm Mon-Sat. Closed Aug. **Map** p103 C6 ㉕ **Antiques**
This shop has an unrivalled selection of prints, gouaches and watercolours. Pride of place goes to watercolours by such masters as Della Gatta, Ducros and Lusieri. Prices run from a modest €100 to more than €150,000.

Bowinkel
Piazza dei Martiri 24 (081 764 4344). Bus C25. **Open** 9am-1.30pm, 4-7.30pm Mon-Fri; 9am-1.30pm Sat. Closed last 3wks Aug. **Map** p103 C6 ㉖ **Antiques**
Bowinkel is Naples' most respected dealer in period watercolours, prints and photographs; it's a lovely place to window-shop even if you can't afford to buy. Overseas shipping can be arranged.

Campobasso
Via Carlo Poerio 17 (081 764 0770). Bus C25. **Open** *July* 10am-1.30pm, 4.30-8pm Mon-Fri. *Sept-June* 10am-1.30pm, 4.30-8pm Mon-Sat. Closed Aug. **Map** p103 C5 ㉗ **Antiques**
Campobasso, one of Naples' leading specialists in antique nativity scenes, is a treasure trove of 17th-century religious artefacts.

Capua
Via Carlo Poerio 48 (081 405715, www.capua cashmere.it). Metro Piazza Amedeo, or bus C25. **Open** 10am-1.30pm, 4.30-8pm Mon-Fri; 10am-1.30pm Sat. *July & 1st 2wks Sept* 4.30-8pm Mon; 10am-1.30pm, 4.30-8pm Tue-Sat. Closed Aug. **Map** p103 B5 ㉘ **Fashion**
Capua's men's and women's cashmere sweaters, priced from €190, are available in a range of fabulous colours. You can also find more affordable gloves, scarves and other accessories.

Chi Cerca Trova
Via Fiorelli 3, Chiaia (081 764 7592). Metro Piazza Amedeo, or funicular Chiaia to Parco Margherita, or bus C25. **Open** *May-Oct* 10am-2pm, 4-8pm

Mon-Fri; 10am-2pm Sat. *Nov-Apr* 4-8pm Mon; 10am-2pm, 4-8pm Tue-Sat. Closed Aug. **Map** p103 C5 ㉙ **Vintage**
This Neapolitan institution is still going strong after more than 20 years. The name means 'seek and you'll find', which is what this place is all about; you can rummage among the crammed racks of clothes for hours and will emerge with bargains galore.

Ciro Ricci
Via Belledonne a Chiaia 23 (081 414698). Metro Amedeo, or bus C25. **Open** 4-8pm Mon; 9am-1.30pm, 4-8pm Tue-Sat. Closed 3wks Aug. **Map** p103 B5 ㉚ **Accessories**
The go-to choice of Naples' most elegant ladies, this squeeze of a shop is stuffed with shoes but is particularly known for its handmade sandals. Choose your model (from simple leather thongs to rhinestone-encrusted numbers); they'll measure your foot and make them up on the spot. From €60 a pair.

Contemporastudio
Via Crispi 50 (081 2479939, www.asadventrella.it). Metro Amedeo, or bus C24. **Open** 10.30am-1.30pm, 4-7.30pm Mon-Fri; 10am-1.30pm Sat. **Map** p103 C6 ㉛ **Jewellery**
See p110 **All That Glitters**.

Farmacia Greco
Piazza dei Martiri 65 (081 418027). Bus C25, C28. **Open** 9am-2pm, 4-8pm Mon-Sat. Closed 2wks Aug. **Map** p103 C6 ㉜ **Health & beauty**
Dott Alessandro Iuliano, the head of this friendly, old-fashioned pharmacy, speaks English.

Galleria Lia Rumma
Via Vannella Gaetani 12 (081 1981 2354, www.liarumma.it). Metro Piazza Amedeo, or bus C25. **Open** 11am-1.30pm, 2.30-7pm Mon-Fri. **Map** p103 C6 ㉝ **Gallery**
Opened in 1971, this blue-chip gallery has brought big names such as Anselm Kiefer, Michelangelo Pistoletto, Marina Abramovic and Andreas Gursky to Naples, as well as nurturing Italian artists like Vanessa Beecroft and Franco Scognamiglio.

IN THE KNOW VIRGIL'S TOMB... OR IS IT?

At the top of a flight of steps in Parco Vergiliano (see *p109*) – and looking like a large dovecote – stands what is controversially called Virgil's Tomb. While Virgil lived in Naples, he died in Brindisi and whether he was brought back here for burial is a question that has spawned no end of debate. The inscription on the tomb translates as: 'Mantua bore me, Calabria took me, Naples holds me.'

EXPLORE

EXPLORE

★ Gemellidapolso
Piazza Amedeo 161, Passeggiata Colonna (081 403512, www.gemellidapolso.it). Metro Amedeo. **Open** 10.30am-1.30pm, 4.30-8pm Mon-Sat. **Map** p103 B3 ❸ **Jewellery**
See p110 **All That Glitters**.

★ Idem
Via Giuseppe Ferrigni 32 (081 247 1169, www.idembags.it). Metro Amedeo. **Open** 10am-1.30pm, 4.30-8pm Mon-Sat. Closed 2wks Aug. **Map** p103 C5 ❸ **Fashion**
Marietta Tramontano's inviting little shop offers a gorgeous selection of chic, original women's clothes and accessories with an ethnic slant: chunky bags in super-soft leather, shoppers in colourful raffia with leather trim, separates in fine cotton and silk, accessories and jewellery. A second branch at Vico Belledonne a Chiaia 12 also sells shoes.

Libreria Feltrinelli
Piazza dei Martiri, Via Santa Caterina a Chiaia 23 (081 240 5411, www.lafeltrinelli.it). Metro Amedeo, or bus C25. **Open** 10am-9pm Mon-Fri; 10am-10pm Sat; 10am-2pm, 4-10pm Sun. **Map** p103 C6 ❸ **Books & music**
Recharge your batteries at this cool, three-storey bookshop and music store. Magazines are on sale next to the basement café, near a small selection of English fiction, and theatre and concert tickets can be bought at the in-store Ticket One outpost.
Other location Via San Tommaso d'Aquino 70, Toledo (081 552 1436).

Livio de Simone
Via Domenico Morelli 17 (081 764 3827, www.liviodesimone.it). Metro Amedeo. **Open** 10am-1.30pm, 4.30-8pm Mon-Sat. Closed 3wks Aug. **Map** p103 C6 ❸ **Homewares/accessories**
Designer-artist Livio de Simone's hand-painted fabrics, accessories and homewares lines feature big, splashy colours and a retro feel that recalls the heady days of *La Dolce Vita*. Very Amalfi Coast.

Maliparmi
Via Alabardieri 44 (081 402249, www.maliparmi. com). Metro Amedeo, or bus C24. **Open** 10am-1.30pm, 4-8pm Mon-Sat. **Map** p103 C5 ❸ **Fashion**

> ### IN THE KNOW PALAZZO DONN'ANNA
>
> This partly derelict building is the reputed site of Queen Joan II's cruel, amorous pursuits in the 15th century. The original building was demolished in 1642 to make way for the palazzo we see now. It's private property, but a polite word at the gatehouse may gain you access to the terrace.

Covetable clothes in statement colours with a mod-ethnic slant in soft jersey silks, wools, fine cottons, silks and linens. Maliparmi also does a great line in shoes and accessories.

Mandara
Via Chiaia 149C (081 417348). Funicular Centrale to Augusteo, or bus R2. **Open** 8.30am-8.30pm Mon-Sat. Closed 1wk Aug. **Map** p103 B6 ❸ **Food & drink**
Temptations abound at one of Naples' finest food shops: mozzarella that's as soft as clouds, beautifully creamy ricotta and excellent cured meats.

★ Marinella
Riviera di Chiaia 287A (081 245 1182, www. marinellanapoli.it). Metro Amedeo. **Open** 6.30am-1.30pm, 4-8pm Mon-Sat. Closed 2wks Aug. **Map** p103 C5 ❹ **Accessories**
Marinella has been providing exquisite, traditional silk ties to the great and the good since 1914.

Mario Portolano
Via Chiaia 140/141 (081 418354, www.mario portolano.it). Funicular Centrale to Augusteo, or bus R2. **Open** 10am-1.30pm, 4.30-8pm Mon-Sat. **Map** p103 B6 ❹ **Accessories**
This artisan business, which began in Naples in 1895, produces exquisite gloves in the softest leathers.

Paola Grande Gioielli
Via Bisignano 7 (081 417308, www.paola grandegioielli.com). Metro Amedeo. **Open** 10am-1.30pm, 4.30-8pm Tue-Sat; 4.30-8.30pm Sun. **Map** p103 B5 ❹ **Jewellery**
See p110 **All That Glitters**.

Sapori e Dintorni
Via Alabardieri 8 (081 400302, www.conad.it). Metro Amedeo, or bus C24. **Open** 8.30am-9pm Mon-Sat; 8.30am-2pm Sun. **Map** p103 C5 ❹ **Food & drink**
The smart new Chiaia branch of this upmarket supermarket has a vast choice of high-quality groceries and fresh produce, a top-end deli counter and in-house bakery, fresh meat and fish. There's a stand selling Niko Romito's famous savoury and sweet doughnuts, a wine shop in the basement that offers tastings and a bistro-style restaurant for lunch.

Studio Trisorio
Riviera di Chiaia 215 (081 414306, www.studio trisorio.com). Metro Piazza Amedeo, or bus R2. **Open** 10.30am-1.30pm, 4-7.30pm Mon-Fri; 10.30am-1.30pm Sat. Closed Aug. **Map** p103 C3 ❹ **Gallery**
Inaugurated by Pasquale Trisorio in 1974 with a show of Dan Flavin's work, this well-established gallery exhibits painting and sculpture, plus photography, video and multimedia installations. It's now run by Trisorio's daughter, Laura, who shows international stars such as Daniel Buren, Rebecca Horn, Martin Parr and Enzo Cucchi. *Photo p106.*

MERGELLINA & PIEDIGROTTA

Further west, the Riviera forks: north of Largo Torretta lies the densely populated district of Torretta; towards the sea are the elegant *palazzi* of Viale Antonio Gramsci. The huge, heavily fortified American consulate stands in its corner. Ahead, the traffic hell of Via Piedigrotta leads to the art nouveau Mergellina railway station.

Before the railway bridge is **Santa Maria di Piedigrotta** (081 669761, open 7.30am-noon, 5-7.30pm daily). A church has stood on this spot, associated with apparitions of the Madonna di Piedigrotta, since the 13th century and the present building is the fulcrum of the feast-day celebrations for the Madonna on 8 September each year (*see p26*). The pavement beneath the bridge is unpleasant and rather isolated, but leads to the rewarding **Parco Vergiliano**.

Hugging the waterfront from Chiaia, Via Caracciolo leads to the marina at Mergellina and its mix of smart yachts and small fishing boats. The *porticciolo* (quayside), with its fantastic views of the city, is a favourite spot for an evening stroll. On the other side of the road from the marina are the 'Chalets' – a ramshackle yet hugely popular assortment of cafés, ice-cream parlours and late-night dives. **Chalet Ciro** is the most famous. From Largo Barbaia (where Naples' shortest funicular ascends to the hillside suburbs above), Via Orazio climbs up Posillipo hill to Naples' most exclusive residential areas.

Back on the waterfront, the church of **Santa Maria del Parto** (Via Mergellina 21, 081 664627, open 6.30-8pm Mon-Sat, 8.30am-1pm, 5-8pm Sun) stands at the head of a long flight of steps (spare yourself the climb by taking the lift at 9B). The church was built by 15th-century poet Jacopo Sannazzaro, whose tomb is behind the altar; its lights guided fishermen home. In the first side chapel on the right, the painting *St Michael Vanquishing the Devil* recalls a 16th-century episode in which an ambitious prelate, Diomede Carafa, was tempted by a local beauty, Vittoria d'Avalos. When she declared her love for him, he commissioned this work; the faces of the archangel and the serpent are those of Diomede and Vittoria.

Via Mergellina becomes Via Posillipo at Largo Sermoneta, where there's a fountain (1635) by Carlo Fanzago, Cosimo's son, named after the now-buried River Sebeto.

Sights & Museums

★ Parco Vergiliano

Salita della Grotta 20 (081 669390). Metro Mergellina, or bus C16, C24. **Open** 9am-1hr before sunset daily. **Admission** free. **Map** p103 D1 ⓮

The flight of steps up to this wonderfully peaceful spot is long and puff-inducing, but once at the top you'll be rewarded with a view into the first-century

AD road tunnel (closed at present) known as the Crypta Neapolitana. Stories abound of the atrocious conditions in this primitive borehole, as cart-drivers fought to control their vehicles in the choking dust, and it must be said that conditions in the modern tunnel beneath it aren't much better.

Restaurants

★ 50 Kalò

Piazza Sannazzaro 201B (081 1920 4667, www.50kalo.it). Metro Mergellina, or bus 140, C16, C24. **Open** 12.30-4pm, 7.30pm-12.30am daily. **Average** €15. **Map** p103 D1 ⓯ Pizzeria

Challenging Naples' more traditional pizzerias, Ciro Salvo's much talked-about 50 Kalò offers what he claims to be a 'more digestible' dough than his competitors; the lighter-than-average-crusts have the punters queueing out the door of this contemporary pizzeria. The menu ranges from traditional marinara and margherita to innovative combos such as courgette flowers and Nero Casertano salami.

Don Salvatore

Via Mergellina 5 (081 681817, www.donsalvatore.it). Metro Mergellina, or bus 140, C16, C24. **Open** noon-3.30pm, 7.30pm-midnight Mon, Tue, Thur-Sun. **Average** €45. **Map** p103 D1 ⓱ Ristorante

Superb antipasti are a highlight at this busy, family-run place on the waterfront: the tempting buffet may include *polpo ai carciofi* (octopus with artichokes) or *calamaretti con uva passa* (baby squid with sultanas and pine nuts). Owner Tonino Aversano is an expert on the history of Neapolitan cuisine, and historical dishes such as *cuoccio* (parrot fish) with parmesan and fresh tomato appear on the menu alongside more recent creations such as scorpion fish in orange. Tonino is also passionate about wine.

Cafés, Bars & Gelaterie

★ Chalet Ciro

Via Francesco Caracciolo (081 669928, www.chaletciro.it). Metro Mergellina, or bus 140, C24. **Open** 7am-3am Mon, Tue, Thur-Sun. **Map** p103 D1 ⓰

Chalet Ciro is one of the great Neapolitan *gelaterie* and locals travel across town to eat here; expect a queue for pastries on Sunday mornings too. After choosing from the vast array of *gelati* and pastries, bag a seat outside and watch the boats sailing by.

Remy Gelo

Via Galiani 9 (081 665752). Metro Mergellina. **Open** 10am-midnight daily. **No credit cards**. **Map** p103 D1 ⓳

Aficionados reckon this widely renowned *gelateria* has lost ground to Bilancione and Chalet Ciro, but Remy Gelo still offers a huge range of ice-creams, sorbets and *semifreddi*. Each one is made on the premises and served up in all manner of different-sized tubs, pots and cones.

EXPLORE

ALL THAT GLITTERS
Naples' new generation of jewellers.

Naples has a long, distinguished history of jewellery design and manufacture, and today's skilled designers and artisans, many of them continuing family businesses, are interpreting the techniques handed down through the generations to suit contemporary tastes.

Mother-and-daughter team Paola Grande and Giulia Di Pace have updated a family tradition of jewellery-making that goes back several generations. Designs are made up in their Naples atelier and sold in an elegant jewel box of a shop in Chiaia, **Paola Grande Gioielli** (see p108; pictured), where you'll find exquisite original pieces in gold, silver and bronze set with precious stones. Look out for the Congiunzioni (conjoined) collection of rings, which can be worn singly or in a bunch for a chunkier look.

Cristiano Barbarulo, another Neapolitan with jewellery in his blood, sells exquisite cufflinks – some designed by him, all made by artisans – at **Gemellidapolso** (see p108). They range from classic to extravagant designs in gold and silver set with coral, lapis lazuli, amber and other precious and semi-precious stones. Geoffrey Rush wore

Barbarulo cufflinks in *The Best Offer* (2013), as did Michael Caine in Paolo Sorrentino's *Giovinezza* (2015).

Hailing from a dynasty of distinguished Neapolitan jewellery makers (grandfather Giuseppe supplied jewels to the royal family in the mid 19th century; father Roberto was an innovative designer during the 1970s, when he worked for Dior among others), Asad Ventrella and his sister Luisa continue the family tradition in their contemporary Chiaia workshop, **Contemporastudio** (see p107). The annual collections – funky, whimsical designs in silver, bronze, aluminium and titanium – have a pop art look and often take inspiration from Naples: sirens, labyrinths, pasta shapes and so on.

Shops & Services

Anna Matuozzo
Viale Gramsci 26 (081 663874, www.anna matuozzo.com). Metro Mergellina, or funicular Mergellina, or bus C12, C18. **Open** 9am-7pm Mon-Fri; Sat by appt only. Closed Aug. **Map** p103 D1 ⑤ Fashion
Matuozzo's handmade shirts for men are the finest that money can buy.

POSILLIPO

As it climbs and heads west, long, wide Via Orazio becomes Via Petrarca, and then, at the top of the hill, merges with Via Francesco Manzoni. It's lined with huge but discreet apartment buildings, some with guards on the gates: these are the homes of Naples' movers and shakers – politicians, lawyers and business magnates. Turn left at the top of Via Manzoni and look westwards for wonderful views over the Bay of Pozzuoli and the site of the former steelworks at **Bagnoli**. As part of the area's redevelopment, the **North Pier** was opened in December 2005. Once the pier where ships unloaded ore and took away finished

steel, it's now thronged with partygoers in summer. It extends out into the Bay of Pozzuoli, towards the isle of Nisida. Further down the hill, turn right up Viale Virgilio for the **Parco Virgiliano** (open 1 May-20 June 7am-midnight daily, 21 June-30 Sept 7am-1am daily, Oct-Apr 7am-10pm daily), not to be confused with the Parco Vergiliano in Piedigrotta (see p109), a horseshoe-shaped park on top of Posillipo Hill with sumptuous views over the Campi Flegrei and a busy clothes market on Friday mornings.

Back at the junction with Via Petrarca, a right turn (uphill) on to Via Francesco Manzoni leads to a Spanish watchtower, the **Torre Ranieri** (1530), one of a chain of towers along the coast; its signals could be seen from Baia. From Largo Sermoneta in Mergellina, cobbled Via Posillipo clatters away from the bathing establishments set along the shoreline, passing the decrepit **Palazzo Donn'Anna** in the eponymous piazza.

Shortly after the municipal bus depot on the right, the moody, grey, faux-Egyptian **Mausoleo** war memorial (Via Posillipo 155, open 9am-1pm daily) overlooks the road from a peaceful garden, shaded by massive pine trees. From Via Posillipo, three twisting lanes lead down to little beaches

EXPLORE

– although they're not for young children or poor swimmers. No buses serve these routes, so it's a long haul back up.

Via Russo passes the presidential summer residence **Villa Rosebery** (open during Maggio dei Monumenti, *see p25*). Via Marechiaro starts where Via Posillipo meets Via Boccaccio, and winds down to a tiny parking area surrounded by fish restaurants. The Calata del Ponticello a Marechiaro leads to a romantic spot overlooking a pebbly beach. A path to the sea on the left of the road, just before **Villa Pausilypon**, descends to the pleasant cove of La Gaiola. There's a small shingle beach and a long quay to swim from.

Via Posillipo continues on from the villa through a cutting in the headland, becoming Discesa Coroglio, then dropping sharply down towards the alternative entrance to the **Grotta di Seiano** and the sprawling, ex-industrial site of the Bagnoli steelworks, now occupied in part by the **Città della Scienza** (*see p127*) and a new pier. The island in the distance, Nisida, is home to a NATO naval support base and a juvenile reformatory, and is strictly closed to the public, although you can walk across the promontory that connects the island to the mainland.

Sights & Museums

FREE Grotta di Seiano & Villa Pausilypon

Discesa Coroglio (081 230 1030, guided tours 081 575 4465). Bus 140 to Capo Posillipo, then C1. **Open** *Guided tours only* 9.30am, 10.30am, 11.30am Mon-Sat. **Admission** free. **Map** p103 D1 51

Once the private entrance to ornate Villa Pausilypon, the Grotta di Seiano is more tunnel than grotto and was built by the architect Cocceius during the first century AD; he also designed the Grotta di Cocceio and the Crypta Neapolitana (*see p109*). Strengthened in 1840 with a series of load-bearing arches, the tunnel stretches for 770m (2,526ft). En route, galleries provide magnificent views over the small Trentaremi Bay, named after the 30 ('*trenta*') rowing boats used by the Romans. The fragile cliff of tuff stone into which the tunnel was bored is prone to landslides, and over the years access to the Grotta has been irregular; for the moment, though, it's open for guided tours.

Through the tunnel and in a magnificent setting on the Posillipo cliffs is Villa Pausilypon, which once belonged to a Roman senator by the name of Publius Vedius Pollio. The site includes the remains of the villa itself and an amphitheatre, which is used for open-air concerts. The ugly, neoclassical villa built on the island was last owned by the Agnelli family; it's reputed to bring bad luck to all who possess it.

Restaurants

Al Poeta

Piazza Salvatore di Giacomo 134-135 (081 575 6936, www.alpoeta.org). Bus 140. **Open** 1-3.30pm, 8pm-midnight Tue-Sun. Closed 2wks Aug. **Average** €40. **Map** p103 D1 52 Ristorante

The Varriale brothers' *ristorante*-pizzeria has a delightfully peaceful setting high up on Posillipo Hill and a loyal local following. Housed in a Liberty *villetta* with a lovely garden set back from the main road with views of the bay, it's all wood, white walls and copper pots inside. The food is traditional: deliciously fresh fish, accompanied by a fine range of wines, and there's good pizza too. Try the linguine with scampi; *paccheri* with fresh tuna, cherry tomatoes, capers and black olives; *rombo* (John Dory) baked in the oven with potatoes; or a succulent steak.

Rosiello

Via Santo Strato 10 (081 769 1288, www.ristoranterosiello.it). Bus 140, C31. **Open** 12.30-4pm, 7.30pm-midnight Mon, Tue, Thur-Sun. Closed 10 days Aug. **Average** €60. **Map** p103 D1 53 Ristorante

Tables are set in a terraced, wisteria-draped garden, high above the restaurant's own lemon grove and vines, from which it makes wine and limoncello. The views over the Bay of Naples are wonderful and the food, although expensive (wood-fired pizza is a cheaper option), is generally good with a fine repertoire of pasta and fish.

> **IN THE KNOW JUST THE TICKET**
>
> For tickets to gigs, sporting events, opera, ballet and theatre, museums and more, contact **Concerteria Schipa** (Via Schipa 23, 081 761 1221, www.concerteria.it) or **Ticket One** in the Feltrinelli bookshop, Piazza dei Martiri (081 240 5411, www.lafeltrinelli.it).

Cafés, Bars & Gelaterie

Bilancione

Via Posillipo 238B (081 769 1923, www.gelateriabilancione.it). Bus 140. **Open** 7am-midnight Tue-Fri, Sun; 7am-1.30am Sat. **Map** p103 D1 54

Staunchly old-fashioned in its ways, this is one of the city's most traditional *gelaterie*. The fantastic ice-creams and mouthwatering sorbets (around 100 in all) attract a loyal following, and the benches outside offer spectacular views across Naples.

Shops & Services

Mirage Day Spa

Via Porta Posillipo 135D (081 769 1436, www.miragespa.eu). Funicular Manzoni. **Open** 9am-9.30pm Mon-Sat. **Map** p103 D1 55 Health & beauty

Facilities include a pool, Turkish baths and a restaurant; there's a range of treatments available.

EXPLORE

Campi Flegrei

Wrapped around the Bay of Pozzuoli to the west of Naples and incorporating the towns of Pozzuoli and Bacoli, the area known as the Campi Flegrei (the Phlegrean or Burning Fields) is an extraordinary area rich in extinct (or not quite extinct) volcanic activity, and Greek and Roman archaeological remains. It's steeped in myth, mystery and weird geological phenomena: hissing fumaroles and bubbling mud baths, rising and falling water levels, the cave of the great oracle Sybil, a fabulous Flavian amphitheatre and the fabled entrance to the underworld. In Roman times, it was a leisure destination for the rich and famous, who built fabulous summer villas with vast spa complexes and mighty ports. All this was a magnet for the grand tourists of the 18th and 19th centuries. Erratic public transport connections to the more far-flung sights present logistical problems. But for those who persevere, the rewards are huge.

Anfiteatro Flavio

Don't Miss

1 Parco Sommersa di Baia Dive beneath the waves for a glimpse of ancient Baiae (p116).

2 Anfiteatro Flavio The third largest in the ancient world (p115).

3 Abraxas Great food, gorgeous setting (p118).

4 Parco Archeologico di Cuma A ramble through history (p118).

5 Riserva Naturale Cratere degli Astroni Climb into the crater (p114).

 EXPLORE

EXPLORE

INTRODUCING THE AREA

These days, the aura of mystery that surrounded the Campi Flegrei has been severely compromised by the *abusivismo edilizio* (illegal building) that has resulted in swathes of the countryside being covered with cement. Many of the place names still have a classical ring, but the reality is much less romantic: **Arco Felice** (happy arch), named after the old Roman aqueduct spanning the road from Pozzuoli to Cuma, can be a traffic nightmare; **Lago Lucrino** (the Lucrine lake, famed for its oyster beds in antiquity) is now fringed by a disco, a supermarket and seafood restaurants. Meanwhile, the reposting of the NATO base from Bagnoli to Lago Patria in 2012 is adding a new dimension (and even more traffic) to the area.

Some areas, however, have been spared. Two volcanic craters (**Monte Nuovo** and **Astroni**) have been transformed into nature reserves, while **Pozzuoli** has been spruced up and is home to a magnificent Roman amphitheatre. **Baia** has a small but spectacular, state-of-the-art museum within its castle walls; and at the end of the peninsula, **Capo Miseno** remains picturesque and sports good beaches on its westward side. And if you close your eyes and use a bit of imagination, places such as the **Cave of the Sibyl**, the **Solfatara** and **Lago d'Averno** still have the power to beguile.

SIGHTS & MUSEUMS

Astroni

Astroni is one of the wonders of the Campi Flegrei: an entire volcanic crater carpeted with Mediterranean vegetation. Tapped by the Romans for its geothermal waters (the baths have never been discovered) and used by Naples' various dynasties as a hunting area from the 15th century to the 19th century, Astroni is now a World Wildlife Fund (WWF) reserve. A landslide after heavy rains in March 2005 blocked the road (near the site entrance) that winds down towards the lakes on the crater floor; visitors have since been channelled down a steeper path through holm oak woodland.

A shady picnic site has been laid out at the bottom of the crater and screened observation walkways have been erected for birdwatchers by the lakeside, although much of the area is so dense in vegetation that twitching here requires a good pair of ears as well as binoculars. Be warned that access by public transport involves a two-kilometre walk through an isolated area and the opening hours are subject to change, so phone ahead.

Riserva Naturale Cratere degli Astroni

Oasi WWF, Via Agnano Astroni 468 (081 588 3720, www.wwf.it/oasi/campania/cratere_degli_astroni). Cumana train to Pianura or Bagnoli, then bus C14 or 20min walk from Pianura station. **Open** varies. **No credit cards. Admission** €6; reductions €4; free for WWF members.

Pozzuoli

Greeks from Cuma founded Dikaiarchia (ancient Pozzuoli) in c530 BC as a bulwark against encroaching Etruscans and Samnites, but few traces of the original settlement remain. The area regained strategic importance in the late third century BC during the Second Punic War, when the Romans were anxious to prevent Hannibal reaching the Tyrrhenian coast from nearby Capua. The hill overlooking the port, now known as Rione Terra, was colonised in 194 BC and the new settlement (Puteoli) rapidly expanded. In Imperial times, Puteoli was a thriving *entrepôt* port, several times larger than Pompeii. Extensive traces have survived, albeit often suffocated by the modern town.

The seafaring tradition is still strong here. Pozzuoli is the closest mainland harbour to the islands of Procida and Ischia, and its ferry port does brisk business. Meanwhile, Neapolitans come here in droves to dine on fresh fish and *frutti di mare* at lower prices than in the city.

Down near the port is the Roman fish and meat market, the *macellum*, commonly known as the **Serapeo** (Temple of Serapis). Its columns are visibly perforated by molluscs, showing that the *macellum* has spent much of its existence submerged in seawater. It's subject to a rising and sinking phenomenon called bradyseism, caused by geological shifts several kilometres below the earth's surface.

IN THE KNOW ANCIENT WINES

Grapes have been cultivated for wine-making in these parts for millennia – Pliny the Elder sang the praises of Falerno wine, made on the coast near Pozzuoli and a favourite of the Roman upper classes. These days, local wines are made principally from two grape varieties, white Falanghina dei Campi Flegrei and red Piedirosso, a grape that was also highly regarded in ancient Rome. Growing conditions are governed by the mineral-rich volcanic soil and the proximity to the sea with its cooling breezes. Falanghina is a fresh, light wine with a subtle fragrance; Piedirosso is light and juicy with a burnt-red colour. The quality of these wines has improved enormously in recent years; to taste them at their best, look out for examples from Contrada Salandra, Agnanum and La Sibilla.

Up on the hill above the port is the site of the original Roman colony, **Rione Terra**, a warren of ancient roads, shops and houses. Parts of the site can now be visited (*see p117*).

North-east of the port, the 40,000-seater **Anfiteatro Flavio** (Flavian amphitheatre) was the ancient world's third largest, after the Colosseum in Rome and Capua's amphitheatre. Rising above the congested roads, railways and ugly modern apartment blocks literally and figuratively, it was built mostly during Vespasian's rule (AD 70-79), though work may have started under Nero. The impressive *carceres* (cells) in the underground area below the arena indicate that the amphitheatre was used for *venationes* – contests involving exotic animals, shipped via Puteoli's port from one of the Empire's distant provinces.

The large *fossa* (ditch) cutting across the arena may have contained the stage scenery, which was raised or lowered depending on the backdrop. The underground cells are open to visitors, and the area around the amphitheatre is scattered with beautifully carved marble fragments found in the Campi Flegrei, a wonderful open-air museum.

For a taste of just how 'burning' the Campi Flegrei still are, walk across the dormant volcanic crater of the foul-smelling **Solfatara** to the east of the town centre. The ancient Romans called the Solfatara 'Forum Vulcani', and visited it with the same strange fascination as modern tourists. From an eerie lunar landscape, wisps of sulphurous steam rise up in fumaroles and boiling mud quivers in broad bubbles. According to locals, breathing in the sulphur fumes deeply does wonders for sinus and lung problems. On the north-eastern side of the crater, entrances to a *sudatorium* (built in the 19th century and now bricked up) form weird, intolerably hot saunas. In recent years, the Solfatara has also made an atmospheric concert venue during the **Pozzuoli Jazz Festival** (www.pozzuolijazzfestival.it) in July, along with the Rione Terra (*see p117*) and Serapeo (*see p114*).

On Via San Gennaro, a few hundred metres south of the Solfatara, the 16th-century **Santuario di San Gennaro** church marks the spot where Naples' patron saint was decapitated. Legend has it that the deed was done beside the second column on the right. The stone used for the beheading is now kept in the first chapel on the right, and the congealed blood turns a bright, healthy red on the days when a vial full of what is said to be San Gennaro's blood liquefies in Naples' Duomo (*see p72* **City of Blood**).

★ Anfiteatro Flavio
Via Terracciano 75 (081 526 6007). **Open** 9am-1hr before sunset Mon, Wed-Sun. **Admission** €4; €2 reductions (tickets valid for 2 days and include entry to Cuma, Museo Archaeologico dei Campi Flegrei & Parco Archeologico e Monumentale di Baia). **No credit cards**.

IN THE KNOW EXQUISITE POOLS

In the town of Bacoli, just south of Baia, lies one of the unsung ancient wonders of the area. The **Piscina Mirabilis** ('Exquisite Pool') is a colossal, vaulted underground reservoir that once formed part of a subterranean aqueduct system supplying water to the Roman naval fleet at Miseno, to the south. It's like a massive underground cathedral and the haunting atmosphere is enhanced by the fact that few visitors ever get this far. To gain access, you have to call the custodian, Signora Immacolata, in advance and fix an appointment (333 573 0225, 333 685 3278, visits 9am-1hr before sunset Tue-Sun).

FREE Santuario di San Gennaro
Via San Gennaro Agnano 10 (081 526 1114). **Open** 9am-noon, 4.30-6pm daily. **Admission** free.

★ Solfatara
Via Solfatara 161 (081 526 2341, www.vulcano solfatara.it). **Open** *Apr-Sept* 8.30am-7pm daily. *Oct-Mar* 8.30am-4.30pm daily. **Admission** €7; €6 reductions (evening visit €15). **No credit cards**.

Baia

From well before the Christian era until the 18th century, **Baia** (possibly named after Baios, a companion of Ulysses who, according to legend, was buried here) was one of Italy's prime holiday resorts, combining all the essential ingredients of sea air, health-giving mineral springs and glorious scenery. Modern Baia consists chiefly of unattractive strip development along the main coast road, with a plethora of bars, restaurants and *gelaterie*. In Roman times, though, it was a different story: wealthy aristocrats (Julius Caesar, Nero and Hadrian, to name a few) built sumptuous holiday villas here and constructed ports for their barges. Although much of ancient Baiae now lies under the sea (the *città sommersa* can be seen from a glass-bottomed boat that operates from the port at Baia; *see p116*), there's still a certain opulence about the site and its natural setting.

Emperor Caligula, who reigned from AD 37 to 41, built a causeway of boats and ships across the stretch of water from Baiae to Puteoli (now Pozzuoli). According to Roman historian Suetonius, this was intended to outdo Xerxes' celebrated bridging of the narrower Hellespont – or as a large-scale engineering feat to terrify the Germans and Britons into submission.

The **Parco Archeologico** is arranged in terraces overlooking the bay. At the top, the view from the Villa dell'Ambulatio gives a good idea

EXPLORE

of the layout. At the end of the *ambulatio* is the *balneum* (bathroom), a jewel of stuccoed artistry. The level below contains a *nymphaeum* (a grotto with a pool and fountain dedicated to the water-nymphs) or perhaps a miniature theatre; further down on the lowest terrace stands the Tempio di Mercurio (Temple of Mercury) and a large *natatio* (swimming pool) with an imposing dome (50-27 BC) that pre-dates the cupola of Rome's Pantheon.

Housing some of the archaeological finds from the area is the **Museo Archeologico dei Campi Flegrei**. It's set in the Castello di Baia, built in the 15th century over the ruins of a Roman fort. Its present look dates from 1538 to 1550. There's a reconstructed *sacellum* (shrine) used for the cult of the emperors, represented here in flattering statues of Vespasian and Titus; the bronze statue of the unpopular Domitian was reworked to depict his successor, Nerva, after he had been deposed. On the upper level is a reconstruction of a *nymphaeum* that was excavated in the 1980s but which lies, together with much of Baiae, under six metres of water. The statues, however, have been brought to the surface, and include a headless Odysseus plying Polyphemus (statue not found) with wine, a favourite theme of Roman sculptors. The rest of the castle is given over to a display of finds from across the Phlegrean Fields. Few of the explanatory panels are in English.

IN THE KNOW SUBMERGED CITY

The gulf of Naples is a brilliant spot for diving enthusiasts, and the **Parco Sommersa di Baia** (*see right*) is as good as it gets. The Centro Sub Campi Flegrei (Via Miliscola, Lucrino, 081 853 1563, www.centrosubcampiflegrei.it) runs both snorkelling and diving excursions to explore the sunken city. The site is only four to five metres below sea level so, on a calm day, snorkelling can be very rewarding; an hour's trip costs €20 including equipment. Diving trips take in the submerged city but also go further afield to the islands of Nisida, Procida and Ischia. These are charged by the dive (€35 for one, €65 for two, €90 for three). Equipment can be rented for €20. Courses are run at all levels by PADI-accredited instructors and tuition is also available in English. Take the Cumana railway to Lucrino; leave the station on the beach side, turn left and walk along the beachfront for 100 metres. The diving centre is part of the Capo Blu lido (open May-Oct 8.30am-6.30pm daily, Nov-Apr 8.30am-5.30pm Sat, Sun), where there's also a bar, sunbeds and umbrellas for hire, and a spa.

North of Baia, the **Lago di Averno** (Lake Avernus) was where Virgil led Dante down into the Underworld ('*Facilis descensus Averna*' – 'The way to Averna is easy' – he said); the *sommo poeta* might think twice about getting his feet wet in its decidedly uninviting waters today. The sulphurous belching from beneath the surface of this crater lake was once said to be potent enough to stop passing birds dead, mid-flap. On the north-western shore, the **Grotta di Cocceio** (closed to the public) leads to a wide, perfectly straight tunnel that runs to the Sibyl's cave in Cuma. In antiquity, Averno was an inner harbour, connected by canals to the sea via the Lago di Lucrino, where stubs of Roman walls and arches can still be seen.

★ Museo Archeologico dei Campi Flegrei

Via Castello 39 (081 523 3310, 848 800288, www.cir.campania.beniculturali.it/luoghi-della-cultura/castello-aragonese-di-baia). **Open** 9am-2.20pm Tue-Sun (last entry 1.20pm). **Admission** €4; €2 reductions (tickets valid for 2 days and include entry to Anfiteatro Flavia, Cuma & Parco Archeologico e Monumentale di Baia). **No credit cards.**

Parco Archeologico e Monumentale di Baia

Via Sella di Baia 22 (081 868 7592, 848 800288). **Open** 9am-1hr before sunset Tue-Sun. **Admission** €4; €2 reductions (tickets valid for 2 days & include entry to Anfiteatro Flavia, Cuma & Museo Archaeologico dei Campi Flegrei). **No credit cards.**

Parco Sommersa di Baia (Underwater City)

Via Molo di Baia (boat trips 349 497 4183, www.baiasommersa.it). **Open** by appt. Closed mid Nov-Mar. **Trips** from €10. **No credit cards.** The Parco Sommersa di Baia can be visited through the cultural association of Baiasommersa. They also arrange scuba-diving trips to various underwater sites. To arrange evening visits, contact the association in advance (prenotazioni@baiasommersa.it). *See also left* **In the Know**.

Cuma

The history of the Greek colony of Cumae is little known, but archaeological remains point to a flourishing settlement that was to have a considerable influence in Italy throughout the classical period. The settlement had extensive trading contacts with the Etruscans, and it was Cumaen Greeks who established further colonies at what would become Naples.

The Romans expanded the Greek site, building a forum to the east and a series of impressive tunnels that linked Cuma to the Lago di Averno, an important inland harbour for the Roman fleet.

RIONE TERRA
Pozzuoli's hidden ancient city.

Volcanic activity during the 1970s led to the mass evacuation of Rione Terra, Pozzuoli's densely inhabited and somewhat insalubrious 'acropolis' overlooking the modern port. As so often happens in these parts, a human tragedy was turned into an archaeological success story: with a massive injection of government funds, archaeologists excavated below the 17th-century *palazzi* and brought much of ancient Puteoli to light.

An underground visitors' walkway leads through the dense network of roads and passages that date, in some cases, from Puteoli's foundation in 194 BC. Much is revealed along the way: *tabernae* (simple restaurants), a *cryptoportico* (underground storeroom) and a *pistrinum* (bakery). On a lower level are some *ergastula* (cells for slaves), with surprisingly erudite graffiti featuring quotes from Catullus, and a frescoed *lararium* (household shrine). Beneath the *decumanus maximus* (the main road leading to the forum) is part of the impressive sewage system that channelled waste water into the sea. At the end of the walkway, visitors emerge just below the 17th-century Duomo that was built around a major Roman temple, its columns revealed by a devastating fire in 1964.

For now, the Duomo and immediate surrounding area can be visited at weekends (10am-noon, 5-7pm Sat, 10am-1pm, 5.30-7.30pm Sun). Access to the rest of the *rione*, via guided tours, has been rather sporadic in recent years. At the time of going to press, the site was due to open for a period of three months; hopefully that will be extended. For more information about opening times call 081 526 6007.

EXPLORE

In Book VI of the *Aeneid*, Virgil describes the fascination exerted by the Antro della Sibilla, the fabled cave of the oracle Sibyl, a prophetess sacred to Apollo. With its unearthly light shafts – the *centum ostia* (100 mouths), as the poet called them – at the end of a dark, 350ft (106m) echo-filled gallery, the cave (or Chamber of the Prophetic Voice) is still an eerily atmospheric place. According to myth, it was here that the Trojan Aeneas received his instructions to descend to the Underworld beneath Lake Avernus (**Lago di Averno**, *see p116*). A landslide in 2014 temporarily closed the cave to visitors (although you can see in from above): ask at the Parco Archaelogico for information.

Apollo, the god of light and divination, was worshipped here, as the temple on the lower level of the **Acropolis** reveals. On the highest level (it's worth trekking up to the top for the sweeping views through the oak woods) is the **Tempio di Giove** (Temple of Jupiter), built in the third century BC but manhandled by Roman refurbishers in Imperial times.

South of Cuma, the Acherusia Palus of old, now **Lago Fusaro**, has a *cascina* (lodge) designed in 1782 by Carlo Vanvitelli, joined by a causeway to terra firma. Beyond Lago Fusaro is Capo Miseno (Misenum), from where Pliny the Younger watched Vesuvius erupt in AD 79.

★ Parco Archeologico di Cuma
Via Acropoli 1 (081 854 3060, 848 800288). **Open** 9am-1hr before sunset Mon, Wed-Sun. **Admission** €4; €2 reductions (tickets valid for 2 days and include entry to Anfiteatro Flavia, Museo Archeologico dei Campi Flegrei & Parco Archeologico e Monumentale di Baia). **No credit cards**.

RESTAURANTS

★ Abraxas
Via Scalandrone 15, Pozzuoli (081 854 9347, 339 223 6700, www.abraxasosteria.it). Cumana rail to Lucrino, then taxi or 20mins walk. **Open** 8pm-midnight Mon, Wed-Fri; 1-4pm, 8pm-midnight Sat; 1-4pm Sun. **Average** €40. Ristorante

It may be off the beaten track (in the hills above Lago d'Averno), but Abraxas is worth seeking out. The menu includes the likes of *bucatini* pasta with rabbit sauce or *spezzatino* (beef stew) slow-cooked in local aglianico wine. If you fancy fish, try the anchovies marinated with mint or pasta with mussels and *cicerchie* (a kind of chickpea). Desserts are delicious, and there's a superb choice of local cheeses and a serious wine list too. The atmosphere is warm and inviting, and there's a lovely garden for warmer weather.

Bobò
Lungomare Cristoforo Colombo 20, Pozzuoli (081 526 2034, www.ristorantebobo.com). Cumana rail or metro line 2 to Pozzuoli. **Open** 12.30-3.30pm, 8.30pm-midnight Mon, Wed-Sat; 12.30-3.30pm Sun. **Average** €50. Ristorante
Set back from the quayside in Pozzuoli, and close to one of the biggest fish markets in Campania, this is the sort of classic restaurant that droves of Neapolitans head to for a hearty Sunday lunch. Fish and seafood delivered daily to the local port go into dishes such as spaghetti with sea urchins or fusilli with clams and earthy porcini mushrooms. The locals hold the 'crudo' platters – hopping fresh raw crustaceans and oysters dressed with a little oil and a squeeze of lemon – in high regard, but be warned: they're no bargain.

Il Casolare da Tobia
Contrada Fondi di Baia, Via Pietro Fabris 12-14, Baia (081 523 5193, 366 536 6025, www.datobia.it). Cumana rail to Lucrino then Torregaveta bus, or bus SEPSA 1 from Piazza Garibaldi to Bacoli. **Open** 1-4pm, 8pm-midnight Tue-Sat; 1-3.30pm Sun. Closed 1wk Aug. **Average** €30. Trattoria
Using local organic produce, owners Tobia and Elisabetta create hearty seasonal meals based on traditional recipes, accompanied by excellent local wines. The set menus (€30) are mainly meat-based, but fish features too. The Friday evening 'steak-outs' are particularly good value at €35 for two people (book in advance). Il Casolare, an *agriturismo*, is set in a 10,000-year-old extinct volcano, and in summer Tobia organises barbecues around the new swimming pool; bring your bathing togs.

★ La Catagna
Via Pennata 50, Bacoli (081 523 4218). **Open** 8-10.30pm Tue-Fri; 1-3pm, 8-10pm Sat; 1-3pm Sun. **Average** €40. Trattoria
Hidden away among the quiet backstreets of Bacoli, this small, family-run trattoria has a fantastic terrace overlooking Capo Miseno. The menu relies on the catch of the day brought in by local fishermen, but could well include *insalata di polpo e patate* (octopus and potato salad), *crochette di baccalà* (salt cod), pasta with lobster or crab, and whole fish with grilled vegetables. Leave room for the wild strawberry flan and a drop of homemade *nocino* (walnut liqueur). It's hard to find, so make sure you know where you're going. Booking is essential.

★ Da Fefè

Via della Shoah 15, Case Vecchie, Bacoli (081 523 3011, www.fefeabacoli.it). Monte di Procida bus from Piazza Garibaldi or Piazza Municipio. **Open** *May* 8.30-11pm Tue-Fri; 12.30-4pm, 8.30-11pm Sat, Sun. *June-Sept* 8.30-11pm Mon-Fri; 12.30-4pm, 8.30-11pm Sat, Sun. *Oct-Apr* 8-11.30pm Tue-Fri; 12.30-4pm, 8-11.30pm Sat; 12.30-4pm Sun. Closed 2wks Jan. **Average** €40. **Ristorante**
With tables laid out by the picturesque port where the Roman fleet once moored, this tiny restaurant serves delicious fish and seafood. Nibble on crispy *crochette di baccalà* (salt cod) while you contemplate spaghetti with fresh anchovies, local green peppers and cherry tomatoes; pasta with *genovese di polipo* (octopus sauce); or giant prawns sautéed with Bacardi. Finish your meal with one of the in-house liqueurs. Féfé is poular with the Neapolitan intelligentsia who make a beeline for the outside tables: book ahead or be prepared to queue.

La Tortuga

Via Molo di Baia 42, Baia (081 868 8878). Cumana rail to Torregaveta or Fusaro, then bus. **Open** 7.30-11.30pm Mon, Wed-Fri; noon-4pm, 7.30-11.30pm Sat; noon-4pm Sun. **Average** €45. **Trattoria**
With tables on the pretty quayside at Baia and a terrace with views of Vesuvius, this little resturant is an excellent place for a reasonably priced fishy lunch. Order *paccheri* (large pasta tubes) with lobster or monkfish, or spaghetti with sea urchins (a local delicacy). There's grilled tuna steak and good *fritto misto* to follow. Wash it all down with a local Falanghina.

INFORMATION

Campi Flegrei Tourist Information Office

Largo Matteotti 1, Pozzuoli (081 526 1481, www. infocampiflegrei.it). **Open** *June-Oct* 9am-3pm Mon-Fri; 9am-7pm Sat, Sun. *Oct-May* 9am-3pm Mon-Fri. Times may vary; check in advance.

GETTING AROUND

The **Artecard** museum and transport ticket (*see p297*) covers the area's major sights. The Cumana train line (*see p291*) and some bus services link the area's major towns. However, public transport between the sites is not very efficient. Visiting the area by car is the best option.

GETTING THERE

By bus

Bus M1B from Piazzale Tecchio in Fuorigrotta passes the Solfatara and the church of San Gennaro, but you'll save time by taking the metro from Piazza Garibaldi or the Cumana railway from Montesanto to Pozzuoli, then taking buses or walking.

By car

Take the Tangenziale ring road westwards out of Naples (direction Pozzuoli) and veer off at the appropriate exit (for Astroni and Solfatara, take exit 11 at Agnano). All sites listed are within a half-hour drive of the centre, traffic permitting.

By train

The Cumana railway (800 211 388, www.eavsrl.it) runs three or four trains every hour from the transport hub of Montesanto in Naples to coastal sites in the Campi Flegrei, terminating at Torregaveta. There are bus connections to the smaller towns from several stops along the line (081 014 1012, www.eavsrl.it). For Baia, Miseno and Cuma, get off at either Torregaveta or Fusaro and catch the bus. For Pozzuoli (amphitheatre, Rione Terra and Solfatara), take the Cumana railway or metro line 2 to Pozzuoli-Solfatara; it's a 1km walk up to the volcano. For Astroni, the most inaccessible of the sites, take the Circumflegrea line to Pianura or the Cumana to Bagnoli then bus C14. It's a 20min walk from Pianura station.

EXPLORE

Abraxas

The Suburbs & Beyond

The cheap cement blocks of post-war urban expansion have pushed the city limits far into the countryside around Naples, and the bucolic charm of yesteryear has today been replaced by unappealing urban sprawl. A long way from the charms of the Centro Storico, this is a side of Naples that tourists rarely see. Nonetheless, there are still a few places worth visiting that have been salvaged from the aesthetic devastation wrought in the 1950s and '60s. The 16th-century monastery of Eremo Santissimo Salvatore perches on its hilltop, as it has done for centuries, and parks and picturesque cemeteries offer welcome respite from the city. The suburbs are also home to large-scale sports and entertainment facilities – namely the gigantic Stadio San Paolo, home ground of Napoli, and the Arena Flegrea. And, incongruously, a fantastic Michelin-starred restaurant.

Stadio San Paolo.

Don't Miss

1 **Parco Urbano dei Camaldoli** Escape the chaos of the city (p122).

2 **Cimitero Monumentale** Resting place of Enrico Caruso and Totò (p122).

3 **Stadio San Paolo** Catch the mighty Blues in Serie A action (p122).

4 **Parco del Poggio di Capodimonte** Green expanse with glorious views (p122).

5 **Sud** Sensational food in the suburbs (p123).

EXPLORE

NORTH-WEST

The opening of the Collinare railway in the 1990s – a considerable feat of engineering – improved access to the city centre from the north-western suburbs, encouraging more construction in what was once Naples' green belt. What's left of the countryside has been preserved in the appealing **Parco Urbano dei Camaldoli** and **Parco del Poggio di Capodimonte**.

FREE Eremo Santissimo Salvatore

Via dell'Eremo 87 (081 587 2519, www.brigidine. org). Bus C44 from Piazza Medaglie d'Oro. **Open** *Church* 10am-noon daily. *Grounds* May-Oct 10am-8.30pm daily. Nov-Apr 10am-5pm daily. *Monastery* by appt only. **Admission** free.

The chapel built here in AD 493 by St Gaudosius was replaced in 1585 by the current church and monastery. The monks' cells were little houses, each with their own garden, and the belvedere affords a high, hazy view over the Bay of Naples. Occupied by monks of the Camaldolese order until 1998 (by which time only three were left), the site was then taken over by the Sisters of St Bridget. A meticulous restoration of the buildings, kitchen gardens and walkways now allows the thriving religious community to cater for religious retreats, with prayer meetings and simple, serene accommodation. Visitors are very welcome, but groups are advised to call before visiting.

FREE Parco del Poggio di Capodimonte

Viale del Poggio 60, Colli Aminei (081 795 3612, 081 795 2442). Metro Colli Aminei or Dante, or bus C66, R4. **Open** *Mar, Oct* 7am-6pm daily. *Apr-June* 7am-7.30pm daily. *July, Aug* 7am-8.30pm daily. *Sept* 7am-7pm daily. *Nov-Feb* 7am-4.30pm daily. **Admission** free.

This unusual park clings to an exposed hillside above the city ring road, offering little protection against sun or heavy rain. There's a dramatic view over the palace at Capodimonte and out across the bay. There are play facilities, large expanses of grass, a lake and lots of seating.

FREE Parco Urbano dei Camaldoli

Via Sant'Ignazio da Loyola (081 770 4930). Bus C44 from Piazza Medaglie d'Oro. **Open** 7am-1hr before sunset daily. **Admission** free.

This park was founded in 1995 – in part to halt the uncontrolled urban development on the upper reaches of the Vomero hill. A number of paths on both sides of Via Rai wander across chestnut-wooded, orchid-strewn slopes, with magnificent views.

NORTH-EAST

When they die, most Naples residents will be laid to rest in a vast cemetery region north-east of the centre, towards Capodichino airport. On Via Santa Maria del Pianto, the **Cimitero Monumentale** (open 7am-5pm daily) houses more imposing, older graves (famous residents include tenor Enrico Caruso and comedian and actor Totò); the newer **Cimitero Nuovo** (Via Santa Maria del Pianto, 081 795 7533, open 8am-1pm daily) is nearby. On busy days, the area outside the graveyards hosts an animated cut-flower market, run under the watchful eye of the Polizia Mortuaria; flower traders have been known to gather flowers from graves and sell them the next day.

A quieter resting place can be found closer to the centre of town, by Piazza Santa Maria della Fede. Despite its name, the **Parco ex Cimitero degli Inglesi** (Park of the former British Cemetery; open 9am-5pm Mon-Fri; 9am-1pm Sat, Sun) was an international and inter-denominational affair. It was closed in 1898, when the remains of the deceased were repatriated or dumped in a common burial ground, and became a park. The larger tombs are still there, though, and this is a corner of a foreign field that will be forever England.

FUORIGROTTA

So called because of its position outside (*fuori*) the two tunnels (*grotte*) into the Mergellina area, the gritty, eastern suburb of Fuorigrotta was developed under the Fascist government during the 1920s and '30s. The wide, regular streets of this downmarket residential district are rather soulless – but there are a few points of note.

Piazzale Tecchio lies at the heart of the district, which is best reached by taking the metro to Campi Flegrei or the Cumana railway to Mostra. The piazza was given a facelift for the 1990 World Cup, and the gigantic **Stadio San Paolo** dominates the scene. On match days, it's a dazzling swirl of sky-blue shirts and scarves.

Beyond, the **Mostra d'Oltremare** was built in 1939-40 to show off 'achievements' in Italy's African colonies. Heavily bombed during World War II, it was rebuilt as a trade exhibition space in 1952. Concerts and festivals are held at the restored 5,000-seater **Arena Flegrea** (52 Piazzale Vincenzo Tecchio 49-50).

SENSATIONAL SUD

Gastronomic brilliance in the suburbs.

Quarto Flegrea, named after its location four Roman miles from Pozzuoli, is a sprawling dormitory town. Its messy, down-at-heel streets hold nothing for the visitor and it's the last place on earth you'd expect to find a Michelin-starred restaurant. And yet, here is Marianna Vitale's **Sud** (Via Santi Pietro e Paolo 8, 081 020 2708, www.sudristorante. it), a beacon of understated contemporary style and gastronomic excellence that has become something of a pilgrimage site for in-the-know foodies from Naples and beyond.

Although she has had stints in kitchens in France and Spain and a year at Michelin-starred Palazzo Petrucci (*see p62*), Vitale is largely self-taught and opened Sud with sommelier Pino Esposito in 2009. The challenging location was chosen for its affordability, says Vitale: 'I knew that it was going to be difficult, but I didn't know for how long'. Not long at all as it turned out; she won a Michelin star in 2012, at the tender age of 32.

Female chefs rarely reach the top of their game in southern Italy. While there are plenty of Mamma figures stirring the ragù in homely *trattorie*, few go beyond this. In Campania, which is home to more Michelin-starred restaurants than most other regions, only one other woman has managed to gain such a gastronomic accolade. But Vitale is dismissive of the challenges she has encountered on her way to the top: 'It's the same for a woman as for a man, a question of long hours and hard grind for us all.'

In spite of its star, Sud is anything but stuffy. The low-key decor allows the glorious food to take centre stage, the busy kitchen is on display, shelves are stocked with interesting bottles, food and wine books lie open on side tables, and the service is professional yet affable.

Vitale's menus are based on affordable, seasonal ingredients and regional traditions – 'the product is the protagonist and it is always recognisable'. Vitale 'contaminates' the classic dishes that her grandmother taught her with modern techniques and the odd ethnic hit, but never strays too far from her roots. An autumn dinner might include an intense, cold soup of red peppers served with marinated anchovies that sing of the sea and the sun; a dreamily light *cheesecake di baccalà* (a delicate soufflé of ricotta rolled in wild fennel seed and topped with salt cod); and inky black *linguine con quinto quarto di calamaro*, using the squidgy inner bits of the squid that are normally discarded. The set menus, from €40 for four courses to €60 for seven courses, are extraordinarily good-value and mark-ups on the wines are admirably low. Tell Pino Esposito that you want to drink local and he will guide you to some of the best wines being produced in the area today.

Vitale is looking for premises closer to the centre of Naples, but for now it's a trek to get out to Sud. If you don't have your own wheels, the only way back to town after dinner is a taxi. But the effort involved makes the end reward all the more satisfying.

EXPLORE

Arts & Entertainment

Children

Like all Italians, the Neapolitans adore children and visiting *bambini* are given a warm welcome by locals, whose smiles and friendly overtures soon break down any language barrier issues. In spite of the relentless traffic and noise, Naples is an extremely child-friendly place. While an overload of church frescoes and more high-minded museums may not appeal, inner-city attractions such as three bona fide castles and the hidden underground secrets of Napoli Sotterranea are likely to prove big hits. Much of Greater Naples provides the perfect playground for children: parks and green spaces abound, clean sea and good beaches are within relatively easy reach, and Pompeii and the Campi Flegrei make for truly adventurous family outings. Finally, small fry will also appreciate two of Naples' finest assets – gorgeous *gelaterie* and a plethora of pizza joints.

SIGHTSEEING

If you've always thought that museums and children don't mix, Naples is a city that can change your perception. The **Città della Scienza** (*see p127*) in Bagnoli should be first on the agenda. Aimed specifically at children, it takes a hands-on approach to science, with all sorts of wacky experiments for kids to try.

For a more traditional take on science, the four university museums housed in the **Centro Musei Scienze Naturali** (*see p48*) are packed with rocks, fossils and stuffed animals. To peep at turtles, seahorses, octopuses and other marine life from the Bay of Naples, visit the **Stazione Zoologica** (*see p102*), a grand old 19th-century aquarium in Chiaia.

Children also enjoy exploring Naples' castles and dreaming of being sword-wielding defenders at the **Castel dell'Ovo** (*see p44*) or **Castel Sant'Elmo** (*see p94*). Those of a more macabre bent will relish dark tales of the dungeons at the **Castel Nuovo** (*see p40*). For high jinks without the history, there are trampolines, carousels and pirate boats at **Liberty City Fun** (*see p127*), located on the outskirts of town.

A tour of Naples' vast network of underground cisterns and chambers at **Napoli Sotterranea** (*see p128*) or the **Galleria Borbonica** (*see p127*) will appeal to any child or teenager with a vivid imagination. Further afield, Portici is home to the **Museo Ferroviario di Pietrarsa** (*see p193*) – an enormous railway museum with plenty of gleaming locomotives to admire.

The volcanic activity of the area is guaranteed to thrill children. In Pozzuoli, you can walk on the crater of a dormant volcano, the **Solfatara** (*see p115*). Boiling sulphurous gases rise continuously from underfoot, as do occasional eruptions of mud. Another exciting place to visit is **Lago di Averno** (*see p116*), also located in the Campi Flegrei. The volcanic lake gets its name from a dark abyss that the ancient Greeks believed to be the entrance to the Underworld.

IN THE KNOW KAYAKING FOR KIDS

An unusual way to visit Naples' beautiful shoreline is by canoe, and **Kayak Napoli** (Lido Rocce Verdi, Via Posillipo 68, 331 987 4271, 338 876 1157) organises excursions for families.

Close by are the remains of the Temple of Apollo and the cave of the Cumaean Sibyl (*see p116*). It was here, according to myth, that the renowned prophetess received messages from the gods. Finally, **Vesuvius** (*see p203*) is a must-see sight, as is the town that it overwhelmed during its AD 79 eruption – the archaeological site of **Pompeii** (*see p198*).

For rainy days, there are several bookshops around town that put on regular activities for kids, and although these are mostly in Italian, they can be fun.

Even the public transport can be fun in Naples: the city's metro stations, effectively open art and architecture museums, are a voyage of discovery for all ages, and the trundling *funicolari* make an original way to get up to Vomero for an ice-cream and a walk in the park.

Museums & attractions

★ Città della Scienza
Via Coroglio 104, Posillipo (081 735 2111, www. cittadellascienza.it). Metro Bagnoli, then bus C1, R1 to Città della Scienza. **Open** 9am-3pm Tue-Sat; 10am-5pm Sun. **Admission** €8; €5.50 under-18s; free under-4s. *Planetarium* €1.50.
This wonderful science museum in a converted 18th-century factory was all but destroyed by fire in March 2013: much of the exhibition space (including the Planetarium) was annihilated. However, the administration has managed to keep at least part of the museum open since, and a new Planetarium

and Museum of the Human Body should be up and running by summer 2016. In the meantime, there are temporary interactive exhibitions, games and scientific curiosities. Suitable for over-twos, it's still a brilliantly hands-on experience.

★ Galleria Borbonica
Vico del Grottone 4 or Parking Via Domenico Morelli, Chiaia (081 764 5808, www.galleria borbonica.com). **Guided tours** 10am, noon, 3.30pm, 5.30pm Fri-Sun. **Prices** vary. **Map** p311 J13.
You can take various tours of this Bourbon-era tunnel and aqueduct complex, which was used as a bomb shelter during World War II – kids will love the cars and motorbikes left over from that period. The Adventure Tour (over-10s) includes a raft ride through a flooded section of tunnel. *Photo p128.*

Liberty City Fun
Via Monteoliveto 48, Volla (081 774 0186, www. libertycityfun.com). Circumvesuviana train to Volla. **Open** 3-10.30pm Tue-Fri; 9am-2pm, 4pm-midnight Sat, Sun. **Admission** free. *Activities* prices vary. **No credit cards**.
This giant complex has trampolines, carousels, pirate boats and rides, a quad track, pizzeria and pool; an area for grown-ups has bowling lanes, billiards and a restaurant. There's live music every Thursday night, and jugglers and magicians at the weekends.

MADRe
For listings, *see p87*.

Museo Ferroviario di Pietrarsa.

ARTS & ENTERTAINMENT

Galleria Borbonica. See *p127*.

Look out for the excellent Sunday family series at Naples' contemporary art museum. Sessions run at various times during the year.

★ Napoli Sotterranea

For listings, *see p68*.

Beneath the city lies Napoli Sotterranea – a thrilling network of tunnels and chambers, built by the ancient Greeks, which can be explored on special tours. The channels and cisterns were integrated into Naples' water supply system and remained in use until the cholera epidemic of 1884; during World War II, some of the tunnels were converted into air-raid shelters.

OUTDOORS

Beaches

When it gets too hot to enjoy the city, the beach is the obvious alternative. Naples' authorities have been cleaning up the sea near the city, so you don't need to go far. To the west, **Posillipo** (*see p110*) has a few rocky beaches but the walk back into town is quite tough. Offshore, just beyond Marechiaro, lies the tiny island of **Gaiola** and its protected marine park (www.gaiola.org). The park authorities run all sorts of activities and courses for kids, including glass-bottomed boat trips and snorkelling expeditions. On the road to Cuma, **Torre Gavetta** has some decent sandy beaches, but its proximity to the (albeit processed) main Naples sewage outlet may be off-putting. Another option on the mainland is the **Campi Flegrei** area (*see p112*), with beaches around Capo di Miseno: Milliscola has full facilities and man-made coves.

For the very best beaches, though, you need to put some distance between you and the city. Some of the cleanest water can be found around the islands of **Ischia** (*see p176*), **Procida** (*see p188*) and **Capri** (*see p156*), and the boat rides out to them are great fun for kids. Alternatively, try the beaches around **Sorrento** (*see p206*) or along the **Amalfi Coast** (*see p220*).

A more adventurous alternative to the beach is **Magic World** (Uscita Tangenziale Licola, Via San Nullo, Localita' Masseria Vecchia, Licola, 081 854 6792, www.magicworld.it, closed Oct-May), a vast water park with slides galore.

Parks

The city's green spaces offer a compendium of lovely views, play areas, colourful gardens and extravagant villas. The most centrally located is the beautiful **Villa Comunale** (*see p104*), which runs along the bay of Chiaia for almost a mile and was built to resemble the Jardin des Tuileries in Paris. The park is also home to the **Stazione Zoologica** (*see p102*), which is Europe's oldest aquarium. At the weekends and during the holidays, there are Falabella horses to ride and family tandem bikes for scooting up and down the pavement parallel to the park and seafront. The nearby Lungomare that runs east along the shoreline is now pedestrianised and is an excellent spot for bike rides and in-line skating.

The calm, green **Parco della Floridiana** (*see p95*) in Vomero is also an ideal family hangout, as is the **Bosco di Capodimonte** (*see p90*). Set to the north of the Centro Storico, the park is the largest in Naples and is home to the royal palace (now the art-filled **Museo di Capodimonte**, *see p90*) of Carlos III de Bourbon. Closer to the centre, don't overlook the lush **Orto Botanico** (*see p87*) – though be sure to call ahead and reserve. At weekends there are often children's theatre shows in the gardens (www.iteatrini.it). The best option for sporty kids is the **Parco Vergiliano** (*see p109*), with an outdoor gym and running track.

PUPPET MASTER

Meet Pulcinella – a not-so-distant cousin of Mr Punch.

Bruno Leone is a *guarattellaro*, the puppet-master who brings the age-old character of Pulcinella to life through performances in theatres and on the streets. Taught by Nunzio Zampella, the last of the great Neapolitan puppeteers, Leone breathes new life into this centuries-old tradition.

Time Out (TO): You learned from the last great interpreter of Pulcinella. How has the art of the *guarattellaro* evolved since then?
Bruno Leone (BL): From Nunzio Zampella, I learned the traditional repertoire of Pulcinella, which to me is a blueprint that can be used to recount any story, transcending space and time. Pulcinella isn't only a character. He's the archetype of humanity, the symbol of people's desire to live. His girlfriend represents life itself, and there are three evil characters that try to divide them: the dog, the Guappo and the policeman – representing the fear of nature, the fear of others and the fear of authority. With these characters it's possible to recreate any tale,

as well as comment on modern-day issues, from 9/11 to the problem of trash in Naples.

TO: Is there a risk that the stories may be too disturbing for a child?
BL: It's interesting that you mention that, because it's true that a few people are worried about Pulcinella. But Pulcinella teaches us that confronting our fears is the only way to defeat them.

TO: Do you often perform outside Italy?
BL: Yes indeed! Travelling with Pulcinella, I was astonished to discover that he had relatives wherever I went. Puppeteers as far away as Brazil, Africa and even a village in China have a puppet that looks like Pulcinella, acts like Pulcinella and even speaks like him, thanks to the *pivetta* – a metal instrument that creates his characteristic clucking sound. The character is a valuable friend to all the children in the world.

For details of shows, visit www.guarattelle.it or contact Bruno Leone on 340 601 5658.

ARTS & ENTERTAINMENT

Film

ARTS & ENTERTAINMENT

Naples holds a vital place in the history of cinema. During the early 20th century, along with Turin, it was the Italian capital of the seventh art; Rome only caught up later. Italy's pioneering female director, Elvira Notari (1875-1946), lived and worked in the city, and the first purpose-built projection hall was constructed here. In fact, the Sala Iride still exists – sadly, though, it now screens only porn. More recently, directors have focused on the city's criminal underworld in films such as *Gomorra* and *Fortapàsc*. These tough semi-documentaries are seen by many as long overdue coming-of-age works, not only for Naples but for Italy as a whole.

NAPLES ON SCREEN

Neapolitan actors, their craft rooted in the deep theatrical traditions of the city, have made monumental contributions to cinema. Every Italian recognises the inimitable Totó (1898-1967), who churned out around five films per year; while Sophia Loren, who grew up in Pozzuoli, became a universal symbol of Mediterranean beauty and picked up two Oscars.

The cinematic careers of actor-playwright Eduardo de Filippo (1900-1984) and his brother Peppino (1903-1980) also reached brilliant heights, often in collaboration with Totó in some of his most exhilarating turns.

Directors here have always tried to capture the essence of this unique, elusive city and its highly complex social fabric. Francesco Rosi (1922-2015) made his name tackling gritty, controversial issues, from political corruption to bullfighting; two of his most famous films, *La Sfida* and *Le Mani Sulla Città* (see p133), were shot in Naples.

The great Vittorio de Sica (1901-1974) was born in Lazio, but grew up in Naples and shot two films in the city – *Ieri, Oggi, Domani* and *L'Oro di Napoli* with Sophia Loren. In 1960, he also acted alongside Loren and Clark Gable in the romantic comedy *It Started in Naples*.

The 1980s, which was overshadowed by a climate of disenchantment and bitterness, belonged to the beloved actor-director Massimo Troisi (1953-1994). His work blended together tough irony and sweetly disarming comedy in films such as *Ricomincio da Tre* (1981) and *Non ci resta che piangere* (1984), which dealt with the fate of southerners in a north-centred economy. His final – and most famous – film was the heartwarming, Oscar-nominated *Il Postino*.

In the 1990s, a new scene arose around the work of young, independent filmmakers such as Antonio Capuano, Mario Martone and Pappi Corsicato. Their work, which depicted a Naples that was hard and pitiless, was squarely aimed at the international mainstream. They also collaborated on a group film, *I Vesuviani*.

CURRENT TRENDS

For Neapolitan cinema, 2008 proved to be a pivotal year. Three significant films were released – *Il Divo* by Paolo Sorrentino; *Gomorra* by Matteo Garrone; and Milanese director Marco Risi's *Fortapàsc*. *Il Divo* won the Prix du Jury and *Gomorra* won the Grand Prix at Cannes. All three films tackle powerful themes pertaining to the social and political fabric of the city, played out against the backdrop of some of its toughest suburbs, and have had a remarkable impact on public opinion.

Neapolitan cinema gained truly international recognition in 2014 when Sorrentino's Rome-based tragi-comedy *La Grande Bellezza*, starring Tony Servillo in arguably his best film to date, won the Oscar for Best Foreign Film, plus a Golden Globe, a BAFTA and a host of other international awards.

CINEMAS

The average price of cinema admission is €8, with discounts offered for students and seniors at certain times of the week – usually on Wednesdays. Midweek nights may be cheaper than weekends.

Astra

Via Mezzocannone 109, Port & University (www.astra.unina.it). Bus CS, R2. **No credit cards. Map** p312 M9.

Located in the heart of the university quarter, this historic arthouse venue has a very irregular programme. It's part of the University of Naples and mornings are devoted to lectures. Its façade comprises part of the ancient Greco-Roman wall.

Filangeri

Via Filangieri 43/47, Chiaia (081 251 2408). Metro Piazza Amedeo. **No credit cards. Map** p311 H13.

The Filangeri's three screening rooms bear the names of the greats of Italian cinema: Rossellini, Magnani and Mastroianni. The programme is devoted to independent – and mainly European – film.

Med Maxicinema

Viale Giochi del Mediterraneo, Agnano (081 242 0111). Cumana rail to Agnano, or bus 152. **No credit cards.**

This is the largest multiplex in the Naples area with 11 screens, from blockbusters to kids' flicks.

Modernissimo

Via Cisterna dell'Olio 59, Centro Storico (081 580 0254, www.modernissimo.it). Metro Dante, or bus 24, R1, R4. Closed 2wks Aug. **No credit cards. Map** p312 K9.

This former theatre was remodelled as a multiplex in 1994, with four screening rooms and a fifth room for videos. The standard fare is blockbusters, but some independents make it on to the bill. Latest release films are shown in their original language (mostly English) on Thursdays.

FESTIVALS

Artecinema

081 414306, www.artecinema.org.

This excellent four-day festival, held in mid October, showcases films and documentaries about modern art. Artists featured in the 20th season in 2015 included Bill Viola, Tracy Emin, Jeff Koons and Man Ray. The opening night is held at the Teatro San Carlo (*see p149*) and successive screenings are staged at the Teatro Augusteo (Piazzetta Duca d'Aosta 263, Via Toledo & Sanità).

ARTS & ENTERTAINMENT

Artecinema.

IN THE KNOW A PLACE IN THE SUN

Launched in 1996, *Un Posto al Sole* (A Place in the Sun) is Italy's longest-running soap opera. By October 2015, it had clocked up 4,351 episodes. Set in Naples, it's based on a *Neighbours*-style formula and focuses on the inhabitants of fictional Palazzo Palladini in Posillipo. But unlike the rose-tinted spectacles of its Australian cousin, *Un Posto al Sole* chronicles real life, weaving crime and social problems into its storylines. The series has become so popular that the name Palazzo Palladini is written next to its real-life equivalent, Villa Volpicelli in Via Ferdinando Russo, on Google Maps. The show is broadcast weekdays at 8.35pm on RAI 3.

Independent Film Show
Museo Nitsch, Vico Lungo Pontecorvo 29D (081 564 1655, www.em-arts.org). Metro Dante or Montesanto, or bus 139, 182, 201, C63, R4.
Held in late June at the belvedere of the Museo Nitsch, this international festival is dedicated to independent experimental cinema.

Napoli Film Festival
Metropolitan, Via Chiaia 149 (www.napolifilm festival.com). **Map** p311 H13.

This annual week-long festival takes place in late September or early October, with screenings at the Institut Français, the Instituto Cervantes, PAN and the Metropolitan. Originally called Modfest, the event has gradually evolved, building up a strong rapport with Hollywood. Stars such as Harvey Keitel, Sigourney Weaver, Cate Blanchett and Miloš Forman have attended and the festival programme is duplicated in New York.

Giffoni Film Festival
Various locations, Giffoni Valle Piana (089 802 3001, www.giffonifilmfestival.it).
The second most important film festival in Italy after Venice was founded in 1971 by Claudio Gubitosi, who is still the director. The festival takes place in July and August in Giffoni Valle Piana, a tiny town near Salerno with streets named after directors and actors. What makes the festival unique is that it concerns itself with children's cinema; even the jury is composed of kids. The festival has a US branch in Los Angeles, run by actor Jon Voight, and an Australian counterpart. François Truffaut declared it 'the most necessary of all festivals'. Numerous directors and actors have participated over the years, including Robert de Niro, Oliver Stone and Meg Ryan.

Venezia a Napoli
Various venues (www.veneziaanapoli.it).
Held in late October, this festival screens films previously shown at the Venice Film Festival at cinemas across the city, including the Filangeri and the Modernissimo (for both, *see p131*).

Giffoni Film Festival.

ESSENTIAL NAPLES FILMS

Passion, grit, complexity – and that's just the location.

Il Postino.

L'ORO DI NAPOLI
VITTORIO DE SICA (1954)
Sophia Loren plays a curvaceous *pizzaiola* cheating on her husband in Vittorio de Sica's enjoyable collection of cinematic short stories. De Sica himself plays a nobleman so hooked on gambling that he's reduced to playing cards with the porter's son. Edoardo de Filippo is 'Professore' Ersilio Micci and Totò is Don Saverio Petrillo, a thug. A chance to see all the Neapolitan greats in one sitting.

LE MANI SULLA CITTÀ
FRANCESCO ROSI (1963)
The late Rosi's tough film follows the irresistible rise of property speculator Nottola – played by Rod Steiger, his voiced dubbed into Italian – as he channels the public building programme on to his own land, shrugs off the collapse of a slum tenement and cold-bloodedly shifts the balance of power in the council to his own advantage. A totally convincing analysis of civic corruption.

L'AMORE MOLESTO
MARIO MARTONE (1995)
Adapted from the eponymous early novel of literary flavour-of-the-year Elena Ferrante, this hard-hitting thriller sees Anna Bonaiuto returning home to investigate the suspicious death of her 70-year-old mother. Martone uses a noir mystery as an intriguing framework to explore feminist, Freudian and social concerns.

GOMORRA
MATTEO GARRONE (2008)
Based on the bestseller by Roberto Saviano, this film is set in the squalid suburbs of Naples. Its tone is of brutal realism, as actors mingle with non-professionals taken from the street, some of whom are genuine denizens of Naples' nightmarish underworld. This is a drama about how ordinary lives and ambitions are impinged upon in a society where the parameters of business, justice and everyday life are defined and warped by the influence of organised crime.

PASSIONE
JOHN TURTURRO (2014)
John Turturro's rapturous love letter to the music and people of Naples, past and present, is a wildly colourful, ecstatic romp around that chaotic, passionate, complex city. Turturro describes the film as 'a musical adventure that comes directly out of the people and the volcanic land they inhabit'. It's great stuff – and features some inspiring location work.

IL POSTINO
MICHAEL RADFORD (1994)
On a quiet little island off the Italian coast, a simple young postman's world is turned on its head when he starts delivering mail to exiled Chilean poet Pablo Neruda. Neapolitan actor Massimo Troisi (who died tragically young during filming) was a modern successor to the city's Pulcinella, with a strong line of melancholy underlying his one-liners. It's filmed on Salina, but the film is Neapolitan in spirit.

Gay & Lesbian

It may not have many LGBT-specific venues, but extrovert, anarchic Naples is a relaxed and open destination for gay travellers. There's a long history regarding transvestites and transsexuals in the city; the former have been an integral part of traditional Neapolitan theatre culture since the 17th century. Today, the gay and lesbian scene is small but active and growing all the time. Locals are generally tolerant, adopting a live-and-let-live attitude – especially in the areas of Piazza Bellini and Chiaia – but it still isn't a good idea to be too physical (although strolling arm-in-arm is perfectly acceptable). Naples' Gay Pride (now known as the Mediterranean Pride of Naples) is held in mid July, with the parade setting off from Piazza Dante. The route takes in Piazza Carità, Via Toledo, Piazza Trieste e Trento and Via Partenope, before finishing up in front of the Castel dell'Ovo with a riotously colourful festival of music and dance.

INFORMATION

Gay associations

Arcigay-Circolo Antinoo

Vico San Geronimo 17, Centro Storico (081 552 8815, www.arcigaynapoli.org). Metro Dante, or bus E1. **Open** 9am-12.30pm Tue, Thur; 5.30-8.30pm Fri, Sun. Closed Aug. **Map** p312 M9.
Based in Bologna, the highly regarded Arcigay organisation (www.gay.it) is Italy's most serious gay lobbying group. Its Naples offshoot organises films and events such as poetry readings, often in collaboration with other cultural associations in the city. The premises house a small bar (*see p135*) and can also provide up-to-the-minute information on bars, clubs and events in town.

Arcilesbica-Circolo Le Maree

Vico San Geronimo 17 (081 552 8815, www.arcilesbica.it/napoli). Metro Dante, or bus E1. **Open** 5-9pm Sat. Closed Aug. **Map** p312 K7.
This organisation is also based at Arcigay (*see above*) and offers information on lesbian events, bars and clubs in Naples and the surrounding area.

WHERE TO STAY

Favourite gay-friendly hotels include the **UNA Hotel** (*see p283*), **Chiaia Hotel de Charme** (*see p279*) and **Decumani Hotel de Charme** (*see p282*), **Romeo Hotel** (*see p277*) and **Hotel Piazza Bellini** (*see p282*). Among options not already listed in this guide, you could try the faux-Baroque flourishes of the friendly **Hotel des Artistes** (Via del Duomo 61, 081 446155, www.hoteldesartistesnaples.it) or the roof terrace and hot tub at **Sweet Sleep B&B** (Via Alessandro Poerio 14, 081 260210, www.sweetsleepbeb.it).

CAFES & BARS

Nearly all of the cafés, bars and restaurants in and around Piazza Bellini are LGBT-friendly (they'd be crazy not to be given the nightly gay influx to the area), as are the bars in the area known as the Baretti di San Pasquale in Chiaia.

Cambio Vita

Via Poerio 100A, Chiaia (081 1957 0395, www.cambiovitastore.it). Bus 140, 151.

Open 8.30am-8pm Mon-Thur, Sat; 8.30am-11pm Fri. Map p311 G13.

This stylish, very gay-friendly café serves a menu of healthy drinks and snacks, and also stocks health foods and organic produce.

★ Fiorillo

Via Santa Maria di Costantinopoli 99, Centro Storico (081 459905). Metro Dante, or bus 201, R4. Open 6am-2am daily. No credit cards. Map p312 L8.

This trendy meeting place faces gay-friendly Piazza Bellini. The place starts to fill up after dinner, when the prime pavement tables soon get snapped up.

Free-id

Vico San Geronimo 19, Centro Storico (081 552 8815, www.arcigaynapoli.org). Metro Dante, or bus E1. Map p312 M9.

The bar at the Arcigay headquarters (*see p134*) serves *aperitivi* on Fridays and Sundays at 6pm (Arcigay membership required).

Ghetto Crime Bar

Via Ferrigni 21, Chiaia (339 107 7754). Metro Amedeo, or bus 128, C24, E6. Open 7pm-3am Wed-Sun. Map p311 G13.

This small, friendly LGBT bar attracts a mixed young crowd and is a great *aperitivo* spot.

Intramoenia Caffè Letterario

For listings, see p71.

A straight meeting place for Naples' intellectuals by day, the Intramoenia – and Piazza Bellini in general – become a catwalk on summer evenings for self-confident gays to compare their tans and show off their designer togs.

Spritz

Via Bisignano 45, Chiaia (335 444547). Metro Amedeo, or bus 128, C24, E6. Open 6.30pm-2am Mon-Thur, Sun; 6.30pm-3am Fri, Sat. Map p311 H13.

Spritz is a particularly gay-friendly cocktail bar.

CLUBS

There are not many exclusively gay or lesbian establishments in the city; instead, most are straight venues that function as gay meeting places or run gay nights one evening a week. There's usually no cover charge, but you're expected to have at least one drink. Your *consumazione* is marked on a slip of paper that you receive at the entrance, and you pay on leaving. Gay men and lesbians mix in many of the same places.

Basement

Via Atri 36/b, Centro Storico (081 1925 2174, www.thebasement.it). Metro Dante, or bus E1, E2.

Open 10pm-3am Mon, Thur; 10pm-6am Fri, Sat; 3pm-3am Sun. Admission €10. Membership required. Map p312 M8.

This underground cruising and fetish venue runs themed nights for a 30s-50s crowd; see the website for full details of the various nights.

Depot

Via della Veterinaria 72, Sanità (081 780 9578, www.depotnapoli.com). Metro Cavour or Museo, or bus 12, 202, C47. Open 10pm-3am Tue-Thur; 10pm-6am Fri, Sat; 6pm-3am Sun. Admission €10 (€7 under-25s Tue-Thur). No credit cards. ID required for membership card to enter.

This is the kind of gay club you'd expect to find in any major European city, with a darkroom, labyrinth, cubicles, sling, leather bar, glory holes, naked parties with masks and more. There's plenty of information on the website.

Macho Lato

Via Abate Minichini, 62, Corso Malta (081 780 3062, 320 199 4834, www.macholato.it). Bus 184, 245, C68. Open 11pm-5am Sat; 10pm-3am Sun. Admission €15 (Sat); €10 (Sun). No credit cards. ArciGay UNO card required.

Weekend cruising bar for muscle-bound, leather-loving bears and the men who appreciate them. Macho Lato (formerly 'Kapsula') also organises regular events and welcomes the whole LGBT community.

Intramoenia Caffè Letterario.

ARTS & ENTERTAINMENT

IN THE KNOW BASKING ON THE BEACH

There are several gay-friendly beaches within easy reach of Naples. In the Campi Flegrei area (see p112), the free spiaggia del Fusaro near Cuma is right by the Lido Fusaro stop on the Circumflegrea train line. Or you could get off at the Marina di Licola stop and head for either Lido Capri (Viale Sibilla 20, 392 244 3060), right by the train station, or Lido Vittoria (Viale Sibilla 24/26, 081 8043910,www.lidovittoria.it) to the north. Super-chic beach club Nabilah (Via Spiaggia Romana 15, Bacoli) is another popular haunt. Although the water quality leaves something to be desired, the huge rocks on the shoreline opposite the Villa Comunale (the Mergellina end) are a popular spot on warm spring and summer days.

One-off events

Details of parties and one-off events (usually held Friday to Sunday) are communicated via *passa parola* (word of mouth) and gay websites, but **Criminal Candy** (*see below*) organises a full calender of events, details of which are posted on its website.

Criminal Candy
338 107 7754/338 751 8195, www.criminal candy.com.
'You can like the life you're livin' or you can live the life you like': so runs the mantra of Criminal Candy, which organises a variety of house and pop dance parties, as well as other events (most take place at weekends) for the gay and lesbian community in Naples. Locations vary.

CRUISING

Centro Direzionale
Map off p313 R6.
After midnight and only by car.
Very dangerous.

Ippodromo di Agnano
After midnight and only by car. Fairly safe.

Via Brin
Map off p313 R9.
After midnight and only by car. Dangerous.

Villa Comunale
Riviera di Chiaia.
During the day, especially in spring and summer. Safe.

SAUNAS

Blu Angels Sauna
Via Taddeo da Sessa, Centro Direzionale (081 562 5298, www.saunabluangels.com). Bus 191, 469, C56. **Open** 1-10pm daily. **Admission** €13 (membership required for entry). **No credit cards.**
The friendly Blu Angels was the first gay sauna in southern Italy and features a Finnish sauna, Turkish bath, hot tub, labyrinth and darkroom, plus a shower and massage service.

SHOPS & SERVICES

Colonnese
Via San Pietro a Maiella 33, Centro Storico (081 459858, www.colonnese.it). Metro Dante or Museo. **Open** 9am-1.30pm, 4-7.30pm Mon-Sat. Closed 2wks Aug. **Map** p312 L8.
This wood-panelled bookshop is full of treasures. There are antiquarian books, modern editions (new and used), prints, postcards, books on Naples and Campania, and gay and erotic literature – along with tomes on witchcraft, featuring potions for impotence, love and jealousy.

Eva Luna
Piazza Bellini 72, Centro Storico (081 033 2513, www.evalunanapoli.it). Metro Dante, or bus 182, 201,R4. **Open** 10.30am-1.30pm, 5-9pm Mon-Sat. Closed Aug. **Map** p312 L8.
This appealing little bookshop and café on pretty Piazza Bellini carries all manner of women's literature, along with an extensive selection of prints and postcards. The shop also hosts regular talks, music and poetry events; check the website to find out what's coming up.

Libreria Feltrinelli
Piazza dei Martiri, Via Santa Caterina a Chiaia 23, Chiaia (081 240 5411, www.lafeltrinelli.it). Metro Amedeo, or bus C25. **Open** 10am-9pm Mon-Fri; 10am-10pm Sat; 10am-2pm, 4-10pm Sun. **Map** p311 H13.
This cool bookshop, music store and café stocks a limited selection of gay and lesbian publications in English. It's also a choice site for discreetly eyeing up the talent.

CINEMAS

No, these aren't arthouse cinemas with erudite gay programming. Venues such as **Agorà** (Via Guantai Nuovi 6, Royal Naples, 081 552 4893) and **Casanova** (Corso Garibaldi 330, Port & University, 081 200441) show heterosexual porn flicks, but also attract gay men. Few tend to see much of the film, though. Be careful in the vicinity of the railway station by the Casanova as it can be quite unsavoury.

Nightlife

The nightlife scene in Naples varies considerably, depending on where you choose to pass your *serata*. From the student-heavy bars and squares of the Centro Storico to the trendy *baretti* of well-heeled Chiaia, there's something to suit everyone's style. Naples' night owls come out to play relatively late, with places only starting to fill up around midnight. Much of the after-dark action takes place in the city's squares and alleys, with large groups of youths gathering in the Centro Storico's Piazza San Domenico Maggiore and surrounding streets, Piazza Bellini and Piazza del Gesù to enjoy a beer and a cigarette: although Italy's ban on smoking in public areas took effect in 2005, it's still widely flouted.

NIGHTLIFE, NAPLES-STYLE

Don't be too surprised when what feels like the entire population of Naples takes to its cars in the suburbs of **Chiaia** (*see pp102-108*) and **Mergellina** (*see p110*) for a few hours of horn-blowing, scooter-dodging (an essential skill in Naples) and furious gesticulating, especially during the summer months. This transit chaos is usually followed by a half-hour *gelato* break, drink or *passeggiata* (stroll), then it's back into the cars. The trendier clubs are to be found here (Chiaia in cooler weather, Mergellina in the summer), with the narrow streets transformed into crowded catwalks where the youth of Naples flirt and strut.

Most of the city's discos and clubs charge an entrance fee, which may or may not include one drink. In some places you'll be given a card that's stamped for every drink you purchase, and requires you to buy at least one drink before leaving the venue. Hold on tight to this card; you'll be charged a fee if you lose it.

Some bars also have small dancefloors where you're welcome to shake your stuff should the mood take you. Sometimes, a membership card (*tessera*) is required for admission; there may be a small fee for the card, but entry is generally free on subsequent visits.

These days, the techno and trance scene has transferred to the aircraft hangar-style **Golden Gate** in Pozzuoli (Via Campana 233, 333 711 3112,

www.goldengatedisco.it). The crowd is usually very young and be warned: you'll never get there and back without a car.

Unless otherwise stated, admission to the venues listed in this chapter is free.

SOUNDS OF THE CITY

It's surprisingly difficult to find a good live music venue in Naples, although lots of bars in the Centro Storico and Vomero squeeze a band or singer into a corner a couple of nights a week. In the summer months, though, the scene comes alive, with *piazze* and parks playing host to local and international acts. Events tend to take place outside the city confines, requiring a taxi ride; keep an eye on posters in the Centro Storico and listings in local newspapers.

Just outside the city, **Duel Beat** (Via Antiniana 2A, Pozzuoli, 329 467 6763) is a cinema turned 'multiclub' featuring an extensive line-up of bands and DJs, plus an exhibition area and restaurant.

Any big names who make it this far south will probably end up in the **Palapartenope** (Via Barbagallo 115, Fuorigrotta, 081 570 0008, www.palapartenope.it); it has a cheap bar, but is utterly devoid of atmosphere. The outdoor, 6,000-seater **Arena Flegrea** at Mostra d'Oltremare (*see p122*) tends to be a better bet. Built by Mussolini and restored in 2001, it now hosts summer concerts on its pleasant marble terraces in a dedicated area known as **Isola delle Passioni** (www.isoladellepassioni.it). Past performers have included the likes of Bob Dylan, Massive Attack, Iggy Pop, Santana, REM and Nick Cave.

Venues

Nightlife venues in Naples are a moveable feast with small bars and clubs opening and closing regularly. There are the reliable stalwarts, but don't be surprised if your favourite haunt from last year has morphed into something else. In cooler weather, the bar and club scene is mostly divided between the Centro Storico, the university area and Chiaia.

The dozens of small bars and bistro-style restaurants with music and DJs in the Centro Storico have a hipster vibe and are crowded with students: Piazza Bellini, Piazza San Domenico and the little piazza in front of the Università Orientale (known locally as Piazza Orientale) are all stuffed with late-night bars and lots of people.

Venues in Chiaia are more upmarket and popular with young professionals and arty types. Cramming the narrow streets around Via San Pasquale, Via Bisignano and Via Fiorelli, they have become known as the '*baretti di San Pasquale*': on warm weekend nights, there are so many people spilling out on to the streets that you have to elbow your way through the throng to move forwards.

In the summer months everything moves to the beach (*see p141* **Hit the Beach**), leaving these central areas puzzlingly empty. Instead, you can check out the bars and restaurants along the Lungomare near the Castel dell'Ovo or hop on the *funicolare* up to the fresher air of Vomero and the many *locali* strung out along panoramic Via Aniello Falcone.

CENTRO STORICO
DJ bars & clubs

★ Galleria 19
Via San Sebastiano 19 (081 1981 0100, www. galleria19.it). Metro Dante, or bus E1, R4. **Open** 10pm-2am Tue, Thur-Sat. Closed May-Sept. **No credit cards. Map** p312 L9/10.
Galleria 19 (formerly Rising South) is one of the most well-designed nightclubs in the city – a long, tunnel-like space with rough stone walls, dotted with comfortable sofas and armchairs. Music sticks to a downbeat/nu-jazz/lounge vibe. During the week, this tends to be a student haunt (there's a dedicated University Party each Tuesday with discounts for students), but come at the weekend,

and you'll find one of the most diverse crowds in the city here. Check online for special events.

Libreria Berisio
Via Port'Alba 28 (081 549 9090). Metro Dante. **Open** 10am-1.30am daily. Closed 1wk Aug. **Map** p312 L8.
You'll find cocktails and dancing among the bookshelves at this lovely bookshop, with its warmly glowing 1950s wood interiors. By day, it sells antique and second-hand books. By night (from 7pm), it transforms into a cute bar and music venue with 101 cocktails on the menu and a rolling events diary that ranges from tango and swing lessons to jazz or DJ sets and dancing.

Superfly
Via Cisterna dell'Olio 12 (347 127 2178). Metro Dante, or bus 24, R1, R4. **Open** 7pm-2am Mon, Wed, Thur, Sun; 7pm-3am Fri, Sat. Closed end July-early Sept. **No credit cards. Map** p312 K9.
This diminutive bar barely has room for the two bartenders and the DJ, never mind the customers. It can get jam-packed within minutes; undeterred, the good-natured crowd spills out into the street. With lounge and acid jazz sounds in the background, it's a great place to go with friends for a chat and a good cocktail. Don't hesitate to ask for your favourite drink; staff are more than happy to mix up bespoke requests.

Live music

Lanificio 25
Piazza Enrico de Nicola 46 (081 658 2915, www. lanificio25.it). Metro Garibaldi, or bus 150, 191, 202, C41, C56, E2. **Open** varies; see website for details. **Map** p313 O7.

ARTS & ENTERTAINMENT

ARTS & ENTERTAINMENT

Lanificio 25 is located in a down-at-heel area close to the Castello Capuana and occupies part of a 15th-century former monastery. The innovative programme at this atmospheric performance space includes an eclectic range of live music (both local and international bands), theatre, dance and contemporary art shows and workshops. It's something of an oasis in the rundown Porta Capuana area: sip a cocktail in the lovely cloister on a warm summer evening and the grind of the city will seem a long way away.

PORT & UNIVERSITY
DJ bars & clubs

Aret' a' Palm
Piazza Santa Maria la Nova 14 (339 848 6949). Metro Università, or bus E1, R2, R4. **Open** 6pm- 2.30am daily. **No credit cards.** **Map** p312 L10.
In Neapolitan, Aret' a' Palm means 'behind the palm' and, sure enough, this small but stylish bar is located near an incredibly tall palm tree on a quiet square in the centre of town. The only live music is when the staff feel inspired to pick up a guitar; otherwise, DJs spin jazz and world music so loud that it's audible even if you sit at one of the tables out on the piazza.

Live music

Kestè
Largo San Giovanni Maggiore 26-27 (081 1936 0932, www.keste.it). Metro Università, or bus E1, R2. **Open** 7pm-2am Tue-Sat. Closed Aug. **No credit cards.** **Map** p312 L9.
Situated just opposite the University of Oriental Studies, Kestè is a bar, café, gig venue and restaurant all rolled into one. The attractive interior is a bit cramped, so tables tend to spill out on to the square. It's an enjoyable place for an aperitivo before going on to eat elsewhere, but it's worth sticking around to check out the live music on Tuesdays, Fridays and Saturdays.

Mamamu
Via Sedile di Porto 46 (320 669 5222). Metro Università, or bus E1, R2. **Open** 10pm-4am Thur-Sat. Closed June-Sept. **Map** p312 M10.

Tiny and usually packed to the rafters, Mamamu has been a gig venue since 1996. Bands are usually (but not always) local, and can be heard from an upstairs seating area if the space in front of the stage becomes too congested – this place is exceedingly popular with the local student population. Admission is free, but you have to get a membership card at the door.

VIA TOLEDO
DJ bars & clubs

Cammarota Spritz
Vico Lungo Teatro Nuovo 31 (320 277 5687). Metro Toledo, or bus E1, R4, C25. **Open** 4.30pm-midnight Mon; 11.30am-midnight Tue-Sun. **Map** p316 K16.
This tiny Quartieri Spagnoli drinking dive may be as basic as they come, but it's always packed to the gills with a lively, eclectic mix of students and arty types. Prices here are ridiculously low: an Aperol spritz (served in plastic cups) is just €1 . Every now and then, the owners chuck a live music session into the mix.

Slash
Via Vincenzo Bellini 45 (081 564 8902, www.slashnaples.com). Metro Dante, or bus 201, C63, R4. **Open** 10am-1.30am Tue-Fri; 6pm-2am Sat; 6pm-1.30am Sun. **Map** p312 L8.
This address has housed a Turkish bath and a brothel in the past, but these days it's a café, bar and art gallery, serving creative food, good drinks and with a mellow mix of lounge, jazz and bossa nova sounds. It's a fine place to kick back and relax during the day (with free Wi-Fi), as well as being a good evening alternative to the often overcrowded bars in Chiaia.

Live music

Bourbon Street
Via Vincenzo Bellini 52/53 (338 825 3756, www.bourbonstreetjazzclub.com). Metro Dante, or bus 201, C63, R4. **Open** 8pm-4am Tue-Sun. Closed May-mid Sept. **No credit cards.** **Map** p312 K8.
Bourbon Street is a large, centrally located jazz venue, with shows every night except Monday. It gets pretty crowded and attracts a cheery mix of bright young things and slightly older jazz buffs. There's a decent range of beers to complement the varied acts that take to the stage.

Galleria Toledo
For listings, see p146.
This hip theatre screens films and, during the cooler months, hosts an eclectic programme of alternative Italian and international bands.

HIT THE BEACH

Summer clubbing means moving outdoors.

For Neapolitan clubbers, summer means the sound of surf mixed with top-quality DJs in one of the many nightclubs along the coast. Inspired by the success of similar ventures in Ibiza, many a lido has realised that the big business starts after the sun goes down.

Although Naples may not rival the Isla Blanca for the quality of its beaches, it can match it for the sheer length of its coastline. Clubs such as **Music on the Rocks** (*see p224*) in Positano have been capitalising on their spectacular location for years, and canny Neapolitan venues are keen to follow suit.

The best example of the evolution from the city streets to the beach is **Arenile** (Via Coroglio 14B, Bagnoli, 081 570 6035, www.arenilereload.com), the closest beach club to the city centre. Once a fairly scuzzy beach in the shadow of the decommissioned steelworks at Bagnoli, Arenile was cleaned up as part of a neighbourhood renovation. It experienced modest success as a beach, until the owners realised that most people were turning up in the evenings to hang around the bar and catch the great sunsets. These days it draws the crowds with live music (BB King, Suzanne Vega and Snoop Dogg have all played here, although the focus is generally indie and dance), followed by a disco on the sand with high-profile DJs such as Fritz Kalkbrenner.

The **Lido Turistico** (Via Lido Miliscola 21, Bacoli, 081 523 5228, www.lidoturistico.com) feels more like a glorified beach bar, where the sea comes almost right up to the row of tables and chairs.

Upping the style ante, **Nabilah** (Via Spiaggia Romana 15, Fusaro, 081 868 9433, www.nabilah.it) is the summer version of Archivio Storico (*see p142*). Inviting sofas are arranged around low, white tables with designer candles, surrounding the DJ console. Sitting on a sofa with a chilled drink in your hand and your bare feet in the sand is a wonderfully decadent experience, and worth the steep bar prices.

These are a handful of the more enduring clubs on the beach, but there are many more (all open in the summer season only). In the Pozzuoli, Baia, Bacoli area, try **Beach Brothers** (Via Dragonara 72, 081 523 3183), the **Neries** 'Soundrink bar' (Via Montegrillo 8, 081 868 7588, www.nereis.it) and the

beautiful **Lost Paradise** (Via Castello 95, 081 1920 0806, www.lostparadisebacoli.it), where there are rooms to rent if you can't make it back to town. Closer to Naples, you could try **Voga** (Via Cordoglio 144), the **Neasy** 'Sea Lounge' (Via Coroglio, 338 925 9852, www.neasy.it) or close neighbour **Riva** (Via Coroglio, 334 833 7581).

A few tips: Neapolitans love to dress up and the beach clubs are pretty smart, so dig out your glad rags. If you're feeling daring, bring your swimming togs and go for a late-night dip – though be sure to stay in the shallows if you've had a few drinks. The major drawback of the beach scene is its relative inaccessibility. That said, Bagnoli is accessible by metro, and the clubs in Fusaro are within walking distance of Torre Gaveta at the end of the Cumana railway line. As for getting home… well, be prepared to dance until dawn!

Music on the Rocks.

Ba-Bar.

VOMERO

In the summer months, Vomero's nightlife scene is largely concentrated along panoramic Via Aniello Falcone, from where the views over the city and bay are stupendous. Bars and pubs compete for space and attract punters trying to beat the heat from down in the city. The wall across the road makes a good perch for chatting and drinking. Among the most popular bars here are **One** (no.354), **Saint Tropez** (nos.336-338), **Baik** (no.372) and **Flame** (no.378), but there are many others; you'll soon get a feel for whether you like the sound of the music and the look of the crowd.

DJ bars & clubs

Fonoteca

Via Morghen 31C-E (081 556 0338, www. fonoteca.net). Metro Vanvitelli, or funicular Chiaia to Via Cimarosa or Centrale to Piazza Fuga. **Open** noon-1am Mon-Thur; noon-2am Fri, Sat; 6.30pm-1.30am Sun. Closed 2wks Aug. **Map** p315 F10.

The legendary Fonoteca made its name as the best record shop in Naples; it now also houses a bar-café

and stays open late. Browse through the large collection of new and used CDs, then grab a beer or a cocktail in the hip bar area. Often heaving with the Vomero cognoscenti, this is an essential stop for music fans.

Live music

Archivio Storico

Via Alessandro Scarlatti 30 (081 1932 1922, www.archiviostorico.com). Metro Vanvitelli, or funicular Montesanto to Morghen or Centrale to Piazza Fuga. **Open** 8pm-1am Tue-Thur; 8pm-2am Fri-Sun. Closed July, Aug. **Map** p315 F10.

A smart, contemporary cocktail/wine bar and restaurant with live music (mostly jazz and blues) on Tuesdays and Thursdays. The same owners run Nabilah (*see p141*) during the summer.

Covo dei Briganti

Traversa Privata San Severino 10 (348 662 0480). Metro Medaglie d'Oro, or bus C47. **Open** 8pm-2am Tue-Thur, Sun; 8pm-3am Fri, Sat. **Map** p315 F6.

It's more of a pub than a DJ bar (with affordable drinks and a menu of steaks and burgers), but Covo

Seventy. See p144.

is packed to the gills at weekends when a DJ spins dance sounds and the heaving dancefloor extends to the tables and bar counter. On Saturday nights there's usually a live band. Crazy fun.

★ Goodfellas
Via Morghen 34B (340 922 5475, www.goodfellas dub.com). Metro Vanvitelli, or funicular Montesanto to Morghen or Centrale to Piazza Fuga. **Open** 8.30pm-2am Mon-Thur, Sun; 8.30pm-3am Fri, Sat. **Map** p315 F10.
Relative newcomer Goodfellas serves up good beer, good food and a mixed bag of live music almost every night of the week – expect anything from rock to jazz. Check the website for the full programme of upcoming events.

New Around Midnight
Via Bonito 32 (388 814 0469, 348 481 1722, www.newaroundmidnight.it). Metro Vanvitelli, or funicular Montesante to Morghen, or bus V1. **Open** 8.30pm-1am Wed-Sun. **No credit cards.** **Map** p315 F9.
New management has recently moved into this longstanding jazz venue and the programming is now in the hands of the Napoli Jazz Fest organisers. There's live jazz – from trad to bossa nova – every evening.

CHIAIA TO POSILLIPO
DJ bars & clubs

66 Fusion Bar
Via Bisignano 58 (081 415024, 328 756 7981). Metro Amedeo, or bus C24, E6, 128. **Open** 6pm-2.30am Mon-Thur; 6pm-3.30am Fri, Sat; 6.30pm-3.30am Sun. **Map** p311 H13.
A key Chiaia nightlife haunt, the crowded 66 Fusion Bar serves cocktails and a buffet in the early evening. But it isn't until later that things really start to swing. The ground floor is home to a large bar, while upstairs there are two VIP lounges with low tables and sofas.

★ Ba-Bar
Via Bisignano 20 (081 764 3525, www.ba-bar.it). Metro Amedeo, or bus C25, 151. **Open** 9am-4am daily. **Map** p311 H13.
It's hard to define exactly what Ba-Bar is; a kind of laid-back literary café/bistro/bar hybrid that opens for breakfast (*see p105*) but stays open until the early hours. With its vintage look and candlelit interior, it's a pleasant place at any time. There's a wide selection of gins and an interesting wine list, plus a menu of snacks and hot dishes. The basement space has a big screen for sports events.

Barril

Via G Fiorelli 11 (393 981 4362, www.barril.it).
Metro Amedeo. **Open** 7pm-2am Tue-Sun. Closed
3wks Aug. **Map** p311 G13.
Barril is a comfortable lounge bar with a decent-
sized terrace garden. Aside from cocktails, there's a
good selection of wines and a menu of cold dishes
if you're still hungry after your aperitivo buffet. The
laid-back soundtrack is mainly super-cool bossa
nova and jazz, perfect for sultry summer evenings.

Be Bop

Via Ferrigni 34 (081 245 1321). Metro Amedeo,
or bus C24, E6, 128. **Open** 6pm-3am daily.
Closed Aug. **Map** p311 G13.
Be Bop opened more than 30 years ago as a homage
to the music of the 1940s, '50s and early '60s. With its
vintage music and decor, it makes a great escape from
the electronic music played in neighbouring bars.
Opening and closing hours don't always stick to the
official version: the owner sometimes skips *aperitivi*
but after-dinner cocktails can last into the small hours.

★ Enoteca Belledonne

Vico Belledonne a Chiaia 18 (081 403162, www.
enotecabelledonne.com). Metro Amedeo, or bus
C25, 151. **Open** 4.30pm-1am Mon; 10am-1.30pm,
4.30pm-2am Tue-Sat; 7pm-2am Sun. Closed 2wks
Aug. **Map** p311 G13.
This upmarket wine bar, with exposed brickwork and
shelves stacked with bottles, is one of Chiaia's best-
loved watering holes. The old-style *enoteca* is wonderfully relaxed and has excellent, reasonably priced
wines by the glass. There's no buffet, but you can order
a plate of cheese or bruschetta to soak up the wine.

Happening

Via Bisignano 2 (www.happeningbar.it). Metro
Amedeo, or bus C25, 151. **Open** 7pm-3am daily.
Map p311 H13.
With its slick contemporary look, the two-level
Happening is a cut above some of the other bars in
the area and offers a great selection of drinks, plus
a decent buffet. Not surprisingly, it's always packed.
The music is excellent too; it's worth pitching up on
Thursdays for the chilled Aperireggae.

Seventy

Via Bisignano 19 (339 286 0214). Metro Amedeo,
or bus C25, 151. **Open** 6.30pm-2.30am Tue-Sun.
Map p311 H13.
With soft lighting, red velvet sofas and dark walls
hung with pictures in gilded frames, the mood at
Seventy is cosy and intimate; service is friendly so.
Aperitivi and nibbles are served from 8.30pm, and a
DJ spins from 9pm Thursday to Sunday. *Photos p143.*

S'move

Vico dei Sospiri 10A (081 1956 7977). Metro
Amedeo, or bus 128, 140, 151, E6. **Open** 7pm-2am
Mon-Thur, Sun; 7pm-4am Fri, Sat. **Map** p311 H13.

After more than two decades, S'move is still one of
the smartest venues in this area, with upmarket decor
and a lively vibe. The area's beautiful people make up
most of the clientele, but it's refreshingly welcoming.
There's no dancefloor as such, but the music (ranging
from Latin to house and techno) encourages even the
glacially cool to shake a limb or two. There's now a
stage for live music (on Wednesdays) and other events.

Spritz

Via Bisignano 45 (335 444547). Metro Amedeo,
or bus C24, E6, 128. **Open** 6.30pm-2am Mon-
Thur, Sun; 6.30pm-3am Fri, Sat. **Map** p311 H13.
Spritz is the neighbourhood's answer to a buzzing
local corner bar, with people using the place as if it
was an extension of home. For all its frenzy, bright
colours and eclectic music choices, a barstool perch
at Spritz feels delightfully cosy. Although the staff
know how to mix more than just a spritz, Aperol, prosecco and orange is still the name of the game here.

★ Trip

Via Martucci 64 (081 1956 8994, www.trip
napoli.com). Metro Amedeo, or bus C24.
Open 7pm-midnight Mon-Thur; 8pm-1.30am
Fri-Sun. Closed Aug.
This large space serves up decent food and drinks,
music, art and photography exhibitions, cinema and
live performances. Weeknights are laid-back, with
extended *aperitivi* and chilled music; at weekends,
the pace picks up with DJs and dancing. There's live
music – often jazz or 'mod Neapolitan' – on Saturdays.
There are plans to open during the day in summer: see
the website for details of upcoming events.

Live music

Barrio

Vico Satriano 10 (335 161 4060, 331 160 5185).
Bus 128, C24, E6. **Open** 7pm-4am Thur-Sun.
Map p311 H14.
This music bar serves up a mixed bag of live music
(rock, jazz, folk) on Thursday and Saturday evenings.
There are DJ sets most Fridays, often with retro
sounds from the 1960s and '70s.

OTHER AREAS

CSOA Officina 99

Via Gianturco 101 (081 734 0853, www.
officina99.org). Metro Gianturco, or bus 193,
172, 175, 192. **Open** 9pm-3am Tue, Fri, Sat. Closed
July-Sept. **Admission** varies. **No credit cards.**
Naples' most famous *centro sociale* (a semi-legally
occupied space), Officina 99 is located in an abandoned factory in the mean streets south-east of
Stazione Centrale. Unlike its sister set-ups the
Brancaleone in Rome or the Leonkavallo in Milan, it
hasn't spruced itself up and remains cold, cavernous
and edgy. But there's fun to be had here. Payment is
voluntary; around €3-€5 for gigs is typical.

ARTS & ENTERTAINMENT

FESTIVAL FUN
What to see, when.

Napoli Teatro Festival.

The number of ongoing festivals in Naples has diminished dramatically in recent years, mainly due to lack of funding, so it's important to scour the local press and events websites for upcoming events. Fingers crossed, ongoing festivals to look out for include the **Ethnos Festival** (www.festivalethnos.it), with its great line-up of world music acts; venues change from year to year, but are generally in the city centre. The **Napoli Jazz Fest** (388 814 0469, 348 481 1722) combines a summer festival on a weekend in late July for mostly young and up-and-coming talent (various venues), and a September season held in the courtyard of San Domenico Maggiore. The organisers also promote two monthly concerts (Jan-Apr) and stage the Sant'Elmo Estate season (www.comune. napoli.it) in July, which includes jazz and swing concerts on the panoramic Piazza d'Armi at Castel Sant'Elmo.

During the summer months, the city promotes an assortment of music, film and dance events (usually with free entrance) and there are plenty of other initiatives too. Check the comprehensive Napoli da Vivere website (www.napolidavivere.it) and English-language Napoli Unplugged (www.napoliunplugged.it).

Jazz events are staged in the Parco Urbano Virgiliano (see p109) on Posillipo Hill, at the Mostra d'Oltremare (see p122), and in the nearby town of Pomigliano d'Arco (081 803 2810, www.pomiglianojazz.com). The **Pozzuoli Jazz Festival** (www.pozzuolijazz festival.it) in late June/July takes place in the atmospheric Solfatara (see p115) and other venues in the Campi Flegrei; and the excellent **Napoli Teatro Festival** (www. napoliteatrofestival.it), held in June, has an 'after-theatre' venue at Castel Sant'Elmo with a bar and live music (mostly jazz, swing, Latin) or DJs. The **Galleria Toledo** theatre (see p146) also stages regular gigs.

Notte Bianca (www.nottebiancanapoli. com), or 'white night', is an all-night festival of music, shows and performances held in every available space in the city. Streets and squares are packed with revellers, and getting between events is nearly impossible (past years have attracted up to two million people). Although it's great fun for punters, city officials invariably grumble about the cost; for a start, the clean-up operation afterwards doesn't come cheap. Check ahead if you're planning to go, in case the event is cancelled.

Performing Arts

The origins of the city's theatrical traditions lie deep in its Greco-Roman past. The famous *commedia dell'arte* evolved from ancient farces and, combined with French influences, gave birth to mainstream Neapolitan theatre. Neapolitan dance – as seen in the whirling tarantella, say, or the more joyful tammurriata – also stems from ancient roots and has evolved along its own uniquely local lines.

Then there is the opera, of course, displayed in all its magnificent gilded opulence at the stately San Carlo, which remains one of Italy's finest opera houses. A distinct style of Neapolitan opera had developed by the early 18th century that made good use of *castratos* and was more concerned with the elegance of the sung melodic line and the expression of emotion than with dramatic validity. Any weakness in the plot was redeemed by the beauty of the music in operas by Alessandro Scarlatti and Giovanni Battista Pergolesi.

THEATRE

Neapolitan theatre is, for many, synonymous with playwright Eduardo de Filippo (1900-1984), whose most famous works include *Questi fantasmi* (*These Ghosts*) – brought to the New York stage as *Souls of Naples* in 2005 by John Turturro. Other key 20th-century Neapolitan playwrights include Viviani, Santanelli, Ruccello and Moscato.

More recent experimental works have been penned by Neiwiller, Martone, Servillo and Salemme – and in 2008, the city launched the **Napoli Teatro Festival Italia** (*see p150*). Yet despite its many rich offerings, the theatre scene in Naples remains a world that is essentially closed to outsiders, unless they can manage fluent Italian – and in many cases, Neapolitan dialect.

Galleria Toledo
Via Concezione a Montecalvario 34, Toledo (081 425037, www.galleriatoledo.org). Metro Montesanto, or bus E2. **Open** *Box office Sept-May 10.30am-1.30pm, 5.30-7pm Mon-Sat. Performances Oct-May 8.30pm Mon-Sat; 6pm Sun.* **Tickets** €15-€20. **No credit cards. Map** p312 K10.

The focus at this small stage is on experimental theatre, but there are contemporary dance shows and concerts too. There's also a good cinema line-up. Check the website for the full programme.

Mercadante
Piazza Municipio 1, Royal Naples (081 551 3396, www.teatrostabilenapoli.it). Metro Municipio, or bus 201, 202, C25, R2. **Open** *Box office 10.30am-1pm, 5-7.30pm Mon-Fri; 10.30am-1pm Sat.* **Performances** 9pm Mon-Wed, Fri, Sat; 5.30pm Thur; 6pm Sun. Closed Aug. **Tickets** €15-€29. **Map** p316 K11.

Naples' beautiful municipal theatre dates from 1779. The main 500-seater theatre hosts high-profile productions of the classics with big-name actors and directors such as Luca Ronconi, Roberto de Simone, Peter Brook and John Turturro, while the 80-seater 'Ridotto' puts on more modern fare.

Nuovo Teatro Sanità
Piazzetta San Vicenzo 1, Sanità (339 666 6426, www.nuovoteatrosanita.it). Metro Materdei, or bus 168, 178, C63, R4. **Open** *Box office (by phone) 10am-8pm daily. Performances 9pm Fri, Sat; 6pm Sun. Closed Aug.* **Tickets** €12.

This new theatre is located in the Sanità, *rione* of the legendary Totò and one of Naples' more challenging neighbourhoods. Housed in the deconsecrated 18th-century church of San Vincenzo, it was dubbed the 'Miracolo della Sanità' by the press when it opened in 2013. Partly financed by Roberto Saviano (author of the hard-hitting *Gomorra, see p133*) and under the artistic directorship of Mario Gelardi (who directed the stage version of the book), it's run by a young collective of actors, directors, writers, designers and technicians. The focus is mainly Neapolitan theatre with a strong commitment to the local community through workshops and youth projects.

Teatro Bellini
Via Conte di Ruvo 14-19, Toledo (081 549 9688, www.teatrobellini.it). Metro Dante or Museo, or bus 139, C63, R4. **Open** *Box office* 10.30am-1.30pm, 4-7pm Mon-Sat; 10.30am-1pm, 4-6pm Sun. *Performances* 9pm Mon-Sat; 5.30pm Sun. Closed Aug. **Tickets** €10-€30. **Map** p312 L8.
This lavishly decorated 19th-century theatre seats 820 and puts on an eclectic programme of everything from Pirandello and Eduardo de Filippo to *Who's Afraid of Virginia Woolf?* and *One Flew Over the Cuckoo's Nest* (in Italian, of course), with the odd dance performance thrown in. There are limited performances during the summer months (May-July).

Teatro Nuovo
Via Montecalvario 16, Toledo (081 497 6267, www.teatronuovonapoli.it). Metro Montesanto, or bus E2. **Open** *Box office* 10.30am-1pm, 5.30pm until performance Tue-Sat; 10.30am-1pm, 4.30pm until performance Sun.* **Performances** *Mid Nov-Apr* 9pm Tue-Sat; 6.30pm Sun. **Tickets** €10-€25. **Map** p312 K10.
Fresh, experimental theatre is the rule here, at the rapid clip of about one production per week. The programme sometimes includes international works, but performances are always in Italian.

CABARET & MUSICALS

Programmes at the **Mercadante** (*see p146*) and a few other theatres feature the odd musical, but more important in terms of Neapolitan tradition is cabaret. On a small, dimly lit stage, with perhaps a chair for a set and minimal make-up and costumes, one or two actors will riff – sometimes crudely – on society's foibles and ills. Neapolitan cabaret reached its peak in the 1970s with an enormously successful trio known as La Smorfia, which gained wide popularity thanks to TV exposure and whose work still enjoys a cult following. The three members, Lello Arena, Enzo Decaro and Massimo Troisi, played on the intolerance of the poor, uncultured youth from the suburbs against the suffocating rhetoric of everything traditional: theatre, culture, religion and politics. The group broke up in 1981 to allow

its members to pursue solo careers; most successful was the much-loved actor and director, Troisi, who died at the age of 41 just after finishing work on *Il Postino*. Today, virtually all cabaret in Naples draws on the group for inspiration. Notable performers include I Ditelo Voi, Ardone-Peluso-Massa, Alessandro Siani, Paolo Caiazzo, Rosalia Porcaro and Rosaria de Cicco.

Portalba
Via Port'Alba, Piazza Dante, Toledo (338 810 5370, www.teatrocabaretportalba.it). Metro Dante or Montesanto, or bus R1, R4. **Open** *Box office* 4-8pm Mon-Sat. *Performances* Mid Sept-June 9pm Fri-Sun. Closed July-mid Sept. **Tickets** €10-€25. **Map** p312 K8.
This tiny space showcases Neapolitan cabaret and also hosts musical events, including evenings of traditional Neapolitan song.

Tam
Gradini Nobile 1, corner of Via Martucci, Chiaia (081 682814, www.tamteatro.it). Metro Piazza Amedeo. **Open** *Box office* 10.30am-1.30pm, 3-6pm Tue-Sat; 4.30-8pm Sun. *Performances* 10pm Thur-Sat; 9.30pm Sun. Closed Aug. **Tickets** €10-€20. **Map** p310 E13.
Cosy, colourful and lots of fun, Tam's cabaret is full-force every weekend, with dinner or bar service an added option. It's very Neapolitan; if you don't understand dialect, you'll probably be lost. Performances aren't held every weekend, so check the website.

Totò
Via Frediano Cavara 12E, corner of Via Foria, Piazza Cavour (081 564 7525, www.teatrototo.it). Metro Cavour, or bus 182, 201, 204. **Open** *Box office* 10.30am-1pm, 4.30-7pm Tue-Sun. *Performances* 9pm Tue-Sat; 6pm Sun. Closed July-Sept. **Tickets** €15-€20. **Map** p312 L7.
Named after the great Neapolitan comic actor, this small theatre specialises in comedy (often accompanied by music) and cabaret.

CLASSICAL MUSIC & OPERA

Composers such as Alessandro and Domenico Scarlatti, Niccolò Iommelli and Giovanni Battista Pergolesi are among the best-known exponents of Neapolitan Baroque music. Musicians in the city continue to pay homage to those traditions. Look out for performances by the excellent **Orchestra Barocca Pietà dei Turchini**; under director Antonio Florio, they have been performing early Neapolitan repertoire on original instruments since 1987, often with singers, and they appear regularly on the programme of the **Associazione Scarlatti**. The **Teatro San Carlo** (*see p149*) also hosts a wide range of classical performances.

ARTS & ENTERTAINMENT

TEATRO SAN CARLO
The city's indomitable opera house.

The opera scene in Naples revolves around the magnificent **Teatro San Carlo** (see p149), designed in 1737 by Giovanni Medrano at the behest of King Carlos I de Bourbon. Rossini, Donizetti and Bellini have all served as director, and many of the greatest operas have seen their debuts here – among them *La Donna del Lago*, *Lucia di Lammermoor* and *Luisa Miller*.

It's the oldest active opera house in Europe and performances have never been suspended – except between May 1874 and December 1876, due to the economic crisis following the Unification of Italy. Not even the devastating fire of 1816 – after which the present-day structure was completed in just ten months – or the tragic events of World War II have succeeded in closing it down.

Dedicated to King Carlos's namesake saint, San Carlo is a place of pilgrimage for opera devotees. Behind its austere façade, the regal grandeur of its design, lighting and decoration have enchanted visitors for centuries. The French writer Stendhal reports having had his eyes dazzled and

soul ravished at the sight of this 'sultan's palace', and famous Grand Tourist Samuel Sharp found it 'as remarkable an object as any man sees in his travels'.

Inside, it seems as if anything that couldn't be covered in red velvet has been gilded. But there was a method to the opulence: the soft fabric enhances the superb acoustics, and it's said that the sound of a piece of paper being crumpled on the stage can easily be heard up in the very last row of the gods.

Other luxurious touches include mirrors in every box, positioned in such a way that the occupants could see the Royal Box without craning their necks. By way of a glance in the mirror, no one would upstage the royals, who, of course, had always to begin the applause. The Royal Box itself is constructed entirely from humble papier-mâché, the material of marionettes, and its extreme fragility has given restorers here headaches for centuries.

Although Neapolitans will don their glad rags for opening nights, dinner jackets are rarely seen at San Carlo, but 'casual' here means stylish and elegant.

Naples' famous **Conservatorio San Pietro a Majella** music school (Via San Pietro a Majella 34, 081 564 4411, www.sanpietroamajella.it) stages regular student performances. The Conservatory is also home to a small museum that holds examples of early instruments and music memorabilia, as well as one of the most important libraries of music manuscripts in the world.

Look out for posters advertising concerts and opera, especially during the summer months when all sorts of performances take place. Advance publicity is often scant and you need to keep an eye open for events. Look in the local papers (*see p295*) for listings or contact the tourist office (*see p297*).

★ Associazione Scarlatti

Piazza dei Martiri 58, Chiaia (081 406011, www. associazionescarlatti.it). Metro Amedeo, or bus C24, E6. **Open** *Box office* 10am-1pm, 3.30-6pm Mon-Fri. **Performances** 9pm (days vary). Closed June-Aug. **Tickets** €15-€25. **Map** p311 H13.

The most important concert society in Naples, the Associazione Scarlatti promotes chamber music concerts mainly in Castel Sant'Elmo and the Teatro di Corte in Palazzo Reale. The roster features a line-up of international and Italian musicians, such as Jordi Savall, the Emerson Quartet, Ramin Bahrami and the Quartetto Cremona.

Centro di Musica Antica Pietà dei Turchini

Via Santa Caterina da Siena 38, Chiaia (081 402395, www.turchini.it). Funicular Centrale to Augusteo, or bus C16. **Open** *Box office* 30mins before performance. *Performances* 8.30pm Fri, Sat. Closed Aug. **Tickets** €10. **No credit cards**. **Map** p311 J12.

This centre for early music focuses firmly on early Neapolitan music. Many performances are held in the church of Santa Caterina da Siena.

★ Teatro San Carlo

Via San Carlo 98F, Royal Naples (081 797 2331, 081 797 2412, www.teatrosancarlo.it). Metro Municipio, or bus C25, R2, E6. **Open** *Box office* 10am-7pm Tue-Sun. *Performances* times vary. Closed Aug. **Tickets** €20-€500. **Map** p316 K12.

Although solidly traditional programming gives the San Carlo a rather staid image, the standard is often exceptional and its reputation as being second only to Milan's La Scala is deserved. Openings here are Neapolitan high-society events (complete with the obligatory anti-fur protesters). Although many go to the opera *per vedere e farsi vedere* (to see and be seen), large chunks of the audience are genuine, diehard opera buffs. Traditionalists at heart, San Carlo-goers can give innovative works a rough ride: if it's not a classic, it has to be very good to escape being rubbished. Still, an increasing number of 20th-century works in recent seasons haven't driven the public away.

The opera season runs from January to December with a pause in late July and August. The *abbonamenti* (subscription) system allows opera-goers to reserve their seats for the whole season. Don't despair, though, as seats can still be found.

The San Carlo also has ballet and orchestral seasons. In summer, performances take place outside – you might catch a ballet in the courtyard at Castel Nuovo or opera in the Arena Flavio in Pozzuoli. The theatre has its own ballet troupe, school, choir and orchestra. It often attracts big-name international soloists, conductors and orchestras.

NEAPOLITAN SONG

The *canzone napolitana* had its heyday in the late 19th and early 20th centuries, when artists such as Enrico Caruso and Gilda Mignonette enjoyed huge popularity worldwide. It was a golden age of song, when poets wrote passionate lyrics and composers set them to soaring melodies. Nowadays, the consummate interpreter of these traditional songs is Massimo Ranieri, whereas Peppino di Capri gets the credit for linking the tradition to rhythms derived from 1950s rock. More recent standout voices include the late Pino Daniele, Nino d'Angelo, Edoardo Bennato and Enzo Gragnaniello, while Roberto de Simone is an important Neapolitan musicologist, composer and director.

The **Nuova Compagnia di Canto Popolare** was formed in 1967, with the remit of preserving the traditional musical patrimony of Naples and the south, from the medieval period to the 20th century. It continues its work today, giving rise to performers such as Peppe Barra, Eugenio Bennato and Patrizio Trampetti, as well as the folk groups Musicanova and Zezi.

Nuova Compagnia di Canto Popolare.

Napoli Teatro Festival Italia.

Teatro Trianon Viviani

Piazza Calenda 9, Centro Storico (081 225 8285, www.teatrotrianon.org). Metro Garibaldi. **Map p313 O8.**

The Trianon was closed at the time of writing but is due to reopen sometime in 2016. The focus will remain on traditional Neapolitan theatre and song, and it's hoped that singer Nino d'Angelo will once again be directing. Inside the theatre, you can see some of the remains of ancient Greek Neapolis.

DANCE

Naples is the land of the tarantella, a sprightly, carefree dance known worldwide – at least in its softer, folkier version. Some say its name came from the city of Taranto in Puglia, while others believe the dance was linked to the bite of the tarantula. Either way, the roots of this strange, frenzied dance have been traced back as far as the Dionysian cults brought over by the Greek colonists who settled in Italy's heel and toe. Today's most famous musician-dancer-singer is Marcello Colasurdo.

Naples also has an important school of classical ballet, which is directed by Anna Razzi and based at the **Teatro San Carlo** *(see p149).* Ballet performances, both classical and modern, are part of the regular programme at the theatre.

FESTIVALS

The city's theatres close down in the hot summer months and performances are held out of doors (and out of town), often in magnificent alternative venues. The most prestigious of all the region's outdoor summer events is the **Ravello Festival** *(see p241),* which runs from June to September. The **Concerti al Tramonto** on Anacapri and the **Pompei Festival** (www.pompeifestival.it) offer more opportunities to hear music and opera in sublime settings.

Napoli Teatro Festival Italia

For listings, see p25.

This excellent itinerant theatre and dance festival, held in June and July, features top-notch Italian and international works (in their original language with Italian subtitles) in venues across the city. The 2015 festival saw productions ranging from Goldoni's *La Bottega del Caffè* to Strindberg's *Miss Julie* and Sarah Kane's *Crave*. The E45 Napoli Fringe Festival runs concurrently, showcasing young companies and performers and new shows.

★ Festa della Madonna di Piedigrotta

For listings, see p26.

For a week during early September, this wonderfully lively festival animates the city with colourful floats, dancing and music: the annual song competition is a major draw.

THE CRUELLEST CUT
The story of Naples' castrati.

Artists are often forced to go to great lengths for their work, but few would make the sacrifices required of a castrato. The practice of castration in order to preserve a boy's pre-pubescent voice into adult life began in the 16th century, initially to provide singers to perform the complex polyphonic church music of the time (women were banned) and later for the new style of opera that arrived in Italy in the early 17th century. Boys, often from poor families willing to sacrifice them for money, were castrated between the ages of seven and nine and underwent a long period of tough voice training. Once they reached adulthood, the high pitch of the voice was accompanied by the greater lung capacity and physical bulk of a fully grown male, so the castrato soprano voice was much more powerful than its female counterpart.

The practice was widespread in Italy, and mid 18th-century Naples became the castrato capital of Europe. The demand from its opera house and four conservatories led to a thriving black market in eunuchs; children were bought by speculators who paid for their surgery (often carried out in appalling conditions) and musical training in the hope that they would make their fortune as opera singers or soloists with choirs in royal palaces and churches.

A small number became international opera stars. The most famous was Farinelli (*pictured*), who was said to have 'seven notes more than the normal voice' (his range was over three octaves). Other celebrated castrati included Senesino and Giovanni Carestini (Cusanino), who were both favourites of Handel. Jonathan Swift reported that 'In London… Senesino is daily voted to be the greatest man who ever lived.'

By the end of the 18th century, fashions in opera had changed and the popularity of the castrato declined except in the Vatican, where the Sistine Chapel continued to employ them until 1903. The last was Alessandro Moreschi, who died in 1924 and made gramophone recordings that provide the only direct evidence of a castrato's singing voice – a strange, rather sad, almost other-worldly sound.

ARTS & ENTERTAINMENT

Escapes & Excursions

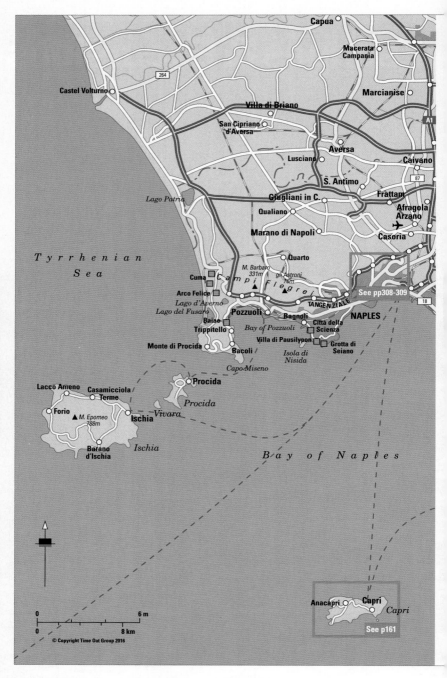

Capua

Macerata
Campania

Marcianise

A1

Castel Volturno

264

Villa di Briano

San Cipriano
d'Aversa

Aversa

Caivano

Lusciano

87

S. Antimo

Frattam

Lago Patria

Giugliani in C.

Afragola
Arzano

Qualiano

Casoria

Marano di Napoli

Tyrrhenian
Sea

Quarto

M. Barbaro
331m

gli Astroni
76m

Campi Flegrei

See pp308-309

Cuma

Arco Felice

TANGENZIALE

18

Lago d'Averno
Lago del Fusaro

Pozzuoli

Bagnoli

NAPLES

Baiae
Trippitello

Bay of Pozzuoli

Città della
Scienza

Villa di Pausilypon

Monte di Procida

Bacoli

Isola di
Nisida

Grotta di
Seiano

Capo Miseno

Procida

Procida

Lacco Ameno

Casamicciola
Terme

Vivara

Forio

M. Epomeo
788m

Ischia

Bay of Naples

Barano
d'Ischia

Ischia

0   6 m

0   8 km

© Copyright Time Out Group 2016

Anacapri

Capri

Capri

See p161

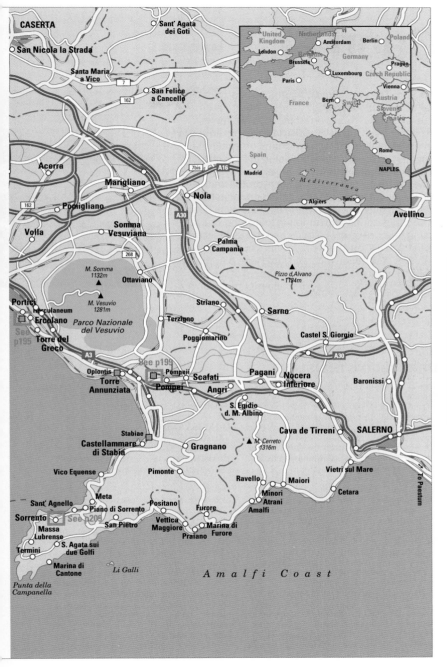

CASERTA

Sant' Agata
dei Goti

San Nicola la Strada

Santa Maria
a Vico   7

San Felice
a Cancello   162

United Kingdom   Netherlands
London   Amsterdam   Berlin   Poland
Brussels   Germany
Paris   Luxembourg   Czech Republic   Prague
Vienna   Austria
Bern   Switz   Slovenia
France   Italy
Spain   Rome
Madrid   NAPLES
Mediterranea
Algiers   Tunis
Avellino

Acerra

Marigliano   7bis   A16

Nola

Pomigliano   162   A30

Volla

Somma
Vesuviana

Palma
Campania

Pizzo d'Alvano
~ 1134m

268

M. Somma
1132m   Ottaviano

Striano

Sarno

Portici   M. Vesuvio
1281m   Terzigno

Herculaneum
Ercolano   Parco Nazionale
del Vesuvio   Poggiomarino

Castel S. Giorgio

Torre del
Greco   A3   A30

See
p195   See p199

Oplontis   Pompeii

Torre
Annunziata   Pompeii   Scafati

Pagani   Nocera
Inferiore

Baronissi

Angri

S. Egidio
d. M. Albino

Stabiae   Cava de Tirreni   SALERNO

Castellammare
di Stabia   Gragnano   M. Cerreto
1316m

Vico Equense   Pimonte

Vietri sul Mare

Ravello   Maiori

Sant' Agnello   Meta   Furore   Cetara
Piano di Sorrento   Positano   Minori
Sorrento   See p205   Atrani
San Pietro   Vettica   Amalfi
Massa   Maggiore   Marina di
Lubrense   Praiano   Furore
S. Agata sui
Termini   due Golfi

Marina di   Li Galli   A m a l f i   C o a s t
Cantone

Punta della
Campanella

Capri

Capri. The very name conjures up heady images of unrivalled glamour, azure seas and eternally blue skies. But this is an island with two faces. In high season, up to 70,000 day-trippers squeeze on to the jagged, 10.4sq km chunk of limestone, clogging its pretty lanes, browsing the kitsch tat in the souvenir shops and ooh-ing and aah-ing at the Blue Grotto before catching the hydrofoil back to the mainland. Beneath this garish surface, though, is a much quieter Capri where elegant villas nestle in secret gardens and rambling footpaths weave round heather-strewn slopes and along deserted coasts. In hilltop Anacapri, farmers cultivate tiny patches of terraced land and local kids play football while their mums mull over the gossip of the day. Capri will bewitch – if you just allow it time to do so.

INTRODUCING THE ISLAND

Traditionally, Capri town has been regarded as chic and urbane; while Anacapri, set on the high ground of Monte Solaro, is more rugged, rural and down-to-earth. Although less pronounced than in the past, the contrast still holds true: luxury hotels and villas cluster around Capri town (which also bears the brunt of the summer tourist invasion), while Anacapri is home to a farming population and is decidedly more low-key.

To fully appreciate the island's charms, you need to bite the bullet and stay at least one night; it's well worth the inevitable expense involved. By day, the Piazzetta, Capri's heart and site of the world's most famous *passeggiata*, is jammed with pedestrians. In the evening, however, as the sky darkens to cobalt and the last of the day-trippers drift down to the port, this stage set of a square is transformed into the Med's most elegant drawing room, and you begin to see what all the fuss is about.

The best time to visit is out of season (May or October). During spring, the carpet of wild flowers adds glorious colour to the scenery but the sea is still cold. Come in late September or early October and the evenings are balmy, the water is still warm and the islanders breathe a deep sigh of relief as the day-trippers are reduced to a trickle. From November to March, Capri practically closes down and only a few hotels and restaurants stay open. But for some, this is the perfect time to savour the simple delights of this magical place.

GOAT ISLAND

This rugged chunk of limestone broke off from the tip of the Sorrentine peninsula at the end of the last Ice Age and has been inhabited since pre-history. The origin of the island's name is much debated, deriving either from *capreae* (a Romano-Italic word meaning 'island of goats') or *kaprie* (Greek for the 'place of the wild boar'). There are no boars around these days, but you might catch sight of the odd goat. The first inhabitants were Neolithic tribes, and then came the Greeks of Cumae and Neapolis (Naples) – Virgil associated it with the Teleboans, a legendary race of Greek pirates.

In 29 BC, Octavian – who was soon to become Emperor Augustus – landed here. Charmed by its beauty, he persuaded the Greeks of Neapolis to take back the already Romanised and larger island of Ischia and give him Capri instead, for use as a private estate. Although he never lived here, Augustus set about building villas and water cisterns, and took an active interest in the island's traditions.

TIBERIUS'S CAPRI

Augustus's successor, Tiberius, ignored the
island for years before finally visiting in AD 27.
He never returned to Rome, spending the last
ten years of his life on Capri. His reign on the
island – absolutist to the point of derangement –
has been the subject of a great deal of historical
embroidery. Suetonius, the scandalmongering
author of *De Vita Caesarum* (Lives of the
Caesars), depicted Tiberius as a misanthropic
reprobate with a predilection for orgies and
debauched erotica. Evidence of prisons,
torture and execution chambers in Tiberius's
villas testify to his other preferred form of
entertainment. Suetonius is, however, almost
the sole literary source for the final years of
the emperor's life, and some believe his account
to be vindictive and one-sided.

After Tiberius's death in AD 37, his 12 villas
crumbled into ruin and the island was forgotten
by the outside world, save as a place of exile for
Roman undesirables. Later it came under the
sway of the Abbey of Montecassino, then of the
Republic of Amalfi. Thereafter it followed the
fortunes of Naples, passing meekly from Anjou
then Aragon to Spanish rule. Never entirely self-
sufficient, the islanders faced starvation many
times, enduring repeated Saracen pirate attacks
as well as the plague. In the 18th century, the
Bourbons hunted here – while the king went
looking for quails, warships circled the island
checking for pirates.

During the Napoleonic Wars, the British
occupied Capri as a bastion against the French
Kingdom of Naples, but some brilliant decoy
tactics by a French invasion force led to its speedy
recapture in 1808. This period saw Austrian
envoy Norbert Hadrawa run off with marbles,
mosaics and valuables from the villas; their
ruins were then plundered to build forts.

INTELLECTUAL INVASION

With its balmy climate and classical past, Capri
soon became less of a military prize and more of
a magnet for artists and intellectuals. The first
hotel, the Hotel Pagano (now La Palma), was
opened in 1822; and after the Blue Grotto was
rediscovered in 1826 by German poet August
Kopisch and local fisherman Angelo Ferraro,
tourists started to roll in. With a reputation as a
haven for Greek and Sapphic lovers, an aura of
licentiousness hung around the island where
Tiberius had supposedly swung both ways
with such abandon.

Capri.

Capri

ESCAPES & EXCURSIONS

IN THE KNOW APERITIVO KNOWLEDGE

If you want to slip into the Piazzetta crowd unnoticed at cocktail hour, make your *aperitivo* of choice a 'spritz'. Originally a Venetian drink but now favoured all over Italy, a spritz is made with either Aperol or Campari plus prosecco and a dash of soda water; it's served on the rocks with a slice of orange. Warning: it may slip down a treat but it packs a punch.

Gay Capri's finest years were the first two decades of the 20th century, when British writer Norman Douglas (whose *South Wind* is still the definitive Capri novel) and perfumed French aesthete Jacques Fersen helped keep the island boys in pocket money. Foreigners, including Fersen and Scandinavian doctor Axel Munthe (*see p168*), began building villas. Writer Curzio Malaparte, a sort of Italian Ernest Hemingway who was famous in the 1940s and '50s, also built a property here. Designed by Adalberto Libera, his brutalist red house on Punta Massullo, Villa Malaparte – which he called Casa Come Me (house like me) – is one of the island's more unusual landmarks. It played host to famous figures such as Jean Cocteau and Albert Camus, and appeared in Jean-Luc Godard's *Le Mépris*; these days, it's open for the occasional art exhibition.

The funicular was built in 1907 and the port opened in the '30s; until then, visitors arrived in rowing boats, among bags of mail and provisions, and were carried ashore to stop their feet getting wet. It was only after World War II, when it was used as an American base, that Capri began to attract billionaires, heiresses, Hollywood stars and jetsetters. Thereafter, a tidal wave of hotel construction destroyed most of Capri's farmland, making it forever dependent on tourism.

Capri Town & Around

Landing in **Marina Grande** in high season can be a stressful undertaking. Day-trippers and touts swarm around the harbour, and the tacky souvenir stores and touristy bars are a far cry from the Capri of your fantasies. To make your escape, join the queue at the ticket desk for bus or funicular tickets; once you've got these, you can squeeze on to a tiny orange bus up to Capri town or Anacapri, or take the funicular to Capri town.

The only reason most people pass through Marina Grande (apart from hopping off and on ferries) is as a jumping-off point for Capri's most famous sight, the **Blue Grotto** (*see p162*). It's worth experiencing, despite the expensive palaver a visit entails; the iridescent quality of the blue light inside is mesmerising.

Midway up the road linking the Marina to Capri town, the bus passes the island's non-Catholic **cemetery** (open 8am-7pm Mon-Sat, 7am-noon Sun). Created in 1878 for the growing

Grand Hotel Quisisana. *See p167.*

community of foreign residents, it's the final resting place of Norman Douglas and Gracie Fields, among others. Far from the tourist trail, it's a good starting point for visitors wishing to explore Capri's free-thinking, artistic past.

The funicular, which offers splendid views as it crawls up the hill, emerges on the piazza at the end of Via Roma, Capri town's access road. Above the funicular station is a terrace with a bar, from which you can drink in the view over the Marina and **Monte Solaro**. A picturesque bell tower separates this antechamber from the Piazzetta (officially Piazza Umberto I): core of the Capri experience, archetype of the perfect Mediterranean island square, and the town's main pedestrian traffic chicane.

In Capri, all roads seem to lead to the **Piazzetta**, the island's drawing room. With its four rival bars (distinguished by colour-coded tables) it's one of the best places at which to see and be seen. Grab a table, order a drink (you only live once), sit back and enjoy the show. Around it run the narrow alleys of the old town, whose vaulted streets, low arches, loggias and courtyards were built as a means of hampering marauding pirates.

On the south side of the square, the main parish church of **Santo Stefano** (open 8am-1pm, 5-8pm daily), with its barrel-vaulted roof, sits pretty at the top of a flight of steps. The present Baroque structure was built on the site of an earlier church; inside, the intarsia marble flooring in front of the main altar comes from the **Villa Jovis** (*see p162*). Legend has it that the painting

of the Madonna in the first chapel on the left was thrown down a cliff by invading Turks, but remained intact. In front of the church, the **Museo del Centro Caprense Ignazio Cerio** (*see p162*) houses relics of Capri's pre-history.

Take Via Madre Serafina from the top of the church steps (keep to the right) and enjoy a wander through medieval Capri. This lane eventually becomes the steep Via Castello, at the end of which is the **Belvedere Cannone**. Named after a French cannon placed here, it used to be known as Malerplatte – painters' square – due to its popularity with German artists, and affords magnificent views over the **Faraglioni** (*see p162*) and **Marina Piccola**.

From the Piazzetta, Via Vittorio Emanuele (the closest Capri comes to a main street) descends past boutiques and limoncello outlets to the **Grand Hotel Quisisana** (*see p167*), doyen of the island's luxury hotels. Continue down Via Federico Serena to Via Matteotti, a curving lane that opens on to an unexpectedly rural scene of olive groves, a medieval monastery and the sea.

The monastery – the **Certosa di San Giacomo** (*see p162*) – can be reached via a walled avenue at the eastern end of Via Matteotti. It was established in 1371 by Count Giacomo Arcucci, powerful secretary to Queen Juana I, who became a monk when he fell from favour in 1386. The Carthusian brotherhood of San Giacomo owned land, grazing and hunting rights to most of the island – bringing it into frequent conflict with islanders. When plague broke out in 1656, the monks sealed themselves

ESCAPES & EXCURSIONS

GOING SWIMMINGLY
Where to take the plunge.

The sea around Capri is heart-stoppingly beautiful, but it can be frustratingly difficult to get to. So here is a round-up of the best places to take a dip. Expect to pay €20-€25 per person per day to gain entrance to one of the lidos listed; the price includes a deckchair or sunbed (umbrellas cost extra) and all of them have bars, a restaurant, showers and changing rooms. Some even have a pool.

Most 'beaches' are rocks or platforms with steps into the sea; if you yearn for sand between your toes, there's always Marina Grande. But if that's too close to the port for comfort, head to the far more pleasant **Bagno di Tiberio** (081 837 0703, www.bagnitiberio. com), a 15-minute walk from the port.

The most exclusive lido of them all is **La Fontelina** (Località Faraglioni, 081 837 0845, www.fontelina-capri.com), with its simple blue-and-white parasols and good restaurant. It's perched on a stone platform on Stella, the first of the Faraglioni islands, and offers stunning views of the Faraglioni rocks. You can get a boat from Marina Piccola or walk down from Punta Tragara.

For small children, **Marina Piccola** is your best bet. Arrive early and you won't pay a penny for your postage-stamp place on its pebbly beach, which has a fine view of the Faraglioni. Otherwise, pay for a lido. **La Canzone del Mare** (081 837 0104, www.lacanzonedelmare.com), co-founded by singer Gracie Fields in 1933, is sandy and popular with families. Nearby **Scoglio delle Sirene** (081 837 0221, www.loscogliodelle sirenecapri.com), positioned on a low, rocky outcrop, has a mellow vibe and a great bar.

Way out on the extreme south-west tip of the island lies Punta Carena: the rocks here face the island's lighthouse, and the stretch of coast includes free beaches as well as lidos, with bars overlooking the bay. The most popular is **Lido del Faro** (081 837 1798, www.lidofaro.com, *see p172*), which seems a world away from the Piazzetta and is as popular with *anacapresi* grandparents as their grandchildren. A sundowner here at the end of a day on the beach is a real treat. A ten-minute bus ride from Anacapri, it's also the starting (or finishing) point for the Sentiero dei Fortini fortress walk (*see p170* **Scenic Splendour**). Another very popular spot is the **Lido Nettuno** (081 837 1362, www. clubnettunocapri.com) by the Blue Grotto.

La Fontelina.

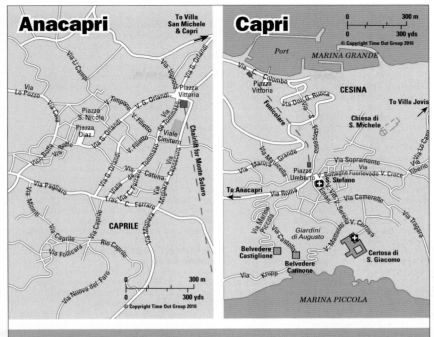

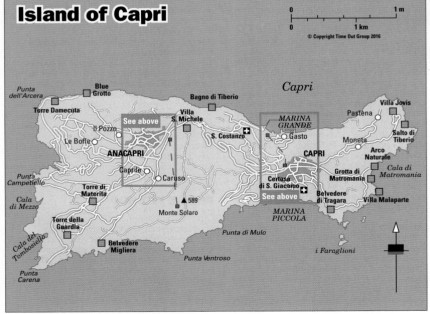

ESCAPES & EXCURSIONS

off to avoid infection instead of tending to the sick; the *capresi* responded by dumping the corpses of plague victims over the monastery wall. Dissolved by Napoleon in 1808, the Certosa became a prison and military hospital.

At the other end of Via Matteotti are the **Giardini di Augusto** (open dawn-dusk daily), a panoramic series of terraced gardens that once formed part of the estate of German arms manufacturer Alfred Krupp. Beyond the gardens stands a monument to Lenin, who stayed in the villa above with Maxim Gorky. Opposite, the Via Krupp (closed indefinitely) is a wonderful hairpin path built in 1902, which winds down the cliff linking the Certosa to the Marina Piccola.

Back up at the Quisisana, Via Camerelle heads east past elegant boutiques and bars to Via Tragara, lined with upmarket hotels. This is the route of the evening *passeggiata* – just long enough to work up an appetite for dinner, and with a wonderful view at the end from the Belvedere di Tragara; the deep red villa standing on the Belvedere that now houses the upmarket **Punta Tragara** hotel (*see p167*) was built by Le Corbusier. From here, there are magnificent views down on to the three rock stacks known as the **Faraglioni**. The outermost stack is home to a species of blue lizard found nowhere else in the world. Freeclimbers are allowed to scale the rocks, with prior permission from the tourist office.

The paved path that descends from this point is one of the best walks on the island (*see p170* **Scenic Splendour**), via the mysterious **Grotta di Matermania** and **Arco Naturale**. The classic excursion from Capri town, however, is the easy hike up to Tiberius's **Villa Jovis** (*see right*). From the Piazzetta, Via le Botteghe leads to a crossroads just below the tiny chapel of **San Michele** (open 10am-4pm daily). Beyond here, the path dawdles past imposing villas and more humble *capresi* dwellings until the houses thin out and the going gets steep. Just before the remains of the villa, **Parco Astarita** is an unassuming but scenic patch of grass under the pines.

Within the Villa Jovis complex is the tiny medieval church of **Santa Maria del Soccorso**, occasionally open for exhibitions. Fersen's neoclassical **Villa Lysis** (081 838 6111, open 10am-1hr before sunset Mon, Tue, Thur-Sun), built in 1905, is further along as the crow flies on Via lo Capo, but you'll need to take a different path at an earlier fork to get there.

Blue Grotto

(081 837 0973). From Marina Grande, take a speedboat (€14, see p174); from Anacapri, take the Grotta Azzurra bus from Piazza della Pace in Anacapri (€1.50) and then transfer to one of the rowing boats (€9) at the jetty. **Open** *1 May-31 Oct* 9am-5pm daily. *1 Nov-30 Apr* 9am-2pm daily. **Admission** €4 plus boat fees. **No credit cards**.

Discovered in Roman times, the Blue Grotto and its famously iridescent light subsequently became associated with evil spirits, and was given a wide berth by locals. That all changed with its rediscovery in 1826, when it became a fêted attraction. If the sea is even slightly rough, trips are cancelled; allow plenty of time as there may be a wait to get inside. *Photos p172*.

Certosa di San Giacomo

Via Certosa (081 837 6218). **Open** *Summer* 9am-2pm, 5-8pm Tue-Sun. *Winter* 9am-2pm Tue-Sun. **Admission** €4.
Recently restored, the Certosa is an atmospheric place. It's partly abandoned, partly given over to municipal uses – including as a school, library, temporary exhibition space and museum dedicated to the lugubrious canvases of German painter and Capri resident Karl Wilhelm Diefenbach. The simple church has a fine 14th-century fresco above the door; among the three praying women to the left of the Virgin is Queen Juana, the monastery's co-founder.

Museo del Centro Caprense Ignazio Cerio

Piazzetta Cerio 5 (081 837 6681, www.centro caprense.org). **Open** 10am-1pm Mon; noon-4pm Tue, Sat; 10am-4pm Wed-Fri. **Admission** €2.50; €1 reductions. **No credit cards**.
The archaeological museum's collections include the fossilised skeletons of long-extinct mammals, unearthed below the Grand Hotel Quisisana.

★ Villa Jovis

Viale Amadeo Maiuri, Via Tiberio (081 837 0381). **Open** *Mar* 10am-2pm Mon, Wed-Sun; *Apr-Oct* 10am-6pm Mon, Wed-Sun. **Admission** €2. **No credit cards**.
The best time to visit Villa Jovis is as soon as it opens, before the bulk of the day-trippers make their way up. Not much is left of the Roman complex, yet it's still imposing in all its splendid, solitary glory. The most impressive remains are those of the huge cisterns in the centre and the long, straight loggia to the north, which ends in the 330m (1,155ft) Salto di Tiberio – the precipice from which the emperor reportedly hurled people who annoyed him. The story may be mere fabrication, but the stunning view across to Punta della Campanella on the mainland is real enough.

WHERE TO SHOP

Capri town is a fashionista's heaven, with a cluster of designer boutiques, although why anyone would spend their time designer-shopping here rather than taking in the sun and sea is a mystery. The big hitters – Ferragamo, Gucci, Fendi, Alberta Ferretti, Cavalli, Prada – are crammed into tiny, prestigious outlets along Via Vittorio Emanuele and Via Camerelle. However, a much more interesting shopping experience is to be had

SAVVY SOUVENIRS
Bag yourself some Caprese classics.

Capri's long-standing artisan tradition means that you can find beautiful, original gifts and souvenirs to remind you that there's more to shopping here than Gucci and Prada. Capri sandals, made famous in the 1960s by jet-setting icon Jackie O, are still one of the best souvenirs to bring home. There are endless factory-made versions, but for the real, hand-made deal, head to **Giuseppe Faiella** (Via le Botteghe 21, 374 678 0079), whose family has been making sandals since 1917, or **Da Costanzo** (Via Roma 49, 081 837 8077). Over in Anacapri, try **Antonio Viva** (Via Orlandi 75, 081 837 3583, www.sandalocaprese.it). Zabattigli, a Caprese version of the rope-soled espadrille, are still made in a small workshop in Anacapri (see p166 **In the Know**).

For local cashmere, seek out **Farella** (Via Fuorlovado 21C, 081 837 5243, www.farella.it, closed Jan, Feb & Sun Oct-Dec, Mar), where four sisters make beautiful shawls, scarves and sweaters in a fabulous range of colours.

Another Capri speciality is limoncello, the potent lemon liqueur which has become the statutory Italian restaurant *digestivo* in the past decade or so. But beware: much of what is sold is mass-produced and synthetic. For an authentic, good quality limoncello, go to **Limoncello di Capri** (Via Roma 85, 081 837 5561, www.limoncello.com, closed Jan, Feb).

Giuseppe Faiella.

Perfume is a big-seller and the limited-production **Carthusia** perfumes – made locally according to old convent recipes – are lovely gifts to take home. Men's products are made with a base of rosemary from Monte Solaro, women's with wild carnation. Of the several shops on the island, the biggest is on Via Camerelle (no.10, 081 837 0529, www.carthusia.it, closed Jan, Feb).

And if you want to pick up the perfect trousers to go with your Capri sandals, visit **Laboratorio Capri** (Via Ignazio Cerio 6, 081 837 6296) to be measured for a bespoke pair.

exploring the artisan tradition that's still going strong on the island (*see above* **Savvy Souvenirs**).

For handbags and luggage made from famous Santacroce leather, no one does it better than Neapolitan masters **Tramontano** (Via Fuorlovado 1, 081 837 4401, www.tramontano.it, closed Nov-Mar); **Intimo Anna** (no.23) stocks lovely underwear and pyjamas.

There's a good *enoteca* and gourmet food shop run by the Capannina restaurant (*see p164*), **Capannina Più Gourmet** (Via le Botteghe 39-41, 081 837 8899, www.capannina-capri.com, closed Feb & Sun Oct-Apr).

Other shops specialise in antiques, ceramics and gifts. The wonderful **Sud Capri Gallery** (Via le Botteghe 4-6, 081 837 0165, closed Jan-Easter) sells household and decorative objects (glass, ceramics and so on), as well as clothes and accessories, all made in Italy. Visitors hankering after the older, loftier Capri of philosophers, poets and artists should visit **La Conchiglia**, a local publisher with 70 or so titles in its catalogue (a few of which are in English translation), all dealing

with the island's history or its literary denizens. Its main outpost (Via Camerelle 18, 081 837 8199, www.laconchigliacapri.com) has a wide array of second-hand books on Capri – many in English – and a good range of antique prints.

WHERE TO EAT

Capri has proud culinary traditions (faithfully recorded by Elizabeth David in the 1950s and '60s), but restaurants on the island tend to cater for the droves of day-trippers that invade daily (although standards have improved in recent years). Prices are high and menus at traditional restaurants tend to offer little more than the usual standards, such as ricotta- and herb-filled *ravioli capresi*, seafood pasta, and baked *pezzogna* (sea bream). These may all be delicious when prepared properly, but they can become monotonous – and often the only alternative is pizza.

Restaurants frequently charge a *coperto* (cover charge) as well as 15 per cent service; menus should clearly state this. It's best to avoid places

JK Place. See p167.

that serve all-day meals or have menus written in five languages, and always ask to see a menu with prices. If you're ordering fish, ask to see it and get an estimated price as they're often sold by weight. Most restaurants close for the winter, but many reopen for Christmas and New Year.

Aurora
Via Fuorlovado 18-22 (081 837 0181, www.aurora capri.com). **Open** noon-3pm, 7pm-midnight daily. Closed Nov-Mar. **Average** €80.
Still up there among the 'see-and-be-seen' restaurants in Capri after a century of business, Aurora is the celebs' hangout of choice. But this bright, modern space with its buzzy pavement terrace is delightfully unsnooty (although prices are steep). The chef creates beautifully presented dishes from a Neapolitan and *caprese* repertoire, such as spaghetti with clams or local *pezzogna* in a potato crust served with spinach. Pizzas with super-thin crusts are a speciality (and more affordable) and desserts are delicious. There's a great tome of a wine list with outrageous mark-ups.

La Capannina
Via le Botteghe 12B (081 837 0732, www. capanninacapri.com). **Open** mid Mar-Oct

noon-3.30pm, 7.15pm-midnight daily. Closed Nov-mid Mar. **Average** €65.
A top celebrity haunt since the 1930s (sightings these days are rather more thin on the ground), this traditional, family-run place is one of the best-known – and most consistent – restaurants on Capri. It delivers textbook renditions of the classics, so expect perfect *ravioli alla capresi, linguine allo scorfano* (linguine with scorpion fish, the house speciality) or a wicked *torta caprese*. The set lunch menus (€22, €28) are good value.

★ Da Paolino
Via Palazzo a Mare 11 (081 837 5611). **Open** 7.30pm-midnight daily. Closed Nov-Mar. **Average** €60.
Da Paolino, one of Capri's most popular restaurants, lies just above Marina Grande. Charmingly set in a lemon grove, it may be full of tourists, but there's good reason as the food is delicious. Dinner here starts with helping yourself at the groaning antipasto table before moving on to excellent pasta dishes such as penne with mozzarella and courgettes, as well as meat and fish dishes that are grilled to order. Room for dessert? Another laden table awaits. Book ahead.

E' Divino
Via Sella Orta 10A (081 837 8364, www.edivino capri.com). **Open** *July* 12.30-3pm, 8pm-1am daily. *Aug* 8pm-1am daily. *Sept-June* 12.30-3pm, 8pm-1am Tue-Sun. **Average** €40.

Hidden down an alleyway, E' Divino makes a quirky, friendly change from the Capri norm and is one of the few places to stay open out of season. It's done out to feel like a typical Capri dwelling: you can choose to eat sitting at a proper table, but it's more fun to perch on a sofa or armchair in one of several living rooms, surrounded by a collection of domestic clutter and potted palms. The menu is mainly meat-and veg-based.

Le Grottelle
Via Arco Naturale (081 837 5719). **Open** *Apr-June, Sept, Oct* noon-3pm, 7-11pm Mon, Wed-Sun. *July, Aug* noon-3pm, 7pm-midnight daily. Closed Nov-Mar. **Average** €45.

On the path leading to the Arco Naturale, half inside a cavern and half perched on a terrace overlooking a verdant slope and the sea, Le Grottelle is hard to beat – especially on a clear, moonlit night. The food is earthy and reliable, with *primi* such as pennette with rabbit sauce followed by roast chicken or, in the evenings, pizza. Finish with the best *torta caprese* (chocolate and almond cake) you're ever likely to taste. The local wines are especially good.

Mammà
Via Madre Serafina 6/11 (081 837 7472, www. ristorantemamma.com). **Open** *Apr-mid Oct* 12.30-3pm, 7.30-11pm daily. **Average** €80.

Expansive chef Gennaro Esposito opened his Capri outpost in 2013 in what was Gemma, Graham

---

IN THE KNOW ISLAND WINES

Grapes have been cultivated to make wine on Capri for almost 3,000 years, using indigenous varieties such as white greco, biancolella and falanghina, and red piedirosso. Vines are grown on steep terraces and picked by hand during late summer and autumn. The final results are becoming increasingly sophisticated and you can sample some of what's on offer at **Vinicola Tiberio** (Via Trieste e Trento 28, 081 837 1261, closed Sun).

IN THE KNOW PICK UP A PAIR OF ZABATTIGLI

Originally humble fishermen's shoes, **Zabattigli** are espadrille-style slip-ons that became popular as 'resort shoes' in the 1960s with film stars, artists and politicians. These rope-soled shoes, with canvas tops, have recently made a comeback and are once again made on the island in a small workshop in Anacapri using traditional methods. They don't come cheap (prices from €90), but they're very comfortable and stylish. Look out for them in the island's chicest shops (www.zabattigli. com). Can't make it to Capri? Try Barneys New York or the Conran Shop in London.

Greene's favourite island eatery. Less elaborate than what's on offer at his two Michelin-starred La Torre del Saracino on the mainland (see p216), the menus here feature local fish and vegetables, cooked to simple perfection and served beautifully in an elegant white-on-white room and terrace. The hand-rolled pasta dishes are particularly delicious, or you could try the unusual risotto of dried figs, pesto and *baccalà* (salt cod). Mammà Pizza (just across the alleyway) is a cheaper alternative.

Pulalli

Piazza Umberto I 4 (081 837 4108). **Open** 10am-3pm, 7pm-midnight Mon, Wed-Sun; 7pm-midnight Tue. Closed Nov-Easter. **Average** €40.
With a tiny terrace situated beneath the clock tower (prepare for noisy chimes), wine bar and restaurant Pulalli offers a hidden ringside perch for the goings-on in the *piazzetta*, plus delicious food and a great choice of Campanian wines. You can just eat a snack, but dishes such as *polpettine di melanzane* (deep-fried aubergine croquettes), citrusy salmon tartare, and a zingy *risotto al limone* served in a half lemon tempt you to go further. Booking is essential for a terrace table.

CAFÉS, BARS & GELATERIE

The island's social hub is the glamorous Piazzetta (Piazza Umberto I), its four bars staffed by elegant waiters in cream-coloured jackets. Although Capri isn't as exclusive as it used to be, almost everyone who's anyone has sipped a drink here.

The oldest of the four bars is the **Piccolo Bar** (081 837 0325) in the corner, open until 2am in high season. The locals' choice, it's good for people who like to watch rather than be watched, especially if you grab one of the tables by the window upstairs. Below the church, **Bar Tiberio** (081 837 0268, closed mid Jan-end Feb & Wed Dec-Feb) attracts a young crowd and visiting

Neapolitans; it has the best cakes and cocktail nibbles. The **Gran Caffè** (081 837 0388, closed Nov-mid Mar), the most elegant, is favoured by tourists; while **Bar Caso** (081 837 0600, closed Jan) serves good *granite* (crushed ice drinks) and is a popular gay haunt. Any one of them affords a perfect vantage point from which to watch the show unfold in what Norman Douglas called 'the world's little theatre'.

The locals have their morning coffee at **Bar Funicolare** (Piazza Diaz, 081 837 0363, closed Dec-Feb & Thur Mar, Apr), next to the cable car entrance. An alternative *aperitivo* spot to the Piazzetta (which some consider just too touristy), with a high people-watching quota, is the chic **Quisi Bar** (closed mid Oct-mid May), the terrace bar of the Grand Hotel Quisisana (see p167).

At **Buonocore** (Via Vittorio Emanuele 35, 081 837 6151, closed Nov-Mar & Tue, Apr-June), sample the famed *caprilù* lemon and almond cakes or the *torta caprese*. The homemade ice-cream is delicious, too, and is served in crisp, freshly made cones. The cool, tiled interior makes the perfect spot for coffee and cake, and the *rosticceria* counter has hot, ready-made dishes to eat in or take away.

Away from the centre, **Bar Lindos** (Via Matermania 2, 081 837 6493, closed Jan, Feb & Sun Oct-Dec, Mar, Apr) is a pleasant resting place en route to Villa Jovis. It's also opposite a supermarket – handy for picnic provisions.

NIGHTLIFE

Capri nightlife revolves around hotels, bars and restaurants. The Piazzetta stays open late and has a lively buzz; there are also a handful of discos and smooth club-bars where there might be some dancing on the tables. The most famous is Guido Lembo's charismatic, enduringly popular **Taverna Anema e Core** (Via Sella Orta 39E, 081 837 6461, www.anemaecore.com, closed Tue, Wed Easter-June, Sept, Oct & Nov-Mar). Opened in 2005, **Pantarei** (Via Lo Palazzo 1, 081 837 8898, www.pantareicapri.it, closed Nov-Mar & Tue in Apr-June, Sept-Oct) a club-cum-lounge bar, restaurant and spa, with plenty of space inside and out for mixing with the beautiful people. Admission is free except on Saturdays, when you'll pay €20.

Capri's cultural scene has quietened down considerably since the days when it was a hub for European intellectuals. Cinephiles have to rely on two cinemas: the **Auditorium** in Capri town and the **Apollo** in Anacapri, which both largely show dubbed foreign films. Modest exhibitions or performances are occasionally held in the **Certosa di San Giacomo** (see p162), the **Museo del Centro Caprense Ignazio Cerio** (see p162) or in upmarket hotels, mainly featuring local artists.

WHERE TO STAY

Capri overflows with chic, and often wildly expensive, hotels; bargains are hard to come by. However, there are a few relics of old Capri left: old-fashioned, family-run *pensioni* (although that category doesn't officially exist these days) that haven't yet succumbed to the temptation to smarten up and still manage to keep prices contained. There are some good new B&Bs too.

Booking well in advance is always a good idea. Check websites, too, as hotels often have special offers, especially in low season. Most close from November to mid March, though some reopen for a week or two over Christmas.

Deluxe

Capri Tiberio Palace

Via Croce 11-15 (081 978 7111, www.capritiberio palace.com). Closed mid Oct-Apr.

With playful, colourful interiors that hark back to the glamour years of the 1960s, the luxurious Capri Tiberio Palace is located at the bottom of the steep lane that leads up to Villa Jovis. Public rooms and the 46 bedrooms and suites are filled with an intriguing collection of vintage travel memorabilia: splash out on one of the terrace suites where the private, sea-facing terraces are as big as the rooms. There's an impressive indoor-outdoor pool, a Sodashi spa, the Terrazza Tiberio restaurant and a retro lounge bar for cocktails.

Grand Hotel Quisisana

Via Camerelle 2 (081 837 0788, www.quisisana. com). Closed Nov-mid Mar.

Set in five acres of gardens, this Capri institution began life in 1845 as a sanatorium (the name translates as 'Here one heals'), but soon transformed itself into the island's top hotel. Behind the cream-and-white neoclassical façade are two swimming pools (one indoor, one outdoor), a shady garden, a gym and a spa. Service is impeccable, but the decor can feel a little anonymous, and the size of the place may leave you cold. Many rooms have magnificent views over the Giardini di Augusto (*see p162*), and there's a good array of restaurants and bars on site. *Photos p158*.

▶ *Whether you're staying here or not, an aperitivo on the terrace of the Quisi Bar is a must (see p166).*

★ JK Place

Via Provinciale Marina Grande 225 (081 838 4001, www.jkcapri.com). Closed Nov-Mar.

Opened in 2007, JK Place is wonderfully stylish and the backdrop for many a fashion shoot. The white clifftop villa was designed by Michele Bönan, who has created a luxurious yet fun feel: think seaside elegance with fur-trimmed curtains and zebra-skin footstools. The lounge area, with a palette of cool greys and vases of lilies, has a library of arty books to peruse. Most bedrooms have views of Vesuvius and Naples, and the relaxing spa area overlooks a lovely infinity pool. Breakfast can be enjoyed on the terrace overlooking the sea and Marina Grande, and the restaurant (though not the pool) is open to the public. It's terribly glamorous, but the vibe is one of a home from home. Staff are exceptionally helpful. *Photos p164*.

Villa Marina Hotel & Spa

Via Provinciale, Marina Grande 191 (081 837 6630, www.villamarinacapri.com). Closed Nov-Mar.

On the road from Marina Grande to the Piazzetta, the five-star Villa Marina has 27 luxury rooms named after famous former visitors to Capri (Douglas, Malaparte, Marinetti, Munthe, Neruda et al). Each room is individually and extremely tastefully styled, perhaps with a mini library or stylish stone 'sharing' bath. Facilities include the on-site Stai spa, an infinity pool and a roof terrace with spectacular sea views. The charming staff couldn't be more helpful, and a shuttle bus transports guests to and from the port and the centre of town.

Expensive

Punta Tragara

Via Tragara 57 (081 837 0844, www.hotel tragara.it). Closed Nov-Mar.

Designed by Le Corbusier in the 1920s as a private villa, this deep pink hotel also served as US headquarters during World War II. It has one of the best views of any hotel on the island. The rooms, each with their own balcony overlooking the Faraglioni, are stylish and grand; the views are breathtaking; and the terrace bar, with its heated seawater pool, is a wonderful spot from which to watch the sun setting. Under-12s are not admitted.

Moderate

Luna

Via Matteotti 3 (081 837 0433, www.lunahotel.com). Closed Nov-mid Apr.

The view is the thing here. Although the Luna is soberly furnished in a slightly old-fashioned style, the cheerful colours of the common areas, peaceful setting and spectacular position overlooking the Certosa and the sea make up for any design shortcomings. The hotel is approached via a pretty walk, shaded by bougainvillea and surrounded by gardens, with an Olympic-size swimming pool and a restaurant (open for dinner only) on a rocky balcony above the sea.

★ La Minerva

Via Occhio Marino 8 (081 837 0374, www. laminervacapri.com). Closed mid Nov-mid Mar.

Away from the crowds, in a prime spot overlooking the sea, the Minerva is a delightfully traditional place with a loyal clientele. With five storeys of flower-filled terraces, charming original architectural detail and better views than its three-star peers, it's easy to see why. The superior rooms have terraces, and deluxe rooms have whirlpool bathtubs and

ESCAPES & EXCURSIONS

private sea-facing terraces. There's no pool, unfortunately, but you can pay to use facilities at one of the neighbouring hotels.

Villa Krupp
Viale Matteotti 12 (081 837 0362, www.villa krupp.com). **Closed** Nov-Mar.
Maxim Gorky used to live in the white house now occupied by the family-run Villa Krupp, and you can see why it appealed: perched above the Gardens of Augustus, the views are breathtaking. Inside, it's delightfully old-fashioned with clean, bright rooms, many of which have terraces with sea views: the terrace (where breakfast and drinks are served) shares the same vista. It's one of the best options in this price range, so book well ahead.

Budget

Hotel Quattro Stagioni Capri
Via Marina Piccola 1 (081 837 0041, www.hotel4stagionicapri.com).
This charming, family-run hotel sits on the bend of the road leading down from Capri to Marina Piccola, and offers the best of both worlds: guests can wander downhill to the beach or meander uphill towards the Piazzetta. There's also a bus stop nearby. Rooms are simple but comfortable, and there are sunny terraces to relax on. Book ahead.

La Tosca
Via Birago 5 (081 837 0989, www.latosca hotel.com). **Closed** mid Nov-mid Mar.
One-star La Tosca is an excellent choice for visitors on a budget. It's spotlessly clean, uncluttered and stylish, and is centrally located in a quiet lane leading down to the Certosa. The 11 bedrooms (many of which have balconies) are large and airy, and continental breakfast is served on a terrace overlooking the sea. Staff are friendly, attentive and very helpful when it comes to making arrangements. This place is very popular, so book well ahead.

RESOURCES

First aid
Guardia Medica *Piazza Umberto I (081 838 1239).* **Open** 24hrs daily.
In a medical emergency, the Guardia Medica will arrange transport to the mainland.

IN THE KNOW GETTING IT RIGHT

If you want to earn street cred on Capri, begin by getting the name right. The correct pronunciation is Ca-pri and not Ca-pree (with the emphasis on the first syllable); practise at home and use liberally once you're there. The locals will love you for it.

Internet
Capri Tech Internet Corner *Bar Gabbiano, Via Cristoforo Colombo 76 (081 837 6531).*

Police
Carabinieri *Via Provinciale Marina Grande 42 (081 837 0000).*

Post office
Via Roma 50 (081 978 5211).

Tourist information
Azienda Autonoma di Cura, Soggiorno e Turismo *Piazzetta Cerio 11, Marina Grande (081 837 0634, www.capritourism.com).* **Open** June- Oct 9am-7pm daily. *Nov-May* 9am-1.30pm, 3-6pm Mon-Sat.
Azienda Autonoma di Cura, Soggiorno e Turismo *Piazza Umberto I (081 837 0686).* **Open** June-Oct 9am-7pm daily. *Nov-May* 9am-1.30pm, 3-6pm Mon-Sat.

Anacapri & Around

Incredibly for such a small island, the first road linking Capri town and Anacapri was only built in 1872. Until then, the two villages led different lives on the opposite sides of the seismic fracture and wall of cliffs that split the island in two.

Set on the cliff's western side at the base of Monte Solaro, the loose-knit cluster of houses that forms Anacapri is interspersed by olive groves and vineyards. A community of farmers and artisans began to form here in Greek times, but only really condensed into a proper village in the late Middle Ages. Anacapri's rural way of life and centuries of physical isolation are reflected in the proud, feisty character of the *anacapresi*, who preferred to work as ships' caulkers for the king of Naples than have anything to do with the *capresi* down below.

The only means of communication between the two villages was the **Scala Fenicia**, a steep flight of around 900 steps built by Capri's first Greek settlers. Still in existence, it leads up from Marina Grande (the island's only proper port, which the *anacapresi* were forced to use even though it was in 'enemy territory') to the tiny chapel of Sant'Antonio, just below Villa San Michele.

When Swedish doctor Axel Munthe first walked up here in the late 19th century, overtaking the village postwoman (who couldn't read), the hostess of Anacapri's one and only inn told him that she had 'once been down to Capri', but it hadn't impressed her much. If rural Anacapri today receives as many visitors as swish Capri town, it's largely thanks to Munthe. His book, *The Story of San Michele*, filled chilly northerners with longing for the 'warm south', bringing the rustic characters of Anacapri vividly to life. Translated into over 30 languages,

ESCAPES & EXCURSIONS

Villa San Michele. *See p171.*

Munthe's memoir continues to sell steadily around the world, more than seven decades after its publication in 1929.

Munthe first set foot on Anacapri in 1874 as a young medical student. It wasn't until 15 years later, when he had become the youngest and most sought-after society doctor in Paris, that he was able to realise his dream of building the clifftop **Villa San Michele**, on the site of one of Tiberius's villas and a medieval chapel. Designed in an eclectic style that mixes Romanesque and Renaissance influences with Moorish trills, the villa and its trim gardens are studded with fragments of classical statuary.

The ruined **Castello di Barbarossa** on the crest above, named after the Greek pirate who destroyed it, is part of the same property; it can be visited on a free guided tour on Thursdays at 5pm (Apr-Oct; places are limited, book a day ahead). The hillside also has a resident population of peregrine falcons; weekend guided tours are organised in spring and autumn (call Villa San Michele for details).

Munthe was the first of a steady trickle of foreign residents who preferred Anacapri's quiet charm to the more glitzy delights of Capri town: writers Compton Mackenzie and Graham Greene had houses here, and Queen Victoria of Sweden had a summer villa at Caprile, just south of the town. Today, the peace and quiet that attracted these escapees is challenged by the busloads of tourists that come to visit Villa San Michele and offload their euros in a slough of tacky souvenir shops. But away from this thankfully limited

outbreak of bad taste, and out of season, Anacapri is an idyllic place in which to see the island's more rural side.

Gateway to the town, and the setting-down point for the buses that connect Anacapri with Marina Grande and Capri town, is little Piazza Vittoria. Most visitors head straight along souvenir-lined Via Capodimonte to Villa San Michele. From the square, the pedestrianised Via Giuseppe Orlandi leads west past the tourist office into the centre of the old town. Halfway down on the right is the **Casa Rossa**, an antiquity-encrusted folly built in 1876 by a former Confederate soldier, JC MacKowen, who wrote one of the first travel guides to the island.

On the left, Via San Nicola leads to Piazza San Nicola, dominated by the church of **San Michele Arcangelo**. Continue down Via Giuseppe Orlandi, past the quaint church of Santa Sofia constructed in 1510 (look out for the carved Pietà) and you reach the pretty district of Le Boffe; with its pavilion-like, round-roofed arches, it's the oldest part of town.

Also worth a visit is the **Parco Filosofico**, on the way to Migliera. You can meander through this 'Philosopher's Park', set up in 2000 by Swedish intellectual Gunnar Adler-Karlsson and his wife, and peruse some 60 quotations by Western philosophers, written in English and Italian on little ceramic tiles.

From Anacapri, two bus routes run west (*see p174*). One goes down to the Blue Grotto (*see p162*), via the remains of **Villa Damecuta** (ask the bus driver to drop you off by the side

SCENIC SPLENDOUR

This most glamorous of islands is also a walkers' paradise.

Capri is home to a network of idyllic footpaths that weave among towering cliffs and past whitewashed villas, all to a background of blue. The following are at their best in spring and autumn. Suitable footwear, suncream, a decent hat and plenty of water are essentials.

ANACAPRI TO THE BLUE GROTTO
Time 1hr. **Grade** easy.
In the cooler seasons, one of the best ways to visit the **Blue Grotto** (see p162) from Anacapri is to walk down to the jetty from where the rowing boats depart and take the bus back. From Piazza Armando Diaz in Anacapri, Via Cava and Via Lo Pozzo lead down to a path that continues past orchards and farms to the parking lot above the Blue Grotto, which is also the bus terminus. Stop for a picnic en route at the **Villa Damecuta** (see p169).

ANACAPRI TO MIGLIERA
Time 45mins. **Grade** easy.
Another good walk from Anacapri is the flat, contour-hugging stroll to Migliera.

Faraglioni islands.

Take Via Caposcuro, to the left of the **Monte Solaro** chairlift (see p171), and continue along it for a couple of kilometres (it soon changes its name to Via Migliera), walking through a landscape that's about as rural as you get on Capri. Stop off for an excellent lunch and a swim at **Da Gelsomina alla Migliera** (see p171). At the end of the path, the Belvedere di Migliera offers spectacular views over the cliffs below Monte Solaro.

I FARAGLIONI, GROTTA MATERMANIA & THE ARCO NATURALE
Time 1hr. **Grade** easy, but a stiff climb; the opposite way round is easier. After the stroll up to **Villa Jovis** (see p162), this classic round trip is easily the best of the paved walks that depart from Capri town. From the **Belvedere di Tragara** (see p162), take either of the stepped paths that head downwards. After a steep turn-off down to the right to the Faraglioni (where there's a small, rocky beach platform), the path continues east around the wooded slopes of Monte Tuoro, with views over the rocky coast and **Villa Malaparte** (see p158).

Soon after the villa, the path turns into a flight of steps that leads up to the **Grotta Matermania**; it's said that the huge cavern was sacred to the cult of Cybele (the Great Mother). The steps continue up to a junction by bar-restaurant **Le Grottelle** (see p165). Turn right here, and in a few minutes you'll see the steps leading to **Arco Naturale**, a limestone arch that was a favourite with Romantic travellers. To head back to Capri town, carry on straight past Le Grottelle along Via Matermania. Before you know it, you're back in the Piazzetta.

FORTRESS WALK
Time 3hrs each way. **Grade** easy.
A marked footpath, dubbed Il Sentiero dei Fortini, has been laid out along the lovely, little-visited west coast of the island: it connects **Punta Carena** and its impressive lighthouse with **Punta dell'Arcera**, not far from the Blue Grotto. You walk past five ruined Napoleonic forts and towers. Bring your swimming gear, as some of the coves along the way are hard to resist. The path tends to be too high to allow easy access to the sea, but there's a small set of steps into the water near the **Punta Campetiello**.

road to the villa). One of Tiberius's 12 imperial villas, it was devastated first by volcanic rain from Vesuvius, then by pillaging troops. Little remains today, but it's a pretty spot for a picnic and is covered in wild flowers in spring. The second bus goes to the lighthouse at Punta Carena, on Capri's south-western tip. Just before the lighthouse is one of the island's less crowded rocky beaches (to be avoided when the wind is blowing in from the west).

For walks from Anacapri, *see p170* **Scenic Splendour**. An easy alternative to hiking up Monte Solaro is to take the *funivia* (funicular) from the station on Via Caposcuro (081 837 1438, www.seggioviamontesolaro.it, open Mar, Apr 9.30am-4pm daily, May-Oct 9.30am-5pm daily, Nov-Feb 9.30am-3.30pm daily). The journey takes 12 minutes and costs €7.50 single, €10 return.

Casa Rossa

Via Giuseppe Orlandi 78 (081 838 2193). **Open** *Apr, May* 10am-5pm Tue-Sun. *June-Sept* 10.30am-1.30pm, 5.30-8pm Tue-Sun. *Oct* 10am-4pm Tue-Sun. **Admission** €3.50. **No credit cards.**
Painted a striking shade of red, the crenellated former home of 19th-century American expat John MacKowen houses a permanent exhibition of landscapes, painted by various artists.

FREE Parco Filosofico

Via Migliera (081 837 1499, www.philosophical park.org). **Open** 9am-1hr before sunset daily. **Admission** free.
Inside the Philosophical Park, meandering paths lead past quotations from great thinkers, inscribed on majolica tiles. It's a peaceful, meditative place.
▶ *Superb restaurant Da Gelsomina alla Migliera (see right) is opposite the park.*

San Michele Arcangelo

Piazza San Nicola (081 837 2396). **Open** *Apr-Sept* 9am-6.45pm daily. *Oct-Mar* 10am-3pm daily. **Admission** €3. **No credit cards.**
Beyond a standard Baroque façade lies an unusual Greek cross nave, enlivened by a delightful octagonal majolica floor dating from 1761. The theme is Eden, complete with Adam and Eve frolicking among ostriches, camels and crocodiles, as well as a few mythical creatures.

Villa San Michele

Viale Axel Munthe 34 (081 837 1401, www.villa sanmichele.eu). **Open** *Mar* 9am-4.30pm daily. *Apr, Oct* 9am-5pm daily. *May-Sept* 9am-6pm daily. *Nov-Feb* 9am-3.30pm daily. **Admission** €7. **No credit cards.**
There might be the odd visitor who tends to agree with writer Bruce Chatwin, who concluded in his Munthe-debunking essay 'Self-love among the Ruins' (reprinted in *Anatomy of Restlessness*) that Munthe's creation wouldn't get more than a passing glance in

Pasadena or Beverly Hills. Still, the views are spectacular, and the villa and gardens are preserved with Nordic tidiness by a foundation whose members are nominated by the Swedish state. Look out for the small Egyptian sphinx that gazes out to sea, which dates from the 11th century BC. It appears on countless postcards and posters. *Photo p169.*

WHERE TO EAT

As usual, avoid anywhere offering a €10 menu for a plate of pasta with salad and a drink or a multilingual menu. For an excellent, traditional breakfast of cappuccino, brioches and sweet croissants straight from the oven, head to **Bar-Pasticceria Ferraro** (Via Orlando 233, 081 837 1216, closed Jan-mid Mar & Wed Oct-May). For a satisfying pizza, try **La Rondinella** (Via Orlandi 245, 081 837 1223, closed Thur & Nov-Mar).

★ Da Gelsomina alla Migliera

Via Migliera 72 (081 837 1499, www.dagelsomina. com). **Open** *Mar, Apr, Oct-Dec* 11.30am-3.30pm Mon, Wed-Sun. *May-Sept* 11.30am-3.30pm, 7-11pm daily. Closed Jan, Feb. **Average** €45.
Far from the madding crowd, this little oasis nestles on terraced farmland among vines and neat rows of vegetables just above Anacapri: the views are stunning and the food lives up to the scenic location. The menu revolves around local classics such as pasta with prawns and asparagus or rosemary-spiked rabbit stew. The homemade *falanghina* is a perfect acompaniment and the tiramisu is superb. It's perfect for a day out with the kids, as it also has a swimming pool and there are seven rooms for rent. Anacapri is half an hour's walk away, but free transfers can be arranged if you call ahead.

L'Olivo

Capri Palace Hotel, Via Capodimonte 2B (081 978 0111, www.capri-palace.com). **Open** 12.30-2.30pm, 7.30-10.30pm daily. Closed Nov-Mar. **Average** €150.

IN THE KNOW SWIMMING IN THE BLUE GROTTO

While most people visit the Blue Grotto on an official tour and in the company of many others, there's an alternative from Anacapri. Pick a calm evening and make your way down the Via Grotta Azzurra to the jetty at the bottom (the pick-up point for scheduled visits). If you wait until after 7pm when the tourist boats knock off, you can quite easily swim into the cave. Only then will the full force of that fluorescent blue hit home, which Neapolitan writer Raffaele La Capria described as 'more blue than any other, blue below and blue above and blue along each curve of its vault'.

Set within one of the island's most prestigious hotels, L'Olivo features impeccable decor (note the cashmere-covered sofas), service and cuisine, plus a delightful terrace overlooking the vast swimming pool. Original chef Oliver Glowig has moved on and today the restaurant is in the highly capable hands of Ischian Andrea Migliaccio, who has been awarded two Michelin stars for his light-handed, creative take on the local cuisine. Expect the likes of *paccheri* pasta with scorpion fish (*scorfano*), sweet green peppers and burrata or roast suckling pig with apricot jelly and lemon-scented fennel cream. The selection of amuse-bouches, home-made breads and petits fours are extraordinary, and the wine list is one of the island's best.

Il Riccio

Via Gradola 4-6 (081 837 1380, www.capri palace.com). **Open** 12.30-3.15pm Mon-Wed; 12.30-3.15pm, 7.30-10.15pm Thur-Sun. Closed Nov-Mar. **Average** €70.

If you're looking for a long, lazy (and very delicious) lunch with a view, head for Il Riccio, which is perched on a cliff near the Blue Grotto and is now owned by the Capri Palace Hotel (*see p173*). Delightfully informal in spite of its Michelin star, it serves wonderfully fresh Bay of Naples fish and seafood dishes (*paccheri* with squid, artichokes and mint, for example) under a wide pergola right over the water. Make sure you leave room for dessert, which is a dangerous, help-yourself affair laid out in the *Stanza degli Tentazioni* (Room of Temptation). For post-lunch snoozes, there are sunbathing platforms carved out of the rock.

NIGHTLIFE, ARTS & ENTERTAINMENT

One of the classic spots on the island for a sundowner is the scenic **Lido del Faro** (Via Punta Carena, 081 837 1798, www.lidofaro.com, closed Nov-Mar; *see p160* **Going Swimmingly**),

Blue Grotto. *See p162.*

which is also home to a decent restaurant. Visitors who want to feel like royalty should try the elegant (and expensive) **Bar degli Artisti**, with its contemporary artworks, in the Capri Palace (*see below*). There are a handful of bars where you can listen to live music: **Club La Lanterna Verde** (Via Giuseppe Orlandi 1, 081 837 1427) is open all year round or try the piano bar of the **Capri Palace Hotel** (*see below*). The **Red Lounge** (Via Giuseppe Orlandi 259, 081 837 3605) is about the only clubby option.

In summer, Anacapri hosts loads of free events – dodgy Italian pop, classical and jazz, outdoor cinema. Ask at the tourist office (*see p174*) for the programme. Villa San Michele (*see p171*) also stages classical recitals and theatre.

WHERE TO STAY

Da Gelsomina alla Migliera (*see p170*) also has rooms for rent (from €115).

Deluxe

Capri Palace Hotel & Spa

Via Capodimonte 2B (081 978 0111, www.capri-palace.com). Closed Nov-Mar.
Perched 300m (984ft) above the sea, the elegant Capri Palace has tailored every detail to chic yet unstuffy perfection. Its cool, cream-hued public rooms and hallways, tastefully decorated rooms, and lovely pool and spa are glamorous yet understated. The catering is equally impressive: there's an unforgettable breakfast buffet, several restaurants (including the superb L'Olivo) and a cool cocktail bar, Bar degli Artisti. Owner Tonino Cacace has filled the hotel with his collection of modern and contemporary art that includes paintings by De Chirico. The bedrooms range from entry-level (but supremely comfortable) doubles to 'art suites', rooms with private pools, a series of pristine blue-and-white Capritouch suites or the presidential Paltrow suite (a mere €8,800 per night) with private roof garden and panoramic pool dedicated to a favourite regular VIP guest. The renowned spa is one of the best in Italy and there are three boats for private use.

Expensive

Caesar Augustus

Via Giuseppe Orlandi 4 (081 837 3395, www.caesar-augustus.com). Closed Nov-Mar.
Transformed into a hotel more than 60 years ago, this luxurious villa is set 300m (1,000ft) above the sea, on a cliff looking out over the Bay of Naples and Marina Piccola. It capitalises on its magnificent setting with a two-tiered infinity pool. The fragrant garden and terraces, and many of the bedrooms, have the same stupendous view. The modern rooms have antique furniture, king-size beds, tiled floors, marble bathrooms and balconies; some also have jacuzzis and private terraces high above the sea.

ESCAPES & EXCURSIONS

Moderate

Capri Suite
Via Finestrale 9 (338 933 1961, 366 368 3927, www.caprisuite.it). Closed Nov-Mar.
A refreshing departure from the traditional Capri norm, this stylish, shabby-chic B&B occupies part of the ex-convent of San Michele complete with faded frescoes and vaulted ceilings. Furnished with a funky mix of vintage and design pieces, and with a deliciously fresh white, blue and yellow colour palette, the two quiet suites share a courtyard, sitting room and kitchen, so this could be a good choice for a longer stay. The deluxe Blue Room has a sunken tub and fireplace in the room plus a vast bathroom with double shower.

Hotel San Michele
Via Giuseppe Orlandi 1/3/5 (081 837 1427, www.sanmichele-capri.com). Closed Nov-Mar.
This large, rose-coloured hotel has the island's biggest swimming pool and is a popular choice for families (it even offers swimming lessons). The decor is comfortable and old-fashioned, and service is friendly. Rooms have views over to Monte Solaro or of the sea, and some have sizeable sun terraces.

Budget

★ Casa Bove
III Traversa Tuoro 9 (081 837 1228, www.casabove.it). Closed Nov-1 wk before Easter.
Occupying a typical, pristine white *caprese* house set in a bucolic garden with magnificent views, this three-room B&B ensures a welcoming home-from-home atmosphere. Gigi is a delightful host, greeting guests as friends and offering warm pastries from a local bakery for breakfast and trips in his sailing boat.

Villa Eva
Via Grotta Azzurra, trav. Via La Fabbrica 8 (081 837 1549, www.villaeva.com). Closed Nov-Feb.
Located on the route from Anacapri to the Blue Grotto, the villa is set in a forest, with fantasy architecture, a stunning garden and a lovely pool. The rooms are spacious and have appealing little patios overlooking the garden. Villa Eva has a deal with a nearby restaurant, and is within walking distance of the swimming platforms near the Blue Grotto and Villa Damecuta (see p169).

Resources

First aid
Guardia Medica *Via Caprile 30 (081 838 1240).*

Internet
Capri Tech Internet Corner *Bar Due Pini, Piazza Vittoria 3 (081 837 1404).*

Police
Carabinieri *Via Caprile (081 837 1011).*

Post office
Viale de Tommaso 8 (081 837 1015).

Tourist information
Azienda Autonoma di Cura, Soggiorno e Turismo
Via Giuseppe Orlandi 59 (081 837 1524, www.capritourism.com). **Open** June-mid Sept 9am-3pm daily. Mid Sept-May 9am-3pm Mon-Sat.

GETTING AROUND

Capri town is closed to all forms of motorised traffic beyond the bus terminus on Via Roma (except for little luggage-bearing electric trolleys, which are also licensed to carry people with disabilities). If you're staying in an upmarket hotel, you should be met at the quay by a porter who'll have your luggage sent up to the hotel. Most of the swankier hotels in Anacapri, and some of the mid-range ones, have their own minibus. Otherwise, the funicular, buses and taxis are all at the end of the quay.

All public transport on the island – including the funicular from Marina Grande to Capri town, but not the Monte Solaro cable car – is covered by the Unico Capri ticket, which comes in three versions: €1.80 for a single trip, €2.70 for an hour on the whole network (allowing you to change at Anacapri for the Blue Grotto, for example) or €8.60 for a day pass. Tickets should be bought from the terminus and shown to the driver on boarding. If you get on at an intermediate stop, tickets can be bought from the driver.

By boat

For the **Blue Grotto** (see p162), you can either take a speedboat from Marina Grande (€14) or take the bus from Anacapri and pick up a small rowing boat at the jetty. A complete circuit of the island (giro dell'isola) is also offered by a number of operators, including **Lasercapri** (081 837 5208, www.lasercapri.com, €18) and **Gruppo Motoscafisti** (081 837 5646, www.motoscafisti capri.com, €18) in Marina Grande.

You can also rent small motorboats from Marina Grande or Marina Piccola (no licence required). Try **Capritime** (329 214 9811, www.capritime.com) for boat hire or trips in a typical Capri boat (gozzo) or a luxury speedboat or yacht. Prices start at €185 for an afternoon on a boat (including captain, fuel and light snacks) accommodating up to six people.

By bus

In high season, be prepared to queue – especially if you get on at the Piazza Roma bus terminus or in Anacapri. The three main services are Marina Grande–Capri (6am-midnight; 6am-2am July-Sept), Marina Grande–Anacapri (6am-7pm; until

10pm to connect with Caremar boats) and Capri–Anacapri (6am-2am). Other routes, with less frequent services, are Capri–Marina Piccola, Capri–Damecuta, Anacapri–Grotta Azzurra (Blue Grotto) and Anacapri–Punta Carena (Faro). Call **ATC** (081 837 6302) for information, or **Staiano Autotrasporti** (081 837 2422, www.staianotourcapri.com) for the Blue Grotto and Punta Carena lines.

By funicular railway

Departures from the station at Marina Grande to Capri town (and vice versa) run every 15mins (6.30am-8.30pm Jan-June, 16 Sept-Dec; 6.30am-11pm July-15 Sept) and are run by **SIPPIC** (081 837 0420); a return trip costs €3.60.

It can get crowded in high season, especially in the early evening when the day-trippers leave; if you need to get to Marina Grande quickly, take the bus or walk (it takes 15-20mins via the path that starts next to the funicular entrance).

By scooter

Given the traffic restrictions and congestion on Capri's narrow roads, scooters aren't necessarily the best way to get around during the high season. Out of season, it's a different story. Try **Noleggio Motorini** (Via Marina Grande 280, 081 837 7941, €50/day, €15/hr) by the port, or on **Piazza Barile** in Anacapri (no.26, 081 837 3888, €55/day, €15/hr).

By taxi

Capri's seven-seat, open-top taxis are unique to the island. Although expensive, there's something innately glamorous about bounding along in one of these vehicles, so try and budget for at least one ride. Allow €17 from the port to Capri town (they can go no further than the taxi rank by the bus terminus in Via Roma) or €23 to Anacapri. Both rates include one suitcase; an extra case costs a flat €5. There are only a couple of vintage cars that serve as taxis left on the island, but they can be booked. There are two taxi companies on the island, in **Capri** (081 837 6657) and **Anacapri** (081 837 1175). You can hail a cab, call or go to the ranks.

GETTING THERE

Naples newspaper *Il Mattino* publishes daily updated timetables of all bus, train, sea and air connections to and from Naples. On Capri, the tourist offices give out a free timetable, updated fortnightly, with sea crossings; these are also posted on the Capri tourist board website (www.capritourism.com). The services mentioned below run daily. *See also p290.*

By helicopter

Anyone really pressed for time can take a helicopter from Capodichino airport in Naples to the heliport at Anacapri; prices start from €1,850 per one-way flight for up to four people. The flight takes about 17mins. Contact **Sam Helicopters** (082 835 4155, 800 915012, www.flywithsam.it).

By sea from the Amalfi Coast

Alicost (089 871483, www.alicost.com) runs ferries and hydrofoils from just before Easter to the end of October between Salerno, Amalfi, Positano and Capri. From Positano, the journey time is 45mins; fares start at €17.70 (Capri–Positano).

By sea from Ischia

Services run all year round, but are most frequent from mid April to mid October. There are four hydrofoils daily. One is run by **Alilauro** (081 991888, 081 497 2238, www.alilauro.it); the other is run by local companies **Rumore Marittima** (www.rumoremarittima.it) and **Capitan Morgan** (081 985080, www.capitanmorgan.it). From mid June to mid September, Alicost also runs connections from Ischia. Fares start at €18.30.

By sea from Naples

NLG Linea Jet (081 837 0819, 081 552 0763, www.navlib.it) and **SNAV** (081 428 5555, www.snav.it) run hydrofoils (hourly in summer) from the central quay of Molo Beverello. Crossing time is around 40mins. **Caremar** (081 837 0700, www.caremar.it) also runs six daily ferries from Beverello all year round, with an extra fast service in high summer. Three are high-speed *traghetti veloci* (60mins); the others take 80mins. Ferries are cheaper, and the only option when the sea is too choppy for the hydrofoils. The last boats leave around 7.30pm (winter) or 9.30pm (summer). Ferries cost €11.20, hydrofoils and fast ferries €16.30-€19 one-way.

By sea from Sorrento

Caremar (*see above*) and **Gescab** (081 428 5555, 081 428 5259, www.gescab.it) *navi veloci* and hydrofoils leave from Sorrento's Marina Piccola for the 25min crossing to Capri (at least half-hourly in summer). There are also less frequent conventional ferries. *Navi veloci* cost €13.20, hydrofoils €15.60-16.80.

By water taxi

Water taxis are operated by **Capri Sea Service** (081 837 8781, www.capriseaservice.com). A private taxi (six people max) from Naples to Capri costs €850; Sorrento to Capri is €650.

Ischia

Legend has it that Typhon, creator of volcanoes, was exiled here and that his struggles to escape from prison (with lots of wailing and sighing) resulted in all the earth's rumblings and hissings that are still so evident. The curative qualities of Ischia's thermal waters first came to the attention of the Romans, but droves of middle-aged Northern Europeans still come to the island today to wallow and the spa industry is flourishing. While this means that too many hotels, restaurants and souvenir shops are geared up to cater for middle-of-the-road tourism, the island also has secret charms (and a life beyond the tourists) that will become evident if you're prepared to stay for a bit; a verdant interior with vineyards and exotic gardens, unspoilt villages, some wonderful hidden restaurants, good out-of-the-way beaches and a spectacularly positioned castle. Like Capri, Ischia has attracted its fair share of high-profile residents over the years; Henrik Ibsen wrote *Peer Gynt* here, WH Auden spent nearly ten years on the island, and English composer William Walton settled in the late 1940s and, with his wife, created the fabulous garden at La Mortella near Forio.

INTRODUCING THE ISLAND

Although the Greeks were the first to arrive on the island, during the eighth century BC, it was under the Romans that Ischia became famous for its thermal waters. Throughout its history, various parts of the island (which is really a complex volcano) have opened up, unleashing devastating lava flows. In 1301, lava inundated the area between what is now Ischia Porto and Ischia Ponte, forcing its inhabitants to flee to Baia on the mainland. When they returned, they crowded on to the **Castello Aragonese** (*see p178*), a fortified rocky outcrop off Ischia Ponte. The Castello was hotly fought over by the Angevins and Aragonese in the 14th century, and remained a place of refuge from marauding Saracens, who first attacked Ischia in the Middle Ages and continued to menace the island until as late as 1796.

When Ischia supported the Parthenopean Republic in 1799, King Ferdinando's British allies soon overran the place. The British had more trouble ousting the French, who occupied Ischia in 1806; the devastation that the British, under Nelson, wreaked in their bombardment of the Castello Aragonese can still be seen.

These days, the island that was once so desperately coveted by the Saracens is again being overrun, this time with luggage-toting visitors and island-hopping yachters, here to sample its relaxing spas, delightful beaches and crystal clear waters.

Note that Ischia's churches tend to open to the public at the discretion of their priests, but most can be visited from around 7am to 11am or noon, and in the late afternoon (5-6pm to 7-8pm). You can always get in immediately before or after Mass (times are posted on the door).

ISCHIA PORTO & ISCHIA PONTE

Once two separate towns, **Ischia Porto** and **Ischia Ponte** (formerly called Villa dei Bagni and Borgo Celsa, respectively) stretch from the ferry port to Castello Aragonese, linked by a busy, tree-lined road. Colourful Porto is one long hotel- and shop-filled agglomeration, whereas Ponte maintains some of its sleepy fishing village charm.

The swift and complex manoeuvring of ferries and hydrofoils in the little port can distract you from the uniqueness of the harbour itself. Until 1854, this was an inland lake in an extinct volcanic crater. But when the island fell under Spanish control, King Ferdinando II was sickened by the smell of its brackish waters and demanded that an opening be made to the sea. Be prepared for traffic jams blocking access to the ferries on busy weekends, during bank holidays and throughout the whole of August.

Overlooking the port, the church of **Santa Maria di Portosalvo**, also built in 1854, was another of Ferdinando's good works. East of the church, the former royal palace is now a military spa, of all things, its gateposts guarded by imposing lions. Across the road, another old spa, the **Antiche Terme Comunali**, now houses government offices and hosts occasional (often mediocre) art exhibitions.

Over on the eastern shore of the port, Via Porto leads past restaurants and bars out to the point at **Punta San Pietro**, dominated by a dark-red underwater research station (closed to the public).

Ischia's (theoretically) pedestrianised main drag, Via Roma, which becomes Corso Vittoria Colonna, is usually packed. Lanes running north of Via Roma lead to the main beach, **Spiaggia del Lido**. Where Corso Colonna meets Via Gigante, you'll find the church of **San Pietro** (also known as Madonna delle Grazie in San Pietro), a Baroque extravaganza with a curving façade.

Just beyond the junction with Via d'Avalos, a gate off the main road leads to the slightly unkempt but beautifully shady gardens of the **Villa Nenzi Bozzi** (open 6.30am-7.30pm daily). Looking uphill from here, the stone pines – those that haven't been sacrificed to creeping construction – are all that remain of the woods planted in the mid 19th century on the great lava flow from Monte Arso; beneath them lies the entire village of Geronda, which was buried in the devastating eruption of 1301. The little chapel of **San Girolamo** (venerated for its splendid painting of the Madonna della Pace) commemorates the disaster.

The eastern end of Corso Colonna, and Via Pontano, run along the dark sands of **Spiaggia dei Pescatori**, where fishing boats pull up among the sunbathers; from here, there's an unimpeded view across to the Castello. At the top of the steps off Corso Colonna, the church

of **Sant'Antonio in Santa Maria delle Grazie** (or Sant'Antonio a Mandra) was built in the 18th century to replace the 14th-century original cut down by Arso's lava flow. Inside are the remains of San Giovanni Giuseppe della Croce, the island's patron saint.

At Via Seminario 26 is the **Palazzo del Vescovado** (the Bishop's Palace). It houses the **Museo Civico** (081 991706, open 10am-noon Mon, Wed, Fri), where early Christian relics and other historic objects are on display. Opposite, Vicolo Marina leads to the 16th-century **Palazzo Malcoviti**; stark and forbidding as you approach, the palazzo hides a pretty flower-filled courtyard behind.

On Via Mazzella, the 17th-century church of **Santo Spirito** (also known as San Giovanni Giuseppe) has a fine 18th-century marble altar. Across the road from here, the **Cattedrale dell'Assunta** (or Santa Maria della Scala) became Ischia's cathedral after its predecessor in the Castello Aragonese was bombarded by the Royal Navy in 1809. The original 12th-century church was replaced in the 17th and 18th centuries, but the 14th-century baptismal font survived, as did the Romanesque wooden crucifix and a 14th-century painting of the Madonna in the right-hand end of the nave.

The building facing the cathedral, Palazzo dell'Orologio, is home to the engaging **Museo del Mare** (*see p178*), where nets, tackle, photographs, stamps and a few posters of films shot on the island chart Ischia's relationship with the sea. Via Mazzella continues to the lovely 1432 **Ponte Aragonese** bridge, and then on to the Castello Aragonese.

The rocky outcrop on which the **Castello Aragonese** sits was fortified in the fifth century BC by Greeks from Syracuse in Sicily. Since then it has been used as a stronghold by Romans, Goths, Arabs and just about every other group that ruled, or tried to rule, Naples. When Monte Arso erupted in 1301, it was within the thick walls of the castle that the locals sought protection.

Alfonso of Aragon fortified the crumbling rock in the mid 15th century, adding the bridge and turning the Castello into an impregnable fortress where the island's inhabitants could take refuge during Saracen attacks. Over the centuries, its influence waxed and waned, leaving a rich historical legacy for visitors to explore.

There's a lift up to the castle's higher levels but, if you're feeling energetic, take the magnificent tunnel hewn through the solid rock by King Alfonso. Paths to the Castello's various churches, exhibition spaces and viewpoints are clearly signposted. Although it's now a tourist draw, the Castello is privately owned and the former ruler's residence at the top of the building is closed to the public. You can, however, stay in the wonderful **Monastero** hotel (*see p180*) at the top.

Giardino Eden.

Around the Bay of Cartaromana, the 16th-century chapel of **Sant'Anna** overlooks rocks thrusting out of the sea. The annual Feast of Sant'Anna (26 July) sees brightly decorated fishing boats and rafts competing for a trophy in the bay, followed by a spectacular fireworks display. Nearby, the square **Torre Michelangelo** may or may not be where the Renaissance genius stayed when attending Vittoria Colonna's court (*see p186*).

★ Castello Aragonese

Via Pontile Aragonese (081 992834, www. castelloaragonese.it). **Open** 9am-sunset daily. **Admission** €10; €6 reductions. **No credit cards**. *See p186* **Castello Aragonese**.

Museo del Mare

Palazzo dell'Orologio, Via Luigi Mazzella 7 (081 981124, www.museodelmareischia.it). **Open** *Apr-June* 10.30am-12.30pm, 3-7pm Tue-Sun; *July, Aug* 10.30am-12.30pm, 7-11pm Tue-Sun. *Sept-Mar* 10.30am-12.30pm Tue-Sun. Closed Feb. **Admission** €2.50. **No credit cards**.

Where to eat & drink

★ Un Attimo DiVino

Via Porto 103 (081 1952 8411). **Open** 10.30am-3pm, 5pm-midnight daily (closed Tue Oct-Mar). **Average** €60.

'A moment of wine' is a wine bar and restaurant owned by Sicilian chef Raimondo Triolo – and what an experience it is. Over 700 wines are available, many of them lining the walls. At this concept restaurant, or 'social experiment' as the chef puts it, there's no menu. Instead, you're treated like a guest in his home as he prepares you a three-course meal from one single fish infused with local, seasonal ingredients. It's a bit pricey and the wait can be long, but it's an experience not to be missed. You can also drop by for a glass of wine and a snack.

★ Bar Calise

Piazza degli Eroi (081 991270/www.barcalise. com). **Open** *Apr-Oct* 6am-2am daily. *Nov-Mar* 7am-midnight Mon, Wed-Sun.
Partially hidden in a pine-filled park and one of the oldest bars in Ischia, Bar Calise has been a hit with locals and tourists for almost a century. Customers flock here for morning coffee, a pastry-based sugar rush in the late afternoon, or a chance to dance or listen to local music on summer evenings. A second Bar Calise can be found near the ticket offices at the Port, and the owners also run a large bar/pasticceria and a disco-pub/pizzeria in Casamicciola Terme.

€ Da Ciccio

Via Luigi Mazella 32 (081 991686). **Open** *May-Sept* noon-3.30pm, 7.30pm-midnight daily. *Oct-Apr* 11.30am-3.30pm, 7.30pm-midnight Mon, Wed-Sun. **Average** €30.

Not to be confused with the bar of the same name found at Ischia Porto, Da Ciccio is a family-run fish restaurant in Ponte. Expect excellent local dishes such as *calamari ripieni* (stuffed squid), *polipetti affogati* (baby squid 'drowned' in tomato sauce) or *fritto misto*. Service is friendly and prices are reasonable.

La Dolce Sosta
Corso Vittoria Colonna 251 (081 991678).
Open 7am-2am daily (closed Mon Nov-Mar).
Be it people-watching, palate-pleasing or piano-listening, La Dolce Sosta is the perfect stop for an *aperitivo*, *digestivo* or afternoon *gelato*. Set along Ischia's main shopping and strolling street since 1952, La Dolce Sosta is not just another bar, it's an institution. There's an extensive menu of cocktails, refreshing summer beverages and decadent desserts. Don't leave the island without sampling one of the artisan *granitas*, *a babà* or the classic Aperol Spritz.

Giardino Eden
Via Nuova Cartaromana 62 (081 985015, www.giardinoedenischia.it). **Open** 1-3pm, 8-11pm daily. Closed Oct-Apr. **Average** €60.
Tucked away in the smart Garden of Eden beach club on Cartaromana Bay, this restaurant (under the same ownership as the wonderful Umberto al Mare in Forio) offers romantic seaside dining at its best. The view is to die for, the food – rich in fresh seafood and local ingredients – is divine, and the staff are courteous, professional and attentive.

Ice Da Luciano
Via Luigi Mazzella 140 (081 012 3228). **Open** *Mar, Apr* 9.30am-9pm daily. *May-Sept* 7.30am-2am daily. Closed Oct-Feb. **No credit cards**.
Ice Da Luciano is popular with locals and an obligatory stop during a *passeggiata* along the Via Mazzella – Ischia Ponte's main drag. Owner Luciano sticks to traditional flavours and is particularly proud of his mint choc chip.

Pizzeria Rosticceria da Gaetano
Via delle Ginestre 27-28 (081 1895 8442, www. pizzadagaetano.it). **Open** noon-3pm, 7pm-midnight daily. **Average** *Pizzeria* €15. *Ristorante* €30.
Tucked away on a shady side street a couple of kilometres south of the port (the walk is uphill, so you may want to take the bus), this is a locals' place. The atmosphere may be no-frills, but the legendary pizza served up in this AVPN (Vera Pizza Napoletana Association) establishment makes it worth the trek.

Ristorante Alberto
Lungomare Cristoforo Colombo 8 (081 981259, www.albertoischia.it). **Open** noon-3pm, 7-11pm daily. Closed Nov-mid Mar. **Average** €50.
Boasting a starry clientele (Gwyneth Paltrow, Kate Moss and the late Anthony Minghella among them), this classic restaurant sits on a platform jutting out over the blue sea: floor-to-ceiling windows make the very best of the views. It serves imaginative versions of local favourites such as *pesce alla maruzzara* (fresh fish fillets with cherry tomatoes). Tasting menus start at €25 for lunch and €40 for dinner.

€ Ristorante Pizzeria Pirozzi
Via Seminario 51 (081 983217). **Open** *Apr-Oct* 12.30-4.30pm, 7pm-2am daily. *Nov-Mar* 12.30-3.30pm, 6.30pm-midnight Tue-Sun. **Average** *Pizzeria* €15. *Ristorante* €30.
Although the pasta and fish dishes are very good, especially the *linguine all'astice* (lobster), locals flock here for Fabio's pizzas; you can watch them prepare a margherita on YouTube. Fried appetisers such as *crochette fritte* stuffed with cheese and ham also go down a treat. If you don't have time for a sit-down meal, you can grab a quick bite from the counter near the entrance.

Where to stay

Hotel Floridiana Terme
Corso Vittoria Colonna 153 (081 991014, www.hotelfloridianaischia.com). Closed Nov-Mar. **Rates** €156-€256 double.
Just off Ischia's main shopping street, the Hotel Floridiana is the perfect base for a stay on Ischia. The hotel has three thermal pools – salt, sulphate and alkaline – and a beauty and wellness centre. Full-board, half-board and B&B accommodation is available, and there's access to a nearby beach. Wi-Fi, though spotty in some areas, is available throughout the hotel.

Miramare e Castello

Via Pontano 5 (081 991333, www.miramare castello.it). Closed late Oct-mid Apr (except 26 Dec-5 Jan). **Rates** €150-€400 double.
As its name suggests, this hotel faces the sea (it's on the beach), and is eyeball to eyeball with the Castello. Rooms are tastefully furnished in shades of blue; rates rise for a sea-view or balcony room. The spa offers weekly pampering packages.

★ Il Monastero

Castello Aragonese 3 (081 992435, www.albergo ilmonastero.it). Closed Nov-Mar. **Rates** €100-€140 double.
Located inside the Castello Aragonese, Il Monastero has one of the finest views in the world – and compared to much of the accommodation on Ischia, it's ridiculously cheap. Most of the 22 rooms have sea views, and there's a lovely patio where breakfast and dinner (by reservation only) are served. Much of the fresh produce comes from the kitchen garden.
► *There's no spa pampering here, but guests are eligible for discounts at the Negombo (see p183).*

★ Il Moresco

Via Emanuele Gianturco 16 (081 981355, www.ilmoresco.it). Closed late Oct-mid Apr. **Rates** €220-€340 double.
The elegant Moresco (part of a group that includes the Grand Hotel Excelsior across the road) lives up to its name with low, Moorish-style arches and wrought ironwork. The gardens are delightful and it's close to the sea, with a thermal pool in a rocky cave nearby. Staff are charming and informative.

La Villarosa

Via Giacinto Gigante 5 (081 991316, www. dicohotels.it). Closed late Oct-mid Apr. **Rates** €150-€225 double.
Immersed in a jungly garden close to the centre of town, this is a homely place with comfortable nooks, antiques in hidden corners, and a fourth-floor dining room with a fine view. There are guest chalets among the greenery, as well as all the usual spa treatments.

The North Coast

CASAMICCIOLA TERME

Ischia's second port, Casamicciola, added '*terme*' (thermal spring) to its name in 1956. As far back as the first century AD, however, Pliny the Elder wrote about the town's Gurgitello spring, where water bubbles out of the earth at 27°C (81°F). Centuries later, Casamicciola came up with the idea of combining luxury hotels and thermal treatments for medical conditions.
By 1883, when the town was razed by an earthquake that killed 2,300 people, a stopover at Casamicciola was an essential part of any

young gentleman's grand tour of Europe. Although a decrease in demand for spa cures has driven many centres out of business, there's still plenty of scope here for soaking, sweating and inhaling the waters from the natural wells and springs bubbling from verdant Monte Tabor above the town. The emphasis is on serious cures rather than beauty pampering (*see p182* **Where to Wallow**).
Despite its ancient roots, most of what you see in Casamicciola today was built after the 1883 earthquake. The seafront is crowded with bars, and the desolate shell of the once-glorious **Pio Monte della Misericordia** spa dominates the central stretch; a market (open 6am-3pm Mon, Fri) sells tacky clothes and fresh produce behind the spa's remains.
One block back from the congested coast road, there's a warren of narrow streets and gaily painted houses. East of the Pio Monte, roads striking inland lead to Corso Vittorio Emanuele, which winds uphill. Via Cretaio (left at the T-junction) heads steadily up towards Monte Rotaro (be prepared for a serious hike or take a taxi). Two kilometres along on the left, there's a metal gate across the entrance to **Bosco della Maddalena**, a volcanic crater. Thick with myrtle and oak trees and criss-crossed by footpaths, it looks like a sylvan glade. It conceals a surprise, though: if you stumble across anything looking like a rabbit hole, you can put your hand inside to feel the volcanic steam the ground exhales.
Corso Vittorio Emanuele continues to Piazza Bagni di Gurgitello. **Terme Belliazzi** (*see p183*) sits above Casamicciola's Gurgitello Spring, which was the location of the thermal baths in medieval times. Further uphill, Via Paradisiello leads to the huge red *municipio* (town hall) that dominates the town. The view from the square in front is stunning. The town council has also taken over Villa Bellavista, where the **Museo Civico** (*see p184*) contains old photos and maps, but this can only be visited with a pre-arranged appointment and at limited times (081 507 2535). Still further up is the church of Sacro Cuore, dating from 1898.

LACCO AMENO

Piazza Santa Restituta and the candy pink-and-white 19th-century church of the same name are the heart of this seaside town, built on the remains of one of Italy's first Greek settlements. The body of Tunisian virgin martyr Restituta arrived on nearby San Montano beach in the fourth century, borne, it was said, by lilies; this miracle is depicted in the church's artworks.
Below, in the **Area Archeologica di Santa Restituta** (closed until further notice for renovation work), are the remains of a fourth-century Christian basilica, a late-antique

Roman necropolis and ovens for ceramic production from the Hellenistic period (the third to second centuries BC).

Uphill from the piazza, the 18th-century **Villa Arbusto** houses the **Museo Archeologico di Pithecusae**, named in honour of Ischia's ancient Greek moniker and home to beautifully arranged artefacts. One of its prize possessions is 'Nestor's Cup', inscribed with probably the oldest transcription of a Homeric verse in existence: it dates from around 740 BC and was used in a burial ceremony. Part of the villa and a second museum on the property are dedicated to the life of film producer and publishing magnate Angelo Rizzoli, who once lived here, while the gardens host summer concerts and art installations.

Heading west out of town, the **Baia di San Montano** has one of the island's best beaches; follow signs to the Negombo (*see p183*) to reach the long, sandy crescent. There's a public area, a section for guests at the Hotel della Baia (*see right*), and another stretch for people who have paid for a session at the spa.

Lacco Ameno's best-known landmark is the *fungo* (mushroom) that sits in the water just off the seafront promenade. Ten metres (33 feet) tall, the chunk of volcanic rock is thought to have been catapulted here thousands of years ago by a rumbling Monte Epomeo.

Area Archeologica di Santa Restituta
Piazza Santa Restituta (081 992442).

★ Museo Archeologico di Pithecusae & Museo Angelo Rizzoli
Villa Arbusto, Corso Angelo Rizzoli 210 (081 996103, www.pithecusae.it, www.museoangelo rizzoli.it). **Open** *Apr-Oct* 9.30am-1pm daily (winter opening hours vary; call to check). **Admission** €5 incl both museums. **No credit cards**.

Where to stay & eat

You'll need to arrange your own transport to reach the best restaurant in Casamicciola, which is located in the hills around five kilometres out of town. At **Il Focolare** (Via Cretajo al Crocifisso 3, 081 902944, www.trattoriailfocolare.it, closed Wed Oct-Apr, lunch Mon-Fri, average €35), the D'Ambra family uses mountain produce such as rabbit, snails, chestnuts and herbs to create wonderfully earthy, flavoursome dishes in a delightfully rustic setting.

Lacco Ameno's seaside restaurants are rather more hit-and-miss, and sandwiches are often a visitor's best bet. Luckily, Ischia's traditional sandwich, the hearty *zingara* (ham, cheese, tomato, lettuce and mayo on a toasted roll), is served in most places.

The **Hotel Marina 10** (Piazza Marina 35, 081 900516, www.marina10.it, closed mid Oct-mid

Apr, €110-€215 double) is just off Casamicciola's main thoroughfare. Its 20 modern rooms have the option of garden or sea views.

Lacco Ameno's **Albergo della Regina Isabella** (Piazza San Restituta 1, 081 994322, www.reginaisabella.it, closed Jan-Mar, €310-€450 double) is a grand hotel – arguably the best on the island – built in the 1950s by Angelo Rizzoli. It has a pool overlooking the beach, a glorious spa centre and a Michelin-starred restaurant, Indaco. **Villa Angelica** (Via IV Novembre 28, 081 994524, www.villaangelica.it, closed Nov-Mar, €55-€90 double) is a beautiful, palm-filled hotel with a thermal pool and massage treatments.

Off the road between Lacco and Forio, the **Hotel della Baia** (Via San Montano, 081 986398, www.negombo.it, closed Nov-Mar, €250 double) is quiet, comfortable and set on one of Ischia's loveliest beaches. Half- and full-board rates include entrance tickets to the famous Negombo thermal park (*see p183*). Further up the road, down a secluded lane, the stately but charming **Mezzatorre** (Via Mezzatorre 23, 081 986111, www.mezzatorre.it, closed mid Oct-mid Apr, €280-€700 double) has an excellent spa, lovely views from the guestrooms, and stone steps leading down to the sea. Visitors in search of luxurious seclusion can book a suite in a separate building, with a canopied bed and private outdoor patio with sunken whirlpool.

WHERE TO WALLOW

Murky waters and miraculous mud.

Ibsen, Garibaldi, Hans Christian Andersen and, long before them, Virgil and Pliny have all taken the waters in Ischia, where the bubbling veins beneath the island's crust made it a spa centre as far back as the eighth century BC. Greek colonists believed that the hot waters could cure mind and spirit, and were convinced that the sulphurous broth had supernatural powers. Later, the pragmatic Romans built their public baths atop the island's hot springs. But the most recent invaders have been tourists, lured by the combination of luxury hotels, spa treatments and lots of sunshine thrown in for good measure.

But were the Greeks right? Ischia's waters are the most radioactive in Europe, and rise from a deep reservoir, mixing sea water and ground water before gushing up in hot springs and fumaroles around the island. The hottest springs are at Monte Tabor, above Casamicciola, where the water bubbles out of the ground at around 160°C (320°F). Don't worry: it's cooled before you bathe in it.

Curative spa treatments here are a serious business. The water, mud and clay from the various springs on the island have different chemical properties, and are appropriate for the treatment of different ailments, from rheumatism and arthritis to respiratory and gynaecological problems. The water itself is a rather murky green, and, by law, treatments

are limited to six days a week (normally mornings only) with a doctor present.

Happily, more hedonistic alternatives are also part of the local spa culture these days. Five-star hotels such as the Regina Isabella (see p181), Il Moresco (see p180) and Hotel Mezzatorre (see p181) offer spa treatments and thermal baths at five-star prices, but the best places at which to indulge in less medicinal therapies are the 'thermal parks' listed below – non-residential resorts often set in magnificent gardens. The entrance fee covers the basic facilities (thermal pools, saunas, beach beds and umbrellas, changing rooms), while spa treatments cost extra. You can wallow in mud, get wrapped up in seaweed, stew in heated caves, have yourself hosed down with pressure jets or just idle in the thermal pools thinking about how you're reducing your cellulite, while checking out (from behind designer sunglasses) the latest swimwear fashions worn by the other guests.

GIARDINI POSEIDON

Via Mazzella, Spiaggia di Citara (081 908 7111, www.giardiniposeidonterme.com). **Open** 9am-7pm daily. Closed Nov-Easter. **Admission** €32 full day; €27 after 1pm; €20 4-7pm.
This grand old spa complex comprises saunas, 21 pools, jacuzzis and a long private beach with umbrellas and sunbeds – all run

Hotel Mezzatorre.

ESCAPES & EXCURSIONS

with firm Teutonic efficiency. A bar on the volcanic cliff-side offers sea views. There are also three restaurants to choose from.

NEGOMBO

Via Baia di San Montano, Lacco Ameno (081 986152, www.negombo.it). **Open** 8.30am-7pm daily. Closed mid Oct-mid Apr. **Admission** €32 full day; €26 after 1.30pm; €22 3.30-7pm.

The Negombo is arguably the best spa complex on the island. Set in a beautiful garden with more than 500 exotic plant species and works of art, it features various thermal and sports facilities, including a number of inviting pools. Guests also have access to the pretty San Montano beach.

PARCO TERMALE APHRODITE APOLLON

Via Petrelle, Sant'Angelo (081 999219, www. miramarearesort.it). **Open** 9am-6pm daily. Closed mid Oct-Easter. **Admission** €25 full day; €20 after 1pm.

Rambling across the headland east of Sant'Angelo, the Aphrodite has 12 pools (each named after a Greek god), as well as saunas and gyms; a boat-taxi from Sant' Angelo port is included in the admission fee. Massages (from €30) and fitness and medical treatments cost extra. Major renovation work is planned for 2016, so check that the spa is open before going.

TERME BELLIAZZI

Piazza Bagni 134, Casamicciola (081 994580, www.termebelliazzi.it). **Open** 7am-1pm Mon-Sat. Closed Nov-mid Apr. **Admission** free.

This slightly dreary shrine to the healthy body is built over ancient Roman pools and offers massages (€16-€45), a dip in the heated pool and whirlpool bath (€25), and mud treatments (€30). The waters here are said to help alleviate respiratory disorders.

TERME DI CAVA SCURA

Via Cava Scura, Spiaggia dei Maronti, Serrara Fontana (081 905564, www.cavascura.it). **Open** 8.30am-6pm daily. Closed Nov-mid Apr. **Admission** €1. **No credit cards**.

In a spectacular natural setting, hewn out of tall cliffs at the end of a long coastal walk, this is a spa for devotees. There's a natural sauna in a dingy cave, grave-like baths with steaming sulphurous water (€14), massages (from €28), and thermal and beauty treatments (from €20). You can also be smothered in thermal mud for €20.

Forio & the West Coast

FORIO & AROUND

The largest town on Ischia, with around 20,000 inhabitants, Forio has some of the island's best restaurants and some of its worst traffic jams. In times past, its problems were much more serious – its exposed position left it prey to attacks by Saracen pirates, so 12 watchtowers were built along the coast. One of them, the late 15th-century Il Torrione, still dominates the town centre with its craggy crenellations. Just off Via Matteo Verde, it's home to the tiny **Museo Civico** and hosts the occasional exhibition. At the eastern end of Via Matteo Verde, you'll find Forio's daily covered market.

There are more than 20 churches in and around Forio, most of which were heavily reworked during the 18th century and none of which observes regular opening hours. The decoration of many of the town's churches and chapels was entrusted to local mannerists Cesare Calise and Alfonso di Spigna.

Standing apart from the town on its headland (where Forio's youth congregate in the evening), the stark, white **Santuario della Madonna del Soccorso** wouldn't look out of place in Greece. It's a mixture of architectural styles (Byzantine, Moorish and Mediterranean), with pretty majolica Stations of the Cross around its steps. Inside, sailors who credited the Madonna with saving them from shipwreck have filled the church walls with ship-shaped votive offerings in her honour. The adjacent square has breathtaking views over the coast.

In Corso Umberto, a church has stood on the site of **Santa Maria di Loreto** since the 14th century; in Piazza del Municipio, much of the **Convento di San Francesco** is now occupied by council offices, but the church can still be visited. In the 17th century, alms were dispensed in nearby **Santa Maria della Grazie** (also known as Visitapovere); in the piazza of the same name, **San Vito** is Forio's parish church.

Just north of Forio, along the road to Lacco Ameno, a sign points left to **La Mortella**, a garden designed by renowned British landscape gardener Russell Page. Having arrived on the island at the end of the 1940s in search of peace and inspiration, composer Sir William Walton and his young Argentine wife Susana set about turning a wild plot of land (described by their friend, Laurence Olivier, as nothing but a quarry) into one of Italy's most opulent gardens. It's a magical spot, where New Zealand tree ferns unfurl with a prehistoric languor alongside heavily scented Amazon waterlilies.

The William Walton Trust, which maintains the garden, also provides accommodation and coaching for young musicians and organises

IN THE KNOW BOOKING A HOTEL

Many hotels on the island offer half-board only (meaning breakfast and dinner are included), especially during the summer, although you may find places offering B&B rates out of season or online. Steep single supplements are almost always applied if you're travelling alone. Many hotels close from mid October to Easter, but these days Ischia is also seen as an off-season destination – some will open earlier or close later if the weather is good.

classical music concerts. During spring and autumn, chamber music concerts are held on Saturdays and Sundays in the indoor Recital Hall; in summer, the Summer Festival of Youth Orchestras symphony concerts are held on Thursdays in the Greek Theatre. Arrive at least half an hour early to be sure of a seat. To get there, take the CS bus from Ischia Porto, Casamicciola or Lacco Ameno or the CD bus from Forio.

A few kilometres further down the lane, through unspoilt Ischian countryside and past a breathtaking belvedere, is Luchino Visconti's villa, **La Colombaia** (Via Francesco Calise 130, 081 987115, www.fondazionelacolombaia.it). The villa was converted into a film foundation, museum and cultural centre, with regular exhibitions and events, but it doesn't operate regular opening hours, so call ahead. Along Via Provinciale Panza (the road leading to Citara), are the **Giardini Ravino** botanical gardens. Rich in cacti and succulents that have been collected by the owner for over 30 years, you'll also see examples of the critically endangered Wollemi pine. The garden is enhanced by interesting sculptures and occasional art exhibitions. Before leaving, try a bit of cactus juice in the charming Cactus Lounge Café or spend a few nights in one of the gardens' 18 mini-apartments (€50-€230 plus final cleaning fee).

Forio also has a sailing school that offers courses for all levels and ages. Lessons at the **Scuola Vela Ischia** (Hotel Villa Carolina, Via Marina 50/55, 997119, www.scuolavelaischia.it, closed Nov-Easter) last four hours, and courses range from five days to two weeks (from €250 per person).

Giardini Ravino
Via Provinciale Panza 140B, Forio (329 498 3923, www.ravino.it). **Open** 9am-sunset Mon, Wed, Fri-Sun. **Admission** €9.

★ La Mortella
Via Francesco Calise 39, Forio (081 986220, www.lamortella.org). **Open** Apr-early Nov

9am-7pm Tue, Thur, Sat, Sun. For concert programme, consult the website. **Admission** *Gardens* €12. *Concerts* €20. **No credit cards**.

Museo Civico del Torrione
Via Torrione 32, Forio (349 911 2360, www.iltorrioneforio.it). **Open** Apr-Oct 10am-12.30pm, 7-10.30pm Tue-Sun. **Admission** €2. **No credit cards**.

Monte Epomeo & the South-west

MONTE EPOMEO & BEYOND

Looming over Forio to the east, **Monte Epomeo** is Ischia's highest point at 787 metres (2,582 feet). It can be ascended by walking up Via Monterone or Via Bocca to one of the poorly-marked paths that lead up through the glorious Falanga forest and on up to the summit.

If Forio's town beaches don't appeal to you, try **spiaggia di Citara** to the south, which has another long stretch of sand – although much of it is monopolised by the fabulous **Giardini Poseidon** (*see p182*).

Sorgeto, another treat of a beach, can be reached from the nearby village of Panza, although it's all too easy to miss the flaking, half-hidden signs. A series of hairpin bends and some long flights of stairs lead down to the rocky cove. In the eastern corner, a thermal spring gushes between the rocks and into the sea; at about 32°C (90°F), it's hot enough to cook an egg. Alternatively, there's normal cold water with hot rock-pool soaking.

Where to stay & eat

Just a few kilometres above the centre of Forio is the secluded hideaway, **Tenuta del Poggio Antico** (Via Bellomo 2, Montecorvo, 081 986123, www.ilpoggioantico.com, closed Dec-Feb, €72-€180 double). With only eight rooms in the main building plus two independent cottages, it's a peaceful alternative to Ischia's larger thermal hotels. A panoramic pool overlooks the bay of Citara and is the perfect spot from which to watch the sunset. Ingredients for breakfast and lunch are picked fresh from the property's garden.

Well south of town, perched on a spectacular peninsula jutting out into the sea between Sorgeto beach and Sant'Angelo, **Hotel Punta Chiarito** (Via Sorgeto 51, 081 908102, www.puntachiarito.it, closed Nov-Dec, €120-€160 double) is another attractive option. Rooms are pleasant, and there's a beautifully landscaped garden with a thermal pool; some bedrooms have kitchens and the restaurant serves good traditional fare.

Although decent hotels may be in short supply in Forio, the same cannot be said of restaurants. Beneath the Soccorso church, **Umberto a Mare** (Via Soccorso 2, 081 997171, www.umbertoamare. it, closed Nov-Mar, average €65) is one of the island's best and offers a menu that relies on the daily catch: maybe spaghetti with fresh anchovies, capers and *pomodorini* or deep-fried giant prawns with a tangy lemon and mint salad. Desserts might include apple pie with cream and chocolate. There's a wonderfully romantic terrace with sunset views and ten bright, cheery rooms (€100-€200 double) if you can't bear to leave.

Miles up a tortuous road leading to Monte Epomeo (and not far from Tenuta del Poggio Antico, *see p184*), **Da Peppina di Renato** (Via Bocca, 42, 081 998312, www.trattoriadapeppina. it, closed mid Nov-mid Mar, average €40) serves great pizza and fantastic meat dishes – including the Ischian-style rabbit with seasonal veg. It's closed for lunch for most of the year, except on selected summer evenings.

Pietratorcia (Via Provinciale Panza 267, 081 907232, www.ristorantepietratorcia.it, closed mid Nov-Mar) is one of Ischia's leading wine producers. Tastings are held on a sunny terrace; samples of three different wines, plus a big plate of cheese and cold meats, costs €20. The restaurant (open lunch & dinner mid Mar-Oct) serves local meat and fish dishes, including *conoglio all'Ischitana* (Ischian-style rabbit). Visits to the wine cellars and vineyard can be arranged from April to mid November.

The South

SANT'ANGELO & MARONTI

Reaching the pretty former fishing village of **Sant'Angelo** can be a traffic nightmare (regular, crowded bus services run from Porto and Forio), but lots of Italians think it's worthwhile. Indeed, this may be the one place on the island where Italians outnumber German tourists. They lounge around in the dockside cafés, or stroll insouciantly along the isthmus joining the jumble of white and blue houses to the *scoglio* (rock). A community of Benedictine monks once lived on the rocky promontory, sowing fields of wheat and barley and planting orchards and vineyards. Today, a ruined watchtower keeps lookout – it was built during the 15th century and restored by the Bourbons in 1741.

From the village, a clifftop footpath hugs the south coast, above the **spiaggia dei Maronti**. Once a two-kilometre stretch of unbroken sand, Maronti has been eaten away by the sea and storms. Of what remains, the eastern end is best for family fun, and can be reached by bus from Barano. To access the western end, where steam

slips out of holes between rocks, take the path leading east out of Sant'Angelo. For the tranquil, deserted coves stranded between the two ends, hire a boat-taxi from Sant'Angelo.

Between Sant'Angelo and Maronti, signs point up a steep valley to the extraordinary **Cava Scura** (*see p183*), a natural hot spring.

THE SOUTHERN VILLAGES

From Sant'Angelo, the SS270 road meanders inland, winding a tortuous route among the leafy, craggy hills to **Serrara**, **Fontana**, **Barano d'Ischia**, and then back to Ischia Porto. Alhough architecturally uninspiring, the southern villages offer superb views over the sea and up to Monte Epomeo. In Fontana, don't be deterred by a steep road marked *strada militare* and *vietato l'ingresso* (no entry). It is, in fact, a perfectly legitimate route up to the path for the summit of **Epomeo**; vehicles can be driven as far as the bar-restaurant before the military zone begins, marked with a metal bar across the road.

The path to the left of the bar leads up to an eyrie-like rock formation at the top (the walk will take about 40 minutes), with a truly breathtaking view over the island. Below is the hermitage and little chapel of **San Nicola di Bari**, hewn out of the rock in the 15th century and occupied until World War II. It opens erratically, in the mornings only; the key is kept by the local priest in Fontana.

From Barano, a narrow road plunges through lush countryside to Testaccio and on towards the eastern end of the spiaggia dei Maronti.

Shortly before the SS270 enters Ischia town, a road to the left leads to **Campagnano**, where the church of **San Domenico** has striking 19th-century majolica decoration on its façade; the view from the village down to the Castello Aragonese is glorious.

IN THE KNOW DIVING

The waters around Ischia, Procida and Vivara are part of the protected Regno di Nettuno marine park (www.nettunoamp.org) and are rich in fish, marine flora and fauna, and even red coral. **Orizzontiblu** (340 425 9162, www.orizzontiblu.net) and **Ischia Diving** (081 981852, 347 432 8583, www. ischiadiving.net) are both based on the harbour in Ischia Port and run excursions within the park; dive sites vary from 10m (33ft) to a challenging 130m (426ft) in depth. Prices start at €35 for a single dive (€70 for two) and equipment hire costs €20 per day. Courses at all levels are run with qualified instructors and packages (some including accommodation) are on offer.

CASTELLO ARAGONESE
The rise and fall of a mighty fortress.

First fortified in the fifth century BC, the rocky outcrop that's home to the **Castello Aragonese** (*see p178*) has been used as a stronghold for centuries. Beleagured locals have long found refuge here, sheltering within the castle's walls when Monte Arso erupted in 1301, and during the Saracen pirate attacks that plagued the island for centuries.

In the 16th century, the castle was home to a brilliant court centred around the beautiful and devout Vittoria Colonna, wife of Ischia's feudal chief, Ferdinando Francesco d'Avalos. Her verses were praised by poet Ludovico Ariosto, her learning by humanist philosopher Pietro Bembo. But it was Vittoria's touchingly platonic relationship with Michelangelo that ensured her lasting fame. 'Nature, that never made so fair a face, remained ashamed, and tears were in all eyes', wrote the artist in 1574, after watching over the dying Vittoria.

By the 18th century, the Castello was home to 2,000 families, 13 churches and a few Poor Clare (Clarisse) nuns. But once they moved out a hundred years later, the castle fell into ruin; what time hadn't destroyed, the British finished off when they bombarded the island in 1809. The crippled fortress later became a prison.

Inside the castle, the 18th-century church of the Immacolata has a stark white interior built to a Greek cross plan, and holds temporary exhibitions. The convent of Santa Maria della Consolazione, founded in 1575, proved a convenient place for families with

more titles than funds to park their dowry-less younger daughters. The girls were consigned to a life of prayer until they died, at which point their corpses were placed sitting upright on macabre thrones in the *cimitero* beneath the convent. The living nuns visited their decomposing sisters daily as a stark reminder of mortality. The nuns remained immured in their convent until 1809.

Built after the 1301 eruption, the ex-Cattedrale dell'Assunta was given a heavy Baroque reworking in the early 18th century; the stucco decorations that survived the British shelling are eerily lovely. Restoration of the crypt revealed frescoes dating from the 13th to 16th centuries, some by the School of Giotto; in 2001, another, much older fresco was found behind one of the walls.

Where to stay, eat & drink

In Sant'Angelo, the **Park Hotel Miramare** (Via Maddalena 29, 081 999219, www.hotel miramare.it, closed Nov-Mar, €240-€260 double) is the flagship hotel of a group that also includes the Casa Apollon next door (same phone number, €160-€192 double). Room rates include entrance to the **Parco Termale Aphrodite Apollon** (*see p183*). The charming **Casa Celestino** (Via Chiaia di Rose 20, 081 999213, www.hotel celestino.it, closed mid Oct-Apr, €120-€170 double) with its 20 pristine blue and white rooms lies on the street leading down to the village and has a good restaurant with a sea-facing terrace. **Casa Gennaro** (Via Provinciale Panza Succhivo 27, 081 907118, www.pensione casagennaro.com, closed Nov-Easter, €40-€80 double) is a simple, rustic but friendly option

set on the road up to Panza. All rooms have fantastic views and delicious meals include fish caught by the owner, plus local wine. Half-board costs just €15 extra per head.

The beautifully situated **Neptunus** (Via Lo Russo 1, 081 904255, www.ristoranteneptunus. com, closed Jan-mid Mar, average €40), perched on a cliff overlooking Sant'Angelo, serves up fresh seafood and the occasional land-sourced speciality such as *coniglio all'ischitana* (Ischian-style rabbit cooked in tomato sauce) if you ring and order in advance.

In the port, **La Tavernetta del Pirata** (Via Sant'Angelo 77, 081 999251, closed Jan-Mar, Wed in Dec, average €50) is Sant'Angelo's hippest bar, and a good place to sink an *aperitivo* or tuck into a seafood feast overlooking the marina where Gianni Versace's mega-yacht was once a fixture; it's open until midnight. When you can't face any more seafood, **Da Pasquale** (Via Sant'Angelo 79, 081 904208, www.dapasquale.it, closed Dec-Mar except New Year's Eve, average €15) will fill you up with good, cheap pizza and beer.

RESOURCES

Hospital
Ospedale Anna Rizzoli *Via Fundera, Lacco Ameno (081 994044).*

Police
Carabinieri *Via Casciaro 20, Ischia Porto (081 991065, emergencies 112).*
Polizia *Via delle Terme (081 507 4701, emergencies 113)*

Post office
Via Luigi Mazzella 46, Ischia Ponte (081 992180).
Via de Luca Antonio 42, Ischia Porto (081 507 4611).

Tourist information
Azienda di Cura Soggiorno e Turismo delle Isole di Ischia e Procida *Banchina Porto Salvo (by the hydrofoil dock; 081 5074231, www.infoischia procida.it).* **Open** 9am-2pm, 3-8pm Mon-Sat. Occasional Sunday openings in summer.

GETTING AROUND
By boat

Capitan Morgan (081 985080, www.capitan morgan.it) organises trips around the island (tickets €13-€20), and day trips to Procida (€15), Capri (€30), the Amalfi Coast (€37), Ponza (€50), Ventotene (€37) and Pompeii (€54). **Ischiabarche** (081 984854, www.ischiabarche.it) can arrange day charters around Ischia (€250-€650) and further afield. **West Coast Ischia** (338 509 9868, www.westcoastischia. it) has 14 locations around Ischia for boat rentals, charters and island tours. **Marina Sant'Anna** (081 985510, www.marinadisantanna.it) offers water taxi services around Ischia Ponte and Cataromana Bay.

By bus

EAV (800 211 388, www.eavsrl.it) runs a highly efficient, if crowded, bus service. The main routes are the *circolare sinistra* (CS), which circles the island anticlockwise stopping at Ischia Porto, Casamicciola, Lacco Ameno, Forio, Serrara, Fontana, Barano, and back to Ischia Porto; and the *circolare destra* (CD), which covers the same route clockwise. The services run every 30mins, with buses every 15mins during rush hour. There are also services from Ischia Porto to Sant'Angelo (every 15mins), Giardini Poseidon at Citara (every 30mins) and Spiaggia dei Maronti via Testaccio

(every 20mins). In addition, minibus services operate within Ischia Porto and Ponte, and in Forio. Buy tickets before boarding; get them (along with bus maps and timetables) at the terminus in Ischia Porto, or at any *tabacchi* or newsstand. Tickets cost €1.20 (single trip), €1.50 (for 100mins), €3.60 (24hrs), €12.60 (weekly) and €33.60 (monthly).

By scooter

Hiring a scooter is an inexpensive, fun way of exploring the island. **Del Franco** (Via Alfredo de Luca 121, Ischia Porto, 081 991334, www. noleggiodelfranco.it) rents out scooters and bicycles. **M Balestrieri** (Via Iasolino 35, Ischia Porto, 081 985691, www.autonoleggiobalestrieri.it) can deliver a set of wheels straight to your hotel. Both charge from €25 per day (and also hire out cars). **Giuseppe di Meglio** (Via Tommaso Morgera 4, Casamicciola, 081 980312, www.ischia-autonoleggio.it) rents scooters from €35 per day.

GETTING THERE
By boat

Several boat companies, including **Caremar** (081 984818, www.caremar.it), **AliLauro** (081 497 2238, www.alilauro.it), **Medmar** (081 333 4411, www. medmargroup.it) and **SNAV** (www.snav.it), run hydrofoil and car ferry services between Ischia (from Porto, Casamicciola and Forio) and the mainland (from Naples Beverello, Naples Mergellina, Naples Porta di Massa and Pozzuoli), plus less frequent ones between Ischia Porto or Casamicciola and Capri, Sorrento and Procida. The trip from Naples Beverello to Ischia takes 95mins by ferry, and costs around €11 for passengers (extra for vehicles), depending on the company. It takes 45mins if you take the hydrofoil (around €18 plus luggage). Caremar is the cheapest and most crowded service. Some companies accept internet bookings, but not credit cards. There may be a service charge for ordering advance hydrofoil tickets, but it's worth it during the busy season (July and, especially, August).

ESCAPES & EXCURSIONS

Procida

Just half an hour's ferry ride from the mainland and with a surface area of barely four square kilometres, Procida may be the smallest island in the Gulf of Naples but it also holds the record for being the Med's most densely populated. At the same time, it's charmingly laid-back, unpretentious and friendly, a perfect foil to Capri's glitz. The local economy once revolved around lemon groves and the sea, but today it relies on tourism: smart cafés line the harbours, yachts moor at the gleaming Marina Grande, and day trippers pack the sandy beaches in August when the coast is heaving. But there's always space to stroll through the island's lemon groves, savour a freshly made *granita di limone* or watch the day's catch being unloaded from the boats.

INTRODUCING THE ISLAND

In the Middle Ages, frequent Saracen attacks forced villagers to flee to the highest point of the island, the **Terra Murata**. The distinctive local architecture, with its steep staircases, arches and loggias, dates from this period.

Procida really began to develop during the 16th century, despite repeated pirate attacks. (In 1544, according to local legend, Barbarossa the barbarian fled the island after a miraculous vision of St Michael in the Terra Murata – but not before indulging in a little rape and pillage.) Medieval Terra Murata was fortified after 1520, but the defence mentality was already fading. Prosperous families from the mainland built summer homes here, shipbuilders constructed family *palazzi*, and the Marina Grande became the centre of the fishing industry.

Procida was a favourite haunt of the Bourbon kings; in 1744 they bought the **Castello d'Avalos** and turned the island into a royal hunting reserve. As you approach Procida by ferry, the view is dominated by the Castello (an Italian Alcatraz until 1986), surrounded by faded, tumbledown fishermen's houses.

Ferries dock in the **Marina Grande** (*see p191*) among the fishing boats. The fish stalls open in the afternoon, selling the day's catch: prawns, red mullet and squid, as well as *misto di paranza* (small fish and crustaceans caught in the trawling nets).

Towards the eastern end of Marina Grande, by the late 18th-century church of **Santa Maria della Pietà** (Via Roma, open 8.30am-noon, 5-8pm daily), steep Via Vittorio Emanuele leads off to the right up into the centre of the island. Some 100 metres (350 feet) further on the left, Via Principe Umberto, with its old houses, leads to **Piazza dei Martiri**, from where you get a good view of the castle and the Terra Murata above, with the enchanting fishing village of Corricella below.

The road continues to climb steeply past the forlorn, abandoned Castello d'Avalos. Built in the mid 16th century, the castle belonged to the D'Avalos family until it was bought by the Bourbon kings in the mid 18th century.

From here, it's not far to the **Porta di Mezzomo** (1563) that leads into the medieval Terra Murata walled village. There are some breathtaking views over Naples and Capri – especially from the hilltop Via Borgo, where the **Abbazia di San Michele Arcangelo** is built on the edge of the sheer rock. Procida's fascinating Good Friday *processione dei misteri* starts here. In what was once a procession of flagellants, a life-size wooden sculpture of the dead Christ, dating from 1754, is carried under a black veil by fishermen from the Abbazia to Marina Grande. It's followed by the other *misteri* (handmade wooden models of religious scenes), carried by the Turchini fraternity, in white habits and turquoise capes, and by children in medieval costume. Close by, the ruins of 16th-century **Santa Margherita Nuova** stand on the Punta dei Monaci.

From Piazza dei Martiri, the sleepy little harbour at **Corricella** is accessed via the Scalinata Scura steps. On the descent, you'll pass by tiny houses massed on the rock, some of which are chic homes for weekenders. The bay, exposed to African winds, has its own mild microclimate, and bananas grow here.

From the western end of Corricella, steps head up to Via Scotti, where 18th-century buildings have vaulted entrances leading to gardens, lemon groves and terraces overlooking the sea. Pick up Via Vittorio Emanuele again to reach the southernmost part of the island.

From Piazza Olmo, Via Pizzaco leads to **Pizzaco**, where a lovely nature walk rounds a crumbling promontory with fantastic views across to Corricella and Terra Murata. One of the island's nicest beaches, **La Chiaia**, is reached from the piazza via about 180 steps. Flagging spirits can be revived at the excellent **La Conchiglia** trattoria.

Via Giovanni da Procida leads from Piazza Olmo to **Chiaiolella**, Procida's main resort – a small marina enclosed by two promontories. On the western side of the island, the kilometre of sand stretching from Chiaiolella to Ciriaccio is Procida's most fashionable (and crowded) beach, the **Lido**. From the southern tip of this pretty bay, a lane leads to a bridge connecting the island to the nature reserve of Vivara (*see below*).

The north-east of Procida, between the lighthouse on Punta di Pioppeto and Punta Serra, takes you off the beaten track (even during high season), with lanes meandering through lemon groves and offering fine sea views. From Piazza Olmo, Via Flavio Gioia leads to a belvedere with an outstanding view over Chiaiolella, Vivara and Ischia. A short path hugs the promontory of Punta Serra, overlooking the sea.

Via Flavio Gioia heads to the old cemetery; below is **Pozzo Vecchio** beach, made famous by Michael Radford's charming film, *Il Postino*. There's a café here in summer. The road (at this point called Via Cesare Battisti) passes a restored 16th-century tower and hamlet, before rambling on past isolated farmhouses and woodlands to the lighthouse; from here, Via Faro leads back to the main road.

Off Procida's south-western tip and reached by a footbridge is the tiny island nature reserve of **Vivara**, inhabited even before Procida: traces of Neolithic remains have been found here. Once a hunting reserve, this is one of the most beautiful

and unspoilt nature reserves in the whole of Italy. More than 150 species of bird live here or migrate through, and it's home to a rare species of rat that walks on its hind legs. Here, too, are the ruins of a hamlet beside the coast and, at the centre of the island, an abandoned manor house with a loggia and an old olive press in the cellar. Vivara is closed to the general public to protect its delicate ecosystem; needless to say, locals have been known to climb through the fence.

The opening of the tourist port in the Marina Grande makes Procida an ideal base for yacht charters. **Blue Dream** (Via Vittorio Emanuele 14, 081 896 0579, www.bluedreamcharter.com) offers day trips, fishing and diving days, as well as several B&B boats in the Marina Grande. **Sailitalia Procida/Bluebone** (Via Roma 10, 081 896 9962, www.sailitalia.it) is another option, and also offers one-way trips such as Procida to Palermo or Tropea. Skippers and crew are available on some boats, and prices range from a low-season week for four at €1,500 to a high-season crewed week at €9,000. They also have a fleet of new catamarans.

FREE Abbazia di San Michele Arcangelo
Via Terra Murata 89 (081 896 7612, www. abbaziasanmicheleprocida.it). **Open** *Apr-Oct* 10am-12.45pm, 3-5pm Mon-Sat. Closed Sun & during religious functions. *Nov-Mar* by reservation only. **Admission** *Church* free. *Museum, library & catacombs* €3. **No credit cards**.
Dating from the 11th century, but remodelled in the 17th to 19th centuries, the abbey has a painting (1699) by Luca Giordano of Archangel Michael on its coffered ceiling. Inside is an 8,000-strong religious manuscript library, a museum containing religious thanksgiving pictures from shipwrecked sailors, an 18th-century Nativity scene, and a maze of catacombs leading to a secret chapel.

★ FREE Santissima Annunziata (Madonna della Libera)
Via SS Annunziata (081 526 1654). **Open** 8.30am-noon, 5-8pm daily. **Admission** free.
Inside is a fascinating collection of devotional ex-votos, painted by grateful sailors saved from storms at sea. November's Festa del Vino is organised by the church committee in the surrounding lanes.

ESCAPES & EXCURSIONS

IN THE KNOW DIVE TIME

Procida's clear waters are great for diving. The **Procida Diving Centre** (Via Marina Chiaiolella, Lido di Procida, 081 896 8385, www.vacanzeaprocida.it) is open year-round (only weekends during winter) and offers courses, equipment hire and excursions with expert instructors.

IN THE KNOW LAND OF LEMONS

Much of Procida is given over to lemon groves that produce a very distinct type of lemon – larger and paler than others found in Campania and with a thicker pith. Along with the ubiquitous *coniglio alla procidana*, they pop up in restaurant menus all over the island, most notably in the unusual and deliciously refreshing *insalata di limoni* – where the ripe lemons are peeled, sliced and dressed with fresh mint, garlic, *peperoncino* and olive oil.

Where to eat & drink

In recent years, the choice and quality of restaurants on Procida have improved, but prices have risen to match. In August and on summer weekends, it's best to book ahead.

Sample the local catch opposite the ferry port at **La Medusa** (Via Roma 116, 081 896 7481, closed Tue, average €28), with a spanking-fresh *zuppa di pesce* followed by delicious *pasta con alici e peperoncini verdi* or *spaghetti ricci di mare* (with sea urchins).

For more inventive fish and vegetable dishes, try **Fammivento** (Via Roma 39, 081 896 9020, closed Mon & Jan, average €25), facing the yacht harbour. Among the dishes is *pasta alla genovese di polipo*; pasta in a fragrant, slow-cooked octopus sauce. **Il Gazebo** (Via Roma 146, 081 810 1071, open for dinner only, closed Tue Sept-June & all Nov, average €40) is a relatively new arrival housed in an ex-fisherman's hut on the port. Dishes include the likes of *spaghetti alla carbonara di mare* (with fish replacing the more usual bacon).

By the church of Santa Maria della Pieta, **Bar Roma** (Via Roma 164, 081 896 7460, closed Tue Oct-Apr) sells great cakes. You can quaff cocktails at **Bar del Cavaliere** (Via Roma 42, 081 810 1074, closed Mon Dec-Mar); or just hang out and wait for the boat at **Bar Grottino** (Via Roma 121, 081 896 7787, closed Wed Oct-Apr), which serves home-made ice-cream and *granite*.

Corricella's **Caracalè** (Via Marina Corricella 62, 081 896 9192, closed Tue & Nov-Dec, Feb, average €35) adds a modern twist to the classics; try *parmigiana di pesce spatola* (silver scabbard fish) or *zuppetta di totani e patate* (baby squid and potato stew).

For a romantic meal, book the free shuttle boat from Corricella to **La Conchiglia** on Chiaia beach (no car access, steps from Via Pizzaco 10, Piazza Olmo, 081 896 7602, www.laconchigliaristorante.com, closed Nov-Mar, average €40) for abundant fresh pasta and excellent seafood straight off the family boat; reservations are required.

Local ingredients and fresh fish inspire the menu at **La Pergola** (Via Salette 10, 081 896 9918, closed lunch, Mon & weekdays mid Oct-Easter, average €30); sample homemade ravioli stuffed with artichokes and ricotta followed by *coniglio alla procidana* (rabbit stew) under the lemon trees.

Where to stay

Hotel rooms are scarce, so book well ahead for peak season. Recent years have seen an increase in the number of good quality self-catering options available on the island and this is an ideal solution for families, budget travellers or those simply craving a bit of privacy.

Procida Holidays (Via Roma 117, 081 896 9594, www.isoladiprocida.it) can arrange accommodation in fishermen's cottages, villas and holiday flats, as well as organising bike hire, boat trips, yacht charters and coastal rowing tours. **Casavacanza** (Via Principe Umberto 1, 081 896 9067, www.casavacanza.net) is another good resource for finding a holiday apartment. **Miratour** (Via Roma 109, 081 896 8089, www.miratour.it) offers a selection of rooms and apartments plus tourist information. There are also half a dozen camping sites on the island; ask the tourist office (*see p191*) for details.

Overlooking Corricella from its cliffside position under the Terra Murata is the romantic **La Casa sul Mare** (Salita Castello 13, 081 896 8799, www.lacasasulmare.it, closed Jan-Feb, €90-€170 double), housed in an 18th-century palazzo with sunny, air-conditioned rooms and terraces with bay views. There are transfers to La Chiaia beach and early evening cocktails.

The charming rooms looking out on to the vineyard and gardens of **La Vigna** (Via Principessa Margherita 46, 081 896 0469, www.albergolavigna.it, closed Jan, €90-€200 double), five minutes' walk from Piazza dei Martiri, offer a haven of tranquillity from the high-season crowds. There's a new pool and a tiny wellness centre offering massage and wine-therapy treatments.

In the centre of the island, near La Chiaia, **Casa Giovanni da Procida** (Via Giovanni da Procida 3, 081 896 0358, www.casagiovannidaprocida.it, €70-€110 double) is a 17th-century farmhouse converted into a stylish B&B. The split-level rooms are air-conditioned and there's a garden.

Hotel Celeste (Via Rivoli 6, 081 896 7488, www.hotelceleste.it, €50-€130 double) is a bright and breezy establishment, set in a lemon grove a short walk away from Chiaiolella beach.

La Rosa dei Venti (Via Vincenzo Rinaldi 32, 081 896 8385, www.vacanzeaprocida.it) offers beautifully fitted apartments year-round, with a two-bed flat costing from €50 to €80 per night. It's set on the island's north coast, amid citrus trees and vines (and a family of donkeys), and has a private rocky beach. The friendly owners also run the local diving school (*see p189* **In the Know**) and organise sailing excursions, food events and grape-picking.

Set in lush gardens, the tranquil **Tirreno Residence** (Via Faro 34, 081 896 8341, www. tirrenoresidence.it) also offers apartments (€40-€110 per night). With free Wi-Fi, plus a free shuttle service to the beaches and centre, it's great value for money. There's also free parking and a panoramic terrace.

Resources

Hospital
Via Alcide de Gasperi 203 (081 810 0510).

Police
Via Libertà 70bis (081 896 8539).

Post office
Via Libertà 72 (081 896 0711).

Tourist information
Azienda di Cura Soggiorno e Turismo delle Isole di Ischia e Procida *Via Antonio Sogliuzzo 72 (081 507 4211, www.infoischiaprocida.it).* **Open** 9am-2pm, 3-8pm Mon-Sat.
The tourist office is on the island of Ischia, but the website also covers Procida.
Pro Loco di Procida *Via Vittorio Emanuele 173 (081 896 9628, www.procida.net).* **Open** *Apr-Sept* 9am-1pm, 3-8pm daily. *Oct-Mar* 9am-1pm, 3-7pm daily.

Getting around

Walking, cycling and buses are all good ways to get around; in summer there are heavy restrictions on private cars and scooters.

By bus
Buses run to all parts of the island. Line 1 departs every 20mins from Marina Grande to Marina di Chiaiolella, operating for most of the night in July and August. Tickets are €1 (buy in advance from *tabacchi* or pay €1.30 on board). The three other lines run every 40mins.

By scooter
Autoricambi Sprint (Via Roma 28, 081 896 9435 www.sprintprocida.com) hires out 50cc scooters from €25 per day, electric bikes from €20 per day and bicycles from €10 per day.

By taxi
Taxis can be hired from Marina di Chiaiolella or Marina Grande (081 896 8785); a tour around the island costs roughly €40. Taxis can also be booked on 338 899 9912 or 368 755 5360.

Getting there

From Naples Beverello/Porto di Massa
Caremar (081 896 7280, www.caremar.it) runs ferries from Naples Porto di Massa (1hr; €9.70) and hydrofoils from Naples Beverello (35mins; €13.20). **SNAV** (081 896 9975, www.snav.it) runs hydrofoils between Naples Beverello and Procida (35mins; €15), and between Procida and Ischia (20mins; €7.50). During the summer, SNAV also runs hydrofoils from Mergellina and Ischia. A midnight ferry from Naples' Porto di Massa is run by **Medmar** (081 333 4411).

From Pozzuoli
Caremar (081 526 2711, www.caremar.it) runs ferries (35mins; €7.20). **Procida Lines 2000** (081 896 0328) runs car ferries (35mins; rates vary according to size of vehicle). **Procidamar** (081 497 2222) runs a passenger boat service (Apr-Oct).

La Vigna.

Pompeii, Vesuvius & Herculaneum

The sight of Vesuvius towering over a wide sweep of bay with the Sorrentine peninsula to the south and Naples to the north has held visitors spellbound for centuries. Add to these natural wonders the wealth of ancient Roman archaeological sites and lovely 18th-century villas, and you have a unique combination. The stark contrast with the harsh realities of life in the Comuni Vesuviani (the towns around Vesuvius) is equally striking in its way and the ugly agglomerations bear all the hallmarks of 21st-century urban blight, with catastrophically high unemployment, apocalyptic traffic and graffiti-daubed public places. But all this only heightens the dramatic effect: sumptuous Roman villas immersed in the quiet countryside overlook demolition-ripe 1950s tower blocks, while lava fields from the 1944 eruption lie wild and deserted, just a few miles from the remains of ruined streets and houses buried in a much bigger blow two millennia before.

INTRODUCING THE AREA

The Etruscans, Greeks, Oscans and Romans have all occupied the lower slopes of Vesuvius, building settlements such as **Pompeii** (*see p198*) and **Herculaneum** (*see p194*), as well as secluded villas like **Oplontis** (*see p197*) and **Stabiae** (*see p203*).

In the 18th century, the Bourbon monarchs built a royal palace, the **Reggia** (*see p193*), in Portici. Wealthy noblemen soon followed suit, building lavish villas between Portici and Torre del Greco in an area that became known as the **Miglio d'Oro** (Golden Mile).

DIGGING DEEP

Using excavation techniques that would make modern archaeologists shudder, the Bourbons carted off statues and frescoes to be exhibited in the Reggia palace. Many works of art were damaged, and others were smuggled out to private collections around the world. The sites still bear the scars of these cavalier excavations, with tunnels bored through ancient villa walls in an attempt to reach the treasures within. Describing a visit to Herculaneum during the 18th century, poet Thomas Gray told his mother how 'the passage they have made with all their turnings and windings is now more than a mile long.'

The archaeological resources of this area are immense. Not only is it home to Pompeii, Italy's third most-visited attraction (after the Vatican museums and Colosseum in Rome), but also to a wealth of lesser sights to which, apart from Herculaneum, are sadly undersold. But there are plans afoot to make these more visitor-friendly and to divert some of Pompeii's 2.6 million annual visitors in their direction.

The five key archaeological sites (Pompeii, Herculaneum, Oplontis, Stabiae and Boscoreale) can be visited on the Campania Artecard circuit (*see p297*). Alternatively, a combined ticket, which costs €22 and is valid for three days, is available at all sites except Stabiae, where entrance is free. There's also a one-day ticket (€5.50) for Oplontis, Stabiae and Boscoreale, and entrance to all five sites is free on the first Sunday of each month for Domenica al Museo, an initiative that began in 2014.

PORTICI

Portici has the dubious distinction of being the most densely populated town in Europe – though the other *comuni vesuviani* can't be too far behind. Left in ruins after Vesuvius erupted in 1631, it was little more than a wasteland when Charles III, Naples' first Bourbon king, gave orders for a palace to be built here. The **Reggia** (royal palace) and its grounds, which are now surrounded by concrete on all sides, give you an idea of what the whole area must have looked like 200 years ago. The town was home to more than 30 villas along the Miglio d'Oro (Golden Mile), and was also the terminus for Italy's first railway line; the old station now houses the excellent **Museo Ferroviario di Pietrarsa**.

★ Museo Ferroviario di Pietrarsa

Via Pietrarsa (081 472003, www.museopietrarsa. it). **Open** 9am-4.30pm Fri; 9am-6pm Sat, Sun. **Admission** €5; €3.50 reductions; free under-6s. **No credit cards**.

The first railway to be built on the Italian peninsula was a modest 7.4-kilometre stretch between Naples and Portici, opened with much fanfare by Naples' King Ferdinando II in 1839. The following year, a railway factory and workshops were installed in an area close to Portici called Pietrarsa ('burnt stone' – apt enough, given its proximity to Vesuvius). The factories remained operational until 1975.

The biggest – and arguably the finest – railway museum in Europe, the Museo Ferroviario di Pietrarsa is a joy, even for non-train buffs. The buildings housing original workshops and lathes have been minimally and tastefully restored. Pavilion A has a superb display of steam locomotives, including a faithful reconstruction of the royal train used for the inaugural trip on the Portici railway in 1839. Across the gardens, Pavilion C showcases the full gamut of 20th-century rolling stock, and an immaculately preserved royal carriage built in 1928. Raised walkways around the carriage allow an excellent view of the plush upholstery and gilded ceilings. The museum's central courtyard has been converted into a Mediterranean garden, with an open-air theatre for summer concerts.

Detailed information about the museum, in English, is available from the reception area. To find the museum, take the Portici exit from the A3 motorway and head down to the coast road (SS145),

turning right towards Naples; the easily missed Museo Ferroviario sign is on the seaward side of the main road in an area called Croce del Lagno. Alternatively, take a train from Naples' Stazione Centrale to Pietrarsa-San Giorgio a Cremano.

★ Reggia di Portici & Orto Botanico

Via Università 100 (081 253 2016, www.centro musa.it). **Open** *Reggia* by appt only (min 15 people) Sept-July 9am-6.30pm Mon-Fri. *Orto Botanico* by appt only (min 15 people) 9am-1hr before sunset Mon-Fri. **Admission** €5; €3.50 reductions; free under-12s. **No credit cards**.

Designed by Antonio Medrano, the Reggia di Portici is the greatest of all the Vesuvian villas. Ferdinando Fuga and Luigi Vanvitelli both worked on it. The vast façade looks out across what was once its own private terraced gardens, cascading down towards the seashore. The lower of the Reggia's two buildings is separated from the upper wing (which looks out towards Vesuvius) by a square. Charles and his son Ferdinando had the spoils from digs at Pompeii and Herculaneum brought here, creating a royal antiquarium of incomparable richness; most of the spoils are now held at the Museo Archeologico Nazionale (*see p82*). On the Vesuvius side of the main road is the Orto Botanico (botanical gardens), an impressive collection of more than 500 species of native and exotic plants, bordered by the holm oak wood where the royals used to hunt. The gardens and museum are off-limits unless you're a group of 15 people minimum. However, the Reggia has also been home to the Naples University Faculty of Agriculture since 1873: to visit the entrance hall and the grand staircase, just wander in.

▶ *For more on architects Medrano, Fuga and Vanvitelli, see pp268-273.*

IN THE KNOW POMPEII OR HERCULANEUM?

It's possible to visit Pompeii and Herculaneum in one long, rather tiring day. But if you have to choose, there's a lot to be said for picking the smaller of the two sites. Herculaneum is compact enough to be able to 'do' in an hour or so, and it offers a particularly vivid picture of what daily life in a Roman town would have been like. Both towns were engulfed in the same volcanic eruption, but while Pompeii was buried under a 10m (33ft) blanket of ash and pumice, its smaller neighbour to the north was encased in compacted layers that cooled into solid rock up to 25m (82ft) deep. For this reason, even organic material such as wooden beams and furniture was preserved, and several houses have kept their upper floors.

ESCAPES & EXCURSIONS

ERCOLANO & HERCULANEUM

Although it rivals Portici for urban squalor and traffic noise, Ercolano also has some sumptuous 18th-century villas and the spectacular ancient site of Herculaneum. You could drive through the postwar construction catastrophe and never notice the splendour, but blot out everything built since 1945 and you're left with some fishermen's huts near the shore, a once-smart late 19th-century main street and assorted *ville* – now crumbling, dilapidated affairs, set in overgrown gardens behind locked, rusting gates.

Because the Reggia di Portici was home to the Bourbon court for several months each year, court hangers-on from all over the Kingdom of the Two Sicilies – anxious to be on hand when honours or cash rewards were distributed – summoned the leading architects of the day to build luxury homes nearby. Soon, the stretch of coast between Naples and Torre del Greco became known as the Miglio d'Oro (Golden Mile). With the absorption of Naples into the United Kingdom of Italy in 1860, the frivolous, worldly *ville* of the Miglio d'Oro became obsolete; the villas' owners sold them to nouveau riche Neapolitan property speculators or simply left them to decay. Many were eventually divided up into flats, while others, such as the spectacular **Villa Favorita** (*see p196*), were boarded up and abandoned for generations.

A handful have been salvaged by the Ente per le Ville Vesuviane (Board of Vesuvian Villas), based in the **Villa Campolieto** (*see p196*). Many of the properties are open to the public and, though the Villa Favorita may have missed out on the Ente's benevolence, its lower park and annexe, the Palazzina del Mosaico, have been restored. The Ente has also given a new lease of life to the **Villa Ruggiero** (*see p197*).

Herculaneum

Herculaneum (Scavi di Ercolano)

Corso Resina (081 732 4311, www.pompeiisites. org). **Open** *Apr-Oct* 8.30am-7.30pm daily (ticket office closes 6pm). *Nov-Mar* 8.30am-5pm daily (ticket office closes 3.30pm). **Admission** €13; €7.50 reductions; free under-18s (EU citizens). **No credit cards.**
Bold letters in the text refer to map (p195).
It was described by the ancients as being *inter duos fluvios infra Vesuvium* ('between two rivers below Vesuvius'), but over the years the topography around Herculaneum has changed beyond all recognition. The rivers have disappeared, the shoreline has moved a kilometre to the west, and the part of Herculaneum that hasn't been excavated lies some 25m (82ft) below the modern town of Ercolano. Descending from Ercolano, emerging from the

tunnels leading into the site and strolling through the ancient town is an extraordinary experience – like entering a time capsule.

The town was probably founded by Greek settlers in the fourth century BC, though most of what can be seen today dates back no further than the second century BC. The town had a grid layout similar to that of its neighbour, Neapolis; at the time of its destruction in AD 79, it had around 5,000 inhabitants. Buried in an airtight layer of solidified volcanic mud (unlike Pompeii, where the volcanic ash took longer to settle and become compressed), organic remains found at Herculaneum have yielded all sorts of insights into everyday life, from diet to clothing and furniture.

Pedestrian access to the site from Corso Resina (just keep heading straight down from Circumvesuviana station on Via IV Novembre) is via an impressive ramp with fine overviews of the Roman town. At the main ticket office halfway down, you should be able to pick up a free site map and a small booklet on Herculaneum in English (or print them out from the website before arrival). At the base of the ramp, site facilities include a bookshop and an audioguide kiosk. From here, you can either follow the footbridge directly across into the site, or take the tunnel leading down to the original shoreline **[A]**, the best place from which to admire the towering volcanic deposits. It was near here that 250 skeletons were discovered in the 1980s. They're believed to be the remains of inhabitants overwhelmed by the surge cloud from Vesuvius as they hoped, in vain, to be rescued by sea. Most of the best-preserved houses (many with upper storeys still intact) are on either side of Cardo IV and Cardo V, perpendicular to the two *decumani* (main roads).

Near the seaward end of Cardo V, an altar and a statue base stand outside the Terme Suburbane (suburban baths, closed at the time of writing) **[B]**; the statue, dedicated to local dignitary Nonius Balbus, is in Naples' Museo Archeologico Nazionale (*see p82*).

In Insula IV, the Casa dei Cervi (House of the Stags, closed at the time of writing) **[C]** was a villa with a prime seafront location and gazebo. It's named after the two sculptures of deer attacked by hunting dogs found in the garden; the ones here now are replicas. Excavated in the early 20th century, Casa dei Cervi suffered less and preserved more of its upper storeys than the houses in Insula II on the north-western side of the site, excavated 100 years before. Nearby are two shops **[D & E]**, identifiable by their broad fronts that accommodated folding wooden screens to separate the shop from the street. The first **[D]** is the Taberna di Priapo (Priapus's Tavern), complete with waiting room, a rather tired-looking fresco and private inner chambers. On the street corner, with large ceramic jars set into marble counters, is one of the town's *thermopolia* **[E]**; these were the fast-food outlets of the ancient world and good places to pick up garum, a fish-based sauce and popular aphrodisiac.

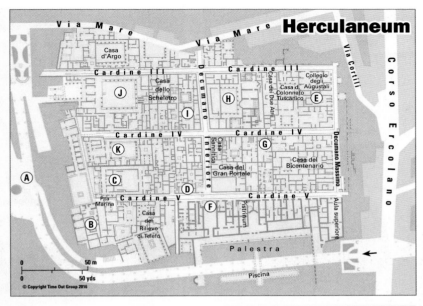

Where Cardo V meets the lower *decumanus* (one of two main roads), two columns mark the entrance to the large *palaestra* (Insula Orientalis) [**F**], where ball games and wrestling matches would have been staged. Two sides of its rectangular peristyle are still largely buried beneath volcanic deposits. Within this leisure complex were two *piscinae* (swimming pools or fishponds): one at the centre of the peristyle, tunnelled out of the rock, which now has a replica of the original bronze hydra fountain; and the other with amphorae for fish farming set into its sides.

The houses in Herculaneum are virtually all named after archaeological finds or architectural peculiarities. The Casa di Nettuno e Anfitrite (House of Neptune and Amphitrite, Insula V) [**G**] on Cardo IV is no exception, taking its name from the beautifully preserved mosaic adorning the wall of the secluded *nymphaeum* at the back of the house. It tells the tale of Neptune and Amphitrite: he saw her dancing with the Nereids on the island of Naxos and spirited her away to be married.

Opposite are the Terme del Foro (Forum Baths, Insula VI) [**H**], with separate sections for men and women. The women's baths have the more attractive and better preserved mosaic flooring; the male section is larger and contains an exercise area and a round *frigidarium*, in addition to the mandatory *apodyterium* (changing room), *tepidarium* and *calidarium* also found in the female section next door. Note the *apodyteria*, with partitioned shelves for depositing togas and belongings, and the low *podia* to use as seating space while queuing.

HERCULANEUM KEY

A	Original Shoreline
B	Terme Suburbane
C	Casa dei Cervi
D	Taberna di Priapo
E	Thermopolia
F	Plaestra
G	Casa di Nettuno e Anfitrite
H	Terme del Foro
I	Casa del Tramezzo di Legno
J	Casa dell'Albergo
K	Casa dell'Atrio a Mosaico

Unusually, the Casa del Tramezzo di Legno (House of the Wooden Partition, Insula III) [**J**] has two atria. This suggests that there were originally two houses here, joined together in the first century AD when one of the emerging class of *mercatores* (traders) perhaps bought out the patrician owner. Note the carbonised wooden screen beyond the marble *impluvium*, separating the atrium from the *tablinum*, where the *patronus*, or master of the house, conducted business with his clients.

Further down Cardo IV is the Casa dell'Albergo (House of the Inn, Insula III) [**K**]. One of the largest buildings in Herculaneum, it was undergoing restoration from previous earthquake damage when it was overwhelmed by the eruption in AD 79. Note

ESCAPES & EXCURSIONS

Herculaneum. See p194.

the small private baths just to the right of the main entrance, with wall decorations in second Pompeiian style. Beyond the atrium is an impressive peristyle enclosing a sunken garden. The trunk of a pear tree was found here, suggesting that the garden may have been an orchard. Pear trees have been replanted here in an attempt to recreate the original vegetation.

Outside the main site, just across the road from the bookshop and cafeteria, is the Villa dei Papiri. It was a luxurious villa, measuring 250m (870ft) from end to end, where a total of 87 sculptures – Roman copies of Greek originals – and more than 1,000 charred but legible papyrus rolls were unearthed. Most of the papyri are the product of a lesser-known Epicurean poet and scholar called Philodemos, and not, as had been hoped, lost works of Aristotle. The magnificent statues are now in the Museo Archeologico Nazionale in Naples (*see p82*) and the villa is closed for restoration with little chance of reopening any time soon.

At any given time in Herculaneum, there are likely to be houses closed or cordoned off, either due to lack of staff or for renovation work. A list of the buildings open to the public is posted at the site ticket office.

Le Ville Vesuviane

The administrative offices of the Ville Vesuviane association are on the ground floor of **Villa Campolieto**. For information and a list of villas included in the association, call in at the office – staff are happy to help. Villa Campolieto, the park of Villa Favorita and Villa delle Ginestre are all used as venues for the **Festival delle Ville Vesuviane** (www.festivalvillevesuviane. it) in the summer, mainly featuring Italian rock and pop artists.

★ Villa Campolieto
Corso Resina 283, Ercolano (081 732 2134, www. villevesuviane.net). **Open** *Office* 9am-2pm Mon-Fri. *Villa* 10am-1pm Tue-Sun. **Admission** €3 (ticket valid for all villas). **No credit cards**.
Designed by Luigi and Carlo Vanvitelli, the Villa Campolieto was built between 1760 and 1775. The circular portico – where a summer concert season is held – has a sweeping view over Ercolano and down to the sea. The villa was closed for restoration at the time of writing, but will reopen in early 2016 with the rooms restored to their original grandeur. For more information and a list of the *ville* in the area, call in at the office on the ground floor, where staff are happy to help.

FREE Villa Favorita Park
Via Gabriele d'Annunzio 36, Ercolano (081 739 3961). **Open** 10am-1pm Tue-Sun. **Admission** free. **No credit cards**.

Dotted with gracious pavilions and teahouses, the Villa Favorita's lower park sweeps down towards the sea and a jetty – all that remains of a Bourbon construction that was the nearest thing Italy had to Brighton Pier. On the seaward side of the park is the restored Palazzina del Mosaico, now used for conferences and accessible on a guided tour. The park makes a spectacular setting for summer concerts and opera performances.

▶ *For details of forthcoming events, check online at www.villevesuviane.net.*

Villa delle Ginestre

Via Villa delle Ginestre 21, Torre del Greco (081 732 2134). **Open** 10am-1pm Tue-Sun. **Admission** €3 (ticket valid for all villas). **No credit cards.**

Once home to poet Giacomo Leopardi (1798-1837), and now a museum dedicated to his life and work, the late 16th-century Villa delle Ginestre is tucked away in the countryside at the foot of Vesuvius. On the main floor is Leopardi's bedroom, complete with its original furnishings, where he wrote *La Ginestra* and *Il Tramonto della Luna*, as well as several multimedia rooms, a small cinema and a wraparound balcony that circles the entire villa. From the roof, you can share the same views over the gardens to Vesuvius and the sea that Leopardi himself would have enjoyed.

Villa Ruggiero

Via Alessandro Rossi 40, Ercolano (081 732 2134). **Open** 9am-1pm Tue-Sun. **Admission** €3 (ticket valid for all villas). **No credit cards.**

The Villa Ruggiero, set slightly back from the main road, was built during the mid 18th century for the baronial Petti family. Note that only the elegant courtyard is on show.

Where to stay & eat

If you want somewhere to stay near Ercolano, comfortable, modern **Hotel Andris** (*see p205*) lies within the Vesuvio National Park to the east of the town and has a good restaurant. Offering a wine list of around 1,500 labels and a weekly-changing menu focused on Campania, stylish new-generation osteria **Viva lo Re** (Corso Resina 216, Ercolano, 081 739 0207, www.vivalore.it, closed Mon & Sun eve, last 3wks Aug, average €30) is an excellent place to recharge the batteries after a visit to Herculaneum (a five-minute walk away). Tuck into the likes of potato and artichoke soup, local swordfish and home-made tiramisù.

TORRE DEL GRECO

Torre del Greco displays much of the urban blight common to all the *comuni vesuviani*. Located in the heart of the volcano's red alert area, its 110,000 inhabitants – known as *corallini* – blithely

press on with business as usual; the manufacture of coral and cameos (hence *corallini*) is a major source of income, along with floriculture. Coral is highly prized in the East Asian market, so the factories are often visited by tour groups. Skilled artists and trainees can be seen at work at the privately owned **APA Coral & Cameo Factory**, which is located conveniently close to the Torre del Greco motorway exit.

The **Museo del Corallo** has fine 18th-century pieces from the Trapanese school and attractive cameos set on malleable lavic stone.

FREE APA Coral & Cameo Factory

Via Cavallo 6 (081 881 1155, www.lpm-apa.com). **Open** 8.30am-6.30pm daily. **Admission** free.

If you can navigate between the tour groups, the quality of the artistry may persuade you to buy.

FREE Museo del Corallo

Piazza Luigi Palomba 6 (081 881 1360, www.isdegni.it). **Open** 9am-1pm Mon-Sat; advance booking required by email (nais048006@istruzione.it). **Admission** free.

The museum – open again after a two-year closure – is located on the first floor of the Istituto Statale d'Arte technical college.

Where to stay & eat

Torre del Greco is home to one of Italy's finest pizzerias, according to a recent article in well-respected Italian food guide *L'Espresso*. **Palazzo Vialdo** (Via Nazionale 081, 081 847 1624, www.palazzovialdo.it, open noon-3pm, 7-11.30pm, average €15 pizzeria, €35 bistro) is actually three eateries rolled into one; bistro, pizzeria, and gourmet sandwich/wine bar. At the pizzeria, you'll find classics such as margherita and marinana (you can choose from no less than five types of local tomato), but there are also more complex combinations such as mozzarella, frisée salad leaves and anchovies. The bistro serves a full menu of both fish and meat options.

TORRE ANNUNZIATA & OPLONTIS

Once a thriving town where Neapolitans spent their summers lazing on black volcanic beaches, Torre Annunziata lost its allure long ago – today it provides plenty of material for the *cronaca nera* (crime news) pages in the local papers. It does have one saving grace, though, the wondrous archaeological site of Oplontis.

★ Oplontis

Via Sepolcri 1 (081 862 1755, www.pompeiisites.org). **Open** *Apr-Oct* 8.30am-7.30pm daily (ticket office closes 6pm). *Nov-Mar* 8.30am-5.30pm daily (ticket office closes 4pm). **Admission** €5.50; €2.75

ESCAPES & EXCURSIONS

reductions; free under-18s (EU citizens). Ticket also valid for Antiquarium di Boscoreale. **No credit cards**.

On the basis of an inscription on an amphora, this villa is thought to have belonged to Nero's second wife, Poppaea Sabina – the prosaically named Villa A certainly has some of the finest examples of the second Pompeiian style of wall painting. Whether or not Poppaea really lived here and indulged her passion for asses' milk baths within its finely frescoed walls, she would have done better to stay with her husband, Marcus Otho, rather than take up with Nero, who arranged for Otho to be posted as governor of the far-flung province of Lusitania (central Portugal). Poppaea eventually became imperial wife number two in AD 62 before – if Tacitus is to be believed – she was kicked to death by Nero three years later while pregnant.

This delightful, under-visited villa amply merits a ramble. As you get your ticket or show your Artecard (*see p297*), you'll be given a helpful site map and a booklet describing each major room or living space. The west wing is right up against the main road; more lies below it, unexplored. West of the reconstructed main atrium (room 1), the walls of the *tridinium* (room 6) contain stunning illusionist motifs. The *calidarium* in the adjoining baths complex (room 3) has a delicate miniature landscape scene surmounted by a peacock in a niche at the far end; the adjacent *tepidarium* (room 4) shows off Roman baths and heating systems: the floor is raised by *suspensurae* (brick pilasters), enabling warm air to pass beneath.

Off the portico on the southern side of the site is an *oecus* or living room (room 8) with spectacular still-life frescoes in the second Pompeiian style; the *cubicula* (bedrooms) nearby have frescoes in the finer, less brash third style. As you leave the warren of *cubicula*, the spaces become more grandiose, culminating with a large *piscina* (swimming pool) fringed, in Roman times, with oleander and lemon trees. The atmosphere of relaxation and contemplation lingers, making this a pleasant antidote to what the poet Horace would have called the *profanum vulgus* (vulgar rabble) down the road in Pompeii.

The site is very close to the Circumvesuviana railway station of Torre Annunziata. Turn left outside the station, right at the first junction and then straight across at the traffic lights. The site is 100m (330ft) down the road on your left. As this is a depressed area, avoid visits in the early afternoon when the streets are deserted. By car, take the motorway exit at Torre Annunziata Nord and follow the brown signposts for 'Scavi di Oplontis'; bear in mind there's no attended parking at the site.

POMPEI & POMPEII

To many Italians, Pompei (the town, as opposed to Pompeii, the architectural site) is a place of pilgrimage. People flock here from all over the south to pay their respects to the Madonna in the

POMPEII KEY

A	Porta Marina
B	Basilica
C	Forum
D	Tempio di Giove
E	Marcellum
F	Terme del Foro
G	Casa del Fauno
H	Lupanare
I	Porta Ercolano
J	Villa dei Misteri
K	Terme Stabiane
L	Teatro Grande
M	Odeion
N	Casa dei Casti Amanti
O	Palaestra
P	Anfiteatro

large, early 20th-century *santuario* on the main square, Piazza Bartolo Longo, praying for the kind of miracle that healed a girl suffering from epilepsy in 1876. Others bring their new cars to have them blessed and secure divine protection; given local driving standards and roads, this seems a wise precaution.

The sheer volume of religious and cultural tourism caught modern Pompei by surprise. Having long reaped the benefits of mass tourism and given little in return, the town now has some nice surprises in store: once-seedy lodgings have given way to well-appointed hotels, and eating out is no longer hit-and-miss, especially if you leave the archaeological site for the town centre.

About three kilometres to the north is the **Antiquarium di Boscoreale**, opened in the 1990s as a permanent exhibition on Pompeii and its environment some 2,000 years ago. Reconstructions show idyllic scenes of wildlife along the River Sarno, now, regrettably, one of the most polluted waterways in Italy.

★ Antiquarium di Boscoreale
Villa Regina, Via Settetermini 15 (081 536 8796, www.pompeiisites.org). **Open** *Apr-Oct* 8.30am-7.30pm daily (ticket office closes 6pm). *Nov-Mar* 8.30am-5pm daily (ticket office closes 3.30pm). **Admission** €5.50; €2.75 reductions; free under-18s (EU citizens). Ticket also valid for Oplontis. **No credit cards**.

Set incongruously in the middle of a 1960s housing development – indeed, that's how the villa here was originally discovered – the Antiquarium documents daily life, the environment and technology in Roman times. Disparate finds ranging from fishing tackle to ceramic cages for rearing dormice (a favourite Roman delicacy) are displayed alongside life-size photos of original mosaics and frescoes from other sites and museums. In the grounds of the museum

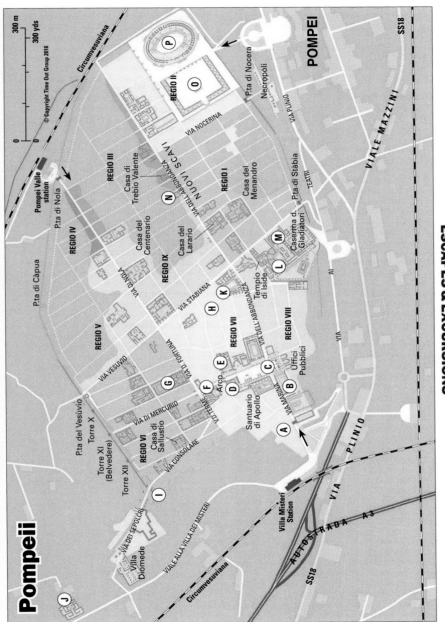

Pompeii

POMPEI

ESCAPES & EXCURSIONS

is Villa Regina (currently closed for renovation work), an ancient farmstead with storage capacity for 10,000 litres (2,200 gallons) of wine. The villa's vineyard has been replanted along ancient rows. The Porta Marina tourist office at Pompeii (*see p205*) will direct you here, though it's best approached via the Circumvesuviana station at Boscoreale, where a skeletal bus service is provided.

★ Scavi di Pompeii

Porta Marina, Piazza Anfiteatro, Piazza Esedra (081 857 5347, www.pompeiisites.org). **Open** *Apr-Oct* 8.30am-7.30pm daily (ticket office closes 6pm). *Nov-Mar* 8.30am-5pm daily (ticket office closes 3.30pm). **Admission** €13; €7.50 reductions; free under-18s (EU citizens). *Audioguide* €6.50; children's version €4.
Bold letters in the text refer to map (p199).
Unlike Rome, where ancient monuments have suffered millennia of weathering, re-use and pillaging, Pompeii had the good fortune (for posterity at any rate) of being overwhelmed by the AD 79 eruption of Vesuvius. The ancient street plan is intact, the town still has its full complement of civic buildings, the houses still have their frescoed walls, and – thanks to painstaking work by generations of archaeologists and vulcanologists – we have a fairly clear picture of what life was like here 2,000 years ago. The picture is still being completed: emergency digs during roadworks on the Naples–Salerno motorway have revealed the full extent of a frescoed leisure complex close to the Sarno river, and the tomb of a Sannite woman, believed to date from 350 BC, was discovered just outside Porta Ercolano in September 2015.

Pompeii came under uncomfortable worldwide scrutiny in November 2010 when the building known as the House of the Gladiators collapsed along with its precious frescoes, apparently due to unusually heavy rainfall. It became a symbol of management incompetence and political neglect – 'a world scandal' shouted the *Repubblica* newspaper; 'a disgrace for Italy' cried President Giorgio Napolitano – and Pompeii declared a state of emergency. Since then, there have been other, less high-profile collapses and tales of financial misdealings, official corruption and protection rackets. But an injection of funds in 2013, partially from the EU, has paved the way for a multi-million euro makeover and talk at government level about how to put the dignity back into Pompeii. Proposals include more efficient staffing, improvements in ongoing maintenance and more visitor-friendly facilities. Eight buildings reopened to the public in 2014, the celebrated Villa dei Misteri reopened the following year and work has started on rebuilding the House of the Gladiators.

For now, though, visitor facilities at Pompeii are still pretty minimal: the site only has one very mediocre bar-restaurant, although there are plenty of places to have a snack or full meal outside the entrances (the quality of the food improves the further you get from the site). The maps supplied at the information booth tend to run out and are not always up to date, but they can be downloaded from the website (*see p201* **Visiting Pompeii**). Signposting is scarce, areas may be cordoned off and wildcat strikes by site guards can mean that entry to the site is blocked without notice: in this case, get on the first Naples-bound Circumvesuviana train and get off at Torre Annunziata to visit Oplontis (*see p197*) or Ercolano-Scavi for Herculaneum (*see p194*).

The Porta Marina [**A**], with its separate entrances for pedestrians (on the left) and animals and light vehicles (on the right), is near the original harbour, hence the name. (The shoreline is now much further away than in antiquity, when a canal is thought to have provided access from the sea to the town.) This gate provided the quickest way of getting to that hub of Roman life, the forum – though as the route was also the steepest, most vehicles would probably have taken one of the other seven gates leading into town.

On the right is the basilica [**B**], Pompeii's law court and stock exchange. These rectangular buildings ending in semicircular apses were the model for early Christian churches.

The forum [**C**] is a rectangular area with a colonnade surmounted by a loggia running along three sides. Plinths at the southern end indicate that a row of large statues once stood here. At the northern end are the remains of the second-century BC Tempio di Giove (Temple of Jupiter) [**D**] with the cone of Vesuvius behind. As Jupiter was head of the Roman pantheon, it was standard practice to dedicate a temple to him (together with Juno and Minerva) at the centre of town. The temple had already suffered severe damage in an earthquake before AD 79.

The elegant, three-columned portico on the eastern side of the forum marks the entrance to the *macellum* [**E**], a covered meat and fish market built in early imperial times.

The *terme del foro* (forum baths) [**F**] are small as Roman baths go, but retain much of the original stucco decoration. Within the *calidarium* is a well-preserved marble *labrum* (fountain) with an inscription in bronze letters around the rim, recording the names of the officials (C Melissaeus Aper and M Staius Rufus) who installed it in AD 3-4, as well as its cost (5,420 sesterces). Except for a short period in early Imperial times, sexes were segregated in all Roman baths; women would have had the morning shift and men the afternoon.

Close to the baths on Via della Fortuna is the Casa del Fauno (House of the Faun) [**G**], named after the small bronze statue in the middle of the marble *impluvium* (the original is in the Museo Archeologico Nazionale; *see p82*). One of the largest and most sophisticated houses in Pompeii, its front section is arranged around two atria; behind is a peristyle with a portico of Ionic columns. Found in the *exedra* (discussion hall) at the far end of the first peristyle, flanked by two *tridinia*, was a million-tessera mosaic (also in the Museo Archeologico Nazionale).

VISITING POMPEII
What you need to know before you go.

Allow at least three hours to visit Pompeii; it will take longer if you intend to see the amphitheatre and the newly restored Villa dei Misteri, which are a good 25 minutes' hike apart. The audioguides offer two-, four- or six-hour itineraries – times that are probably an underestimate if you choose to listen to the optional in-depth information supplied. The Pompeii Sites website (www. pompeiisites.org) has a page that lists which buildings are open when. At the time of going to press, the *terme suburbane* (suburban baths) near the Porta Marina, the Casa del Menandro (House of Menander) near the theatre and the Casa degli Amorini Dorati (House of the Gilded Cupids) were open from 9.30am to 5.20pm daily.

Ask for a site map and free information booklet from the information booth at the Porta Marina entrance (they tend to run out at the Piazza Anfiteatro entrance). Alternatively, save time and download the map and guide from the website before you visit. Afternoon visits to the site pay dividends, as the crowds start to thin out. The Circumvesuviana railway station at Pompei Scavi-Villa dei Misteri is opposite the main Porta Marina entrance to the site; just inside, the forum is a good place to get your bearings.

There's very little shade at Pompeii and the sun can be merciless in the summer months. It's best to visit on an overcast day; if this isn't possible, take precautions by carrying plenty of drinking water and wearing a sun hat.

It's thought to depict the Battle of Issus in 330 BC, fought between Alexander the Great and the Persian emperor Darius III. Artists from the Ravenna School of Mosaics have now completed a faithful replica of this remarkable mosaic in situ, so you can see where it would have been displayed.

Outside the city walls, through the attractive Porta Ercolano [I] leading towards Herculaneum and Neapolis, the Villa dei Misteri (Villa of Mysteries) [J] reopened in March 2015 after two years of restoration, mainly focused on the wall paintings and floors. The frescoes in the *tridinium* depict – experts believe – a young woman's initiation into the cult of Dionysus: there are ten scenes of vivid intensity, thought to have been copied from a local artist from a Hellenistic original of the fourth- or third-century BC. The villa was a working farm for much of its existence; the wine-making area is still visible at the northern end.

Stroll down the main street (Via dell'Abbondanza) from the forum towards the amphitheatre and the town takes on a different feel. The shops here can be identified by their broad entrances for easy access from the street. Private houses had *fauces* (narrow passages) – security was a problem in ancient Pompeii, and inhabitants went to great lengths to protect themselves and their property.

The Terme Stabiane (Stabian Baths) [K] are a much larger complex than the forum baths, with the exercise area in the middle surrounded by the male and female sections. The stuccoed vault in the men's *apodyterium* (changing room), with its images of nymphs and cupids, is particularly well preserved.

There are also two cases containing gruesome plastercasts of Pompeii inhabitants; a graphic reminder of the last-minute agonies suffered by those who failed to escape in time. The technique of pumping liquid cement into the voids left when the victims' bodies decayed was pioneered by Giuseppe Fiorelli in the 1860s. If these have merely whetted your appetite, head over to the Orto dei Fuggiaschi (Garden of the Fugitives) near the amphitheatre, where whole families were overwhelmed and re-emerged as casts two millennia later.

The Lupanare [H] is believed to have been the ancient city's only purpose-built brothel (*lupa* is latin for she-wolf). The explicit wall paintings within have long attracted visitors.

To the south is the theatre complex. The Teatro Grande [L] seats about 5,000 and – like so many theatres in the ancient world – enjoyed a stunning backdrop, in this case the Sarno river plain in the foreground and the heights of Mons Lactarius (Monti Lattari) behind. This second-century BC theatre underwent a great deal of restoration in antiquity, unlike the adjoining smaller Odeion or Theatrum Tectum [M]. The semicircular *cavea* (seating area) was truncated at both ends to facilitate the building of a permanent roof, which would have offered welcome shade to Pompeii's concert-goers. Opera and ballet productions are now staged at the Teatro Grande for the new Pompei Festival (www.pompeifestival.it), launched in 2014 with a production of Puccini's *La Bohème*.

North of Via dell'Abbondanza, excavations continue around the Casa dei Casti Amanti (House of the Chaste Lovers; closed for restoration) [N]. The house has yielded important evidence about life immediately prior to the eruption. Earthquake damage from AD 62 had been repaired, and the inhabitants were trying to patch up cracks from recent tremors, perhaps days before the AD 79 eruption; the rooms were being replastered and painted by teams of craftsmen at the moment Vesuvius erupted. In the rapid getaway, tools were downed and plaster abandoned. The donkeys – turning the grindstone and milling wheat in the adjoining bakery – were left to their fiery fate.

The large *palaestra* [O], a rectangular porticoed exercise area dating from the Augustan period, was reopened in 2015 after a five-year restoration. At the gym's southern portico is the new permanent exhibition of Moregine frescoes accompanied by a sound installation. West of here are recently planted vineyards that use grape varieties and training systems thought to have been employed in ancient times. Villa dei Misteri 2002 was snapped up at dizzying prices.

By Roman standards, the *anfiteatro* (amphitheatre) [P] was small, seating about 20,000. Entertainment would probably have been limited to gladiatorial combat, with occasional *venationes* (contests with wild animals) or *naumachiae* (mock sea battles). Though gladiators had a fairly short life expectancy – it was considered an occupation for slaves and social outcasts – records do exist of the odd volunteer signing on for combat. The amphitheatre preserves a fair amount of its seating area, divided into three sections, with a series of *vomitoria* (entrances) near the top.

Where to stay & eat

Conveniently close to the amphitheatre entrance of the Pompeii archaeological zone, the four-star **Hotel Forum** (Via Roma 99, 081 850 6132, www.hotelforum.it, from €80 double) is thankfully set back from the main road. **Il Principe** (Piazza Bartolo Longo 1, 081 850 5566, www.ilprincipe.com, closed Mon & 3wks Jan, average €40) serves ancient recipes gleaned from classical authors. If you make it to dessert, try the exquisite cassata Oplontis, with honey and goat's milk ricotta. Michelin-starred **President** (Piazza Schettino 12/13, 081 850 7245, www.ristorantepresident.net), closed Mon in winter & Jan, average €50) is located between the *scavi* and the *santuario* and serves modern Campanian dishes such as pasta with clams, bitter *friarielli* greens, raw prawns and candied lemon peel: the wine list is formidable. For something simpler (and some excellent pizza), head for **Ristorante Carlo Alberto**, just opposite Il Principe (Via Carlo Alberto 15, 081 863 3231, www.ristopizzacarloalberto.it, average €20).

CASTELLAMMARE DI STABIA & STABIAE

Famed for its spa, shipyards and *biscottifici* (biscuit factories), Castellammare has not only been bypassed by the coast road, but has also suffered gradual industrial decline over the past 30 years. Although the shipyards are once again humming with activity, and there's a swish new tourist port full of yachts, the transport infrastructure and pedestrian access will have to be massively improved before ancient Stabiae's archaeological heritage can be fully exploited. Castellammare is served by rail, and there are hydrofoil and ferry services to Capri; there's also a *funivia* cable car up Monte Faito, but it's closed at present with no word as to when it will reopen.

Monte Faito
Stazione Circumvesuviana, Castellammare di Stabia (081 879 3097, www.vesuviana.it).
With its pleasant walks through shady beech woods, Monte Faito provides an escape from the heat in the steamy summer months. From the top, the views over the Bay of Naples are nerve-tingling. Robins retreat here in summer from the coast, and the distinctive calls of nuthatches can be heard as they flit from tree to tree. Plants tend to flower much later than down on the coast; for late spring orchids, look in the clearings and in the more exposed areas below the cable car station.

The upper *funivia* station is the start of hiking trails across to Positano: allow five to six hours, take good maps and water, and be prepared for plenty of ups and downs. There are also low-key circular routes through the beech forest. The path from the *funivia* to the chapel of San Michele, about 3km away, climbs 170m (595ft); you'll be rewarded with splendid views of Vesuvius and the Sarno valley.

At the time of writing, the *funivia* had been closed for a year with no reopening date in sight. However, you can also reach the summit of the mountain by car from Castellammare or from Vico Equense on the Sorrentine Peninsula.

FREE Stabiae (Scavi di Castellammare)

Via Passeggiata Archeologica (081 871 4541).
Open *Apr-Oct* 8.30am-7.30pm daily (last admission 6pm). *Nov-Mar* 8.30am-5pm daily (last admission 3.30pm). **Admission** free.

'Ash was already falling, hotter and thicker as the ships drew near, followed by bits of pumice and blackened stones, charred and cracked by flames: then suddenly they were in shallow water, and the shore was blocked by debris from the mountain. For a moment my uncle wondered whether to turn back, but when the helmsman advised this he refused, telling him that Fortune stood by the courageous, and they must make for Pomponianus at Stabiae.'

So reads Pliny the Younger's account of his uncle's ill-fated attempt to rescue Pomponianus, a friend living 5km south of Pompeii at Stabiae – modern-day Castellammare di Stabia. Pliny wouldn't recognise today's coastline, which extends much further out to sea than it did in AD 79. Nowadays, too, decidedly unlovely postwar urban development rises where his uncle would have encountered shallow water, and the seaside settlement where Pomponianus may have lived is perched on the bluff of a hill called Varano, almost a kilometre inland.

The archaeological site of Stabiae was partially explored and plundered by the Bourbons 200 years ago: some Roman wall paintings left behind were deliberately defaced to enhance the value of artworks removed to adorn the king's palaces. It fell into further disrepair as resources were siphoned off to unearth Pompeii in the 18th and 19th centuries, and it was only in the 1950s that the site began to recover from centuries of neglect – although the 1980 earthquake set the work back.

Two villa complexes can be visited: Villa Arianna and Villa San Marco. Both are set just off the Passeggiata Archeologica, the road that skirts around the south-eastern side of Castellammare. For these sites you really need a car, and a skilled navigator to pick out the faded signs pointing to the villas. The ground plans are complex, because of additions and extensions carried out in antiquity, and partly because they were designed to fit the lie of the land. Named after a fresco depicting King Minos's daughter Ariadne, who helped Theseus out of the labyrinth after he killed the Minotaur, Villa Arianna is the oldest structure on the hill. Dating from the first century BC, it was renovated and extended in the first century AD. New rooms relating to the villa's thermal complex, and two rooms that originally opened on to the villa's atrium and contain well-preserved wall paintings, were opened to the public in 2015.

Although the frescoed decorations are less spectacular in Villa San Marco, it would have made a pleasant summer retreat for a wealthy Roman magnate. The location was ideal: far away from the imperial intrigues on the other side of the Bay of Naples in Baiae, yet reasonably close to main thoroughfares linking large urban centres such as Pompeii and Nuceria (now Nocera). With its 30m (98ft) *natatio* (swimming pool) flanked by rows of plane trees and enclosed on three sides by a peristyle, this was a place for enjoying *otium* (relaxation) to the full.

Where to stay

The **Towers Hotel** (SS 145 Sorrentina, km 11, Località Pozzano, Castellammare di Stabia, 081 872 2477, www.towershotelsorrento.com, €120-€240 double) is an impressive conversion of an old cement factory with wonderful views of Vesuvius and the Bay of Naples, luxury accommodation and excellent facilities.

Set in verdant gardens, within walking distance of the Stabian villas, the **Grand Hotel La Medusa** (Via Passeggiata Archeologica 5, 081 872 3383, www.lamedusahotel.com, €120-€265 double) is a renovated fin-de-siècle villa, providing the perfect antidote to the hustle and hassle down in the *comuni vesuviani*.

VESUVIUS

Before Pompeii and Herculaneum were all but obliterated on 24 August AD 79, Vesuvius was a very different mountain. Possibly as high as 2,000 metres (6,600 feet), it was covered with thick vegetation; few people suspected they were living close to a major geological hazard.

Today's residents – about 700,000 live in the 13 *comuni vesuviani* around the base and on the lower slopes of the 1,281-metre (4,203-foot) volcano – opt to be as blissfully unconcerned by this threat as their counterparts 2,000 years ago. They're not about to abandon the fertile volcanic soil: the slopes produce wine (Lacryma Christi, which has shaken off its downmarket reputation thanks to some state-of-the-art wineries), and the area's small, pointed *piennolo* tomatoes (delicious on pasta) earn tidy profits for local farmers. Besides, there are few visible reminders of the danger. Vesuvius does not spew lava like Etna, or eject ash like Stromboli. It lost its *pennacchio*, or plume of smoke, in 1944, and the lava fields created by previous eruptions are gradually being colonised by vegetation, giving the volcano a deceptively benign appearance.

The authorities have abandoned the idea of mass resettlement, and the main focus now is on swift evacuation in the event of an eruption. Given the numbers of people involved and the current state of the road network, early warning of any eruption is critical. That's where the

Vesuvius.

of San Sebastiano al Vesuvio up to the Bourbon observatory. Much of the park, though, is fenced off for security reasons: forest fires (often started deliberately to free up land for building projects) have wrought considerable damage in recent years, and access to certain areas is now only granted for scientific purposes.

Vesuvius is at its best in early summer, in particular in May or June, when the upper slopes are awash with colourful wild flowers (look out for the leggy Mount Etna broom and red valerian) and nightingales, whitethroats and blue rock thrushes are marking out their territory with prolific song. Start your visit first thing in the morning, and avoid windy days when conditions on the exposed rim can be harsh.

By far the best way to approach is from the Circumvesuviana train station at Ercolano. Just outside the station to the left is the Vesuvio Express office (see p205), which organises an efficient collective taxi service up to the car park. For €10 per person, a minibus ferries you as far up as vehicles can go, allows about 80-90 minutes for the ascent and descent, then completes the return trip – which means a visit could take as little as three hours out of your day.

Once at the car park at Quota 1,000 (1,000 metres above sea level), the standard half-hour route to the cone zigzags along a well-kept path up the mountain's western flank. Although the inside of the crater itself is off limits, there's a good view of steaming fumaroles and stratified pyroclastic deposits on the other side of the crater rim. Fight your acrophobia and peer down into the crater; enterprising plants have moved in, joining several bird species.

Also on the road up the western slope of the volcano, the **Museo dell'Osservatorio Vesuviano** offers a broad overview of the geology of the volcano and the threats it poses, as well as some Heath Robinson-style seismographs from the 19th century. It's housed in the old Bourbon observatory, a distinctive Pompeiian-red building that has survived the ravages of at least seven eruptions.

Osservatorio Vesuviano comes in. The institute, which has monitored Vesuvius's activity since 1841, has warned that the volcano could erupt any time between 20 and 200 years from now. The longer it lies dormant (the last eruption was in 1944), the greater the risk.

When the volcano does blow, scientists believe it will not be ash fallout or lava flow that pose the greatest danger to the locals and the landscape, but a surge cloud of the kind that rolled down the mountain in AD 79 at an estimated 65 to 80 kilometres per hour and produced the ultimate open-air *calidarium*. Reaching a temperature of 400°C, it caused the widespread devastation still evident today.

Vesuvius is now a national park and a UNESCO Biosphere Reserve. But of the 400,000 visitors who trek up to the rim of its cone and peer down into the depths of the crater 200 metres (700 feet) below, few currently stay to enjoy the wilder side of the volcano. The park authority (www. parconazionaledelvesuvio.it) has marked out footpaths; one of the best goes from the town

★ Cratere del Vesuvio

(081 771 0939, www.parconazionaledelvesuvio.it/ grancono). **Open** *Mar, Oct* 9am-4pm daily. *Apr-June* 9am-5pm daily. *July, Aug* 9am-6pm daily. *Nov-Feb* 9am-3pm daily. **Admission** €10; €8 reductions; free children under 1.2m. **No credit cards**.
Trips to the volcano's crater are suspended during bad weather or when fog descends.

FREE Museo dell'Osservatorio Vesuviano

Via Osservatorio (081 610 8560, www.ov.ingv.it). **Open** *by reservation only* Apr-July 9am-4pm Mon-Sat, 10am-4pm Sun. Sept-Mar 9.30am-4pm Mon-Sat, 10am-4pm Sun. Closed Aug. **Admission** free.

Look for signs to the Osservatorio at 600m (2,000ft) above sea level, just behind the Eremo Hotel.

Where to stay & eat

You wouldn't expect to find a stylish, modern hotel on the slopes of Vesuvius, but the **Hotel Andris** (Via San Vito 130, 081 777 1312, www. andrishotel.it, €65-€85 double) is just that. Immersed in the Vesuvius national park, a few kilometres from the Ercolano archaeological site, it has 23 rooms, a good restaurant (average €28) and a pool with views down to the coast.

On the southern slope of the volcano (and convenient for Pompeii) lies *agriturismo* and wine estate **Le Lune del Vesuvio** (Via Vicinale Lavarella, Terzigno, 081 828 2420, www.vini forno.it), where you can taste a range of wines (including Lacryma Cristi) and feast on the likes of spaghetti with local *piennolo* tomatoes at the restaurant (menus from €25). For the 2016 season, there will also be four B&B rooms.

TOURIST INFORMATION

Azienda Autonoma di Cura, Soggiorno e Turismo *Via Sacra 1, Pompei (081 850 7255, www.pompeiturismo.it).* **Open** 8am-3.40pm Mon-Fri.

Ufficio di Informazione e di Accoglienza Turistica *Via IV Novembre 82, Ercolano (081 788 1243).* **Open** *June-Sept* 9am-6pm daily. *Oct-Apr* 10am-5pm daily.
The Ercolano office can also provide information on neighbouring Portici.

Ufficio di Informazione e di Accoglienza Turistica *Porta Marina entrance, Pompeii archaeological site (081 857 5347, www.pompeii sites.org).* **Open** *Apr-Oct* 9am-5.30pm daily. *Nov-Mar* 9am-3.30pm daily.
This Pompeii tourist office can also provide information on Torre del Greco, Torre Annunziata and Castellammare di Stabia.

GETTING THERE
By bus

Run by **ANM** (www.anm.it), bus 157 from Via Brin goes to Ercolano. But given the traffic hell and route complexities, the train is a far better bet.

Vesuvio Express (081 739 3666, www. vesuvioexpress.it) runs a minibus to the car park on Vesuvius from the Ercolano Circumvesuviana station (€10 return). Alternatively, a local **Trasporti Vesuvian** bus (081 963 4420, 081 963 4418) starts from Piazza Anfiteatro in Pompei, stops at Piazza Esedra near the motorway toll booth and at Ercolano train station, then winds its way to the top (€2.70 each way). Check return times, and say if you need to stop at the Museo

dell'Osservatorio. **EAV** (081 014 1012, www.eavslr.it) runs a bus service from Piazza Piedigrotta in downtown Naples to Vesuvius twice a day each way; and **Tramvia** (www. tramvianapoli.com) runs a vintage tram bus (€10 each way) from the Stazione Marittima to Pompeii and Vesuvius.

By car

Most sites are fairly close to the A3 Naples–Salerno motorway. For Herculaneum, take the Ercolano exit and follow the signs to Scavi di Ercolano. For Oplontis, exit at Torre Annunziata Sud, turning right when you hit the first main road. Follow signs to Scavi di Oplontis. For Pompeii, if travelling from Naples take the Pompei Ovest exit from the A3 motorway (Pompeii is beside this exit). From Salerno, take the first Pompei exit.

For Vesuvius, coming from Torre del Greco or Ercolano, just follow the signs to the Parco Nazionale del Vesuvio.

For Boscoreale, exit at Pompei Ovest and follow signs to the Antiquarium (or ask for directions from the helpful information office at Porta Marina in Pompeii, *see left*).

For Stabiae, take the Castellammare di Stabia exit from the A3 and follow the signs to Sorrento (not Castellammare). Take the first exit (Gragnano) from the Sorrento road; the Passeggiata Archeologica starts at the junction (opposite) where the exit road meets the main Gragnano–Castellammare road.

You'll have to pay to park at Herculaneum and Pompeii; Stabiae and Boscoreale have free parking.

By train

The major sites are all served by the Circumvesuviana railway (800 211 388, www. eavsrl.it). If you're travelling from Naples to Pompeii, take the Naples–Sorrento line and get off at Pompei Scavi–Villa dei Misteri. The swish new Naples-Sorrento Campania Express, inaugurated in May 2015 and also run by EAV, was designed with tourists in mind. Leaving from Naples Porta Nolana and only stopping at Naples Piazza Garibaldi, Ercolano-Scavi, Pompei-Villa dei Misteri and Sorrento, it is much faster than the squalid old Circumvesuviana trains and comes complete with a multi-lingual hostess. Tickets cost €15 return (or €10 with the Campania ArteCard).

The other Pompei station lies on a different line and is closer to the amphitheatre entrance.

Boscoreale (Boscoreale station) requires a considerable amount of legwork and is very poorly signposted; for Stabiae (Via Nocera station, Castellammare), you need to take bus 1 Rosso from near the station.

Sorrento & Around

Sorrento may have been an obligatory stop for Grand Tour travellers during the 18th and 19th centuries, but its powers of seduction were already acknowledged in ancient times. The Greeks are believed to have settled the area in around the sixth century BC and they founded Surrentum, the 'city of the sirens'; it was here that Odysseus was lured by the seductive song of these mythical creatures with the heads of women and the bodies of birds. He was only saved by having himself tied to the mast of his ship and filling the sailors' ears with wax. These days, while it may have a vaguely passé air, Sorrento is an undeniably pretty resort and remains hugely popular; it makes a welcome escape from chaotic Naples and an excellent base for exploring the area.

INTRODUCING THE AREA

Viewed from Naples, the Sorrentine Peninsula resembles a gnobbly, outstretched finger pointed at Capri, which lies off its tip like a Modigliani head. Magnificently placed on the northern shore of the peninsula atop steep cliffs and facing Naples and brooding Vesuvius across the bay, the resort town of Sorrento is backed by the limestone ridge of the Monte Lattari mountains. Their lower slopes are home to citrus orchards and olive groves, with tiny towns and villages nestled in the folds. Well-kept footpaths zigzag across the peninsula, offering fantastic walking opportunities (*see p214* **Head for the Hills**), quite different from those round the corner on the celebrated Amalfi Coast. It has been said that the Sorrento and Amalfi coasts were made by two separate gods: one sweet-tempered, the other irate. Sorrento's is Arcadia; Amalfi's the abyss.

In Sorrento, pretty tiled cupolas and multi-coloured pontoons compete with brilliant geraniums and wisteria, the bluest of seas, the greenest of hills, the yellowest of limoncellos and the pinkest of sunburned flesh for your attention. In a truly democratic tourist mix, the socks-and-sandals brigade shuffles alongside sashaying local sophisticates, beer-and-tattoo Brits, day-tripping Neapolitans and chichi wedding parties. As is often the case in the Bay of Naples, it's not

an easy matter to go for a swim here (*see p219* **Bathing Beauties**). If it's a watery holiday you're after, opt for a hotel with its own pool – or be prepared to walk or pay to use a lido.

The area around Sorrento has been inhabited since prehistoric times, as the remains displayed in museums in **Vico Equense** (*see p213*) and **Piano di Sorrento** (*see p213*) show. Etruscans who moved in from the north in the sixth century BC found Greek settlers already in residence, and an uneasy and often violent co-existence ensued until the decline of Etruscan influence in the fifth century BC. When the Romans routed the Greeks, the remaining Etruscans and the local Samnite tribes during the late fourth century BC, they transformed the peninsula into a sought-after holiday destination, building luxury villas along the coast from Castellammare di Stabia to **Punta della Campanella** (*see p217*).

As the Roman Empire in the west wavered and finally fell, the Goths stampeded along the peninsula, razing small towns as they went. Sorrento, on the other hand, passed formally into the control of Rome's Eastern Empire, ruled from Byzantium (Constantinople). Harried by Lombards, who had established their southern Italian headquarters in nearby Benevento, as well as power-hungry Amalfi on the other side of the peninsula, and later by marauding Saracen pirates from north Africa, the Sorrentines fought hard to keep their independence. However, the Normans (who arrived in the 12th century) were too powerful for them. The towns of the peninsula were absorbed into the southern Italian kingdom, their fate inextricably linked to that of Naples.

Sorrento

Sorrento became particularly popular with the British between 1943 and 1945, when it was used as a convalescence centre for soldiers; word spread, and it has remained a haven ever since. In spite of this, the town is still very Italian and makes a viable – and cheaper – option as a base for seeing the Amalfi Coast.

The grid plan of the streets stretching west from Piazza Tasso is almost all that's left of Greek and Roman Surrentum; the Normans destroyed much of the Roman fortifications. Most of what remains lies inside the 15th-century walls, and is reached from the traffic-clogged Via degli Aranci ring road. Parts of the old city walls are incorporated into the Parco Ibsen.

As late as the 16th century, these defences were crucial for the town (and the whole peninsula) as they were subject to attacks by Saracen pirates from across the Mediterranean. On 13 June 1558, the north African marauders sacked Sorrento; a chain of lookout towers, many of which still stand today, were subsequently built along the coast.

The final stretch of the Vallone dei Mulini (Valley of the Watermills) was another natural border of the city, running from Piazza Tasso to Marina Piccola. The ruined mill on **Piazza delle Mure Vecchie** remained in use until the early 1900s. A more complete picture of how the city once looked can be seen at the **Museo Correale di Terranova**, where 18th- and 19th-century paintings depict rustic scenes, crumbling town gates and wild, unspoilt coasts.

While Sorrentine youths tend to congregate in the soulless Piazza Lauro, their elders gather in **Piazza Tasso**. Bar tables cluster on the pavement, and the evening *struscio* (stroll) begins and ends here; the surrounding streets of the Centro Storico are closed to traffic between 8pm and midnight daily. Sorrento's most famous literary luminary, Torquato Tasso (1544-95), author of the epic poem *Gerusalemme Liberata* (Jerusalem Delivered) and pastoral drama *Aminta*, lends his name to the town's busiest square; his statue overlooks proceedings. A balcony on the northern side of the piazza offers views of the dark ravine that leads to **Marina Piccola**, the port from which ferries and hydrofoils depart for Capri and Naples. Stairs lead down from here towards the dock.

Leading out of the south-western corner is the narrow Via Pietà. At no.24, the early 15th-century

Palazzo Correale has an impressive door and arched upper windows; head into the courtyard next to the **Terranova** shop to admire its 18th-century majolica-tiled wall. The windows of the 12th-century **Palazzo Veniero** at no.14 are framed with pretty Byzantine designs.

Via Pietà emerges on to Corso Italia by the Romanesque **Duomo**. The cathedral is surrounded by a bishop's palace, now occupied by church offices. From here, Via Sersale leads to the remains of the Roman southern town gate and a stretch of 15th-century wall. Corso Italia heads on, lined with smart shops, past a small park, art gallery Villa Fiorentino (no.53) and the relatively quiet Piazza Veniero, before curving round the cliff towards **Capo** (*see p216*). Turn right down Via Tasso to reach the narrow, souvenir shop-packed **Via San Cesareo**. Here you can pick up examples of the intarsia for which Sorrento was famous in the 18th century, as well as bottles of the omnipresent limoncello.

One block to the east, where Via Cesareo intersects with Via Giuliani, the arched **Sedile Dominova**, with its fading frescoes, was a 15th-century open-air meeting place. Here the aristocracy discussed local policy; their coats of arms can be seen around the walls. In an ironic twist of fate, the Sedile is now the front porch of a working men's club; pensioners gather there to play cards and chew the fat.

Parallel to Via Cesareo, Via Santa Maria delle Grazie changes name several times as it runs west towards the **Museo Bottega della Tarsia Lignea**, set in the carefully restored 18th-century Palazzo Pomarici Santomasi. Its private collection of intarsia, which sits alongside paintings and photos of old Sorrento, is extensive and beautiful. The ground floor, meanwhile, is dedicated to modern interpretations of the craft.

Several blocks to the north-east, Via Veneto gives on to the **Villa Comunale**, a small but leafy park overlooking the Bay of Naples to Vesuvius, with steps down to the lidos (*see p219* **Bathing Beauties**) and a pleasant bar. Further along Via Veneto is **San Francesco** church; beside its entrance, a small 14th-century cloister with pretty ogival arches and a garden hosts art exhibitions, music recitals and civil weddings.

Nearby Piazza Sant'Antonino is named after Sorrento's patron saint, whose tomb can be admired in the atmospheric 18th-century crypt of the **Basilica di Sant'Antonino** (open 7am-noon, 4-7pm daily). Though heavy with Baroque features, the basilica stands on the site of an earlier church. An 11th-century door is surrounded by Roman remains, and there's an impressive Nativity scene inside, as well as ex-votos from shipwrecked sailors and two whale's jawbones hanging in the front porch; Sant'Antonino, the protector of those at sea, supposedly saved a child swallowed by a whale.

ESCAPES & EXCURSIONS

ESCAPES & EXCURSIONS

Duomo.

Via Marina Grande and narrow, craft shop-lined Via Sopra le Mura lead to the confusingly named **Marina Grande** (it's smaller than the Marina Piccola). This was once the heart of the fishing village of Sorrento; however, the natural deep-water harbour of the Marina Piccola made a more suitable dock for ferries, and the focus shifted. Over the past few years, it's been spruced up a bit: the tall multicoloured houses have been given a lick of paint, and several new restaurants and bars have opened along the quayside. But it still has plenty of old-world charm and is much quieter than up in the main part of town; stray dogs sleep under seafront benches, kids play football in front of the tiny church of **Sant' Anna** (worth checking out for the glass cabinets of ex-votos) and fishermen mend their nets. In fact, it probably looks pretty much as it did when Sophia Loren was here in the 1950s filming *Scandal in Sorrento*. Its dark, volcanic sand beach is popular with locals, but there are better spots to swim and sunbathe elsewhere (*see p219* **Bathing Beauties**).

FREE Duomo (Santi Filippo e Giacomo)
Corso Italia (081 878 2248). **Open** 8am-12.30pm, 4.30-9pm daily. **Admission** free.
The Romanesque cathedral that once occupied this site was largely rebuilt in the 15th century. Despite the Duomo's Gothic appearance, its brick-red façade is fairly modern. The three-aisled interior has 16th- and 17th-century paintings in its chapels and on the ceiling. The bishop's throne (1573) is a jigsaw of ancient marble fragments; the choir stalls are adorned with fine examples of local intarsia work.

Museo Bottega della Tarsialignea
Via San Nicola 28 (081 877 1942, www.museo muta.it). **Open** *July-Sept* 10am-1pm, 4-7.30pm Mon-Sat. *Oct-June* 10am-1pm, 3-6.30pm Mon-Sat. **Admission** €8; €5 reductions; free under-12s.
In the mid 18th century, Sorrento became famous for its intarsia, avidly collected by the Neapolitan royal family and grand tourists alike. In addition to its excellent collection of intricately inlaid objects in natural and stained woods, the museum seeks to revive the tradition, and its shop sells contemporary interpretations of marquetry furniture.

★ Museo Correale di Terranova
Via Correale 50 (081 878 1846, www.museocorreale. it). **Open** *Apr-Oct* 9.30am-6.30pm Mon-Sat; 9.30am-1.30pm Sun. *Nov-Mar* 9.30am-1.30pm Tue-Sun. **Admission** €8; €3 reductions. **No credit cards**.
Alfredo and Pompeo Correale, the last male heirs to the title of Count of Terranova, left their grand 18th-century family villa and collection of local art and artefacts to the town in the 1920s, and this museum was opened to hold it all. The archaeological section, with finds from around town, is on the ground floor; upstairs are views of 18th- and 19th-century Sorrento, as well as local furniture, porcelain, time-pieces and clothing. Beyond the camellia garden lies a lookout point with a beautiful view across the bay.

Where to shop

Corso Italia is packed with clothes shops: the cheaper stores are east of Piazza Tasso, whereas the more upmarket boutiques (MaxMara, Emporio Armani, Furla) are to the west.

Pretty craft shops line tiny Via Sopra le Mura, while Via Cesareo and its continuation Via Fuoro are the obvious places for souvenirs, particularly limoncello – if you want to see the stuff being made, head downtown to **I Giardini di Cataldo** (Corso Italia 267, 081 878 1888, www.igiardini dicataldo.it), where you can wander through the old lemon grove before sampling delicious, refreshing granita and limoncello.

For local produce, drop into **Terranova** (Piazza Tasso 16, 081 878 1263, www.fattoriaterranova.it). **Raki** (Via San Cesareo 48, 329 877 7922, www.raki sorrento.com) produces superb artisan ice-cream using seasonal ingredients – pineapple and basil or orange and mango in summer; figs, almond and bay or salted caramel in cooler weather.

For marquetry souvenirs, try the workshop of **Salvatore Gargiulo** (Via Fuoro 33, 081 878 2420, www.gargiuloinlaid.it).

Where to eat & drink

While much of the food served in Sorrento tends to be unremarkable and geared towards tourists, standards are rising. Locals usually head for the hills to eat, but good food can be found in the centre; the better restaurants are quite pricey, but there's a fair choice of less costly options.

Popular café-bar **Il Fauno** (Piazza Tasso 13-15, 081 878 1135, www.faunobar.it) is open year-round, until 1.30am (midnight low season) – though the price for great people-watching is decidedly brisk service. Meanwhile, pizza-lovers head to late-opening **Da Franco** (Corso Italia 265, 081 877 2066) opposite the Giardini di Cataldo; delicious, ridiculously cheap pizzas make up for the plastic cups, paper plates and snappy service.

For people in search of ye olde English style, there are plenty of rather uninspiring pubs. The other-worldly **Circolo dei Forestieri** or 'Foreigners' Club' (Via Luigi de Maio 35, 081 877 3263, closed Nov-Mar), situated next to the tourist information office, also draws expats with its wonderful terrace views and an all-day menu of snacks and more substantial fare. For fine dining, head either to **Il Buco** or out of town to Gennaro Esposito's wonderful **Torre del Saracino** (see p216).

★ Il Buco
Il Rampa Marina Piccola 5 (081 878 2354, www.ilbucoristorante.it). **Open** 12.30-2.30pm, 7.30-11pm Mon, Tue, Thur-Sun. Closed Jan. **Average** €80.
The name of this relaxed, Michelin-starred restaurant – 'the hole' – refers to its setting in the brick-vaulted

ESCAPES & EXCURSIONS

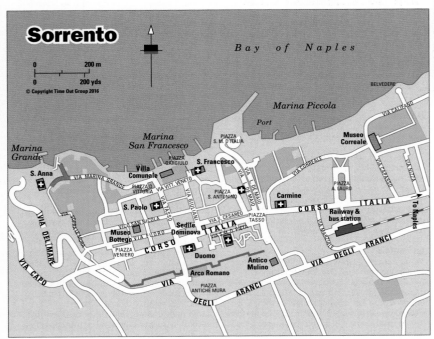

The name of this relaxed, Michelin-starred restaurant – 'the hole' – refers to its setting in the brick-vaulted cellars of an old convent. In summer, the outdoor tables are a lovely spot at which to sample the mostly fish-based, modern Italian menu that chef Peppe Aversa so deftly prepares for guests using seasonal, locally-sourced ingredients and an abundance of fresh herbs. Service is professional and courteous, and the wine list has some affordable options.

Delfino

Via Marina Grande 216 (081 878 2038). **Open** noon-3.30pm, 6.30-10.30pm daily. Closed Nov-Mar. **Average** €50.

The decor of the family-run Delfino is smartly nautical, a suitable choice given that most of the restaurant is built right over the water. It serves top-notch fish – you can't go wrong if you follow the delicious, complimentary tomato-topped bruschetta with a plate of *calamarata Delfino* (the house pasta with clams, courgettes and shrimps) or the grilled catch of the day, which is sold by weight. Wash it down with a carafe of house white or something a little more extravagant from the long list.

Donna Sofia

Via Talagnano 5 (081 877 3532, www.ristorante donnasofia.com). **Open** noon-3.30pm, 7pm-midnight daily (closed Mon Dec-Feb). **Average** €45.

Named after Sofia Loren, this restaurant sits in a lemon grove around a kilometre from Sorrento, but you'll be picked up – and dropped off again – at your hotel. Once seated, you'll be offered a glass of prosecco while you mull over a menu that includes the likes of deep-fried courgette flowers, spaghetti with prawns and pistachios, and fish in a salt crust. Desserts are all home-made: try the white chocolate flan with a citrus sauce.

Da Emilia

Via Marina Grande 62 (081 807 2720). **Open** noon-3pm, 6.30-10pm daily. Closed Nov-Mar. **Average** €30.

With its sunny wooden deck set over the rocks at the eastern end of Marina Grande, this much-loved trattoria is a perfect spot for a relaxed lunch. Emilia is no longer with us, but her family continues to serve up reliable, mostly fishy staples such as *alici fritti, spaghetti alle vongole* and grilled calamari. They don't make coffee here, but you can transfer to the family bar next door for your caffeine shot.

La Fenice

Via degli Aranci 11 (081 878 1652, www.ristorante lafenicesorerento.com). **Open** noon-2.45pm, 7-11.45pm Tue-Sun. Closed 2wks Feb. **Average** €30.

Close to Sorrento's main drag, Corso Italia, La Fenice is a good stop for pizza, pasta and fresh fish. The welcome is warm, the service efficient and the food (lemon risotto served in a whole lemon shell, pizza baked in a wood-fired oven) freshly prepared: check out the fish display as you go in for the day's catch. It's popular with locals, so expect things to liven up as the lights go down.

Ristorante La Favorita

'O Parrucchiano' dal 1868 Corso Italia 71 (081 878 1321, www.parrucchiano.it). **Open** noon-3.30pm, 7-10.30pm daily (closed Wed Nov-Mar). **Average** €40.

This vast glasshouse restaurant (it seats around 500) has been run by the same family since 1868 and is laid out across a series of steep terraces planted with luscious greenery and flowers not far from the Duomo. At the top is a beautiful garden where yet more tables are laid out under a lemon arbour lit by fairy lights. Sure, it's touristy, but the locals come here too and the food is mostly decent, sometimes very good: expect warm calamari salad, *paccheri pasta 'al profumo di mare'* or bream in a citrus sauce, served by crusty old waiters in dapper white jackets.

€ Zi'Ntonio

Via Luigi de Maio 11 (081 878 1623, www. zintonio.it). **Open** noon-3.30pm, 6pm-midnight daily. **Average** €20.

Occupying a rustic, wood-beamed dining room plus an adjacent brighter, more modern space, this friendly family trattoria serves good wood-fired pizzas and reliable fish dishes such as *scialiatelli allo scoglio* (with mixed seafood) and *souté di cozze* (a kind of mussel stew), plus meaty choices such as fillet steak cooked in Barolo wine.

Arts & nightlife

Sorrento's largely tourist-centred economy rules out a truly vibrant cultural scene, and most of the city's night-time entertainment consists of strolling up and down the traffic-liberated centre eating ice-cream, or relaxing in bars and watching others do the work. In summer, lots of temporary venues open up – keep your ear to the ground.

At the **Fauno Notte Club** (Piazza Tasso 1, 081 878 1021, www.faunonotte.it) you can dance until dawn. Popular with local night owls, **Insolito** (Corso Italia 38E, 081 877 2409, www.insolito sorrento.it) is a contemporary cocktail bar that turns into a dance space with DJ after 11pm.

Sadly, the respected Sorrento Festival no longer exists and it hasn't been replaced with anything that can be called regular. However, concerts are held in the summer months in the Chiostro di San Francesco (when it's not being used for weddings) and in the church of San Paolo in Via Tasso. The **Sorrento Piano Festival** (081 807 4033, www. sorrentotourism.it) had its first season in 2015, with free concerts from May to early July in San Paolo. Check with the tourist office (*see p212*) for upcoming events. The world-class **Ravello Festival** (www.ravellofestival.com) is accessible from Sorrento with a little effort.

Bellevue Syrene.

2588, www.hoteltramontano.it, closed Feb, €170-€272 double), where he wrote *Ghosts*. Byron also stayed here, and GB de Curtis penned his famous 'Torna a Surriento' on the terrace overlooking the Bay of Naples. For less flush visitors, mid-range hotels can disappoint. We've listed the better central choices, and a few budget options. Further out, Sant'Agnello is a quieter alternative – and boasts one of the area's top hotels.

Campsites include the **Nube d'Argento** (Via Capo 21, 081 878 1344, www.nubedargento.com, closed Jan-Feb, €8-€12 per person, €5-€10 tent), which has a decent pool and restaurant. It also offers wooden 'bungalows' (chalets) that sleep up to six and cost from €50-€70 for two people. The town's smart, modern youth hostel, **Ostello delle Sirene**, is at Via degli Aranci 160 (081 807 2925, www.hostellesirene.net, closed 3wks Nov, €16-€30 dorm bed, €45-€80 double).

Bellevue Syrene

Piazza Vittoria 5 (081 878 1024, www.bellevue.it). **Rates** €270-€350 double.
Built on a cliff edge on the site of a second-century BC villa, the Bellevue has been a hotel since 1820, hosting royalty, writers and countless celebrities. Elegant yet modish, it benefited from a recent makeover by local interior designer Marco de Luca; antiques, frescoes and vaulting are set off by stylish pastel tones. Rooms with a sea view are at a premium, but you'll be happy to pay up when you wake to a pure blue sea and Mount Vesuvius. The garden rooms are also lovely, and there are fabulous views from the restaurants. A flight of steps (or a handy lift) will whizz you down to the beach, and there's a pool and beauty centre.

Casa Astarita

Corso Italia 67 (081 877 4906, www.casastarita. com). **Rates** €70-€130 double.
Occupying part of a 19th-century palace, the Astarita sisters' charming B&B has seven individually decorated rooms; ask for a room at the front, as the back is notoriously noisy. There's also a lovely breakfast and sitting room, with a library and a majolica-tiled fireplace. The atmosphere is relaxed – help yourself to home-made cakes and limoncello. Its central location on busy Corso Italia, just along from La Favorita (*see p212*), makes this a very popular pad.

Grand Hotel Excelsior Vittoria

Piazza Tasso 34 (081 877 7111, www.exvitt.it). **Rates** €240-€550 double.
In the hands of the Fiorentino family since 1834, the grandest of Sorrento's grand hotels has seen numerous royals and celebrities pass through its lobby over the years. The most famous tenor of all time, Neapolitan Enrico Caruso, stayed here the week before his death in 1921. Set in five acres of orange and lemon groves, it oozes peace and tranquillity in spite of its central location. Spacious, individually decorated bedrooms are dotted with period furniture

Teatro Tasso

Piazza Sant'Antonino 25 (081 807 5525, www.teatrotasso.it). **Open** *Box office* 9.30am-1pm, 4-9pm daily. **Shows** *Apr-Oct* 9.30pm daily. **Admission** €50 (incl dinner); €25 (incl cocktail).
Teatro Tasso's programme leans heavily towards the kind of *folkloristico* musical variety shows that require no knowledge of Italian culture. Watch out for the season of summer shows entitled 'Sorrento Musical'. Cheesier than mozzarella.

Where to stay

Sorrento's best hotels are genuinely splendid and, if your bank account is up to the strain, you can have a classic Grand Tour experience. Henrik Ibsen spent six months at the **Hotel Imperial Tramontano** (Via Vittorio Veneto 1, 081 878

ESCAPES & EXCURSIONS

and have delightful terraces overlooking the sea or the gardens. There are several restaurants, as well as a holistic centre and the wonderful park to explore.

Grand Hotel La Favorita

Corso Italia 71/77 (081 8782031, www.hotel lafavorita.com). **Rates** €189-€259 double.

This pleasant five-star hotel makes up for not being located right on the sea by offering competitive rates. There are gleaming marble hallways and sitting rooms, an airy lounge bar with terrace and a large roof garden with a pool and impressive views over the bay to Vesuvius. The restaurant moves up here from May to late September. All but three of the 85 pristine, comfortable rooms have balconies; if you want a sea view you need to book one at the top.

€ Hotel Mignon Meuble

Via Sersale 9 (081 807 3824, www.sorrento hotelmignon.com). **Rates** €70-€100 double.

This charming little hotel, just behind the Duomo, is now run by the original owner's son and has had a recent facelift. The 22 rooms have all been spruced up and are now done out in smart blue and white, and there's a new, sunny breakfast area leading to a terrace and patch of garden. All rooms have air conditioning and street-facing rooms are soundproofed.

★ La Minervetta

Via Capo 25 (081 877 4455, www.laminervetta.com). **Rates** €150-€400 double.

This chic boutique hotel is just ten minutes' walk from the town centre – but it feels leagues away in terms of peace and quiet. Twelve bright, individually designed rooms have huge picture windows with views of the Bay of Naples and glowering Vesuvius. There's a magnificent sun terrace for breakfast and drinks, and a sunny lounge area with an eclectic collection of shells, paintings, ceramics, books and magazines. A plunge pool overlooks Marina Grande, which you can reach via a long staircase. The enormous breakfasts are the stuff of legend.

Palazzo Jannuzzi

Vico S. Aniello 39 (081 877 2862, www.palazzo jannuzzi.com). **Rates** €100-€140 double.

This smart, modern 12-room boutique B&B is located right on top of Bar Fauna with most rooms overlooking busy Piazza Tasso. Yet another project of local designer Marco de Luca, it's filled with his characteristic bright colours and bold stripes against a gleaming white background. Rooms are spacious and well-equipped; the two at the top have kitchenettes and large terraces. Rates are very reasonable for Sorrento.

★ Palazzo Marziale

Piazza Francesco Saverio Gargiulo 2 (081 807 4406, www.palazzomarziale.com). **Rates** €90-€200 double.

This lovely 15th-century family palazzo has seven beautifully appointed rooms and a romantic gourmet restaurant. Each room is filled with fine antiques

and pictures, and decked out with parquet flooring, billowing silk curtains and gorgeous marble bathrooms. Thoughtful details include embroidered linen sheets, tea and coffee trays, and robes and slippers. Prices are surprisingly affordable.

★ Parco dei Principi

Via Rota 1, Sant'Agnello (081 878 4644, www.grandhotelparcodeiprincipi.net). **Rates** €130-€250 double.

Just beyond Sorrento's town centre, this hip hotel has a distinctly nautical feel. It was designed – building, furniture, fittings and all – in shades of blue and white by architect Giò Ponti in 1962, and staying here is rather like being on the set of a stylish '60s Italian film. The modernist floor tiles are arranged in a different design in every room. There's also a seawater pool, sauna, private beach and lush botanical garden. A free shuttle service takes you to the Piazza Antiche Mura, where the local bus stops.

▶ *For more of Ponti's bold signature style, check into the Royal Continental in Naples and ask for a room on the Giò Ponti floor; see p277.*

Resources

Hospital

Santa Maria della Misericordia *Corso Italia (081 533 1111).*

Internet

Insolito Café *Corso Italia 38/E (081 877 2409).* **Open** 8am-4am daily.

Police

Carabinieri *Via Bartolomeo Capasso 11 (081 878 1010).*
Polizia di Stato *Vico III Rota 14 (081 807 5311).*

Post office

Corso Italia 210 (081 877 0834).

Tourist information

Azienda Autonoma di Soggiorno di Sorrento e Sant'Agnello *Via Luigi di Maio 35 (081 807 4033, www.sorrentotourism.com, www.info sorrento.it).* **Open** *Oct-Apr* 8.30am-4pm Mon-Fri. *May-Sept* 8.30am-8pm Mon-Sat; 9am-1pm Sun.

Getting around

Four red and orange bus lines serve the Sorrento area, and run from 5.30am to midnight. Line A goes from Massa Lubrense to Capo di Sorrento via Meta; line B goes from the port at Marina Piccola to the centre/station; line C goes from the port at Marina Piccola to Sant'Agnello; and line D plies between Marina Grande and the centre. The terminus is in front of the Circumvesuviana station, on Piazza Giovanni Battista de Curtis. For information on **Getting there**, *see p218*.

Car & scooter hire

Hertz *Via Capo 8 (081 807 1646, www.hertz.it).* **Open** *Apr-Oct* 8.30am-1pm, 2-8pm Mon-Fri; 9am-1pm, 4-8pm Sat; 9.30am-12.30pm, 4-8pm Sun. *Nov-Mar* 9am-1pm, 2-6pm Mon-Fri; 9am-1pm Sat.
Jolly Servizi & Noleggio *Corso Italia 3 (081 878 2403/www.jollyrent.com).* **Open** *Mar-Oct* 9am-1pm, 4-8pm daily. *Nov-Feb* 9am-1pm, 4-6pm Mon-Fri; 9am-1pm Sat.

East from Sorrento

PIANO DI SORRENTO TO SEIANO

Since the building and tourism boom of the 1950s and '60s, what was once a collection of fishing and farming villages, punctuated by the odd stately holiday villa, has become one big urban sprawl – albeit a very pretty one. East of the town is a long, low, whitewashed conurbation of hotels that absorb Sorrento's overflow, many of which have the pretty gardens and sports facilities that more central hotels don't have the space to offer. If you're looking for a hotel in the town centre, check the location carefully or you may end up out here.

Sant'Agnello's traffic-clogged main street is little more than a funnel into and out of town; more pleasant is the almost-coast road, which cuts past beautiful villas – many of them converted into hotels – and their flower-filled gardens, just a block back from the sea.

Piano di Sorrento still retains the feel of a separate town. On the coast road, set in the 18th-century Villa Fondi, the **Museo Archeologico Georges Vallet** (Via Ripa di Cassano 14, 081 808 7078, closed Mon) offers free admission and contains archaeological finds from the Sorrentine Peninsula: artefacts from necropolises, arrow-heads and pre-Roman pottery. In summer, concerts and romantic soirées are held here. A tortuous track leads down to the little harbour, **Marina di Cassano**, whose beach is encroached upon by boats from one of the peninsula's few remaining economically significant fishing fleets.

Meta di Sorrento boasts the area's longest stretch of sand, the **spiaggia di Alimuri**. It's named after a Saracen pirate captain called Ali, who came ashore in the mid 1500s and died (*muri*) there in fierce fighting with the locals. Until a century ago, Meta's marina moored one of Italy's largest shipping fleets. It's now another bustling modern suburb, with hotels and cafés on *piazze*. In a square on the main road, the **Madonna del Lauro** basilica (open 7am-noon, 4-7pm daily), with its low, tiled dome and neoclassical façade, was rebuilt in the 18th century, but is believed to stand on the site of a temple to Minerva.

After Meta, there's a slight lull in the urban sprawl before reaching the village of **Seiano**,

where the 16th-century chapel of **Santa Maria delle Grazie** (closed to the public) has a medieval fresco over its front door. You'll also see the 18th-century church of **San Marco**, which has the highest dome on the peninsula.

VICO EQUENSE

Coast road and railway line then cross the breathtaking viaduct over the Murrano river to Vico Equense. Less touristy than Sorrento, Vico is a lovely place to escape the crowds and mix with the locals. Then known as Aequana, the town was founded by the Romans, who used its sunny slopes for cultivating grapes – before the Goths razed it in the fifth century. (The area's wine production has since moved uphill to **Gragnano**, where a tasty, slightly fizzy red is still produced.) The town of Vico Equense was resurrected in the 13th century by King Charles II of Anjou.

Castello Giusso, which now houses privately owned apartments, looms over the town. Its fanciful crenellations are a 19th-century addition to the original medieval building of 1284; the Renaissance section above was added in the mid 16th century. To the south, in Via Puntamare, the church of **Santissima Annunziata** (open 9.30-11am Mon, Thur, Sat, 10-11am Sun) overlooks a dramatic drop to the sea, making it an essential photo opportunity. The Annunziata was Vico's cathedral until the bishopric was abolished in 1799, when the incumbent, Michel Natale, was hanged for his over-enthusiastic support of the Parthenopean Republic. His portrait is missing from the collection of medallions of former bishops in the sacristy; instead, there's a painting of an angel with a finger raised to its lips, inviting onlookers to draw a veil of silence over Natale's unwise allegiance. Gothic arches from the original 14th-century church are in the side aisles.

Along Viale Rimembranza, the Baroque church of **San Ciro** (open 8.30am-noon, 4.30-7.30pm daily) has a pretty tiled dome. Nearby, the **Museo Mineralogico Campano** (Via San Ciro 38, 081 801 5668, www.museomineralogico campano.it, closed Mon, admission €2) has a tremendous collection of minerals, with a very impressive selection from Vesuvius. Inside the town hall, artefacts from a local necropolis (seventh- to fifth-century BC) are displayed in the **Antiquarium Aequano** (Palazzo Municipale, Corso Filangieri 100, 081 801 5752, contact the tourist office next door for entry).

Below the town centre to the east, **Marina di Vico** has a short pebbly beach with a handful of restaurants. To the west, the harbour at pretty **Marina di Equa** allows access to long stretches of sun-worshipping space at **Pezzolo** (where ruins of a first-century AD villa are visible) and **Vescovado** to the east, and **Calcare** to the west; the imposing ruin at the far end of Calcare beach

HEAD FOR THE HILLS

The peninsula is a hikers' paradise.

Trek up and down between Sorrento's Marina Piccola and the centre a couple of times, and you may well decide that walking in the area is really not your thing. If steep slopes don't stress you out, though, you'll find that the beautiful and seemingly inaccessible hills around Sorrento afford some glorious hikes and some even more glorious views. Often invisible from the road, footpaths criss-cross the area from **Castellammare di Stabia** (*see p202*) to Salerno and Punta della Campanella.

Most paths are colour-coded and, in general, easy to follow. Some tracks are maintained by the Club Alpino Italiano (CAI) mountaineering association, which marks routes with red-and-white paint flashes on rocks, walls, lampposts and the like. Paths vary dramatically in difficulty. The further you stray from habitation, the less well defined they become; once in a while, you may even end up having to cut across someone's vineyard or olive grove.

HALF-DAY WALKS & EASY STROLLS

Sorrento is a starting point for several pleasant walks. For one, take the Via Capo west out of Sorrento as far as

Capo di Sorrento (or get the bus a few stops), then turn right down to the Roman **Villa di Pollio Felice** and continue on across the wooden bridge as far as the **Bagni della Regina Giovanna** (*see p216*), where you can stop for a swim. Another walk begins by the Sorrento Palace Hotel, where you take the Via Crucis steps (marked out with the Stations of the Cross). The path continues as far as **Sant'Agata** and then on to the **Deserto monastery** (for both, *see p227*). The views from Sant'Agata are stunning, spanning the Bay of Naples and the Gulf of Salerno (hence the town's full name, Sant'Agata sui Due Golfi). Either walk can be done in a morning.

If you have the legs for it, carry on from Sant'Agata to the **Marina di Crapolla**, on a path that winds steeply down the hillside to a tiny pebble beach. Aside from the path, the beach is only accessible from the sea, so you're likely to have it all to yourself. The 12th-century church of San Pietro is just behind you, and some Roman walls remain on the beach itself.

People who are good with heights but not so good with uphill hikes can take the regular Circumvesuviana train to Castellammare, then the *funivia* (cable car) up to the top of

Sentiero degli Dei.

Monte Faito (Apr-Oct). The ride is stunning and can be combined with a pleasant, level stroll around the summit (the second highest in the area after Vesuvius).

DAY-LONG WALKS

If you have an entire day to spare, embark on a dramatic coast-to-coast walk. The first goes from **Puolo** to **Crapolla**, stopping for a break in Sant'Agata just past the halfway mark. The climb is long and fairly relentless, but the views provide ample reward. Slightly shorter is the walk from **Marina della Lobra** to **Marina del Cantone**. It's no less strenuous, but most of the ascent is in the first hour, leaving you with a long, gradual descent across the spectacular Positano side of the peninsula. Neither walk is recommended for people with bad knees.

More serious walkers will want to try the **Alta Via dei Monti Lattari**, which stretches from **Colli di Fontanelle** above Positano down to **Punta della Campanella**. Said to be a former shepherd's path down from the hills into Sorrento, it's marked by a red-and-white line. It takes at least a day to walk the length of the path, and it's best to break your journey with a stopover in Massa or Sant'Agata.

The area's other long path is the **Sentiero degli Dei** (Pathway of the Gods). Considerable confusion abounds as to its exact start and end points; the official view is that it leads from Bomerano to Nocella. Meandering as it does along the pinnacle of the mountains – with a sheer drop on either side at times – it's easy to see how the path got its name. This is definitely not one for the faint-hearted.

PUNTA DELLA CAMPANELLA

Many of the best walks in the area pass through the Punta della Campanella national park and marine reserve, which was founded in 1997 with the aim of protecting the date shell mollusc (*dattero del mare*) from being harvested out of existence. The park has flourished, despite strong opposition from property developers and powerboat owners. Its name comes from the bell (*campanella*) here that was rung to warn residents when marauding pirates were sighted.

The best entry points to the park are in the towns of Termini or Nerano. From **Termini**, a long, gentle two- to three-hour walk winds its way down to Punta della Campanella. You're only five kilometres from Capri, and the enchanting island seems close enough to touch. A Greek temple once stood on the tip of the peninsula, although the ruins you can see today are of a second-century

Baia di Jeranto

Roman villa and 14th-century bell tower. From **Nerano**, head south to Punta Penna and Punta di Montalto, with its Napoleonic lookout tower. There's a tiny beach at Capitello on the **Baia di Jeranto** (*see p217*) – possibly the most spectacular swimming spot in the area.

More information on the park is available from **Ente Parco Punta della Campanella** (Via Roma 29, Massa Lubrense, 081 808 9877, www.puntacampanella.org, open 9am-1pm Mon, Wed, Fri, 9am-1pm, 3-6pm Tue, Thur).

NEED TO KNOW

In spring or autumn, watch out for sudden, heavy rain showers. Some of the ravine-like paths can become blocked up with leaves and debris, and stone paths can become slippery. In summer, many of the paths have little or no shade for long stretches. Wear a hat, bring suncream and carry plenty of drinking water.

Be aware, too, that Italian farmers sometimes leave large, aggressive dogs to roam freely around what they perceive to be their land. Although they may bark loudly, they rarely bite.

The best places for information on walks are the tourist offices in **Sorrento** (*see p212*) and **Massa Lubrense** (*see p218*). The website www.giovis.com is also useful.

ESCAPES & EXCURSIONS

was part of a centuries-old lime quarry that closed down in the late 19th century. Marina di Equa itself has a Saracen watchtower, and is home to one of the outstanding restaurants in the area, the wonderful **Torre del Saracino**, as well as lots of bars.

Head inland and uphill from Vico Equense to the *casali* (hamlets): **Moiano** is a starting point for walks in the **Monte Faito** area and across to Positano; **Massaquano** is home to the haunting, Giotto-style 14th-century frescoes of the chapel of **Santa Lucia**.

Where to eat & drink

Vico Equense is home of 'pizza by the metro', thanks to the endeavours of **Gigino Pizza al Metro** (Via Nicotera 15, 081 879 8426, www. pizzametro.it, open noon-1am daily, average €15). It's a great barn of a place, popular with busloads of tourists and large Neapolitan families. Stretch-pizzas of all imaginable varieties are served here; order slices of a length to match your appetite. The town is also home to the friendly **Gelateria Latteria Gabriele** (Corso Umberto I 5, 081 879 8744, www.gabrieleitalia.com, closed Tue), with its 1960s decor. Try the alpine strawberries and mulberry granita. A superb range of local cheeses and *salumi* is also available. In central Vico, **Al Buco** (Via Roma 19, 081 801 6255, closed Mon, average €20) is the ideal trattoria: good pasta, good pizza and delicious desserts.

In Marina di Equa, the **Torre del Saracino** (Via Torretta 9, 081 802 8555, www.torredel saracino.it, closed Sun eve, mid Jan-mid Feb, average €90, set menus from €120) more than deserves its two Michelin stars. Larger-than-life chef Gennaro Esposito creates some of the best food on this (or any) coast: exquisitely presented seafood antipasti, home-made pasta and the freshest of seafood – octopus, squid, shrimp, anchovy – cooked to perfection in all manner of creative ways. A Saracen watchtower guards the romantic patio where dinner is served.

Just outside Vico, on the road towards Sorrento, lies what many consider to be the best food shop in Campania. Annamaria Cuomo and Salvatore Da Gennaro's deli **La Tradizione** (Via R Bosco 696, 081 8028437) in Seiano is an Aladdin's cave of food and wines, showcasing the very best artisan foods the region has to offer.

Where to stay

Down a sharp drop off the coast road just east of Vico Equense, the nautical-themed **Hotel Capo La Gala** (Via Luigi Serio 8, 081 801 5757, www. hotelcapolagala.com, closed Nov-Mar, €150-€215 double) is a stylish, romantic hideaway with an excellent restaurant; take the Circumvesuviana train to Scrajo Terme (Apr-Sept). The balconies

of its 18 tasteful rooms overhang the wave-battered rocks below, while the pool is filled with mineral-rich water from the nearby Scrajo spring.

Perched above Vico in Santa Maria del Castello, off Via Bosco, **Agriturismo La Ginestra** (Via Tessa 2, 081 802 3211, www.laginestra.org, €70 B&B, €85 half-board, €110 full-board) has simple, bright rooms in a pink farmhouse, with spectacular views and delicious organic home-cooking (non-residents can eat here if they book).

Resources

Tourist information
Azienda Autonoma di Cura Soggiorno e Turismo *Corso Filangieri 100, Vico Equense (081 801 5752, www.vicoturismo.it).* **Open** *May-Sept* 9am-8pm Mon-Fri; 9am-1pm, 2-5pm Sat; 9.30am-2pm Sun. *Oct-Apr* 9am-8pm Mon-Fri; 9am-1pm, 2-5pm Sat.

West from Sorrento

CAPO & AROUND

Heading west from Sorrento is a totally different experience than the built-up area to the east. You can take the **Citysightseeing Sorrento** bus (081 877 4707, www.sorrento.city-sightseeing.it, ticket €12, Apr-Oct daily), which runs a hop-on, hop-off service around the Sorrentine Peninsula from Piazza de Curtis (the Circumvesuviana train station) every two hours. The developers have yet to reach this dramatically beautiful and wild chunk of the peninsula, in part due to the inaccessibility of its roads and the dramatic lie of the land. Towns are hemmed in by lemon and olive groves, and the air in spring and summer is full of the pungent perfumes of wild garlic, myrtle and broom.

The first stop out of Sorrento is the small village of **Capo di Sorrento**, overlooking Marina Grande, where Maxim Gorky's stay at the **Villa Il Sorito** in the 1920s and '30s is commemorated by a plaque on the front wall. A little further on, a high-walled path leads off the coast road to the right (north). Edged by romantic fields of lemon trees and asphodels, it leads to what is known locally as the **Bagni della Regina Giovanna** (Baths of Queen Joan). The medieval queen is said to have bathed here in what was once a sumptuous Roman villa, possibly built by Pollio Felice. The ruins that dot the headland, surrounding a deep seawater inlet, are much easier to interpret after a visit to the **Museo Archeologico Georges Vallet** in Piano di Sorrento (*see p213*). The outcrops of brick are a good place on which to sit and contemplate the sweep of the coast to Sorrento.

Beyond Capo, a pretty road drops down to the tiny **Marina di Puolo**, where, at the end of a long walk down from the car park, there's a lovely sandy beach backed by a string of small bars and restaurants; it's a good spot for a swim. More citrus orchards and olive groves (nets to collect the falling fruit are stretched out between the trees from October to December, then rolled up and left between the trees in multicoloured swathes) line the coast road from here to the lively town of Massa Lubrense and beyond.

MASSA LUBRENSE & BEYOND

Massa comes from the Lombard word for settlement, *mansa*, although the area was already known in ancient times. Lubrense is derived from the Latin word *delubrum* (temple); temples to Hercules and Minerva existed in the vicinity. The village has 23 outlying hamlets in its verdant sprawl, along with numerous churches and convents; a famous walk that leaves the centre on the nearest Saturday to 25 April visits them all. A haunting Easter procession, starting in Vico Equense, also terminates here.

There's a great view across to Capri from the belvedere in **Largo Vescovado**. On the other side of the square stands the former cathedral of **Santa Maria delle Grazie** (open 7am-noon, 4.30-8pm daily). It dates from the early 16th century, although it was reworked in 1769. The chapel of **Sant'Erasmo**, to the left of the main altar, is believed to stand above a temple to Hercules. Directly opposite the church, a road leads down to the attractive hamlet of **Marina di Lobra** (take a scenic shortcut down the first downward flight of steps right from the road; you may, however, want to hitch a lift or wait for the infrequent bus on the way back up).

Halfway down the road, the church of **Santa Maria di Lobra** (open very irregularly; ask at the monastery) has a pretty yellow-and-green tiled dome, a 'miraculous' 16th-century Madonna and Child over the altar, and a cool, homely cloister with a tiled well-head. There was once a temple here, too, probably dedicated to Minerva. The place has a charming, lived-in feel. The adjoining monastery now houses a small, quiet guest house, the **San Francesco Relais** (081 878 9323, www.sanfrancescorelais.it, €50-€90 double), with simple rooms and sea views. Weather permitting, breakfast is served in the garden or cloister.

From Massa's main square, a road north-west (that soon swings south) heads to the tiny village of **Santa Maria Annunziata**, home to a rarely opened church, the ruins of the 14th-century **Castello di Massa** and the wonderfully rustic **La Torre** restaurant. A well-marked walking trail runs from Massa to Annunziata. It's worth taking it, not only for the walk itself but also to see the **Villa Rossi**, where Joaquim Murat

holed up after the Battle of Capri and signed the capitulation that put an ignominious end to French rule in Naples.

The coast road out of Massa swings past the church and cemetery of **San Liberatore**. It's a final resting place of incredible beauty on the edge of a cliff, with Capri – once part of the mainland – tantalisingly close on the other side of the bay. The little whitewashed chapel dates from 1420, although it has been heavily restored.

In ancient times, the coast road continued as far as the temple to Minerva on **Punta della Campanella**. Nowadays it curves inland a couple of kilometres short of the point, heading to the small town of **Termini**. A nondescript place with a marvellous view, Termini is the starting point for walks around Punta della Campanella, down to the Amalfi Coast and along the crests of the peninsula.

The lane that heads south opposite the church leads to the chapel of **San Costanzo**; the walk takes around 40 minutes. The chapel is a stark white construction, rarely open; the view down towards the very tip of the peninsula at Punta della Campanella and the Baia di Jeranto immediately to the north is awe-inspiring. From the same point, another path (grey and green stripes; 90 minutes) follows the headland out to the Saracen watchtower on Punta della Campanella where there are the remains of a Roman villa. The path for **Punta Penna**, with access to Jeranto Bay, begins in Nerano.

Where to eat, drink & stay

Accommodation in and around Massa Lubrense was pretty low-key until the arrival of the spectacular **Relais Blu** (Via Rocanto 60, 081 878 9552, www.relaisblu.com, closed Nov-Mar, €245-€495 double), with 11 luxurious, beautifully designed rooms, all with sweeping views of the sea. There's a pool and an excellent restaurant where Roberto Allocca's creative take on Mediterranean cuisine has won him a Michelin star. Cookery courses are also on offer. The four-star **Hotel Delfino** (Via Nastro d'Oro 2, 081 878 9261, www.hoteldelfino.com, closed Nov-Mar, €140-€280 double) is a good, more traditional bet and it offers similarly spectacular views, a pool, a good restaurant and direct access to the sea below.

Family-run **Hotel La Primavera** (Via IV Novembre 3/G, 081 878 9125, www.laprimavera.biz, closed mid Jan-mid Feb, €60-€100 double) has 16 clean and simple rooms, most with balconies and some with sea views. The restaurant serves excellent seafood (average €35).

If you fancy a stay in a Saracen watchtower-turned-*agriturismo*, book in at the **Torre Cangiani** (Località Vigliano, 081 533 9849, www.torrecangiani.com, €70 double), where farmer Aldo and his wife Matilde will take care of you.

Massa's premier restaurant is the **Antico Francischiello da Peppino** (Via Partenope 27, 081 533 9780, www.francischiello.com, closed Wed Nov-Mar, average €50), serving traditional seafood and local cheeses. Rooms with a view are available at the adjoining hotel (€90-€100 double).

In Marina di Lobra, the **Piccolo Paradiso** (Piazza Madonna della Lobra 5, 081 808 9540, www.piccolo-paradiso.com, closed mid Nov-Feb, €88-€134 double) is a more upmarket option, with a swimming pool and scuba diving on request. It also handles the very simple monks' cells for rent at the monastery opposite (€28 per person B&B).

At **La Torre** in tiny Annunziata (Piazzetta Annunziata 7, 081 808 9566, closed Jan, Feb, average €30), Maria Mazzola cooks up a storm with her traditional fish and meat dishes. The antipasti are legendary (one portion is enough for two), after which you can move on to *paccheri* with sea urchins. There's a pretty patio and, just across the piazza, a wonderful terrace with breathtaking views of Capri.

Resources

Tourist information
Proloco *Viale Filangieri 11, Massa Lubrense (081 533 9021, www.massalubrenseturismo.it).* **Open** *Apr-Sept* 9am-1pm, 4-8pm Mon-Sat; 9am-1pm Sun. *Oct-Mar* 9am-1pm daily.

Getting there
FROM NAPLES AIRPORT

Autolinee Curreri Service (081 801 5420, www.curreriviaggi.it) runs eight coaches in each direction daily between Capodichino Airport and Sorrento, stopping at Vico Equense, Piano, Meta and Sant'Agnello; tickets cost €10.

IN THE KNOW RIDE THE CAMPANIA EXPRESS

Much quicker – and infinitely more pleasant – than the Circumvesuviana train service for Sorrento is the new **Campania Express** service operated by EAV (www.eavsrl.it). Running between Naples' Porta Nolana station and Sorrento, with stops along the way at Herculaneum and Pompeii, the journey time is 50 minutes and tickets cost €15 return (€10 with a Campani Art Card). Passengers are greeted by multilingual 'hostesses' and promotional videos of the area. The service was being trialled during summer 2015; if it's deemed successful, it will continue in 2016. Fingers crossed.

BY BUS

Sita (089 405145, www.sitasudtrasporti.it) runs a coastal bus service with routes from Sorrento across the peninsula to the Amalfi Coast. Services are frequent in high season, running roughly hourly 6.30-8.30am and 5-7pm, and half-hourly 8.30am-5pm.

The Sorrento–Meta di Sorrento–Positano–Amalfi route has an hourly service (approx 6.30am-8pm), leaving from outside the train station. Services are hourly (6am-10.30pm) on the Sorrento–Massa Lubrense–Sant'Agata sui Due Golfi route, but only a few go on to Nerano, Marina di Cantone and Marina di Lobra. Check timetables at tourist offices and bus stops.

BY CAR

Take the A3 motorway to Castellammare di Stabia, then follow the SS145 south-east around the peninsula. Take the SS142 to pass through Vico Equense, Piano and Meta, or stay on the SS145 as it swings inland towards Sant'Agata sui Due Golfi. An unnumbered road forks east along the peninsula through Massa to Termini, before rejoining the SS145 at Sant'Agata. Inland roads vary greatly in quality; all have hair-raising bends (sound your horn).

BY HYDROFOIL/FERRY

Alilauro (081 497 2238, www.alilauro.it) and **Navigazione Libera del Golfo**, or NLG (081 5520763, www.navlib.it) run hydrofoil services between Naples' Molo Beverello port and Sorrento. Services run all year, weather permitting (€12.30 single; 40mins). **Caremar** (081 892 123, www.caremar.it) has a ferry service to Capri from Sorrento (€13.20 single; 25mins) and NLG (*see above*) runs a 'Jet' boat to Capri (€16.80 single; 20mins). There are also services in high season from Sorrento to the Amalfi Coast, stopping at Positano and Sorrento, run by **Gescab** (081 807 3024, www.gescab.it), but these are notoriously mercurial, so check at the tourist office.

BY TRAIN

Sorrento is the terminus of the lumbering **Circumvesuviana** railway (081 772 2444, www.vesuviana.it), which can be picked up from Naples' train station on Piazza Garibaldi; services run every 30 minutes (more frequently at rush hour) in both directions and take 75 minutes. The train stops at Ercolano, Pompeii, Vico Equense, Meta, Piano and Sant'Agnello. The last Naples-Sorrento train leaves at 9.39pm, and from Sorrento back to Naples it's 9.37pm. A Naples–Sorrento ticket costs €3.60 single or €4.50 for a ticket that's valid for 180 minutes on public transport in the two towns.

BATHING BEAUTIES

Where to dip your toes in the deep blue sea.

Sorrento may be a seaside resort, but it's not that easy to take a dip in the remarkably clear water, and there's often a hefty price tag attached. Sandy beaches are few and far between, so swimming here mostly takes place from colourful, stilted pontoons built out over the water – and you usually have to pay for the privilege.

The **spiaggia di San Francesco** is accessed from the Villa Communale park. You can either walk down a steep, stepped path or take the lift from the corner of the park (€1). At the bottom, pontoons have been built to enlarge the small beach and huts, while parasols and loungers create a vibrant mass of colour against the enticing blue of the sea. There's also a scrap of 'free beach' that's usually packed with noisy locals playing frisbee and football. But it's OK if you just want to have a swim.

The average price for entry to a lido for two including sunloungers and umbrella is around €35 per day and all have bars and/ or restaurants serving snacks and full meals. Chic, white **Marameo** has floating sunbeds,

four-poster loungers, a restaurant and lounge bar, while family-friendly **Leonelli's** offers a strip of beach and a 'water gym course'. To get away from the crowds (and pay a bit less), head to **Bagni Salvatore** on the far left under the hotel Bellevue Syrene.

Another possibility – and one that's pretty popular with the locals – is the beach at **Marina Grande** (*see p208*), which is mostly free. Any lidos here are cheaper than at San Francesco: **Tony's Beach** on the left has just had a chic revamp and offers the usual loungers and umbrellas, as well as a good restaurant. If you fancy a walk before your swim, climb up to Capo, then down to **Bagni della Regina Giovanna** (*see p216*), where there's clean water and good snorkelling.

Alternatively, **Marina di Puolo** (*see p217*), along the coast to the west, has a lovely curve of shingly beach (much of it 'free') and shallow, crystal-clear water. East of Sorrento, try the **spiaggia di Alimuri** (*see p213*), **Pezzolo**, **Vescovado** and **Calcare** (*see p213*), **Scrajo Terme** (near Vico Equense) or pretty **Marina di Lobra** (*see p217*).

ESCAPES & EXCURSIONS

Marina Grande.

The Amalfi Coast

There's no denying that the Costiera Amalfitana is one of the most beautiful, dramatic stretches of coastline in the world. A combination of dizzying views, dazzling colours and an elusive, yet hugely seductive, sense of glamour attracts droves of visitors from across the globe. Blasted from solid limestone cliffs in 1852, the celebrated Amalfi Coast Drive – the corniche road officially known as Strada Statale 163 – winds from Positano to Vietri sul Mare around towering cliffs and deep gorges, through whitewashed villages and lemon groves, rising and dipping above a shimmering sea. John Steinbeck described this rollercoaster as 'carefully designed to be a little narrower than two cars side by side' in a piece he wrote for *Harper's Bazaar* in 1953, and little has changed since then.

INTRODUCING THE AREA

An intriguing mix of sophisticated, jet-set chic and rudimentary, rural lifestyle characterises this legendary corner of Campania. Beyond the five-star hotels, Michelin-starred restaurants, superyachts and chauffeur-driven Mercedes, much harsher realities exist. In the hills, around scattered villages, farmers cultivate small plots of steeply terraced land while their wives make cheeses; down on the coast, tiny fishing communities struggle to make a living.

As a visitor, it's all too easy to drop a serious amount of cash in this impossibly gorgeous area. The views – and a dip in the sparkling azure sea, if you choose the right place – may be free, but the high life comes with a heavy price tag. There are also plenty of B&Bs, homely *trattorie* and good public transport links, though. With a little careful planning, a holiday here needn't break the bank.

But back to that narrow 'road of a thousand bends'. Ironically, when you're on it, you'll find it impossible to fully appreciate the ravishing scenery; you'll be concentrating too hard on the twists ahead, and on the cars, bikes and three-wheeled vans coming towards you. Remarkably, fatal accidents are almost unheard of since the bends are so frequent, and the traffic so heavy, that there's rarely a chance to build up speed. The public SITA bus offers a decent alternative

to the car and its drivers know this stretch of road better than anyone. As a passenger, you'll have all the time you need to savour the superb views of jagged rocks, Saracen towers, deep blue waters and terraced gardens tumbling down to the pastel-painted houses below – many equipped with cliff-edge swimming pools. Just make sure you get a seat on the seaward side.

After the land, there's the Mediterranean. The locals' seafaring passion – and close relationship with the soil – are genuine sentiments, not merely folklore dished up for tourists; there's real pride in the region's eventful past. The diminutive city of Amalfi was once a major maritime power, and so important that its crest still sits alongside those of Genoa, Pisa and Venice on the Italian naval ensign. It's often said that the compass was invented in Amalfi and that the first set of maritime laws was passed here. The former is dubious, the latter a matter of record. Such ingenuity was born of the necessity to regulate Amalfi's bustling commerce, and to combat the Pisans and the Saracen pirates drawn to its wealthy shores.

Historically, the only practical way to mount an invasion of its imposing cliffs was from the sea, and even today hopping from town to town on a boat is often more convenient than by bus or car. Better still, though arduous, is to walk. A well-signposted network of paths extends along the whole coast, from short village-to-village strolls to a spectacular long-distance footpath, the Alta Via dei Lattari, that follows the ridge dividing the Amalfi Coast from the Bay of Naples. The footpath numbers in the text refer to the official CAI (Club Alpino Italiano) numbers, and should be written on markers along the way. The CAI's excellent Monti Lattari map and walking guide can be found in local bookshops and *tabacchi*.

Positano

When John Steinbeck arrived in Positano to write his article, he found a pretty little fishing village, known only to a few arty – and mainly Italian – cognoscenti. But the word was out; the *Dolce Vita* set moved in, and during the mid 1960s it was briefly more fashionable than Capri.

Described by artist Paul Klee as 'the only place in the world conceived on a vertical rather than horizontal axis', today Positano is home to just short of 4,000 souls – in summer, though, that number swells to many, many more. But in spite of the crowds, it remains a beguiling and impossibly picturesque place. Its cubed, pastel-hued houses, with their sun-drenched, bougainvillea-draped terraces tumbling down the mountainside and closing around the beach, is a little like an open-air stage set.

Positano's brief moment of glory came in the 12th and 13th centuries when its merchant fleet gave rival Amalfi a run for its money. But centuries of subsequent decline forced three-quarters of the population to emigrate to America in the mid 19th century, and even today it's said that Columbus Avenue in New York has more *Positanesi* than Positano.

The dramatic topography that made life here so difficult is seriously photogenic, and almost every house has a clear view over the top of the one in front. But with the views come hefty bills. Like Capri, Positano has deliberately priced itself out of the package tour market. More than two-thirds of its hotels are three-star or above; in high season it's nearly impossible to find a double room for less than €150 a night, unless you've booked weeks or even months in advance.

In summer, the narrow streets and alleys are often blocked by tourists squeezing their way up and down, red-faced from the climb. Restful it isn't, and with the nakedly money-hungry and surly demeanour of staff in the more touristy shops and restaurants – plus the dearth of real attractions other than wonderful views – Positano can soon feel like a trap. Off-season, when the town and its inhabitants have room to breathe, the magic is much more obvious.

Directions here are either up or down, unless you're in a car – in which case they're round and round for hours. The SS 163 coast road hugs the

contours in the upper part of town, where it goes by the name of Via Marconi. From the town hall to the west, the one-way Viale Pasitea descends in a series of curves to Piazza dei Mulini, then changes its name to Via Cristoforo Colombo and climbs again to rejoin the coast road on Positano's eastern edge. These are the only roads open to traffic; in summer, the lower one is permanently clogged with cars hunting for parking spaces. Strong legs will get you around the town centre faster than a set of wheels – though if you can't face the climb, there's a regular, circular bus service.

From Piazza dei Mulini – where the traffic-free zone starts – narrow, shop-lined Via dei Mulini runs down to the beach past the parish church of **Santa Maria Assunta** (open 8am-noon, 4-8pm daily). It has a brightly-coloured majolica dome, and a 13th-century burnished gold Madonna and Child above the main altar.

The beach, **Marina Grande**, is a neat strip of fine grey pebbles with colourful fishing boats pulled up at one end, serried ranks of umbrellas and sunbeds belonging to the private beach concessions at the other. To the right, looking seawards, is the quay for boat services to Amalfi, Capri, Naples and Salerno. From the western end of the beach, steps lead up to a path that winds around the side of the cliff to the smaller, rockier, but popular beach of **Fornillo**, set in a bay guarded by two ancient watchtowers.

Perched above Positano lie the tiny villages of **Montepertuso** and **Nocelle**. Until a few years ago, the road ended at Montepertuso so the inhabitants of Nocelle either took the mule track to get home or walked straight up the 1,865 steps from Positano. Nowadays, the SITA bus serves both places, terminating in Nocelle. You still have to walk down nearly a hundred steps to reach the village after getting off the bus, but its scattered, rustic houses have breathtaking views.

Nocelle is an access point for one of the Amalfi Coast's great hikes. The Sentieri degli Dei, or 'Pathway of the Gods' (*see p214* **Head for the Hills**), goes up the side of a sheer cliff to the narrow pass of Colle di Serra, from where there's an easy descent to Bomerano and **Agerola** (with buses to Amalfi). The spectacular hike isn't particularly difficult, although some walking experience, a good head for heights, and plenty of water and sunblock are essential.

Where to eat & drink

Positano has lots of restaurants, although many are geared towards tourists; 'budget' in these parts is a relative term. For drinks and snacks to eat in or take away, **La Zagara** (Via dei Mulini 10, 089 875964, www.lazagara.com, open mid Mar-Oct daily) is a cheap and cheerful option in a central location. It's a piano bar and café with a glassed-in verandah, scenic patio immersed in greenery, and

an inner *salotto* with a fireplace for chilly days. The pizzas, cakes and pastries are all home-made and delicious. There's live music in the evenings and free Wi-Fi. Just above the beach, **Capricci** (Via Regina Giovanna 12, 089 812145, www.capriccipositano. it, open daily) makes good pizzas, plus sandwiches and other snacks, to eat in or take away.

Bar Bruno
Via Cristoforo Colombo 157 (089 875392).
Open *Easter-Oct* 12.30-11pm daily. **Average** €45.
The views from the narrow pavement terrace of this family-run trattoria, located on the high coastal road, are as good as any in Positano, and the food doesn't disappoint either. The all-day menu covers old favourites (pasta with *frutti di mare, spaghetti alle vongole*), plus a few more unusual choices such as fish gratin baked on lemon leaves. It's a wonderful spot for dinner on a warm summer evening.

★ La Cambusa
Piazza Vespucci 4 (089 875432, www.lacambusa positano.com). **Open** *Easter-Oct* noon-midnight daily. **Average** €45.
Positano stalwart La Cambusa (meaning 'galley') was established in 1970. It serves good fish and seafood, prepared in a wide variety of ways – fried,

grilled, roasted, baked and in soups and pastas – and offers a prime people-watching view of the beach from its handful of terrace tables. If you stick to simple *primi* (*spaghetti alle vongole*, for example), followed by a salad, it's quite affordable too.

★ Da Adolfo
Spiaggia di Laurito (089 875022, www.daadolfo. com. **Open** *May-mid Oct* 1-4pm daily. **Average** €30.
Although Adolfo's beach shack has well and truly been discovered by tourists, it's still a fantastic place for a laid-back lunch and prices are contained. Set just above tiny Laurito beach, a ten-minute boat hop from Positano (book ahead and wait on the pier for the *gozzo* with the red fish on it to pick you up), the food is fresh and vibrant: marinated anchovies, mozzarella grilled on lemon leaves, *zuppa di cozze* (mussel soup) and grilled catch of the day. Wash it down with the house sangria and sleep off the consequences on one of the loungers crammed on to the tiny patch of sand.

★ Next2
Via Pasitea 242 (089 8123516, www.next2.it).
Open *Easter-Oct* 7-11pm daily. **Average** €50.
The look and vibe at sleek Next2 in the upper part of town may be contemporary, but the food is firmly rooted in local traditions, with stalwarts such as

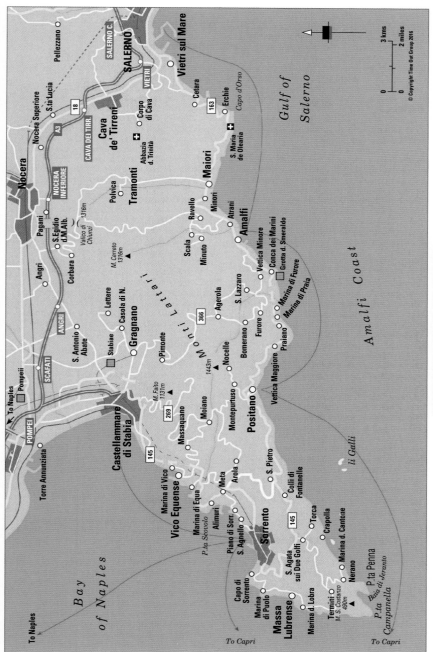

pizzella fritta (small, deep fried pizza) and *totani e patate* (squid and potato stew) alongside ravioli stuffed with shrimps and aubergine, and griddled *ricciola* (amberjack) dressed with a minty sauce. Homemade desserts are a treat and the wine list includes lots of local labels. There's a pretty patio bar for pre- or post-dinner drinks too.

Il Ritrovo

Via Montepertuso 77 (089 812005, www.ilritrovo. com). **Open** noon-midnight daily. Closed 7 Jan-mid Mar. **Average** €35.

The quiet village of Montepertuso, set high above Positano, is a world apart from the coastal chaos and this restaurant, with its panoramic terrace, courteous service and free shuttle service from Positano and back, is a fine place for a reasonably priced meal. The menu highlights seasonal veg and meat from the family farm (although there are plenty of fish choices too), so you'll find deep-fried courgette flowers, ravioli with porcini mushrooms, and fillet steak accompanied by grilled peppers and aubergine.

Nightlife

The beachfront is lined with bars, most of them overpriced. At the eastern end of Marina Grande, **Music on the Rocks** club is located in La Rada restaurant (Grotta dell'Incanto 51, 089 875874, www.musicontherocks.it, open until 4am daily, closed Nov-Mar). Here, you'll be treated to smooth piano bar music and, later, a disco tune or two.

The **Africana** (089 874858, www.africana famousclub.com, open Easter-mid June & Sept Sat, mid June-Aug daily; *photo p230*) is the coast's most celebrated club – not that there's a great deal of competition. It reopened in 2011 after a major refit. Situated right on the water between Positano and Amalfi, just west of Marina di Praia, it was a VIP hangout in the 1960s and has its very own rocky cove with a glass dancefloor, so you can watch the sea crashing below as you bop. An access road leads down, found between the 21km and 22km markers on the main road. Otherwise walk round the cliff from Marina di Praia. When the club is open, buses run from Amalfi and Positano; there are also boats from Amalfi, Maiori, Minori, Positano and Salerno.

IN THE KNOW BEAN FEAST

The inhabitants of Montepertuso turn out in force on the last Saturday in August to celebrate the humble bean, or *fagiolo*. Stalls full of beans and other gastronomic specialities line the narrow streets of the town, and restaurants and food stands showcase bean-based dishes served by waiters in traditional garb.

Where to stay

★ Casa Buonocore

Via Cristoforo Colombo 77 (089 875085, www.casabuonocore.com). **Open** Apr-Oct. **Rates** €220-€240 double.

A classy B&B occupying a lovely old family palazzo, Casa Buonocore lies atop more than 70 steps just above Piazza dei Mulini. Six gorgeous rooms, each very different from the next, are done out in restful shades with pops of brightly coloured fabric and ethnic touches: one has a vast terrace with 360° views. Lit by Moroccan lanterns at night, there's a pretty, Vietri-tiled breakfast terrace with oranges and lemons in pots, and a cosy sitting room for cooler evenings. The beach is a mere stroll away.

€ Casa Cuccaro

Via Pizzillo 4, Nocelle (089 875458, www.casa cuccaro.it). **Open** Mar-Oct. **Rates** €75-€85 double. **No credit cards.**

Walkers will appreciate the setting of this friendly B&B. Occupying an old village house in Nocelle, it's located steps from the famous Sentiero degli Dei footpath (*see p215*). But it will also appeal to anyone who shuns the crowds down on the coast; up here, all is calm and the views are magnificent. From the bar and breakfast terrace at the top of the house, you can see along the coast to Capri. The eight sunny bedrooms, all with their own terrace or balcony, share the view.

La Fenice

Via Marconi 8 (089 875513, www.bbfenice.com). **Rates** €155 double. **No credit cards.**

A sort of low-budget San Pietro (*see p225*), this charming B&B sprawls up a series of verdant terraces on either side of the main coast road. There are seven whitewashed rooms in the main villa (three with terraces), with a further eight built into the side of the cliff below. There's a pretty swimming pool and hot tub, and a path descends to a small, semi-private beach. It's not at all bad for the price, though you'll need to bring cash to cope with the no credit cards policy. A three-night minimum stay is required from April to October. Parking is €16 per day.

Palazzo Murat

Via dei Mulini 23 (089 875177, www.palazzo murat.it). **Open** Apr-Oct. **Rates** €200-€330 double. Located in the centre of the old town, this elegant 18th-century mansion once belonged to Joachim Murat, King of Naples and Napoleon's brother-in-law. The deluxe rooms in the original palazzo, with Bourbon-era antiques and four-posters, are larger and more atmospheric, but the modern rooms in the newer wing, which extends through the beautiful gardens, are significantly cheaper – some have balconies with sea views. The gorgeous entrance patio is a haven of peace and birdsong off the crowded main drag into town and makes a perfect spot for an evening *aperitivo*. The hotel's highly rated Al Palazzo restaurant lays out tables in the garden in warm weather and serves up Mediterranean cuisine with a twist. A smart new pool and free boat trips up and down the coast complete the picture.

★ San Pietro di Positano

Via Laurito 2 (089 875455, www.ilsanpietro.it). **Open** Apr-Oct. **Rates** €450-€820 double.

Carlo Cinque built his spectacular villa into the side of a rocky promontory just east of Positano. Over the years, more rooms were added and the idea of turning this remarkable feat of engineering into a hotel took shape. Today, it is one of the most exclusive in Italy. Indeed, from the road, the only evidence of its presence is a discreet sign and a tiny chapel. From here, a lift descends to the lobby, which opens on to a hibiscus-strewn terrace with breathtaking views. Its 62 rooms spill down the hillside, beautifully decorated in sunny colours with gleaming tiles and gorgeous fabrics, each with a private terrace (some huge). A second lift whisks you through the rock face to the private beach, tennis court and Carlino restaurant, where you can feast on the freshest fish and seafood. Back up top, the Michelin-starred Zass restaurant has tables laid on a candlelit terrace and offers dishes whipped up by Alois Vanlangenaeker. The hotel is still immaculately run by Cinque's family, with a huge amount of charm, and service is wonderfully attentive. A complimentary shuttle bus runs round the clock and free boat excursions are available; the hotel also hosts cookery classes.

Le Sirenuse

Via Cristoforo Colombo 30 (089 875066, www.sirenuse.it). **Open** Apr-Oct. **Rates** €506-€1,430 double.

Everything about the former private villa of the Marchesi Sersale is tastefully done, from its aristocratic Pompeian red façade to the majolica-covered panoramic terrace, with its pocket-sized swimming pool and oyster-and-champagne bar – one of *the* places for an *aperitivo* in Positano. The exquisite, antique-filled rooms exude a lived-in elegance and all – bar the standards – have sea views and balconies. Matteo Temperini's confident, subtly creative cooking has won him a Michelin star at the restaurant, La Sponda, where tables are laid on a terrace overlooking the twinkling lights of the town (or, in cooler weather, in a vaulted room lit with candles galore). There's a small gym, a contemporary spa and a fleet of boats – including a vintage Riva – for exploring the coast.

Villa La Tartana

Vicolo Vito Savino 6/8 (089 812193, www. villalatartana.it). **Open** Easter-Oct. **Rates** €170-€190 double.

The pristine white Tartana, brilliantly located just above the beach, has 12 fresh, comfortable rooms with painted headboards, colourful tiled floors and balconies; €20 extra will get you a full frontal of the sea. Public rooms are limited to the lemon yellow

Palazzo Murat.

reception and sitting area, and a small breakfast room with terrace, but you'll be spending most of your time working on your tan; beach towels are supplied free.

€ Villa Maria Antonietta

Via Cristoforo Colombo 41 (089 875071, www. villamariaantonietta.com). **Open** mid Mar-Dec. **Rates** €70-€150 double.

Run by brother-and-sister team Giuseppe and Carla, this neat, good-value little hotel offers seven simple, clean, air-conditioned rooms with new bathrooms. Upstairs rooms have French windows while those on the ground floor have small, sea-facing terraces. Breakfast is served on the terrace.

Resources

Hospital

Croce Rossa Italiana Viale Pasitea 246 (089 811912). **Open** 24hrs daily.

Internet

La Brezza Net Art Café, Via del Brigantino 1 (089 875811, www.labrezzapositano.it).

Post Office

Via Guglielmo Marconi 318, Località Chiesa Nuova (089 875142).

Tourist Information

Azienda Autonoma di Soggiorno e Turismo, Via Regina Giovanna 13 (089 875067, www.azienda turismopositano.it). **Open** *Apr-Oct* 9am-6pm Mon-Sat; 9am-2pm Sun. *Nov-Mar* 9am-2pm Mon-Sat.

Getting around

By boat

From a booth on Positano's main beach, **Lucibello** (089 875032, www.lucibello.it) runs boat trips to Capri, the Grotta dello Smeraldo (*see p230*), and up and down the coast, as well as to the Li Galli islets and some of the more inaccessible beaches and coves. There is also a fleet of boats for hire, with or without a skipper, plus canoes and pedalos.

By bus

A local bus service departs from Piazza dei Mulini, taking an anticlockwise circuit of Via Colombo, Via Marconi and Viale Pasitea every 15 minutes, 8am-10pm (winter), 8am-midnight (summer). A less frequent service serves the villages of Montepertuso and Nocelle. For details of services in Positano, contact **Flavio Gioia** (089 813077, www.flaviogioia.com).

An **UnicoCostiera** ticket will save you money and a lot of travel headaches. It's an integrated ticket that can be used on all public transport on the Amalfi Coast and Sorrentine peninsula (SITASUD and EAV buses, and Circumvesuviana trains) in all 20 of the coastal *comuni*, including Agerola, Amalfi, Maiori, Massa Lubrense, Minori, Positano, Ravello, Salerno and Sorrento. Tickets are sold at SITA and Circumvesuviana ticket

Quattro Passi. *See p228*.

ESCAPES & EXCURSIONS

offices and cost €2.50 for 45 minutes, €3.80 for 90 minutes, €7.60 for 24 hours and €18 for three days. See www.unicocampania.it for more details.

Getting there

By boat

Hydrofoils run by **Travelmar** (089 872950, www. travelmar.it) zip between Amalfi, Capri, Positano and Salerno one to six times a day, depending on the time of year. **Alicost** (089 811986, www. alicost.it) runs two hydrofoils per day (Apr-Oct) from Salerno to Capri, stopping at Amalfi and Positano. **Gescab** (089 234892, www.gescab.it) runs a service between Positano and Capri. From Capri, there are regular services to Naples.

By bus & train

SITA (089 405145, www.sitasudtrasporti.it) runs buses from Sorrento to Amalfi and Positano. Take the Circumvesuviana railway from Naples and change at Meta, just before Sorrento, where you can hook up with the service. Buses to Amalfi and Sorrento from Positano stop at the top of Via Colombo and the top of Viale Pasitea, outside the Bar Internazionale (Via Marconi 164). Bus tickets can be bought from the bar, or at the Bar-Tabacchi Collina (Via Colombo 3-5).

To reach Positano from Naples airport, catch the **Curreri** bus (081 801 5420, www. curreriviaggi.it) to Sorrento (eight daily) and change for SITA services as above.

By car

Take the A3 motorway to Castellammare di Stabia, and follow signs to Sorrento. At Meta, 4km east of Sorrento, take the SS 163. Alternatively, take the slower but more scenic SS 145 Nastro Azzurro route up and across the mountainous peninsula from the western edge of Sorrento, passing through Sant'Agata dei Due Golfi at the top. From Salerno, take the SS 163, which runs the length of the Amalfi Coast.

West of Positano

Administatively part of the province of Naples, the spectacular rocky coastline further west of Positano has few hotels or historical sites and only a sprinkling of tiny villages. Although most are well back from the shoreline, until relatively recently they were only accessible by boat. Even today, the road descends to the sea in just one place, **Marina del Cantone**, where you'll find a pebbly beach lined with bars and restaurants.

It's this remoteness that makes the coast between **Punta della Campanella** (*see p217*) and Positano worth exploring, and it's a sobering thought that this is what the entire Amalfi Coast must have looked like before it was invaded by mass tourism in the 1950s. The lack of roads is the walker's gain as there are some beautiful paths down to hidden coves and wild headlands, plus the western section of the Alta Via dei Lattari – for serious walkers only – which traverses the coast (*see p214* **Head for the Hills**). Rather surprisingly, given its remoteness, this stretch also has some excellent restaurants.

Set in a dip on the ridge dividing Sorrento from the sheer southern coast, **Sant'Agata sui Due Golfi** (named for its elevated position dominating the gulfs of both Naples and Salerno) was a favourite summer resort for well-off Neapolitan families in the 18th and 19th centuries. It doesn't look like much today, cars vying with agricultural equipment for parking places outside the 17th-century church of **Santa Maria delle Grazie** (open 8am-1pm, 5-7pm daily), which has

ESCAPES & EXCURSIONS

a monumental, multicoloured, inlaid marble altar. But there are two very good reasons for a stopover. One is the Michelin-starred **Don Alfonso 1890**. The other, much more modest, reason is the convent of **Il Deserto**, a kilometre north-west of the town along a signposted road. A forbidding bunker built by the Carmelite order in 1679, and now occupied by a closed order of rather cross Benedictine nuns, Il Deserto (081 878 0199, open 10am-noon and 5-7pm daily) has a belvedere with a view across the peninsula that defies description. Entrance is free but contributions towards the convent's upkeep are appreciated. From Sant'Agata, Via Torricella leads south-east to **Torca**, a tiny village with terrific views over the coast. On the headland to the west are the remains of a 12th-century abbey; on the beach stands a ruined Roman villa. The islet of Isca, just offshore, was owned by the famous Neapolitan playwright Eduardo de Filippo.

The road from Sant'Agata heading south-west to Termini, the jumping-off point for **Punta della Campanella** (see p217), is viewless. Beyond the hamlet of Caso, a side road on the left winds down to the pretty village of Nerano and the seaside resort of **Marina del Cantone**, which has one of the longest beaches on the southern side of the peninsula. This is not necessarily a blessing, as Cantone seems to have expanded into a resort without passing through the limbo of planning permission. Nonetheless, it's still small-scale and has a certain low-key charm.

The best way to get a feel for the contortions of the coast at close hand is to hire an outboard motor boat from the **Nautica O' Masticiello** hut (081 808 1443, www.masticiello.com, open May-Oct) in the main square. For €70, you'll get three hours in a small boat – enough to get as far as Positano and still have time to explore coves and inlets, many of them inaccessible from land, along the way. Marina di Cantone also has an excellent diving centre, **Diving Nettuno** (Via Vespucci 39, 081 808 1051, www.divingsorrento. com, open mid Mar-Oct), offering courses and guided dives, and the resort makes a good springboard for the breathtaking natural beauty of the **Baia di Jeranto** to the west.

This untouched, sandy bay can be reached either by boat from Marina di Cantone (shop around on the beach for the best price) or via a marked footpath (no.39) from the church in Nerano. East of Cantone, **Torca** is a three-hour walk away, along a stunning – and strenuous – cliff-hugging section of the Alta Via dei Monti Lattari long-distance path. For more on walking in this area, see p214 **Head for the Hills**.

East of Sant'Agata, the Nastro Azzurro road wends its spectacular 14km way to Positano. Over the pass of San Pietro, where the road across from Sorrento joins the Nastro Azzurro, the Amalfi Coast proper comes into view.

Where to eat, drink & stay

Sant'Agata is a good, low-key base for exploring the Sorrentine peninsula and the Amalfi Coast, especially if you're a walker. Set just outside the village, **Agriturismo Le Tore** (Via Pontone 43, 081 8080637, www.agriturismosorrentoletore. com, €90-€110 double) is a working olive farm that produces award-winning olive oil and offers eight simple but pretty bedrooms, plus two apartments, in an 18th-century stone farmhouse. Delicious evening meals and generous breakfasts are prepared by the owner, Vittoria.

In Sant'Agata, **Lo Stuzzichino** (Via Deserto 1, 081 533 0010, www.ristorantelostuzzichino.it, average €35) offers a much more rustic, but still excellent, alternative to Michelin-starred **Don Alfonso 1890** (see p241 **The Importance of Being Ernesto**). Overseen by wine buff and personable owner Mimmo de Gregorio, the menu of traditional, expertly prepared dishes includes a near-perfect *melanzane alla parmigiana* (much lighter than most), lemon-spiked ravioli, and succulent chicken *alla cacciatora* with tomatoes, mushrooms and aubergines. The well-priced wine list showcases local producers.

Tiny Marina del Cantone has two Michelin-starred restaurants. The rather formal **Taverna del Capitano** (Piazza delle Sirene 10, 081 808 1028, www.tavernadelcapitano.it, closed Nov-Feb, average €80) is headed by chef Alfonso Caputo, who works wonders with seafood and local garden produce. Upstairs are 14 bright, airy rooms (€180 double).

Cantone's other hot culinary contender, with two Michelin stars, is **Quattro Passi** (Via Vespucci 13N, 081 808 2800, www.ristorante quattropassi.com, closed Nov-Feb, average €90; *photos p226*), a more relaxed option set in large grounds just above the village. A stylish place with the heart of a family restaurant, it's known for its attention to vegetables, which are all home-grown. Starters could include *tortellini cacio e pepe* with clams and wild fennel; then fish tempura with green tomato gazpacho and burrata cheese as a main. The cellar – dug into the *tufa* stone – is a cave of oenological wonders. There are also six simple double rooms (€150) and three suites (€180), surrounded by a terraced olive grove.

Lo Scoglio (Piazza delle Sirene 15, 081 808 1026, www.ristoranteloscoglio.com, average €40) is another popular spot, open all year round and with a terrace right over the water. Run by the same family since 1956, it's also famous for its vegetables, grown on the family plot. Signature dish *spaghetti alle zucchine* has been served up to luminaries such as the Sultan of Brunei and Steven Spielberg.

A boat shuttle service, or an easy, 20-minute cliffside walk, takes you to the pretty little cove of **Recommone** to the east. Quieter and less touristy than Marina del Cantone, it boasts a smart little beach club, **La Conca del Sogno**, with a friendly restaurant (Via San Marciano 9, 081 808 1036, www.concadelsogno.it, closed Nov-Easter, average €45) which offers excellent fish dishes and some good wines. Finish your meal here with a glass of *finochietto* (wild fennel liqueur). There are recliners for sleeping it off, and a handful of bright, sunny rooms too (€130-€180 double).

Resources

See p226.

Getting there

See p227.

Positano to Amalfi

Before Ferdinando II of Naples commissioned the Strada Amalfitana, the now famous coastal road connecting Positano with Vietri and Salerno, most of the settlements along this stretch of coast were accessible only by sea or tortuous mountain tracks from the other side of the Sorrentine peninsula. Originally built to accommodate horse-drawn traffic, the narrow road is known today as the SS 163 and is plied by lorries, buses, tourist coaches and swarms of private cars; it's hardly surprising that the going can be agonisingly slow, especially in summer.

Heading east of Positano, the road winds around steep gullies towards **Vettica Maggiore** and **Praiano**, which merge into one another on either side of the Capo Sottile promontory. Neither place has much of a centre, and both are often lumped together as Praiano. Vettica has a small beach and one of the coast's more interesting churches, **San Gennaro**, its dome and bell tower clad with colourful tiles, the subject of many a photo. The wide piazza in front of the church is popular with local kids for ad hoc

Conca dei Marini. *See p230.*

football games and offers far-reaching views back along the coast to Positano and beyond. There's also a diving centre, **Centro Sub Costiera Amalfitana** (Via Marina di Praia, 089 812 148, 329 687 4980, www.centrosub.it).

Praiano proper, on the eastern side of the promontory, is a low-key alternative to Positano. It has a charming seaward extension to the east, tiny **Marina di Praia**, a fishing cove consisting of a scrap of beach pinched between two high rock walls. There's just enough room for a few boats, a handful of houses and a couple of bar-restaurants. For exploring the contorted coast between here and Amalfi, you can hire a boat from the **Sibilla** boat concession down on the quay (089 874365, 334 3078344, www.lasibilla.org). A path around the cliff to the right leads past the **Il Pirata** bar and restaurant to the retro-groovy **Africana** club (*see p224*).

IN THE KNOW ANNA AND ROBERTO

A few metres above sea level in Marina di Furore stands a little stone fishing hut named Villa della Storta, once owned by Oscar-winning actress Anna Magnani. She lived here for the few days in 1948 that it took to shoot her part in *L'Amore*, or rather, the first of its two parts – *Il Miracolo*. The film's director, Roberto Rossellini, was Magnani's lover at the time. You can visit the atmospheric little house if you ask at bar-restaurant Al Monazeno (*see p231*).

The jagged coastline between here and Conca dei Marini is the wildest stretch of the Costiera – nowhere more so than at the **Vallone di Furore**, a deep gorge two kilometres beyond Marina di Praia. Such an unrepentantly steep feature is called an *orrido* ('horrid') and its seaward opening is the nearest Italy comes to a fjord. There's a viaduct over the gorge; the Mediterranean Cup high-diving championship takes place here every July. Given the view, it's impossible to park on the viaduct at any time of year. But there's a steep footpath alongside leading down to Marina di Furore. It's an even tighter squeeze than Marina di Praia, with a few rock-hewn fishermen's huts and a scattering of boats on the narrow beach.

These days the hamlet is an **Ecomuseo** ('Ecomuseum'), its clutch of houses, old paper mill and hermitage restored to include a small museum on paper-making, a herbarium and a bar-restaurant (*see p231*). There are no set opening hours; for more information call 089 874100 or visit www.ilfiordodifurore.com.

Back on the coast road, just before Conca dei Marini, the big tourist pull of this stretch is the **Grotta dello Smeraldo**. From the car park on the road above, a lift descends into the cave, where visitors are decanted into box-like rowing boats. Alternatively, you can take a boat trip from Positano or Amalfi. The Emerald Grotto was discovered in 1932, ending Capri's hundred-year grotto monopoly. Cave buffs will say that it's a pale imitation of that island's **Blue Grotto** (*see p161*), but the translucent blue-green light that filters in from an underwater crevice is pretty enough, and it's a lot cheaper than its rival.

Beyond the headland of **Capo di Conca**, the bay of Amalfi appears at last in all its glory. The sprawl of houses on the hillside to the left is **Conca dei Marini** (*photos p229*), which once had a merchant fleet to rival those of its more muscular neighbours, Positano and Amalfi. The upper part of the town is accessible from the Agerola road, which forks off sharply to the left just past the random collection of houses that call themselves (confusingly) **Vettica Minore**, a couple of kilometres before Amalfi. If you've had enough of the glitz and crowds of the Costiera, this road offers a worthwhile detour – though it's not a short one, and unless you want to press on to Naples, the only way back is the way you came. It begins by heading west, passing the long, barrel-vaulted profile of the **Convento di Santa Rosa**. This was formerly a house of Augustine nuns, famous as the inventors of the *torta di Santa Rosa* – a concoction of flaky pastry, blancmange and dried fruit traditionally eaten on 30 August, Santa Rosa's feast day. Nowadays, the convent houses a luxury hotel (*see p232*).

Rising gently up through the contour lines, the road continues around the upper part of the Vallone del Furore to **Furore** itself, a rugged

Africana. *See p224.*

village that – like so many in these parts – lacks a centre. It does, however, boast some unexpected murals and modern sculptures, and also produces some of the Amalfi Coast's best wine. For a taster, head for pioneering wine-maker Marisa Cuomo's **Gran Furor Divina Costiera** winery (Via Giovambattista Lama 14, 089 830348, www.marisacuomo.com). From precarious vineyards planted on near-vertical slopes come the indigenous grapes for the award-winning wines produced here; visits take place between March and August and can be booked via the website. It's not all grapes, though, as Furore is also rightly celebrated for its tiny, intensely flavoured cherry tomatoes (*pomodorini a piennolo*).

Beyond the village, the road snakes up to the ridge in a series of bends before spilling out into the fertile upland plain of **Agerola**, a collection of agricultural settlements, cut off by rugged terrain from the Costiera below and the Vesuvian plain beyond. Up here, soft-eyed brown Agerolese cows provide milk for delicious cheeses such as the ovoid *Provolone del Monaco* and *fior di latte agerolese* (cow's milk mozzarella), while farmers produce much of the fruit, meat and vegetables that end up in swanky Amalfi restaurants.

Grotta dello Smeraldo

1km west of Conca dei Marini on the main coast road. Information: APT Amalfi (089 871107, www.amalfitouristoffice.it). **Open** 9am-4pm daily. **Admission** €5. **No credit cards.**

Where to eat, drink & stay

Just east of Praiano, cool, contemporary **Casa Angelina** (Via Gennaro Capriglione 147, 089 813 1333, www.casangelina.com, closed Nov-Mar, €355-€415 double) features whiter-than-white rooms, most with terraces or balconies, and all with spectacular sea views past Positano to Capri; common areas are splashed with bright, modern artworks and designer furniture. There's a rooftop gourmet restaurant, two pools, a spa and a cigar bar, while the hotel has its own beach and boat. Four romantic rooms are housed in ex-fishermen's huts just above the beach, more than 200 steps below the main hotel. Breakfasts are spectacular.

On Praiano's main drag, you'll find the **Tramonto d'Oro** (Via Gennaro Capriglione 119, 089 874955, www.tramontodoro.it, closed Nov-Feb, €100-€250 double). It's a friendly hotel with clean rooms – most of which have sea views – decent food, and a rooftop pool overlooking the coast and the San Gennaro church. Hidden away below the coast road in Praiano, **Hotel Le Sirene** (Via San Nicola 10, 089 874013, www.lesirene.com, closed Nov-mid Mar, €80-€100 double) is a simple, pretty establishment with a stone-flagged courtyard, neat bedrooms, and views over olive trees and kitchen gardens to the sea. The rooftop terrace is a bonus, as are the friendly owners.

Back on the main street, scenic **La Brace** (Via Gennaro Capriglione 146, 089 874226, www. labracepraiano.com, closed Wed mid Oct-mid Mar & all Nov, average €40) offers simple, good-value seafood dishes such as *scialatielli* with seafood sauce or salt-crusted seabass, as well as excellent Neapolitan pizza baked in a wood-fired oven.

Taking the steps down to the beach from Piazza San Gennaro, you'll eventually come across **La Gavitella** (089 813 1319, www.ristorante lagavitella.it, closed Nov-Mar, average €45). The terrace overlooking the sea is lovely for an *aperitivo*, before you tuck into fresh fish and pasta. **Il Pirata** (Via Terramare, 089 874377, www. ristoranteilpirata.net, closed Nov-Easter, average €35), accessed by boat or via the cliff path from Marina di Praia, enjoys similarly wonderful views and serves linguine with sea urchin sauce and other fishy treats at tables laid out over the rocks.

At **Trattoria da Armandino** (089 874087, www.trattoriadaarmandino.it, closed Nov-Mar, average €35), also in Marina di Praia, dishes such as succulent grilled swordfish steak drizzled with the local mint-spiked dressing are served right on the quayside under towering cliffs. Marina di Furore's tiny bar-restaurant **Al Monazeno** (Via Anna Magnani, 349 0772544, www.monazeno-fiordo-furore.com, closed Nov-Mar, average €35) is one of the more unusual places in which to have lunch or dinner on the Costiera. Set at the foot of yet more towering cliffs, overlooking the tiny scrap of beach, it serves snacks and hot dishes such as *tubettoni* pasta with squid, a Furore speciality. On the road above, towards Positano, **La Locanda del Fiordo** (Via Trasita 9,

IN THE KNOW AMALFI'S PAPERMAKERS

Amalfi has been a centre for papermaking since the 13th century. Its natural setting, wedged into a gorge that opens on to the sea, was perfect: steep hillsides meant gushing streams, providing a reliable source of power to drive the machinery. The Amalfitani learned to make paper from the Arabs, producing *bambagina* – a thick, heavy parchment fashioned from cotton and linen rags. A century ago the area was still full of paper mills, but there are only a couple left today. You can still buy the paper with its characteristic ragged edges and beautiful watermarks; it makes a handsome souvenir. To find out more, visit the **Museo della Carta** (see *p234*), housed in a 15th-century paper mill.

089 874813, www.lalocandadelfiordo.it, €90-€200 double) is a classically stylish B&B with an entrance at road level and rooms (each named after an Italian screen diva) on two rock-hewn terraces below, where steps descend to the sea.

From its clifftop perch dominating Conca dei Marini, the **Monastero Santa Rosa** (Via Roma 2, Conca dei Marini, 089 8321199, www.monasterosantarosa.com, closed Nov-mid Apr, from €400 double) can claim to have some of the best views on the coast, none more so than from its spectacular heated infinity pool, set in terraced gardens. The 20 cool, luxurious bedrooms were fashioned from the monks' cells; there's a fabulous spa and a gourmet restaurant where chef Christoph Bob cooks up a storm with the likes of linguine with fresh anchovies and wild fennel. Those monks will be turning in their graves.

In Vettica, **Vettica House** (Via Maestra dei Villaggi 92, 089 871930, www.hostelscalinatella.com, closed Nov-Mar, €60-€140 double, €27-€35 dorm) has some of the best budget accommodation on the Costiera along with stupendous views. Run by the family that owns A' Scalinatella hostel in Atrani (see *p236*), it's a cluster of simple rooms (from doubles to six-bed mixed dorms) carved into the rock above a lemon orchard. Be warned: it's a stiff climb up 270 steps from the nearest bus stop on the Furore/Agerola road. Phone ahead for precise instructions on how to get here; the owner may even come to meet you on his scooter.

For sustenance, a good bet is the **Hostaria da Bacco** (Via Giovambattista Lama 9, 089 830360, www.baccofurore.it, closed Jan & Feb Mon-Thur, average €40), located a stone's throw from Marisa Cuomo's winery (see *p230*). It draws customers up from the coast with its refined home cooking, which uses plenty of local produce and seafood

in signature creations such as *ferrazzuoli alla nannarella* (spiral pasta with swordfish, capers and pine nuts). You can sample the succulent Agerola cheeses here and finish off with *cicale di furore* (little cakes made from almond and locally harvested prickly pears). There are staggering views from the terrace and the serious wine list includes some 500 labels from all over Italy; where better to sample Marisa Cuomo's very special Fior d'Uva? If you can't face the cliff-hugging drive back, there are 18 simple rooms (€80-€100 double).

Resources

See also p226 and p237.

Internet
Dimensione Futuro, Via Gennaro Capriglione 27, Praiano (089 874420).

Getting there

The villages can all be reached by bus or car from **Positano** (see *p221*) or **Amalfi** (see *below*).

Amalfi & Atrani

Fringed by lemon trees, Amalfi is a pretty tourist resort that spills over on to the coast and lines both sides of the steep, fertile Valle dei Mulini. Between the ninth and 12th centuries, this was a glorious maritime republic. In its prime, Amalfi had 70,000 inhabitants, and many more lived abroad in merchant colonies scattered around the Mediterranean from Tunis to Beirut.

On land, Amalfi's dominion extended over the whole of the Sorrentine peninsula and beyond. At sea, it had few rivals; its navy protected the republic's independence and won battles for allies such as the Lombards and the Duchy of Naples. The republic survived at least nominally from 839 until the devastating Pisan raids of 1135 and 1137. Then, gradually, a Venetian-style system of government was adopted, led by a doge elected by a council consisting of the menfolk of the town's most important families. Amalfi coined its own money and made its own laws; its maritime code, the *Tavole Amalfitane*, was recognised across the Mediterranean until well into the 16th century.

Mercantile prosperity continued even after the end of the republic. But an earthquake in 1343 destroyed most of the old town – Amalfi didn't really recover until the 19th century, when its illustrious past and spectacular setting began to attract literary and artistic travellers from northern Europe. The **regata storica delle Antiche Repubbliche Marinare** – a ceremonial boat race between Amalfi, Genoa, Pisa and Venice – is a reminder of the golden age, held on the first Sunday in June.

Amalfi's narrow, high-sided streets and alleyways mean it's always shady, even in the blazing sunshine. The tourist office can supply you with a map, but it's just as rewarding to strike out up steps and side alleys – it's amazing how quickly you can lose the crowds.

On the seaward side of the pretty, cream-coloured town, the port, bus terminus, bars and restaurants jostle for space on the waterfront. To the east lies a decent grey shingle beach – packed in summer – although better bathing spots are tucked away in a series of coves and beaches (marked 'Spiagge') to the west, served by a circular ferry service from the main quay.

Dominating the hillside to the west are the collonaded halls of the Capuchin convent, now a luxury hotel. Along Corso delle Repubbliche Marinare, which follows the shoreline eastwards out of town, are the post office and the tourist office; just around the corner, in a palm-shaded piazza, stands the Municipio, or town hall, which houses the small Museo Civico. The sweep of the bay ends in a medieval watchtower that houses the **Luna Convento** restaurant; the hotel of the same name (*see p235*) occupies a former Franciscan convent on the other side of the road.

The sea-facing Piazza Flavio Gioia is dominated by a statue of Flavio himself, who not only didn't invent the compass, as the plaque at his feet claims, but may never even have existed. The Porta Marinara gate here leads into the old town. Before you pass through it, have a look at what remains of Amalfi's shipyard, the **Arsenale della Repubblica**, beneath an arch to the left of the gate which now houses the **Museo della Bussola**. This was where huge galleys, with more than 100 oars, were built by teams of shipwrights. The central Piazza del Duomo is dominated by Amalfi's colourful **Cattedrale**. A masterpiece of the Arab-Norman style, it's reached – like everything in this region – by a steep staircase. The jazzy façade is a dubious reconstruction of the early 13th-century original; most of it was added after part of the church collapsed in 1861. The pretty, free-standing campanile, dating from 1276, is the real thing, having been tampered with very little over the course of the centuries. Underneath a lofty porch, the central bronze doors of the Duomo were cast some time before 1066 by a Syrian master and carried back by a local shipping magnate's fleet. The inscription explains that they were donated to the republic by Pantaleone di Mauro Comite, head of the Amalfitan colony in Constantinople.

Crowded with pavement bars and cafés, Piazza del Duomo is a good place in which to rest, refuel and maybe flick through a copy of *The Duchess of Malfi*. To the north, Via Genova and Via Capuano lead up through an increasingly quiet residential part of town, where the sound of fast-flowing water can be heard everywhere, even at the height of summer. This deep valley – the Valle dei Mulini – was the site of some of Europe's first papermaking factories, powered by a series of watermills; one, at Palazzo Pagliara, has been turned into the **Museo della Carta**.

The wild, upper part of the Valle dei Mulini (take the road that skirts the eastern side of the valley) is well worth exploring. In its further alpine reaches, the valley becomes the Vallone delle Ferriere, named after the ironworks (*ferro* means 'iron') that drew their power from the gushing waters, like the paper mills downstream.

In the days of the republic, quiet and charming **Atrani** (*photo p236*) was an upmarket residential quarter and remains a good place to escape Amalfi's crowds. It's less than a kilometre east, round the headland, accessible on foot via the web of staircases that straggle across the hill. Atrani was razed by the Pisans in 1187 and today feels more workaday than its neighbour. It has a busy fishing port and some good examples of local architecture, with a maze of arches, long pedestrian tunnels, staircases and barrel-vaulted houses on different levels. Space is so tight here that the main coast road sweeps across the centre on a viaduct whose arches separate the port from the pretty main square, Piazza Umberto I.

The little church of **San Salvatore de' Bireto** (open May-Oct daily, Nov-Apr Sat & Sun), at the top of a flight of steps on the opposite side of the piazza, was where the investiture of Amalfi's doges took place; its name derives from the *berretto*, or 'ducal cap'. Its bronze doors were a gift, in 1087, from the same Amalfitan merchant in Constantinople who commissioned the doors of Amalfi's Duomo. They can now be seen in the parish church of **Santa Maria Maddalena** (open Sun am for Mass), which rises high above the road to the east. The dome is a classically colourful example of local style; inside, the original Romanesque was swept aside in a Baroque makeover, but there are some marvellous wooden statues of roasting sinners on the wall.

High above the town to the west, the 13th-century church of **Santa Maria del Bando** (open Sept only; ask at the town hall on Via dei Dogi) perches on a narrow ledge halfway up a vertical cliff below the Torre dello Zirro, a medieval watchtower that locals say is haunted.

★ Duomo di Amalfi (Cattedrale di Sant'Andrea)

Piazza del Duomo (089 871324). **Open** *Mar* 9.30am-5.15pm daily. *Apr-June, Oct & 26 Dec-6 Jan* 9am-6.45pm daily. *July-Sept* 9am-7.45pm daily. *Nov-24 Dec* 10am-3.45pm daily. Closed 7 Jan-Feb & 25 Dec. **Admission** *Cathedral* free. *Chiostro del Paradiso* €3. **No credit cards.**

The cathedral's interior, recently restored to reduce some of its Baroque excess, is nonetheless a bit of a disappointment in comparison with the Romanesque

ESCAPES & EXCURSIONS

Marina Grande.

simplicity of its cousin in Ravello (*see p242*). Remnants of the original church furniture include the two *amboni* ('pulpits') flanking the main altar, some ancient columns, and a beautiful mother of pearl cross (another piece of Crusader loot).

Don't miss the delightful Chiostro del Paradiso, entered through a door at the left end of the porch in front of the Duomo. Built in 1266 as a burial ground for the members of Amalfi's aristocracy, this cloister, with its Moorish-style arches and central garden, is a reminder of the glory days of the maritime republic.

A door leads from the cloister into the Cappella del Crocefisso, the only part of the church to have survived more or less intact from the 12th century. Glass cases hold treasures belonging to the diocese, including a bejewelled mitre made for the Anjou court of Naples in 1297.

From the chapel, with its faded 14th-century frescoes, stairs lead down to the crypt dedicated to St Andrew, whose mortal remains were stolen from Constantinople in 1206. The sarcophagus that contains the saintly remains oozes a 'miraculous' fluid that the locals call manna (it's actually a plant extract).

Museo della Bussola e del Ducato Marinaro di Amalfi

Largo Cesareo Console 3 (089 871170, www. museoarsenaleamalfi.it). **Open** *9am-1pm, 4-7pm Tue-Sun.* **Admission** €2. **No credit cards**.
The Museum of the Compass and the Maritime Duchy of Amalfi is housed in the vaulted halls of the ex-arsenal and documents Amalfi's glorious history

as a once-mighty maritime republic. The collection includes examples of the earliest navigational instruments, such as the compass that revolutionised explorations of the oceans towards the New World. Among the ancient parchments, codices and manuscripts is a facsimile of the *Tabula de Amalpha*, Amalfi's code of maritime law.

Museo della Carta

Palazzo Pagliara, Via delle Cartiere 23 (089 830 4561, www.museodellacarta.it). **Open** *Mar-Oct 10am-6.30pm daily. Nov-Feb 10.30am-3.30pm Tue-Sun.* **Admission** €4 (incl guided tour in English). **No credit cards**.
Housed in a 15th-century paper mill, this museum tells the history of Amalfi's ancient papermaking industry with displays of tools, machinery, paper samples and a good, clear audiovisual presentation.

Where to shop

Food is a big draw in Amalfi, especially anything to do with lemons. **Pasticceria Andrea Pansa 1830** (Piazza del Duomo 40, 089 871065, www. pasticceriapansa.it, closed Jan) uses this local fruit in any number of inventive ways: candied rind, *frolla* (a ricotta-filled pastry dome), sticky *delizia al limone* cakes. Almond-lovers will also appreciate the delicate *paste di mandorla*. The same owners also run the lovely **Cioccolateria** (Piazza Municipio 12, 089 873291, www.andrea pansa.it, closed Sun Oct-May). For more intoxicating treats, head for the tiny corner outlet of **Antichi Sapori d'Amalfi** (Piazza del Duomo 39, 089 872062, www.antichisaporidamalfi.it) closed Tue Nov-Mar). They make their own limoncello and other fruit liqueurs.

Paper is the other traditional industry; the best place at which to view and buy some of the high-quality paper still made hereabouts is **La Scuderia del Duca** (Largo Cesareo Console 8, 089 872976, www.carta-amalfi.it, closed Sun Oct-May). It's a cave of wonders with a good selection of books on Amalfi and the surrounding area, some in English.

Where to eat

★ La Caravella
Via Matteo Camera 12 (089 871029, www. ristorantelacaravella.it). **Open** *Sept-June* noon-2.30pm, 7-11pm Mon, Wed-Sun. *July, Aug* 7-11pm Mon, Tue; noon-2.30pm, 7-11pm Wed-Sun. Closed mid Nov-Dec. **Average** €85.
Opened back in 1959, La Caravella was the first restaurant in the Campania region to be awarded a Michelin star, and still holds it own among stiff competition. The two-room restaurant has no view, but the superb food (mainly fish and seafood), extensive wine list and attentive service make up for that in spades. If you can't decide between the lemon leaves stuffed with swordfish and grilled with fennel sauce or *pesce del golfo in crosta di sale* (local fish in a salt crust), try the tasting menu; be sure to finish with the legendary hot lemon soufflé. If it was good enough for Jackie Kennedy...

Eolo
Via Pantaleone Comite 3 (089 871241, www. eoloamalfi.it). **Open** *Apr-June, mid Sept-Oct* 12.30-2.45pm, 7-10.30pm Mon, Wed-Sun. *July-mid Sept* 7-10.30pm Mon, Wed-Sun. **Average** €75.
With its sophisticated menu and romantic little terrace overlooking the beach, this is a place for a special treat. The young chef plays variations on a traditional theme with outstanding results, serving seasonal treats such as tagliolini with red mullet and wild fennel, and a soufflé version of the classic *insalata caprese* with mozzarella, tomatoes and basil. A heavyweight wine list seals the deal.

Marina Grande
Viale delle Regioni 4 (089 871129, www. ristorantemarinagrande.com). **Open** *Mar-June & Sept-mid Nov* noon-3.15pm, 6.30-10.30pm Mon, Tue, Thur-Sun. *July, Aug* daily. **Average** €55.
The Esposito family's restaurant and bathing establishment has stood on this spot on Amalfi's main beach since 1939, but current patron Giampaolo has given both the menu and the decor a contemporary makeover. To a background of lapping waves and cool jazzy sounds, you can sample the chef's take on the local seafood: risotto with clams, artichokes and

garlic butter; sea bass served with vegetable rösti and courgette flowers; or a light, crispy *fritto misto*. This is also a popular beach club, so you can rent sunbeds and spend the day here.

★ A' Paranza
Traversa Dragoni 2, Atrani (089 871840, www.ristoranteparanza.com). **Open** 12.30-3pm, 7.30-11.30pm Mon, Wed-Sun (daily in summer). Closed 2wks Dec. **Average** €45.
Set on a side street just off Atrani's main square, this little upmarket trattoria is a fine place for traditional seafood and offers a fantastic array of fishy antipasti. That could be followed by *paccheri al ragù di pesce* (with its rich, fish-based sauce), perhaps, or catch of the day *'in acqua pazza'* (tomato and herb broth). Finish with delicious homemade desserts such as ricotta and pear flan. The crisp white wines from nearby Tramonti make a perfect accompaniment.

€ Trattoria dei Cartari
Piazza Spirito Santo 5 (089 872131). **Open** *Jan-July, Oct-Dec* noon-3pm, 6.30pm-1.30am Tue-Sun (daily in Aug). **Average** €25.
For simple, authentic Amalfitana cuisine and good prices, this friendly trattoria is a good choice. Situated high on the road that leads up to the Valle dei Mulini, it's far enough from the town centre not to be overrun with tourists. It also attracts lots of locals, especially at weekends when the terrace is full of family groups. Order a plate of fried local anchovies while you peruse the menu of favourites such as *spaghetti alle vongole, paccheri* with monkfish sauce and *fritto di calamari e gamberi*.

Nightlife

The only disco of note in town is **RoccoCo'** (Via delle Cartiere 98, 089 873080, closed Mon-Thur & Sun, Nov-Mar), a rather cheesy place with occasional guest DJs, some way up the valley. Otherwise, jump on a boat to the **Africana** (*see p224*). On summer nights, Atrani's pretty Piazza Umberto I, with its bars and restaurants, morphs into quite a lively hangout. **Bar Risacca** (Piazza Umberto I 16, 089 872866, www.barlarisacca.it, closed Mon Oct-Apr) is the favourite lounging spot; have breakfast here before heading under the arches to the beach, try the bruschetta at lunchtime, or enjoy the evening cool over a spritz. In high season, it's open until 3am daily.

Where to stay

Luna Convento
Via Pantaleone Comite 33 (089 871002, www.lunahotel.it). **Rates** €220-€290 double.
Five minutes from the centre of Amalfi, this tastefully converted, 13th-century former monastery has whitewashed walls, vaulted ceilings and a delightful Byzantine cloister where breakfast is served in

summer. Previous guests include Wagner, Ibsen, Mussolini and Tennessee Williams. Over the road is a Saracen tower which houses the restaurant: the pool is carved out of the rocks beneath. Rooms are bright and comfortable (some with sea views), and desk staff are helpful. Parking is €20 per day.

★ € Residenza del Duca

Via Mastalo II Duca 3 (089 873 6365, www. residencedelduca.it). **Rates** €90-€140 double.
Located in an old palazzo just off the main drag, this lovely little hotel offers six handsomely furnished rooms with fine fabrics, original beamed ceilings and excellent rates. Rooms have rooftop or sea views and one has a private terrace, well worth the small extra charge. Showers come with massage jets, and there's air-conditioning and Wi-Fi throughout. Breakfast is served on a flower-filled terrace in summer.

★ Santa Caterina

SS Amalfitana 9 (089 871012, www.hotel santacaterina.it). **Rates** €347-€847 double.
A kilometre west of central Amalfi, the clifftop Santa Caterina enjoys breathtaking, uninterrupted views of the coast. Expect sunny, spacious rooms with hand-painted majolica floors, marble bathrooms and terraces with sea views. The hotel is surrounded by its own terraced garden, verdant with lemon trees and bougainvillea, where two self-contained suites hide (the Romeo and Juliet suite is the most spectacular). Sunlight floods the gleaming white public rooms and dining terrace, where a splendid breakfast is served. From the spacious hall, a lift takes guests down to the private beach, pool and one of two on-site restaurants where you can tuck into the likes of wood-fired pizza or chargrilled scampi overlooking the sea. There's also a fitness centre and beauty treatments, including the signature 'lemon massage'.

€ A' Scalinatella

Piazza Umberto I 5/6, Atrani (089 871492, 338 473 9200, www.hostelscalinatella.com). **Rates** €27-€35 dorm; €60-€90 double.
The charming, laid-back village of Atrani has no hotel as such. It does have this budget operation, though, with a couple of hostel-style dormitories in a house off the main street, plus a scattering of double rooms and mini apartments all over the village. From April to September, breakfast is served at

Atrani. *See p233.*

the Scalinatella bar in the main square, which is also where new arrivals should check in (before 2pm if possible). Open all year, A' Scalinatella is a meeting point for backpackers and independent travellers otherwise poorly served on the Amalfi Coast.

Villa Lara

Via delle Cartiere 1 (089 873 6358, www.villa lara.it). **Rates** €90-€195 double.

Access to this six-room gem, which is housed in a 19th-century villa set among vineyards and lemon groves in the quiet, upper part of Amalfi, is via a lift carved out of the rock face. The bright, modern rooms have Vietri tiled floors and beamed ceilings, and look down over the town to the sea; one even has a sunken hot tub. Breakfast is served on a beautiful terrace by the friendly owner, Nello Rispoli, who is full of helpful advice for guests.

Resources

Police

Piazza Municipio (089 873 6210, 089 871 633).

Post Office

Corso delle Repubbliche Marinare 33 (089 830 4811).

Tourist Information

Azienda Autonoma di Soggiorno e Turismo Corso delle Repubbliche Marinare 27 (089 871 107, www.amalfitouristoffice.it). **Open** *May-Oct* 9am-1pm, 3-8pm Mon-Sat. *Nov-Apr* 9am-1pm, 3-6pm Mon-Fri; 9am-1pm Sat.

Getting around

By boat

The main quay by the bus terminus is the hopping-off point for regular boats to the western beaches, marked 'Spiagge', which leave at least every hour (9am-5pm daily June-Sept, €3 return).

By bus

Amalfi's bus terminus is in Piazza Flavio Gioia on the waterfront. Local services run to Pogerola, Ravello and Scala. Tickets can be purchased at the SITA outlet in Largo Scoppetta, next to the bus terminus, or *tabacchi*. For information on **UnicoCostiera** tickets, *see p226*.

Getting there

From Naples airport

Take the Curreri bus to Sorrento (there are 10 daily) and change for the SITA bus to Amalfi. If you don't like winding roads, you can also take the bus into Naples Centrale train station and catch a fast train from there to Salerno, from where you can pick up the SITA bus to Amalfi.

By boat

From April to October, it's possible to travel to Amalfi from Naples via Capri. But unless you want to spend some time on the island, it's cheaper and quicker to get the regular boat from Salerno. **Travelmar** (089 872950, www.travelmar.it) runs ferries from Piazza della Concordia and the Molo Manfredi quay in Salerno to Amalfi and Positano (Apr-Oct only). **Cooperativa Sant'Andrea** (089 873190, www.coopsantandrea.com) runs between Amalfi, Salerno, Positano, Minori, Maiori and Capri.

By bus

SITA buses make the cliff-road journey between Amalfi and Salerno, with hairpin bends aplenty. For Naples, there are two main options: via Agerola (15 daily) or via Vietri (four daily). Or take the Circumvesuviana train from Naples and change at Meta for the Sorrento–Amalfi bus. For times and information, go to www.sitasudtrasporti.it. Note that Sunday services on these lines are infrequent.

By car

From Naples, leave the A3 motorway at the Angri exit, just past Pompeii, and follow signs through the urban blight to the Valico di Chiunzi pass and Ravello. Equally scenic, but much longer, is the SS 366 route, which crosses from Castellammare di Stabia via Gragnano, Agerola and Furore, to emerge on the coast road 2km west of Amalfi. From Salerno, take the SS136 road.

By train

There's no Amalfi Coast line; the nearest station is Vietri, at the eastern limit of the Costiera, served by only a few very slow trains. It's better to go to Salerno station (40 minutes from Naples) and continue either by boat or SITA bus.

East of Atrani

Some say that the real Amalfi Coast road ends in Amalfi and that the stretch between here and Salerno is little more than a traffic jam. However, if you have time to explore, you'll find that the area has low-key, authentic charms.

Minori, three kilometres east of Atrani (or a pleasant hour's hike from Ravello down an ancient staircase) is by no means picturesque in the Positano sense, but it's a pleasant little place with a small beach that justifies a stopover, not least for Sal de Riso's excellent pastry shop (see p239). If you're heading east, this is also one of the few Amalfi Coast towns to have a relatively flat centre, nestled between high valley walls.

In the middle of a warren of houses, the **Villa Romana** is the only archaeological site on the Costiera that's open to visitors. Excavations began in 1951 but were held up by a catastrophic flood in 1954 that consumed not only the villa but much of Minori and neighbouring Maiori. The property, arranged around a large *viridarium* ('courtyard garden'), must have belonged to a rich nobleman; it's generously proportioned, and traces of first century AD frescoes remain on the walls of many of the rooms. Upstairs, an antiquarium contains relics found here and at two nearby sites.

Above **Bar de Riso** lies the **Basilica**. The church is dedicated to the patron saint of Minori, St Trofimena, whose feast day is celebrated on 13 July by a flotilla of boats.

Just around the next headland, **Maiori** nestles in a floodplain that has been a continual source of danger to its inhabitants, but has also given them space to expand. In the 11th century, the town was girded with walls and used as a shipbuilding centre for the Amalfi Republic. Today, it's the Costiera's only truly nondescript tourist resort, packed with modern hotels built after the 1954 flood. It does have the coast's longest beach, though, a historic gem of a hotel in the **Casa Raffaele Conforti**, and gourmet restaurant **Torre Normanna**.

From Maiori, a side road winds up the Valle di Tramonti to the 656m (2,152ft) Valico di Chiunzi pass. Also accessible from Ravello, it offers far-reaching views right across the construction-plagued Sarno plain to the menacing bulk of Vesuvius. Like Agerola (see p230), **Tramonti** is not a single village, but a series of communities scattered over a fertile upland plain surrounded by mountains (hence the name 'between the mountains'). It's known for its farm produce, cheese, honey and excellent wines, along with baskets woven from the branches of the local chestnut trees. The cold north wind that Amalfi mariners called the *tramontana* howls out of the encircling mountains; the word has become the standard Italian term for a biting northerly.

The coast road east of Maiori negotiates the rocky **Monte dell'Avvocata**, providing spectacular views along the coast. A short distance beyond the 39km road marker, steps on the left lead up to the rock-hewn chapel of **Santa Maria de Olearia** (open by appointment, 089 814201). Also known as the Catacombe di Badia, the chapel is one of the more unusual holy sites on the coast, and well worth a visit if you can find a place wide enough to leave the car, or persuade the bus driver to set you down. Two hermits were the first to occupy this site in 973; their shrine became a Benedictine abbey, squeezed between the towering rocks, which still has some atmospheric if faded 11th-century frescoes.

Beyond the little fishing cove of **Erchie**, with its pretty beach watched over by a Saracen tower (look for the access road on the eastern side of the valley, after the main road has rejoined the shore), the coast road winds along to the authentic, workaday village of **Cetara**, once the eastern limit of the Amalfi Republic. Offering a taste of what the area must have been like before the tourist invasion, it still has a salty, frontier town feel and is home to the only remaining working fishing fleet on the Costiera, which roams the whole Mediterranean in search of shoals.

With its small beach and medieval watchtower, and the honest, unprettified houses that line its single street, Cetara has a different feel from the other towns on the coast – in spite of the familiar vertical shape. Its excellent restaurants (see p237 **In the Know**) are another incentive to visit.

East of Cetara, the road hugs the coast, passing below what is left of the massive hotel at Punta Fuenti. For years, this illegally built blot on the landscape was at the centre of a struggle between environmental pressure groups and local politicians, who feared a domino effect – and the end of lucrative backhanders – if it were shown that what went up could indeed come down. Finally, in 2000, the bulldozers moved in.

Further east, on the site of the Etruscan town called Marcina, **Vietri sul Mare** is the capital of southern Italy's handcrafted ceramics industry. Although pottery has been made here since Roman times, the locals had lost their touch by the early 20th century. German ceramicists moved into the area and got the industry going again, and today the town is heaving with shops selling the ubiquitous, multicoloured breakables that you see in every bar, hotel and restaurant up and down the coast. In **Raito**, the town adjacent to Vietri, the **Museo Provinciale della Ceramica** (Torretta Belvedere di Villa Guariglia, 089 211835, closed Mon, admission free) traces the history of the local ceramic industry in detail and is housed in the beautiful Villa Guariglia, where summer jazz and classical music concerts are sometimes held (ask at the Vietri tourist office).

There are pretty examples of local majolica tiles on the dome of the 18th-century church of **San Giovanni Battista** (open 7.30-10.30am, 5.30-8pm daily). Inside, look out for the ceramic Stations of the Cross and the brightly coloured statue of Christ. The beach at Marina di Vietri, with its seaside bars and *gelaterie*, is a popular summer attraction.

Villa Romana & Antiquarium

Via Capodipiazza 28, Minori (089 852893). **Open** 8am-7pm daily. The antiquarium closes an hour before sunset. **Admission** free.

Where to shop

If you'd like to invest in the work of local artisans, visit Maiori's **Sandali Tipici** (Lungomare Amendola 38, 089 851595, www.sandalitipici. com) for handmade sandals.

Cetara's **Cetarii** (Via Largo Marina 48, 089 261863, www.cetarii.it) stocks bottles of high-quality *colatura di alici* (the celebrated anchovy sauce), jars of local tuna preserved in oil, tuna roe, anchovies and other local products.

In Vietri, housed in a striking, Gaudí-esque building designed in the 1950s by Paolo Soleri (a pupil of Frank Lloyd Wright), the **Ceramica Artistica Solimene** (Via Madonna degli Angeli 7, 089 210243, www.ceramicasolimene.it) is an Aladdin's cave of an outlet shop stuffed with ceramics bargains. The colourful, handpainted pieces with naive animal designs make wonderful gifts and can be shipped home.

Where to eat, drink & stay

Near Minori, the best accommodation is the **Agriturismo Villa Maria** (Via Annunziata, 089 877197, www.agriturismovillamaria.it, €90-€110 double). It's halfway up a mountain (call Maria's husband Vincenzo to pick you up from outside Bar de Riso), so the views over Minori and the coast are fabulous, and the only sounds you'll hear are a braying donkey or twittering birds. The rooms are simple but pretty and spotlessly clean; each has its own little terrace. Maria cooks up a storm using produce from the terraces that fan out down the mountain. If you can't get a room, at least try to come for lunch or dinner.

Down in town is the famous **Bar de Riso** (Piazza Cantilena 1, 089 853618, www.salderiso.it, closed Oct-May), which sits between the main square and the busy Lungomare. Run by the De Riso family since 1908, the bar serves confectionery created by Salvatore, whose cakes (*sfogliatelle, babà*) and homemade ice-cream are renowned – Sal has written books on the subject. Grab a seat outside and enjoy your treat with an excellent coffee or *granita di caffè*.

It's not obvious from the cement-lined waterfront, but Maiori also has a historic centre, though floods and other catastrophes have pared it back. Just off pedestrianised Corso della Regina, on an ancient arched street, stands the rather faded, but still charming **Casa Raffaele Conforti** (Via Casa Mannini 10, 089 853547, www.casaraffaeleconforti.it, closed Jan, Feb & Nov, €65-€130 double). Lovely fresco ceilings, antique furniture and gilded mirrors set the tone at this nine-room hotel that occupies the second floor of a crumbling 19th-century townhouse.

The Proto brothers' elegant **Torre Normanna** (Via Diego Taiani 4, 089 877100, www.ristorantetorrenormanna.it, closed 10-30 Nov & Mon Dec-Mar, average €80) offers some of the best food on the Costiera plus fabulous views; no surprise that this is a popular wedding venue. It occupies the largest and oldest Norman watchtower on the coast, where four brothers serve up expertly executed fare – perhaps sea bass sautéed in lemon and capers with *broccoletti*. The wine list offers a wide choice, but if you stick to something local the bill for a superb meal will be relatively contained.

In Cetara, **Acqua Pazza** (Corso Garibaldi 38, 089 261606, www.acquapazza.it, open Mar-May, Sept & Oct Tue-Sun, June-Aug daily, Nov-Feb Thur-Sun, closed one month early each year, average €55), located down by the harbour, is one of those restaurants fans like to keep quiet about. Chef Gennaro Marciante prepares fresh, locally caught seafood with the minimum of fuss. The in-house *colatura di alici*, along with a little raw garlic, parsley and a dash of olive oil, is used to

ESCAPES & EXCURSIONS

dress steaming linguine. But you'll also find *paccheri* pasta with tuna roe and *provolone del Monaco* cheese, linguine with sea urchin and candied lemon peel, and delicious puds such as citrus tart. Book well ahead, especially if you want one of the terrace tables in summer.

Overlooking the main square, the **San Pietro** (Piazzetta San Francesco 2, 089 261091, www. sanpietroristorante.it, closed Tue & Jan, Feb, average €45) is Cetara's other temple to seafood. Excellent *primi* may include *paccherini* with fresh anchovies and wild fennel, or risotto with tuna roe and courgette flowers. You can follow this with a plate of crispy deep-fried anchovies or a locally caught tuna steak with cherry tomatoes, capers and olives. It's a little more formal than Acqua Pazza, but the food is delicious and the *piazzetta* is a lovely place to sit on a summer's evening.

Swish **Hotel Cetus** (Corso Umberto 1, 089 261388, www.hotelcetus.com, €140-€260 double) is built into the cliffside just outside Cetara; its 37 fresh, sea-facing rooms have jazzy tiled floors and terraces or balconies. There's a good restaurant and a private beach too.

For lovers of five-star luxury, stylish **Hotel Raito** (Via Nuova Raito 9, 089 763411, www. hotelraito.it, €275-€319 double) in Vietri sul Mare will do the job. Set a few kilometres outside the town centre (a shuttle service is provided), the hotel has a lovely pool overlooking the bay, a gourmet restaurant (Il Golfo), a wellness centre and a beach, accessed via a flight of steps. There's even a helipad and boat dock.

For an excellent and reasonably priced lunch or dinner, Vietri's **Evù** (Via Diego Taiani 1, 089 210237, www.ristorantevu.it, closed Sun eve in Jan, average €30) is a stylish, good-value option specialising in pasta and fish dishes, some with an innovative twist . It's small and popular with the locals – book ahead.

The pizzas at **I Due Frattelli** (Via Molina di Vietri Km.49, 089 761300, www.iduefratelli.it, pizzas from €7), in the northern part of Vietri, come in two sizes, 700g and a whopping 1kg.

For more accommodation options, **Salerno** is located at the furthest end of the Amalfi Coast but is only four kilometres from Vietri sul Mare. It also has the advantage of decent rail and ferry links.

Resources

Tourist information
Associazione Autonoma di Soggiorno e Tourismo *Corso Regina 73, Maiori (089 877452, www.aziendaturismo-maiori.it).* **Open** 9am-1pm, 2-6pm Mon-Sat; 9am-1pm Sun.
Centro Turistico ACLI *Piazza Matteotti, Vietri sul Mare (089 211285, www.ctavietri.it).* **Open** *Oct-Apr* 10am-1pm, 4-7pm Mon-Fri; 10am-1pm Sat. *May-Sept* 10am-1pm, 5-8pm Mon-Fri; 10am-1pm Sat.

Getting there

By boat
Cooperativa Sant'Andrea (089 873190, www.coopsantandrea.com) runs frequent Salerno–Amalfi–Maiori–Minori–Positano ferry services, Apr-Oct.

By bus
The regular Amalfi-Salerno SITA bus (half-hourly in rush hour, hourly thereafter) stops in all the localities mentioned above, and more besides.

By car
Take the Vietri exit from the A3 motorway; from here, the SS 163 coast road winds its way west.

By train
The station at Vietri sul Mare is served by only a very few, very slow trains. Most of the time, it's quicker to go straight to Salerno station (40mins from Naples) and continue by SITA bus.

Ravello

Ravello is the jewel in the coastal crown. The ravishing town that André Gide declared to be 'nearer to the sky than it is to the shore' sits atop a mountain buttress 350m (1,148ft) above the sea, refined and aristocratic, removed both in body and soul from the frantic hubbub below.

Like Amalfi, the town was once much larger and richer. Since the days of the Grand Tour its once elegant *palazzi*, secluded villas, dreamy gardens and magnificent views have attracted a steady stream of A-list writers, artists and musicians, all inspired by its romantic, melancholy sense of decayed nobility. Wagner, Liszt, Virginia Woolf and the Bloomsbury Group all spent time here; DH Lawrence wrote parts of *Lady Chatterley's Lover*; Graham Greene stayed in Ravello while writing *The Third Man*; Gore Vidal took up residence in his sumptuous private villa, La Rondinaia, for many years.

Even today in high season, when the coach parties hit Ravello and troop dutifully around, it's easy to find peace. Turn a corner in the old town, or visit the lovely gardens in the early evening, and you'll be alone once more. Once the crowds have gone, there's a real feeling of otherworldly serenity, best savoured with an overnight stay.

Overshadowed through most of its early history by Amalfi, Ravello still grew rich on trade. In the 13th century it counted as many as 36,000 inhabitants, but its fall from grace was dramatic. While Amalfi took to fishing, papermaking and iron foundries, in Ravello the post-boom decline – to its present population of around 2,500 – was so swift that parts of the town look frozen in the 14th century. And that's a central part of the charm.

THE IMPORTANCE OF BEING ERNESTO
Star chef nails it at Sant'Agata.

Quiet Sant'Agata sui Due Golfi may be an unassuming sort of place, but it is home to one of Italy's most celebrated restaurants, the two Michelin-starred **Don Alfonso 1890** (Corso Sant'Agata 11, 081 878 0026, www.donalfonso.com).

Founding father Alfonso Iaccarini has now passed the culinary reins to his son, Ernesto, while wife Livia and other son Mario work front of house. Like his legendary father before him, Ernesto's food is based on produce from the family's organic farm at Punta Campanella, plus other local fish and meat. The set menus come in at €145 or €170 and typical dishes include risotto flavoured with citrusy *cedro*, sea urchin, scampi and sea algae; or rolled turbot in a herby bread crust with mozzarella, garlic and shallot purée. Heavenly desserts and petits fours complete the picture.

You can sleep it off in one of the suites (€280-€500), refurbished by Sorrentine designer Marco de Luca and beautifully

appointed with antique furniture. Breakfasts are out of this world, and there's a pool, tours of the vast wine cellar, trips to the family farm and a cookery school to keep guests occupied. Don Alfonso 1890 opens seasonally (Apr-Oct).

If possible, don't drive to Ravello. The main non-residents' car park beneath Piazza del Duomo is expensive, even with a 50 per cent reduction for guests of any of the town's hotels, and other spaces are hard to come by. It's better to take the bus from Amalfi or even take one of the steep but quiet footpaths from Amalfi, Atrani or Minori.

From Atrani, the Ravello road winds up the Valle del Dragone and, doubling back on itself just before a long tunnel, enters the town at **Santa Maria a Gradillo** (normally closed, but you can try asking at the Duomo). The church is a pretty 12th-century Romanesque structure, whose bell tower is a good example of the Arab-Sicilian style, and whose charming interior has been stripped of distracting ornament. The lanes that skirt the church on the right and left both end up in Piazza del Duomo, the civic heart of Ravello, and the **Duomo**, with its imposing bronze doors, intricate high pulpit and light-flooded interior. Its crypt contains the **Museo del Duomo**, a better-than-average collection of late imperial and medieval fragments.

Ravello's other must-sees are its celebrated villas. Both are historical assemblages – the work of expat Brits who came, saw and did a bit of gardening. **Villa Rufolo**, entered via the 14th-century tower to the right of the Duomo, is named after its original 13th-century owners, the Rufolo family, who amassed a fortune acting

as bankers for, among others, Charles of Anjou; they're mentioned in Boccaccio's *Decameron*. It was bought in 1851 by Sir Francis Neville Reid, a wealthy Scot, who rescued it from its semi-derelict state. Romantically restored, its lovely gardens inspired Wagner's *Parsifal*.

In Wagner's honour, a world-class series of concerts – mostly classical and jazz – is held here in the summer, along with the occasional dance performance. Showcasing both Italian and international performers, the famous **Ravello Festival** (www.ravellofestival.com) is an eclectic season of mostly open-air events running from the end of May until early September. The gardens of Villa Rufolo are the main venue, but concerts are also held in Oscar Niemeyer's New Energy Auditorium (*see p239* **In the Know**).

Ravello's other garden estate, the enchanting **Villa Cimbrone**, is one of the highlights of the coast and well worth the ten-minute trek from the centre of town along Via San Francesco and Via Santa Chiara.

Back in Piazza del Duomo, the stepped lane by the side of the tourist office leads up to Via dell'Episcopio. Veering to the left, this becomes Via San Giovanni del Toro, site of Ravello's most upmarket hotels, and where the **Belvedere Principessa di Piemonte** provides a great view over the coast to the east. Further along on the left, opposite the fabulous **Hotel Caruso**,

ESCAPES & EXCURSIONS

the church of **San Giovanni del Toro** has preserved much of its original 12th-century appearance. Its mosaic-encrusted pulpit, built for the local Bovio family, rivals those in the Duomo, with another Jonah-swallowing whale and deep blue-green plates of Arab workmanship embedded in the centre of mosaic circles. In a niche in the sacristy is a rare 12th-century stucco statue of Santa Caterina, with traces of the original paintwork. Although a lengthy restoration has finished, the church remains closed at the time of writing; ask at the tourist office for the latest information.

If even the slow pace in Ravello is proving too fast, head up to **Scala**, a sleepy little village perched on the opposite side of the Dragone valley. Older than either Amalfi or Ravello, and once almost as prosperous, Scala is now the sort of place where the arrival of the grocery van is a major event. It has a fine **Duomo** dedicated to San Lorenzo (open 8am-noon, 5-7pm daily), with a 12th-century portal and an interior that conceals a few gems beneath its Baroque facelift. The wooden crucifix over the main altar dates from 1260; to the left is the Gothic tomb of the Coppola family. Note among the figures on the canopy above the tomb that of the rabbi who – according to an apocryphal gospel – had his hands lopped off when he gave the Virgin Mary's coffin a shove.

Scala is the starting point for various walks. The most ambitious (no.51) takes two hours to complete, heading via the peak of Il Castello to Casa Santa Maria dei Monti, with a magnificent view over the Sorrentine peninsula. An easier option is to continue past the Duomo to the hamlet of **Minuto** (whose apt name translates as 'tiny'), served by six buses a day from Amalfi and Ravello. The road ends just above the pretty 12th-century **Chiesa dell'Annunziata** (open Sunday morning for Mass; otherwise knock on the first door on your left down the steps from the road and ask the custodian for the key). Inside are ten ancient granite columns and some fine Byzantine frescoes in the crypt. In the square in front of the church is a drinking fountain and, behind this, a path descends to Amalfi via the little medieval village of Pontone; allow around 40 minutes.

Duomo di Ravello & Museo del Duomo

Piazza del Duomo (089 858311, www.chiesa ravello.com). **Open** *Church* 9am-noon, 5.30-8pm daily. *Museum* 9am-7pm daily. **Admission** €3. **No credit cards**.

Also known as the Cattedrale di San Pantaleone, the Duomo was founded in 1086; little remains of its original façade, which was reworked in the 16th century. Far more interesting are its magnificent central bronze doors, divided into 54 bas-relief panels that tell the stories of the saints and the Passion. Barisano da Trani, who designed them in 1179, was undoubtedly influenced by the Oriental Greek style.

The interior was given a Baroque reworking in 1786, but in the early 1980s the courageous decision was taken to rip it all down and restore the church to something close to its late 13th-century appearance. Halfway down the central aisle, two pulpits are set face to face. The *pergamo* ('high pulpit') was commissioned by a scion of the local Rufolo family in 1272; six lions support the spiral columns holding it up, decorated with mosaics depicting birds and beasts. The simple *ambone* ('low pulpit') opposite was donated by Costantino Rogadeo, the second bishop of Ravello, in 1130. Its mosaics of Jonah being swallowed by the whale (on the right) and regurgitated (on the left, with a little wave for his fans) are symbols of the Resurrection. To the left of the main altar is the chapel of San Pantaleone, Ravello's patron saint. It contains a phial of his blood, which is said to liquefy on 27 July each year and stay liquid until mid September.

Down in the crypt is the Museo del Duomo, whose assorted ancient remains include first-century and second-century rose marble urns, fragments of the original 12th-century floor, and a delicate marble bust of Sichelgaita della Marra (wife of Nicola Rufolo, who paid for the *pergamo* upstairs).

★ Villa Cimbrone

Via Santa Chiara 26 (089 857459, www. villacimbrone.com). **Open** 9am-30mins before sunset daily. **Admission** €7. **No credit cards**.

Though records of a villa on this site date all the way back to the 11th century, the current building is mostly the work of Lord Grimthorpe, the designer behind the mechanism that makes London's Big Ben tick in time. He bought it in 1904. In its heyday in the 1920s, the villa and its glorious garden was a favourite haunt of the Bloomsbury Group; later, Greta Garbo and conductor Leopold Stokowski used it as their love nest.

To see inside the actual villa, you'll need to check into the luxurious **Hotel Villa Cimbrone**, but the gardens can be admired by all. Roses, camellias and exotic plants line the lawns and walks, which are less formal than those of Villa Rufolo. There's a pretty faux-Moorish tearoom and – one of the high points of the visit – a scenic viewpoint, the Terrace of Infinity, lined with classical busts. The view, which stretches along the coast for miles, is considered to be the finest on the Amalfi Coast.

Villa Rufolo

Piazza del Duomo (089 857621, www.villarufolo.it). **Open** 9am-8pm daily (closes 5pm on concert days). **Admission** €5. **No credit cards**.

By the time Scotsman Sir Francis Neville Reid bought it in 1851, the Rufolo family villa and its surrounding garden were little more than tangled ruins. The house was reborn as an eclectic mix, although certain parts – notably the charming, double-tiered Moorish cloister – were not tampered with too much. But it's really the gardens that draw people here, with their geometric flowerbeds amid Romantic ruins.

ESCAPES & EXCURSIONS

When Wagner saw them in 1880, he knew he'd found the magic garden of Klingsor, the setting for the second act of *Parsifal*.

► *For more on the Ravello Festival, see p241.*

Where to shop

Limoncello opportunities abound but two good sources are **I Giardini di Ravello** (Via Civita 19, 089 872264, closed Sun), which also makes its own extra virgin olive oil, and **Ravello Gusti & Delizie** (Via Roma 28-30, 089 857716, closed Wed & Thur pm Jan-Mar), a tiny shop that also has a selection of wine and deli treats.

Ceramics are the best bet for serious shoppers, although don't expect rock-bottom prices. Giorgio Filocamo's **Museo del Corallo** (Piazza Duomo 9, 089 857461, www.museodelcorallo.com, open 10am-noon, 3-5pm Mon-Fri) not only sells jewellery fashioned from coral and shells, but also houses a wonderful family collection of coral dating from Roman times to the last century.

Where to eat & drink

★ € Babel

Via Trinità 13 (089 858 6215). **Open** *mid Mar-mid May, Oct & Nov* noon-3.30pm, 6.30-11pm Mon, Wed-Sun; *mid May-Sept* noon-3.30pm, 6.30-11pm daily. **Average** €25.

This small, laid-back contemporary wine bar, deli and exhibition space is a welcome – and affordable – addition to Ravello's all-too-touristy eating and drinking scene. The short menu of snacks and more substantial dishes changes regularly, but you'll always find a selection of bruschetta plus platters of local cheeses and meats, as well as choices such as Italian-style gazpacho (with burrata and pistachio pesto) or a warm salad of pan-fried prawns and rocket.

Cumpà Cosimo

Via Roma 46 (089 857156). **Open** noon-3.30pm, 6-11pm daily. Closed Mon in Jan. **Average** €35.

Nettie Bottone's popular trattoria is usually crowded with tourists and prices are high for such a rustic place, but the food is good and portions are generous. Fill up on the *misto di primi*, a quintet of homemade pasta dishes – it's enough for two. The meat-based *secondi* such as *salsiccia al finocchietto in mantello di provola* (fennel-flavoured sausage covered in cheese) are excellent and so they should be; the owners also run the butcher's shop next door. The homemade wine is drinkable and cheap.

Ristorante Pizzeria Vittoria

Via del Rufolo 3 (089 857947, www.ristorante pizzeriavittoria.it). **Open** 12.15-3pm, 7.30-11pm daily. *Nov-Apr* closed Tue. **Average** €30. **Pizza** from €6.

The family-run Vittoria offers excellent pizza baked in a wood oven and lots more besides: linguine with

rocket and walnut pesto, lemon risotto with shrimps and mullet roe, or entrecôte of beef with porcini mushrooms. The dining room is plain, and the lack of windows feels a little oppressive, but there's a pretty terrace out the back. Prices are reasonable.

★ Rossellinis

Palazzo Avino, Via San Giovanni del Toro 28 (089 818181, www.palazzoavino.com). **Open** 7.30-10.30pm daily. Closed Nov-Feb. **Average** €120. **Menus** €85, €95.

Now headed by Michelin-starred chef Michele Deleo, who took over from Pino Lavarra in 2013, Rossellinis continues to be one of the coast's top tables. The dining room is formal, with heavy drapes and regency chairs, but the terrace, with its spectacular views, is more relaxed. Either way the food is extraordinary. Deleo's dishes are firmly rooted in the traditions of his native Campania, but combined with the use of herbs and spices, modern technical wizardry and spectacular presentation, the results are original and memorable. An exciting amuse-bouche paves the way for a journey through the likes of steamed lobster served with aubergine 'caviar', asparagus risotto with burrata and scampi carpaccio, John Dory in an olive crust, or suckling pig prepared three ways with a *scarola pizzetta*. Desserts and petits fours are suitably theatrical, and the award-winning sommelier will help you navigate the 75-page wine list. Add exemplary service and you have perfect celebration dining.

Where to stay

Hotel Caruso

Piazza San Giovanni del Toro 2 (089 858800, www.hotelcaruso.com). **Open** Apr-Oct. **Rates** €715-€924 double.

Perched on a clifftop high above the sea, and inhabiting an 11th-century palazzo, the Caruso is one of the most talked-about hotels in Italy. Its guestbook positively bulges with celebrity signatures, from Humphrey Bogart and Truman Capote to Jackie Kennedy. Pampered guests spend cocktail hour on the terrace, taking in the panoramic views through Norman arches, or admiring the hotel's 18th-century frescoes. The glamour factor is off the scale, with a heated infinity pool, opulent suites, an impossibly chic piano bar and sublime views. The alfresco Belvedere restaurant serves top-notch food.

Hotel Rufolo

Via San Francesco 1 (089 857133, www.hotel rufolo.it). **Open** Mar-Dec. **Rates** €160-€290 double.

DH Lawrence started work on *Lady Chatterley's Lover* while staying at the Rufolo in 1926, and although it has since undergone major renovation, the latest completed in 2011, the stunning views down the coast from its garden terrace are the same. Most of the guest rooms also have sea views (the standards overlook the garden) as does the large pool; a leisurely backstroke will allow you to admire the remains of the Villa

ESCAPES & EXCURSIONS

Palazzo Avino.

Rufolo (*see p242*) next door. Centrally located with a restaurant and spa, it's also one of the few hotels in Ravello to have its own parking.

★ Hotel Villa Cimbrone
Via Santa Chiara 26 (089 857459, www.villa cimbrone.com). **Open** Apr-Oct. **Rates** €330-€660 double.

Book a room at this luxurious hotel and you get a chance to wander around one of Italy's most famous gardens in peace after the paying visitors have left. Many of the villa's rooms are museum pieces in their own right, with frescoes and antique furniture. Tiles from Vietri add local character and the library, with its huge stone fireplace, is wonderful. Until a few years ago, the villa had few modern conveniences, but now there's air-conditioning, satellite TV and internet access. Its Flauto di Pan restaurant has recently been awarded a Michelin star and is a magical lunch spot, even if you're not staying. The lack of car access still makes it difficult to reach, but there are few more romantic hideaways on the Amalfi Coast.

Palazzo Avino
Via San Giovanni del Toro 28 (089 818181, www.palazzoavino.com). **Open** Apr-Oct. **Rates** €440-€800 double.

This 12th-century, pink-hued palazzo offers lovely views from many of its 43 lavishly appointed rooms and suites, although only a handful have private terraces. There are restaurant and pool terraces, an open gym and spa, and a smart beach club down on the rocks with a shuttle bus down and back. Michelin-starred Rossellinis (*see p243*) is a romantic spot for a very special dinner.

Palumbo
Via San Giovanni del Toro 16 (089 857244, www.hotelpalumbo.it). **Rates** €295-€392 double.

Almost next door to Palazzo Avino (*see left*), the Palumbo, housed in rambling 12th-century Palazzo Gonfalone, has the atmosphere of a rather grand (if a tad faded) private house. Filled with precious antiques and pictures, it's built round a once-open, Moorish inner courtyard with ancient stone columns and a dazzling tiled floor. The guestrooms have views, private balconies and bags of character – at least those in the main house do; the four contemporary suites in the annexe less so. There's a garden and a terrace where meals are served in the summer.

★ Torre dello Ziro
Via delle Cartiere 6 (089 873503, www.torre delloziro.com). **Rates** €120-€140 double.

On the main road halfway between Ravello and the coast (about 20 minutes' walk from town or the sea), this stylish little B&B has six sunny, beautifully furnished bedrooms, valley views to a slice of sea far below and a surprisingly peaceful terrace garden for breakfast and lounging. Signora Lella is a warm and

welcoming host and a wonderful cook. Breakfast includes homemade cakes, tarts or muffins, jams and freshly squeezed orange juice. Prices are good for such a stylish venue and include parking.

Villa Amore
Via dei Fusco 5 (089 857135, www.villaamore.it). **Rates** €100-€140 double.
This characterful old villa is one of Ravello's best budget options. There are 12 clean, simple rooms; all but two have frontal sea views and all have either a balcony or terrace. There's free Wi-Fi in the communal spaces. Breakfast and lunchtime snacks are served on a terrace with head-spinning views.

Villa Maria
Via Santa Chiara 2 (089 857255, www.villa maria.it). **Rates** €170-€245 double.
This converted villa has a lovely shady garden. Most of the 23 rooms are spacious, and all are simply furnished. In summer, meals with ingredients from the villa's organic garden are served alfresco. Friendly owner Vincenzo Palumbo also runs the nearby Hotel Giordano (Via Santissima Trinità 14). Villa Maria guests can use the heated pool and free parking there.

Resources

Police
Carabinieri, Via Roma 1 (089 857150).

Post office
Via Roma 50 (089 858 6611).

Tourist information
Azienda Autonoma di Soggiorno e Turismo
Via Roma 18bis (089 857096, www.ravellotime.it). **Open** *Apr-May* 9.30am-6pm daily. *June-Oct* 9.30am-7pm daily. *Nov-Mar* 9.30am-4pm daily.

Getting around

By bus
A SITA bus runs at least hourly (less frequently on Sundays) from Piazza Flavio Gioia in Amalfi to Ravello (6am-10pm, 25mins). In Ravello, the bus sets down and turns around just before a short road tunnel; walk through this to Villa Rufolo and Piazza del Duomo. The bus then stops, and turns around, in front of the church of Santa Maria a Gradillo, and continues to Scala, on the other side of the valley, before making the return journey to Amalfi (some services stop at Scala before Ravello). Six buses a day continue beyond Scala to San Pietro and Minuto. For information on UnicoCostiera tickets, *see p226.*

Getting there

Ravello is best approached from Amalfi by bus (*see above*). If you're driving, follow the signs leading off the coast road.

In Context

History

Who hasn't ruled the roost here?

TEXT: ANNE HANLEY

Greeks, Germans, Romans, Spaniards, French, Austrians and even Poles have all influenced, for better or (more often) worse, the city of Naples. Some suggest that the succession of invading rulers has contributed to the eccentric characteristics of its citizens, from the Neapolitan's sense of an eternal underdog status to a widely held mistrust of rulers, including the state, and even the emergence of and continued support for 'their own' in the form of the omnipresent Camorra. Indeed, the rise of the Camorra originally came about to 'protect' weak peasant farmers from greedy landowners… with a few conditions to make it worth the *camorrista*'s while. Another telling influence in forming the Neapolitan character – besides an abortive revolt against taxation on food in the 17th century – was the plague in that same century, as well as numerous cholera outbreaks centuries later. Add to that the perpetual threat that Vesuvius poses, and it's little wonder that life in this city has become singularly rough and ready, decidedly helter-skelter.

Odoacer deposes Romulus Augustulus.

IT'S ALL GREEK

In the eighth century BC, a small band of adventurers from the Greek island of Euboea set up a trading station near what is now Lacco Ameno (see p180), on the island they called Pithekoussai (Ischia). Ischia's volcanoes were rumbling at the time, driving some of the less courageous newcomers across the bay to Cuma (see p116) on the mainland. There, they soon began to build trade links around the Mediterranean basin.

Infinitely more sophisticated than the tribes that had long populated the lush hinterland and sparser mountain region beyond, the Greeks made Cuma the area's most powerful city. The addition of a sibyl – a prophesying voice of the gods – in a local cave added to its clout. Confident in their control of the area, the Cuman Greeks spread down the coast, founding Parthenope (near Pizzofalcone, see p43) in c680 BC, Dikaiarchia (Pozzuoli, see p114) in c530 BC, and Neapolis ('New Town') in 470 BC; the Greeks' grid pattern of the streets can still be seen in central Naples.

Yet as the Cuman Greeks were extending their sphere of influence, so too were the Etruscans. From their power base in Tuscany, these highly advanced people spread southwards from the ninth or eighth centuries BC, establishing their southern capital at Capua in about 600 BC. Conflict was inevitable between two such dynamic groups, and battles were fought at Cuma in 524 and 474 BC, both won by the Greeks. The clashes exhausted the strength of the two rivals, leaving them prey to the encroaching Samnites.

WHEN NOT IN ROME

Shepherds and fighters, the Samnite hill people took Capua in 424 BC and Cuma in 421 BC. Into this scenario stepped another tribe with a mounting lust for land and power: the Romans. Around 340 BC, the Romans began the job of bringing the Samnites to heel. By 328 BC they had turned on Neapolis, laying siege to the city; it held out for two years before grudgingly handing itself over to the conquerors. The city was forced to supply ships and men for Roman naval battles, and its assimilation into greater Rome sent its economy into a deep depression that was to last for centuries.

Neapolis continued to grow in population and cultural importance, while still clinging to its Greek identity and language. As all things Hellenic became fashionable in republican Rome, wealthy Roman offspring were often dispatched to the southern city for their education, while their parents soaked up the balmy climate in holiday villas along the coast from Cuma to Sorrento. To make communication and transport easier, the Appian Way (Via Appia), the first major Roman highway, was begun in 312 BC.

HANNIBAL & EMPIRE

The idyll suffered the occasional brutal interruption. In the Second Punic War (218-201 BC), the Romans battled Hannibal's Carthaginian forces back and forth across the plains of the Neapolis hinterland; during the Roman Civil War (88-82 BC), Sulla occupied Neapolis and massacred a large proportion of its inhabitants during his triumphal march on Rome, where he was to rule as dictator from 82 to 79 BC; and in 73 BC, runaway slave Spartacus established the headquarters of his slave army on the slopes of Mount Vesuvius, and set out on rampages up and down the Italian peninsula.

But by the time the Roman Empire was established in 27 BC, Neapolis was once again a centre of learning, attracting writers, teachers and holidaymakers. Virgil lived here for many years, composing the *Georgics*, and died here, so some believe; the sybaritic General Lucullus built a home where Castel dell'Ovo now stands (*see p44*).

Although the city flourished under the Empire, it wasn't so in the surrounding region, where agriculture was hit hard by imports of cheaper grain and oil from Rome's new possessions in Africa and Spain. In the largely abandoned areas around the Volturno estuary to the north of the city and Paestum to the south, malaria was rife. By the time Vesuvius erupted in AD 79, burying many surrounding towns beneath a layer of lava and ash, Pompeii was already little more than a ghost town, having suffered a devastating earthquake some years before.

VANDALISED BY GOTHS

As the Empire declined, so did Naples and its environs, which from the early fifth century were prey to attacks by Goths and Vandals. The latter razed Capua in 456, and the former won and lost Naples itself several times during the fifth century, despite works to strengthen the walls in 440. It was in Naples that the Western Roman Empire truly came

to an end when the last emperor – Romulus Augustulus, imprisoned by the Goth King Odoacer – died in 476.

In Byzantium (Constantinople), the Eastern emperor Justinian was keen to assert his power over Italy. In the 530s he dispatched his prize general, Belisarius, to do the job. In 536, Naples' walls held Belisarius at bay for three weeks. Then one of the general's men spotted a water conduit leading into the city and a handful of crack fighters crawled inside. Attacked from within and without, Naples fell.

The Byzantines continued to harry the increasingly demoralised Goths until 553, when the last Goth ruler was killed. The following year, Naples became a Byzantine-controlled duchy, with dukes, magistrates and military leaders appointed by the Eastern emperor's Italian representative, the Exarch of Ravenna. By 645, this tight rein had loosened, and a Neapolitan by the name of Basilio became the city's first native duke.

With a population of 40,000, Naples was flourishing once again, its importance growing in inverse proportion to that of declining Capua. Yet marauding invaders continued to threaten the area. In 568, the Germanic *longobardi* (Lombards) swept across the Alps, taking northern Italy without much of a struggle and moving swiftly down the peninsula. Their sieges of Naples – in 581, 592 and 599 – were largely unsuccessful, though much of the Campania region, including Capua and, in 625, Salerno, fell to them. At the same time, Naples was beset from the sea by Saracens. In the ninth century came the Franks, who were sworn enemies of the Neapolitans.

INDEPENDENCE DAY

Uninterested in territorial aggrandisement, the little duchy was content to ensure its own independence by playing off its conflicting allies (Byzantium and the Pope in Rome) and foes (Lombards, Franks and Saracens) against one another, sealing secret pacts, and balancing loyalty against distance, coherent policy against tactical advantage.

While Naples played Machiavellian games to keep the wolves from the door, the city was growing in beauty and wealth. Churches were built, schools were founded, and artists and goldsmiths worked furiously to decorate the proud duchy. In the mid tenth century, with

Saracens attacking from the sea and disgruntled Byzantines besieging from the landward side, Duke John III still found time to dispatch monks to libraries around Christendom to copy manuscripts sacred and profane to enrich his splendid collection. Industry and trade flourished, with Neapolitan textiles in great demand.

Beyond Naples and the lands directly under its control, things started to look up for the Lombard-dominated territories after the Germanic overlords converted to Roman-style Christianity in the seventh century. Firmly settled in their southern dominions, the Lombards embarked on a bout of building and learning, especially in their capital at Benevento. By the eighth century, however, divisions were appearing in the united Lombard front, as Salerno grew in importance and wealth. In 849, Benevento and Salerno split, weakening the Lombard position. Capua, too, became a separate principality in the tenth century.

Not far from Salerno, Amalfi had emerged as a law unto itself, resisting Lombard encroachment, slipping out of the control of the Duchy of Naples and continuing to swear fealty to Byzantium – an invaluable trading partner for this growing sea power.

THE CRAFTY NORMAN CONQUEST

This fragmented state of affairs was soon to come to an end. In a final show of strength in 1027, the Lombard Prince Pandolf IV of Capua seized power in Naples, helped by Neapolitan barons keen to oust the reigning Duke Sergio IV. Holed up in Gaeta, Sergio turned to an unruly band of Normans who had strayed into southern Italy. He married his sister to their leader, Rainulf Drengot, then made him the Count of Aversa. The combined Neapolitan and Norman force soon drove the Lombards out of Naples.

With Aversa – a small town situated to the north of Naples – as a power base, the Normans grew in number as more compatriots arrived from France, grew wealthier through mercenary activities, and became increasingly power-hungry. In 1062, they took Capua; in 1073, Amalfi. In 1077, Lombard Salerno fell to Robert Guiscard ('the Crafty') – a member of the powerful Hauteville (Altavilla) family, who made the city his mainland capital.

The Normans besieged Naples for two years, to no avail. Robert set his sights on Byzantium, but died in his bid to oust the Eastern emperor. His brother Roger concentrated his efforts on southern Italy, most of which was firmly under Norman control by 1130, the year when his son was crowned Roger II, King of Sicily. The Norman monarch demanded that Duke Sergio VII of Naples recognise him as sovereign. Sergio obliged, then recanted, joining an anti-Norman League that scored numerous bloody victories against the French interlopers. Having identified Naples as the centre of opposition, Roger laid siege after siege to the city, but was driven back by inclement weather and disease.

Sergio, having made another of his temporary pledges to support Roger, died fighting for the Normans in October 1137. The Neapolitan people turned to the anti-Norman Pope Innocent II for help, holding out against the Norman king for a further two years. But when Innocent was taken prisoner by the Normans, Naples was left with little choice; in August 1139, a delegation vowed to support the Sicilian crown in Benevento.

Despite the lengthy struggle, the final capitulation was not an unpopular one. When Roger visited Naples in autumn 1140, 30,000 joyous people turned out to greet him. Roger was impressed by the great houses and lavish churches; outside the city walls, trade flourished in two separate ports. With its incorporation into the Kingdom of Sicily, though, Naples was overshadowed by Palermo. A model of stability and efficiency, the Norman kingdom was highly centralised, leaving little scope for independent action by its constituent parts. The Neapolitan nobility – for centuries a thorn in the side of the ruling dukes – swore fealty to the Norman crown in exchange for land and privileges.

The Norman conquest coincided with a period of high agricultural production in the Campanian countryside and explosive growth in the shipping trade; relative peace and prosperity also meant a livelier market for the city's artisans. This general wellbeing may explain Naples' loyalty to Roger's vacillating grandson Tancred, when his throne was contested by the more dynamic Heinrich Hohenstaufen of Swabia, son of Holy Roman Emperor Friedrich Barbarossa and son-in-law of Roger.

THE GERMANS ARE COMING

After Tancred's death in 1194, Heinrich became king of Sicily and punished Naples by ripping down its walls. Three years later he died, leaving a three-year-old heir. Still smarting from its punishment, Naples entered into the dynastic struggles of the German emperors, wholeheartedly backing the claims of Otto IV of Brunswick over those of the baby king Friedrich II. The city decided to recognise Otto as sovereign, sticking by him through papal excommunications and various routs on the battlefield.

It was a wonder, then, that the victorious Friedrich, when he was safely on the thrones of the Holy Roman Empire and southern Italy in 1214, decided to invest so much in Naples and treat it with such munificence. Although his brilliant and artistically astonishing court remained in Palermo, he rebuilt Naples' fortifications and made the city an intellectual centre of his Italian kingdom, establishing a new university.

Roger II, King of Sicily.

Nothing, however, could erase Naples' historic hatred of the Hohenstaufen family. In 1251, after the death of Friedrich II, the city rose up against attempts by his son Conrad to assert control. With the backing of Pope Innocent IV, it declared itself a free commune, resisting sieges until 1253, when the imperial forces broke through.

When the emperor died the following year, the commune was briefly re-established. In 1258, Conrad's illegitimate brother Manfred became king of Naples, but the Neapolitans seized the first possible opportunity to discard their Hohenstaufen sovereign. Charles of Anjou had hardly completed his invasion of Sicily in 1265 before the city rushed to pledge its loyalty to the newly arrived French dynasty.

ANJOU AND ARAGON

In order to set themselves apart from their predecessors, the Anjous moved the capital of their Italian kingdom from Palermo to Naples, though the realm continued to be called the Regno di Sicilia. New buildings went up, and merchants and craftsmen from across Mediterranean Europe flocked to the booming city. Charles I (who reigned over all southern Italy 1265-82) had the Castel Nuovo built, and a wealthy, well-planned quarter grew up around it.

In Sicily, things didn't go so smoothly for the Angevin kings. Resentful at the removal of the capital from their soil, as well as at harsh taxes imposed by the newcomers, Sicilian barons began plotting with Pedro III, king of Aragon, to overthrow Charles. The rebellion went into top gear on Easter Monday 1282, when French soldiers were killed after vespers outside a Palermo church; over the following night, in a riot that became known as the *vespri siciliani*, 2,000 French people were killed. The ensuing Vesper Wars dragged on until 1302, raging through Sicily and up and down the southern mainland, until Charles finally acknowledged that Sicily was lost and was reduced to ruling the southern Italian mainland.

Naples thrived as the Anjous sought to make the city a fitting capital for their dynasty. Under the third Angevin king, Robert (reigned 1309-43), the Castel Sant'Elmo (*see p94*) was built. However, the city's success caused lasting harm to the area around it. Naples' port expanded exponentially, sounding the death knell for former naval powers such as

IN CONTEXT

Amalfi, Gaeta and Salerno. While the primarily agricultural regions immediately surrounding the city capitalised on the food demands of the growing populace, the foothills of the Apennines became increasingly poor and depopulated, and diseases such as malaria flourished in the marshy districts around the mouth of the Volturno, and in the Sele valley south of Salerno.

Naples' relationship with its French rulers was loyal, though never unquestioningly so. When András of Hungary, husband of the beautiful and highly intelligent Queen Juana I (reigned 1343-81), was murdered in 1345, the Neapolitan people caught and wreaked vengeance on his suspected murderers. King Lajos I of Hungary suspected, however, that Juana might have had something to do with his brother's demise and invaded Naples in 1348. Juana remedied the situation by fleeing to her county of Provence, and selling her city of Avignon to the Pope in return for absolution for any misdemeanours she might have committed. In 1352, she returned to Naples to a rapturous welcome. Thirty years later, when Juana backed the anti-Pope Clement VII, her own people rose up to overthrow her in favour of her cousin Charles III of Durres (reigned 1381-86), a champion of Pope Urban VI.

THE STRUGGLE FOR POWER
When Charles's son Ladislas (reigned 1386-1414) died, the Neapolitans defended his sister, Joan II (reigned 1414-35), against her second husband Jacques de Bourbon, who tried to wrest power away from her. They also backed Joan's chosen heir, her cousin René of Anjou (Good King René of Provence) against the claims of Alfonso 'the Magnanimous' of Aragon (King Alfonso V of Sicily), whom she had previously adopted, then disinherited.

But Alfonso was more than a match for René, whom he drove out of Naples shortly after Joan's death. Southern Italy was one kingdom again, and a long period of Spanish control had begun. With his leech-like crowd of Catalan followers, Alfonso (reigned 1442-58) failed to ingratiate himself with his Neapolitan subjects, despite his lenient treatment of a city that had fought tooth and nail to prevent him taking its crown. His illegitimate son Ferdinando (also known as Don Ferrante, reigned 1458-94) won some hearts when he ejected the overbearing freebooters

and championed the arts and trades of the expanding city. However, Naples' powerful barons continued to oppose the Aragonese presence; some even persuaded France's King Charles VIII to occupy the city in 1494. But the Neapolitan people rose up against French domination, reinstating King Ferdinando's grandson, Ferdinando II (known as Ferrandino) to the throne.

On Ferrandino's premature death the following year, the people pressed for the crown to be given to his young widow Joanna, sister of Spain's King Ferdinando 'the Catholic'. The barons, on the other hand, conspired to place Ferrandino's uncle Federico (reigned 1496-1501) on the throne. This enraged France and Spain, which marched on Naples in 1501.

ENTER THE HABSBURGS
When the French arrived first, Federico hoped to salvage something for himself by agreeing to hand over Naples and part of his realm to the French King Charles VIII. But when the great Spanish General Consalvo di Cordoba appeared at the city walls in 1503, the people promptly let him in, and Spain's King Ferdinando added the Neapolitan crown to his already impressive list of titles, reigning from 1503 to 1516.

Ferdinando visited his new acquisition in 1506, conferring privileges on the nobles and the *piazza* – the people – and leaving behind him the first of a long succession of viceroys who would be feared, hated and mistrusted for the next two centuries. With the arrival of the viceroys, the locals' say in the running of their own affairs greatly diminished. The parliament served almost exclusively to rubber-stamp cynically named *donativi* – not in fact donations, but crippling taxes. Even the barons were deprived of their near-omnipotence. During his term of office, Pedro di Toledo (viceroy 1532-53) had no qualms about imprisoning or even executing nobles who had previously enjoyed impunity.

REIGN FROM SPAIN
Although violent Neapolitan protests halted attempts to introduce the Spanish Inquisition, and the city reaped some benefit from the viceroys – especially Toledo, responsible for vast redevelopment to improve living standards in the city, building the now

disreputable Quartieri Spagnoli (see p76) – Spanish rule did little to improve Naples' lot. In the early days, the city did profit from the extraordinary economic boom resulting from the Spanish conquest of the New World. Still, the inflation-fuelled slump that ensued hit hard in a city with no strong trade infrastructure. The slump was accentuated by short-term administrators with little interest in stamping out the endemic corruption in the realm's bureaucracy, and by chronic crime levels in the unpoliced countryside (which often failed to produce enough food to feed the population).

Yet it was on this depressed part of its dominions that Spain depended to finance its European wars. Taxes were levied on just about every commodity or transaction: on flour and bread, on tobacco, on rents, on hemp and on imported metals. Even ransoms paid to release Neapolitans from Turkish pirates were subject to tax. But the levy most certain to set the city aflame was the one on fruit and vegetables.

SAY YOU WANT A REVOLUTION

The tax sparked the worst uprising to hit Spanish-controlled Naples. In 1647, Neapolitans rallied behind a 27-year-old fisherman from Amalfi called Tommaso Aniello (known as Masaniello), who headed a bloody revolt until his assassination. Masaniello was pro-king but anti-levy. His task of leading the undisciplined mob was rendered all the more difficult by a vacillating viceroy, the Duke of Arcos. The Duke promised to suspend the tax but didn't, armed the people then sent his troops to gun them down, and pledged greater clout in parliament to the masses while stationing troops to cover the retreat of the barons' henchmen after they had murdered Masaniello. By April 1648, the Neapolitans had grown tired of the upheaval. Endlessly optimistic, they settled for a new viceroy – the Count of Oñate – and a promise of more reasonable taxes in future.

At the beginning of the 17th century, Naples was Europe's biggest city, with a population of over 300,000. The plague that ravaged the area for six months in 1656 left three-quarters of the population dead. But the rest of Europe, sinking deeper into dynastic struggles and other wars of succession, had little time to worry about the devastation caused by disease in this poverty-stricken outpost.

THE END OF THE LINE

When it became clear that the last of the Spanish Habsburgs, Carlos II (Carlo V of Naples, who reigned from 1665 to 1700), would die childless, various crowns needed to be reassigned. England, France and Holland agreed that Spain and the Spanish Netherlands should pass to the Austrian Habsburg Archduke Karl (younger son of the Holy Roman Emperor, Leopold I), with Naples and Sicily going to France. But Carlo rejected this arrangement: he had been persuaded by his Bourbon brother-in-law, King Louis XIV of France, that only a Bourbon would keep Spanish dominions intact.

On Carlo's death in 1700, Louis' grandson Philippe of Anjou became Felipe V of Spain, sparking a continental conflict that would last from 1701 to 1714. When France backed Felipe and invaded the Spanish Netherlands, Britain, Holland and Austria formed an anti-French alliance. But when Archduke Karl unexpectedly became Holy Roman Emperor Karl VI in 1711 after the death of his older

Tommaso Aniello.

Carlos II (Carlo V of Naples). See p255.

the British envoy of the time, Horace Mann) by shooting the eyes out of birds in the Gobelins tapestries in the Pitti Palace and whisking courtiers' wigs off with strategically placed hooks and lines. Elisabetta had sent her teenage son, with a 40,000-strong army, to occupy her family's dominions in Parma and Piacenza. He was also to take over Tuscany on the death of Gian Gastone Medici. But when the Bourbons entered hostilities with Austria, Elisabetta set her sights somewhat higher. Shortly after his 18th birthday, she ordered her son to mobilise his army and take 'the most beautiful crown in Italy'.

Don Carlos's procession south was largely good-natured and mostly unimpeded. Austria failed to reinforce its embittered, over-taxed city of Naples, and he entered the city in triumph in May 1734. In July 1735, having expelled the Austrians from the whole of southern Italy, he was crowned Carlo III of the Kingdom of Sicily. Although the Peace of Vienna (1738) obliged him to cede Parma, Piacenza and most of Tuscany to Austria, he was confirmed as king of an independent southern Italian realm. Finally, Naples was a capital again, with a king it could call its own.

THE AGE OF ENLIGHTENMENT

With the Age of Enlightenment in full swing, the king (supported, from 1737, by his wife Maria Amalia of Saxony, upon whom he doted) transformed his capital into a city worthy of the times. Although he was no opera lover, he built one of Europe's finest theatres, the San Carlo (see p42). Although he was no scholar, he established the Biblioteca Nazionale. Under Carlo's rule, the excavation of Herculaneum and Pompeii got underway. The 16th-century Palazzo Reale was extended and refurbished (see p40). To pursue his passion for hunting, Carlo had magnificent palaces built at Portici, Capodimonte and Caserta. To house the city's poor, he built the enormous Albergo dei Poveri (see p85).

The death of the Austrian emperor in 1740 plunged Europe into war again. Unwillingly, Carlo was prevailed upon to back the Franco-Spanish-Prussian alliance contesting the accession of the late emperor's daughter Maria Teresa to the Austrian throne. Once the redoubtable empress had secured her crown (and Naples had been forced to capitulate in humiliation to her British allies, who

brother, the allies baulked at fighting to extend his power and dominions still further. Sick of the succession of Spanish viceroys, and hoping for their own independent monarch in the shape of a minor Habsburg, Neapolitan nobles sought Austrian victory in the War of Spanish Succession. The Neapolitan people, as much at loggerheads with their nobles as ever, were happy to support Spain's new Bourbon king, and Felipe V was given a tumultuous welcome when he visited the city in 1702. In 1707, however, Austrian forces occupied southern Italy, and Naples once again found itself with a series of Habsburg-appointed viceroys at its helm.

Succession in Poland caused the next major European shake-up (1733-35), pitting Russia and Habsburg-controlled Austria (in favour of Augustus III) against the Franco-Spanish Bourbon alliance (which backed Stanislav I, father-in-law of France's Louis XV).

'THE MOST BEAUTIFUL CROWN IN ITALY'

When the War of Polish Succession broke out, the squat, ugly, but likeable Spanish Infante Don Carlos, younger son of Felipe V and the scheming Elisabetta Farnese, was in Florence, amusing himself (according to threatened to bombard the city from the sea in 1742), Carlo could settle back down to the business of running his kingdom.

In 1759, he abdicated and returned to Spain, to succeed his father as King Carlos III. As he did, he left his eight-year-old son Ferdinando under the tutorship of his most trusted adviser, Tuscan lawyer Bernardo Tanucci. Tanucci had been instrumental in seeking to introduce bureaucratic and fiscal reforms into the shambolic state, though the continued power of the feudal barons limited his success. Even more resounding was his failure to provide Ferdinando with a monarchical education.

When the highly educated and strong-willed Maria Carolina, daughter of the Austrian empress, arrived in Naples to marry the young king in 1768, she was shocked. He played with toys, spoke coarse local dialect, enjoyed rough games with low-class youths and hated anything bookish. Ferdinando was, however, most impressed by his clever young wife, whose orders – especially in matters of state – he accepted unquestioningly.

BRITISH NAVAL HERO STEPS IN

With the birth of her first son in 1777, Maria Carolina entered the Council of State, as was stipulated in her marriage contract. From this position of strength, she was able to engineer the downfall of her arch-enemy Tanucci.

In 1778, she adopted as her favourite John Acton, a wandering British naval hero, who may have become her lover. Born in France, Acton had made vast improvements to the Tuscan navy before being summoned to modernise Naples' neglected fleet. In Spain, King Carlos was furious that a subject of his enemy, Britain, should be gaining influence in his former realm. Indeed, Acton was apt to pass classified information from the queen's lips to the British ambassador, Sir William Hamilton, and steered Naples into an iron-clad alliance with Britain. He served Naples faithfully, however, displaying rare honesty and organisational powers in the midst of ministers who were known for their inefficiency. He may also have attenuated the worst excesses of the queen's hysteria following the outbreak of the French Revolution. For Maria Carolina the revolution was shock enough, but the execution of her sister Marie Antoinette in 1793 was too much.

Naples entered enthusiastically into the anti-French alliance. A Neapolitan army of 60,000 troops occupied French-held Rome on 27 November 1798, with the triumphant King Ferdinando at its head. But Karl Mack, the Austrian general who led the Neapolitan forces, proved to be a bungler. When France's General Championnet marched back into Rome 11 days later, the Neapolitans fled, with the French at their heels.

A RIGHT ROYAL RETREAT

In Naples, news of the defeat was greeted by the fiercely royalist masses with ferocious attacks on those Neapolitan liberals who had championed French ideals of liberty and equality. The massacre ended only as the French entered the city, and the Repubblica Partenopea was declared in January 1799.

The royal family, with Acton, fled to Sicily on board Admiral Horatio Nelson's ship the *Vanguard*. In Naples, efforts – confused and botched – by Republican leaders to introduce pro-equality reforms failed to impress the poor, who took advantage of the early

Elisabetta Farnese.

withdrawal of the French military to rise up and force liberals to take refuge in the city's forts.

Further south, the queen's envoy Cardinal Fabrizio Ruffo led his rag-tag Christian Army of the Holy Faith up the boot of Italy, in a bloody campaign to oust the French and their sympathisers. In June, the Republican leaders agreed to a capitulation, the terms of which were promptly ignored by Nelson and King Ferdinando. More than 200 executions – including the royalist-turned-rebel Admiral Francesco Caracciolo – were carried out.

Naples was a minor player on the European chessboard, and easily sacrificed by allies in general disagreement over how to cope with the vast Revolutionary and then Napoleonic armies descending on them. When France beat Austria at Marengo in 1800, becoming the dominant European power on land and debilitating Naples' chief ally, the kingdom bartered its independence for those parts of Tuscany that still belonged to the Neapolitan crown. Only Britain stood by the little kingdom; but with French troops poised in Rome, this friendship was more a red rag to a bull than any guarantee that there would be no invasion.

FRENCH EMPEROR, KING OF NAPLES

In 1805, Austria suffered another crippling defeat on the battlefield at Austerlitz, and French forces under Joseph Bonaparte occupied Austria's ally Naples on 14 January 1806. The royals fled to Sicily and Joseph was declared king of Naples, replaced on the throne by Napoleon's brother-in-law Joachim Murat in 1808, when Joseph was crowned king of Spain.

Try as they might, the Napoleonic rulers failed to win the hearts of the fiercely royalist southern Italians. The numerous reforms introduced under French rule were, on the face of it, to the advantage of the people: feudalism was abolished and land redistribution begun; absolute power was wrested from the hands of the Neapolitan aristocracy and the towns of Campania grew in status and importance. Murat gave the city its Orto Botanico (botanical garden, see p87) and made efforts to stamp out southern Italy's endemic banditry.

Though their weak-willed ex-monarch Ferdinando dithered in Palermo – under the thumb of British ambassador Lord William Bentinck, who first forced Ferdinando to promulgate a democratic constitution,

and then to send his by now fanatically scheming wife Maria Carolina into exile in Austria in 1811 – the Neapolitan masses remained doggedly hostile to the French, rising up against them on innumerable occasions. They were also singularly unimpressed by Murat's efforts to create a united Italy when Napoleon's star waned.

During ten years of French rule, Naples' rightful monarch spent much of his time hunting in the Palermo hinterland, while the British – the only power that could have reinstated him in his capital – used Sicily as their Mediterranean power base.

KINGDOM OF THE TWO SICILIES

At the Council of Vienna in 1816, Europe's victorious conservative monarchies confirmed Ferdinando as Naples' ruler; he took the new title of King Ferdinando I of the Kingdom of the Two Sicilies. The old king received a rapturous welcome when he returned to Naples. But he and his successors misjudged the changing times, and the enthusiasm soon paled.

Ferdinando responded to the demands of the shadowy Carbonari liberal reform movement (a secret society seeking a unified Italy) by promulgating a parliamentary constitution in 1820. However, he then stood contentedly by as his reactionary ally Austria sent troops into his kingdom to quash these dangerous signs of anti-absolutism. Ferdinando died in 1825; his successor, Francesco I, had shown early signs of liberal leanings, but these soon disappeared when he took the throne.

Ferdinando II, who became king in 1830, managed to bring Naples' huge public debt under control. He also helped the poor at the behest of his first wife, the saintly Maria Cristina of Savoy, and initiated a series of important public works, including the completion of the Portici railway, Italy's first, which opened in 1839. But the king was as committed to absolutism as his predecessors had been. Liberal movements were watched by an efficient spy network, and all revolts were ruthlessly put down, sometimes before they even began.

GARIBALDI TAKES THE BISCUIT

In 1847-48, when the city of Naples joined the more openly rebellious Sicily in demanding a constitution, Ferdinando granted it, but then

THE ULTIMATE GRAND TOUR?

Naples is no newcomer to the tourist trail.

During the 17th, 18th and early 19th centuries, no young gentleman's education was complete without a 'grand tour' – a lengthy jaunt through the cultural capitals of contemporary and classical Europe, including, of course, Naples. Not only was Naples a magnetic stopover for resting (and playing) on the tourist's adventurous slide down the Italian peninsula, it was also one of the greatest epicentres of ancient culture.

The rich, newly discovered archaeological heritage of Pompeii and Herculaneum combined powerfully with the awe-inspiring beauty of the bay and the smouldering backdrop of Vesuvius – the killer volcano that had, at the same time, ensured that so much of ancient culture would be preserved for future generations.

Some attribute the famous phrase 'See Naples and die' to the brilliant German grand tourist Goethe. Could he have been referring to the city's perpetual sense of danger under the glowering Vesuvius? Or, more likely, to the

sense of ultimate beauty the place evoked, whereby a kind of mystic sublimation of life itself seems to occur? Goethe had this to say about his reaction to the place: 'I can't begin to tell you of the glory of a night by full moon when we strolled through the streets and squares to the endless promenade of the Chiaia, and then walked up and down the seashore. I was quite overwhelmed by the feeling of infinite space. To be able to dream like this is certainly worth the trouble it took getting here.'

The light-suffused gouache paintings from the era reveal how grand tourists perceived the city. They were merely the postcards of the age, brought home by the dozen by every visitor, but now the originals grow more precious every year. Reproductions decorate sweet boxes and hotel walls everywhere you look: day scenes with peasant folk doing an impromptu tarantella, say, or night scenes with fishing boats bobbing on a ruddy sea, reflecting erupting Vesuvius's flaming display.

IN CONTEXT

played moderate and extreme liberal camps off against each other until he could justify dissolving the bickering parliament in 1849.

Ferdinando II's son Francesco II (reigned 1859-60) came to the throne in mid-Risorgimento, as Piedmontese troops fought to oust the Austrians from northern Italy. Each victory for these Italian unification forces was greeted with joy in Naples, but the new king still couldn't see that his harsh repression of liberalism could not continue. It was becoming clearer – even to those who had backed the Bourbons so enthusiastically – that Italian unification could only bring change for the better. With unification troops having taken Sicily and much of the southern mainland, Francesco agreed to the introduction of a constitution in June 1860. It was too little, too late. The city's residents turned out en masse to welcome unification general Giuseppe

Garibaldi, with an enthusiasm boosted by the fact that he had established his credentials as a royalist, rather than a republican. When Garibaldi entered Naples on 7 September 1860, banners hanging from every window showed the cross of the Piedmontese royal family, the Savoys. On 21 October the city voted overwhelmingly in favour of joining a united Italy ruled by Vittorio Emanuele II of Savoy.

It was to be ten years before the Unification of Italy was complete – with the capture of Rome. For Naples, integration into the national fabric meant that any faint glory that still clung to the once-flourishing capital evaporated. It was Rome that the Unification leaders aspired to, and Rome was now to be designated capital of the newly united realm. Despite some housing reforms instituted after a devastating cholera epidemic in 1884, Naples languished in growing neglect and poverty.

The aerial bombardment of Naples during World War II.

DON'T MENTION THE WAR

Naples' strategic importance – as a port, and as the gateway from southern to northern Europe – was only fully recognised once again during World War II; this time it was to the city's detriment. Aerial bombardments tore through its historic centre and waterfront, while its incomparably rich state archive was destroyed by the city's German occupiers.

The Germans were ejected in an uprising known as Le Quattro giornate di Napoli (the four days of Naples). Between 27 and 30 September 1943, residents of Naples paved the way for the arrival of the Anglo-American forces. When the Allies finally entered the city's blackened shell, they found Neapolitans eking out the most pitiful of livings. The injection of Allied food and funds – coupled with Allied reliance on underworld figures to get things done – served more to fuel

the black market and crime than to put the city back on its feet.

Reconstruction was carried out in an unregulated, lawless fashion; in the early 1970s, an official enquiry found that almost none of the post-war buildings in the Naples area – a large majority of them horrendous eyesores – had acquired planning permission. Beset by local government corruption, high crime and unemployment rates, and decaying urban infrastructure, Naples had entered one of its darkest ages.

RETURN OF THE KING?

Although the monarchy was abolished in 1946, Vittorio Emanuele (son of the last King Umberto II, who claims to be the Prince of Naples and head of the House of Savoy) returned to Italy in 2002, having spent most of his life in exile. He soon became embroiled in charges of criminal association, corruption and exploitation of prostitution. In 2007, he requested 260 million euros in compensation from the State in return for the family's years of exile, and the restitution of the family's confiscated properties. He was acquitted of all charges in 2010, but no compensation was paid.

No one in Naples (or anywhere in Italy for that matter) took his claim seriously, and compared to the economic and social problems that the city was living with at the time, it was laughable. The notorious rubbish crisis came to a head in 2007: by the end of that year, Naples was drowning under more than 100,000 tons of putrifying refuse after landfills, already at bursting point, were closed down. Coupled with its reputation for lawlessness, the city was creating more reasons for tourists to stay away.

But there was hope: in June 2011, youthful ex-prosecutor Luigi de Magistris was voted mayor, running for office on a law and order platform along with proposals for relaunching Naples as a major European capital. While his popularity has taken a nosedive since his election, de Magistris is credited with having finally solved the rubbish problem and introducing the controversial ZTL (Zona di Traffico Limitato) to the Centro Storico to curb carbon emissions. He also pedestrianised much of the Lungomare for the 2012 America's Cup. Four new metro stazioni dell'arte have opened and the Duomo stop is due to completed in late 2016. On the face of it, at least, Naples is finally cleaning up its act.

IN CONTEXT

Painting in Naples

Strokes of genius.

TEXT: VICTORIA PRIMHAK

If Naples' dramatic setting is a gift for landscape artists, the fluctuations in the city's fortunes have also left their mark on Neapolitan painting. Over the centuries, great artworks were commissioned and then lost – Giotto's frescoes in the Castel Nuovo, say – as tastes and rulers changed. For centuries, the Church and ecclesiastical orders were the foremost patrons of art. Across the ages, though, the paintings in the city's churches have been neglected, stolen or damaged. In some cases, only what was hidden for centuries, underground or beneath layers of paint, survived; only in recent decades have serious restoration efforts begun. The city's rulers also left their mark on Naples' artistic output. In the 17th century, the Spanish viceroys developed an insatiable appetite for local works; sadly, many of these left Naples with their owners. During his four-year term, Count Olivares amassed enough art to fill 40 ships; today, much of his collection graces the Museo del Prado in Madrid. Naples' great families also put together private collections, many of which were broken up as noble fortunes declined in the 19th century. In a few cases, they were left to the state and can now be found in the Museo di Capodimonte and the Certosa-Museo di San Martino, or religious institutions such as the Pinacoteca Girolamini and Pio Monte della Misericordia.

Museo di Capodimonte.

CLASSICAL ART

Naples and the Campania region are home to some of the world's greatest examples of classical art. Much of it – including mosaics from Pompeii and marble and bronze statues from Herculaneum – can be seen in the Museo Archeologico Nazionale (*see p82*). But there's plenty still in situ (or nearby). The frescoed slabs from the Tomba del Tuffatore (480 BC), now in the museum in Paestum, are the only surviving examples of classical Greek painting in Magna Grecia. The detail of two male lovers intent on their conversation in the banquet scene, and the image of the diver – perhaps symbolic of the sudden passage from life to death – have come to symbolise Greek culture in Italy.

The heights of Roman figurative art can be seen in the wall paintings in Pompeii (at Villa dei Misteri and Casa dei Vettii, *see p200*), with their warm, intense tones dominated by the russet-brown colour known as Pompeian red.

It is difficult, however, to spot a truly local tradition in these classical examples. Only with the coming of Christianity did Campanian art really take off, reflected in the frescoes and mosaics decorating the catacombs of the city. The paintings in San Gennaro (*see p90*) date from the second century AD, when Christianity was a clandestine cult.

The lack of a gold background, use of classical elements and figures collocated in space differentiate the local early Christian art from the Byzantine tradition, although the influences gradually mingled.

The domination of Naples by foreign powers was inevitably reflected in art. The arrival of the Angevins in the 13th century led to an initial decline in local art, as painters and architects were imported first from France and then from other parts of Italy. **Pietro Cavallini** was brought from Rome; his refined use of colour and calm naturalism can be seen in the frescoes (1309) that decorate the Brancaccio chapel in San Domenico Maggiore (*see p59*) and the church of Santa Maria Donnaregina (*see p73*).

Giotto arrived from Florence and worked as court painter from 1328 to 1334, tasked with decorating Castel Capuano (*see p65*), Castel Nuovo (*see p40*) and Santa Chiara (*see p59*). Though only traces of his own work remain, he influenced many local painters. His Neapolitan pupil **Roberto di Oderisio** (active 1340-70) continued Giotto's experimentation with space and perspective in the fresco cycle of Old Testament stories in Santa Maria Incoronata (*see p36*). In the same church, Oderisio offers an arresting glimpse of Angevin court life in *The Sacraments* and

José de Ribera's *Drunken Silenus*.

The Triumph of the Church (1352-54). But power struggles in the late 14th century halted the innovations in Neapolitan art. Few examples remain from the period, in which the late Gothic style prevailed; the most notable are frescoes in San Giovanni a Carbonara (*see p87*) by **Leonardo da Besozzo** and **Perinetto da Benevento**.

The Renaissance touched Naples around 1450 with the advent of Alfonso of Aragon, who brought Aragonese and Catalan culture to the city. **Niccolò Antonio Colantonio** (active in Naples 1440-70), the most important Neapolitan painter of the 15th century, was to fuse the Flemish and Burgundian traditions left over from the last of the Anjous with the new Renaissance spirit. His extraordinary capacity for reproducing Flemish painting can be seen in *St Jerome in his Study* (1445) in the Museo di Capodimonte (*see p90*); the tiny books on the shelves and the objects on the saint's desk need a magnifying glass to be appreciated properly.

In the early 16th century, Naples' Spanish viceroys were little more than transient bureaucrats, uninterested in commissioning art. The task of patronising the arts fell to the new monastic orders that arrived in the city from the 1530s. In the monasteries, emotional and tortured Mannerism

dominated. The Mannerist style of the Sienese **Marco Pino** (c1525-c1587) can be seen in the brilliance of the twisted figure of Christ in San Domenico (1564, *see p59*); his later paintings for Santi Severino and Sossio (1571-77, *see p48*) were tempered by his knowledge of Spanish figurative painting.

A GOLDEN AGE

Counter-Reformation fervour and immense sums of money spent building and decorating churches and monasteries provided a fertile climate for the golden century of Neapolitan art. Religious commissions were a counterpoint to a troubled period scourged by earthquake, volcanic eruption, epidemics, famine and riot, and the repressive regime of the Spanish viceroys.

Few of the founders of the so-called Neapolitan School were actually Neapolitan. **Michelangelo Merisi da Caravaggio** (*see p91* **Caravaggio on Canvas**), the most influential, fled to Naples in 1606. His theatrical intensity, stark naturalism and vivid contrasts struck a real chord with the local passionate temperament. His super-realistic *Flagellation* (in Museo di Capodimonte) and *Seven Acts of Mercy* for the Pio Monte della Misericordia revolutionised the tired Mannerist tradition. He paved the way for the creation of a

Neapolitan school of Caravaggisti. His follower **José de Ribera** (c1588-1652) was born near Valencia, but spent his working life in Naples. His sensational style and bold originality quickly caught on among the Spanish viceroys and religious orders, and his sadistic martyrdoms became the last word in religious taste. Ribera's taste for vivid narrative was sometimes grotesque, as in *Drunken Silenus* (Capodimonte), but he gradually developed an extreme pictorial elegance with refined colours, which can be seen in the *Pietà* (1637) in the Certosa-Museo di San Martino. In contrast, from the 1630s there was a move towards a neo-Venetian painterliness and Bolognese classicism, evident in the intimate works of **Massimo Stanzione** (c1585-1656), who was to decorate the most important Neapolitan churches, including the Certosa-Museo di San Martino, Gesù Nuovo (see p58) and San Paolo Maggiore (see p69).

Mattia Preti (1613-99) brought new life to the city in his four-year stay, by his use of light as the basis of composition. His extraordinary use of colour, light and shadow is best seen in the *Stories of the Lives of San Pietro Celestino and Santa Caterina di Alessandria*, painted for the nave of San Pietro a Maiella (see p69). Local boy **Luca Giordano** (1634-1705), moving from airy, Baroque visions to iridescent rococo, dominated the scene for nearly 50 years. Known as *Luca fa presto*

('Luca does it quickly'), he was a prolific painter. He banged out thousands of paintings and, well into his 70s, completed the frescoes in the Certosa-Museo di San Martino in just a few days. **Francesco Solimena** (1657-1747) merged naturalism and the influence of Preti and Giovanni Lanfranco (1582-1647).

The **Certosa-Museo di San Martino** (see p98) is a splendid compendium of Neapolitan Baroque. Artists vied for commissions from the fabulously rich but famously stingy Carthusian monks. With works by Caracciolo, Stanzione, Ribera, Lanfranco and Giordano, the chapel is a unique gallery of 17th-century Neapolitan painting.

Artemisia Gentileschi (1593-c1652), who lived in Naples from 1630 until her death, experimented with dramatic chiaroscuro effects. Her *Judith Beheading Holofernes* (Museo di Capodimonte) had a great impact on Neapolitan painting. (The victim of a well-publicised rape, Artemisia often dwelt on the theme of female vengeance.)

The flourishing, passionate atmosphere of the city affected its artists, most notably the larger-than-life **Salvator Rosa** (1615-73), an artist, poet, actor and musician who painted romantic battle scenes, *banditi* and the poetic landscapes that were particularly popular in 18th-century England, creating a mythic view of the south of Italy, eagerly investigated by Gothic novelists and travellers on the grand tour.

IN CONTEXT

Museo di Capodimonte.

Artemisia Gentileschi's *Judith Beheading Holofernes*.

CAMPANIA ON CANVAS

Landscape painting reached the height of its popularity in the 18th century, when the taste for the picturesque, the classical and the sublime made the spectacular scenery around Naples, the bay islands and the classical sites a must for the grand tourist (*see p259* **The Ultimate Grand Tour?**). The most popular image was the panoramic or bird's-eye view of Naples from the sea. Vibrant, lustrous portraits of the city painted in 1700 by **Gaspar Van Wittel** (c1652-1736) – a few of which remain in the Certosa-Museo di San Martino – revolutionised landscape painting, with their synthesis of naturalism and the Dutch School. The warm Neapolitan light and local colour inspired him to combine reality and humanity in scenes such as *Largo di Palazzo* and *Galleys in the Port*.

With the growth of Romanticism, foreign painters were drawn to lyrical, emotional Naples. Vesuvius fast became a favourite theme, embodying the heroic and diabolic in a blend of the picturesque and the sublime. Frenchman **Pierre-Jacques Volaire** (1729-1802) captured this spirit in his dramatic *Eruption of Vesuvius with the Bridge of the Maddalena*, now in Capodimonte. **Joseph Wright of Derby** (1734-97), known for his vivid experiments with light and shadow, also painted Vesuvius erupting.

Not all collectors wished to experience such strong emotions. A market grew for standardised, sentimental images of Naples in gouache. In the 19th century, artists expressed their individual, contemplative interpretations of the Bay of Naples. Dutchman **Antonio Pitloo** (1791-1837) infused his real-life landscapes (some now in the Certosa-Museo di San Martino) with natural colour and life, inspiring the Posillipo school. **Giacinto Gigante** (1806-76), many of whose works are in Capodimonte, was the leader of this school, where impressions of an idyllic landscape are depicted in delicate, romantic fashion. **Filippo Palizzi** (1818-99) continued to experiment, contrasting natural colours, light and contours (in the Certosa-Museo di San Martino).

Perhaps most interesting of all was the Welsh painter **Thomas Jones** (1742-1803). Having been a mediocre painter of British landscapes, Jones came to Naples in 1776 and stayed until 1783, during which time he painted a series of tiny pictures recording small, intimate details of the city. *A Wall in Naples* is nothing but that, with a hint of sky in the background and some forgotten washing on a small line hanging from a tiny window. It's a scene that could have been painted yesterday. Almost anticipating later painters such as Edward Hopper in his evocation of daily life in almost deserted cityscapes, Jones is now considered to be one of the first modern painters; some of his paintings can be found in London's National Gallery.

IN CONTEXT

Thomas Jones's *A Wall in Naples*.

Architecture

In Naples, every storey tells a story.

TEXT: VICTORIA PRIMHAK

The brooding silhouette of Vesuvius looms large over Naples and is visible for miles around. Look closer and you'll find its presence surrounds you in the very stone of the buildings: yellowish *tufo*, a soft eruptive stone, bombarded by volcanic gases, is the fabric of the city; grey-black *piperno* is fast-cooled lava, used in ornamental detail; and darker *pietra lavica* is slow-cooled lava, slabs of which make up the roads. Besides the mighty volcano, countless settlers have left their mark over the centuries, from the ancient Greeks to the Spanish; World War II bombs, unscrupulous developers and earthquakes did their best to blow it all away in the 19th and 20th centuries. Even before the modern age, Naples had major problems. By the 1500s, lack of space was one. Moving the city walls outwards failed to solve the problem, so Neapolitans built upwards instead. The poor lived in tiny, street-level *bassi*, and the upper classes occupied the light, airy, first- and second-floor *piano nobile*. In this city of layers, every building tells the story of its people.

TRACES OF GREECE AND ROME

The temples in Paestum and the sanctuary of the Sybil in **Cuma** (see p116) testify to the existence of thriving Greek communities in Campania. Nothing more remains of the original settlement of Paleopolis, but the chequerboard plan of Neapolis (founded by the Greeks around the seventh century BC) can still be clearly seen from the belvedere of **San Martino** (see p94). The Roman *decumani* (main roads) – now Via Anticaglia, Via dei Tribunali and Spaccanapoli (see p58) – intersected from north to south by *cardines* (smaller roads), followed the original Greek layout. The Greek *agora* (marketplace, later the Roman forum) stood near today's Piazza San Gaetano; sections of the Greek walls can be seen just below street level in **Piazza Bellini** (see p67).

Centuries of construction have overlaid the remains of the Roman city, but they're still there: there's a fascinating glimpse of market life beneath **San Lorenzo Maggiore** (see p69) and the **Duomo** (see p67), and an area of Roman baths has been incorporated into the museum behind **Santa Chiara** (see p59). Other relics found their way into later buildings: two columns and marble bases from a temple to Castor and Pollux can be seen in the 16th-century façade of **San Paolo Maggiore** (see p69).

The kind of prosperous town planning that passing centuries obscured in the city is very much in evidence at **Pompeii** (see p198) and **Herculaneum** (see p194). But the Campania Felix of the Romans is dotted with other, smaller reminders of the extent to which this region, with its mild climate and spectacular landscape, was prized in ancient times. There are sumptuous homes in **Castellammare di Stabia** (see p202), **Capri** (see p156) and near **Sorrento** (see p207), as well as temples at **Baia** (see p115) and vast amphitheatres in Pozzuoli and Capua Vetere.

CHRISTIAN BUILDERS

When Emperor Constantine embraced the cult of Christianity in AD 313, its followers came out of hiding and built places of worship near the burial sites of their early saints. Taking the Roman basilica (a meeting place with columned porticos outside) as their model, the Christians turned them sideways and inside out, putting the entrance at one end and the columns in the interior to form side aisles. Paleo-Christian basilicas can still be seen above the catacombs of **San Gennaro** (see p90) and in the fourth-century **Santa Restituta**, incorporated into the Duomo (see p67) in the 13th century.

During the early Middle Ages the real stratification of the city began, with new constructions going up above the Greek and Roman ones around the *agora* and forum in Piazza San Gaetano. These in turn made way for later buildings; nothing remains of the civic architecture of the period. Further south, the early Middle Ages are better represented: the religious architecture along the Amalfi coast, in **Ravello** (see p240) and **Salerno**, is a harmonious mix of Byzantine and Romanesque styles.

EARLY RENAISSANCE

In the 11th century, the Normans made Palermo the capital of their southern Italian kingdom, and Naples became a quiet political backwater. But the city expanded west towards **Castel dell'Ovo** (see p44) when Roger II made the castle his Neapolitan citadel, as well as inland when Roger's son William built **Castel Capuano** (see p65) to house his humanist court, peopled by artists and architects.

The new king chose **Castel Nuovo** (see p40) as his home, sending for the Mallorcan Guillermo Sagrera in 1449 to oversee alterations. Sagrera produced a trapezoid plan with five huge towers, inspired by similar buildings in Provence and Catalonia, and designed the Sala dei Baroni, with its magnificent, lofty vaulted ceiling. But the crowning glory of the early Renaissance in Naples was the **Arco di Trionfo**, a double arch flanked by Corinthian columns, celebrating the virtues and power of the Aragon dynasty, between the two high towers of the entrance to the Castel Nuovo. Its style is clearly Tuscan, showing just how quickly Sagrera's Catalan-Majorcan manner became interwoven with Italian influences.

The same Tuscan flavour was popular with Neapolitan nobles: **Palazzo Maddaloni** (Via Maddaloni 6), for example, has a Renaissance portal and a smooth, rusticated, yellow and grey *tufa* façade (contrasting with late Gothic elements such as the low arches in the courtyard, the vestibule and arch behind);

the diamond-pointed rustication of the façade of the church of **Gesù Nuovo** (see p58) was originally the fortified front of a palace. The Tuscan influence reached its apex in the **Palazzo Gravina** and the Brunelleschi-style chapels in **Sant'Anna dei Lombardi** (see p77) next door.

SPANISH STYLE

The arrival of troops from the recently united Kingdom of Spain in 1503 changed the face of the city. The fortifications of Castel Nuovo were beefed up, a task that took 30 years, and a new city wall with polygonal bastions was built from Via Foria to Castel Sant'Elmo, and east along the seafront to protect Naples from attack from the sea.

In 1540, the most avid builder of all the Spanish viceroys, Pedro de Toledo, ordered an opulent new palace, more or less where today's Palazzo Reale stands. To cope with a chronic lack of housing (the population had almost doubled to 220,000 inhabitants in 50 years), he extended the walls to increase the city area by a third. Illegal shantytowns were razed to make way for new quarters, and an impressive thoroughfare, **Via Toledo** (see p76), was created to link the old and new parts of town. On the hillside to the west of Via Toledo, the **Quartieri Spagnoli** (see p76) was built to house Spanish troops; as demand

for housing grew, the single-storey dwellings rose to four or five floors.

THE BAROQUE

The extravagant flourishes of the Baroque appealed to the Neapolitan imagination, and few employed them more extensively than Cosimo Fanzago (1591-1678), the city's most prolific church architect, who spent 33 years revamping the **Certosa-Museo di San Martino** (see p94). The **Guglia di San Gennaro** (see p65) epitomises his decorative exuberance; the gruesome bronze skulls on the façade of the church of **Santa Maria delle Anime del Purgatorio ad Arco** (see p70) show him in glummer Counter-Reformation mood.

The advent of the Bourbon dynasty in 1734 produced a rash of imposing civic buildings, which gave Naples a veneer of modernity without imposing any true order on its architectural chaos. Among the crop of ambitious architects was Ferdinando Fuga; only one-fifth of his design for the **Albergo dei Poveri** poorhouse (see p85) was ever completed, but even so it was Europe's largest civic construction. The restored central section provides a tantalising glimpse of his dream. Meanwhile, Giovanni Antonio Medrano designed the **San Carlo** opera house (see p149), which made Naples one of Europe's musical capitals, and the **Palazzo Reale** at

IN CONTEXT

Palazzo Maddaloni.

Capodimonte (*see p90*). Luigi Vanvitelli gave the city the imposing Foro Carolino, today **Piazza Dante** (*see p82*), though his crowning glory – and perhaps the finest product of the Neapolitan Baroque – was the Reggia at **Caserta** and its glorious gardens.

Indeed, it was the Bourbon love of the countryside (and hunting) that gave the architects of the day their grandest canvas. Medrano began work on the Reggia at **Portici** (*see p193*), later to be replaced by Fuga and Vanvitelli; the royal palace sparked a building boom along the coast south of Naples, on the so-called **Miglio d'Oro** (*see p193*). The nobles' villas were built with two aspects – one up to the live volcano, the other down to the sea.

Two other 18th-century notables were Ferdinando Sanfelice and Domenico Antonio Vaccaro, who designed many of the city's private and religious buildings. Sanfelice's work was an organic but lively blend of decorative stucco and stonework that was imitated across the city. His 'flying staircases' in **Palazzo Sanfelice** (*see p85*) and **Palazzo dello Spagnolo** (*see p85*) are spectacular. Vaccaro's touch is best seen in the cloister of **Santa Chiara** (*see p59*), a splendid tiled affair in shades of blue and yellow.

SPECULATION AND 'RENEWAL'

In the early 19th century, the city's French rulers introduced neoclassical touches in **Piazza del Plebiscito** (*see p36*). This style was continued by Ferdinando I, on his restoration, in the church of San Francesco di Paola (*see p41*), which was designed by Pietro Bianchi. Nobles fled the crowded centre, building seafront palaces along the **Riviera di Chiaia** (*see p102*); up on the hill of Vomera, the simple, two-storey **Villa Floridiana** (*see p95*), with its English-style garden, was built for Lucia Migliaccio, the morganatic wife of King Ferdinando.

Urban renewal projects – designed to impose some order on Naples' haphazard development – degenerated into wholesale destruction of poorer but nonetheless historic areas of the old city centre. Set up with the best of intentions in 1839, the Consiglio Edilizio (building council) soon became a vehicle for rampant speculation. Clearance of the city's ancient slums started in Via Duomo, radiating out to the bay, and an entire nave of the basilica of **San Giorgio Maggiore**

(*see p59*) was destroyed. Plans to hack a new road through the 15th-century **Palazzo Cuomo** sparked uproar; the philanthropist Prince Gaetano Filangieri financed the rebuilding of the façade 20 metres (66 feet) further back, at the same time designing the interior to accommodate his extensive art collection.

The eclectic, revivalist style of Anglo-Italian architect Lamont Young dictated the fashion in the late 19th century. His creations range from the neo-Gothic **Palazzina Grifeo** (Parco Grifeo 37) to the pseudo-Tudor **Castello Aselmeyer** (Corso Vittorio Emanuele 166). Young's sense of the weird and wonderful caught on. Neo-medieval and Chinese-style villas can still be seen along Via Posillipo, whereas art nouveau decoration flourished in buildings for the new, rich professional classes around **Vomero** (*see p92*) and Via dei Mille.

A cholera epidemic in 1884 gave unscrupulous speculators further scope. The Società per il Risanamento, owned by northern bankers, built straight, 'clean' streets by ruthlessly razing not only insalubrious slums, but 57 historic *fondaci* (merchants' yards, shops and lodgings) and medieval and Renaissance buildings. Before their destruction, the slums were recorded for posterity by painter Vincenzo Migliaro, whose works can be seen in the Certosa-Museo di San Martino (*see p94*).

Between the two world wars, the country's Fascist regime made its mark on Naples. The **Palazzo delle Poste e Telegrafi** (*see p76*), with its sleek black-and-white marble façade and rectangular steel windows, and other monumental public buildings in Piazza Matteoti, are prime examples of totalitarian art deco. The white Stazione Marittima was a paean to classicism, and the **Mostra d'Oltremare** (*see p122*), blending gardens, water features and exhibition spaces, extolled the regime's colonial pretensions. Rationalist architect Adalberto Libera built the groundbreaking **Villa Malaparte** (*see p158*) in 1939 on Capri, a brick-red house perched on a rocky promontory: a dramatic flight of steps led to a flat roof terrace, where its owner used to cycle.

BOMBS, BUILDINGS AND… BOATS?

Allied bombs did immense damage to Naples' Centro Storico during World War II

IN CONTEXT

– as did the retreating German forces. Ironically, painstaking restoration work returned to the city such gems as the church of Santa Chiara, which was rebuilt to its original specifications and without its later Baroque trappings.

Elsewhere in the city, however, bomb sites gave way to a concrete jungle. Naples' sole skyscraper, the inappropriately named Jolly Hotel, which stands just off Piazza del Municipio, was permitted by Mayor Achille Lauro in the 1950s, as was the rebuilding of the railway station at Piazza Garibaldi. The havoc wreaked by construction magnate Mario Otieri inspired film director Francesco Rosi's searing indictment, *Le Mani sulla città* (Hands Over the City; *see p133*) of 1963. Not all postwar architecture was without charm, though. After the devastation of Santa Lucia, Giò Ponti, a pioneer of modernism, was hired to create the **Royal Continental** hotel (*see p278*) in 1954 and, in 1962, the **Parco dei Principi** in Sorrento (*see p212*), now one of the world's hippest hotels. In **Vietri sul Mare** (*see p238*), the Ceramica Artistica Solimene, a ceramics factory designed by Paolo Soleri, a student of Frank Lloyd Wright, is an undulating wall of green and orange ceramic-covered columns.

Unregulated and unchecked, the concrete sprawl spread beyond the city limits, making the fortunes of ruthless property developers. In Portici, 18th-century villas were engulfed by modern apartment blocks, which were built in the shadow of the decidedly non-dormant Vesuvius. Huge council estates, built in the 1970s outside Naples to house the city centre's poor, became crime-ridden ghettos. Meanwhile, the coastline and islands were riddled by unlicensed villa development for holiday homes.

Gradually the tide turned, as local authorities started greening what was left or promoting ambitious renewal projects. Concrete carbuncles, such as some of Scampia's notorious tower blocks – named Le Vele ('the sails') after the shape of the buildings – have been knocked down, as has the incomplete Hotel Fuente on the cliffs of the Amalfi Coast.

Sadly, Naples was wounded further by the 1980 earthquake – some historic buildings are still shored up with iron chains – and yet again the council turned a blind eye to building work in the rush to rehouse people, much of which remains in legal no-man's land.

HOPE FOR THE FUTURE

The 1980s brought an ambitious project to extend the city eastwards. However, the **Centro Direzionale** (*see p122*), designed by Japanese architect Kenzo Tange (who was also behind the **Romeo Hotel**; *see p277*), was unappealingly isolated on marshy land near the city's prison and a derelict industrial area. Now home to offices, law courts and residential property, it was the intended site of the *municipio* and NATO's new Allied Forces Southern Europe HQ – but both ideas were summarily shelved, and many of the buildings remain underoccupied. By day it's still shiny and upbeat; after dusk it becomes dangerous.

Sustainable town planning is the buzzword for 21st-century Naples. In 2005, two museum developments brought a buzz to the city's art scene: contemporary art museum **MADRe** (*see p87*) was created within the Donnaregina monastic complex, with Portuguese architect Alvaro Siza at the helm; and **PAN** (*see p102*) opened up in the 17th-century Palazzo Carafa di Roccella. In 2008, the **Museo Hermann Nitsch** (*see p77*), another space dedicated to the contemporary arts, was opened up in an ex-power station in the Sanità.

Although plans to convert abandoned industrial buildings and warehouses on the seafront seem to have been shelved for the moment, the central station has been given a serious makeover. The city centre section of the extension of the underground railway system is within sight of being finished, too, though the completion of the Municipio stop has been partly impeded by the exciting – if problematic – discovery of Roman shipyards.

A drive to rescue decrepit buildings and once-stately *piazze* has also changed the face of this long-suffering city, whose Centro Storico holds UNESCO heritage status for the unique beauty of its architecture. The roadworks that have blighted the areas immediately surrounding Piazza del Municipio and Piazza Garibaldi are near completion, and **Monumentando** (www.monumentando napoli.com), an innovative new project aimed at finding private funding to restore 27 of the city's monuments through commercial advertising, got underway in 2014 and has already completed four restorations.

IN CONTEXT

Essential Information

Hotels

Tourist numbers have risen steadily in recent years and Naples' accommodation scene has responded accordingly. The biggest change has been the number of B&B options, but there's also an increasing number of small hotels and guesthouses. Any visit to Naples will involve both good and bad surprises, and where you rest your weary head after a long day navigating around this confounding – and often exhausting – city can make all the difference. There's something for every budget, but rest assured that your euro buys more in Naples than it would in, say, Venice or Florence. At the upper end of the scale, grand, old-fashioned five-stars compete with luxurious new boutique establishments set in gracious, antique-filled *palazzi*. Then there are the elegant, Liberty-style villas on the edges of the Centro Storico, with their fine period details and garden oases, plus a burgeoning selection of design hotels.

WHERE TO STAY IN NAPLES

Every area in the city has its own distinctive flavour. For good restaurants, raw energy and true *napoletanità*, the **Centro Storico** and **Via Toledo & La Sanità** are the best options.

For an arty vibe and doorstep access to nightlife, bars and restaurants, and boutique shopping, **Chiaia to Posillipo** will work well, while **Royal Naples** combines romantic views and the city's most upmarket accommodation. These two locations are also handy for the ports of Mergellina and Beverello, for a quick getaway to the islands.

If you prefer leafy peace and quiet, retire to the less hectic, mostly residential **Vomero** district, set on the hill above the centre. For budget lodgings, the **Port & University** area is the best bet.

Check exactly where a hotel is before you book: it may not have good transport links or could be in an 'iffy' spot. A more expensive hotel in a central, safer area could save on taxis and make for a more relaxed stay in the long run.

For destinations outside Naples, refer to individual chapters in the **Escapes & Excursions** section (*see pp156-245*).

PRICES & CLASSIFICATION

Italian hotels are classified by the one- to five-star system; B&Bs, residences and *affittacamere* (rooms for rent) aren't classified at all and standards vary wildly. It's never a bad idea to ask to see your room before registering: if the desk clerk has your passport and credit card, it's much harder to negotiate. Wherever you stay, it's always best to confirm prices and your reservation before you arrive, and to bring a print-out of the email with the agreed terms to avoid any problems when you come to check out.

Accommodation rates in Naples are substantially lower than in Rome, Florence and Venice, although bargains are thinner on the ground than they used to be as tourist numbers rise. As a general rule for this guide, **Deluxe** means that a standard double room in high season will cost from €300 per night. **Expensive** means that it will cost between €200 and €300 per night. **Moderate** means €100 to €200 per night. **Budget** will come in at under €100. Higher room categories may cost substantially more. Prices include continental breakfast, unless otherwise stated. Remember that it always pays to check hotel websites, as well as booking engines, as the best prices will nearly always be available online. Always book ahead in high season.

ROYAL NAPLES

Deluxe

★ Excelsior

Via Partenope 48 (081 764 0111, www.excelsior.it). Bus 128, 140, 154, E6. **Rooms** 130. **Map** p316 K15.
Royals, film stars and jet-setters have all walked the Excelsior's sumptuously decorated halls and corridors. A Neapolitan landmark, it exerts a heady glamour – helped by its enviable position overlooking the bay, with Vesuvius as the backdrop and the Borgo Marinari opposite. Each room is different, though all share a fin-de-siècle polish. The top-floor restaurant, La Terrazza, offers breathtaking views, and there's a bar on the ground floor for a pre-dinner tipple.

★ Grand Hotel Vesuvio

Via Partenope 45 (081 764 0044, www.vesuvio.it). Bus 128, 140, 154, E6. **Rooms** 160. **Map** p316 K15.
Built in 1882, when the Santa Lucia seafront was created in a huge redevelopment, the Vesuvio was completely destroyed during World War II and rebuilt in 1950 with the addition of two extra floors. Royalty, world leaders, opera singers and

Hollywood actors – Queen Victoria, Grace Kelly and Oscar Wilde, to name a few – have all stayed in its stately rooms and opulent suites over the years. The place is looking a little faded these days, but that's all part of the charm. On the top floor is a roof-garden restaurant named after Enrico Caruso, a favoured guest. A room overlooking the Castel dell'Ovo is a must and the wonderful spa completes the civilised picture.

Romeo

Via Cristoforo Colombo 45 (081 017 5008, www.romeohotel.it). Metro Municipio or Università, or bus 151, 154, or tram 1.
Rooms 83. **Map** p316 M11.
When this contemporary five-star hotel, designed by the late Kenzo Tange, opened in 2009, there were plans to spruce up and redevelop the Port area. These plans have never materialised and the Romeo remains a beacon of upmarket style in a dingy and (after dark) rather threatening area. The location is quite central, though, and Piazza del Municipio and the Centro Storico are within easy walking distance. Inside the high-tech glass-and-steel edifice, lavish public rooms are stuffed with contemporary art and antiques, while bedrooms are luxuriously appointed with the sleekest of fittings and endless gizmos. There's a rooftop pool, a huge spa and a Michelin-starred restaurant, Il Commandante (*see p55*). The ground-floor sushi bar is a good bet if you want a change from pizza.

Romeo.

Royal Continental

Via Partenope 38-44 (081 245 2068, www. hotelroyal.it). Bus 128, 140, E6. **Rooms** 400. **Map** p311 J15.

Built in the 1950s by modernist architect Giò Ponti, the Royal Continental may not grab everyone at first. However, it's functional and extremely comfortable, and staff are great. It's favoured by business people, who probably don't have the time to appreciate its wonderful seafront location overlooking the Castel dell'Ovo. There's a delightful 1950s swimming pool on the roof and a variety of smart room styles to choose from – the ones on the first floor are perfectly restored time capsules of Giò Ponti's upbeat style.

Expensive

★ Cigliegina

Via Imbriani 30 (081 1971 8800, www.cigliegina hotel.it). Metro Toledo, or bus C25, R2. **Rooms** 14. **Map** p315 H7.

Luxury boutique hotel the 'Little Cherry' is on the third floor of an old palazzo close to the shops of Via Toledo and the port area. The soothingly cool, white interior makes a perfect escape from the dust and grime of the city. The 14 comfortable bedrooms, decorated in crisp blue and white, are enlivened with splashes of red and have plenty of luxurious touches, including superb Hastens mattresses and linen sheets, robes and slippers. Grey marble bathrooms come with Etro bath goodies. You can even see a slice of Vesuvius from the window of the junior suite. There's a large roof terrace with a breakfast bar, hot tub and sun loungers, plus views that stretch from San Martino to the Sorrentine peninsula.

Hotel Santa Brigida.

Hotel Santa Brigida

Via Santa Brigida 6 (081 1933 8206, www. hotelsantabrigida.it). Metro Municipio or Toledo, or bus C25, R2. **Rooms** 12. **Map** p316 K2.

Just off the busy shopping street of Via Toledo and close to the Centro Storico, this architect-designed hotel opened in 2013. The minimalist interiors are done out in moody shades of grey and mauve, with contemporary art and monochrome photos on the walls. The individually styled bedrooms all have slick, open-plan bathrooms; one has a bed suspended from the ceiling and another has a sunken bath. The breakfast buffet is sumptuous and includes fresh cakes baked in-house daily.

Miramare

Via Nazario Sauro 24 (081 764 7589, www. hotelmiramare.com). Bus 128, 140, 154, E6. **Rooms** 18. **Map** p316 L14.

The hotel Miramare occupies an aristocratic Liberty villa dating from 1914. It became a hotel in 1944, but became famous in the 1950s when its restaurant and piano bar, the Shaker Club, drew top-name Italian and international singing stars. Small and family-run, it has a friendly, welcoming atmosphere. Breakfast is served on a roof-garden terrace with breathtaking views over the bay and Vesuvius. Rooms vary in size – it's worth investing in one with sea views. Guests get a 10% discount at nearby restaurants La Cantinella and Il Posto Accanto.

Moderate

Chiaja Hotel de Charme

Via Chiaia 216, 1st floor (081 415 555, www.hotel chiaia.it). Metro Municipio or Toledo, or bus C25, E6, R2. **Rooms** 27. **Map** p311 J12.

Tucked away off a courtyard, the former home of the Marchese Nicola Lecaldano (whose distinguished-looking portrait hangs in the lobby) is now a friendly and elegant hotel. The location – on a pedestrian street between Piazza Trieste e Trento and Piazza dei Martiri – is brilliant and it's pleasantly quiet. The conversion of a former brothel next door has added an additional eight rooms, each named after one of the women who worked there; there's even a list of 'services' offered. Rooms are well appointed and dotted with antiques; staff are helpful. Cakes and pastries are offered each afternoon at teatime.

Hotel San Marco

Calata San Marco 26 (081 552 0338, www. smhotel.it). Metro Municipio, or bus C25, R2, R4. **Rooms** 13. **Map** p316 L11.

The San Marco is conveniently located just off Piazza del Municipio, near the main port and a stone's throw from the major sights, shops and restaurants. The entrance is a bit dreary, but the rooms are comfortable enough, with double-glazing and air-conditioning. The occasional antique adds a bit of character and the bathrooms are new.

ESSENTIAL INFORMATION

HOTEL PALAZZO ESEDRA

NAPOLI

UN NUOVO ALBERGO, LA QUALITÀ DI SEMPRE.

Luna Caprese B&B

Via Chiatamone 7 (081 764 6383, 339 271 2392, www.lunacaprese.net). Bus 128, 140, 151, 154, C25. **Rooms** 7. **Map** p311 J14. *See p284* **B&B Bonanza**.

Mercure Napoli Angioino Centro

Via Agostino Depretis 123 (081 552 9500, www.accorhotels.com). Metro Municipio, or bus C25, R2, R4. **Rooms** 89. **Map** p316 L11.

Modern and comfortable, albeit somewhat anonymous, the Mercure is ideally located for forays into the Centro Storico, as well as quick getaways to the islands or the Amalfi Coast: it's just five minutes to the port at Beverello (and the airport bus). Rooms are air-conditioned and soundproofed, business facilities are available and there's a convenient, good-value underground parking lot nearby. The third-floor terrace for breakfast and *aperitivi* with full-on views of the Castel Nuovo is a bonus.

★ MH Design Hotel

Via Chiaia 245 (081 1957 1576, www.mhhotel.it). Bus R2. **Rooms** 20. **Map** p316 K12.

Run by two brothers, this handsome boutique hotel is decorated in calm, neutral hues, and has an appealingly airy feel. The long entrance hall sets the tone, leading away from bustling Via Chiaia and into a serene domain, punctuated by tasteful contemporary art. The guestrooms are understated yet plush, and the skylit breakfast room and bar on the top floor complete the sense of quiet comfort.

Orsini 46

Via Generale Orsini 46 (081 764 3790, 335 710 9484, www.orsisni46.it). Metro Municipio, or bus 128, 140, 154. **Rooms** 3. **Map** p316 K14. *See p284* **B&B Bonanza**.

Palazzo Turchini

Via Medina 21/22 (081 551 0606, www.palazzo turchini.it). Metro Municipio, or bus C25, R2. **Rooms** 120. **Map** p316 L11.

This elegant 18th-century building was formerly a royal orphanage and famous music conservatory. The sixth-floor breakfast room and terrace have lovely views towards Castel Nuovo. Bedrooms are beautifully fitted out in an elegant, contemporary style, and are well insulated against the noise outside. Staff are friendly and discreet.

Budget

★ Bella Capri Hotel & Hostel

Via Melisurgo 4, Gate B, 6th floor (081 552 9265, www.bellacapri.it). Metro Università, or bus 151, 154. **Rooms** 14. **Map** p316 M11.

Set half a block from the main port, with views of Capri and Vesuvius (ask for a room with a balcony), this cheerful, modest establishment enjoys an ideal location for trips round the bay and exploring the city sights. Friendly staff bend over backwards to be helpful, and there are special deals for island trips and excursions. The unpretentious rooms are comfortable, if a trifle noisy.

Palazzo Turchini.

▶ *Upstairs is a busy youth hostel with dorm beds from €15 per person in a mixed room; call the hotel for details.*

CENTRO STORICO
Expensive

★ Costantinopoli 104
Via Santa Maria di Costantinopoli 104 (081 557 1035, www.costantinopoli104.it). Metro Dante, or bus E1, 204, R1. **Rooms** 19. **Map** p312 L8.
A delightful boutique hotel, this Liberty villa is a tranquil retreat in the heart of town, close to the social hub of Piazza Bellini. It was converted from an aristocratic palazzo, with stained-glass windows and wrought-iron gates; there's a small, sun-filled garden where guests can enjoy breakfast or a drink beside the charming pool. Bedrooms are stylish and individually decorated; some have private terraces. There's a complimentary supply of limoncello and nocino for guests.

★ Palazzo Decumani
Via del Grande Archivio 8 (081 420 1379, www.palazzodecumani.com). Metro Dante, or bus E1, E2. **Rooms** 28. **Map** p312 N8.
A relatively recent addition to the Centro Storico hotel scene, and a good choice if you want to be in the thick of things, this designer boutique hotel is housed in a meticulously restored belle époque building. Inside, the sumptuous public areas are scattered with contemporary art. Bedrooms are over the top (there are so many velvet pillows piled on the bed, you may wonder where you're supposed to sleep), but soothingly comfortable nonetheless. The staff are very helpful and a superb breakfast buffet is another boon.

Moderate

Caravaggio Hotel di Napoli
Piazza Cardinale Sisto Riario Sforza 157 (081 211 0066, www.caravaggiohotel.it). Metro Cavour, or bus E1, E2. **Rooms** 18. **Map** p312 N7.
Occupying a restored 17th-century building, the Caravaggio's creamy colour scheme and exposed stonework give it a pleasantly airy feel. Bedrooms are modern and comfortable, albeit a little short on personality; some have a jacuzzi. It stands just behind the Duomo, opposite the Guglia di San Gennaro, so the view is charming; there's also a small roof garden. Staff can be a little prickly, but otherwise it's a good bet.

★ Decumani Hotel de Charme
Via San Giovanni Maggiore Pignatelli 15, 2nd floor (081 551 8188, www.decumani.com). Metro Piazza Cavour, or bus R2. **Rooms** 23. **Map** p312 M9.
This hotel is in the heart of old Naples, close to Santa Chiara and a stroll away from the lively university

quarter. Rooms are elegantly appointed and decorated with tasteful antiques – as you'd expect in a historic palace, once home to the last bishop of the Bourbon Kingdom of Naples. The high point is the ballroom, decorated from floor to ceiling with lavish frescoes. In spite of the palatial surroundings, the atmosphere is convivial.

★ Donna Regina B&B
Via Luigi Settembrini 80 (081 446799, 339 781 9225, www.discovernaples.net). Metro Cavour, or bus E1, E2, 203. **Rooms** 3. **Map** p312 N6.
See p284 **B&B Bonanza**.

★ Hotel Piazza Bellini
Via Santa Maria di Costantinopoli 101 (081 451732, www.hotelpiazzabellini.com). Metro Dante or Museo, or bus 139, 182, 201, C63, R4. **Rooms** 48. **Map** p312 L7.
A few steps from the buzzy nightlife of Piazza Bellini, this sleek, modern hotel inhabits the six floors of an elegant old palazzo wrapped around a beautiful courtyard garden laid out with chairs and sofas. The modern, uncluttered bedrooms vary in size and shape, but all are variations on the same stylish theme with parquet floors, contemporary furnishings and gleaming bathrooms. The duplex rooms are great for families; top-floor terrace rooms have fabulous views over the city. There's a vaulted breakfast room where you can leave your scribblings on a huge blackboard. The lovely courtyard is a perfect place to wind down with a drink after a long, hot day's sightseeing.

Neapolis
Via Francesco del Giudice 13, off Via Tribunali (081 442 0815, www.hotelneapolis.com). Metro Dante or Cavour. **Rooms** 18. **Map** p312 L/M8.
Located in the Centro Storico, close to buzzy Piazza Bellini, the friendly Neapolis is a decent, modestly priced choice. Little extras include a computer in every room with free internet access. Windows are soundproofed, but the walls are a little thin; still, you'll wake up to an ample breakfast buffet. The adjoining Locanda del Griffo (same owners as Neapolis) serves good Neapolitan food; hotel guests receive a 10% discount.

Budget

Duomo
Via Duomo 228 (081 265988). Bus E1, E2. **Rooms** 10. **Map** p312 N8.
Run by three brothers, this quiet little hotel is an ideal base for sampling the action in the old quarter. Furnishings are plain but have a polished feel, and guestrooms are generally spacious and decorated in cheerful colours. There's no air-conditioning, but the ceiling fans are reasonably effective. For breakfast, you'll head out to one of the many excellent bars in the area.

Hotel Piazza Bellini.

PORT & UNIVERSITY

Expensive

Hotel Una

Piazza Garibaldi 9/10 (081 563 6901, www. unahotels.it). Metro Garibaldi, or bus E2, R2, 460. **Rooms** 89. **Map** p313 P8.

Part of a Florentine chain of business-centric hotels, the Una occupies a tall, renovated 19th-century building on the corner of Piazza Garibaldi and Corso Umberto I. An oasis of calm after the gritty chaos outside, its airy rooms feature tufa stone panels, pale green or Pompeiian red walls, and understated Neapolitan motifs and prints. Staff are polite and amenable, and the restaurant serves food all day. In warmer weather, the restaurant and bar move up to the roof terrace, from where you can survey the city.

Budget

Europeo & Europeo Flowers

Via Mezzocannone 109C (081 551 7254, www. sea-hotels.com). Metro Università, or bus E1, R2. **Rooms** *Europeo 17. Europeo Flowers 8.* **Map** p312 M9.

Close to Spaccanapoli, the university district and the Centro Storico, the friendly Europeo hotels offer good value and have been upgraded recently. The cheerful rooms now have air-conditioning and flat-screen TVs as well as more basic amenities; those at Europeo Flowers feature modern flora and fauna frescoes, while the top-floor Europeo rooms are themed around European capitals. Neither hotel serves breakfast, but there are plenty of nearby eating options.

Suite Esedra

Via Cantani 12, off Corso Umberto I (081 287451). Metro Garibaldi, or bus 202, 460, R2. **Rooms** 17. **Map** p313 O8.

The cosy Esedra is handy for the Centro Storico, the port and the railway station. Rooms are individually decorated with astronomy motifs; the Venus suite, with its private rooftop plunge pool, is a delight. The hotel has only one drawback: it overlooks the thundering, traffic-jammed and somewhat insalubrious Corso Umberto I.

VIA TOLEDO & LA SANITÀ

Expensive

Mediterraneo

Via Ponte di Tappia 25 (081 797 0001, www. mediterraneonapoli.com). Metro Toledo or Municipio, or bus C25, R2. **Rooms** 228. **Map** p316 K11.

Now part of the Renaissance chain, this stylish, centrally located hotel is very convenient for exploring Naples' major shops and sights. Catering mainly for business people (there are eight conference rooms), its bedrooms are comfortable with contemporary

B&B BONANZA
Brilliant budget beds in Naples.

In recent years, B&Bs have been popping up everywhere in Naples. These range from really lovely rooms furnished with family antiques in glorious old *palazzi* to spartan squats offering little more than a bed, some hanging space and a shared bathroom. Some of them don't even offer breakfast. Prices vary accordingly, but on the whole you can expect to pay €80-€120 in high season for a double room in a good B&B including breakfast.

There are six comfortable, air-conditioned rooms at the appealing **Cappella Vecchia 11** (see p288), which has understated, colourful decor and modern art on the walls. The quiet, elegant Chiaia district makes an excellent holiday base. Another good bet in Chiaia is the **Chiaia B&B** (see p288), run by the charming Maria Luisa Giannini, who offers three beautifully decorated rooms – each with a Neapolitan theme – on the second floor of a residential building. There's a comfortable communal area with use of a kitchen and washing machine. Breakfast is served on the pretty roof terrace or in your room. There are also three apartments for longer stays.

Just a short stroll from the Lungomare and not far from the Castel dell'Ovo, the **Luna Caprese B&B** (see p281) occupies a large fourth-floor apartment in a 17th-century palazzo and offers a mix of rooms (some of which sleep three or four) and self-catering

studio apartments. Furnished with antiques, sofas and oriental rugs, it has the feel of an elegant private home. Owner Arnaldo Cotugno is a font of local knowledge.

Manuela and Gabriele Nannini's **Orsini 46** (see p281) enjoys an enviable position near the seafront just east of the old Santa Lucia neighbourhood – two of the three elegant, sunny rooms have sea views. There's a comfortable sitting area and guests have use of a small kitchen. Breakfast includes bacon and eggs on request.

At **Donna Regina B&B** (see p282), near the MADRe contemporary art museum (see p87), a hearty and delicious breakfast (plus traditional Neapolitan dinner if you book in advance) is served in a lovely old tiled kitchen in what was originally part of a 14th-century monastic complex. Filled with antiques and modern art, the rooms are charming, and guests are welcome to relax in the elegant sitting room. **Villa Bruna B&B** (see p285) is another gem, on the main road up the hill between the Museo Archeologico and Capodimonte. It may seem rather out of the way, but there are good bus links and a nearby lift will take you down to La Sanità. The delightful little Liberty-style villa has a sunny garden, where breakfast is served. Each of the three rooms is charming and cosy.

For details of more B&Bs in Naples, see www.bed-and-breakfast.it.

Chiaia B&B.

decor; breakfast is served on the lovely roof ter-race restaurant overlooking the bay and Vesuvius. There's also a cocktail and piano bar in the foyer.

Palazzo Caracciolo

Via Carbonara 111/112 (081 016 0111,
www.hotel-palazzo-caracciolo-naples.com).
Metro Cavour, or bus 182, 201, 203, E2, C47.
Rooms 238. **Map** p312 N6.

Part of the M brand of the Accor chain, this magnif-icent palazzo dates from 1300 when it was a castle: the central cloister – now a seating, bar and restau-rant area – dates from that era. The bedrooms wrap around the courtyard and are done out in soft grey and white with classy touches of burnished silver: two of them have private terraces. The restaurant serves up Neapolitan classics with a modern twist.

Moderate

Il Convento

Via Speranzella 137A (081 403977, www.hotel
ilconvento.com). Metro Toledo, or bus C25, R2.
Rooms 14. **Map** p316 K11.

Housed in a former convent dating from 1600, this hotel has been restored with an eye to the building's origins – beamed ceilings, unadorned creamy white walls and grey stone floors dominate – but without sacrificing guest comfort. The rooms (or 'cells', as they're known) are spacious and some have a small ter-race. The hotel, set just off busy Via Toledo, is handy for the port and all main sights. Don't be put off by the address – the Quartieri Spagnoli are quite safe these days. There are discounts for family groups.

Hotel 241 Correra

Via Correra 241 (081 1956 2842, www.correra.it).
Metro Dante, or bus 139, 182, 201, C63, R4.
Rooms 12. **Map** p312 K8.

This popular boutique hotel bills itself as the city's first 'art hotel', and it's certainly a colourful place. The entrance lies behind an iron gate, leading to a walkway facing a vast tufa wall. Inside, the walls are painted in reds, oranges and blues. Large, slickly modern rooms are painted in more pop art colours; service is equally warm. Breakfast is served on the small, more conventionally decorated terrace.

Budget

Toledo

Via Montecalvario 15 (081 406800, www.
hoteltoledo.com). Metro Toledo. **Rooms** 22.
Map p311 J11.

Neapolitans may shudder at the thought of staying in the Quartieri Spagnoli, but the area's reputation for crime far outstrips reality today. So long as you don't parade your diamond tiara after dark, you're unlikely to encounter any problems. The three-floor, 17th-century palazzo that houses the Toledo has been handsomely restructured, with a pretty roof

garden and views over the Certosa-Museo di San Martino and Castel Sant'Elmo. The pedestrianised shopping area of Via Toledo is just a few steps away.

Villa Bruna B&B

154 Via Santa Teresa degli Scalzi (081 544 2079,
www.bedandbreakfastvillabruna.com). Metro
Materdei, or bus 168, 178, C63, R4. **Rooms** 3.
Map p312 K5.
See p284 **B&B Bonanza**.

CAPODIMONTE
Moderate

Culture Hotel Capodimonte

Salita Moiariello 66 (081 459000, www.
villacapodimonte.culturehotel.it). Bus C63.
Rooms 55.

Although it's some way from the centre of the city, this modern, four-star hotel is worth considering if you're driving (there's free parking on site) or are an art lover: the Museo di Capodimonte is nearby. Approached along a narrow lane, the hotel is immersed in a luxuriant garden high above the city with views that take in the bay, Vesuvius and the Sorrentine peninsula; the best of the large, comforta-ble rooms make the most of the panorama with large windows. There's a restaurant and a shuttle service to the Centro Storico.

VOMERO
Moderate

Hotel Cimarosa

Via Cimarosa 29 (081 556 7044, www.hotel
cimarosa.it). Metro Vanvitelli, or funicular
Montesanto to Via Morghen, Centrale to
Piazzetta Fuga or Chiaia to Via Cimarosa.
Rooms 16. **Map** p315 F10.

Stylishly transformed from a simple *pensione* to a hotel by its architect owner, Sergio Arpaia, the Cimarosa is pleasantly located in quiet, central Vomero. There are plenty of shops and restaurants nearby, not to mention the Certosa-Museo di San Martino (*see p94*), and it's just a short funicular ride from the centre. Eight of the 16 rooms have sea views. All are spacious and individually decorated, with an airy, solidly contemporary feel; the two Superior Plus rooms have very swish bathrooms.

★ Weekend a Napoli

Via E Alvino 157 (081 578 1010, www.weekend
anapoli.com). Metro Quattro Giornate, or funicular
Chiaia to Cimarosa or Centrale to Piazza Fuga.
Rooms 7. **Map** p314 E9.

The owners of this delightful boutique hotel, set in a Liberty villa in quiet, leafy Vomero, offer the warmest of welcomes and lots of useful local advice. There are seven beautifully furnished bedrooms

Santa Lucia.

(plus two self-catering options for longer stays), a comfortable sitting room and a flower-filled garden. Breakfast includes home-made cakes and jam, and cooking lessons followed by dinner are available.

CHIAIA TO POSILLIPO

Expensive

Grand Hotel Parker's
Corso Vittorio Emanuele 135 (081 761 2474, www.grandhotelparkers.com). Funicular Montesanto to Corso Vittorio Emanuele, or bus C16. **Rooms** 82. **Map** p310 E12.

A favourite with 19th-century British travellers, Parker's has a long, august history. Despite some dark days (it was requisitioned by troops during World War II and damaged by the 1980 earthquake), the building has now been restored to its original grandeur. Crystal chandeliers, antiques, paintings and statues abound, and there's a library of antique volumes. The rooms are lavishly furnished and comfortably equipped, and there's a plush spa. The two restaurants (one on the roof terrace) serve good international food. Specify when booking to ensure you get a room with the famous view.

▶ *Excellent restaurant Veritas (see p105) is just a few doors up the road.*

★ Hotel San Francesco al Monte
Corso Vittorio Emanuele 328 (081 423 9111, www.sanfrancescoalmonte.it). Funicular Centrale to Corso Vittorio Emanuele, or bus C16. **Rooms** 45. **Map** p315 J10.

This hotel was converted from the Santa Lucia al Monte convent, founded in 1557 by the Minori Conventuali monks. The building is a warren of twisting stairways, long corridors, arches and little windows, with features such as the monks' refectory, old confessionals and a nativity scene reminding you of its origins. The bedrooms – once severe monastic cells but now comfortable and well-appointed– all have views over the bay and lovely bathrooms. The USP is the fabulous roof terrace that includes a lovely pool sculpted into the rock with shaded seating areas. Lunch is served up here in the summer and the sweeping views take in the whole city, the bay and Vesuvius.

Santa Lucia
Via Partenope 46 (081 764 0666, www.santalucia. it). Bus 140, 152, C25. **Rooms** 96. **Map** p316 K15.

Built in 1900, this classic hotel enjoys marvellous views over the bay. The furnishings are sober and traditional, the atmosphere is quiet and relaxing, and the staff are very professional. It's situated opposite the Castel dell'Ovo and the Borgo Marinari, with its many bars and restaurants.

Micalò.

Moderate

Ausonia

Via Caracciolo 11 (081 682278, www.hotelausonia napoli.com). Metro Mergellina, or bus 140, C12, C16, C18. **Rooms** 10. **Map** p310 C15.
Set in a residential building on the seafront, this little hotel has a great location in Mergellina. There are no sea views, as the hotel faces an inner courtyard, but its hands-on owner has brought the sea to you: the rooms are cheerfully decorated with nautical motifs and paraphernalia. Old-fashioned and quirky, it's also perfectly spick and span; equally importantly, it's quiet.

Chiaia B&B

Via Palasciano 17 (081 658 3667/www.chiaia baiabb.it). Metro Piazza Amedeo, or bus 140, C9, C10. **Rooms** 3. **Map** p310 E13.
See p284 **B&B Bonanza**.

★ Micalò

Riviera di Chiaia 88 (081 761 7131, www.micalo. it). Metro Mergellina, or bus 140, 151, C12, C18, R7. **Rooms** 9. **Map** p310 D14.
This designer boutique beauty, hidden behind a 17th-century façade on the Riviera di Chiaia, is owned by English ex-pat Michelle Lowe. The rooms – some of which have sea views – are decorated in cream and white with liberal use of natural materials; wood, pale Trani marble slabs and pure linens on the beds. Splashy contemporary art livens it all up. An excellent breakfast, plus drinks and snacks, are served in the stylish Art Bar. The location close to the boutiques and vibrant nightlife of Chiaia, as well as the seafront at Mergellina with its fish restaurants, is great.

Paradiso

Via Catullo 11 (081 247 5111, www.hotelparadiso napoli.it). Funicular Mergellina to Sant'Antonio, or bus C21. **Rooms** 72.
Now owned by Best Western, the Paradiso is situated high on the hill of Posillipo, away from the city. From this idyllic perch, you can see right across the bay, then survey the traffic hell below and heave a sigh of relief that you're not in it. The rooms are airy and bright, and many have little private terraces. Views from the restaurant are lovely – especially when dusk falls and the lights twinkle around the curve of the bay.

Budget

Cappella Vecchia 11

Vico Santa Maria a Cappella Vecchia 11 (081 240 5117, www.cappellavecchia11.it). Metro Amedeo, or bus C45, E6. **Rooms** 6. **Map** p311 H13.
See p284 **B&B Bonanza**.

CAMPI FLEGREI
Moderate

★ Villa Giulia
Via Cuma Licola 178, Cumae (081 854 0163, www.villagiulia.info). **Rooms** 6.
A kilometre from the sea and 20km (12 miles) from central Naples, this beautiful farmhouse offers rooms and apartments. It feels worlds away from chaotic Naples, set in lush gardens with an inviting pool and sunny terraces overlooking Ischia and nearby Cuma. The charming owners offer cookery courses to guests. To reach the villa by car, take the Tangenziale Ovest in the Pozzuoli direction then exit at junction 13, signposted Cuma. See the website for detailed directions.

Villa Medici
Via Nuova Bagnoli 550 (081 762 3040, www.hotel-villamedici.com). Metro Campi Flegrei, then bus C9 or Cumana line to Agnano. **Rooms** 15.
A charming three-star hotel in a converted Liberty-style villa, Villa Medici is well placed for forays into the Campi Flegrei as well as central Naples. Various well-equipped rooms and apartments are available, many with kitchenettes, and there's a pretty garden and pool. There are special seasonal offers and good discounts for family groups.

Budget

Averno
Via Montenuovo Licola Patria 85, Arco Felice Lucrino, Pozzuoli (081 804 2666, www.averno.it). Bus CTP M1 from Piazza Garibaldi.
This large and well-equipped campsite in the Campi Flegrei is a fair hike from Naples, but only a couple of kilometres from the beach. There are one- or two-bedroom bungalows if you don't fancy sleeping under canvas, plus facilities galore. There's a restaurant and bar; a semi-Olympic pool, children's pool and a hot pool filled by thermal waters; plus a disco, tennis and go-karts. An extra charge applies to certain activities.

★ Vulcano Solfatara
Via Solfatara 161, Pozzuoli (081 526 2341, www.solfatara.it). Metro Pozzuoli, or bus SEPSA 1 from Piazza Garibaldi.
Half an hour from town on the metro and handy for the ferry port at Pozzuoli, this is the most convenient campsite for visiting Naples and the surrounding area. It's also right on the leafy fringes of the bubbling, fuming Solfatara crater (*see p115*). The site has facilities including a handy bar-restaurant, a shop and swimming pool, and there are also bungalows for rent.

Getting Around

ESSENTIAL INFORMATION

ARRIVING & LEAVING

By air

Aereoporto Internazionale di Napoli (Capodichino) is 7km or 10mins from Stazione Centrale rail station, 20mins from the ferry and hydrofoil ports. **Alibus** (800 639525, 081 763 1111, www.anm.it) runs a direct bus from the airport (the bus stop is about 50m from the entrance) to Stazione Centrale (Piazza Garibaldi) and Piazza Municipio (near the ferry port). Buses leave every 20-30mins, 6.30am to 11.30pm daily. Return buses leave Piazza Municipio from 6am to 12.12am daily. Tickets are €3 (€4 on board). The fixed **taxi** fare to central Naples is €16.

Aereoporto Internazionale di Napoli 081 789 6111, *toll-free within Italy 848 888 777, www. aeroportodinapoli.it, www.gesac.it.*

Major airlines
Alitalia 06 2222, *www.alitalia.com*
BA 199 712266, *www.ba.com*
EasyJet 848 887766, *www.easyjet.com*

By boat

Timetables for water transport around the Bay of Naples appear daily in *Il Mattino* and on the not always accurate www.campania trasporti.it. The airport website includes up-to-date ferry and hydrofoil information (www. aeroportodinapoli.it/in-arrivo/ aliscafi-e-traghetti).

Ferries and hydrofoils depart regularly from Naples' port, Molo Beverello, heading to the islands (from €11 for Ischia) and Sorrento (€11), as well as from the smaller port at Mergellina to the islands.

Alilauro 081 497 2238, *www.alilauro.it.*
Caremar 081 551 3882, *www.caremar.it.*
MedMar 081 333 4411, *www.medmargroup.it.*
Navigazione Libera del Golfo 081 552 0763, *www.navlib.it.*
SNAV 081 428 5555, *www.snav.it.*

Ferry services to Palermo (daily) and Sardinia (once or twice weekly) are run by **Tirrenia** (www.tirrenia.it). SNAV also runs a daily hydrofoil to

Palermo. **TTT Lines** (800 915365, 081 580 2744, www.tttlines.info) sails from Molo Beverello to Catania. Hydrofoils to Capri, Ischia and Procida, run by SNAV and Alilauro, also leave from Mergellina, 1.5km from the main port.

MedMar and Caremar car ferries also leave for Procida and Ischia from Pozzuoli, 12km north-west of Naples.

By bus

Most long-distance buses arrive at and depart from Piazza Garibaldi. **CLP** (081 251 4157, www.clpbus.it) runs to cities in Campania, in other parts of Italy and in continental Europe. **CTP** (800 482644, 081 700 1111, 081 700 5104, www.ctp.na.it) and **SITA** (081 752 7337, 089 386 6711, www.sitabus.it, www.sita sudtrasporti.it) serve destinations around Naples and Southern Italy, as well as Tuscany and the Veneto.

By rail

Naples' three mainline stations are Campi Flegrei, Mergellina and the main station, Stazione Centrale.

Stazione Centrale
Piazza Garibaldi (89 20 21).
Map p313 Q7.
Most trains come and go from here, including the Alta Velocità high-speed service to Rome and the new Italo trains. Trains also depart from Piazza Garibaldi station (two levels below the main station), which is used by some long-distance services as well as the regional metro.

PUBLIC TRANSPORT

Public transport in Naples takes the form of buses (including a fleet of eco-friendly Liliputian models that negotiate the narrow streets of the Centro Storico), trams, metro, funiculars and overland trains serving suburban routes. The metro system, with its *'stazioni dell'arte'* (*see pp268-273*), is worth exploring just to ogle the spectacular art installations. And now, with the opening of more stations, it's becoming the best (and fastest) way to get around the city. For getting away from Naples, there are narrow-gauge trains to the south-east and the west, or ferries and hydrofoils to all points around the bay. Apart from

that, count on walking (or taking a taxi); city buses are very crowded and tend to get stuck in traffic.

Fares & tickets

Urbano Napoli tickets (UNA) are required for travel within the city limits. There are two types: TIC (integrated or combined) tickets and agency-issued tickets (relevant to the transport company concerned).

TIC tickets are valid on all modes of public transport within the city limits except the Alibus. The single (*orario*) integrated ticket costs €1.50 and is valid for 90 minutes; it allows you to take multiple journeys within the time limit. The daily (24hr) ticket for unlimited travel is €4.50.

Agency-issued tickets from ANM and EAV start at €1 and are valid for a single journey on the agency's mode of transport only. If you don't know the system well, it's easy to get caught out by this. For example, Metro lines 1 and 6 are run by ANM but Line 2 is run by the Ferrovie dello Stato, so you can't use a €1 ticket if you want to switch from line 1 to line 2. Spot checks are quite frequent and you'll be fined if you have the wrong ticket, so buy an integrated ticket if you're in any doubt.

Tickets can be purchased at most newsstands, *tabacchi* and ticket machines in stations; they must be purchased before boarding (except Alibus) and time-stamped in the validation machines.

Buses

Traffic makes bus travel in Naples a pain: you're often quicker walking. Still, the dedicated bus lane on Corso Umberto can make bus travel to places between San Carlo opera house and Stazione Centrale viable. The bus can also be an option when travelling to Mergellina and Posillipo (from Santa Lucia or Riviera di Chiaia). For lost property, *see p295*.

Bus services are run by **ANM** (800 639 525, 081 763 1111, www.anm.it). There's no central bus station, but the main transport hubs include Piazza Garibaldi, Piazza Cavour, Piazza Municipio and Piazza Vittoria. Electronic signs at bus stops give waiting times. Before taking a bus, buy tickets at a *tabacchi* or newsstand and stamp them in the machine on board. Enter buses through the front or back doors, and exit through the central ones; before your stop, press the red button.

Metro

Naples' Metro system, operated by **ANM** (800 639 525, 081 763 1111, www.anm.it), is the fastest way to get around parts of Greater Naples. For lost property, *see p295*.

Red M signs indicate a station. Tickets are sold at *tabacchi* and at machines in every station. *See p290* for ticket prices.

The Metro system has been in the throes of expansion for decades, with new lines and stations opening frequently. The latest to be up and running are Toledo, Università and, most recently, Municipio, which opened in June 2015 (although the concourse has yet to be completed; *see pp268-273*).

Also now officially part of the system are two older, narrow-gauge overground railways, one heading west and the other snaking in the other direction round the bay; both are fairly ramshackle. The **Circumvesuviana** (800 211 388, www.eavsrl.it) leaves from its own terminus on Corso Garibaldi. Trains run south-east to Oplontis, Pompeii, Herculaneum and Sorrento (6.09am-9.39pm). The **Ferrovia Cumana** (800 211 388, www.eavsrl.it) runs services from Piazza Montesanto to Campi Flegrei (5.20am-9.41pm).

The new **Campania Express** Naples–Sorrento train service, run by EAV (www.eavsrl.it), was launched in May 2015 and ran until mid October. Geared at tourists, it only stopped at Herculaneum, Pompeii and Sorrento, and cost €15 return. Hopefully, this clean, efficient service will continue in the future.

Funiculars

Three of the four trundling funicular railways (Centrale, Chiaia and Montesanto) take you to the Vomero, while the Mergellina funicular takes you to Posillipo. Kids love them and they're a quick, painless connection between the city centre and Naples' hill districts. Maintenance work on the Centrale line is expected to close down the route for six months from summer 2016.

TRAINS

Italy's high-speed train services are superb and new lines have cut travel times between the major hubs considerably. The average journey time between Naples and Florence

is now just 2.5hrs, Milan 4hrs 15mins, and Rome just over 1hr. The trains are supremely comfortable and offer free Wi-Fi, and Italo services even have a cinema car. First-class tickets include drinks and snacks. If you book well in advance online, fares can be very reasonable.

Most FS trains and all Italo trains come and go from **Stazione Centrale** (*see p290*). Below the street-level main station are two further levels: on the first is the entrance to the Circumvesuviana line (*see left*) and on the second is Piazza Garibaldi station.

Fares & tickets

Tickets for both FS and Italo trains can be bought at stations, from the ticket office or ticket machines. Italo (which runs high-speed services from Naples to Salerno, Rome, Florence, Bologna, Milan and Venice) has its own dedicated ticket desks and machines. Expect long queues and temperamental technology. You can also buy tickets from travel agents with the FS or Italo logo or from www.trenitalia.it or www. italotreno.it; both sites have English versions. You pay with a credit card and you'll receive an email with a booking code that should be presented to the inspector on the train (on your smartphone, tablet or on a print-out). Under-12s pay half the adult fare and under-4s travel free as long as they don't occupy a seat. Reservations can be made up to 15mins before departure.

Train fares in Italy are cheaper than in the UK, and various fares may be available on any given route. On high-speed (*alta velocità*) Freccia Argento and Freccia Rossa trains and Italo services, fares are often much lower if you book in advance online. Prices are directly related to distance travelled and, as a rule of thumb, the longer the journey time between any two points, the cheaper the ticket will be. The slow local trains are prefixed R (Regionale) or RV (Regionale Veloce) and are remarkably cheap. Intercity (IC) trains are a bit faster and cost a little more. Frecce trains are the fastest (some travel at up to 300km/h) and most expensive. Freccia Rossa and Freccia Argento bookings include a reserved seat.

If you have a regular ticket, you must stamp it in one of the yellow machines at the head of each platform before boarding or face a fine. If you forget to do this, find the conductor (*capo treno*) as soon as possible in order to waive the fine.

Ferrovie dello Stato (*892021, 06 6847 5475 from outside Italy, www.trenitalia.it*). **Open** 24hrs daily.

Italo (*060708, 06 8937 1892 from outside Italy, www.italotreno.it*). **Open** 6am-11pm daily.

TAXIS

Taxis can be found at signposted ranks; otherwise, call the numbers below. Authorised white taxis have the city's emblem on the front doors and rear licence plate, and a meter. Steer well clear of unauthorised taxi drivers, who may demand exorbitant sums for short journeys.

As you set off, the meter should read €3.50. There's a €4.50 minimum charge per trip. On Sundays, holidays and rides between 10pm and 7am, the minimum charge becomes €6; 50¢ per piece of luggage in the boot, and an extra €4 from the airport and €3 back.

You can avoid confusion by using the fixed rates posted on the tariff card in the back of the taxi (also in English). Each driver must display this list: if you don't see it, ask for the '*elenco di tariffe predeterminate*'. You must ask for the fixed rate before setting off; if you don't, the meter system will kick in. You'll be given a receipt with both the origin and destination written on it. There are fixed rates to and from the airport, central station and port, plus most of the major tourist areas in the city. The rate between Capodichino and Stazione Centrale, for example, is €16; between Stazione Centrale and Molo Beverello it's €11. Fixed rates include luggage.

Cab drivers may try to hike fares, so ensure the meter is on. If you suspect you're being ripped off, make a note of the driver's name and number from the photo ID in the cab; do it ostentatiously and the fare is likely to drop to its proper level. For lost property, *see p295*. Complaints can be lodged with the drivers' cooperative (the phone number is displayed on the outside of the car) or the **Servizio Programmazione, Promozione e Controllo Servizi di Trasporto Pubblico** (081 1997 9674).

When you phone for a cab, you'll be given a geographic location followed by a number and a time, as in '*Treviso 14, in tre minuti*' ('Treviso 14, in three minutes'). The driver should put the meter on as you get in; a call supplement of €1 will be added. Most taxis accept cash only; a few take credit cards.

Consortaxi (081 552 5252, www.consortaxi.it), **Free Taxi** (081 551 5151) and **Partenope** (081 560 6666,

ESSENTIAL INFORMATION

www.radiotaxilapartenope.it) are generally reliable. Some taxi firms run fixed-rate trips outside Naples at reasonable prices: return to Pompeii for €90, say. Many drivers speak English, making the trip a kind of guided tour.

DRIVING

EU visitors can drive on their home country's licence; an international licence is advisable for non-EU citizens. When driving, remember:

● The law insists you wear a seat belt and carry a hazard triangle and reflective safety jacket in your car; scooter riders and motorcyclists must wear helmets.

● Keep your driving licence, insurance documents, vehicle registration and photo ID on you at all times; if you're stopped by the police, you may be fined if you can't produce them.

● Flashing your lights means that you won't slow down or give way, and want the person in front of you to switch lanes.

● Neapolitans often ignore red lights, so approach junctions with caution. If traffic lights flash amber, give way to the right.

● Italians drive on the right.

Reasons not to drive

● Large swathes of central Naples are now designated ZTL (Zona di Traffico Limitato) areas where cars are permitted to enter only between 6pm or 7pm and 7am (although some are accessible to scooters or motorbikes). In some areas (Piazza Gèsu and surrounding streets and the Lungomare in front of Castel dell'Ovo, for example), vehicles are banned altogether. If you do arrive in Naples with a car, leave it in a garage (*see right*) for the duration of your stay and use either public transport or taxis. For more details (in Italian), refer to www.comune.napoli.it.

● In summer, traffic around Sorrento and along the Amalfi Coast is horrific, as tour buses wind their way along narrow coastal roads. Local day-trippers make things even worse at weekends.

● On the islands, roads are packed in the summer. You can't take cars to Capri, so use public transport or walk on tiny Procida. Car rental on Ischia is relatively cheap, but you can't take the car off the island.

Breakdown services

National motoring groups (Britain's AA or RAC and the AAA in the US)

have reciprocal arrangements with the **Automobile Club d'Italia** or ACI, which offers a 24hr emergency breakdown service (803 116, 081 725 3811, www.napoli.aci.it).

Car hire

The minimum age for renting an economy car is 21; you must be 25 to rent a more powerful car.

Avis *Airport (081 780 5790, www.avisautonoleggio.it).* **Open** 7.30am-11.30pm daily. **Other locations** Via Piedigrotta 44 (081 761 8354); Via Partenope 13 (081 240 0307); Piazza Garibaldi 92 (08 128 4041).

Europcar *Airport (081 780 5643, toll-free 199 307030, www.europcar. it).* **Open** 7.30am-11.30pm daily. **Other location** Corso Meridionale 60/62 (081 764 9838).

Hertz *Airport (081 780 2971, www.hertz.it).* **Open** 7.30am-11.30pm Mon, Wed, Sun; 7am-11.30pm Tue, Thur-Sat. **Other locations** Stazione Centrale (081 202860); Stazione Mergellina (081 761 2168).

Maggiore *Airport (081 780 3011, www.maggiore.it).* **Open** 7.30am-11.30pm daily. **Other location** Stazione Centrale (081 287858).

Thrifty *Airport (081 231 1200, www.thrifty.it).* **Open** 7.30am-11.30pm daily. **Other location** Stazione Mergellina (081 761 2168).

Parking

Parking in Naples is a nightmare. Blue lines on the road mean residents park for free and visitors pay (€1-€2/hr) at the pay-and-display machines. Elsewhere, spaces are up for grabs – though look out for signs saying *passo carrabile* (access at all times), *sosta vietata* (no parking). Disabled parking is marked off with yellow lines. 'Zona rimozione' (tow-away area) means no parking and is valid for the length of the street or until the next tow-away sign with a red line through it.

Illegal 'parking attendants' operate in many areas, offering to look after your car for €1 or so.

Via Brin Parking *Via Brin & Via Volta, Port & University (081 763 2855, www.anm.it). Bus 3S, 194, 195, C81, C82, C89, CS.* **Open** 24hrs daily. **Rates** €1.30/4hrs; 30¢ each successive hr; €7.20/24hrs. An 800-car facility between Stazione Centrale and the port (Porto exit

from the ring road or motorway). Buses for Molo Beverello leave every 15mins. However, this is not a great neighbourhood and it's a long way from the tourist areas. **Parcheggio Morelli** *Via Domenico Morelli 40, Chiaia (081 1913 0220, www.quickparking.it).* **Open** 24hrs daily. **Rates** €4/hr; €36/24hrs. The 230 hourly parking spaces are used by some 2,000 cars a day. It's more expensive than Via Brin, but the architecturally spectacular Morelli is centrally located.

CYCLING

Once almost unheard of as a way to get around the city, cycling in Naples is on the rise. Initiatives to support cyclists are helping the situation – a 10km bike path between Piazzale Tecchio in Fuorigrotta and the Lungomare has been laid out, and the municipal **Bike Sharing Napoli** programme (www.bikesharing napoli.it) ran very successfully during summer 2015 and will hopefully be repeated. The **Naples Bike Festival** (www.napolibike festival.it) has also become an annual early summer event. The fast and furious traffic in some parts of the city makes cycling a risky business, to say the least, but the parks, the abovementioned bike path and the pedestrianised Lungomare heading west from the Castel dell'Ovo are all very pleasant for a bike ride. Be aware that bike theft is rife.

WALKING

It's perfectly possible to explore Naples on foot – for the tourist areas, at least. For the hillier parts of town, there are funiculars and a couple of elevators. For the densest part of the Centro Storico, walking is really the only way to get around.

TOURS

CitySightseeing Napoli (081 551 7279, www.napoli.city-sightseeing.it) offers multilingual city tours in open-top double-decker buses. The Art Tour and the Bay of Naples Tour depart roughly every 45mins from Piazza Municipio. Tickets (valid 24hrs) cost €22 for adults, €11 for under-15s and €66 for a family of five. At weekends, there's a San Martino Tour from Piazza Municipio every 2hrs, but you have to pre-book. There's also a new Centro Antico Tour in a smaller open-top bus that leaves Piazza Gésu every 20mins, 9.30am-5.10pm. Hop on and off as you please.

Resources A-Z

TRAVEL ADVICE

For up-to-date information on travel to a specific country – including the latest on safety and security, health issues, local laws and customs – contact your home country government's department of foreign affairs. Most have websites with useful advice for would-be travellers.

AUSTRALIA
www.smartraveller.gov.au

CANADA
www.voyage.gc.ca

NEW ZEALAND
www.safetravel.govt.nz

REPUBLIC OF IRELAND
foreignaffairs.gov.ie

UK
www.fco.gov.uk/travel

USA
www.state.gov/travel

ADDRESSES

Addresses are written with the number following the street name, as in Via Toledo 23. The number after the word '*int*' (short for *interno*) is the flat or apartment number. '*Scala*' and '*piano*' numbers refer to staircase and floor numbers.

AGE RESTRICTIONS

At bars, beer and wine can be consumed from the age of 16, spirits from 18. You must be over 18 to drive and over 21 to hire a car. Over-14s with a licence can ride a moped or scooter with a 50cc engine.

ATTITUDE & ETIQUETTE

Churches are best visited in sober attire, but minor lapses from tourists are usually tolerated. Some churches discourage sightseeing on Sundays and during Mass.

Southern Italians have a me-first attitude when driving, boarding a bus or approaching a counter. Many banks and post offices now have a number system to keep the rabble at bay. Hanging back doesn't pay off. Note who's last in the queue when you enter a shop, and when it's your turn, be firm.

BUSINESS

Couriers

DHL *199 199345, www.dhl.it.*
FedEx *199 151119, www.fedex.com.*
UPS *02 3030 3039, www.ups.com.*
TNT *199 803868, www.tnt.it.*

Office services

Giovanna Pistillo *Vico Prota 9 Mercogliano, Avellino (338 760 5324).* Translating services.
Mail Boxes, Etc *Via Cervantes 55, Piazza Municipio (081 580 0256).* Posting, shipping, copying.

Useful organisations

British Chamber of Commerce for Italy *St Peter's English Language Centre, Via Crispi 32, Chiaia (081 683 468, www.scuolastpeters.com).*

CONSUMER

If you have a problem, your only recourse is the police at the Questura in Via Medina or at the central train station, where you'll need to fill out a form with the help of an officer with limited English.

CUSTOMS

EU citizens don't have to declare goods that have been brought into or out of Italy for personal use, as long as they have arrived from another EU country. Visitors are also allowed to carry up to €10,000 in cash. For all non-EU citizens, the following limits apply:

● 200 cigarettes or 100 small cigars or 50 large cigars or 250g of tobacco.
● 1 litre of spirits or 2 litres of wine.
● 50ml of perfume, 250ml of eau de toilette.
● gift items not exceeding €430 (€150 for under-15s).

DISABLED TRAVELLERS

Naples' narrow streets are tricky for people who can't flatten themselves against a wall to let cars by, and cobblestones – and badly repaired roads – are tough on wheelchair suspension. Where street-to-pavement ramps do exist, they're likely to be blocked by a car.

Old buildings often have narrow corridors, lifts that are too small for wheelchairs and inaccessible toilets. Things are slowly improving, with lifts, ramps and disabled-adapted toilets being installed in museums, restaurants and stations.

On Capri, there are small electric carts to get luggage and people up and down. The main paths are steep, but at least there are no stairs. However, getting up to town from the

LOCAL CLIMATE

Average temperatures and monthly rainfall in Naples.

	High (°C/°F)	Low (°C/°F)	Rainfall (mm/in)
Jan	12/54	4 / 39	116 / 4.6
Feb	13/55	5/41	85/3.3
Mar	15/59	6/43	73/2.9
Apr	18/64	9/48	62/2.4
May	22/72	12/54	44/1.7
June	26/79	16/61	31/1.2
July	29/84	18/64	19/0.7
Aug	29/84	18/64	32/1.3
Sept	26/79	16/61	64/2.5
Oct	22/72	12/54	107 / 4.2
Nov	17/63	9 / 48	147 / 5.8
Dec	14/57	6 / 43	135 / 5.3

port will involve help up the steps to the funicular and buses aren't disabled-friendly.

Upmarket hotels in major resorts cater best to special needs; cheaper hotels and *pensioni* can be trickier.

Transport

Hydrofoil and ferry lines (*see p290*) have begun to adapt for wheelchairs. Book ahead to ensure the ferry isn't an older model.

In Naples, city buses 180, C12, C14, C16, C38 and R2, marked with a wheelchair symbol, have extra-large central doors, access ramps and a space where a wheelchair can be secured. Elsewhere, the situation varies; contact local tourist offices or bus companies for information.

Naples' Stazione Centrale has a *Direzione servizi alla dienteia* (customer services office) near platform five. It can provide information for disabled travellers (081 567 2991, 7am-9pm daily), take reservations (min 24hrs prior to departure) and provide wheelchair assistance and access. Passengers must be at the office at least 45mins before the train departs.

Useful organisations

SuperAbile *800 810810, www. superabile.it.* **Open** *Phone enquiries* 9am-7pm Mon-Fri; 9am-1pm Sat. Italy-wide information on hotels, restaurants and job opportunities for people with disabilities.
Turismo Accessibile *www.turismoaccessibile.it.* Information on disabled access at hotels, restaurants, museums and more, in and around Naples.

DRUGS

If you're caught in possession of illegal drugs, you'll be brought before a magistrate. If you convince the judge they were for personal use, you may be let off with a fine or ordered to leave the country. Anything more than a tiny amount pushes you into the criminal category; couriering or dealing can land you in prison for up to 20 years.

Sniffer dogs are a fixture at most ports of entry into Italy; customs police will take a dim view of visitors entering with even the smallest quantities of narcotics.

ELECTRICITY

Most wiring systems work on 220V. Two-pin adaptor plugs are sold at electrical shops or airports.

EMBASSIES & CONSULATES

Many countries have embassies in Rome, but Naples' consulates can provide emergency help (although some countries such as Canada and the UK have closed down their consulates in the city). For a full list, check the phone book under *Ambasciati/consolati*.

USA *Piazza della Repubblica, Mergellina (081 583 8111, www. naples.usconsulate.gov). Metro Mergellina, or bus 140, C12, C18, C24.* **Open** 8am-noon Mon-Fri for emergency walk-in service; for non-emergency needs, there's an online appointment booking system. **Map** p310 D14.

EMERGENCIES

See also **Accident & emergency** (*see below*) and **Police** (*see p296*).

Ambulance 118
Carabinieri (national/military police) 112
Car breakdown (Automobile Club d'Italia) 803 116
Fire brigade 115
Polizia di Stato (national police) 113

GAY & LESBIAN

Arcigay Napoli *Vico San Geronimo 19, Centro Storico (081 552 8815, www.arcigaynapoli.org). Bus C25, E1.* **Open** varies. Closed Aug. **Map** p312 M9.
Information, advice and events for the gay, lesbian, bi, transgender and transsexual communities.

HEALTH

EU nationals are entitled to free medical care with a **European Health Insurance Card (EHIC)**. British travellers can apply online at www.dh.gov.uk. Using an EHIC, however, condemns you to dealing with the intricacies of the Italian health bureaucracy; for short-term visitors, it's generally better to take out health cover under private travel insurance. Non-EU citizens don't qualify for free healthcare and should take out private medical insurance before leaving home. The British and US consulates have lists of English-speaking doctors.

Accident & emergency

The following Naples hospitals provide 24hr emergency (*pronto soccorso*) services. Details of

emergency treatment outside Naples can be found under Resources in the Escapes & Excursions chapters.

Cardarelli *Via Cardarelli 9, Vomero Alto (081 747 1111). Metro Colli Aminei, or bus C38, C40, C41, C44, C76, R4.*
Santobono *Via M Fiore 6, Vomero (081 220 5111, 081 220 5734). Metro Medaglie d'Oro, or bus C41, C44, V1.* **Map** p314 E8.

Contraception & abortion

Condoms are sold in supermarkets or over the counter at chemists. The contraceptive pill is available at pharmacies, although a doctor's prescription is required.

Abortion is legal if performed in public hospitals; health or financial hardship criteria must be proven.

Each district has a *Consultorio familiare* (family-planning clinic), which EU citizens with an EHIC (*see left*) are entitled to use. Ask at any chemist for the nearest clinic.

AIED *Via Cimarosa 186, Vomero (081 578 2142, www.aiednapoli.it). Funicular Montesanto to Via Morghen, Centrale to Piazzetta Fuga or Chiaia to Via Cimarosa, or bus 128, C31, C36, V1.* **Open** 9.30am-1pm, 3.30-7pm Mon-Fri. Closed 2wks Aug. **Map** p314 E10.
Check-ups, contraception advice and smear tests at a private clinic.

Dentists

In the case of dental emergencies, make for one of the hospital casualty departments (*see above*). For non-emergency treatment, try these English-speaking dentists.

Dott Francesco Olivieri *Via Carducci 6, Chiaia (081 245 7003).* **Open** 9am-9pm Mon-Fri.
Dott Massimo Palmieri *Via Giulio Palermo 80 (081 1935 3550).* **Open** 9am-noon Mon, Wed; 3-7pm Tue, Fri.

Pharmacies

Any *farmacia*, marked by a red or green cross, can give informal advice for simple ailments and make up prescriptions. Standard opening hours are 8.30am-1pm, 4-8pm Mon-Fri, 8.30am-1pm Sat. Every pharmacy should have a list by the door indicating the nearest pharmacies open outside normal business hours. Some levy a small surcharge when the main shop is shut and only the late-night counter is open.

STDs, HIV & AIDS

AIDS Helpline *800 019 254.*
Open 1-6pm Mon-Fri. Information in Italian on tests and prevention.

Helplines

Alcoholics Anonymous *335 194 9586, www.alcolistianonimiitalia.it.* An English-speaking support group meets at the Anglican/Episcopal Christ Church (*see p296*).
TelefonVerde Droga e Alcol *800 63 2000.* 24-hour drugs helpline. Italian only.

ID

Under Italian law, you're required to carry photo ID at all times. Hotels will ask for a document (passport or ID card) when you check in. They'll take your details and should return the ID immediately.

INTERNET

Up to three hours' free Wi-Fi per day is available in the main piazzas and parks in Naples (including Piazza Dante, Piazza Bellini and Piazza Bovio) via Napoli Cloud City. The first time you log on, you must register and create a password.

There's no shortage of cafés and bars around Naples offering free Wi-Fi, and even small towns in the provinces or on the islands will have an internet café or, at worst, a bar with a cranky computer.

LEFT LUGGAGE

At **Naples Airport**, the luggage storage office (081 789 6555, open 5am-10pm) is on the first floor of departures near security control. The daily rate is €7 per bag.

The luggage storage office at Naples' **Stazione Centrale** (081 567 2181) is open 7am-8pm daily. Prices start at €6 per bag, max weight 25kg. There are no left luggage facilities at Campi Flegrei or Mergellina stations.

In **Capri**, the luggage storage office (081 837 4575, open 9am-6pm daily summer, 9am-5pm daily winter) is operated by Caremar ferries at the port in Marina Grande. The rate is €3 per item.

In **Sorrento**, the tourist office (*see p212*) may watch your bag during opening hours.

LEGAL HELP

For legal advice, first go to your embassy or consulate (*see p294*).

LOST PROPERTY

If you lose anything valuable, go immediately to the nearest police station (*see p296*) to make a *'denuncia'* (statement).

If you leave anything on city buses or the metro in Naples, go to the *capolinea* (terminus) of the route and ask there. Failing that, phone the helpline (800 639 525 from Naples, 081 763 2177 from outside Italy, open 7am-8pm Mon-Sat). For items left on SITA buses, call 089 386 6701 or 089 386 6711, or see www.sitabus.it.

The lost property office at Naples Airport (081 789 6237, 081 789 6765) is open 9.30am-1.30pm, 2.30-4.30pm Mon-Sat (until 1.20pm in Aug).

MEDIA

Magazines

With naked women often on the covers, Italy's 'news' magazines are not always distinguishable from soft porn at the newsstands. Despite appearances, *Panorama* (centre right-ish) and *L'Espresso* (centre left-ish) provide a good round-up of the news. For *Hello!*-style scandal with lots of sex and glamour thrown in, try *Gente*, *Oggi* or the execrable *Novella 2000* and *Cronaca Vera*. *Internazionale* (www.internazionale. it) puts together an excellent digest of the previous week's global press.

Newspapers

Italy's newspapers are unsnobbish, blending serious news with well-written, often surreal, crime and human-interest pieces. Sports coverage in the dailies is extensive; if you're not sated, try sports rags *Corriere dello Sport*, *La Gazzetta dello Sport* or *Tuttosport*. Finance and business is covered by *Il Sole 24 Ore* and *Italia Oggi*.

Corriere della Sera *www.corriere.it* To the centre of centre-left, this solid, serious but often dull Milan-based daily is good on crime and foreign news, and has a Thursday colour supplement. Its Neapolitan insert, 'Corriere del Mezzogiorno', has good local entertainment listings.
Il Mattino *www.ilmattino.it* Naples' major daily, *Il Mattino* sits firmly on the political fence. National news is thoroughly covered, but there's only superficial coverage of international affairs.
La Repubblica *www.repubblica.it* This centre-ish, left-ish paper is good on the Mafia and the Vatican, and comes up with the odd major scoop

on its business pages. It has a fairly exhaustive Naples section.

Television

Italy has six major networks – three owned by the state broadcaster RAI (**RAI 1, RAI 2, RAI 3**) and three belonging to ex-Prime Minister Silvio Berlusconi (**Rete 4, Canale 5, Italia 1**). The content is dominated by ghastly variety shows with dancing girls and horribly acted TV dramas. There's the odd exception, such as Rai's wonderful Sicily-based crime series *Commissario Montalbano*. For local interest, try Rai 3's set-in-Naples soap *Un Posto al Sole* (*see p132*). News and current affairs programmes vary in standard: Rai 3 is the most left-leaning (and serious) of the channels. Foreign films are always dubbed.

Radio

There are three state-owned stations: **RAI-1** (90.6FM, www.radio1.rai.it), **RAI-2** (93.7FM stereo, www.radio2. rai.it) and the excellent **RAI-3** (99.4FM, www.rai3.rai.it).

Radio Capital *104.5FM, www. capital.it.* Classics and hits from the UK and US, with lots of home-grown goodies thrown in.
Radio Kiss Kiss Napoli *103.0FM or 99.2FM, www.kisskissnapoli.it.* Hits from Italy and abroad, and live broadcasts of Napoli football games.
Radio Monte Carlo *91.6FM or 98.6FM, www.radiomontecarlo.net.* Plays a good mix of US and UK hits with some Italian tunes thrown in. Nick the Night Fly's jazz-lounge Montecarlo Nights spot from 10pm is worth tuning in for.

MONEY

The Euro is legal tender in Italy. By law, you must be given a receipt (*scontrino fiscale*) for any transaction. Even if places try to avoid giving you a receipt for tax reasons, it's your right to ask for one.

Banks & ATMs

Most banks are open 8.20am-1.20pm, 2.45-3.45pm Mon-Fri. Banks are closed on public holidays, and usually close around noon the day before a holiday. Most have cash machines (*bancomat*) that allow you to withdraw money with major cards. In more out-of-the-way places, ATMs may be switched off at night and at weekends. Always be alert when withdrawing money.

ESSENTIAL INFORMATION

Bureaux de change

Bureaux de change (*cambio*) are plentiful at the airport, around the Stazione Centrale, on the port side of Piazza Municipio and near major tourist sites. Rates are not usually as good as at the banks, but *cambio* are conveniently located and stay open later. When changing money, bring a passport or other ID. Rates vary and you can pay as much as €10 for each transaction. Beware of places with 'no commission' signs: the rate of exchange may be terrible. Many banks will give cash advances against a credit card, though they may refuse if you don't have a PIN.

Main post offices also have exchange desks. Commission is €2.58 plus 1.5% for cash transactions up to €1,032.91; traveller's cheques are not accepted.

San Paolo/Banco di Napoli
Via Toledo 177/178, Toledo (081 792 4567, 081 791 1111). Metro Toledo, or bus 201, E1, R4. **Open** 8am-4pm Mon-Fri. **Map** p316 K11.
Travelex *Departures 081 780 1825, Arrivals 081 780 9107.* **Open** *Departures* 6am-9pm daily. *Arrivals* 8am-11.30pm daily. Money can be transferred here from any Travelex branch in the world.
Western Union *c/o Space, Piazza Garibaldi 69, Port & University (081 207 597). Metro Garibaldi, or bus 191, 192, 194, 195, C40, R2.* **Open** 9am-6.30pm Mon-Fri; 9am-3pm Sat. Closed 2wks Sept. **Map** p313 P7.
Money sent here should arrive within an hour. The sender pays the commission.

Lost/stolen credit cards

Phone one of the 24-hour emergency numbers listed below:

American Express
800 864 046.
Diners Club *800 393 939.*
Mastercard *800 870 866.*
Visa *800 819 014.*

OPENING HOURS

Most shops are open roughly 8.30am-1pm, 4-7/8pm Mon-Sat, though many stores now open on Sunday mornings in the tourist and shopping districts of Via Toledo and Chiaia. Many shops are closed on Saturday afternoon and Monday morning. Office hours are similar, but only Mon-Fri. Bars generally open from early morning until

around midnight, and also open on Sunday for part of the day.
See p295 for bank opening hours, and *see below* for post office hours.

POLICE

See also p294 **Emergencies**.

Questura Centrale *Via Medina 75 (081 794 1111, emergency 113). Metro Municipio, or bus R2, R4.* **Map** p316 L11.

POSTAL SERVICES

The Italian postal service is pretty reliable these days. Most post-boxes are red and have two slots – marked '*per la città*' (for the city) and '*tutte le altre destinazioni*' (everywhere else).

The postal service promises delivery within 24hrs in Italy, three days for EU countries, and four or five days for anywhere else in the world. A letter of 20g or less within Italy costs 95 cents, to other EU countries €1, and to the US €2.20.

The costlier *Postacelere* promises two- to three-day delivery abroad, and allows you to track the progress of your letter or parcel online. Registered mail ('*raccomandata*') starts at €3.50. It may assure delivery, but is no guarantee of speed. Private couriers (*see p293*) are quicker, but more expensive.

Post office

Palazzo Centrale della Posta, Piazza Matteotti 2, Toledo (081 790 4744, www.poste.it). Metro Toledo, or bus 201, R4. **Open** *Sept-July* 8.20am-6.30pm Mon-Fri; 8.20am-12.30pm Sat. *Aug* 8.20am-1.30pm Mon-Fri; 8am-12.30pm Sat. **Map** p312 L10.

RELIGION

You can hear Catholic Mass in English at the church of **Gesù Nuovo** (*see p58*; 5pm Sun).

Anglican/Episcopal *Christ Church, Via San Pasquale a Chiaia 15, Chiaia (081 411842). Metro Piazza Amedeo, or bus 128, 140, C12, C18, C24, C25, C27.* **Services** 10.30am Sun. **Map** p311 F13. A hub for the English-speaking community.
Baptist *Chiesa Battista, Via Foria 93, Sanità (081 578 4037, 081 751 8294, www.chiesabattista.net). Metro Cavour, or bus 12, 182, 184, 201, C51, C52.* **Services** 11am Sun (in English & Italian). **Map** p312 N6.
Jewish *Comunità Ebraica, Via Santa Maria a Cappella Vecchia 31,*

Chiaia (081 764 3480, www.napolie braica.it). Metro Amedeo, or bus 140, C12, C18, C24, C25, C27, E6. **Services** 9.30am Sat (times may vary so check in advance). Closed 3wks Aug. **Map** p311 H13.

SAFETY & SECURITY

Street crime is common in Naples. Pickpockets and bag-snatchers on foot and on scooters are active in main tourist areas and sites in the surrounding region. Be especially attentive when boarding buses and boats, and when entering museums. If you're a victim of any crime, go to the nearest police station to make a '*denuncia*' (written statement). *See also p295* **Lost property**.

Always take precautions. Look as if you know what you're doing and where you're going, and don't carry a wallet in your back pocket. Keep some small bills and change to hand rather than pulling out a large wad of cash to pay for something.

If you stop at a pavement café or restaurant, don't leave bags or coats on the ground or draped across a chair. Wear bags and cameras across your chest or on the side away from the street so you're less likely to fall prey to a motorbike-borne thief (*scippatore*). Don't wear expensive jewellery or watches. Finally, only take registered, marked taxis.

SMOKING

Smoking is theoretically banned in public offices, bars, restaurants, on public transport or in taxis. For the most part, the law is ignored; still, times are changing and smokers may put out their cigarettes if you diplomatically point out the *vietato fumare* (no smoking) sign.

Tabacchi

Tabacchi or *tabaccherie*, identified by signs with a white T on a black or blue background, are the only places where you can legally buy tobacco products. Most *tabacchi* keep shop hours, but those attached to bars are open later. Many have cigarette machines outside for when the shop is closed (9pm-7am).

STUDY

Naples' universities are the **Università Federico II** (www.unina.it), founded in 1224; the modern **Seconda Università di Napoli** (www.unina2.it); and the **Istituto Universitario Orientale** (www.iuo.it).

Language classes

Centro Italiano *Vico Santa Maria dell'Aiuto 17, Centro Storico (081 552 4331, www.centroitaliano.it). Metro Università, or bus 201, C57, E1, E2, R4.* **Open** 9am-4.30pm Mon-Fri. **Map** p312 L10.

TELEPHONES

Dialling & codes

To make an international call from Italy, dial 00 (or '+' from a mobile phone), then the country code, then the area code (for calls to the UK or Ireland, omit the initial zero) and then the individual number.

To call Naples from abroad, dial your country's international access code (or '+' from a mobile phone), then 39 for Italy and 081 for Naples, followed by the individual number.

All Italian phone numbers must be dialled with their area codes, even if you're phoning from within the area. All numbers in Naples and its province begin 081; this includes Pozzuoli, Ischia, Capri, Sorrento and Pompeii. It doesn't include Positano and Amalfi, which are in the Salerno province, area code 089.

Mobile phones

The main service providers in Italy are **TIM** (Telecom Italia), **Tre** (Three), **Vodafone** and **Wind**.

TIM *www.tim.it.*
Tre *www.tre.it.*
Vodafone *www.vodafone.it.*
Wind *www.wind.it.*

Public phones

There are fewer and fewer public phones in Naples these days, and many of those that do exist are permanently out of order. Most public phones only accept phonecards (*schede telefoniche*), although newer models may accept credit cards. Phonecards (€3, €5 and €10) can be bought at post offices and *tabacchi* plus some newsstands and bars.

TIME

Italy is 1hr ahead of GMT, 6hrs ahead of New York, and 9hrs behind Sydney. The clocks are moved forward 1hr in spring (*ora legale*) and back 1hr (*ora solare*) in autumn.

TIPPING

In Italy, tipping is discretionary. You don't need to leave anything for poor service. However, a tip – rarely more than 10% – is appreciated everywhere (and expected in more sophisticated eateries).

Upmarket restaurants (and a growing number of cheaper ones) will add a service charge of 10-15% to your bill.

Rounding your fare up to the nearest euro will make taxi drivers happy. In resorts, where maids and waiters work seasonally, tips are especially welcome.

TOURIST INFORMATION

Tourist offices

Ente Provinciale del Turismo (EPT) *Piazza dei Martiri 58, Chiaia (081 410 7211, www.eptnapoli.info). Bus 140, C12, C18, C24, C25.* **Open** 9am-2pm Mon-Fri. **Map** p311 H13. **Other locations** Stazione Centrale, by platform 24 (081 268 779); Capodichino airport, on ground floor in arrivals terminal (081 789 6734).
Azienda Autonoma di Soggiorno Cura e Turismo di Napoli *Via San Carlo 9, Royal Naples (081 402394, www.inaples.it). Bus C25, R2.* **Open** 9am-5pm Mon-Sat; 9am-1pm Sun. **Map** p316 K12. **Other locations** Piazza Gesù Nuovo, Centro Storico (081 551 2701); Galleria Umberto (opposite Teatro San Carlo), Royal Naples.

Campania Artecard

If you intend to stay in Naples (or the surrounding area) for several days and see multiple sights, this combined ticket (3, 7 or 365 days) is good value. Cards can be bought from all major museums and archaeological sites, the information point at Stazione Centrale or online (www.campaniaartecard.it).

The **3-day Naples Card** (€21; €12 18-25s) gives free entrance to a choice of three museums or sights and discounts of up to 50% from the fourth day on. It also includes free travel on the public transport system (buses, trams, metro, funiculars, Circumvesuviana and Cumana trains) within the city.

The **3-day Regional Card** (€32; €25 18-25s) widens the choice of sights to include Campi Flegrei, Pompeii and Herculaneum. It gives free entrance to two sights plus discounts from the third onwards. It also includes free transport on the UNICOCAMPANIA network.

The **7-day Regional Card** (€34) offers free entrance to five sights of your choice and discounts from the sixth on. Transport is not included.

The **365-day Regional Card** (€43; €33 18-25s) offers two free visits per year to the listed sights (all the major ones) plus a 50% discount on any others. Transport is not included.

The card is activated on admission to the first sight or (if applicable) on the first journey using the UNICOCAMPANIA network.

VISAS

For EU citizens, a passport or national identity card valid for travel abroad is sufficient. Non-EU citizens must have full passports. Citizens of Australia, Canada, New Zealand and the United States do not need visas for stays of up to 90 days. In theory, all visitors are required to declare their presence to the local police within a few days of arrival in Italy unless they are staying in a hotel (or B&B) where this will be done for them. In practice, you don't need to do this unless you decide to extend your stay and apply for a *permesso di soggiorno* (permit to stay).

WHEN TO GO

Naples sizzles in July and August, and humidity levels can be high. On the islands and coast, sea breezes make the heat more bearable. Spring and autumn are usually warm and pleasant but with some heavy showers. March and October can be wonderful times to visit the islands: they're very quiet but you still stand a decent chance of catching some warmth. From November to February, it's usually crisp with some sun, but with long spells of dreary weather. In winter, there's often a dusting of snow on Mount Vesuvius.

WOMEN

The *maschilista* (macho) southern Italian male can be daunting for the female traveller, but he is, as a rule, more bark than bite. Common sense will get you out of most scenarios.

Avoid lodging or lingering in the area around Stazione Centrale/Piazza Garibaldi; it's bad enough in the day but really horrible at night. On the other hand, you're quite safe in the Centro Storico. The safest places to stay are Royal Naples and Chiaia.

At tourist sights, there's a good chance that would-be Romeos will approach young women without male companions. Perfect the art of saying 'no'. A joking tone will be much more effective than reacting in an aggressive or upset fashion. To get back to your hotel late at night, catch a taxi (*see p291*).

ESSENTIAL INFORMATION

Further Reference

BOOKS

The Ancients

Allan Massie *Augustus, Tiberius, Caesar* Popular rewrites of history.
Suetonius *De Vita Caesarum* (Lives of the Caesars) Ancient muck-raking by a highly biased Roman historian.
Virgil *Georgics* Written during his stay in Naples.

Art & history

Harold Acton *The Bourbons of Naples* A lively historical romp that focuses on the reign of Ferdinand I.
Mary Beard *Pompeii* A scholarly yet absorbing account of life in the Roman city before the eruption.
Bruce Cutler *Seeing the Darkness: Naples, 1943-1945* The city during World War II.
Electa Guides *Naples* An architectural guide.
Paul Ginsborg *A History of Contemporary Italy* Fine introduction to postwar Italy.
Michael Grant *Eros in Pompeii: The Erotic Art Collection of the Museum of Naples* An exploration of erotic imagery in ancient Pompeii.
Jordan Lancaster *In the Shadow of Vesuvius* Cultural history of Naples.
Mary Lefkowitz & Maureen Fant *Women's Life in Greece and Rome* Riveting stuff: topics range from ancient gynaecology to choosing a wet nurse.
Donatella Mazzoleni *Palaces of Naples* Some 30 estates and palaces explored.
Frank J Palescandolo (trans.) *The Naples of Salvatore di Giacomo* Work by the Neapolitan poet.
Roberto Saviano *Gomorrah* A powerful first-hand account of the Camorra and its activities.

Cuisine

Carla Capalbo *The Food and Wine Guide to Naples and Campania* An information-packed foodie tome.
Arthur Schwartz *Naples at Table: Cooking in Campania* A gastronomic trip to Campania.
Pamela Sheldon Johns *Pizza Napoletana!* A history of pizza.

Fiction

Norman Douglas *South Wind* A celebration of Bacchic goings-on.

Elena Ferrante *The Neapolitan Novels* Set in and around Naples, this story of an extraordinary friendship between two women fills four volumes. From one of Italy's most acclaimed authors.
Robert Harris *Pompeii* The cataclysmic events of 79 AD.
Susan Sontag *The Volcano Lover* A postmodern bodice-ripper that centres on the Nelson-Hamilton trio.

Travel & biography

Giacomo Casanova di Seingalt *The Story of My Life* The libertine's autobiography includes 18th-century Naples.
Johann Wolfgang von Goethe *Italian Journey* The poet's 18th-century travel diary.
Shirley Hazzard *Greene on Capri* Memoirs of a postwar Capri resident's meetings with the writer.
Dan Hofstadter *Falling Palace: A Romance of Naples* An artfully constructed memoir about the author's love of the city.
Norman Lewis *Naples '44* Experiences of an intelligence officer in wartime Naples.
Axel Munthe *The Story of San Michele* The Swedish doctor's life, times and love affair with Anacapri.
Susana Walton *Behind the Façade* Bloomsbury moves to Ischia.

FILMS

L'amore molesto *dir Mario Martone* (1995) Adapted from the eponymous early novel of current literary celeb Elena Ferrante.
Il Decameron *dir Pier Paolo Pasolini* (1970) Features Neapolitan locations and dialects.
Fellini Satyricon *dir Federico Fellini* (1969) The maestro's take on the ancient picaresque fragment by Petronius.
Gomorrah *dir Matteo Garrone* (2008) Film version of Roberto Saviano's book (*see left*).
Le Mani sulla Città *dir Francesco Rosi* (1963) Political corruption drama that captures the essence of Naples.
Napoli d'altri tempi *dir Amleto Palermi* (1938) Composer renounces fame and fortune for anonymity in Naples.
L'Oro di Napoli *dir Vittorio de Sica* (1954) Tales of Neapolitan life, starring Sophia Loren and Totò.

Polvere di Napoli *dir Antonio Capuano* (1998) Update of *L'Oro di Napoli*.
Il Postino *dir Michael Radford* (1994) Oscar-winning drama.
Le Quattro giornate di Napoli *dir Nanni Loy* (1962) Oscar-nominated war drama.
Souls of Naples *dir Vincent Monnikendam* (2005) Documentary: Naples, in splendour and adversity.
Totò, Peppino e la… malafemmina *dir Camillo Mastrocinque* (1956) Three brothers and a naughty girl.
Viaggio in Italia *dir Roberto Rossellini* (1954) A couple's relationship, set against the backdrops of Naples and Capri.

MUSIC

Edoardo Bennato *Non farti cadere le braccia* Still producing hits after 30 years.
Eugenio Bennato *Taranta Power* Southern Italian folk songs.
Pino Daniele *Terra Mia* Melodic blues.
Nuova Compagnia di Canto Popolare *Lo guarracino* Folk outfit.
Luciano Pavarotti *Favourite Neapolitan Songs* All the classics.
Daniele Sepe *Spiritus Mundi* Eclectic saxophonist.
Spaccanapoli *Lost Souls* A modern take on tarantella.
Il Tesoro di San Gennaro *I Turchini di Antonio Florio* Sacred music in early 18th-century Naples.

WEBSITES

Culture, museums & events

www.campaniartecard.it
All about the Artecard.
www.comune.napoli.it
The Naples City Council's site.
www.eptnapoli.info The tourist board's excellent site.
www.infocampiflegrei.it
www.napolisworld.it
www.napoliunplugged.it
Excellent site, updated regularly

Listings

www.napolidavivere.it
www.spaccanapolionline.com
http://napolinews.too.it
www.napoli.com
www.nottambulando.it

Glossary

Amphitheatre (ancient) oval open-air theatre
Apse large recess at the high-altar end of a church; adj apsidal
Atrium (ancient) courtyard
Baldacchino canopy supported by columns
Baptistery building – often eight-sided – outside church used for baptisms
Baroque artistic period from the 17th to 18th centuries, in which the decorative element became increasingly florid, culminating in Rococo (qv)
Barrel vault a ceiling with arches shaped like half-barrels
Basilica ancient Roman rectangular public building; rectangular Christian church
Bas-relief carving on a flat or curved surface where the figures stand out from the plane
Byzantine artistic and architectural style drawing on ancient models, developed in the fourth century in the Eastern empire and developed through the Middle Ages
Campanile bell tower
Capital the decorated head of a column (*see below* Orders)
Cardine (ancient) secondary street, usually running north–south
Caryatid supporting pillar carved in the shape of a woman
Castellated (building) decorated with battlements or turrets (*see also* Crenellations)
Cavea semicircular step-like seating area in an amphitheatre (qv) or theatre
Chapter room room in monastery where monks met for discussions
Chiaroscuro painting or drawing technique using no colours, but shades of black, white and grey
Choir area of church, usually behind the high altar, with stalls for people singing sung mass
Coffered (ceiling) with sunken square decorations
Colonnade row of columns supporting an entablature (qv) or arches
Confessio crypt (qv) beneath a raised altar
Crenellations battlements and/or archery holes on top of building or tower
Cupola dome-shaped roof/ceiling
Crypt vault beneath the main floor of a church

Cryptoporticus underground corridor
Decumanus (ancient) main road, usually running east–west
Domus (ancient) Roman city house
Embrasure a recess around the interior of a door or window; a hole in a wall for shooting through
Entablature section above a column or row of columns including the frieze and cornice
Ex-voto an offering given to fulfil a vow; often a small model in silver of the limb/organ/loved one to be cured as a result of prayer
Fresco painting technique in which pigment is applied to wet plaster
Gothic architectural and artistic style of the late Middle Ages using soaring, pointed arches
Greek cross (church) in the shape of a cross with arms of equal length
Hypogeum (ancient) underground room
Impluvium (ancient) cistern in the middle of a courtyard to gather rainwater, funnelled into it by a sloping roof with a hole in the middle
Insula (ancient) city block
Intarsio technique by which patterns or pictures are made in wooden surfaces by inlaying pieces of different-coloured wood
Latin cross (church) in the shape of a cross with one arm longer than the other
Loggia gallery open on one side
Mannerism High Renaissance style of the late 16th century; characterised in painting by elongated, contorted human figures
Marquetry wooden inlay work, also known as intarsio (qv)
Narthex enclosed porch in front of a church
Nave main body of a church; the longest section of a Latin-cross church (qv)
Necropolis (ancient) literally 'city of the dead'; graveyard
Nymphaeum (ancient) grotto with pool and fountain dedicated to the Nymphs, female water deities; name given to ornate fountains with grottos in Renaissance architecture
Ogival (of arches, windows and so on) curving in to a point at the top
Orders classical styles of decoration for columns, the most common being the very simple Doric, the curlicued Ionic and the leafy, frondy Corinthian

Palaestra (ancient) wrestling school
Palazzo large and/or important building (not necessarily a palace)
Parlatorio a convent or monastery's reception room or room for conversation
Pendentives four concave triangular sections on top of piers supporting a dome
Peristyle (ancient) temple or court surrounded by columns
Piazza (or largo) square
Pilaster square column, often with its rear side attached to a wall
Portal imposing door
Portico open space in front of a church or other building, with a roof resting on columns
Presbytery the part of a church containing the high altar
Proscenium (ancient) stage; arch dividing stage from audience
Reggia royal palace
Reliquary receptacle – often highly ornate – for holding and displaying relics of saints
Rococo highly decorative style fashionable in the 18th century
Romanesque architectural style of the early Middle Ages (c500-1200), drawing on Roman and Byzantine influences
Rustication large masonry blocks, often roughly cut, with deep joints, used to face buildings
Sacristy the room in church where vestments are stored
Sarcophagus (ancient) stone or marble coffin
Spandrel near-triangular space between the top of two adjoining arches and the ceiling or architectural feature resting above them
Stucco plaster
Succorpo similar to a crypt (qv), underground space beneath the apse (qv) of a church
Tablinium (ancient) private study
Tessera small piece of stone or glass used to make mosaic
Transept shorter arms of a Latin-cross church (qv)
Triclinium (ancient) dining room
Triumphal arch arch in front of an apse (qv), usually over the high altar
Trompe l'oeil decorative painting effect to make surface appear three-dimensional
Tufa volcanic stone widely used in building

ESSENTIAL INFORMATION

Vocabulary

Although the hotel and restaurant staff in resorts around Naples will have some grasp of English, don't expect anyone in shops or bars to manage any more than prices in anything but Italian. Naples itself is getting used to receiving many more tourists these days and you'll find English (or a version of it, at least) spoken much more widely than in the past.

ITALIAN & NEAPOLITAN

Italian is spelled as it's pronounced, and vice versa. Grammar books will tell you that the stress falls on the penultimate syllable, but this is not a failsafe rule.

Pronunciation

Vowels

a – as in ask
e – like *a* in age (closed e)
or *e* in sell (open e)
i – like *ea* in east
o – as in hotel (closed o)
or hot (open o)
u – as in boot

Consonants

c and *g* both go soft in front of *e* and *i* (becoming like *ch* and *g* in *check* and *giraffe* respectively). Before a vowel, *h* is silent. An *h* after *c* or *g* makes them hard, no matter which vowel follows. Doubled consonants, like those in *cappuccino*, are emphasised by lingering on those syllables.

gl – like *lli* in mi*lli*on
gn – like *ny* in ca*ny*on
qu – as in *qu*ick
r – always rolled
s – either as in *s*oap or in ro*s*e
sc – like *sh* in *sh*ame
sch – like *sc* in *sc*out
z – can be *ds* or *tz*

Neapolitan

Neapolitan dialect is something more than an accent but less than a language, spoken habitually between Neapolitans of all ages and classes; even other Italians don't generally understand a word of it.

Neapolitans tend to…

…leave off the ends of words: *buona ser'* (*buona sera*)
…turn *d* into *r*: *domenica* (Sunday) becomes *rumenica*.
…replace some *e* sounds by *ie*: *tiemp'* (*tempo*, time/weather) or *apiert'* (in Italian *aperto*, open).
…replace some words beginning *pi* by a very hard *ki* sound: *cchiù* (in Italian *più*, more).
…replace a hard *sc* (like *sk* in English) with a soft, English-style *sh*: *scusate* (excuse me) becomes a drunken-sounding *shcusate*.
…make *a* sounds longer than other Italians: *Napule'* (Neapolitan for Naples) is *Naapule'*.
… turn *v* into *b* and double consonants: *che volete?* (what do you want?) *becomes ca' bbulit'?*

Other hints

Bene (well) becomes *buono* (good).
Indefinite articles: *un/uno* (a/an, masculine) become *nu/una* (a/an, feminine) '*nu ggelat'* (*un gelato*, an ice-cream).
Definite articles: *il/lo* (the, masculine) become *'o/la* (the, feminine): *'o ggelat'* (*il gelato*, the ice-cream).

ENGLISH/ITALIAN/ NEAPOLITAN

Basics

hello/goodbye (informal) ciao; *uè uè*
hello (informal) salve; *ttà ppost'?*
good morning buon giorno
good evening buona sera
good night buona notte
please per favore, per piacere
thank you grazie; *grazie assje*
you're welcome prego; *nun' fà nient'*
excuse me, sorry mi scusi (formal), scusa (informal)
I'm sorry mi dispiace; *nun'l'aggia fatt' a ppost'*
I don't speak Italian (very well) non parlo (molto bene) l'italiano; *non parl' buon' l'italian'*
I don't/didn't understand non capisco/non ho capito; *n'aggio capit'*

how much is (it)? quanto costa?
open aperto; *apièrt'*
closed chiuso
where is? dov'è?; *a ro'sta?*

Transport

bus autobus
coach pullman
train treno
underground railway metropolitana (metro)
platform binario
ticket/s biglietto/biglietti
a ticket for… un biglietto per…
one way sola andata
return andata e ritorno

Eat, shop, sleep

a reservation una prenotazione
I'd like to book a table for four at eight vorrei prenotare una tavola per quattro persone alle otto
breakfast/lunch/dinner colazione/pranzo/cena
the bill il conto
is service included? è compreso il servizio?
that was poor/good/(really) delicious era mediocre/buono/ (davvero) ottimo
I think there's a mistake in this bill credo che il conto sia sbagliato
more/less ancora/di meno
shoe/clothes size numero/taglia
a single/twin/double room una camera singola/doppia/ matrimoniale
a room with a (sea) view una camera con vista (sul mare)

Days & nights

Monday lunedì; *lunneri*
Tuesday martedì; *mart'rì*
Wednesday mercoledì; *miercul'rì*
Thursday giovedì; *gioveri*
Friday venerdì; *vierneri*
Saturday sabato; *sabbat'*
Sunday domenica; *dumenec'* or *rumenica*
today oggi; *ogg'*
tomorrow domani; *diman'*
morning mattina; *matin'*
afternoon pomeriggio
evening sera; *ser'*
night notte; *nott'*
weekend fine settimana, weekend; *fine semman'*

Numbers

0 zero, **1** uno, **2** due, **3** tre, **4**
quattro, **5** cinque, **6** sei, **7** sette,
8 otto, **9** nove, **10** dieci, **11** undici,
12 dodici, **13** tredici, **14** quattordici,
15 quindici, **16** sedici, **17** diciassette,
18 diciotto, **19** diciannove, **20**
venti, **30** trenta, **40** quaranta, **50**
cinquanta, **60** sessanta, **70** settanta,
80 ottanta, **90** novanta, **100** cento,
200 duecento, **1,000** mille.

EATING OUT

Antipasti

Alici marinate anchovies
marinated in lemon or vinegar
with oil, garlic, chilli and parsley.
Antipasti di mare a selection of
(usually) cold, cooked seafood such
as octopus, squid, clams, smoked
swordfish and marinated sardines,
or *frittelle di cicinielli* – delicious fried
patties of tiny, transparent fish.
Antipasti misti/di terra
a selection of salamis, hams,
cheeses and olives.
Bruschetta toast with chopped
tomatoes, garlic, basil and oil, or,
occasionally, aubergine or olive paste.
Fritto misto all'Italiana deep-
fried breaded mozzarella bites,
deep-fried pizza dough, potato
balls (*crocchè*), rice balls (*arancini*)
and courgette strips.
Funghi trifolati cooked, diced
mushrooms with garlic, chilli
and parsley.
Involtini di peperoni cooked
peppers, rolled and filled with
cheese and breadcrumbs.
Mozzarella e prosciutto
mozzarella and parma ham.
Prosciutto e fichi parma ham
and figs.
Prosciutto e melone parma
ham and cantaloupe melon.
Soutè di vongole sautéed clams.
Impepata di cozze steamed
mussels with black pepper,
lemon and toast.

Pasta

Alla barese with broccoli.
Alla bolognese tomato and
ground beef sauce.
Alla genovese thick onion and
meat (veal) sauce.
Al nero di seppia in squid ink.
**Alla puttanesca, alla bella
donna** with tomato, capers, black
olives and a touch of chilli.

**Alla Santa Lucia, alla bella
Napoli, alla pescatora** with
seafood and shellfish.
Alla siciliana with tomato,
aubergine, basil and mozzarella.
Alla sorrentina with tomato and
mozzarella, or provola.
Alle vongole with clams (specify
in bianco if you don't want your
clams cooked with tomato).
Al sugo tomato and basil sauce.
Con fagioli e cozze with beans
and mussels.
E ceci with chickpeas, sometimes
creamed.
E patate, con provola with
potatoes and smoked mozzarella.
Ragù thick tomato and meat sauce.

Other first courses

Gattò di patate potato pie with
mozzarella and ham or salami.
Sartù di riso baked rice with
tomato sauce, mozzarella, peas
and small meatballs.

Pesce & frutti di mare (fish & seafood)

Aragosta lobster.
Astice crayfish.
Bianchetti whitebait.
Calamaro ripieno stuffed squid.
Frittura di paranza small, local
deep-fried fish.
Gamberi prawns.
Mazzancolle very large prawns.
Mussillo marinato marinated
cod-like fish.
Orata a kind of bream.
Pezzogna locally caught type of
sea bream (blue-speckled).
Pignatiello seafood soup served
with fingers of toasted bread.
Polipo affucate/affogato literally
'drowned octopus', cooked in an
earthenware dish with a little
water and tomato.
**Purpietielle/purpo/polpo/
polipo** octopus.
Scampi langoustine.
Seppie in umido similar to *polipo
affucate*, but with cuttlefish.
Telline clams, sweeter than *vongole*.
Totano similar to squid.
Vongole veraci local clams.

Carne (meat)

Carne alla pizzaiola meat served
with a tomato and oregano sauce.
Carne al ragù slow-cooked beef
in tomato.
Involtino a small roll of beef (or
aubergine, *involtini di melanzane*)
stuffed with ham and cheese.

Polpette meatballs, usually in
tomato sauce.

Contorni (vegetables)

Fagiolini all'agro cooked green
beans with garlic and lemon.
Friarielli broccoli rabe.
Melanzane a funghetto diced
aubergine with tomato and basil.
Melanzane alla brace chargrilled
aubergine dressed with garlic, chilli
and parsley.
Peperoncini verdi long, sweet
green peppers cooked in tomato
and basil.
Peperoni in padella pan-fried
peppers (often with capers and
black olives).
Parmigiana di melanzane fried,
sliced aubergines baked with tomato
sauce, mozzarella and basil; often
ordered as a starter.
Pizza di scarole salty pie prepared
with scarola.
Scarola 'mbuttit'/'mbuttonat'
stuffed endive (usually with capers,
pine nuts and olives).
Zucchine alla scapece deep-fried
sliced courgette with vinegar and
fresh mint.

Formaggi (cheese)

Caciovallo ewe's milk cheese.
Caprese mozzarella, tomatoes
and basil.
Fior di latte mozzarella made with
cow's milk, as opposed to buffalo.
Mozzarella in carrozza deep-
fried mozzarella, sandwiched
between two squares of bread.
Mozzarella fritta deep-fried,
breaded mozzarella.
Provola smoked mozzarella.
Provola alla pizzaiola provola
cooked in tomato and basil sauce.
Scamorza hard cow's milk cheese,
usually grilled.

Methods of cooking

All'acqua pazza (fish) simmered
in water, flavoured with tomato,
garlic and parsley.
Al gratin oven-baked with a
topping of breadcrumbs, often
in a béchamel sauce.
Al sale (fish) encrusted in sea salt.
Con pomodoro al filetto cooked
with fresh cherry tomatoes.
In bianco cooked without tomato.
Indorato e fritto deep-fried with
flour and egg.
Macchiato 'stained' with a touch
of tomato.

ESSENTIAL INFORMATION

Index

INDEX

Maps

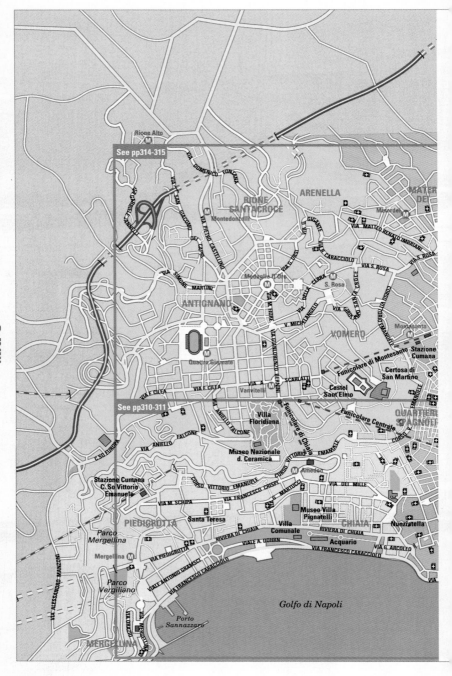

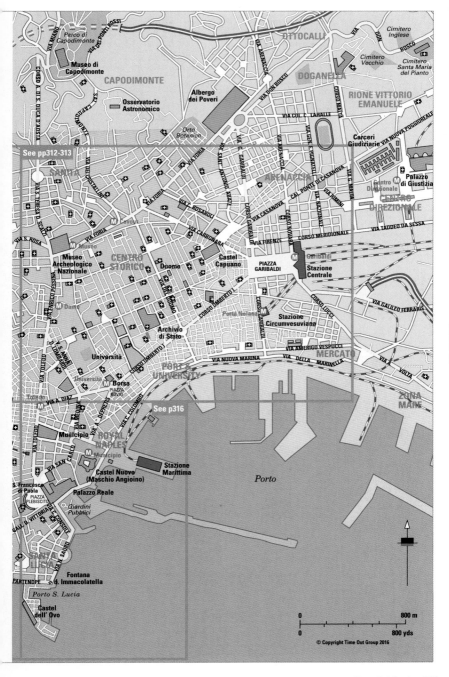

MAPS

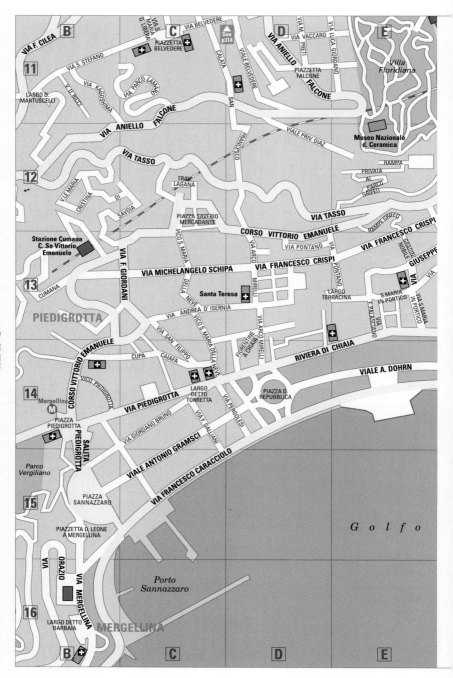

MAPS

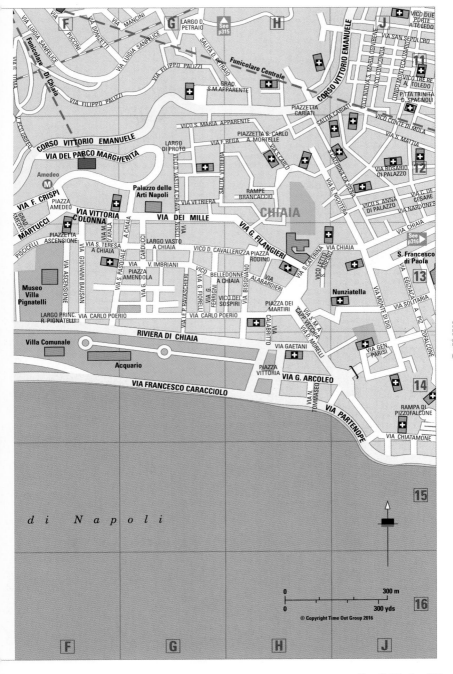

MAPS

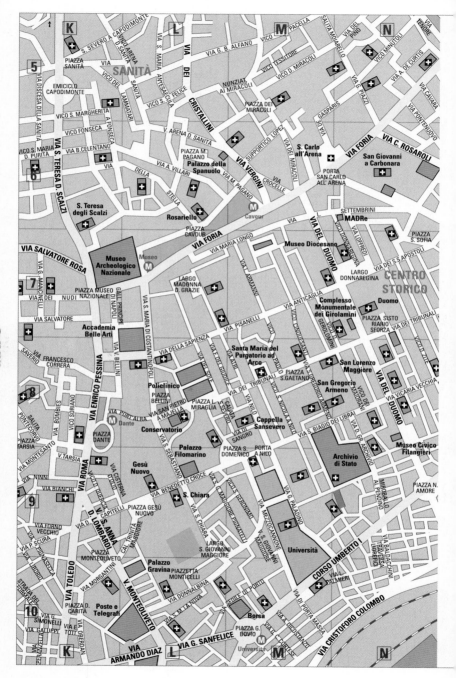

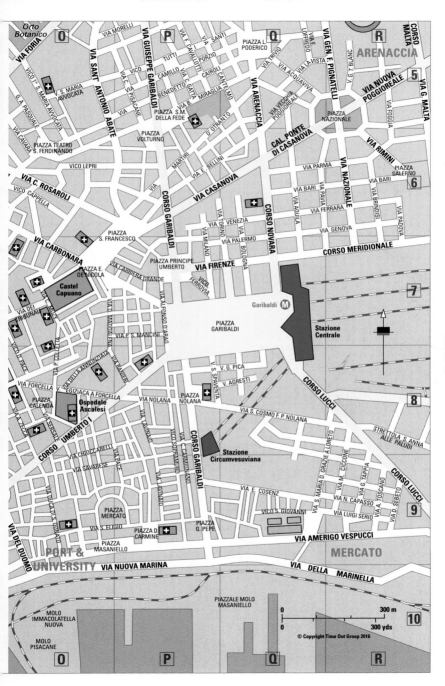

MAPS

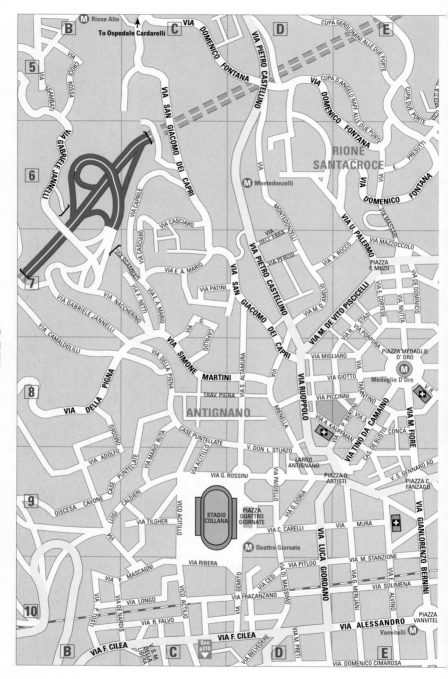

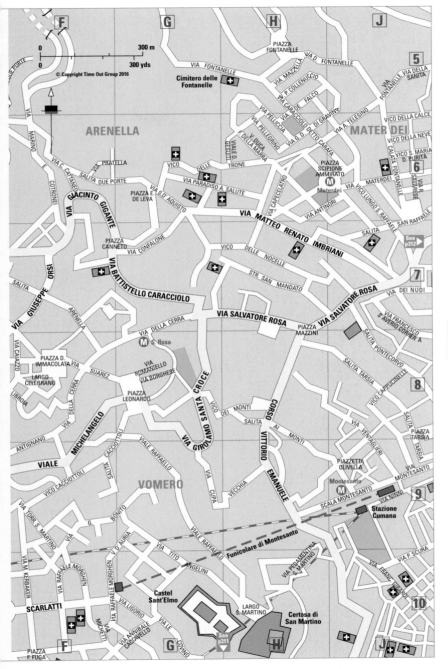

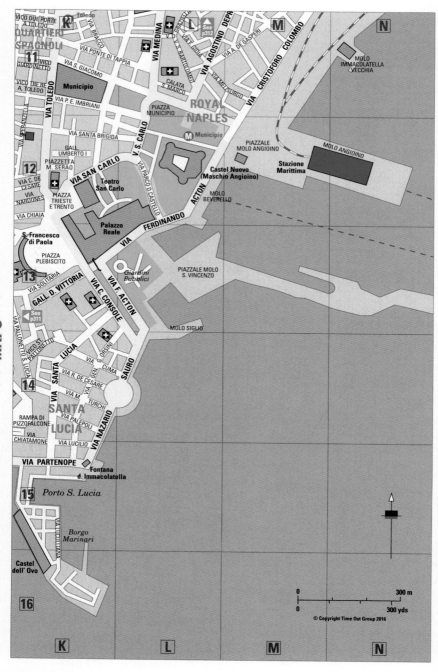

Street Index

STREET INDEX

STREET INDEX

rete metropolitana e tratte ferroviarie urbane
underground and urban railways map